THE WPA GUIDE TO
KENTUCKY

D0762603

THE WPA GUIDE TO
KENTUCKY

*Compiled and Written by the Federal Writers' Project
of the Work Projects Administration
for the State of Kentucky*

F. Kevin Simon, Editor

Foreword by Thomas D. Clark

THE UNIVERSITY PRESS OF KENTUCKY

Editorial and Sales Offices: The University Press of Kentucky
663 South Limestone Street, Lexington, Kentucky 40508-4008

96 97 98 99 00   5 4 3 2 1

Library of Congress Cataloging-in-Publication Data

Federal Writers' Project of the Work Projects Administration for the
State of Kentucky
The WPA guide to Kentucky / compiled and written by the Federal
Writers' Project for the State of Kentucky ; F. Kevin Simon, editor ;
foreword by Thomas D. Clark.
    p.   cm.
Includes bibliographical references and index.
ISBN 0-8131-1997-9 (cloth : alk. paper). —ISBN 0-8131-0865-9
(paper : alk. paper)
    1. Kentucky. 2. Kentucky—Guidebooks. 3. Automobile travel—
Kentucky—Guidebooks. I. Simon, F. Kevin, 1952- . II. Title.
F451.F45 1996
976.9—dc20   96-24751

Contents

Part I. Kentucky: The General Background

Part II. Cities and Towns

Part III. Highways and Byways

Part IV. Appendices

List of Illustrations

ix

III. *Architecture* 42

IV. *Industry: Transportation* 56

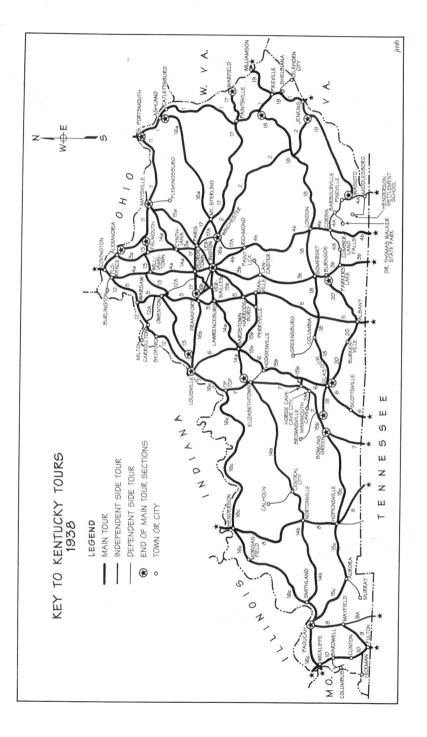

KEY TO KENTUCKY TOURS
1938

LEGEND

MAIN TOUR

INDEPENDENT SIDE TOUR

DEPENDENT SIDE TOUR

⊛ END OF MAIN TOUR SECTIONS

○ TOWN OR CITY

List of Maps

Foreword

THOMAS D. CLARK

The Great Depression of the 1930s caught Kentucky in a vulnerable moment. With the economy in a state of chaos, social and cultural conditions were undergoing transition from an intensely rural-agrarian society to a dawning urban age. A special survey committee in 1932 found the condition of Kentucky's schools "doleful," much of the state's population lived in geographical isolation, and in the eastern coalfields a virtual state of labor war existed. Altogether the Depression thrust upon the Commonwealth an all but impenetrable pall of frustration and defeat.

But changes were under way. The New Deal, largely through the Civilian Conservation Corps, was lowering barriers of isolation by building telephone lines and conditioning old carriage and wagon roads for use by the automobile and motor truck, weaving a web of improved highways. The last vestiges of the nineteenth-century system of toll roads and bridges were being erased. For the first time in Kentucky's history, a series of touring routes could be outlined and used by motorists. Tourism was becoming a significant social and economic force in Kentucky, as elsewhere in America. Portions of the Kentucky population that had been sealed away from the "outside" could now travel outward, and other Kentuckians could travel into hitherto inaccessible corners of the state.

In the midst of the fury that surrounded the creation of New Deal agencies in Washington, D.C, in the 1930s, someone proposed a project to aid the thousands of writers, artists, and photographers whose situation was desperate for lack of employment. Out of this idea grew the Federal Writers' Project of the Work Projects Administration (also known as the Works Progress Administration) and the proposal for a series of guidebooks for the forty-eight states and for many cities and towns.

No one in Washington, of course, had even a glimmer of an idea how many writers were "out there." In the case of Kentucky, the 1930s were a less than golden literary era. Elizabeth Madox Roberts of Springfield and Irvin S. Cobb of Paducah were near the end of their

xvii

productive years. In Louisville, Alice Hegan Rice and Eleanor Mercein Kelly were no longer writing. Younger writers, such as Jesse Stuart, Harriette Arnow, James Still, A.B. Guthrie, and Henry Hornsby, had not begun their serious writing careers. Not a half dozen historians were publishing. In fact, Kentucky was in the literary doldrums between a distinguished older era and the birth of a new one.

It was against this background that the proponents of the American Guide Series put forth their idea as a fitting public works project within the Federal Writers' Project. The Kentucky Writers' Project was placed under the direction of Dr. Urban R. Bell with the political blessings of Senator Alben Barkley and his ardent supporter, George Goodman, the Administrator of the Kentucky Work Projects Administration. Bell, a former Disciples of Christ minister, was the author of one or two published essays but of no books. Of those who worked under him, many had only limited writing and publishing experience. What the great majority of WPA "researchers" brought to their relief jobs were anticipation and energy. They came and went, gathering and recording bits of historical information and folklore wherever they could find them. Then as now, the miracle is that a book emerged from this tangle of good intentions.

The project's central office was located in Louisville, with a sub-office in Lexington. Bell assembled a skeleton staff of secretaries and began the task of selecting potential researchers and writers from the bulging WPA rolls. Meanwhile, from that covey of imaginative souls in Washington there poured forth, almost monthly, new ideas and directional changes displaying little realistic sense of the literary talent, latent or otherwise, "out there." Ultimately, the central objectives for the Writers' Project simmered down to gathering data on slavery and post-slavery times, collecting folklore and the history of local institutions, and creating guidebooks for the states, localities, and towns.

So far as I know, I am the only surviving contributor to the WPA guide to Kentucky. I was at the time director of the Kentucky Historical Records Survey, a sister endeavor. Both projects were administered and financed from the central office. Thus it was that I became involved in the Writers' Project and the guidebook.

The actual writing of the book was done largely by university professors, newspaper reporters, and others with special knowledge of Kentucky. It would now be challenging to identify all the contributions made by non-WPA writers. Those of the WPA researchers and writers are found mostly in the tour sections and in the companion books on Louisville, Lexington, and Breathitt County. No doubt they contributed many of the anecdotal and personal vignettes that appear in these volumes.

The research and writing of the guide consumed an inordinate amount of time, survived the onslaught of a veritable flood of instructions and counterinstructions from Washington, and required the expenditure of vast amounts of human energy. But at last, in 1939, the text was ready for publication. Dr. Bell delivered the manuscript to the president of the University of Kentucky, Dr. Frank L. McVey, who in turn instructed me to read it and make sure it contained nothing that would embarrass the university.

Certainly the text was innocuous enough with the exception of a section describing, in nauseating detail, a spitting contest on a Maysville sidewalk. It was defended as a colorful bit of local folklore, but our insistence that it be deleted prevailed.

The only other controversy arose when Henry Youtsey of Covington called on President McVey to demand that his name not be mentioned in the book. Youtsey had served several years in prison for conspiracy to assassinate Governor William Goebel in 1900, but by the 1930s he was active in church affairs in his community. Although the Goebel tragedy was mentioned several times in the book, Youtsey's name was not, so his fears were groundless.

Rereading this almost forgotten guidebook after the passage of six decades amounts to a vicarious journey into another age. In a sense, its publication in 1939 was a lifting of the curtain of despair that had enveloped the state to reveal a brighter and perhaps more prosperous future. For all Kentuckians with even a glimmer of interest in the past, republication of this volume opens vistas on a Kentucky that was still largely agrarian in both economy and cast of mind. In its pages, one can again journey over narrow roads and come upon toll gates along the way and at stream crossings; find main roads and streets lined with country hotels, drug stores, and soda fountains; discover honest-to-goodness hardware stores where one could buy a good pocket knife or a wagon and mule. This was a time when commercial drummers representing the great wholesale houses of Louisville, Cincinnati, and St. Louis still swarmed through the countryside, and when, through a touch of romance on the part of the Postal Service, fourth-class post offices still stood at every crossroads cluster of homes.

The guide to Kentucky, like the other state guidebooks, is definitely dated. Therein lies its merit. Running like threads through the text and the photographic illustrations are local historical clichés that in themselves constitute important documentation of an age when the Kentucky mind was turning to politics, economics, institutional status, and some frustration with the social and cultural levels of the Commonwealth—a revealing gauge of the social and physical conditions in that "other Kentucky."

The files of the Writers' Project may yet be dredged for clearer insights into the Great Depression era. Certainly this has been the case with the information on slavery and folklore. Ultimately the WPA writers and researchers may have been important largely as gleaners of fugitive information about Kentucky's people, their folklore, traditions, and customs, and even their trivia. Collectively the gatherings of notes, stories, and factual and hearsay materials give a distinctive dimension to that moment of Kentucky's travail. The files await full exploitation by more mature researchers with broader perspectives who will be able to draw out the kernels of fact and to realize more fully the dream of those who established the Federal Writers' Project.

The WPA guide to Kentucky, if not a landmark in local literary history, is a documentary guide to past sights and scenes. For me, reading it again after all these years has been a sentimental journey back into a seminal moment of history.

Introduction

It is now sixty years since work began on the WPA guide to Kentucky. In 1939, after three years of preparation, the volume appeared in bookstores across the Commonwealth. Produced as part of the Federal Writers' Project's American Guide Series, the *Guide* offered knowledgeable insights to Kentucky's history and peoples, informative profiles of the state's leading cities, attractive photographs, and detailed driving tours across the Kentucky countryside. The first printing of the 489-page book sold out quickly. Demand proved steady, and subsequent editions kept the book in print well into the 1940s. This public response lent credence to a reviewer's claim that "the book is a worthy contribution [to Kentuckiana] and will long be appreciated."[1]

The passage of time has not dulled the appeal of the Kentucky guidebook. Its original allure endures, enhanced by the book's importance as a chronicle of Kentucky at mid-century. The book's pictures, narrative, and descriptions comprise a fascinating window on the past. That past, though ever more distant, has yet to vanish completely. Despite more than a half-century of demographic change and commercial development, the Kentucky countryside still greets the traveler's eye much as it did in the 1930s. Likewise, familiar landmarks abound throughout the colorful descriptions of the state's towns and agricultural regions. Perhaps most striking is the lasting relevance of many of the guidebook's motor tours. The interstate highway system bypassed much of the state, leaving Kentucky's rural routes and surrounding countryside to pass the decades relatively untouched by the ravages of time and the effects of modernization. Hence, the inveterate traveler of Kentucky's back roads will find the *Guide* a superb escort to a Commonwealth at once contemporary and unmistakably reminiscent of an earlier time.

As Kentucky writers began their labors in a state wracked by the Great Depression, few anticipated the lasting interest their work would generate. The Federal Writers' Project was, first and foremost, a unique relief program created in 1935 as part of the Works Progress Administration (WPA). Indeed, the Federal Writers' Project was but one component in a group of projects that became known as Federal

One. Federal One, or Federal Project One as it was alternatively known, was comprised of the Federal Music Project, the Federal Theater Project, the Federal Art Project, the Historical Records Survey, and the Federal Writers' Project. These programs promoted culture through work relief for people involved in the arts. Within months of Federal One's creation, thousands of jobless artists eagerly abandoned relief rolls for gainful employment in creative activities sponsored by the federal government.

President Franklin D. Roosevelt named Harry Hopkins to head the WPA. Chief among Hopkins's assistants were two southerners, Aubrey Williams of Alabama and Ellen S. Woodward of Mississippi; both proved ardent supporters of Federal One programs. The Federal Writers' Project itself was directed by New Yorker Henry G. Alsberg, a former theater producer and newspaper journalist. Shortly after assuming his duties Alsberg exulted that "for the first time in the history of the United States writers are working for the government as writers."[2] The *New York Times* later agreed, saying, "The result will be the greatest collection of source material on the United States in existence plus a living for some thousands of writers."[3] By April 1936, Alsberg directed more than 6,600 writers, of whom approximately 40 percent were women. Ultimately, they produced more than a thousand books and pamphlets. Most of these writers toiled in state writers' projects.

The Connecticut Writers' Project developed what came to be regarded as the prototype guidebook. Based on Connecticut's early efforts, American Guide Series editors adopted a format to be followed by each of the state writers' projects; Kentucky was no exception. Each state book was divided into three distinct sections. The first section offered detailed essays describing a state's history, folklore, social life, racial and ethnic groups, geology, economy, and geography. The second section, often the briefest in the more rural southern states, presented descriptions of the state's leading cities and towns. The carefully annotated motor tours in section three became a trademark of the series. The tours augmented a descriptive text, making it a veritable Baedeker to a particular state. This popular segment concluded most guidebooks, though some added a brief chronological list of significant events in state history.

The Kentucky Writers' Project was directed by Dr. Urban R. Bell. A native of Paducah, Bell oversaw a staff of about fifty researchers, writers, editors, and photographers. Their work operated on three levels. At the local level as many as one hundred field workers took photographs, interviewed Kentuckians, and gathered research material. State workers, headquartered in Louisville, revised and condensed the material into a draft volume. The draft was forwarded to Washington for final editing prior to publication. By the time this volume was completed in 1939, federal funding no longer existed to publish the book. The University of Kentucky thereupon assumed sponsorship of the project. President Frank McVey's foreword in the original edition underscored the university's pride in associating itself with Kentucky's contribution to the series.

McVey's faith was not misplaced. The American Guide Series made a lasting contribution to American letters and cultural life, while nurturing the talents of many notable writers. Nowhere did this effort prove more successful than in the South. In some southern states, guidebook editors turned to established writers for contributions. Virginia's Douglas Southall Freeman and Kentucky's Thomas D. Clark made important contributions to their states' guidebooks. Though no memorable novelist emerged from the Kentucky Writers' Project, important southern authors came to the fore elsewhere. Notable in this group were Louisiana's Lyle Saxon, North Carolina's Paul Green, Arkansas's Vance Randolph, Florida's Zora Neale Hurston, and Mississippi's Eudora Welty. Interestingly, Welty contributed photographs, rather than prose, to the Mississippi guidebook. Despite Henry Alsberg's urgent pleas for the inclusion of African Americans in the state writers' projects, southern editors often resisted in accordance with the region's prevailing social mores. Hurston, a prominent figure in the Harlem Renaissance, was a significant exception. Southern African Americans such as Ralph Ellison, Richard Wright, and Arna Bontemps participated in the Federal Writers' Project but did so as part of programs outside their native region.[4]

The Federal Writers' Project was but one of many New Deal programs with direct ties to thousands of Kentucky's citizenry. Prominent Kentuckians also were closely associated with New Deal matters. Senator Alben W. Barkley championed the New Deal throughout the period; from 1938 on the Paducah native shepherded significant legislation through Congress in his capacity as Senate majority leader. Kentucky's delegation to the U.S. House of Representatives included many ardent New Dealers, none more so than Louisa's Fred M. Vinson. As United States solicitor general, Maysville's Stanley Reed consistently argued the legality of key New Deal programs before the United States Supreme Court. In 1938, President Roosevelt named Reed to the

Supreme Court. At the White House, Marvin "Mac" McIntyre of La
Grange served as FDR's appointments secretary, while Bourbon
County's Edward F. Prichard Jr. assisted as an important though lower
ranking New Deal advisor. Robert Worth Bingham, publisher of the
Louisville Courier-Journal, threw his paper's support behind the New Deal
while offering significant financial contributions to Roosevelt's
presidential bids. For his editorial and financial support, Bingham
received the coveted appointment of ambassador to the Court of St.
James's. Without question, Kentuckians exerted distinct influences on
New Deal policies.

Those policies were made manifest in every part of the Commonwealth. Road and building construction could be found in all Kentucky counties. The Civilian Conservation Corps planted trees and
undertook erosion projects throughout Appalachia. Murals painted
by federally employed artists adorned public buildings throughout the
state. TVA projects arose in western Kentucky. Rural electrification
benefited hundreds of thousands of Kentuckians.[5] Farmers and urban laborers alike felt the impact of the New Deal as unemployment
declined and incomes rose. This, then, was the context in which the
WPA guide to Kentucky appeared.

Underpinning all New Deal programs was the crucial element of
hope. New Deal leaders, especially President Roosevelt, never ceased
to reassure Americans that action would alleviate suffering and despair, thereby creating favorable conditions in which the nation's in-
herent greatness would ultimately prevail. The American Guide Series
was an ideal expression of that outlook. The books prompted Americans to learn more about their country and encouraged them to take
to the roads for a first-hand look.

The WPA, and along with it the Federal Writers' Project, came to an
end in 1943. The exigencies of World War II demanded that precious
resources be expended in other areas. Still, the FWP proved a durable
achievement. It nurtured important writers, employed thousands of
deserving Americans in productive pursuits in a time of need, and
produced works of lasting value. The American Guide Series fulfilled
its mission by creating guidebooks for all forty-eight states and
numerous cities, counties, and towns. When President Roosevelt
formally ended all WPA projects, he commended its work and extended
it an "honorable discharge" from government service.[6]

Decades later there is still much to be learned from this guidebook
to the Bluegrass state. This reprint edition is an exact reproduction of

the 1939 three-part text. It carries with it the prose style of the day, and some of its social views bear the unmistakable marks of an era gone by. Importantly, the guide is a tangible expression of the past, a vivid snapshot in time that beckons today's Kentuckians. For many, it represents a Kentucky that persists in living memory. For others, it recounts a time in which parents or grandparents grew to adulthood. Whether read in a comfortable easy chair or from behind the wheel of an automobile, the WPA guide to Kentucky continues to offer readers an enchanting, informative view of a state and its people that have grown more fascinating with the passage of time.

F. KEVIN SIMON

NOTES

1. *Journal of Southern History* 7 (Nov. 1941): 580.

2. Jerre Mangione, *The Dream and the Deal: The Federal Writers' Project, 1935-1943* (New York: Avon, 1972), 97.

3. *New York Times,* November 10, 1938.

4. John Egerton, *Speak Now against the Day: The Generation before the Civil Rights Movement in the South* (New York: Knopf, 1994), 99.

5. For a detailed discussion of the New Deal in the Commonwealth, see George T. Blakey, *Hard Times and New Deal in Kentucky, 1929-1939* (Lexington: University Press of Kentucky, 1986).

6. "Final Report on the W.P.A. Program, 1935-1943," Box 309, Records of the WPA in Kentucky, Kentucky Department of Libraries and Archives, Frankfort.

Preface

A commonwealth, in its most vital aspects, expresses itself through its people, whose characteristics distinguish but do not separate them from their neighbors. The differences need not necessarily be ethnic, but it is likely that speech and customs and points of view may be traced to an ancestry, itself marked and enduring. This is evidently the case with the people of Kentucky. It is not by idle chance that they admit with pride, sometimes with arrogance, that they are not the same as those who face them on the northern side of the Ohio River.

It follows that a guidebook to Kentucky should be something more than pages devoted to its natural wonders, climate, products, and history. It should seek to catch that spirit, indefinable but very real, which has transformed Stephen Foster's "My Old Kentucky Home" into something like a national ballad, poignant and tender, with personal appeal for Kentuckians. To retain that atmosphere, to make the Kentuckian, his land, and his background more understandable to those outside the State, has been one endeavor in the present volume. Another, and perhaps more useful purpose, has been to tell the Kentuckian himself of the natural resources that are his heritage, to invite him to take stock, as it were, of the opportunities which lie at his door.

But the State is well worth the attention of the visitor who travels to enjoy and to learn. It is primarily rural, and its one large city, Louisville, lies on the northern boundary. It has its "rocks and rills" of surpassing beauty, the remains of an untamed wilderness. It is for this reason most of all that this book, like its forty-seven companions, includes numerous meticulously detailed tours through the State, carefully traveled and checked for accuracy. This section of the Guide should be helpful to visitors and instructive for stay-at-homes.

The research and the industry which have gone into this work, cannot be too gratefully acknowledged. The book is submitted with modesty, and also with intimate satisfaction in the co-operation without which it could never have been completed.

Specialists, many of whom volunteered their services, read and criticized all copy prepared by the editorial staff; in some cases they prepared the more technical articles. State representatives, formally appointed by several organizations, have been consulted in the preparation of the Guide. These include the Kentucky Chapter of the American Institute of Architects, the Association of American Railroads, and the National Bus Traffic Association with the concurrence of the National Association of Motor Bus Operators, and the American Hotel Association.

The editors acknowledge with gratitude the help given by specialists in various fields: Rexford Newcomb, Dean of the College of Fine Arts and Applied Design, University of Illinois, who wrote the article *Kentucky Architecture;* T. D. Clark, Department of History, University of Kentucky, for the article *Kentuckians, Who and What They Are;* C. J. Bradley and S. E. Wrather, Department of Agriculture, University of Kentucky; Grant C. Knight, Department of English, University of Kentucky; Frank T. McFarland and Hansford T. Shacklette, Department of Botany, University of Kentucky; Gordon Wilson and L. Y. Lancaster, Western Kentucky State Teachers College; H. J. Thornton, editor of the Louisville *Board of Trade Journal;* Andrew K. Rule, Presbyterian Theological Seminary, Louisville; and Kincaid Herr, associate editor, *L. & N. Magazine.*

Acknowledgment for assistance in securing and preparing material is also made to Joe Hart, Louisville *Courier-Journal;* C. W. Jackson, Louisville Central Negro High School; M. E. Ligon, Department of Education, University of Kentucky; Neil Plummer and Victor Portmann, Department of Journalism, University of Kentucky; Edward W. Rannells, Department of Art, University of Kentucky; Lucien Beckner, formerly a member of the State staff of the Federal Writers' Project; Adele Brandeis, State Director of the Federal Art Project; the Standard Printing Company, publisher of *Mammoth Cave and the Cave Region of Kentucky,* for permission to use material; David W. Maurer, Department of English, University of Louisville; Preston Hinebaugh, Ohio Horse Breeders' Association; and Donald Kays, Department of Animal Husbandry, Ohio State University. Many others, too numerous to list, have assisted in various ways.

It is our hope that the interest and pride that all have taken in the preparation of the Kentucky *Guide* will be justified.

U. R. BELL,
State Director

General Information

Railroads: Baltimore & Ohio R.R. (B&O); Chesapeake & Ohio Ry. (C&O); Cleveland, Cincinnati, Chicago & St. Louis Ry. (Big Four, N. Y. Central System); Chicago, Indianapolis & Louisville Ry. (Monon Route); Frankfort & Cincinnati R.R. (F&C); Flemingsburg & Northern R.R. (F&N); Illinois Central R.R. (IC); Louisville & Nashville R.R. (L&N); Mobile & Ohio R.R. (M&O); Nashville, Chattanooga & St. Louis Ry. (NC&St.L); Pennsylvania R.R. (PRR); Southern Ry. (Southern) *(see Transportation map).*

Bus Lines: Blue Ribbon Lines, Gibbs Bus Line, Greyhound Lines, Meadors & Allen, Mohawk Stages, and Southern Limited furnish scheduled interstate service. Many other lines furnish intrastate service.

Air Lines: American Airlines (Cleveland, Fort Worth, Los Angeles); Eastern Airlines (Chicago, Miami) *(see Transportation map).*

Highways: Fifteen Federal highways. Even numbers run east and west; US 60 is transcontinental. Odd numbers run north and south. State highway patrolled. Gas tax 6¢. *(See State map for routes.)*

Motor Vehicle Laws (digest): Maximum speed, 40 m.p.h., not enforced; greater speed permitted when practicable; residential sections and curves, 20 m.p.h.; congested areas, 15 m.p.h. No licenses required for nonresidents over 16 yrs. of age provided driver has a home State license. Hand signals must be used.

Warning: Persons charged with operating motor vehicles in Louisville while drunk or under the influence of liquor upon conviction will be fined $19 and sentenced to nine days' imprisonment. From such penalties the law allows no appeals, age, sex, color or social pretensions notwithstanding. Sternly enforced.

Prohibited: Operation of automobiles by persons under 16 yrs. of age unaccompanied by person over 21 yrs. of age. Parking on highways (*see General Information for large cities for local traffic regulations*).

Recreational Areas and Accommodations: Mammoth Cave National Park (*see Tours 7 and 6*): two new modern hotels, rates from $1; guides compulsory, available day and night, fee of $2 covers admission, no tax; open all year; temperature in cave remains 54° F. throughout year. Cumberland Falls State Park (*see Tours 3 and 4*), open May 15–Oct. 1, overnight camping, 25¢; State-owned DuPont Lodge, rate per day from $2; Moonbow Inn, per day from $1.50; 15 cabins, rate per day per couple $2, 75¢ for extra lodgers; modern conveniences. Butler Memorial State Park (*see Tour 12*), May 15–Oct. 1, boating on Lake Butler 25¢; fishing 25¢; overnight camping 25¢; cabins. Columbus-Belmont State Park (*see Tour 10*): recreational facilities and cabins. Levi Jackson Wilderness Road State Park (*see Tour 4*): overnight camping 25¢; fishing and swimming 25¢; cabins, picnic grounds, camping, all improvements. Pine Mountain State Park (*see Tour 4A*): open-air auditorium, picnic grounds, observation tower. Natural Bridge State Park (*see Tour 2*): Hemlock Lodge, cabins, auto bridge. Audubon Memorial State Park (*see Tours 8 and 16*): shelter houses, picnic tables, tearoom and lake. Dawson Springs State Park (*see Tour 14*): picnic grounds, trails, shelter house. Blue and Gray State Park (*see Tour 20*): golf links, cabins, shelter houses, picnic tables and ovens, lake. Pioneer Memorial State Park (*see Tours 5 and 15*): museum, cabins in the fort, Lincoln Chapel. Blue Licks Battlefield State Park (*see Tour 15*): overnight camping 25¢, museum, open-air auditorium, trails. Cumberland National Forest: 992,605 acres; camps. Admission to recreational areas, adults 10¢, children 5¢, except Pioneer Memorial State Park—adults 25¢, children 10¢ and Blue Licks Battlefield State Park—adults 15¢, children 5¢; Cumberland National Forest, no charge.

General Accommodations: Few in eastern Kentucky except in larger towns; adequate elsewhere in State.

General Service for Tourists: AAA in larger towns, also *Courier-Journal* in Louisville. When road conditions are doubtful, information should be obtained at nearest filling station, especially in eastern Kentucky.

Poisonous Snakes and Plants: Rattlesnakes, copperheads, and cottonmouth moccasins are uncommon except in southern and northwest section of the State and in cypress swamps. Poison ivy and poison sumac common in wooded areas.

Climate and Equipment: Summer travelers should be prepared for very warm weather, especially in July and August. Spring days are intermittently cool and warm, with frequent showers and late snow flurries. Topcoats needed. Winters generally cold, with heavy frosts and sometimes snow. In mountainous areas the snow glazes into dangerously slippery ice and extreme caution is necessary, especially on the north side of hills. Frozen dirt edges of mountain roads should be avoided.

Fish and Game Laws (digest): Game fish defined as black bass, trout, crappie, rock bass or goggle-eye.

Open Season for Fishing: All months except May.

Fishing License: Nonresident, $2.50. Seven-day nonresident fishing, $1.

Limits: Black bass and trout limit, 10 per day, not more than 20 in possession at one time; unlawful under 11 in. Crappie limit 15 per day; not more than 30 in possession at one time; unlawful under eight in.

Open Season for Hunting (dates inclusive): Quail, Nov. 24–Jan. 9; wild turkey and imported pheasant protected at all times, no open season; doves, 12 M. to 6 P.M., Sept. 1–Dec. 15; woodcock, Nov. 15– Dec. 31; jacksnipe, wild duck, and wild geese, State law in conflict with Federal regulations—comply with Federal regulations. English sparrows, great horned owl, sharp-shinned hawk, crow and crowblackbird, not protected; deer and elk protected at all times, no open season; rabbit, Nov. 25–Jan. 9; squirrels, Aug. 1–Nov. 1; woodchuck or ground hog, not protected; beaver, raccoon, mink, otter, skunk and opossum lawful to kill Nov. 15–Dec. 31.

Hunting License: Nonresident, $10.50. Resident, $1.00.

Limits: Quail, 12 per day, season limit 75, penalty for violation $15 to $50 per quail; doves, 15 per day; woodcock, 6 per day, not over 24 in possession at one time.

Calendar of Events

(nfd means no fixed date)

Jan.	4th Mon.	Princeton	Farm Bureau Meeting
	nfd	Louisville	Band and Orchestra Clinic
	nfd	Louisville	Louisville Art Association Exhibition
Feb.	3rd Mon.	Mayfield	Mule Day
Mar.	4th Mon.	Murray	Mule Trading Day
Apr.	nfd	Bowling Green	Academic Music Festival
	nfd	Louisville	Physical Education Festival
	nfd	Louisville	Boy Scout Circus
	nfd	Louisville	Easter Monday Charity Ball
	nfd	Louisville	Junior League Fashion Show
	nfd	Louisville	Kentucky Education Association Meeting
	nfd	Louisville	State Spelling Bee (in connection with K. E. A. meeting)
	nfd	Lexington	Keeneland Races
	nfd	Morehead	Foster Festival
	nfd	Murray	Academic Music Festival
	last wk or 1st wk of May	Louisville	Spring Meet at Churchill Downs
May	1st Sun.	Scottsville	Allen County Singing Convention
	1st wk	Lexington	University of Kentucky Garden Day
	2d wk	Louisville	Kentucky Derby Festival
	2d Sat.	Louisville	Kentucky Derby, Churchill Downs
	4th Sun.	Benton	Old Southern Harmony Singing Festival

May	30	Paducah	Boy Scout Circus
	nfd	Kentucky	State Federation of Music Clubs Meeting
	nfd	Bowling Green	Music Festival
	nfd	Lexington	High School Music Contests
	nfd	Louisville	Garden Tours
	nfd	Louisville	Kennel Club Spring Show
	nfd	Pineville	Music Festival and Band Concert
	late May or early June	Pineville	Mountain Laurel Festival
June	7	Frankfort	Boone Day Celebration
	12	Springfield	Lincoln Marriage Festival
	15	Parksville	"Blessing of the Berries" (festival in connection with the raspberry crop)
	2d Sun.	Near Ashland	American Folk Song Festival: Traipsin' Woman's Cabin
	nfd	Covington	Latonia Races
	nfd	Paducah	Strawberry Producers' Revel
	nfd	Beaver Dam	Strawberry Carnival
	nfd	Louisville	Annual Board of Trade Outing
July	4	Bardstown	Stephen Collins Foster Festival
	16	Harrodsburg	Kentucky Pioneer Memorial Celebration
	2d or 3d wk	Louisville	Boat Regatta
	nfd	Louisville	State Tennis Tournaments
Aug.	nfd	Crestwood	Kavanaugh Camp Meeting
	nfd	Louisville	Fall Market Week
	nfd	Near Henderson	Dade Park Races
Sept.	2d or 3d wk	Louisville	State Fair, State Fair Grounds
	last wk	Quicksand	Fall Festival
	nfd	Louisville	Junior League Fashion Show

Sept.	nfd	Middlesboro	Tri-State Fair
	nfd	Stanford	Historical Pageant
Oct.	1st wk	Louisville	No-jury Exhibition of Fine and Practical Arts (for Kentucky and Southern Indiana)
	1st Sun.	Scottsville	Allen County Singing Convention
	last wk	Louisville	Fall Meet at Churchill Downs
	nfd	Barbourville	Dahlia Show
	nfd	Lexington	Annual Trotting Races
Nov.	11	Louisville	Armistice Day Parade and Celebration
	last wk	Lexington	Tobacco Festival
Dec.	nfd	Louisville	Associated Industries of Kentucky Meeting
	nfd	Richmond	Oratorio Music Festival

Part I

Kentucky: The General Background

KENTUCKIANS

KENTUCKY is far from being a unified region. Though known as the Bluegrass State, it divides into three sections which differ as sharply in geography, culture, economic activity, and social habit as if they were widely separated areas. These are the Bluegrass, the Eastern Mountains, and Western Kentucky. Each is populated by people who have adjusted themselves to their environment, and who in the process have developed habits and attitudes differing markedly from those of their fellows in the other divisions. Literature concerning Kentucky often fails clearly to identify the section which forms its locale, and readers unacquainted with local conditions are apt to mistake a single section for the State as a whole.

Except for Louisville, Kentucky has no large industrial centers. Most of its 2,900,000 people dwell in small rural communities. Like other agrarian folk they bear the mark of their association with the soil. The rural Kentuckian, whether clad in faded overalls or imported woolens, is an individualist. The rustic lolling at the street corners of towns and villages may give every evidence of being lost or out of place; but try to get the better of him in a trade and often he will prove master of the situation. He may be ragged, dirty, and ignorant, but he is still endowed with something of the unawed self-reliance and resourceful wit of the pioneer.

Wherever a Kentuckian may be, he is more than willing to boast of the beauties and virtues of his native State. He believes without reservation that Kentucky is the garden spot of the world, and is ready to dispute with anyone who questions the claim. In his enthusiasm for his State he compares with the Methodist preacher whom Timothy Flint heard tell a congregation that "Heaven is a Kentucky of a place." After describing the material and cultural well-being of the State, the Kentuckian is likely to begin on its brilliant history. But, unless he is engaged in historical research, the native son's history of Kentucky does not chiefly refer to the part played by the State in the westward expansion of the Nation, to the frontier democracy established by pioneer

3

statesmen on Kentucky soil, or to the State constitution that was framed at a time when it was difficult to gain majority approval for any act of polity. The native son has not pursued his subject through the trying decades of the nineteenth century, nor has he given much thought to the State's role in the twentieth. History, to him, centers on his family. When his ancestors crossed the Appalachians, the family was the core of community life, and the Kentuckian has never lost sight of the importance of his family attachment. His main personal concern is his family's welfare. Many Kentuckians, especially women, spend much time searching genealogical records, not to prove themselves descended from prominent persons, but from sheer love of becoming familiar with their personal pedigrees.

The Kentuckian's love of family is often illustrated in the way in which politicians elected to office give public jobs to their kinsmen. In many instances the victorious Kentucky politician honestly fails to understand why there is anything blamable in such conduct. When a kinsman needs a job, "nepotism" is only a word. And it is difficult to place a limit on a Kentuckian's sense of kinsmanship. Parents, grandparents, brothers, sisters, aunts, uncles, and cousins are part of any family pattern; but to the list of a Kentuckian's cousins there seems no end. There are not only first and second cousins; there are cousins even to the tenth degree removed. It is sometimes said that every mountaineer is related to every other mountaineer; but the same observation applies to a considerable extent to people everywhere in the State.

Next to his family, a Kentuckian's home community occupies the place of importance in his fancy. When viewed from a national standpoint the State itself is of major importance, but on his home ground a Kentuckian never forgets his native county. He may move to Lexington, Bowling Green, or Louisville during his mature years, but he continuously looks with reverence upon the place of his birth. Visitors to many Kentucky communities will be impressed in finding there some of the important relics of American history. Not only have local historians and anthropologists collected important historical relics, but they have also armed themselves with much historical information concerning their community's place in history. A traveler can, if he is lucky, locate the places where "D. Boon cilled a bar on this tree in 1760"; where John Fitch "invented" the steamboat; where Kit Carson was born; where Joseph Bruen built a locomotive; where the first railroad of the West was built; where scores of battles were fought; where

Abraham Lincoln and Jefferson Davis were born; where "Uncle Tom" was sold; where courthouses were scarred by bullets from feudists' guns, and innumerable other points of interest. All of this colorful background is grist to the local historians' mill, and it is used to good advantage.

The average Kentuckian may appear a bit confused in his knowledge of history, but he is firmly certain about current politics. Kentucky cannot claim first place in political importance, but it tops the list in its keen enjoyment of politics for its own sake. It takes the average Kentuckian only a matter of moments to dispose of the weather and personal health, but he never tires of a political discussion. Perhaps the most obvious thing about Kentucky politics is the fact that there it is a continuous campaign. Telegraph poles, fence posts, and trees are seldom free of political posters. It is not at all unusual to see campaign workers pulling the tacks out of old posters and using them in nailing up new ones. If politics ceased to be practical, Kentuckians would lose an excellent excuse for having community picnics, fried chicken dinners, and fish fries. Even the famed Kentucky burgoo would lose much of its flavor. Perhaps few indoor pastimes yield such keen enjoyment as predicting the future turn of political affairs.

Notwithstanding the fact that its white population, like that of most Southern States, is "Nordic," Kentucky's course in the Civil War was unlike that of the South in general. The State persisted in remaining neutral, while at the same time it contributed many soldiers to both the Northern and the Southern armies. When the war ended, Kentucky was left in a sharply divided state of mind. Where other Southern States were unanimously Democratic, Kentucky's voters were divided between the Democratic and Republican parties. This division still prevails in varying degree, and at times lends an interesting complexion to State politics.

In matters of culture Kentucky has been forced, with other Southern States, to change its course completely. It was slow to adopt the idea of public education, and it was not until after the Civil War that the idea of common schools became thoroughly entrenched in the Kentucky mind. There was no real antagonism to this idea before the war, but a convincing precedent was lacking. When pioneer parents were rearing large families on the frontier, they accepted the idea that their family was solely their own responsibility, and that, if it was educated, they had to pay the bill individually. Even yet there is opposition to public schools on this ground. However, Kentucky has progressed to the point of accepting common schools as a necessity. Not only has the public school experienced its most progressive years since the war, but so, likewise, have institutions of higher learning. The University of Kentucky is a post-war institution, and so are teachers' colleges. During the past three decades the number of illiterates has been greatly reduced. Where communities were once denied the privilege of public education, they now have fairly well-equipped schools.

Where public schools have made rapid strides, other cultural agencies have thrived. Towns and villages are establishing libraries and are making available, through local and State agencies, literature which heretofore had been denied to isolated readers. There are several institutions engaged in collecting and preserving historical materials and Kentuckiana. These agencies are beginning to make up for the losses which Kentucky has experienced in the past. Never before have Kentuckians been so conscious of the cultural possibilities of their State.

Kentuckians have never neglected the pleasures of life. From the time when his forebears hunted through the woods by day and danced about the campfire at night, the Kentuckian has been a sporting, pleasure-loving individual. Following the Civil War, travelers through the State remarked that the trains were forever crowded with light-hearted passengers either going to, or coming from, a dance. Racing, baseball, and football have enjoyed considerable prestige. Horse racing is accepted as a matter of fact. When natives of other States see Kentuckians poring over racing forms on Saturday and crowding into churches on Sunday, it is hard for them to understand the apparent incongruity. Yet it is this devotion to both piety and pleasure which is, perhaps, the most distinguishing characteristic of the people of modern Kentucky.

NATURAL SETTING

KENTUCKY, lying on the western slope of the Alleghenies, is bounded on the north by the northern bank of the Ohio River, on the northeast and southeast by West Virginia and Virginia, on the south by Tennessee, and on the west by the Mississippi River. Its greatest length, east to west, is 425 miles; its greatest breadth 182 miles. The total area is 40,598 square miles, including 417 miles of water surface.

"A peculiar situation exists at the extreme southwest corner," the *U. S. Geological Survey Bulletin 817* states, "where, owing to a double bend in the Mississippi River, there is an area of about 10 square miles belonging to Kentucky that cannot be reached from the rest of the State without passing through a part of Missouri or Tennessee."

The State's topographic variations are mainly the result of slow or rapid erosion, according to the degree of resistance encountered in particular rock strata. The mountains in the sandstone region, the occasional deep gorges or underground drainage systems in the limestone area, and the swamp flats and oxbow lagoons in the far western part of the State, indicate the force, extent, and direction of erosive processes. Reelfoot Lake, in the far southwest, resulted from the earthquake of 1811–12. It is the only lake of importance in Kentucky, although the edge of the Highland Rim Plateau in the southwest is pocked with numerous small bodies of still water. These are sinkholes which have choked with vegetable matter and retained the water that drained into them.

The Ohio and Mississippi Rivers flow west and south, and form the State's main drainage channel. The Cumberland River, except for a small portion in the south-central region, the Big Sandy, the Licking, the Kentucky, the Green, the Tradewater, and the Tennessee Rivers follow the general northwest slope of the Allegheny Plateau. About 3,000 miles of river course are navigable.

Kentucky has six natural physiographic regions: (1) Mountain, (2)

Knobs, (3) Bluegrass, (4) Pennyrile, (5) Western Coal Field, and (6) Purchase.

The Mountain region, containing 10,450 square miles, is the remains of a great westerly sloping plateau which has been cut by streams into a region of narrow valleys lying between sharp ridges. The Cumberland and Pine Mountain ranges, near the southeastern border, are "erosion" mountains carved from the upturned edges of hard sandstone. Between them lies the Middlesboro Basin, in which are the State's highest mountains. Here are the Cumberland and Pine Mountain ranges, with the Little and Big Black Mountain ranges between. The highest point in the State is at Big Black Mountain, 4,150 feet above sea level, in Harlan County on the southeastern boundary line. To the west and northwest the mountain crests gradually lower until they merge with the uplands of the Bluegrass and the Pennyrile; the elevation drops from about 2,000 feet in the southeast to less than 800 feet along the western rim. The lowest point in the State is 257 feet above sea level, near Hickman in Fulton County, at the extreme southwest.

The larger streams in the Mountain region have some wide flood plains with alluvial and rock terraces. Wind gaps, such as Cumberland Gap, and the water gaps, like the Breaks of Sandy, are of frequent occurrence. The surface rocks are sandstones and shales, with practically no limestones. The valley soils are deep and yield excellent crops. Soils on the ridges are thin and easily washed away during cultivation.

The Knobs region is bounded on the inner side by the rolling Bluegrass downs, and on the outer by the escarpments at the edge of the mountain region in the east, and of the Pennyrile in the west. It has the appearance of an irregular plain out of which rise many erosive remnants of the Mountain and Pennyrile plateaus. The knoblike shapes frequently seen in these remnants have suggested the name of the region. The escarpments, also considered part of the Knobs, rise from 200 to 500 feet above the drainage and cover an area of about 2,200 square miles. The Kentucky and the Ohio Rivers are the only navigable streams here. The soils, composed largely of weathered shales, erode rapidly when cultivated, and for this reason large areas remain wooded. While not rich, they will yield good crops under proper cultivation. The larger part of the Cumberland National Forest lies in the eastern Knobs.

Within the encircling arms of the Knobs on one side, and the Ohio River on the other, lies the Bluegrass region, about 8,000 square miles

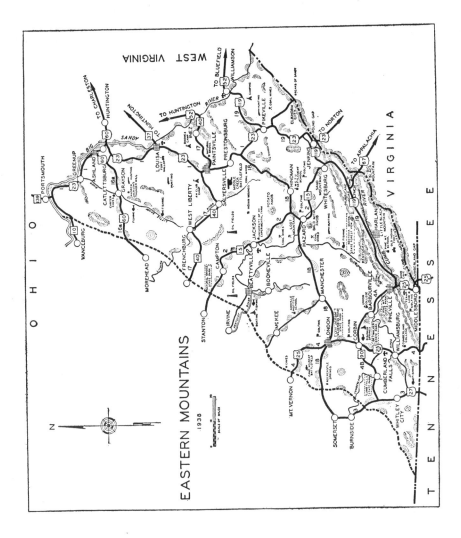

EASTERN MOUNTAINS

1938

SCALE OF MILES

in extent. It is a gently rolling upland, from 800 to 1,000 feet above sea level. Almost everywhere it is cleared of its original forests and is either cultivated or in pasturage. A few open, grass-swarded woodlands remain, especially around the more pretentious manors; and there are uncleared glens and dells where the smaller streams fall rapidly from the high downs to the main streams.

This region is divided into three sections, differentiated by their underlying Ordovician limestone: the inner Bluegrass, the Eden shale belt, and the outer Bluegrass. The first, about 2,400 square miles, has the richest soils due to the underlying limestones with their high phosphate content. Its surface is very gently rolling. The second, about 2,500 square miles, lies as a broad belt around the inner Bluegrass, and is underlain by limestone not so rich in phosphorus, and with a large shale and silica content. Its soils, while good, are easily eroded, producing steep slopes and V-shaped valleys. The third is like the first, but the soils on the whole are not quite so rich.

The large area lying at the southern end of the central plain, of which the Bluegrass region is the northern section, is known as the Pennyrile. Pennyrile takes its name from the local pronunciation of Pennyroyal, an annual plant of the mint family, which grows luxuriantly in this region. It comprises about 7,800 square miles, and is separated from the valleys of the western Knob and southern Mountain regions by an escarpment which, in the Knob area, is called Muldraugh's Hill. The eastern portions of the region rise 600 and 700 feet above sea level, but they drop gradually on the west to about 400 or 500 feet, as they approach the Purchase in the southwest and the western coal fields along the Ohio. The streams cut broad valleys except in the karst or sinkhole areas, where only the larger streams flow on the surface.

The scenery of the Pennyrile is varied from gently rolling farm lands to cliffs and scarps, and from open fields to forested rocky hillsides. The sinkhole part of the region was originally known as the Barrens, because the first settlers found it almost completely lacking in trees and were unable to discover water for themselves and their stock. The lack of trees was the result of continual forest burnings by the Indians to make grasslands upon which the buffalo might feed, and the water scarcity was caused by underground drainage. Neither condition resulted from any barrenness of soil. After white men gained control of the region, it was reforested.

Waters, either surface or underground, are abundant. In the underground drainage courses are thousands of miles of subterranean passages including Mammoth Cave. The soils are principally residual, varying from sandy and silt loams in the east to the limey, phosphorous soils in the west. Frequent coatings of loess or windblown deposits are found on the uplands, and alluvial clays or gravels along the Tennessee and Cumberland Rivers.

The Western Coal Field, an area of about 4,680 square miles, is bounded on the north by the Ohio River and elsewhere by the Pennyrile. The region is characterized by sandstone and wooded ridges, rock shelters, and cliffs. However, the proportion of level lands is so much greater that the Western Coal Field in some places resembles the prairie States. Some valuable timber remains and there are large areas in which second growth timbers are flourishing. On the uplands the soil is a yellow silt loam, thin where hilly, but deeper elsewhere. Transported soils cover the bottom lands.

The Purchase (2,569 square miles), so named from the fact that it was bought from the Chickasaw Indians, is bounded by the Tennessee, Ohio, and Mississippi Rivers, and the Tennessee State Line. The general topographic relief is the lowest in the State. Gently rolling uplands and wide flood plains are the rule along the larger streams. Stream bluffs, cypress swamps, oxbow lagoons, and an occasional deep erosive gully are common sights. The soft rocks of the region erode rapidly. Transported soils cover the Purchase except in a narrow strip, just west of the Tennessee River, where residual soils are found. Yellow-brown silt loam is prevalent.

The average annual rainfall in Kentucky is about 45 inches, which places the State within the humid belt—so important for agriculture and manufacturing. The climatic changes from north to south account for a difference of approximately one week in the growing seasons. Periods of excessive rainfall or drought are rarely great enough to effect serious damage to crops.

The climate of the whole State is temperate and healthful. The mean annual temperature is around 60° F. In the summer months it ranges from 75° F. in eastern Kentucky to 78° F. in the west; and in the winter around 36° F. in all sections. Temperatures of 100° F. are very rare, but marks of 80° F. and above have occurred even in midwinter. Below-zero temperatures occur with moderate frequency in December, January, and February, and −28° F. has been experienced twice in the eastern half during the past 60 years.

The last killing frosts generally occur from April 15 to 23 and the first from October 13 to 21. The growing season is from 174 to 189 days. In the eastern part of Kentucky the average number of rainy days is about 118 a year—5 to 9 in each of the fall months from September to November, inclusive, and 10 to 13 for each of the other months. The average number of rainy days in the west is about 104, of which the months from September to November inclusive have 5 to 8, and the other months from 8 to 12. Prevailing winds are from the south and southwest, with north and northwest winds frequent in winter. Seven to ten miles is the average hourly wind velocity.

Animal Life

The animal life of Kentucky is representative of areas as far apart as the marshes of Louisiana and the forests of New England and southern Canada.

Two large groups of fauna that once were common to the State have now disappeared: prehistoric, or Pleistocene mammals, skeletons of which have been found in various parts of the State but chiefly at Big Bone Lick in Boone County; and species that were killed off or driven away in the course of the settlement of the State. In the first class were mastodons, mammoths, giant wolves, beaver, elk, and moose. Early travelers and explorers were greatly impressed by the giant bones, and often wrote extravagant stories about them. Even more interest attaches to the animals that were almost fabulously plentiful when the settlers came. The bison, or buffalo, grazed the central plains of the Barrens and Bluegrass in numbers comparable with those of the Great Plains west of the Mississippi. It is thought that this species disappeared from the State about 1820, soon after the settlement of the Jackson Purchase. The beaver was less abundant here than farther north, but it survived in small numbers until a generation ago. Hairraising stories are still told about the panther or puma (locally called "painter"), once fairly common but now extinct in the State.

The wild turkey, still found in small numbers in remote places, particularly in the eastern mountains and other wooded sections, may be re-established in the State and National parks and the larger forests under proper protection. The area considered most suitable for this purpose in western Kentucky is the Coalings, a wild, wooded tract between the Tennessee and Cumberland Rivers, now taken over by the Federal Government.

Stories told about the passenger pigeon a hundred and more years ago sound impossible today although "pigeon roost" is found in place names in practically every part of the State. Alexander Wilson, in the Shelbyville area, estimated in 1810 that he saw millions of birds in one day. Audubon, in 1813, on his way to Louisville from Hardinsburg, counted 163 flocks in 23 minutes. Enormous areas in the various parts of the State were used by this species for nesting places. Wilson described one on the upper part of Green River, above the site of Greensburg; Audubon pictured another near the mouth of Green River not far from Henderson.

Another species, long a mark for hunters and therefore almost destroyed, was the Carolina Louisiana parrakeet, which the Audubon societies are protecting in the Everglades of Florida. In earlier days this beautiful little parrot was found in abundance around sycamore groves, salt licks, and fields of cockleburs. The ruffed grouse, hunted intensively from the very beginning of the settlement, still exists in small numbers. The prairie chicken, once found in many sections, disappeared after the Barrens and the Jackson Purchase were opened to settlement.

While game birds like the prairie chicken and the wild turkey soon became scarce around the settlements, most of the songbirds have increased enormously. In earlier days ravens also were common; now only the wildest areas of the mountains harbor them. The chimney swift and the nighthawk, on the other hand, have greatly profited by the coming of civilization. The swift, formerly nesting in hollow trees, has thoroughly adapted itself to chimneys, and the Kentucky Ornithological Society has no record of any nesting in trees within the memory of the present generation.

Almost 300 species of birds have been observed in Kentucky, most of them in land habitations. The great marsh country on the Kentucky-Tennessee border, north of Reelfoot Lake, is the breeding ground of American egrets, great blue herons, snakebirds, double-crested cormorants, and other waterfowl. Huge flocks of waterfowl pass over the State in their migrations, and can sometimes be seen on streams and ponds. On a "wet-weather lake" near Bowling Green, observers have counted 36 species of waterfowl.

Of the 150 to 175 species of birds found in Kentucky in an average year, about 15 are winter residents, including the white-throated and white-crowned sparrows, the slate-colored junco, the golden-crowned kinglet, and the yellow-bellied sapsucker. Numbered among the summer residents are the catbird, brown thrasher, bronzed grackle, crested flycatcher, Bachman and grasshopper sparrows, and Kentucky and yellow warblers. The shy warblers are represented by more than a dozen types that spend the summer here. The mockingbird, bluebird, cardinal, bluejay, Carolina chickadee, tufted titmouse, and towhee are among the 35 to 40 well known species that remain throughout the year.

The United States Bureau of Biological Survey states that "observers in the Mississippi Valley probably witness the passage of greater numbers of varieties of birds than can be observed in any other river valley of the world." The area south of the mouth of the Ohio River is part of the great wintering grounds of the waterfowl; the Ohio River from Louisville up as far as Catlettsburg is another concentration area. Ornithologists at the Falls of the Ohio, at Louisville, have recorded in recent years nearly all the species of waterfowl that visit the State. The migration routes follow the Ohio, Mississippi, and Tennessee Rivers; land birds, particularly the warblers, have another great route through central Kentucky, a little to the east of Mammoth Cave, along what the geologists call the Dripping Springs Escarpment.

Small mammals exist in surprisingly large numbers, especially in the rocky areas. Red and gray foxes, minks, muskrats, raccoons, opossums, red and gray squirrels, cottontail rabbits, marsh rabbits (in the Purchase), and hosts of smaller species are found nearly everywhere. In the Jackson Purchase the large marsh rabbit and an occasional otter are still seen and in central Kentucky the woodchuck is common. The caves are thickly populated with bats and many kinds of rodents.

Over a hundred species of fish have been found in Kentucky. Of the game fishes, the one most closely identified with Kentucky (particularly the Barren and Green River section) is the muskallonge, known locally as jackfish or jack salmon. Three of the bass group, the large- and small-mouth and the Kentucky, are found throughout the State. Many other fishes are widely distributed: the crappie, bluegill, rock bass, drumfish or white perch, red horse, white sucker, and buffalo. Two kinds of catfish—channel and blue—are often taken; some are very large specimens. Among the species of interest principally to ichthyologists are the eel, the spoonbill, the sturgeon, minnows of many

I. THE NATURAL SETTING

BREAKS OF SANDY

CUMBERLAND FALLS

CUMBERLAND GAP

KNOB COUNTRY

KENTUCKY RIVER PALISADES

SKYLINE NATURAL BRIDGE, CUMBERLAND NATIONAL FOREST

LOOKING UP THE OHIO TOWARD CLOVERPORT

THE KENTUCKY RIVER AT CAMP NELSON

ECHO RIVER IN MAMMOTH CAVE

GOTHIC AVENUE IN MAMMOTH CAVE

RUINS OF KARNAK IN MAMMOTH CAVE

CHIMNEY ROCK, NEAR DANVILLE

species, darters, and the several blind and semi-blind species of cave fish.

The efforts of the State game and fish commission to safeguard and restore wild life resources have met with much success. Stationed everywhere are vigilant wardens, who not only protect game, but also educate the people in the proper uses of woodland and streams.

The State has introduced deer, quail, and fish wherever conditions seem favorable, and the Federal Bureau of Fisheries maintains a station and breeding pond at Louisville, from which thousands of fish are distributed annually throughout the State. In eastern Kentucky the State has 12 game refuges where deer, bear, fur bearers, turkey, ruffed grouse, and quail are propagated; and two fish hatcheries where the species best adapted for the region are produced. In central Kentucky are 22 game refuges for upland game birds, pheasants, and fur-bearing animals, and one fish hatchery for black bass. The bass hatchery at Herrington Lake was one of the first to produce black bass under artificial conditions. In the near-famine years fish are seined from the overflowed lands in the Purchase and distributed where needed.

Amphibians, numerous and widely distributed, include the congo snake or blind eel (*Amphiuma means*), several species of waterdogs and salamanders, including the wicked-looking hellbender; bullfrogs, green frogs, leopard frogs, many varieties of tree frogs, and two species of toads. Common turtles are numerous, as are the alligator, snapping, soft-shelled, pond, and land varieties, and the well-known box or Carolina terrapin. Only four poisonous species of snake have been recorded: the timber rattler, copperhead, cottonmouth, and coral. Of these, the first two are widely distributed; the cottonmouth is apparently confined to the Purchase, and the coral, a southern species, is found only along the Tennessee border. Nonpoisonous snakes are much more plentiful. The blacksnake and its near relatives, the pine, the bull, and the chicken snake abound, and this is true also of the king snake and several species of water snakes. The brown or fence lizard, like the six line lizard or scorpion, is known everywhere. Less known are the several varieties of skinks and the fabulous glass or joint snake, which can shed its tail when attacked. All the lizards are useful and harmless. Several species of crawfish, clams, and snails are known to most fishermen and hunters.

Plant Life

Kentucky flora ranges from sub-boreal in the Eastern Mountains to semi-tropical in the Mississippi River bottoms. Each of the State's six topographic and geologic regions has its peculiar type of flora; and in each of these regions are minor floral divisions, resulting from variations in elevation, moisture, soils, exposure, and the work of man.

The most varied plant life occurs in the Eastern Mountains, where clearing and cultivation have not disturbed the native flora. Here are found the large-leafed rhododendron, azalea, blueberry, huckleberry, ferns in great profusion, and the magnolia. Throughout the highland region the rhododendron is at its loveliest in June; and in this month, over all the rockier parts of the mountains, the mountain laurel or calico-bush is in bloom. Perhaps the loveliest flower in the mountains is the great laurel, or mountain rosebay (*Rhododendron catawbaiense*), which covers hill and cliff with bell-shaped, rose-purple flowers, seen in full bloom only in the protected ravines of the Pine Mountains.

Four species of magnolia—the great-leafed, the small-leafed cucumber tree, the ear-leafed, and the umbrella tree—bloom in late May or early June. The waxy gloss of their leaves and their huge, but delicate, pure white, sweet-scented blossoms give them a tropical appearance. Again in the fall they catch the eye with their crimson seed cones.

An aberrant member of the magnolia family, the tulip tree, called yellow poplar in Kentucky, grows in all parts of the State. In May and June it produces dainty chalices of green, tinted with orange. Because of its value for lumber, the supply of larger specimens has been depleted.

In May and June the mountains bloom with trillium, bloodroot, bluebell, wildginger, dogtooth violet, sour-wood, firepink, mosspink, groundpink, violet, bluet, dogwood, crab apple, dwarf-iris, yellow and pink lady-slipper, and dozens of other species. From early summer to the first frosts, the long growing season brings from blossom to maturity the wild strawberry, serviceberry, haw, wild grape, persimmon, and papaw. Edible nuts for winter consumption include the

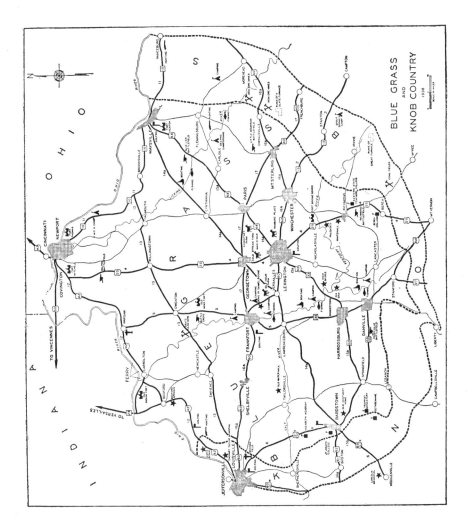

BLUE GRASS
AND
KNOB COUNTRY
1938

chestnut, chinquapin (both rare today), beechnut, hazelnut, walnut, and hickorynut.

Visitors to the Bluegrass region who expect to find the color of its famous grass blue in the summer months are disappointed. Only in May do the blue anthers of its blossoms give the grass a distinctly steel-blue tint. It grows luxuriantly in the limestone phosphorus soils of the Bluegrass region and sporadically in the limestone soils of the Pennyrile but does not prosper elsewhere. In its chosen habitat bluegrass is unequaled as turf and for pasturage, but it is rarely cut for hay. On many farms in central Kentucky it is grazed every month of the year.

Few untouched wild spots are left in the Bluegrass region. Park-like lawns and open, grassy woodland patches surround the farm houses; but along steep banks and in the deep dells much of the original flora of the region survives. Here, in spring, are hidden the purple trillium, springbeauty, dwarf-iris, pink catchfly, bloodroot, stonecrop, columbine, and ferns of every sort. Dogwood and redbud spread their lacy, tinted draperies over the vernal slopes. Later in the summer, purple, white, and blue asters and hosts of other blossoms cover the rocks and find foothold in every pinch of soil between them. In the fields and open places goldenrod vies with bridal-wreath aster in the autumn. Along the streams the artichoke, a sunflower with edible roots, and the goldenglow, very like the artichoke in size and color, cover the bottom lands and banks with gold. Tall purple composites, the ironweed and meadow beauty (deer grass), grace the open woodlands or low meadows.

In the Eden shale soils of the Bluegrass several species of red-haw flourish; these are white with blossoms in the spring, and in the fall are hung with the red berries that children string into long necklaces and belts. When unmolested the red-haw grows from ten to twenty feet high, but cattle browse it to the size of bushes, a fact that suggests their usefulness as hedges.

Old fields in the acid soils and even in the more alkaline soils of the Pennyrile are sometimes covered with clumps of broomsedge, a grasslike plant that grows green in the spring and brown in autumn. When growing thick, it looks like a field of grain and is eaten sparingly by the livestock. Farmers consider it a pest, however, and often burn over patches of the weed.

Everywhere are the climbing vines—grapes, wistaria, trumpetvine, Virginia creeper, and poison ivy. Poison ivy, which smothers fence posts along the highways, grows rankly wherever it finds support. Its three-fingered compound leaves, greenish flowers, and white berries are easily identified, especially in the morning when the plant is covered with dew.

Western Kentucky may be divided into two broad floral grounds: the upland division, represented by hill or knob land; and the lowland or river valley division. The upland flora, although more widely distributed, is less luxuriant than that of the lowland. Extensive ranges of oak forests cover many of the knobs, their rich green foliage making a shady habitat for herbaceous plants. Early spring bedecks these forests with the golden yellow buttercup, the toothwort, springbeauty, and the delicate rue anemone. The birdsfoot violet, the most beautiful native kind, often carpets a gravelly knoll.

Deep, moist ravines are canopied by sugar maple and beech, where the rich humus yields the trim wake-robin, in tones of brown and green, and the ever popular Indian turnip (Jack-in-the-pulpit). The bloodroot, bellwort, Solomon's-seal, Greek valerian, waterleaf, wild sweet William, butterfly weed, trout lily, numerous violets, and other plants furnish a continuous sequence of blossom in the spring. Perhaps the greatest beauty of these woods is at the flowering time of the dogwood and redbud, everywhere abundant.

In summer the dryness of the soil in this area reduces the number of flowering plants. For the most part, plants either make their growth and flower in the spring, or wait until the approach of autumn. Then the roadsides are bordered with goldenrod, the royal purple ironweed, and the sky-blue wild ageratum. Entire fields are covered with a sea of gold as the yellow tickseed comes into flower. Several species of asters herald the approach of frost, as the hills are transformed almost overnight into masses of glowing color.

The overflow lands of the lowland area support a tropical luxuriance of vegetation, particularly in the wooded parts. Trees attain a larger growth here than in the uplands. Nearly all the eastern North American oaks are represented, even the southern willow oak, and there are, in addition, several varieties of hickory (including the pecan), species of ash, besides the maple, willow, cottonwood, sycamore, sweetgum, blackgum, and many others. The picturesque river birch, with its thin, papery bark hanging in shreds, stands out in bold contrast to the smooth silver maples with which it often grows.

Early spring flowers are not abundant, but summer and fall bring a wealth of color as the Indian pinks, the milkweeds, ruellia, cardinal flower, great blue lobelia, spider lily, and aster and goldenrod come into

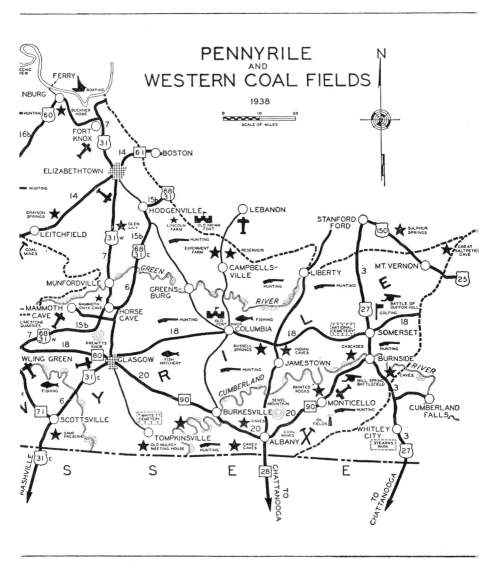

prolific flower. Marshy places are fringed with the swamp rose, halberd-leafed hibiscus, swamp privet, and button bush, and covered with yellow pond lily and lotus. The Ohio, Mississippi, and lesser rivers, by their meanderings, have formed numerous oxbow lakes that furnish ideal conditions for the spread of the bald cypress. These beautiful trees, with their "knees" protruding from the surface of the water, often cover large areas. Festoons of catbird grape hang from the lower branches and climb over the smaller shrubs, extending to the water's edge.

Kentucky lies in the great hardwood forest region between the Alleghenies and the western prairies. Before white settlement, three-fourths of the State was covered with forests unsurpassed in eastern North America for the size of individual trees and the density of the cover. Giants six, eight, and ten feet in diameter were not uncommon. The larger varieties were yellow poplar (tulip tree), sycamore, oak, chestnut, and walnut. It is told that some of the hollow sycamores were so large that families were known to have camped in them until they could build cabins. Today not over one-fourth of the State can be called forested and very little of this is primeval, nearly all having been cut over for timber.

Their attractiveness and the ease of settlement upon them led to the early clearing of limestone lands in the Bluegrass region. Today about 90 percent of these lands are denuded. The western limestone lands of the Pennyrile and the delta lands of the Purchase are about 30 percent forested. The most densely forested areas, amounting to 60 or 70 percent of the area, are in the valleys of the Big Sandy, Upper Licking, Kentucky, and Cumberland Rivers, all in eastern Kentucky. In the latter area the timber is chiefly composed of oak, chestnut, and yellow poplar; in the rest of the State it runs to oak and hickory, except along the lower Ohio and the Mississippi flood plains, where hardwoods peculiar to river bottoms prevail.

Kentucky's forests have brought their owners considerable wealth, but commercial exploitation was practically at an end by the close of the last century. Today the State's forests are still producing moderately, but not as they did when great sawmills stood on all the larger streams and logs by the millions floated down in the spring and fall freshets. As most of the steeper land in Kentucky is better adapted to the production of trees than to other uses, the tendency is to conserve forest stands and to cut the timber scientifically, but no thorough State-wide system of conservation has been adopted. Only in one or

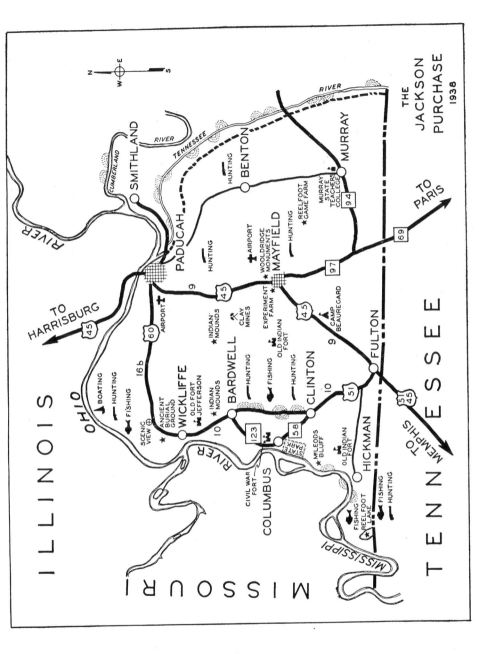

two small areas is reforestation being attempted, where some of the private landholding companies and individual owners have begun to reforest their cut-over lands. The establishment of the Cumberland National Park in eastern Kentucky offers the greatest promise of forest conservation. This park will contain over a million acres, of which much is forested, and the rest already is being replanted. The Federal example points to the necessity for a State forest policy that will increase timber resources, offer a measure of protection against the too rapid run-off of storm water, and restore the natural balance in wild life which reckless exploitation has destroyed.

Geology and Paleontology

The oldest outcropping rock formations in Kentucky are of the Mid-Ordovician period, an early division of the Paleozoic era, hundreds of millions of years ago when only the simplest forms of marine life existed. Cambrian rocks, those from the earliest period of the Paleozoic, are exposed nowhere in the State, but from a deep well drilled at Nicholasville in Jessamine County fossil remains of trilobites, small oval-shaped marine animals, known to have lived in the Cambrian, have been taken.

The Ordovician period, when shell-forming sea animals flourished, is well represented in both surface and subsurface formations. In the vast ocean covering this region lived sponges, corals, moss animals, brachiopods, sea lilies, chambered shells (cephalopods), primitive forms of snails (gastropods), clams (pelecyrods), and buglike creatures, the trilobites. Tiny gastropods, *Cyclora minuta,* were so numerous that their fossil remains in the limestone have been mined as phosphate rock. The lime and phosphorus of these shell-forming sea creatures account in large measure for the fertility of Kentucky soils, especially of the Bluegrass region, with which the Ordovician deposits are practically co-extensive. The limestone and shales of this area are estimated to be half a billion years old.

Through the massive limestone of Central Kentucky the Kentucky River and its tributary, the Dix River, have cut deep gorges. Gently rolling hills, occasional caverns, sinkholes, and countless springs are phenomena resulting from erosion and internal water drainage.

At the beginning of Silurian time—following the Ordovician age and lasting a relatively brief twenty-five million years—an ancient sea invaded Kentucky from the Gulf of Mexico, permitting the immigration of southern types of corals, crinoids (a class to which sea lilies belong), and simple shellfish. About the middle of that age the waters of the North Atlantic invaded the area, bringing many new forms. In this complex of older life forms and newer developing ones are found chain corals, honeycomb corals, cup corals, and organ-pipe corals —all named for peculiarities of shape, crinoids of many kinds, and new species of shellfish. Trilobites were on the decline and disappeared during the Pennsylvanian period.

The limestones of the Devonian, the next period, have preserved about the same number of genera of corals, crinoids, and brachiopods as are found in the Silurian. Cephalopods, with chambered shells, and the mosslike and branching bryozoans are common. During this age, which is marked by the rise of fishes and the appearance of amphibians, there were sharks in Kentucky's waters; the ostracoderm, a great fishlike creature, has left its remains. The oldest known land flora also made its appearance on Devonian lands.

Considerably more than a fourth of Kentucky is underlaid by limestones, shales, and sandstones of the Mississippian system. These formations date from the beginning of the Carboniferous period, which was to last somewhat over one hundred million years and exhibit a flora of primitive scale trees, tree ferns, huge mosses, early forms of flowering plants and, from this world of luxuriant vegetation, the development of amphibians. Among the new creatures was a genus called Archimedes, so named from its resemblance to the screw of Archimedes. From the stem of this living screw, lacy curtains extended, inhabited by thousands of microscopic bryozoan animals. Fossils of the decorative Pentremites, the so-called fossil "hickory nut," are found in abundance in some of the limestones in the Pennyrile. Fossil sharks' teeth are the only evidence of vertebrates of the period in Kentucky.

The limestones of the Mississippian period are responsible for the odd feature of the landscape known as the Land of Ten Thousand Sinks, with its extensive subterranean drainage. From the evidence of existing river channels, cutting deeply through Mississippian strata and subsequently filled with sandstone of the Pennsylvanian period, it may be deduced that the Mississippian period witnessed a vast uplift followed by a subsidence of the region.

The Pennsylvanian, or great coal age, is represented in the surface formations of both the eastern and western coal fields of Kentucky. These are sandstones, shales, occasional limestones, and numerous coal seams. The lower sandstone outcrops along the outer edges of both areas and has been sculptured by erosion into natural bridges, rock castles, and water falls. Natural Bridge and Cumberland Falls are notable among these. The Pennsylvanian shales in places bear the imprint of the abundant plant life of the period. The shale roofs of some of the coal mines are decorated with fossil tree trunks, showing bark patterns and the traces of leaves. The sandstones also exhibit the Lepidodendrons, Sigillaria, and other coal-forming trees, a flora that vanished with the end of the Carboniferous period in its last stage, the Permian. The animal fossils of the Pennsylvanian resembles those of the Mississipian.

The close of the Paleozoic era, an eon of some 350 million years, saw the rise of the ancient lofty Appalachian Mountains, of which the ancestral Pine and Cumberland Mountains formed western outposts.

So far as Kentucky is concerned, there is a hiatus in the rock record, extending from the end of the Paleozoic to the last period of the Mesozoic. Triassic, Jurassic, and Commanchean rocks do not occur, and those of the Cretaceous period show no marine fossils. Dinosaurs or other spectacular creatures of this age of reptiles may have wandered into the area during this time, but neither fossil remains nor footprints have been found.

The Tertiary period, which introduced the age of mammals, found the Purchase Region of coastal plain bordering an enlarged Gulf of Mexico. Cassias, figs, maples, laurels, oaks, walnuts, willows, papaws, gums, yews, hickories, and other contemporary flora thrived. In these forests roamed the giant ground sloth, giant wolves, and other carnivora.

The Quaternary includes the quite recent glacial period, traces of which (in the Illinoian stage) are found ten to twenty miles south of the Ohio, from the Big Sandy to the Kentucky Rivers. Louisville, in part, and other cities of the northern border are built on a glacial Ohio River outwash of sand and gravel. Big Bone Lick in Boone County is named from the leg bones of mammoth and mastodon that mired down at this place. It is possible that cave dwellers lived and hunted at the edge of the slowly retreating ice cap. In any event, within a few thousand years man made his appearance in the forests of this region and the modern era was ushered in.

There are geological and paleontological collections in the University of Kentucky at Lexington, in the Louisville Free Public Library, and in many other Kentucky institutions of higher learning.

ARCHEOLOGY AND INDIANS

THE MANY mounds, forts, cave shelters, and burial fields in Kentucky show that the prehistoric population must have been fairly large for savages. It was diverse in culture and probably had many separate origins.

Aboriginal remains are found in every county in the State. The eastern mound area covers the heart of the Bluegrass region and extends northeastward to the Ohio River. This fertile and well watered land was heavily timbered in prehistoric times. It is characterized archeologically by the great number and large size of its Indian mounds, many of them associated with village sites, and by other structures which have been called forts. The popular notion that the mound builders were a race differing from the American Indians has no facts to support it. They were doubtless the ancestors of some of the historic Indians.

The mounds were originally of various shapes and sizes but have been altered through weathering and the changes caused by agriculture. This is especially true of mounds which were not high and stand in cultivated fields. With each plowing the earth has been removed from the top and spread out at the base until the original shape has been destroyed. Often the surface for many yards around is strewn with flints, bones, and broken pottery upturned by plow and harrow.

Some of these mounds were constructed centuries ago; others are quite recent. Certain tribes of modern Indians were building mounds when the first whites arrived. Sometimes intrusive burials indicate that later tribes used the mounds after the original builders had disappeared. All mounds were not used for the same purpose—they were erected for ceremonial or sacrificial purposes, or for the burial of the dead; and some perhaps represent nothing more than the dirt roof of a lodge or the gradual accumulation of camp refuse.

The remains of camp and village sites, usually found in the vicinity of mounds, are often extensive and show long occupancy. The features by which a site is recognized is the sporadic occurrence of broken

II. HISTORIC PAGES

DANIEL BOONE'S ARRIVAL WITH NORTH CAROLINIANS;
MURAL IN POST OFFICE, LEXINGTON

LINCOLN MEMORIAL, NEAR HODGENVILLE

PIONEER MEMORIAL, HARRODSBURG

BIRTHPLACE OF ABRAHAM LINCOLN, MEMORIAL

OLD CAPITOL, FRANKFORT

THE CAPITOL, FRANKFORT

OLD FAYETTE COUNTY COURTHOUSE, LEXINGTON

INTERIOR FEDERAL HILL, "MY OLD KENTUCKY HOME," NEAR BARDSTOWN

FEDERAL HILL, "MY OLD KENTUCKY HOME"

ASHLAND, HOME OF HENRY CLAY, LEXINGTON

JOHN HUNT MORGAN HOME, LEXINGTON

JEFFERSON COUNTY COURTHOUSE, LOUISVILLE

bits of flint artifacts, potsherds, or bone fragments scattered over the surface. The midden of a village is usually one foot deep, though it may attain a depth of several feet.

The life of the mound builders may be reconstructed, to some extent, from the artifacts found in the mounds. Agriculture is shown in the hoes; fishing in the fishhooks and fish scales; hunting in the bones of many a beast; sports in the almost obliterated race tracks and play-grounds; child-like vanities in the personal ornaments; industry in the laboriously fashioned tools and in the carved pipes and gorgets.

The rock shelter area extends throughout the knobs and eastern mountains and swings south and west of the Bluegrass to portions of west central Kentucky having a similar topography. In this area erosion has formed many vertical cliffs from 50 to 200 feet high in which are rock shelters, known locally as rock houses. Numbers of these shelters are several hundred feet long and from 30 to 60 feet high, and many are quite dry. Into these, primitive man carried wood for fire and animals for food. Ashes and bones have accumulated in layers sometimes 10 feet deep. Each layer contains a record of con-temporary life and is well preserved, for no water has entered the shelters and the dry ashes have prevented bacterial action. Bone, shell, gourd shards, textiles and leather have been found in excellent condition.

Not all the sites are of the same age, nor do all have the same amount of accumulated debris; but the series of artifacts, burial customs, and apparent steps in the development of culture are so nearly identical in the shelters investigated that it is reasonable to suppose that all have a similar story of occupancy.

The western Kentucky rock shelter area embraces the headwaters of the Green River and extends northward to the Ohio River. The cliff shelters found here differ from those in the cliff dwelling area. They are merely overhanging rock strata or ledges of sandstone or limestone, offering protection over a relatively small space. The cliffs are usually not more than 30 feet high, and the actual shelters, while numerous, are individually small—no larger than would meet the need of a single family. The shelters were often so small that the ashes had to be periodically swept out, and their accumulation formed a talus at the foot of the cliff below, which grew deeper and broader as occupancy continued. Burials of men, women, and children were often made in the ashes and debris swept from the shelter. There is no known evi-dence of cremation. Bone and shell were used extensively; a few slate pendants, shell and bone beads, and other ornaments have been found.

The distinguishing feature of the sandstone sites is the hominy hole used for grinding corn. At every site, from one to five or six of these conical holes are found either in the shelter floors or in large sandstone boulders. A hominy hole is from four to ten inches in diameter at the top, tapering to perhaps three inches at the bottom and varying in depth from one to three feet. Associated with the hominy hole is a bell-shaped pestle, lashed to a staff several feet long, and used pointed end downward, with which the corn was ground by percussion. A number of pestles were left in these hominy holes by their users. Crude hoes, the hominy holes, and pestles suggest a horticultural people. They are not to be distinguished from the rock shelter dwellers of the eastern mountains, and their cultural connections are uncertain.

The cliff dwellings were in continuous use from a remote period until the advent of white men. The lowest ash beds have no pottery of any kind, no flint implements, and only the crudest forms of hammerstones; large broken animal bones, mingled with mussel shells, nut hulls, and fish scales, form a considerable portion of the refuse. Upper or later levels show gourd shards, grooved axes, and very crude limestone hoes, indicating the beginning of agriculture. Woven textiles and moccasins of both textiles and leather have also been found in the upper layers. Crude potsherds occur only in the top six inches of the ash, and a few sites have yielded paddle-marked shards. The cliff dwellers used shells as spoons and scrapers, and made a characteristic bone awl from the shoulder blade of the deer.

Many burials of women and children occur in the ash beds, but such burials did not prevent later occupancy of the site. Although dozens of ash beds have been investigated and scores of bodies of women and children have been found, there is no evidence of a burial of an adult male. The question of what was done with deceased adult males may have been answered by the discovery, in one site in Wolfe County, of some 57 artifacts associated with the almost entirely burned bones of what appears to have been an adult male. These bones and artifacts are preserved, just as found, in the museum of the University of Kentucky. Future investigation may show that adult males were cremated.

In the southeastern mountain area are many mounds, but they are not as numerous as in the neighboring central mound area. Here, too, are rock shelters in which the aboriginal people lived and left artifacts. Plowed fields have yielded artifacts of flint and other stones and vestiges of villages may be seen in a few places. The soil was capable of producing maize abundantly but the roughness of the country doubtless interfered with settlement.

An area embracing a portion of north central Kentucky includes evidence of aborigines of unknown cultural affinities. This occupation is indicated by burial sites containing stone cists of two to six burials, usually situated on high hill crests. The graves are covered with a double row of flat stones set on edge and touching each other at the top. Other stones are then leaned against this first row, and sometimes an area of 10 feet square is covered with sloping stones.

Along part of the Ohio River in Kentucky are a few larger mounds associated with village sites, some of which have yielded material of Fort Ancient culture; this would be expected from its contact with the Fort Ancient area in Ohio and with the eastern mound area in Kentucky, to the eastward. The Fort Ancient culture is probably Siouan.

Kentucky caves were inhabited by prehistoric man, but how far he dates back in time is, at present, an unanswerable question. The term "cave dwellers" is used to designate those ancient people whose remains are found in caves and who apparently lived in them. Primitive man could hardly have found a more satisfactory type of shelter. The part of the cave near the mouth was commonly occupied, and caves which had good rooms close to the entrance were favorite dwelling places. The inhabitants also used the most remote passages, for in the deepest and most inaccessible chambers they left evidence of their presence. The caves, like the mounds, represent more than one group of people. After one group deserted them, a new group would move in.

The reason for burial in the caves may have been religious belief, or long-established custom, or a desire to protect the graves, or merely the fact that the floor of the cave was never hard or frozen, and was easy to excavate when the outside ground was not. Whatever the reason, its existence is fortunate, for cave burials have proven conducive to preservation of remains, and thus they give illuminating glimpses of ancient life.

Ash beds are found on the floors of caves, but it is often difficult to tell whether they were made by ancient residents or modern hunters. On the walls are marks and decorations; since weathering is very slow in such protected places, these marks may be ten or a thousand years old. Hidden in crevices are pots containing paint or pigment, but little is known of the men who left them there.

South and west of the western Kentucky rock shelter area, along Green River in its passage through McLean, Muhlenberg, Ohio, and

Butler Counties, is the Shell Mound area. It is distinguished by great shell heaps near the riverbanks, consisting of gastropod and mussel shells mixed with animal bones and camp refuse. The size and number of these mounds suggest a large population or a long-continued occupation. The shell beds are often ten to twelve feet deep, and many of them are several acres in extent. The most important archeological investigation within this area was made by C. B. Moore at Indian Knoll, where many skeletons and certain characteristic artifacts were discovered. The circular pattern of graves at this site is unlike that in the surrounding territory. The artifacts indicate a people living wholly by fishing and hunting. There is no evidence of agriculture and, beyond the mounds themselves, no evidence of permanent occupation. It is possible that these shell mounds are evidences of the oldest human occupancy in this area of the State.

The stone grave area, lying between the Tennessee and Green Rivers, is very rich in prehistoric remains—earth mounds, large village sites, and cemeteries. Stone grave cemeteries are fairly numerous, and some are fairly extensive. A stone grave is made by setting six to eight stones on edge, carefully joined to form a box; in this the body in the flesh is buried at full length. Usually the stone graves were lined at the bottom and covered at the top with flat stones. At one site they were found under mounds which contained crematory pits and ossuaries of a group of unknown culture.

These stone graves are generally devoid of artifacts, although sometimes they contain small mortuary vessels of pottery. At the head or foot of the individual within the stone grave are extended burials and many burials of bones. Thus on such sites there is evidence of at least two methods of disposal of the dead. Because of a dearth of artifacts the cultural connections of these people are uncertain.

Within this area, built upon a stone grave cemetery seemingly at a later date, a village site has been found and a group of sixty or more mounds, many of which have proven to be crematory pits for burning the bones of the dead. Remains show the practice of cremation, strongly suggestive of some members of the Siouan linguistic stock, and collections of jumbled human bones are found, often within the same mound. Such ossuaries often contain the bones of hundreds of individuals, packed into small, stone, chimney-like vaults, similar to the crematory pits. Here again were two methods of dealing with the dead. Artifacts found in this association are few, the most characteristic being pottery "elbow" pipes. These pipes and burial customs are similar to those described by Gerard Fowke in Missouri.

The third culture within this area has been called the Gordon or Tennessee-Cumberland aspect, first described by Meyer in the Cumberland River region of Tennessee. This culture is distinguished by the erection of earth mounds over the sites of buildings or temples. The remains of these buildings, which were made of wattlework between posts driven into the earth, show that they were destroyed by fire and covered with earth while the fire was yet burning. Over this a new structure was erected which, in time, went the way of the first. Generally the mounds show several levels of occupation. Remains of maize are found in the temple sites, indicating that the people of this culture practiced agriculture. They made pottery, producing distinct and attractive types, many of which show outside influence. One characteristic form is a textile-marked vessel of large size, commonly called a salt pan. Shards of such vessels are found in great number in the dirt forming the mounds that cover the sites of burned buildings.

While, in places, these earth mounds are found near the stone grave cemeteries, not all are so situated. Some of the larger sites show fulllength burials in the flesh, accompanied by a variety of artifacts. The occupancy of this area by so many different peoples complicates the problem of identification; on the other hand it has increased the stratification of artifacts and culture customs.

The *Jesuit Relations* recounts that the Five Nations, or Iroquois, in New York, got guns from the Dutch about 1630 and turned on their less advanced neighbors to the north, south, and west with such fury that by 1690 the present States of Ohio and Kentucky were depopulated, their inhabitants having fled across the Mississippi River or to the southeast.

About 1645–1650 a group of these fugitives from the upper Ohio began to cross the present State by the Athiomiowee, or Warriors' Trace. They were overtaken by their Iroquoian foes, but fortified themselves and drove them back. In Virginia they defeated Colonel Howard Hill and killed the chief of his Indian allies, Totopottomoi, a successor to Powhatan. The Virginia records call these fugitives Rickohockans and later Occaneechos. Others of these same people turned down the Ohio—called the Acansea River on early French maps —and the Mississippi, and finally settled on the Missouri and Arkansas Rivers.

Between 1715 and 1725 a number of the Piqua band of Shawnee returned from the South and built a town, Eskippakithiki, in the southeastern part of Clark County. There they remained for some time until they moved to Ohio and took sides with the French in the campaign against Braddock.

In 1736 the French took a census of the Ohio Valley and credited the Shawnees, in the Carolina region, with a strength of 200 men. This was probably only for the Shawnee town of Eskippakithiki, for the Van Keulen map of 1720 shows a trail from the present Illinois, crossing the Ohio near the mouth of the Kentucky River, and passing by the site of Eskippakithiki, to Cumberland Gap, which is labeled, "The route which the French take to trade with Carolina."

Peter Chartier, a half-breed Shawnee trader, the son of Martin Chartier, was in Kentucky in the late seventeenth century. He had his chief post at the Shawnee town on the Pequea Creek in Pennsylvania, and probably reached out for trade with his Shawnee kinsmen in Kentucky. In 1745, he was reprimanded by the Governor for selling liquor to the Indians, and accepted a captaincy in the French service and fled down the Ohio River, taking with him 400 Shawnee warriors and their families. Having robbed all the English traders they met, they went to their kinsmen at Eskippakithiki, where they stopped until the fall of 1747. After making trouble in the South for several years, they drifted back, stopping at the present Shawneetown, Illinois, until they were allowed to return to their British allegiance and their old homes. Chartier fled to the French in Illinois.

About 1729 Shawnees, Delawares, and Mingoes built Lower Shawneetown on the western side of the Scioto River at its mouth. A suburb of this backwoods capital was built on the Kentucky side, now Fullerton, and some trading posts were established there by Colonel George Croghan, and others. This town and its Kentucky suburb were deserted just before the French and Indian War. Eskippakithiki and Lower Shawneetown were the last Indian settlements in Kentucky.

HISTORY

KENTUCKY was the first State to be organized west of the Appalachian Mountains. At the mountain barrier the westward movement of American immigrants had come to its first halt, but there was a lively curiosity about the land beyond to the west.

In 1642 a company of English adventurers, Walter Austin, Rice Hoe, Joseph Johnson, and Walter Chiles, petitioned for "leave and encouragement to explore westward." Whatever their intentions may have been, they failed to use their grant. Twenty-seven years passed before the subject of western exploration was again discussed in the Virginia Assembly. A permit was granted in 1669 to John Lederer, a German adventurer and personal friend of Governor Berkeley, to explore westward. He made three trips into the Blue Ridge, passing through the neighborhood of what is now Lynchburg, but accomplished little. In 1671, Colonel Abram Wood, commandant of Fort Henry at Petersburg, Virginia, sent Thomas Batts and Robert Fallam into the western ranges to find the "ebbing and flowing of the rivers on the other side of the mountains in order to reach the South Seas." This expedition reached the Ohio Valley, but the English were not much impressed with the findings. Two or three years later, however, they discovered that the French were active in the western country beyond the mountains. The English became intensely interested when the French, by virtue of the Mississippi voyages of Jolliet and Marquette in 1673 and of La Salle in 1682, claimed all the region drained by the Mississippi River and its tributaries. James Needham and Gabriel Arthur were sent into the West in 1673. Needham was killed, but Arthur made his way into northeastern Kentucky with the Indians and may have been the first Englishman on Kentucky soil. English interest in the trans-Allegheny region lagged for 70 years and was confined to the cis-Allegheny frontier.

In 1742 John Peter Salley (or Salling) led a party from Virginia to the banks of the Ohio River. One or two of the men were killed, and Salley was captured by French adventurers and sent to prison, first at

Natchez, and later in Cuba and France. He finally returned to Charleston, South Carolina. Salley's adventure stimulated a fresh interest on the part of the English in the Ohio Valley. Seven years later Pierre Joseph Celoron, Sieur de Blainville, set out from Quebec to lay claim for the French to all the land between Quebec and New Orleans. The news of this expedition aroused the English whose Colonial officials took steps to make counter claims. Land companies were organized and plans were made at once to send surveyors beyond the mountains to lay out claims to large tracts of lands for prospective settlements. The Loyal Land Company at Charlottesville, Virginia, secured a grant of 800,000 acres and dispatched an expedition westward under Dr. Thomas Walker in 1750. The party left Charlottesville on March 6 and came to a wide pass in the Allegheny wall on April 13. Walker refers to the pass in his journal as "Cave Gap" through which his party passed on their way to within a short distance from what is now Barboursville. Here the expedition established its base for operations, explored the eastern mountain range of Kentucky for several weeks, and left the country on June 20, 1750.

The next year Christopher Gist, a frontier scout and explorer, was employed by the Ohio Land Company to visit the West. He traveled through passes in the neighborhood of modern Pittsburgh and made his way through Indian trading villages down the Ohio River to the Kentucky country. In March 1751 he visited Big Bone Lick, and headed for the great Falls of the Ohio River, now Louisville, but friendly Shawnee Indians warned him of hostile tribes encamped about the falls. Gist turned back, passing over the mountains to North Carolina.

The settlement line along the Virginia and Carolina frontiers grew more and more populous from 1751 to 1786. The settlers were anxious to move westward to new and more fertile lands, but the country was involved in the French and Indian War from 1755 to 1763 and it was dangerous. It appeared for a time that the land which is now Kentucky would fall to the French, but the tide turned at last, and on February 10, 1763, the Treaty of Paris was signed. The English got possession of the land east of the Mississippi River, but to the disappointment of the frontiersmen, King George III issued the proclamation of 1763 forbidding settlers to move beyond the line of watershed in the Appalachian highlands.

Despite the King's proclamation, scouts of one kind or another brought back from the West thrilling stories of the new country. Mrs.

Inglis, with a German woman companion, came into the northern Kentucky country as captives of the Indians, from whom they escaped almost miraculously. The so-called silver miners, led by John Swift, were in Kentucky from time to time during the 1760's. A legend prevails to this day that Swift and his companions mined large quantities of silver in Kentucky and many communities yet claim the site of the Swift silver mines.

The "long hunters," so called because of long periods of time spent by men of the eastern frontier settlements in hunting across the mountains, began to invade the Kentucky country. Among them were John Raines, Uriah Stone, John Finley, Henry Skaggs, and Daniel Boone. Boone's fame has grown with the passage of time until he has become, in legend at least, the chief figure of the early Kentucky frontier days. His life is symbolical of the western movement in American history.

Born in Berks County, Pennsylvania, in 1734, Boone had moved with his parents in 1750 to the western part of North Carolina, on the Yadkin. He was restless by nature, and in 1766 entered upon a career of exploration that first took him as far south as St. Augustine, Florida. Returning to North Carolina, he was influenced to go West by John Finley's stories of Kentucky, and crossed through Cumberland Gap. But instead of reaching the Bluegrass country he spent the winter of 1767 in the tablelands of eastern Kentucky, and returned to North Carolina. In May 1769, Boone, Finley, and several companions started for Kentucky. They spent the summer hunting in the cane lands and before they realized it winter was upon them. When their stores were broken into by the Indians in December and a number of horses were stolen, the party broke up, and Finley with three of his companions returned to North Carolina.

Meanwhile, Squire Boone, a brother of Daniel, and a companion had come out to Kentucky. The two brothers hunted for a year, and wandered over the country from the Big Sandy to the Cumberland Rivers. It was during these years, 1769–1771, that Daniel Boone acquired information about the Kentucky country that later made him a valuable scout.

The next whites to appear in Kentucky were the land surveyors sent out by land companies and speculators. Captain Thomas Bullitt led one such party to the Falls of the Ohio River in June 1773, where he made a survey of the lands where Louisville now stands. At the same time the McAfee brothers were surveying lands up the Kentucky

River. James Harrod led another surveying party in 1774 to the neighborhood now known as Harrodsburg.

No settlement had been established as yet, but immediately after the Indian disturbances had been settled by the Dunmore War, speculators laid plans to claim vast surveys in the West. The best known of these speculative ventures was the Transylvania Land Company, organized in 1773 as the Richard Henderson Company, under the leadership of Judge Richard Henderson of North Carolina. He and his associates, Colonel Nathaniel Hart and others, made a treaty with the Cherokee Indians on March 17, 1775, at Sycamore Shoals on the Watauga River, granting the whites possession of all the land south of the Ohio River, north of the Cumberland River, and west of the Appalachian ranges. Henderson also purchased a tract that reached from Cumberland Gap to the south bank of the Cumberland River. Daniel Boone and thirty companions were dispatched immediately to Kentucky to blaze the trail, and locate suitable river fording places. Henderson and his party followed and in May 1775, the settlement at Boonesboro was begun.

Harrodsburg, of Virginia origin, was also settled in early 1775. The founding of St. Asaph Station and Boiling Springs followed immediately. Judge Henderson issued a call on May 23, 1775, to all these forts to send delegates to Boonesboro for the purpose of making laws to govern the settlements. The nine laws passed by this meeting are sometimes called the first legislative acts passed by a Kentucky Legislature, though this is not strictly true.

Rivalry soon developed between the Virginia and North Carolina settlements. George Rogers Clark, a young Virginian who had recently come West, called a meeting at Harrodsburg on June 6, 1776, of all the Kentucky forts to discuss a course of procedure. Clark and John Gabriel Jones were selected as delegates to go to Williamsburg and present their problems to the Virginia Legislature, but they arrived too late to go before the assembly. Clark, however, was able to secure an appropriation of 500 pounds of gunpowder for the protection of Kentucky.

Clark and Jones learned, while in Williamsburg, that Richard Henderson and his associates were attempting to secure recognition of their colony. The Harrodsburg delegates, thereupon, decided to remain in Virginia until the assembly convened in the fall in order that they might protect the rights of the Harrodsburg settlers. It was largely through their influence that the Transylvania Land Company was declared illegal, and that Kentucky County was created out of Fincastle County on December 6, 1776. The name Kentucky was first used officially by Virginia at this time.

When Clark and Jones returned to Kentucky they found many settlers moving into the West. The Indians, however, were a constant menace, and Clark realized that if the Kentucky settlements were to survive, a military drive would have to be made beyond the Ohio. He therefore sought the permission and assistance of the Virginia Assembly and Governor Patrick Henry to attack the Indians and the English in their stronghold beyond the Ohio River, and won approval of his plans in December 1777. Starting out from Virginia, Clark went to the Redstone settlement near Pittsburgh to recruit troops for his western expedition. At the same time he dispatched an agent to the Watauga settlements in Tennessee for the same purpose. Both Clark and his agent were disappointed in the number of troops secured. Instead of 350, which he wanted, he got less than 200, and many of them objected to fighting beyond the Ohio River. Clark, nevertheless, proceeded to Corn Island in the Ohio, opposite the site on which Louisville stands today.

The expedition started secretly in June 1778 for Kaskaskia, and took the town by surprise. This successful coup was followed by a similar one against the town of Cahokia. In the fall Governor Hamilton arrived at Vincennes, the main French post in the northwest, with a large force of British and Indian troops, and the British flag was raised over the village. Hamilton thought he was perfectly safe in Vincennes, but in February 1779 Clark and his troops took Vincennes by surprise and captured the fort. The Indians were thus driven back temporarily from Kentucky and the American frontier was extended to the Mississippi River.

In the meantime Kentuckians were having Indian troubles at home. Daniel Boone and his salt-making companions were captured at the Lower Blue Licks February 7, 1778, and carried away to Detroit where he was adopted as a son of Chief Black Fish. He lived happily with the Indians for a time, but when he heard that the French-Canadian, De Quindre, was plotting with the Indians to attack Boonesboro, he returned to that settlement to prepare for the attack. The Indians under the command of De Quindre appeared before the fort and demanded its surrender; the demand was refused and the attack repulsed. The Kentucky settlements were saved.

The British and Indians made a second major attack in 1782, strik-

ing at Bryan Station on August 15. Four days later the Kentuckians
pursued them to the banks of the Licking River. On a limestone road
in a ravine at Blue Licks occurred one of the bloodiest battles ever
fought on the frontier. Though the Americans were defeated, this was
the last battle of any significance fought against the Indians on Kentucky soil.

As the Kentucky country became more settled and Indian skirmishes
became less frequent, the settlers grew tired of living in stockades.
County organizations and taverns began to spring up. The Falls of
the Ohio, which became Louisville, was surveyed in 1773 by Thomas
Bullitt; Boonesboro was incorporated in 1779; Washington and Maysville soon followed; the plan for the town of Lexington was adopted
in 1781. The Kentuckians soon began to consider separating their
territory from Virginia and becoming one of the States of the con-
federation. They first met in Danville December 27, 1784, to discuss
the matter formally; ten conventions were called before an independent
State was created. (In the meantime the Constitution of the United
States was written and ratified.) Many reasons for a separation were
discussed in these conventions: objections to Virginia taxes, inability
of Kentuckians to adapt Virginia laws to local situations, the refusal
of Virginia to permit Kentuckians to pursue Indians beyond the Ohio
River, and the fact that all cases appealed to higher courts had to be
carried back to Richmond for trial. Some people demanded that Kentucky become simply an independent State and have nothing to do
with the Union, some wished to become a part of the Spanish Empire,
some to remain a part of Virginia. Others demanded recognition as
one of the States of the Union. The long, bitter struggle finally came
to an end in the framing of a constitution at Danville in April 1792.
On June 1, 1792, Kentucky was admitted as a State into the Union.

The new government was inaugurated June 4, 1792, in Lexington.
General Isaac Shelby, by common consent, was chosen to be the first
Governor. The Sheaf of Wheat Tavern in Lexington became temporarily the statehouse, and the legislature met for its first session in a
capitol building of logs. Its first task was to select a permanent site
for the State Capital; December 8, 1792, Frankfort was so designated.

Kentucky's first constitution was modeled to some extent on the
National Constitution. All white males over 21 years of age were
permitted to vote, the Governor and senators were elected by an elec-
toral college, slavery was protected, and a bill of rights of 27 divisions
was attached. It failed, however, to provide for a public school system.

In 1799 a second constitutional convention was held, and a new constitution was adopted. It created the office of Lieutenant Governor, and made all State officers subject to direct election by the people. An interesting provision prohibited a minister of the Gospel from serving in the capacity of a lawmaker. Slave owners were afraid that ministers would attempt to pass abolition legislation.

Kentucky became deeply involved in the famous French conspiracy at this time. When Charles Edmund Genet landed at Charleston, South Carolina, on April 8, 1793, he dispatched his agents to the western country. George Rogers Clark was given a high commission in the French Army of the Mississippi Valley. Liberty poles were erected in many towns and Kentuckians hailed one another as "Citizen." Although the conspiracy was put down, the citizens of the State continued to favor the French. In 1798 they protested against the Alien and Sedition laws passed by the Adams government in Philadelphia. John Breckinridge, of Kentucky, in co-operation with Thomas Jefferson, drafted the famous series of resolutions setting forth what they believed to be State rights. There was much public debate on the question and popular opinion became overwhelmingly Republican. George Nicholas, of Lexington, a keen constitutionalist, vigorously attacked the Federalist laws. Henry Clay delivered his first significant speech in Kentucky politics on the question of States' rights. But when Jefferson was elected President of the United States, Kentuckians forgot their attack upon the National Constitution.

Between 1800–1804, the issue of trade rights on the lower Mississippi River was settled by the Louisiana Purchase. Kentuckians had lived in constant fear that the temperamental Spanish officials would remove the American right of deposit, and that Kentuckians would be unable to sell their products southward. In 1802 their fears were realized, and the Spanish canceled the right of deposit. The situation was relieved, however, when Louisiana passed into American hands in 1803.

Hardly had Kentuckians ceased rejoicing than they were involved, innocently, in another national scandal. Aaron Burr, who had killed Alexander Hamilton in a duel, came to the State and plotted much of his proposed independent republic in the Southwest. Many prominent Kentuckians became involved in the plot. Burr was twice brought to trial in the Federal Court of the District of Kentucky, but was released both times as not guilty of the charges of treason preferred against him.

When the excitement about the Burr conspiracy had somewhat subsided, Kentucky became agitated over the possibility of a war with England. News reached Kentucky in 1807 of the *Chesapeake* and *Leopard* affair. Public opinion in favor of war ran high, and the local press cried out loudly against England. The State legislature passed laws forbidding the use of certain British laws and citation of British cases in court. Realizing the temper of the public mind, the politicians who sought office began to agitate the question of expanding American territory. Henry Clay and Richard M. Johnson were elected to Congress on an expansionist platform. Henry Clay even went so far as to advocate the annexation of Canada. By 1811 Kentuckians virtually demanded war with England. When war was formally declared in 1812, Kentuckians advanced rapidly to the area about Detroit. A large part of the American forces at the Battle of the Thames consisted of Kentucky militiamen under the command of Gov. Isaac Shelby and Congressman Richard Mentor Johnson. When Gen. Andrew Jackson defeated the British forces at New Orleans on January 8, 1815, 5,500 Kentuckians were present, under Generals Thomas and Adair.

After the War of 1812 Kentuckians turned their attention to more constructive interests. Western manufactures were increasing because British goods were off the American market from 1805–1815. Kentucky hemp, cloth and rope manufacturers especially enjoyed a flourishing trade, and butchers, distillers, salt-makers, and cabinetmakers were prosperous. Land prices advanced and Louisville, Lexington, Maysville, Covington, Carrollton, Paducah, Henderson, and Hickman were rapidly becoming busy trade centers. River boatmen began to clamor for a canal around the Falls of the Ohio at Louisville. A company was chartered by the State legislature in 1805 for this purpose, but the work was delayed and the canal was not completed until 1829. The first successful steamboat trip on western waters was taken by the *New Orleans* to New Orleans in 1811 by Captain Nicholas Roosevelt. About 1815 a steamboat, the *Enterprise,* came up the river from New Orleans and thereafter the steamboat business began to thrive. By 1860 Kentuckians were supplying the Southern States with the most of their manufactured goods.

With prosperous conditions, there came a demand for improved banking facilities. Kentucky at the time had a system of State banks to which was entrusted the responsibility of issuing currency, but the amount issued was insufficient for the successful conduct of business.

III. ARCHITECTURE

DIAMOND POINT, HARRODSBURG

SHROPSHIRE HOUSE, GEORGETOWN

LIBERTY HALL, FRANKFORT

WILMORE GARRETT RESIDENCE, NEAR LEXINGTON

MC AFEE HOUSE, NEAR HARRODSBURG

OLD KEENE PLACE, NEAR LEXINGTON

FAIR OAKS, NEAR HARRODSBURG

SCARLET GATE, HOME OF JAMES LANE ALLEN, NEAR LEXINGTON

CLAY HILL, HARRODSBURG

MANSION MUSEUM, HARRODSBURG

CARNEAL HOUSE, COVINGTON

WICKLAND, BARDSTOWN

THE ORLANDO BROWN HOUSE, FRANKFORT

STAIRWAY, OLD CAPITOL, FRANKFORT

By 1818 the demand for an increase in the number of banks was so great that the Bank of Kentucky was expanded to include more than 40 branches. Each branch bank was given the authority to issue its own currency. In a short time, however, the lack of control over the volume of currency issued led to general financial confusion, and to depreciation in value of currency. The situation became so acute that in December 1819, the general assembly passed a law granting a stay of execution for 60 days. This relief was not sufficient to stem the tide. In February 1820, all debtors were given a moratorium of two years. A test case was carried to the courts, and the circuit court of Bourbon County declared the law unconstitutional. Later, the State court of appeals upheld the local court and the legislature declared that the courts were thwarting the will of the people. A struggle between the legislative and the judicial branches of the government continued until 1829, when the court was finally absolved of all the charges made against it.

The legislative-judicial struggle over the banking question created two political parties in Kentucky. In the Presidential campaign of 1824 one of the four candidates in the field was Henry Clay of Kentucky, who was defeated; but, as Speaker of the House of Representatives, he was a powerful factor in deciding whom Congress should select for the next President. The Kentucky General Assembly had instructed Clay to support Jackson, but he disobeyed instructions and supported John Quincy Adams. This brought about another break in Kentucky politics; the Clay supporters became Whigs and the Jackson supporters became Democrats. This alignment prevailed until 1860.

The institution of slavery was a political issue in Kentucky from 1792 to 1865. Slavery had been transferred to the West as a part of the social organization of the State, but it was not an economic success. Lack of transportation facilities made large-scale tobacco culture unprofitable in the early years; and the cultivation of hemp and grain and the breeding of livestock were not adapted to slave labor.

After 1820 many Kentucky farmers moved to the Cotton Belt where they could employ their slaves with profit. Others sold off their surplus supply of Negroes to the southern planters. When the War between the States broke out, Kentucky had approximately 225,000 slaves. The State was divided into two distinct economic units. The Bluegrass counties, in which slavery existed to the greatest extent, quite generally favored the southern economic system. The poorer counties and the larger urban centers were quite generally opposed to slavery.

Originally the chief criticism of slavery came from the churches and the clergy. The slaveholders were constantly on guard against this opposition, and since they exercised more political influence than the clergy, they succeeded in building a wall of protective legislation about the system of slave labor. Between 1820 and 1835 the American Colonization Society, of which Henry Clay was president, made considerable headway in Kentucky. At the same time outside abolitionists began to attack Kentucky slavery; this caused much hard feeling in the State, and probably did more immediate harm than good. The institution of slavery also found severe critics within the State. Cassius M. Clay, a native of Madison County, and publisher of the *True American*, a newspaper in Lexington, condemned Kentucky slavery very bitterly.

Other live issues were at stake in antebellum days. When Henry Clay died in 1852 he left behind him the wreckage of the Whig party, and no leader to take his place. Local politicians began to inject into their speeches the questions of religion and nationalities. Catholics were condemned along with all foreigners. The Sons of America, or Native Americans as they called themselves, attempted to keep possession of the reins of local government. A riot in Louisville in 1855, known as "Bloody Monday," resulted.

In the Presidential election of 1860 Kentucky voted against its two native sons, Abraham Lincoln and John C. Breckinridge, and gave its majority support to John Bell of Tennessee, who proposed to save the Union at any cost. Unlike her southern neighbors the State refused to be stampeded into secession. Although Kentucky was a slave State and considered itself Southern, it leaned toward the idea of maintaining the Union intact. Commerce and agriculture had become the chief interests. When war broke out, both sides looked upon Kentucky as a valuable prize, and both sides disregarded its neutrality.

During the early part of 1862 western Kentucky was the scene of most important operations between Northern troops under the command of Grant, McClellan, and Thomas, and the Southern troops under the command of Johnston, Polk, Buckner, Crittenden, and Zollicoffer. Union victory at Mill Springs, where Zollicoffer was killed January 19, opened the way into Eastern Tennessee. In 1863 the Confederates under Braxton Bragg and Kirby Smith made a drive into central Kentucky. Bragg received the surrender of the garrison at Munfordville on September 17. He then moved northeastward through Bardstown, and at Perryville stumbled into one wing of the Union command under General Don Carlos Buell. Here on October 8 was fought the battle of Perryville, the bloodiest encounter in Kentucky history. The result was a draw. Bragg retreated, leaving Buell in possession of the field. This marked the end of any serious attempt by the Confederates to gain possession of Kentucky.

Guerilla warfare was carried on in many sections of Kentucky. The famous bushwhacker, Quantrill of Missouri, transferred his activities to Kentucky and kept local communities in a state of excitement. So vicious did this guerilla warfare become that Governor Bramlette was compelled to organize a home guard for the protection of local communities.

When peace came in 1865 Kentucky firmly believed that it would resume its peaceful pursuit of developing agriculture and industry, but such was not to be the case. The carpetbaggers realized that the Negroes, many of whom were concentrated in Louisville in the Federal camps, offered a good opportunity for political advantage. Farmers were frightened into believing that they would be completely robbed of labor. Pamphlets were issued inviting foreigners to come to the State. Even Chinese coolies were sought as a solution to the labor problem. The State refused to ratify the thirteenth and fourteenth amendments. By 1871 conditions had become more or less normal; Kentuckians gradually forgot the war and turned to the problems of industry, agriculture, politics and temperance.

The lower South, which had been Kentucky's most important market, had been depleted by the war. Louisville merchants were the first to realize the situation, and sent ex-Confederate soldiers as salesmen into the South to help re-establish the crossroads stores. These drummers were instructed to sell goods at all cost. Wholesale houses were generous in their credit to southern merchants. They not only thoroughly canvassed the South, but Louisville financiers backed the extension of the L. & N. R.R. into the South. Consequently Kentuckians soon recovered much of the trade which they had lost in the war, and the State's industry once again became an important factor in the economic development of the South.

Agriculture presented a more difficult problem. Many Kentucky farmers depended upon a single cash crop, tobacco, and with each succeeding panic following 1865, Kentucky tobacco farmers, like southern cotton farmers, became virtually bankrupt. This difficulty led to the organization of various farmers' movements—granger organizations, the Farmers' Alliance, and finally the Populist party. The Populists demanded tariff reforms, regulation of transportation agencies, establishment of agricultural schools, a more satisfactory distribution of the national medium of exchange, more reasonable farm credits, higher agricultural prices, and the framing of a new State constitution in 1890. This constitution, in effect today, reflects the philosophy of the Kentucky Populist party of 1890.

Agricultural issues in the State were not all settled peacefully. From 1907 to 1909 there raged in the dark tobacco belt a "night-riders" war which resulted in many fatalities. The reign of general lawlessness prevailed in the State for more than a year, until it was ended by the State militia, called out by the Governor. Agrarian troubles were largely back of bitter partisan politics that prevailed in Kentucky the latter part of the nineteenth century. The gubernatorial election of 1899 was fiercely fought. William Goebel of Covington opposed William Sylvester Taylor, a western Kentuckian, and John Young Brown. When the votes were counted it was found that Taylor had won by a majority of more than 2,000 votes. The supporters of Goebel contested the election. While the legislature was considering the matter, Goebel was shot by an assassin (January 30, 1900). The legislature at once declared Goebel Governor, but he died on February 3. Kentucky was almost in a state of civil war; for several months it had two Governors and two governments. The Democrats won in the end, and J. C. W. Beckham succeeded the assassinated Goebel as Governor. Several years were required to allay the bitter partisan feeling that was engendered by this affair.

Since 1909 Kentucky has pursued a fairly steady and progressive course, in spite of the fact that Democrats and Republicans have fought each other bitterly and alternated in political power.

Kentucky did its part in the World War by furnishing 75,043 men and meeting its quotas in money subscribed. Men were encamped and trained at Fort Thomas, Camp Zachary Taylor, and Camp Knox. The latter was not dismantled after the war and on January 30, 1932, it became a permanent post of the U. S. Army and officially named Fort Knox. The gold vault of the U. S. Treasury is located on the reservation. Capt. Samuel Woodfill, a Kentuckian, was cited by General Pershing as the outstanding soldier of the war; Woodfill and Willie Sandlin were awarded Congressional medals of honor for heroism. Of the men who were drafted and enlisted, 70 to 80 percent passed their physical examinations and were accepted for Army service.

One of the outstanding achievements of the twentieth century in the

State is the development of good roads, under a State highway commission. By 1920 the highway system was well enough organized to take over a large primary system of highways. The effects of improved highways in Kentucky upon the general character and welfare of the people cannot be overestimated. Not only have the highways speeded up commerce and travel, but they have tended to break down sectionalism. With primary roads in every county, it is no longer strange to see people from the remote eastern and western sections of the State strolling the streets of Louisville as nonchalantly as if they had lived there all their lives.

In the 50 years following the first census of 1790 the population increased more than tenfold—from 73,677 to 779,828. It numbered 1,858,635 in 1890 and 2,614,589 in 1930. Only 30.6 percent of the 1930 population was classified as urban.

Kentucky's government has recently been completely modernized, but this has been done without touching the constitution itself and with only a few optional alterations in the county structure. Increasing difficulties with a government that tried to operate in an industrial era, on a constitution descended from Kentucky's former slave-owning agricultural status, led to the appointment of an efficiency commission in 1926. This body made a two-year study of the State's governmental needs, and recommended widespread changes, but controversies over their adoption disrupted the State for another ten years. In 1934 the executive offices were reorganized under Governor Ruby Laffoon, but this reorganization proved too cumbersome. After two years another exhaustive study was made that resulted in the Shields-Nickell Governmental Reorganization Act, approved March 7, 1936.

The important changes in this reorganization were the creation of a department of welfare, expanded powers of the department of health, consolidation of the State tax commission and the department of revenue and taxation into a single department of revenue, added powers of the efficiency department to improve the civil service, and the creation of a new department of conservation. Finally, there was added to the State government the legislative council, a modern unit in American government in operation now only in a few States. The function of this council is purely advisory. It examines and reports on the working of the existing legislative machine, prepares and submits programs for the general assembly, and promotes interstate comity.

The present Kentucky government follows the traditional American system of three branches—executive, legislative, and judiciary—all responsible directly to the votes of the citizens. Citizenship qualifications are simple. Any person not an idiot or insane, who is over twenty-one years of age and has resided in the State one year, in the county six months, and in the voting precinct sixty days next preceding election, is qualified to vote; except that any person convicted of a felony forfeits his right of franchise, unless he is pardoned by the governor. There are no other qualifications.

The two units of local government are the county and the city. The county government today is an interesting survival from Colonial times, when its forms were borrowed more or less directly from England. Counties have their own courts which administer governmental functions; they collect and spend their own revenues and in general regulate their affairs as they please, subject only to the restrictions of the general assembly which, as has been pointed out, is restricted by the constitution from interfering with major phases of local administration. The government is administered entirely by courts with the county judge as the executive. He is elected by the county at large and presides over the county court. Beneath this court the county is divided into magisterial districts, each with a justice of the peace in authority. These justices compose the fiscal court of each county, with rather indiscriminate legislative and judicial powers.

Kentucky cities have their own government, independent of their surrounding counties, and responsible only to the State. The legislature divides the cities into six classes, according to population, and provides debt limits and general forms of government for each. Three forms of city government are established, and variations from these are allowed by special legislative enactment: the standard mayor-council form, commission government, and the city manager plan.

The constitution of Kentucky, which covers all forms of government and of legislation throughout the State, is subject to alteration through two methods. An amendment may be proposed in either branch of the general assembly at a regular session, and if agreed to by a three-fifths vote of both branches, may be submitted to the voters of the State for adoption. Ninety days must elapse between the legislative adoption of the amendment and its submission to popular vote; and not more than two amendments may be voted on at any one time. If a widespread revision of the constitution is demanded, a general constitutional convention of delegates, equal in numbers to that of the house of representatives, may be authorized by the general assembly. The convention remodels the constitution and submits it to popular vote.

Kentucky has its State flag, its State flower, its State bird, and its State song. The flag is Kentucky blue with the seal of the Commonwealth encircled by a wreath of goldenrod in the center. The State flower is the goldenrod, the bird is the Kentucky cardinal, the song is "My Old Kentucky Home, Good Night," by Stephen Collins Foster.

AGRICULTURE

THE EARLY development of Kentucky was entirely agricultural, and at first only those trades incidental and necessary to farming received attention. Lumbering, mining, and manufacturing had to await the development of agriculture. Isolated from markets and sources of manufactured goods, farmers produced nearly everything consumed by their families, and each farm was largely a self-contained and self-supporting economic unit.

Sugar and hardware had to be imported from the beginning, and at first were paid for with pelts. When farm production began to exceed consumption, farmers sought means of exchanging their surplus products for the articles they had to buy. A system of country merchandising based upon exchange of products developed, and farming for the market began.

Prohibitive freight costs over the Appalachian Mountains made eastward shipment uneconomic for all except commodities of high value in proportion to bulk and weight. The Ohio and Mississippi Rivers, which border Kentucky for more than 700 miles, and tributaries of the Ohio that flow across and through the State, give Kentucky more miles of major navigable streams than any other State. With a mountain barrier to the east and a water route down the Ohio and Mississippi to New Orleans and the Gulf of Mexico, river transportation reached a high stage of development, especially after the coming of the steamboat. This profoundly affected agriculture, and partly accounts for the high rank of Kentucky as an agricultural State for approximately seventy-five years preceding the War between the States. In 1839 Kentucky was first in the production of hemp, second in the production of both corn and hogs (with Tennessee ranking first), fourth in the production of oats and rye, and one of the leading tobacco, wheat, and beef producing States. The influence of Kentucky farmers, represented in Congress by Henry Clay, contributed to the establishment of a protective tariff. Competition of imported fibers with hemp induced Kentucky farmers to endorse the policy of protection.

Properly speaking, commercialized farming dates from about 1825, when the first market for tobacco in hogsheads was opened at Louisville. Before this time Kentucky tobacco was shipped direct from the farm to New Orleans. Naturally, production was confined to areas adjacent to navigable rivers. Western Kentucky, with an abundance of navigable streams, enjoyed transportation facilities superior to other parts of the State, and consequently became the State's center of tobacco culture. Subsequently, tobacco production of the dark type was so concentrated in this area that it became known as the "Black Patch."

Even before Kentucky became a State, tobacco shared with hemp the distinction of being one of the two crops grown commercially. Tobacco had long been the leading money crop in North Carolina and Virginia, and settlers from these States continued its culture. The variety grown was dark and heavy, similar to the present-day dark-fired type. It was believed in the early years that only virgin ground would grow good tobacco. Common practice, therefore, was to clear fresh acreage for the crops each year. Practically all land used for tobacco was originally covered with hardwood forests; but there was no market at that time for timber cleared to make room for tobacco, and great quantities of walnut, cherry, chestnut, hickory, oak, and poplar timber were cut and burned as waste.

Tobacco production increased rapidly after 1825, and by 1865 Kentucky was producing more of this crop than any other State in the Union. White burley was first raised near Higginsport, Brown County, Ohio, in 1864, from seed produced in Kentucky. Rapid spread of this tobacco throughout central Kentucky more firmly fixed tobacco as the key product in the farm economy of the State. Until the coming of white burley, tobacco had not been grown to any extent in central Kentucky. Development of railway facilities, high content of calcium and phosphorus in the soils of central Kentucky, and the fact that burley found a good market as both smoking and chewing tobacco, stimulated the rapid increase of tobacco raising in that area. Tobacco production grew rapidly after 1865, and until recent years Kentucky ranked first among the States in its culture. Lexington is the world's largest loose-leaf tobacco market.

Formerly grown exclusively in the Bluegrass region, burley is now raised in 110 counties of the State. The 1933 crop, the last which preceded production control, was 250 million pounds. In addition to burley, four types of dark tobacco—Dark-fired, One-sucker, Green

River, and Stemming—are grown in 33 western counties. Dark tobacco, with the exception of the finest dark-fired, used in the manufacture of snuff, is largely exported.

One-third to one-half of the annual cash income of Kentucky farmers
is derived from tobacco. The ease with which it lends itself to a one-
crop system of farming has had much to do with establishing it as a
chief product of the State. Because of long-continued dependence on
tobacco as their major money crop, Kentucky farmers are reluctant to
diversify their crops or to adopt more modern practices in tobacco culture. But there has been an economic collapse in the dark-tobacco
areas in Kentucky since the World War, because of curtailed foreign
demand; and as a result, dairying, poultry farming, small fruit orchard-
ing, and legume production are developing in those areas.

Cotton, the chief crop produced with slave labor, was never grown
to any large extent in Kentucky. Hemp growing, the second farm
enterprise in point of time, and tobacco production afforded the most
profitable opportunity in Kentucky for the use of slave labor.

The first crop of hemp was grown near Danville in 1775. When it
was found that hemp grew so well in the Bluegrass region, its growth
was discontinued in the Eastern States, and from 1840 to 1870 practically all of the hemp produced in the United States was grown in
Kentucky. In pioneer days hemp fiber was used for the homespun
cloth woven by the wives and daughters of early settlers. Soon the
fiber was used in making rope, twine, and sacking, particularly to bind
cotton bales; in the War of 1812 rigging and even cables were made of
it for Perry's fleet on Lake Erie. A lively export trade, in addition to
the healthy domestic demand, developed, clearing through New Orleans. As has already been pointed out, protection demanded by hemp
growers in Kentucky resulted in the adoption of the protective tariff
system in the United States. The replacement of sailing vessels by
steamships and the free import of various substitutes for hemp fiber
caused rapid decline in hemp culture after 1860, and the crop is now
not commercially important. Practically the entire national supply of
hemp seed for fiber is now produced in the narrow valleys of the Kentucky River and its tributaries near High Bridge. The story of hemp
and the significance of its production to Kentucky has been fasci-
natingly described in a novel, *The Reign of Law*, by James Lane Allen.

Not only did the early settlers know how to grow tobacco, they also
knew how to make whisky. Because of its high value in proportion to
bulk and the ready market for it at New Orleans, whisky early became

a favored product in the rye and corn regions of Kentucky. Probably the bulk of the State's rye grown before 1860, and a large part of its corn, were utilized in whisky making. Water from Kentucky springs and wells was found to be especially suitable for liquor, and the result is that the distilling industry, in several ways, has affected agricultural practice. Distilleries afforded a local market for small grains, and from year to year farmers hoped to sell all or part of their grain to distilleries at a profitable price. Thus the distilling industry tended to perpetuate the growing of small grains in many localities long after farmers might have turned to other crops. Since the repeal of prohibition, distilleries have again become consumers of local grain and are also important sources of slop feed for beef cattle and hogs.

Horses were used as work stock in the American Colonies long before mules. In 1783, George Washington, believing that mules were superior to horses for work on southern farms, imported jacks from Europe and sent them on a stud tour of the South. Henry Clay was prominent in establishing and developing the mule industry of Kentucky, and in 1827 and 1829 made significant importations of jack stock from Spain. Until the end of the century, Kentucky led in raising mules. Tennessee and Missouri, also important mule-producing States, obtained their foundation stock from Kentucky.

Every American knows of Kentucky bluegrass which thrives in peculiar soil conditions, particularly in the Bluegrass region, where the soil contains phosphorus, lime, and other minerals in such combination as to make the grass especially excellent food for livestock. As soon as the superior feeding qualities of pastures in central Kentucky were recognized, the region became the center of light horse breeding.

Exclusive of horses, it is estimated that $30,000,000 is invested in Bluegrass horse farms and improvements; that employees are paid $1,500,000 annually, and that $2,000,000 of supplies are purchased. Bluegrass pastures contributed to the early development of improved breeds of beef cattle. The Shorthorn in particular received attention, and outstanding specimens, often selling for thousands of dollars, were shipped to foreign countries as well as to other sections of the United States. A somewhat similar improvement developed in sheep breeding, particularly with the Southdown and Cheviot breeds. The Bluegrass specializes in furnishing quality spring lambs for early marketing; these command a high price, since competition for them is keen.

Dairying, during the past decade, has grown almost phenomenally in Kentucky. Though there has been a national decrease in the number of cows, the number in Kentucky has increased. Condenseries have been built at several points, and full advantage has been taken of mild, open winters and long grazing seasons. Collapse of dark-tobacco prices, urban population growth, increasing appreciation of the value of milk as a food, and other factors have contributed to the growth of dairying. In several very commendable respects Kentucky dairymen have shown marked initiative. Union was the first county in the United States to rid itself of scrub bulls. A State-wide campaign to test and weed out tubercular dairy cows has been so successful that all the 120 counties are rated tubercular-free. A State campaign to eradicate Bang's disease, or contagious abortion, among dairy cows is now well advanced. The United States Department of Agriculture actively cooperates in the campaign against tuberculosis and Bang's disease by partially reimbursing farmers for cattle which have to be killed.

Corn is normally the crop of greatest value grown in the State, but little is usually marketed as such, since the bulk is fed to livestock. Hay, which is also a high value crop, is mostly fed to livestock. Jefferson County is one of the most important agricultural counties, ranking with Aroostook County, Maine, in the production of potatoes; it leads all Kentucky counties in onions and onion sets, and is a large producer of orchard and small fruits. McCracken County leads in raising strawberries, other small fruits, and peaches; while in Henderson and a few other counties are several large commercial apple and peach orchards.

Kentucky leads in the production of bluegrass, orchard grass, and lespedeza seed. Poultry and pork production are important, and Kentucky hickory-cured hams enjoy a reputation that is becoming nationwide. The production of sorghum molasses holds promise of future development. In northern, southeastern, and selected areas of western Kentucky, honey is produced on a commercial scale. Some cotton and sweet potatoes are grown, chiefly in the Purchase; and large quantities of vegetables and truck crops are produced around Louisville and the Kentucky area near Cincinnati, Ohio.

Kentucky farmers, attempting to speak collectively concerning agricultural problems, have subscribed to a series of farm movements. The Grange reached its peak in Kentucky in 1875, at which time there were 1,493 granges with a membership of 52,463. The Agricultural Wheel, active in Kentucky in the late eighties and early nineties, established co-operative stores, a co-operative mill, and a co-operative tobacco association in Webster and Henderson Counties. During the existence of the American Society of Equity, 1904–1914, a large percentage of the tobacco of the State was marketed co-operatively. Kentucky farmers have also participated in the work of the Farmers' Alliance, the Farmers' Union, and the Burley Tobacco Growers Co-operative Association, which was organized in 1920 but later abandoned. The Farm Bureau is organized in sixty counties with a membership, in 1937, of 13,500.

Of the total population (2,614,589) in 1930, almost 70 percent was rural, and two-thirds of this number, or 1,174,232, were actually living on 246,499 farms. Farm value of crops and livestock produced in 1929 was approximately $275,000,000; in 1935 gross income from farms was $166,433,000, including Government benefit payments of $7,259,000. The ten leading farm products are corn, tobacco, dairy products, poultry, vegetables and truck, hay, hogs, sheep, beef cattle, and fruit. Although statistics are not available, it is probable that production of horses and mules should be listed as one of the ten most important farm enterprises.

Since its establishment in 1885, the Kentucky Agricultural Experiment Station, co-operatively maintained at Lexington by the State and Federal Governments, has vitally influenced the agricultural and rural life of the State. No valuation in dollars can be placed on the worth to farmers of improved agricultural practices initiated upon recommendations of this agency. Nor can any estimate be made of the additional farm income resulting from improved varieties and breeds of plants and animals, control and prevention of diseases of animals and plants, eradication and control of insect pests, and marketing and farm organization. All these activities have been developed by the experiment station. The increasing significance of this organization's work is indicated by the maintenance of branch stations at Princeton and Quicksand, and five experimental fields at other points in the State.

Farmers have become increasingly conscious of the need for conservation. Work in this field is carried on by the State department of agriculture, Smith-Hughes teachers of vocational agriculture, various State boards, commissions, and agencies, and, lately, through the Agricultural Adjustment Administration and the agricultural conservation program—the Tennessee Valley Authority, Farm Security Administration, Civilian Conservation Corps, Farm Bureau Federation, and other bodies.

TRANSPORTATION

OWING largely to natural barriers, and partly to the demands of interstate commerce, Kentucky's lines of trade and communication by land developed north to south rather than east to west. Pioneer Kentucky lay in the path of the great migrations from Virginia and the South to the West, and commerce between Lakes and Gulf was borne along its bordering waterways. But mountains formed an effective barrier to trade and transport eastward.

For nearly a century, except for the Wilderness Road through Cumberland Gap, the only transport route common to the three sections of the State—mountains, Bluegrass, and western hills and downs—was the Ohio River, tributaries of which reach back into the hills. So completely was the eastern third of the State cut off from the central and western sections that within its isolation developed a type of Kentuckian who was an enigma to the lowlanders. In the 1890's and 1900's rails were laid into the coal country in the eastern part of the State, and many extensions of the coal-carrying lines were made thereafter. In the course of this development the Chesapeake & Ohio connected Ashland and Lexington with a branch line. But even today the only direct rail route from Kentucky to the eastern seaboard is that of the main line of the C. & O., which follows the valley of the Ohio to Cincinnati.

As motor highway transport has advanced, progress has been made in penetrating the eastern section. Two U. S. highways now traverse the area, and a growing network of modern roads is steadily reducing its former isolation. Transportation in its motorized form is making Kentucky a homogeneous State.

Waterways and trails, naturally, were the first travel routes. The southern section of the trail, or trace, from Maysville to Cumberland Gap was the route by which most early white settlers entered the present State of Kentucky. Known in pioneer days as the Wilderness Road, this section today forms part of US 25E, extending southeast

IV. INDUSTRY: TRANSPORTATION

WATER FRONT, LOUISVILLE

COAL MINER

MODERN COLLIERY

STRIP MINING

COAL MINE

MISSISSIPPI RIVER AT COLUMBUS

ALONG THE PINEVILLE-HARLAN ROAD

DIX DAM, HERRINGTON LAKE

BARDSTOWN DISTILLERY

TOBACCO MARKET

MULE DAY

CHAIR MAKERS

from Corbin to Cumberland Gap. North of Corbin the Federal highway roughly follows the old trace to Maysville.

The waterways served well as commercial routes to the West and South, but trade with the East was developed laboriously. Drovers, in the early days, found it profitable to collect cattle and hogs, herd them over the mountain routes to the East, and return bearing supplies in demand among Kentucky settlers.

The trails were improved slowly and unsatisfactorily, mostly through the construction of toll roads by private enterprise. Maintenance was poor, and a writer of the early nineteenth century was frank in declaring that it was easier for an immigrant to reach Kansas from the eastern seaboard than to reach Kentucky. Nonetheless, stagecoach traffic had an early beginning. An advertisement in the *Kentucky Gazette* of August 9, 1803, announced that John Kennedy had started a stage line from Lexington, Winchester, and Mount Sterling to Olympian Springs, a famed resort in Bath County.

Toll roads persisted in the State until late in the century, when users began to protest with threats and later with organized raids to destroy the tollgates. "Shun" pikes, too, were constructed, over which traffic might detour to avoid the gates.

Many migrants from Pennsylvania or Virginia found it feasible to float down the Ohio River to their new homes at Limestone (Maysville), the Falls (Louisville), Yellowbanks (Owensboro), or other settlements. Most of the larger cities of the State are situated on the Ohio, partly as a result of the impetus given their growth when the river was the main artery of trade and travel, and partly because of the natural advantage of their position as centers of interstate traffic by rail, and as markets and distribution points.

The Kentucky boatman of the early nineteenth century belonged to a distinct social class. Tradition pictures him as a robust, rowdy braggart, inured to drudgery and danger, and much given to snorting, slapping his thigh, and proclaiming himself a "half-horse, half-alligator man," a "snapping turtle," or a "child of calamity." He was schooled in disaster, so there was some truth in the last term; at one time the term "Kentucky boatman" had to be pronounced with a smile if no hard feelings were implied.

The flatboats, keelboats, and "broadhorns" used in the river trade gradually gave place to the steamboat, which first stirred western waters in 1811. Within a few decades the steamboats dominated as cargo carriers as well as passenger carriers on the Ohio and Mississippi; and broadhorns, flatboats, and rafts appeared for the most part at floodtime, when back-country folk took advantage of the freshets to float crops or lumber to market on craft of their own making.

One of the earliest railroads west of the Alleghenies was the Lexington & Ohio, now part of the Louisville & Nashville Railroad. It was chartered January 27, 1830, and was opened for traffic August 15, 1832. At its opening, it was a line six miles long, extending from Lexington to Frankfort, with rolling stock hauled by horses; a terminus on the Ohio had purposely been left unsettled. It was 1851 before the L. & O. reached the river, and by that time it had undergone several reorganizations. However, it initiated railroad construction in Kentucky.

On March 5, 1850, the Louisville & Nashville Railroad secured a charter for a route between the cities designated in its corporate name. The first train over the route ran on November 1, 1859. The line proved extremely useful to the Federal forces during the War between the States.

Following the war, railroads became an obsession with numbers of Kentucky towns. Some of the lines built in the flush of railroad fever have been abandoned and their names forgotten. Others, planned to serve a functional need, have endured either as independent lines or as links or branches of larger systems. Today the Lexington & Big Sandy forms part of the Chesapeake & Ohio, and several short lines operate as part of the L. & N.

Unusual in character among railroads is the Cincinnati, New Orleans & Texas Pacific Railway, constructed and owned by the city of Cincinnati, Ohio. Chartered in 1871, by 1881 it had constructed 340 miles of track connecting Cincinnati with Chattanooga, extending through Kentucky and Tennessee. At present it is operated under lease by the Southern Railway System.

A glance at a railroad map of Kentucky shows that most of the major transportation systems in Kentucky touch it only along the Ohio River. Further examination reveals, however, that the State is quite adequately served, except for a comparatively small part of the south central section, by the systems named above, together with the Illinois Central and a number of smaller lines. Although some counties are completely without rail facilities, the railroad and the motor bus in combination leave few areas without modern transport of some kind. There are today in Kentucky approximately 3,821 miles of track, owned or operated by more than twenty railroads. Of this mileage all but about 165 miles is either owned or operated by class 1 railroads.

Electric railroads, or interurbans, as they were more generally called, enjoyed a brief prosperity at the beginning of the present century. With the exception of the electric lines connecting Louisville and New Albany, Indiana, and Cincinnati, Ohio, and its sister cities of northern Kentucky included in the Greater Cincinnati area, there are no interurbans in Kentucky today. The appearance of the private automobile foreshadowed their end, the motor bus made it certain, and the depression delivered the final blow.

As the railroads gradually evolved into the present-day efficient carriers of freight and passengers, river traffic languished. Passenger travel by river has almost entirely disappeared, although some excursion boats are still operated. Volume-freight traffic on the Ohio and Mississippi is gaining, however, under the program being carried out by the Corps of Army Engineers and the Inland Waterways Corporation, operating the Federal Barge Lines.

The introduction of the automobile intensified, in Kentucky as elsewhere, the demand for better roads. The constitution adopted in 1890 had prohibited the State from expending funds on highways, but this provision was removed in 1909. In 1912 a State highway commission was created, and in 1914 the legislature authorized a system of roads connecting county seats. This act was modified in 1920 by an act providing for a primary system of State highways aggregating 4,000 miles. There are now (1939) 62,633 miles of roads within the State. Approximately 500 miles of improved roads are being added annually by the State highway commission, in addition to improved mileage added by the various counties.

Since 1920 improved highways have encouraged the growth of a network of bus lines that covers the entire State. Interstate buses are well designed and equipped, and local buses are becoming more comfortable and modern. The largest bus center in Kentucky is Lexington, which is the hub of a system of fine highways in all directions, over which local and interstate coaches carry hundreds of passengers daily.

Air travel in Kentucky is still in the embryonic stage of development. The only important commercial airport in Kentucky is Bowman Field, in Louisville, used by American Airlines and Eastern Airlines. It is an important stop on the American Airlines route from Cleveland to Los Angeles, by way of Louisville, Nashville, Dallas, and Fort Worth; and on the Eastern Airlines route from Chicago to Miami, by way of Indianapolis, Louisville, and Jacksonville. Many municipalities maintain airports for local air traffic, chiefly of the air taxi type.

MANUFACTURING AND MINING

KENTUCKY'S industries are widely distributed. Much the greater part of the State's factory output issues from the towns along the Ohio River but both eastern and western Kentucky are rich in minerals, though the east far outyields the west in tonnage. Yet Kentucky is rightly regarded as being primarily an agricultural State. The value of factory and mine products is nearly three times that of crops and livestock, but, according to the U. S. Census of 1930, more than 340,000 Kentuckians were gainfully employed on farms, while about 203,000 were gainfully employed in mines, shops, and factories. Interest in agriculture is strong even in the State's industrial centers; and the Kentuckian becomes more excited over a killing frost or a rainy spring than over Dow-Jones averages or the Bedeaux system, and takes more interest in thoroughbred foals than in the latest model punch press. Something of the native temperament seems to have found expression in Kentucky's favorite industries, for the Bluegrass State is most popularly known as a producer of fine rye and bourbon whiskies, and of rich, sweet smoking and chewing tobacco. In quantity of whisky produced it leads the Nation, and in tobacco it is outranked by only two States.

Colonization of Kentucky involved transplanting not merely people but an economy capable of serving community life. Men of numerous trades, professions, and businesses joined the rush to the West, bringing with them their tools and experience.

Isolated from markets and sources of supply, Kentucky was not slow in putting to use the abilities of its pioneer craftsmen. Activities essential to life in the new settlements developed with the clearing of the land. Salt-making, tanning, gristmill construction, gunpowder manufacture, lead molding, iron smelting, and the production of nails, rope, linen, woolen cloth, and paper were among the early industries. The trade in furs, first product of the region, expanded into an exchange and export business that warranted highways across the mountains, and that became a potent argument in favor of the Louisiana Purchase and the opening of the Mississippi.

Tools and equipment for replacement had either to be made on the spot, in the early days, or packed in over long, difficult trails. This accounts for the early development of smelting and forging, antedating by nearly a century the rise of the State's present steel industry. In the 1800's Lexington was a thriving industrial town with 58 manufacturing establishments representing 13 industries. Twelve of the plants were cotton mills, four were hat factories, and four were carriage works. The difficulty of transporting unprocessed grain to market was an incentive to distilling. Georgetown had a distillery as early as 1789, and in 1810 two thousand stills were operating in the State. By that time Kentucky also had nine linseed oil mills, 63 gunpowder plants, and 267 tanneries. Small enterprises and trade limited to the immediate locality were the rule, but every town was eager to outdo the rest. Among the aspiring commercial and industrial centers Lexington early established its leadership.

Rapid settlement created a demand for manufactures that for a time ran ahead of production, and this stimulated plant expansion to a point where surpluses became a plague. The clamor for free navigation of the lower Mississippi grew stronger. In 1803 the United States purchased the Louisiana Territory. The opening of the river sent an increased flow of goods toward New Orleans, and loosed forces which in time were to disrupt and reorganize the economy of the Republic. When, in the second decade of the nineteenth century, the first steamboat appeared on western waters, the Ohio's importance as an artery of commerce was vastly increased. The river towns began to flourish as centers of manufacture and trade after 1820, and inland towns correspondingly declined. The Bluegrass, forced to move its goods over highways, could not compete with the river towns, with navigable waters for heavy freight transportation at their doors. Louisville, at the Falls of the Ohio, prospered as the transshipping point for cargoes from both up and down the river, and had the added advantage of cheap power from the falls.

Hemp, cotton, woolen, and linen mills prospered in early times. Even in the 1860's American sailing ships were equipped with rope from the Bluegrass, and Great Lakes schooners provided a market for a considerable time after. The great cause of decline in the State's hemp industry was the replacement of sailing ships with steamships in the final decades of the century, and the decline was accelerated when, after the war with Spain, sisal and other fibers were placed on the free list of imports. A single hemp factory continued to operate at Frankfort as late as 1937. Cotton, woolen, and linen factories underwent a similar decline.

The extension of railroad lines into the interior of the State in the final half of the century stimulated lumbering, mining, and manufacture in some of the more retarded areas; but elsewhere they failed to stimulate the expansion of established industries or promote the development of new ones. Mainly, the railroad strengthened the dominant economic position of the best-situated river towns. One by one the small factories of the interior towns moved or ceased operation. Today only a few remain. Portable lumber mills now work the cut-over lands for stock for barrel staves and similar special forms. Industries in which proximity to raw supplies is important, like quarrying, brick and tile making, and mining, are represented by plants here and there.

The few small factories surviving in the interior have profited, like the local merchant, from improved highways and motor-truck transportation. The motor truck has made it practicable for manufacturing plants in large industrial centers to maintain branch supply houses at well-chosen points in the interior, through which local dealers may be restocked frequently with goods in quantities suited to their needs. At the same time the motor truck has enabled the local manufacturer greatly to extend his market area. Livestock, tobacco, horticultural and dairy products, and a variety of other local commodities now find their way to market by highway.

The concentration of large-scale industries along the Ohio makes the economic map of the State a wide agricultural zone, with an industrial fringe along its northern border. The State's tobacco crop is processed in major part in the factories at Louisville, and this city also produces the bulk of Kentucky's whiskies. A number of distilleries, however, making brands that have been established in the market for many years, continue to operate at their original locations in the Bluegrass and Pennyrile, and west as far as Owensboro.

Most Ohio River towns prospered during the War between the States as supply centers for the armies of the North; this was especially true of Louisville and Covington. The railroads brought prosperity mainly to the already flourishing river cities, which became division terminals and distribution and transshipment points because of the natural advantages of their locations. Kentucky capitalists chose to invest in further development of their home territory, and this tendency still persists, serving in a degree to stimulate legitimate industry and restrain wildcat speculation. The results of this policy are evident today in the wide variety of the small-scale industries in the river towns. Cabinet making, organ building, shoe production, and the manufacture of wire cloth are but a few of the many industrial activities of the valley. Often the plants were started as small shops by craftsmen who landed from river boats in the 1830's or 1840's with little baggage except the tools of their trades.

Following the War between the States Louisville became Kentucky's leading industrial city, and first among cities east of the Mississippi and south of the Mason and Dixon Line in volume and total of manufactured products and wages. Ashland and Newport have become minor centers of steel manufacture. Covington's industrial pattern is characterized by variety. Owensboro and Henderson, distribution centers for the western Kentucky coal fields, have developed extensive marketing connections for their agricultural and horticultural products as well as for their manufactured specialties, which include textiles and electrical supplies. Paducah, like Louisville, a rail-terminal town, is known chiefly for its locomotive repair shops and as a river-boat construction center.

Kentucky's manufacturing establishments in 1933 numbered about 1,700. Wages paid totaled about $62,000,000, and the value of product was about $500,000,000. Approximately three-fifths of the output by value issued from Louisville. In all, about 70,000 wage earners were employed.

Kentucky's liquor distilleries in 1935 produced about 197,000,000 gallons of spirits, mainly bourbon, corn, and rye whiskies, with a value of approximately $60,000,000. Total wages to 7,500 distillery workers were $4,825,806; more than $11,000,000 was spent for grain supplies; and the bill for cooperage was more than $4,500,000. The industry maintains a stock of between four hundred million and five hundred million gallons in process of aging, representing an investment of $150,000,000. The State's 57 active bonded distilleries produced 43 percent of the Nation's distilled liquor output in the fiscal year 1937.

Kentucky's tobacco industry, first in dollars-and-cents importance in the State's economy, processed 343,865,000 pounds of leaf, grown mainly in the central, southern, and western sections, in 1937. Of this total, about 270,000,000 pounds were burley—which forms the bulk of the average American cigarette—and 55,000,000 pounds were dark tobacco, used in cigars, pipe and chewing tobaccos, and snuff. The value of the crop to the producers was $64,990,000.

Considerable quantities of Kentucky's dark tobacco are exported. Cigarette production in the State was 11,742,614,000 in 1937—an increase of 140,000,000 over that of 1936. This placed the State third in cigarette output. It is first in burley production and third in production of processed tobacco.

Meat packing in Kentucky centers around the Bourbon Stock Yards in Louisville. In this industry Kentucky leads the southeastern area of the Nation. Livestock and other raw supplies valued at more than $13,000,000 were processed in Kentucky packing plants in 1935. Flour and grain processing, railroad rolling-stock repair, petroleum refining, and bread making are other major industrial activities in Kentucky, and more than sixty other industries contribute to the total annual product value of $300,000,000 to $500,000,000.

Kentucky's mineral production is at present confined to coal, petroleum, natural gas, fluorspar, limestone, rock asphalt, and a number of minor substances like the finer plastic and refractory clays and clays commonly utilized in tile making.

In earlier times a number of other minerals were produced locally which are now supplied from more economical sources outside the State. Early settlers in the Kentucky area obtained their salt from the licks frequented by deer, boiling the water from the salt springs until only the solid content was left. In Mammoth Cave and elsewhere deposits of saltpeter were processed for gunpowder by leaching. Lead was found in quantities sufficient for local purposes, and iron ore of good quality was mined in the eastern part of the State. Commercial iron mining was carried on near Ashland as late as the 1870's.

Early in the nineteenth century coal began to be mined in the mountains and shipped by barge to Lexington, Louisville, and other towns for use in both forging and heating. The western fields early developed a trade in coal with New Orleans. Limestone from cliffs along the Kentucky River—"Kentucky marble"—was used to construct both public and private buildings; the old capitol at Frankfort exhibits the natural beauty of this stone. Plastic clays found in scattered deposits in central and eastern Kentucky provided the settlers with material for earthenware, and brick and tile clays found everywhere in the State served for the construction of many homes.

Modern coal mining began to develop in the 1870's, when a blast furnace was blown in at Ashland, now important for iron and steel, using ore and fuel of local origin. Cheaper ores from Missouri and later from the Mesabi Range in Minnesota made iron mining uneconomical in Kentucky, but coal mining in the Big Sandy Valley developed steadily. Coal mines in both the eastern and western parts of the State found a market in the growing industries along the Ohio. Rail connections with Great Lakes ports later widened the market for Kentucky coal.

Mining operations in the later industrial period were at first carried on in the crude style traditional of development by individuals of limited means. Farmers or lessees opened small tunnels, leaving pillars of coal for supports to save the expense of timbering. Coal was hauled by wagon to the barges. But gradually the railroads penetrated the mountainous coal country, and after 1900 coal mining became a big-capital industry (*see Labor*).

Coal production in Kentucky rose from 169,000 tons in 1870 to an average of more than 30,000,000 tons between 1916 and 1920, mainly because of expanding markets and rail transportation. Production in the eastern fields mounted to more than 60,000,000 in 1929, and dropped to 35,000,000 tons at the low point of the depression starting in 1930. In 1936 production had risen to an estimated 47,570,000 tons, with a value at the mine mouth of $65,956,000. One-ninth of this total tonnage is utilized for coke production, mostly outside the State.

Kentucky petroleum production was 5,628,000 barrels in 1936, with a value of $6,000,000. The value of natural gas produced was $17,730,000 at the point of consumption.

The output of fluorspar, from which fluorite—necessary in modern steel manufacture—is obtained, is about 80,000 short tons a year. This is about half the national total. Total annual production of Kentucky minerals, by value, is about $100,000,000.

LABOR

KENTUCKY labor, both white and Negro, has always been almost wholly native born. Its development has been essentially rural and ties in closely with lumbering and river transportation.

In early times, settlers from Virginia, the Carolinas, and Maryland dominated the Bluegrass and the Pennyrile. Many of their slaves were skilled craftsmen, who worked, when not employed at home, for people who paid their masters for their services. Thus they were a source of income to their owners, and as such were assured a degree of security against sale.

Coincidentally, the use of white labor was developing. Many early settlers, especially those from Pennsylvania and other Northern States, took up land in the mountains, where slavery was impracticable. Restricted by nature in its agricultural development, the mountain area soon had an excess of white labor that migrated to the lowlands and competed there with the labor of slaves, which was never sufficient to meet the demand. In earlier times white labor was largely engaged in logging in the great river valleys, and in clearing and farming the cut-over lands. The two processes went hand in hand; and the disappearance of marketable timber left a surplus of white laborers who, when they did not settle down to farming, either "followed the timber" or migrated to other parts of the State. Such was the general situation after the War between the States, when coal mining, oil production, and other industries widened the field of labor and extended it throughout Kentucky.

Of great importance in the developing labor situation was the early rise and subsequent decline of industrial centers. Lexington, a thriving manufacturing center in the 1800's, was plagued with piled-up surpluses and a lack of outlets. The decline of the city's manufacturing, which began about 1825, is illustrative of a process then taking place throughout the State: small community industries were being relocated at places convenient for land-and-water transfer, and in such places a population was growing which was essentially urban in outlook.

With the development of the Ohio River as a major artery of commerce between the Ohio Valley States and the West and South, trading and industrial river ports grew up in which the older Kentucky tradition had little part. The Middle East and the South fought for Kentucky's developing trade, and for a time the South prevailed. But between 1830 and 1860 the Middle East, by weight of numbers, increased its influence and won out. Migrants pouring down the Ohio settled in the river towns, and to their northern traditions were added the traditions of craftsmen who emigrated from Germany in large numbers after the Revolution of 1848.

The labor traditions of Covington, Newport, Louisville, Paducah, and other river towns are largely of such derivation. The late-comers—first as journeymen, later as the owners of shops—set the pattern of labor conditions that prevailed up to the time of the War between the States. Long hours were the rule. Most workmen supplied their own tools. Employers furnished space and materials and found a market for the goods. Wages, affected in many cases by slave competition, were low, but the prospect of a worker's becoming head of his own shop tended to head off union agitation.

The pre-war record of labor unionism is short and vague. In the 1830's seven trade unions were in existence in Louisville. The tailors organized in 1835. Sometime in the 1850's the carpenters of Hopkinsville formed a union along co-operative lines, and those at Ashland and Paducah followed suit. There is no further record of union activities until after the war. Out of the chaos of the War between the States rose the unionism of modern times.

Disbandment of the armies sent masses of men into the labor market to seek work. Kentucky had its full quota, and in addition had the problem of employing the masses of freed Negroes.

Many Negroes collected in Louisville and other industrial towns, competed for jobs, and by their numbers depressed wages. They found work in semiskilled pursuits, or served as doormen, porters, cleaners, servants, hotel attendants, and the like. In more recent times the Negro's field of occupation has widened, and there are Negroes today who own small industries or are members of the professions. But the problems of Negro employment, housing, and wages in the main are still unsolved.

The war was followed by the decline of the hemp industry, which formerly had given off-season work in the mills to farm labor. The slack in employment was taken up by an expansion of tobacco growing, a development that entailed an expansion in curing, warehousing, and marketing. White and Negro labor was attracted to the tobacco centers, where it found quarters in the low-rent areas, worked in the warehouse in the fall and winter, and hired out in the growing season to planters who collected and delivered their daily quota of field hands. The pattern is the same today. Their gregarious habits of living and working have resulted in little or no movement to organize on the part of the farm laborers, who form a large proportion of the working population of the State. The total farm population in Kentucky is 1,307,816, according to the *Statistical Abstract of the United States* for 1936; persons classified as family labor number 414,222, and those classified as hired help number 36,915. Many farmers belong to cooperative organizations, but there is little if any organization among farm workers, Negro or white.

The movement toward labor unionism in Kentucky, feebly defined at best, disappeared during the war period 1861–65. In the war years labor was in demand, wages were high, and betterment through cooperative effort, the working principle of the early unions, lost its appeal. It took a depression—that of the 1870's—to bring to life the idea of group action among the workers. The Kentucky union movement took form in local craft unions, the aim of which was mutual self-help for the immediate benefit of workers and their families. At first the unions of the 1870's gave no special emphasis to collective bargaining, but tried instead to resume action on co-operative lines. Efforts were made to provide employment for jobless workers by co-operative means, and the Knights of Labor established stores (in 1880) and at least one tobacco company (at Earlington), the profits of which were divided equally among capital, labor (the laborer usually supplied the capital by stock purchases), and the Knights of Labor (as the promoting and fostering organization). Failure of the Knights of Labor to live up to its promise as an instrument for bettering conditions resulted after 1886 in loss of membership, and it disappeared from the scene. The American Federation of Labor then came to the fore, with a program of better working conditions, shorter hours, and fair wages; most local unions, whether affiliated with the Federation or not, followed the same line.

Most labor disputes during this period hinged on wages, but union recognition grew in importance as an objective. Employers' associations were forming and growing, and the fight against unionism was carried on ruthlessly. According to A. E. Suffern, during a coal strike starting in November 1900, in Hopkins County, operators secured an injunction forbidding the United Mine Workers of America to supply strikers with food.

The change in union aims, noted above, was made in response to technological and organizational changes in industry out of which developed the present industrial order.

After the southward expansion from the Ohio River of railroads connecting the Deep South with the North, the river towns, notably Louisville, Covington, and Paducah, became centers of labor unionization activity. A wage cut early in the summer of 1877 provoked a railroad strike, in which demonstrations were suppressed by police action. The strike, which coincided in time with others throughout the Nation, was apparently under local leadership and was fought out over issues involved in the relations between the Louisville & Nashville Railroad and its employees. Other strikes, local in significance and effect, at times have interrupted the generally amicable relations of labor and capital, but persuasion and appeal to reason have often ended a dispute peaceably.

The period of industrial expansion ending with American entry into the World War was marked by the passage of laws fostered by the unions. Among these laws were measures widening the field and limiting the hours of women's labor, specifying the industries and limiting the hours of labor for minors, and providing protection for workers in hazardous occupations and compensation for workers injured in the line of duty. The influence of the unions has continued to grow, but the State as a whole is far from unionized, largely because of the peculiar characteristics of many of its industries, chief among which is the production of tobacco. Besides this deterrent factor, the tradition of self-sufficiency operates outside the Ohio River towns against active labor organization based on current union conceptions of the relation between capital and labor.

Especially striking has been the expansion of Kentucky's coal industry. The State's coal production in 1870 was only 169,000 tons; in 1900 it reached 5,182,000 short tons. Coal mining gave work to men of the mountain areas, where lumbering had become a minor industry and where farming, above the subsistence level, was difficult. But until the end of the century the mines were small, individually owned, and manned by local labor. Many operators worked side by side with their men.

After 1900 mining rapidly became mechanized, especially in the east-

ern part of the State. Railroad branches were built into the coal country and large capital investments and corporate ownership became the
rule.

Shortly after the World War, with living costs increasing, the workers
in Kentucky, as elsewhere, began to organize for higher wages. Wage
strikes of steel workers in Newport and of coal miners in the western
part of the State during the 1920's, and the bitterness engendered by
the struggles, are still remembered in those areas. In the steel industry
the Amalgamated Association of Iron, Steel and Tin Workers did little
more than collect dues. If union men displayed militancy, as they did
in Newport when the militia appeared with a tank and enforced a cur-
few law, that was their own affair. The Newport Rolling Mill Company (since absorbed by Armco) and the Andrews Steel Company
drove the unions from their mills, membership dropped, and many
locals ceased to exist. Events in Harlan County since 1931 emphasize
a condition unlike that prevailing generally in Kentucky industry or
elsewhere in the Kentucky coal industry.

Natural advantages favoring cheap coal production in Harlan were
seized upon in 1910 by local enterprise. Capital was secured, a railroad was built, and in 1911 the first coal was shipped. Men flocked
in from the surrounding hills to work at the mines, and the population
of the county increased at an extraordinary rate. Mountaineers, drawn
from their hill farms by the high wages, or what seemed so to them,
came to the mines to work, to live in company shacks, to trade in company stores, and to be policed by company guards.

Limitations imposed on workers became irksome, but it was not practicable to resist the rulers of the county, who were mainly intent on protecting their income and on blocking all organization that might
threaten it. Labor unions were told peremptorily to keep out, and the
Harlan County Coal Operators' Association showed that on this point
it meant business. In the course of five years of operator rule Harlan
County became known as "Bloody Harlan," and labor conditions there
became popularly identified with those in Kentucky as a whole.

After two years of increasing unemployment, unionization of large
numbers of miners was effected by the United Mine Workers of
America. Strikes that developed were met with the usual strikebreaking
tactics, including intimidation and worse by company police and the
importation of non-union employees. One strike brought the "Battle of
Evarts" on May 5, 1935, in which two deputy sheriffs in the employ

of mine owners were killed and a dozen or more miners were killed or reported missing. Something like civil war followed.

Attempts by private organizations to learn the facts and provide relief for out-of-work miners were repressed by the operators and authorities. Beginning in 1931 the violation of the rights of miners, organizers, investigators, and relief workers resulted in many protests, but no action was taken by the Government until the La Follette Civil Liberties Committee started an inquiry in 1935. This inquiry was still in progress when the Wagner Labor Relations Act, affirming the right of workers collectively to bargain through a union of their own choosing, became law. The National Labor Relations Board subsequently issued an order to "cease and desist" from interference with unionization against the operators' association.

The order was ignored by the mine owners, and indictments on charges of conspiracy to deprive citizens of their constitutional rights were returned against 23 members of the operators' association, against a like number of individual heads of the companies involved, and against 21 deputy sheriffs allegedly in company employ. Feeling in Harlan ran so high that venue in the case was changed to near-by London, Laurel County. The trial began May 16, 1938, and ended August 1 with a disagreement of the jury. Action for retrial was halted when the operators signed an agreement on September 1 which substantially satisfied the miners' demands.

The years since the World War have brought difficult problems to the unions. A policy of working constructively with business organizations and with State and Federal Governments has lessened the impact of depression. Organized labor in the State today is for peace in the labor movement, improvement of labor and social laws, and a more comprehensive educational program within the ranks of labor.

THE NEGRO

APPROXIMATELY 226,240 or 7.8 percent of the 2,900,000 people in Kentucky are Negroes. They live for the most part in the inner Bluegrass area, of which Lexington is the center, and in the better farming sections of the Pennyrile around Hopkinsville. Despite their relative numerical unimportance, Kentucky Negroes are an integral part of the State's life and have contributed notably to its development.

In 1751, when Christopher Gist came into the Kentucky country in search of lands for the Ohio Company, his only attendant was a Negro servant. Fifteen years later a mulatto slave was one of a party of five exploring this region. A few of the pioneers from Virginia brought their slaves when they migrated to the West, but as a rule the earliest settlers did not own slaves, since they were poor and slave property was a luxury. Such slaves as were brought into the Kentucky country in the early days were usually affectionately attached to the household through long years of service. In accounts of Indian raids slaves are reported as loyal and daring. One of them, Monk, owned by Colonel William Estill, was an expert in making gunpowder and a preacher of ability, listened to by both Negroes and whites.

Though slavery, as an institution, was slow in becoming established, there were more than 12,000 slaves by 1790, and their number increased during the next 40 years. In 1833, when a quarter of the total population was Negro, it was thought prudent to legislate against further importation of slaves. Thereafter the proportion of Negroes to whites decreased.

This was partly because of the profitable traffic with sections of the Deep South where cotton, cane, rice, and other crops dependent on slave labor were raised. Another factor was the Underground Railroad, so named—according to one version of the origin of the term—by a Kentuckian. Fostered by Northern money, directed by shrewd, resourceful men, it spirited fugitives across the Ohio River into the friendly shelter of Ohio and Indiana. Despite the reputedly mild and patriarchal character of slavery in Kentucky, Negroes took advantage of the opportunity thus offered to gain their freedom. The State's loss in slave property has been placed at not less than $200,000 annually, in the decades immediately preceding the War between the States.

Since the State did not secede from the Union, its slaves were not freed by the Emancipation Proclamation, but by the Thirteenth Amendment, enacted on December 18, 1865. The State legislature passed a civil rights act, repealing the old slave code, in February 1866.

In reality the slave system was not ended by legislation but by enlistment. Negroes deserted from the fields, or were forcibly taken, to serve in the Union Army. The historian, E. Merton Coulter, states that "10,000 slaves left the State during the year 1863; slaves enlisted at the rate of a hundred a day, and after the war, were freed at the rate of 500 a day." The 1860 census showed 236,167 Negroes in the State, of whom 10,684 were free; the census of 1870 showed 222,210 Negroes.

Though losing steadily in ratio, Negro population has gained in numbers and changed in distribution. During the World War there was considerable migration to the North, where labor was at a premium. Then and later a shift set in from the poorer farms to the State's industrial centers—principally to Louisville, Covington, Newport, and Ashland—and to the mining regions. In 1930 approximately half of Kentucky's Negro population was urban. Of the 109,479 Negroes on farms, 9,104 were listed as operators; 4,175 of these owned their farms, 4,914 were tenants, and 15 were managers.

The proportion of those gainfully employed is high, and their occupations are varied. The 1930 United States Census lists a total of 106,572 gainfully employed, including 7,346 in coal mines, 3,414 in railroads, 2,239 in building construction, 2,226 chauffeurs and truck and tractor drivers, 1,473 laborers, porters, and helpers in stores, and 1,222 waiters (men and women).

In the "white collar" class, the census lists 39 Negro college presidents and professors, 86 trained nurses, 25 lawyers, 37 dentists, 129 doctors, 727 clergymen, and 1,615 teachers. The need for expansion of Negro activities in these occupations is shown by the fact that there is 1 trained nurse for every 2,828 Negroes, 1 lawyer for every 9,142 Negroes and 1 doctor for every 1,752 Negroes in the State.

Two large Negro insurance companies are located in Louisville, facing each other on Walnut Street. There are three Negro newspapers in the same city: the *American Baptist,* the *Louisville Leader* and the *Louisville Defender.*

In ante bellum days most of the free Negroes lived in Louisville, and attempts were made to provide education for them. The Freedmen's Guild took charge of such efforts after the war, and in a short time established 35 schools with 58 teachers, many of them Negroes. There was, however, no public provision for financing these schools and tuition fees were necessarily low. Private generosity had to be depended on for funds, and northern Negroes contributed a great share of the donations.

In 1866 a law was passed providing that the proceeds of all Negro taxes should be divided equally between Negro schools and Negro paupers. The principle of equality in education was incorporated in the constitution of 1891, perhaps as a result of agitation in 1873 and a threat of appeal to the State and Federal courts for equal school advantages. During the present century educational facilities for Negro children have improved.

In one institution only—Berea College—have Negroes in Kentucky been permitted to attend school with whites. But this practice was discontinued in 1904 when the law prohibiting "mixed" schools was passed. A division of property and endowment was effected, and Lincoln Institute, a high school for Negroes, modeled on Berea, was established in Shelby County.

The Louisville Municipal College for Negroes is an outgrowth of Simmons University, founded in 1873 by the General Association of Colored Baptists of Kentucky as the Kentucky Normal and Theological Institute. In 1920 a proposal for a million-dollar bond issue for the University of Louisville was defeated, largely because it did not have the support of the Negro electorate. The proposal, with provisions for earmarking $100,000 of the issue for the advancement of higher education for Negroes in Louisville, was resubmitted in 1925 and passed. Simmons University was purchased, renamed the Louisville Municipal College for Negroes, and opened as part of the University of Louisville on February 9, 1931. The institution is now recognized as a four-year college, and has the highest scholastic rating of any Negro institution in the State.

The only other State-supported institution of higher learning in the State is the Kentucky State Industrial College at Frankfort. Since no State institution granting master's and higher degrees admits Negroes, the Anderson-Mayer Aid Act, passed in 1935, requires the State to defray expenses of Negro students wishing to secure advanced degrees in institutions outside the State.

The church is to a considerable degree the center of social life for the Kentucky Negro. The first Negro church in Kentucky was the Methodist Episcopal Zion Church, organized in Louisville in 1816. It was not until after emancipation, however, that the Negro church developed, for the Negro slave generally attended his master's church, worshiping in a gallery set aside for the purpose. Sometimes separate Negro services were held in schoolhouses and vacant church buildings, and gave rise to preachers who achieved more than local fame. Josiah Henson, a slave in Davies County, preached widely in both America and England after escaping from bondage. He is best known as one of the many prototypes of Harriet Beecher Stowe's "Uncle Tom." Total State membership of Negro churches today is 127,126; the Baptist, with 83,837 members, the African Methodist Episcopal, with 10,492, and the Colored Methodist Episcopal, with 7,715 are the three major denominations.

In politics the Kentucky Negro has been traditionally Republican, but in recent years he has supported the Democratic party. In Louisville, Lexington, Hopkinsville, and Paducah the Negro vote is often a decisive factor. As has been noted above the Negro vote was largely responsible for the establishment of the Louisville Municipal College for Negroes, and other advances for Negroes in the educational field have been won through the ballot box. Phil Brown, Kentucky's outstanding Negro in politics, was appointed Commissioner of Conciliation, in the United States Department of Labor in April 1921 and served in this capacity until November 1923. Representative C. W. Anderson, Jr., a Negro of Louisville, has served in the State legislature since 1933.

Housing facilities for Negroes, long a reproach to property owners and to those in authority, are improving. Many fine homes, well maintained, are owned and occupied by Negroes. The Federal Housing Administration completed one Negro project, College Court in Louisville, in 1937 and has others under immediate consideration.

In all the wars fought since Kentucky became a State, the Negro has played his part with credit and distinction. Approximately 23,700 Negroes served in the War between the States; hundreds saw service in the Spanish-American War, and 12,580, or more than 14 percent of the Kentuckians in the World War, were Negroes.

Among Kentucky Negroes who have won distinction in their chosen fields are Bishop Alexander Walters, civic and political leader; Allen Allensworth, chaplain of the Twenty-fourth Infantry; Charles Young,

Twenty-fourth Infantry; Isaac Murphy, famous jockey; Roland Hayes, the singer, a native of Georgia, but resident in Louisville; Stephen Bishop, one of the explorers of Mammoth Cave; Joseph Seamon Cotter, the poet, and his son, Joseph Seamon Cotter, Jr., also a poet; Ernest Hogan, showman and one of the popularizers of "jazz"; and H. C. Russell, Negro specialist in the United States Office of Education.

RELIGION

CHURCH membership in Kentucky has increased at a rate faster than that of the population. Almost one-half of the people of the State—approximately a million—are church members today, while only about one person in 12 claimed membership in 1800.

The different religious sects, of which there are nearly 60, show great disparity in size and represent divisions and subdivisions within some of the major denominations. The Baptists, the largest single group, have a total membership of 425,000, of which 300,000 are in the Southern Baptist Convention and the remainder in nine other Baptist divisions. The Catholics come next in point of numbers, with 180,000 members, followed by the Methodists with 170,000 members distributed among eight subdenominations. The Disciples of Christ (better known in Kentucky as the Christian Church) have a membership of 122,000, and the Presbyterians (subdivided into five groups) number 52,000. The remaining 50,000 church members are found in more than 50 smaller organizations.

The religious history of the State falls roughly into four periods: the time of pioneering, the decades of the Great Revival beginning in 1797, the period dominated by the slavery issue and the War between the States; and what may be considered the modern epoch, following reconstruction and extending to the present. As the story unfolds, the growth of the different denominations and their relative status today, as well as the underlying causes of their schisms, become clear.

Pioneering days were marked by the missionary zeal of the first pastors and circuit riders and, conversely, by a general indifference to religious matters on the part of the general populace. An Episcopalian minister, the Reverend John Lythe, preached the first sermon of which there is any record in 1775. The first recorded preaching by a Baptist minister took place at Harrodsburg the following year, but Baptist services were probably held before that. Increasing religious activity came in the 1780's. Three Baptist churches were established in 1781 at Severn's Valley (now in Elizabethtown), Cedar Creek, and

Gilbert's Creek; the first Methodist church west of the Alleghenies was organized near Danville in 1783; and during the following year Reverend David Rice settled there to take charge of three associations with about twenty churches. By this time the Presbyterians had organized their first presbytery with twelve churches, and a Roman Catholic church had been built at Holy Cross near Rohan Knobs. In 1789 there were three Methodist circuits; the first annual conference of Methodists was held near Lexington in 1790. When Kentucky became a State in 1792 there were forty-two churches with a combined membership of 3,095.

But despite this apparent activity of organized religion, morals were at low ebb at the end of the eighteenth century, according to the accounts of eyewitnesses. Frontier conditions and general religious indifference throughout the country at this time would seem to give credence to these contemporary estimates. The time was ripe for the Great Revival.

The first signs appeared in 1797 when James McGready, a Presbyterian minister, came from South Carolina to take charge of three churches in Logan County. By 1800 the revival spirit had swept over the entire State and the adjoining territory. The period was marked by a wave of religious excitement that found expression in the revivalist or camp meeting type of service and led to a dramatic increase in church membership.

One striking psychological phenomenon associated with the revival meetings (and indeed with similar meetings today) is known as the "jerks." People were seized with violent convulsions, the head jerking spasmodically from side to side. Some fell into a coma-like state; others rolled on the ground, jumped and ran, danced, barked, gave way to hysterical laughter, or had trances and visions. A high tide of emotionalism swept over the meetings and kindled a flame of religious fervor.

The Presbyterians, among whom the revival movement first showed itself, failed to profit by it. Instead, they split on the rock of doctrinal and practical differences. The revival spirit, as it spread through the State, created a demand for preachers that could not be met by the number of trained ministers available. Opportunities opened up by the awakening religious interest had to be lost, or men who lacked the formal qualifications for the task had to be licensed to preach. The Cumberland Presbytery, immediately responsible for carrying on the revival, took the latter way out of the dilemma, and was dissolved by its synod. Appeal was made to the General Assembly of the Presbyterian Church in 1809 without success, and as a result the Cumberland Presbyterian Church was formed as an independent denomination in 1810. By 1829 it had grown so rapidly that it organized a general assembly of its own with eighteen presbyteries.

Matters of doctrine offered an even more formidable stumbling block and led, indirectly, to the formation of the Church of the Christian Disciples (the Christian Church). Barton W. Stone, minister in charge of two Presbyterian churches in Bourbon County, visited the Logan County revival in 1801 and was so impressed that he decided to organize a similar meeting of his own. Held at Cane Ridge in August, it drew crowds variously estimated all the way from 10,000 to 25,000. Excitement and emotional fervor rose to a high pitch, and the Cane Ridge meeting is commonly regarded as the peak of the Great Revival. Stone and his followers (the Stonites) found it difficult to reconcile the part played by human reaction in salvation with the Calvinistic emphasis on the doctrines of election and predestination, and this got them into trouble with the Presbyterian Synod of Kentucky. Suspended in 1803, they first formed the independent Springfield Presbytery, but almost immediately threw over the background of allegiance to the parent denomination and adopted the simple name "Christian."

The Baptists, unlike the Presbyterians, took full advantage of the Great Revival to add to their ranks. In the three years, from 1800 to 1803, they enrolled 10,000 members, and by 1820 had more members than all other denominations combined. But trouble was brewing. Thomas Campbell and his son Alexander, originally Presbyterians, had joined the Baptists when differences of doctrine forced them out of the Presbyterian fold in 1813. They became an influential force among the Baptists of Kentucky and by 1830 had drawn as many as 10,000 adherents away from the Baptist ranks. Their followers (the Campbellites) held the Armenian views and sought to promote a simple evangelical Christianity. In 1832 two men representing the Stonites and the Campbellites were sent through Kentucky to bring these two groups together. They were largely successful and effected a union resulting in the organization of the Christian Church —which may be regarded as a sect formed of members of the Presbyterian and the Baptist Churches.

Methodism was peculiarly open to the influence of the Great Revival. Its numbers grew rapidly and it prospered; not until later did it, too, suffer dissensions and divisions.

The Catholics were untouched by the revival, but were perhaps affected by the general awakening of interest in religion. The first diocese, which originally included Tennessee and all the Northwest Territory, was organized at Bardstown in 1808. The first bishop, Benedict Joseph Flaget, had his residence in a log cabin (still preserved) at St. Thomas, near Bardstown, and began building the first cathedral west of the mountains at Bardstown in 1819. It was not until 1841 that the see was transferred to Louisville.

The Shakers, though they did not come directly under the influence of the revival, were drawn to Kentucky by it. Organized as an offshoot of Quakerism in England, the Shaker Society had been brought to America in 1775 by "Mother Ann" Lee, and was first centered in New York. Its members believed in strict and simple living, in prophecy, and direct spiritual guidance. Thus they were attracted by reports of the revival, and thought, probably, that Kentucky would offer congenial soil for Shaker beliefs and practices. For a time the Shakers prospered in their new home, and had two establishments of which one, known as Shakertown or Pleasant Hill, is still well preserved. By about 1850, however, the society began to decline. Shakerism in Kentucky is of historic interest but it is not part of the present-day picture. There are still a few Shakers in America, but none are left in the State.

What may be considered the third period in Kentucky's religious history reached its climax during the War between the States. It saw divisions over the slavery issue within the major denominations, and reflected the trend of secular events which so bitterly divided the Nation.

The Presbyterians, already disorganized by the revival, were further divided in 1837 by a general schism of the Presbyterian Church over doctrinal matters into Old School and New School Presbyterians. The latter organization was confined largely to the North and became outspokenly antislavery. But there were enough Southern members, including the Kentucky Presbytery of Lexington, to cause these to withdraw in 1857 to form the United Synod of the South, with six synods, twenty-one presbyteries, and about 15,000 members. In 1864 the United Synod of the South joined the Presbyterian Church of the Confederate States (which had split off from the Old School Church in 1861) to form the Presbyterian Church in the United States, now popularly known as the Southern Presbyterian Church. Since Kentucky was a border State, the war divided the Presbyterians cruelly, and created chaos in their ranks. The Southern churches cut themselves off completely from Northern affiliations, and this wound has not yet been entirely healed.

The Baptists and Methodists also split on the slavery question. As early as 1844 the Baptist associations of the South, including those in Kentucky, withdrew from the triennial convention to form their own organization, the Southern Baptist Convention. In the same year the Methodists decided on an amicable separation, and the Methodist Episcopal Church, South (Southern Methodist Church) was organized in Louisville in May 1845. Of its 460,000 members in 1846—in the entire South—125,000 were Negro. But by 1860 there remained fewer than 50,000 Negroes, and ten years later these withdrew to form the Colored Methodist Episcopal Church.

With the slavery issue settled and the War between the States behind them, the denominations which split on these national issues have shown a growing tendency, not yet altogether successful, to mend the schisms of that period. A gradual development of tolerance, and of social and philanthropic activities, mark the fourth (or present) period of Kentucky's religious history.

The picture of religious life today may be drawn briefly. There are, all told, more than 7,000 churches in the State. Though only about 16 percent are urban, these claim approximately 40 percent of the entire church membership. More than 50 percent of all Negroes in Kentucky are church members; the Baptist group—numbering 90,000 —is larger than all other Negro church groups combined.

The Baptists, as stated above, are the largest single religious group. They are found in every county except those of the extreme northeastern section. In many counties they constitute half (or more) of the church membership, and are especially strong along the southern border and in the southeastern section. The Southern Baptist Convention has as yet shown no inclination to reunite with other Baptist groups, possibly because of the fundamentalist issue.

Catholic church membership is unevenly distributed. Thirty-four counties in the southwest and along the southern and eastern borders report no Catholics, while 115,000 of the total 180,000 are in Jefferson, Campbell, Nelson, and Kenton Counties.

Of all the denominations divided by the slavery issue, the Methodists have shown the strongest tendency toward reconciliation with the Northern Conference. In 1925 a plan for the organic reunion of the Methodist Episcopal Church and the Methodist Episcopal Church,

South failed by a narrow margin of the combined votes of lay and ministerial members of the Southern Church, while the vote in the Methodist Episcopal Church itself was overwhelmingly in favor of union. In April 1938, at a meeting of the general conference in Birmingham, Alabama, a plan of union was adopted by a majority of 334 affirmative votes to 26 opposing votes. The plan provided for a uniting conference to be held on April 26, 1939, for the purpose of harmonizing and combining provisions now existing in the disciplines of the uniting churches. At a conference held in Kansas City, Missouri, in June 1939, the three branches of Methodism were united under the name "The Methodist Church."

The Presbyterians are still divided into the Presbyterian Church in the United States with 22,000 members; the Presbyterian Church in the United States of America, with 16,000 members; the Cumberland Presbyterians with 11,600 members; and the Colored Cumberland Presbyterians and the United Presbyterians with 1,370 members. There are, however, many indications of effort to unite northern and southern elements.

The Protestant Episcopal Church is comparatively small. More than half of its 13,000 members are in Jefferson and Breckinridge Counties and 75 of the 120 counties report no members. Jewish congregations are likewise small. Of the 15,500 Jews in the State, 12,500 are concentrated in Louisville.

Camp meetings, revivals, baptisms, and other outdoor religious gatherings, which formerly were an important factor in the religious life of the State, have almost entirely disappeared except in the Kentucky highlands. Here customs change slowly, and, even with better roads and churches, these activities are still conducted with great fervor. One of the oldest institutions of its kind in the Southern Methodist Church is the Kavanaugh Camp Meeting near Crestwood, 18 miles from Louisville. Founded more than 60 years ago by Bishop H. H. Kavanaugh, the meeting has been held here annually except for a short period when the camp was closed. Before there were any buildings on the grounds everything was of a primitive nature. Benches were built in a grove of oak and beech trees; tents were used to lodge those who wished to remain for the entire meeting. Later a pavilion, a dining hall, dormitories, and about twenty cottages were added. Today the camp is equipped with modern conveniences. Speakers of national prominence deliver addresses at the meetings, which are interdenominational.

EDUCATION

PIONEER Kentuckians were often unlettered, according to the standards of formal education, but they respected learning. Wherever stockades were erected, cabins within them were set apart as schools in which the more literate members of the community taught the "three R's," often from memory.

In 1775, before the first church and the first court of justice were established, the first school was opened in the fort at Harrodsburg. The teacher, Mrs. William Coomes, taught the beginners to read and write from paddle-shaped pine shingles inscribed with the alphabet, and from Bible texts. At McAfee's Station, near Harrodsburg, there was a school in 1777. John McKinney taught at Lexington "between fights" with wildcats and Indians. At Boonesboro, at Logan's Station —wherever a cluster of cabins appeared—schools were established, presided over by teachers who sometimes knew little more than their pupils. With low pay, often in tobacco—which was legal tender— bear bacon, buffalo steak, or jerked venison, these pioneer teachers eked out a precarious existence.

The schoolhouse was a cheerless log hut, lighted through oiled paper stretched over an opening that served for a window. Books were few, but there was always the Bible, supplemented by hand-written texts.

Numerous private schools were established between 1780 and 1800. At Lexington, John Filson, Kentucky's first historian, conducted a private academy until his death in 1788; Elijah Craig, a pioneer Baptist minister, established a school for his congregation at Georgetown; and Salem Academy at Bardstown, under John Priestly, became one of the leading schools in the State. Schools at this time were primarily for boys, who were taught arithmetic, surveying, geometry, bookkeeping, a smattering of English grammar, and a little Latin—if they were destined for the law or medicine. The private schools opened by the French immigrants offered languages, music, deportment, and "fancy" dancing.

There were also "female" academies, which corresponded to finishing schools and specialized in such subjects as "ornamental" literature, poetry, and fancy and practical needlework, in addition to reading, writing, and grammar. Girls were considered cultured if they were accomplished dancers, and could make samplers and speak a little French.

Early efforts at elementary education were definitely individualistic, and followed the motto that governed Indian fighting: "Every man to his man, and every man to his tree." The first constitution, adopted in 1792, made no mention of education. On the other hand, higher education was recognized as the responsibility of the State soon after the Revolution. In 1783 the Virginia Legislature set aside confiscated Tory land in the County of Kentucky "for a public school or seminary of learning." As a result, Transylvania Seminary, later to become the first university west of the Alleghenies, was opened as a grammar school at Crow's Station, afterward Danville, in the double log cabin of "Father" David Rice. He was the school's first teacher at a salary of three pounds sterling a year—one-half to be in cash and the rest in corn, tobacco, and pork. In 1788 the seminary was moved to Lexington, which was at that time the most important frontier settlement of the West. Transylvania later developed and prospered sufficiently to make Lexington the literary capital of the region. A large majority of the influential men in the early history of Kentucky and the West are related to this institution in one way or another.

In 1788 there came the first suggestion, from an anonymous Lexington correspondent, that a public school system should be established. The system proposed the division of counties into districts, in each of which a public school was to be located. The opposition of the private academies, however, prevented the materialization of the plan. At Georgetown and Bardstown, and in Mercer and Madison Counties, new private schools were opened.

In 1794 Kentucky Academy, the first public school authorized and incorporated by the Kentucky Legislature, was established through a State endowment of 6,000 acres of land at Pisgah, near Lexington. George Washington and John Adams each contributed $100 to this institution. Bethel Academy, the first Methodist institution of learning in the Mississippi Valley, opened in Jessamine County in 1798. The precedent set by the Methodists was quickly followed by other denominations. The legislature then provided endowments of 6,000 acres of land to each county in the State for the purpose of establishing seminaries that were somewhat more restricted in educational scope than colleges. In order to raise $1,000 with which to meet preliminary expenses, each county was allowed to operate lotteries.

Notwithstanding the development in higher education, common school instruction still followed the pioneer principle that education should be diffused downward from college to the masses. By the end of the second decade of the nineteenth century, fifty-nine county academies, favored by generous legislatures, were chartered. The majority of Kentuckians, however, failed to give adequate financial support to the State-endowed county academies, and by the outbreak of the War between the States, only one of them was left.

The period 1820–1850 was one of extremes in the development of education. Incompetent trustees of academy endowments frittered away assets; visionary legislatures set up educational funds, only to raid them for any emergency which arose; forward-looking men wagged an admonishing finger at those in places of responsibility; Governors addressed legislatures, and the press at times vigorously argued in behalf of the uneducated masses. Meanwhile, religious denominations were establishing or getting control of colleges, seminaries, and academies throughout the State; but this contributed little if anything to elementary education.

The general educational level in 1830 was revealed in a school report from 78 out of 83 counties. Of a total of almost 140,000 children in the State between the ages of five and fifteen years, only 31,834 were attending school. In the county with the best record only one-half of the children were at school.

The State's leaders, concerned over the situation, organized the Kentucky Educational Society in the early 1830's to arouse public sentiment. Realization of the need for education spread, and when the Federal Government adopted the policy of distributing surplus land revenues among the States in 1836, education shared in Kentucky's $2,000,000 windfall. A fund of $850,000 was set aside to found and sustain a general program of public education. A law, sponsored by Judge W. F. Bullock, of Louisville, was passed by the legislature on February 16, 1838, establishing the first public school system. The income from the fund was to be distributed among the counties according to the number of children of school age, and school districts were empowered to tax citizens to an amount equal to the sum received from the State. The system also provided for a State board of education, division of the State into districts containing 30 to 50 children, appointment of five commissioners of education for each county and five trustees for each district.

The cause of general education was retarded by the fact that the prosperous patronized private schools and the poor were indifferent. Agitation continued. One writer suggested that not only should the poor be educated, but poor parents who needed the labor of their children should be compensated for the time their children spent in school.

By 1840, two years after the public school system had come into existence, the first real public school census was made. Only 32,920 children were reported in school, while the school-age population had increased by more than 40,000. There were 42,000 persons over 20 years of age in the State who were unable to read. Counties with as many as 2,000 children of school age reported none in school attendance, while the best records again showed only one-half the children in school. Still the legislature and elected officials bickered over school funds and policies.

In 1847, when Robert J. Breckinridge became superintendent of education, the situation changed. Due to his efforts the new constitution, adopted in 1849, contained a clause protecting educational funds. By 1853 the common-school law was in operation in every county of the State, even though first-class teachers could not always be obtained with the funds available.

Then came the War between the States, and much of the ground gained was lost.

In 1869 there were 4,447 schools with 169,477 children in attendance out of a total of 376,868 of school age. Nine years later there were still 226,323 children out of school. In 1883 more than 250,000 people—15 percent of the Commonwealth's population—could not read.

But it must be remembered that Negroes had not been classed as citizens until after the emancipation of slaves; that Negroes almost without exception had no schooling during slave days and that adequate school facilities for Negroes did not exist for many years thereafter. With this great group of illiterate children added to the population it appeared that the list of illiterate citizens in the State had grown alarmingly when such was not the case.

Increasing funds went into common-school education and the citizens fought illiteracy under such slogans as "We Want a Pen in Every Hand in Kentucky." At one time as many as 100,000 illiterates were being instructed by volunteer teachers.

V. EDUCATION: RELIGION

OLD CENTRE, CENTRE COLLEGE, DANVILLE

MOUNTAIN SCHOOL OF NATURAL STONE, A WPA PROJECT

BEREA COLLEGE, BEREA

KENTUCKY SCHOOL FOR THE DEAF, DANVILLE

THE UNIVERSITY OF KENTUCKY, AIRVIEW

TRAPPIST MONASTERY, GETHSEMANE

AUDUBON MUSEUM, HENDERSON

GIDDINGS HALL, GEORGETOWN COLLEGE

GUEST HOUSE, SHAKERTOWN

DOORWAY TO GUEST HOUSE, SHAKERTOWN

SHAKER CEREMONIES

SHAKER CEREMONIES

ST. JOSEPH'S CHURCH, BARDSTOWN

MUD MEETING HOUSE (*c.* 1806), NEAR HARRODSBURG

Kentucky's educational system received its most progressive boost in the "Educational Legislature" of 1908 and 1909. Funds were increased for the support of schools, and State and county funds were combined and distributed on a basis which equalized opportunities for each county. From 1908 to 1936 important changes were made in the whole school system: the school laws were clarified and placed in a single codification in 1934; the Council of Higher Education was organized; the University of Kentucky was made head of the educational system and given responsibility for graduate training; the other State colleges were entrusted with the responsibility of teacher training and undergraduate work in general. Today (1939) Kentucky has the lowest rate of illiteracy of any of the southern States, and State support to its public schools compares favorably with that of the Nation.

Keeping pace with the development of common-school education, facilities for higher education have also progressed. The University of Louisville, the oldest public institution of higher learning in the State, was founded by the city council in 1837. A branch of the university, the Louisville Municipal College for Negroes, offers a regular four-year college course. The Kentucky State Industrial College is the only other State-supported institution of higher learning for Negroes in the State.

The University of Kentucky was founded as the Agricultural and Mechanical College in 1866, under provisions of the Congressional Morrill Land-Grant Act. It opened with an enrollment of 190 students. The present resident enrollment is 3,825, not counting students in correspondence and extension courses.

There are four State teachers colleges, at Richmond, Moorehead, Murray, and Bowling Green. Among the privately endowed institutions are Transylvania, Centre, Asbury, Union, Georgetown, Winchester, Kentucky Wesleyan, and Berea. Most of the fifteen junior colleges in the State are supported by religious denominations.

Not until 1911 was a concentrated effort made to establish a program of adult education. In that year Mrs. Cora Wilson Stewart founded the "moonlight schools" in which adults were taught to read and write. Her project led to the appointment of Governor McCreary's "illiteracy commission" in 1920.

The public school system is now supported by State appropriations amounting to approximately $11.65 per capita, in addition to county appropriations and funds derived from taxes on public properties for schools. Approximately 655,186 Kentucky children, or 86 percent of those between the ages of six and eighteen years, were enrolled in public and private schools in the school year 1934–1935. In 1935 there were 848 high schools in the State, 773 for white children and 75 for Negroes.

In co-operation with the Works Progress Administration and the Public Works Administration, modern school buildings have been constructed and old buildings have been improved in practically every county in the State. The adult educational program of the Works Progress Administration has done much to solve the problem of illiteracy.

FOLKLORE AND FOLK MUSIC

THE CONVENIENT and pithy term for the mountain people of Kentucky, "our contemporary ancestors," does not indicate the origin of the customs, beliefs, and peculiarities which persist among them. For they too had ancestors. These were, for the most part, British, and of the soil. Just as today many a mountaineer has never been ten miles from his birthplace, so also his forebears remained at home. They were sturdy men and women, steeped in traditional ways, independent and as little humble as possible. The mountaineer is that way too. He cares neither for ease nor for soft living. He is hospitable. "Welcome, stranger, light and hitch," is the salutation, and the stranger is bidden to take "d—n near all" of whatever the table offers. A hunter by race, he is first of all a poacher, in arms against such as would deny him the right to take game where he may find it, a trait dating back to the time of Robin Hood in England. His speech is reminiscent of this older land and people. Labeled as "a survival," the mountaineer in reality is on the defensive, protecting himself against later comers and strange ideas. "I wouldn't choose to crave this newfangled teachin' and preachin'," he says. "All I ask is to be let alone. I was doin' middlin' well. The hull kit and bilin' can go to the devil."

Mountain dialect reflects the Anglo-Saxon origin of the mountain people; obsolete forms found in Shakespeare and the King James version of the Bible are in common use. "Clumb," "writ," and "et" for climbed, wrote, and ate are sound enough if you go back a few centuries. "Buss" for kiss, "pack" for carry, and "poke" for pocketbag and the like are pure Elizabethan.

Shakespeare said "a-feared," as does the mountaineer today, and "beholden" is common to both. "His schoolin' holp him mighty," says the proud mountain father; King Richard of England said, "Let him thank me that holp to send him thither." "Hit's right pied," shouts the mountain boy when the snake he has stoned puffs up and mottles.

But he probably never read of "meadows trim with daisies pied," or heard of the Pied Piper of Hamelin. When he sings, the mountaineer "rolls a song," and his expression, "he looks like the hind wheels of bad luck," is so expressive that only the carping student would seek to trace its heritage.

Folklore is found not only among the mountaineers but in every county in the State, in town and in city. In the mountains, however, because of close-knit family and community ties, it is part of everyday life. Songs and sayings are more than quaint and queer; they have living reality. How much of the folklore is Scotch or Welsh, English or Irish, cannot readily be known.

The sense of something evil pervades mountain superstition; the devil is a personage, as real as he is malicious, as easily foiled as in *Faust*. The formula is common, and Satan is sent packing as surely by the sacred words "in the name of the Father and the Son and the Holy Ghost" as, in European story, by the sign of the Cross. Stories of people seeing the devil are accepted, and such an experience might almost be described as normal. It does not appear that belief in the "little people," so widespread in Ireland, was carried to Kentucky; few cases of children being "fairy-struck" exist. There is bedevilment rather than enchantment.

Hard by the headwaters of Hell-fer-Sartain is the Devil's Jump, a small branch, its course cluttered throughout by a confused mass of boulders and rocks. Here the devil, skipping in haste from hilltop to hilltop, his apron loaded with rocks with which he proposed to burden the land, "busted" his apron string and dropped the cargo into the stream below. To the present day an unusual scattering of rocks will be met with the exclamation: "The Devil must have broken his apron string hereabouts."

Leslie County has the usual legend, based on a common Old World theme, of a wager for the soul of a human being. The devil challenged a gunsmith to a shooting match with the soul of the craftsman as prize. Singularly enough, the gunsmith won. He had the scare of his life, however, and never after could he be persuaded to return to his bench and fashion fine guns.

Among these people, who are not of the twentieth century, nor want to be, strange things are everyday happenings, and witchcraft is taken as a matter of course. Witches, however, are quite another story; they no longer belong. But they are feared just the same. From ante bellum days come superstitions given to white children by their Negro mammies. This is the origin of the wholesome dread of "hoodoo" or "voodoo" signs.

Weather signs are deferred to and planting determined by the phases of the moon. If you don't hang a bread-sifter on the doorknob at night, you'll find witches in the bread in the morning. "If it comes, it no comes; if it no comes, it comes" means that if the crow comes the corn will not grow; if the crow doesn't come, the corn will. Along the Upper Middle Fork of the Kentucky River every hamlet and county seat has its ancient teller of tales, grateful for a good listener.

Old World backgrounds and traits of Kentucky's pioneers are reflected in the tunes and songs handed down from generation to generation— historical and sentimental ballads reminiscent of a time long past. "Queen Jane" tells how Henry VIII followed Jane Seymour to the grave: "Six went before, four carried her along. King Henry followed with his black mourning on." Dating back to the fifteenth century mysteries is the "Cherry Tree Carol," built around the story of Joseph and Mary in the Apocrypha. This song was discovered by Josephine McGill of Louisville, one of the first to collect and harmonize songs in this particular field. "Lord Randal" tells the story of the poisoned lover, a universal theme; the "Maid and the Gallows Tree" brings in the ransom motif; while "Barbara Allen," "Lord Thomas," "Fair Annet," "Sweet William," and "Lord Lovel" lament the girl who loved and died.

There is a more contemporary, defiant note to the well-known lines:

> Way up on Clinch Mountain I wander along;
> I'm as drunk as the devil—
> Oh, let me alone.

A variant is more plaintive:

> Go away, old man, and leave me alone,
> For I am a stranger
> And a long ways from home.

With a Miles Standish touch, another ballad tells of a young fellow in love who, going to sea, leaves a friend to kiss his sweetheart good-by. Eventually he returns to find friend and sweetheart married:

> Jack, you selfish elf,
> The very next girl I learn to love,
> I'll kiss her for myself.

A distinctive type of song was characteristic of the camp meetings, the literary form resembling the popular ballad or song. "Old-Time Religion"—of indefinite length—and "The Old Ship of Zion" are typical camp meeting songs, sung by both white people and Negroes in Kentucky.

One of the earliest of Kentucky's social and educational activities was the singing school. No place was too remote for the singing class that met in the church or schoolhouse. The songs were always religious and were usually found in a book for sale by the teacher. Two of the earliest singing schoolbooks were the *Kentucky Harmony,* in use by 1816, and *Supplement to Kentucky Harmony,* published in 1820. Both were written in four-shape notation and compiled by Ananias Davisson, a singing-school teacher, born somewhere on the border line of Maryland and Virginia; they contained a large number of songs popular in the rural South. The first fifteen pages of *Kentucky Harmony* were devoted to Preface, Rudiments, General Observation, "A Remark or Two at the request of several Refined Musicians," "Lessons for Tuning the Voice," and directions for the construction of a metronome. The 144 pages of tunes were all in four-part harmony. Part I contains "plain and easy tunes commonly used in time of divine worship"; Part II, "more lengthy and elegant pieces," used in "singing schools and private societies."

The *Kentucky Harmonist,* published about 1817, was compiled by Samuel Lytler Metcalf (1798–1856) whose home was Shelbyville, Kentucky. He began teaching singing school when a mere boy, and the proceeds of several editions of the *Kentucky Harmonist* enabled him to complete his medical education.

In 1835 appeared the first edition of *Southern Harmony,* written and published by "Singin' Billy" Walker—perhaps the most widely known of the shape-note song books and still used at "Benton's Big Singing." The last of its many editions, which appeared in 1854, has recently been reproduced in facsimile.

Kentucky Negro spirituals resemble those of other Southern States, but nearly every section has its own slight variations of the same songs as well as actual new ones. So characteristic are the Negro's own harmonic arrangements and words, that his songs may be considered native folk music. His ability to convey emotion in a few powerful, one-syllable words is unparalleled. Beautiful, simple, and generally plaintive, the spirituals are the unique expression of the Negro's experience, and a distinct contribution to the development of Kentucky music.

Another type of Kentucky song is known as a play-party game. Singing is unaccompanied; clapping of hands and stamping or patting of feet are often added. Such games as "Chase (or Shoot) the Buffalo," "Skip to My Lou," "Pig in the Parlor," and "Over the River to Charley" are good examples. These folk games have died out of general usage in Kentucky, but have been revived at school, community gatherings, and camps.

Breakdowns, or dance tunes, are known everywhere. There are two kinds, sung and instrumental. The former is often the same as the play-party game, except that it is used as a square dance. The second type of breakdown calls for a fiddler, usually with the accompaniment of a banjo picker or guitarist. The string band, now known to the radio as a "Hillbilly" band, is made up of a variety of instruments: fiddle, banjo, guitar, bass viol, mandolin, accordion, castanets, or any available musical contrivance. Old songs and ballads are sung regularly by students at Berea College, Hindman Settlement School, Pine Mountain Settlement School, and elsewhere. Several public events in the State are held annually with the primary object of preserving Kentucky's folk music. Among these is the American Folk Song Festival, sponsored by the American Folk Song Society, founded by Jean Thomas of Ashland. On the second Sunday of June of each year, in front of the "Traipsin' Woman's" cabin in a picturesque hollow of the foothills of Kentucky, mountain people gather to present a program of primitive songs and dances. The annual singing convention at Benton, Marshall County, held on the fourth Sunday of May, recently celebrated its fifty-fourth meeting. Kentucky folk music is now reaching an audience outside of the State, through the radio and activities of musicians such as John Jacob Niles, who gives concerts and lecture recitals in Europe as well as America.

KENTUCKY THOROUGH-BREDS

W HEN Daniel Boone in 1775 brought to the Virginia Legislature a resolution to improve the breed of horses over in Kentucky County, he was voicing a determination that has persisted in the Bluegrass. And the Bluegrass has made Kentucky celebrated throughout the world for its fine horses.

The resolve alone would not have been enough, however, if the Bluegrass did not have a mild climate and 1,200 square miles of cherished land around Lexington peculiarly fitted to be the nursery of thoroughbreds. The long, easy roll of the land, with its firm, dry turf undisturbed by plows and harrows, with its pools of water and its clumps of open woods, seems to please the eyes and feet of both horses and men. Underneath this Bluegrass turf is a layer of rare Ordovician limestone, a shell deposit laid down millions of years ago when the region was an ocean floor. This limestone gives to the water and grass a high phosphorus and calcium content which builds light, solid bones, elastic muscles, and strong tendons in the horses that feed and drink here. Under these ideal conditions are developed the prime requisites of the Thoroughbred—strength and fleetness. As a result, Kentucky-bred horses make up one-half of the winners on first-class American tracks, and a large majority of Derby firsts.

Kentucky has always been interested in horse racing and horse breeding. The first settlers in the Bluegrass were men from Virginia and the Carolinas, who brought with them over the mountains and down the rivers on flatboats strong, fast horses, tended affectionately and with care. As early as 1788, six months after the first edition of the *Kentucky Gazette* was printed, there appeared the first Kentucky stallion advertisements. One of them reads, in part:

The famous horse Pilgarlic, of a beautiful colour, full fourteen hands three inches high, rising ten years old, will stand the ensuing season on the head of Salt

River at Captain Abe Irvins, Mercer County, and will cover mares at the very low price of ten shillings a leap, if the money is paid down, or fifteen at the expiration of the season; and twenty shillings the season in cash, or thirty shillings in good trade. . . .

None of these first stallions was good enough to improve the breed; but after about fifty years of importing sires and brood mares, Kentucky began to produce great Thoroughbreds.

The first Thoroughbreds were English products. In England the strong, heavy Norman horses that had carried armored knights into battle were relegated by changing times to the fields, and the qualities of the light, fleet animals from the East were sought. Three great Eastern sires were imported into England—the Byerly Turk about 1685, Darley's Arabian in 1704, and the Godolphin Arabian in 1730. Crossed with native mares, they produced the English Thoroughbred, a peerless runner. In England the Thoroughbred was improved until there were the three great stallions, Herod (1758), Eclipse (1764), and Matchem (1748), who established the three dominant male lines to which all Thoroughbreds belong.

America imported its first thoroughbred, Bull Rock, son of the Byerly Turk and grandson of the Arabian, in 1730. Within the next thirty years Virginia and the Carolinas had excellent Thoroughbred stock. Messenger was brought to America in 1768, and Diomed, winner of the first English Derby, in 1799. Messenger was crossed with American Thoroughbreds and native mares to produce the standard-bred, or light-harness horses—trotters and pacers which, like the Thoroughbred, found their best home in the Bluegrass. The third of the light breeds for which the State became renowned is the American Saddle Horse, which developed after Denmark (an American thoroughbred foaled in 1839) was crossed with standard-breds and thoroughbreds. This breed, known for beauty, intelligence, and show qualities, is Kentucky's own.

During the War between the States Kentucky horses were demanded by both factions. Owners subsequently found their stables empty, and interest in breeding at a low ebb. Since it was costly to ship horses East and South for big money, Colonel Lewis Clark was sent to England to study breeding methods and to investigate the Derby, England's great sporting event. The result was the first Kentucky Derby, held at Louisville in 1875. Aristides galloped home for a purse of $2,850. The mile-and-a-half event (now a mile-and-a-quarter) was worthy of the Kentucky product. Succeeding Derbies focused attention on the State, and several wealthy Eastern owners, Milton Sanford and August Belmont among others, bought large estates and moved their stables to the Bluegrass where some of the best-known sires in America —Man o' War, The Porter, Sir Galahad III, Blue Larkspur, and many others—are spending their last days in the velvet. Every year about 15,000 people follow the arrow from Lexington to pay their respects to "Big Red," as Man o' War is affectionately called. Though insured for half a million, and guarded day and night, he likes nothing so much as retrieving a hat thrown across the paddock. His 25-foot strides soon discouraged competition and he was retired early. He once was clocked at 43 miles an hour during a workout, and his size and strength were such that he seemed never to tire. "Chicago" O'Brien, one of the greatest of plungers, once bet $100,000 on him to win $1,000. Smasher of five world records, his "get," including War Admiral, Crusader, Mars, American Flag, Edith Cavell, and Scapa Flow, are nearing the two-and-a-half million mark in winnings on the American turf.

From the Bluegrass have come many of the great moneymakers of the track, among them Equipoise (d. 1938), the third highest stake winner in America, who earned $338,000; Gallant Fox, who took purses of more than $328,000; and Seabiscuit, who in 1938 passed the $340,000 mark.

The horse farms range in size from less than a hundred to two or three thousand acres. Many of the larger ones are financed by industrial fortunes. Despite spectacular individual earnings, such establishments rarely enrich their owners. Ten thousand dollars is a fair price for a yearling colt of distinguished parentage, and two thousand more each year will keep him in the pink; but even if he shows the stuff Derby winners are made of, he may never return his investment. The hazards of disease, injury, lack of speed, and temperamental obstacles, all unite to keep Thoroughbred breeding a sporting proposition.

A visitor in the Bluegrass sees stone walls and white plank fences rising and falling on an ocean of dark rich green to enclose paddocks and fields and formally beautiful homes, immaculate barns and Negro cabins as precisely arranged as in a blueprint. Great elms, and maples —trees that sheltered early settlers as they made their way across the Great Meadow—interrupt the endless flow of green pasture. An ingenious device on the gates makes it possible to open them from an automobile. The driver, if he is lucky, may be asked by a grinning stable boy to wait a few moments; then he sees a group of colts coming over a hill on their spindly legs. Prancing along, they are ushered gently on to a felt carpet that has been laid across the hard rock. "Horses first!" is the primary rule on the horse farm.

The larger stables maintain a Tack Room, which is decorated with ribbons and silver cups and may have a bar. The Tack Room actually is designed to contain halters, stirrups, spurs, reins, and other horse equipment.

The story is told of a man who, seeing one of the thoroughbred stables for the first time, suddenly removed his hat and said in awed tones, "My Lord! The cathedral of the horse." The varnished stalls with polished metal trim and the tanbark aisles without a wisp of fallen hay are as neat as the cabin of a steamship. A stable boy leads out his royal charge. His attitude is that of a colored mammy toward the "white chile" in her care. He croons and chuckles, argues and cajoles, but never uses a whip. It is generally conceded that the horse "knows more than a pin-headed boy." Yet the stable boys and exercise boys have been carefully selected for their tact, skill, and disposition. Usually one man to every three horses is employed in the racing stables and one to ten on the breeding farms. There may be exercise boys, grooms who rub down the satin coats, jockeys, foremen, blacksmiths, veterinarians, bookkeepers and cooks, as well as a manager and trainer.

Methods of training and stable routine vary, but precision is the keynote of all stables. Colonel E. R. Bradley, of Idle Hour Farm, has a record sheet posted on the door of each stall where twice daily the horse's temperature, the amount of food he has eaten, and other facts of his behavior are recorded. The record is discussed with the veterinarian each night.

During the spring about 70 per cent of the brood mares on a farm will foal. Each receives the care of a maternity ward patient, for nothing must go wrong with the Thoroughbred baby. He spends his first summer in carefree fashion near his mother, and very soon his slender legs have grown sure and he loves to run. His feet are trimmed and watched for the slightest injury. He has been weaned at about 5 to 6 months, and is now becoming accustomed to a diet consisting mainly of crushed oats, with corn, bran, salt, and flaxseed in judicious quantities. Doses of cod-liver oil give him resistance to colds and help to build up his strength.

His first lessons begin early; he is broken to the halter when a few weeks old; as a yearling, about July, he learns the feel of bit, bridle, and halter shank. Slowly he becomes accustomed to the tack he must carry as a race horse. When he can be led around the stall thus equipped, he is ready for the paddock, where he learns to obey the commands of his rider.

New Year's Day is always his first birthday, though he may be actually only seven or eight months old. He may make his exciting debut any time after his second birthday. Since he is born to race, he may instinctively know the procedure. At first the boy lets him go along easily and observes his reactions to the track. By this time it is known whether the colt is calm or nervous, high-spirited or dignified, stubborn or tractable.

On a cool autumn day the yearling goes to work. For a few weeks he walks, trots, and canters up to as much as three and a half miles a day. He gets a few speed trials, generally at one-quarter mile. After his trials, he is let down until February 1, unless he is going to winter racing.

If the Thoroughbred comes from a long line of sprinters, he will probably never be nominated for the Derby, but he has plenty of opportunities at distances shorter than that famous mile-and-a-quarter. By his second winter, perhaps the most important molding period, he has usually given some indication of his racing possibilities. Sometimes he is three before all these things are determined. His speed, action, and conformation (the extent to which he approaches the level of excellence for his breed) do not always explain his performance; authorities agree that there are traits bequeathed him in the conglomerate blood of his forebears. Awkward little colts are often purchased on their pedigrees and on the expectation of development. The training period usually places the Thoroughbred in the company he shall keep; only a few are stars, but almost all take their places somewhere between Belmont and the "leaky-roof" circuits. More and more Thoroughbreds are seen in polo teams; some are sold for saddle horses or hunters. Before being placed at stud, regardless of his brilliant ancestry, a stallion has usually established his reputation on the race track, for his own capabilities should be proved to avoid perpetuating any possible weakness in the line.

Some weeks before the seasonal sales, the breeder selects the most attractive colts and fillies for a regime of diet and grooming that will enable them to appear to the best advantage. Picking a great race horse out of a string of yearlings is a gamble. Samuel Riddle paid

$5,000 for Man o' War because the youngster "had a look"; today he stands at stud for that amount.

The new owner is usually given the privilege of naming the colt—which must be done before March 1 of his two-year-old year. This is no simple matter. There can be no duplicates within a 15-year period, and with approximately 5,000 foals registered annually in the American Stud Book, ingenuity is taxed strenuously. Any number of names may be submitted to the Jockey Club; the owner is notified of the one allowed. Colts may be given names inspired by their ancestry, or associated with speed, courage, stamina, supremacy, luck, heroism, or plain whimsy. When Colonel Bradley bought the colt Bad News, he inquired why that name was attached to the animal. Said the owner, "I've always heard that bad news travels fast." Bradley had such good luck with his first two horses, Bad News and Brigade, that he gave all the others "B" names. In the colorful history of the Kentucky Derby he is the only owner who has taken four Derby firsts. Many Kentuckians will bet on the Bradley entries as a matter of course. Once a Negro admirer of the Colonel declared he would name his expected baby for the Derby winner. After two Bradley horses came down the track to take top honors, twin offspring in Louisville were promptly named Bubbling Over and Baggenbaggage Jones.

The language of the horse barns is simple. The size of a horse is measured in "hands"; a "hand" is four inches. An average horse of the light breed stands between 15 and 16 hands, as measured at the wither. A "foal" is a suckling colt or filly. "Filly" applies to a female four-year-old or less; "colt" applies to a male of the same years. A "maiden" is a race horse that has never placed first in a race. The term "stud" applies to the entire plant of a horse-breeding farm—land, buildings, and livestock. "Imp." before a horse's name means that it is not American-born, but imported. Racing time is written "1:34 2/5," and is read "one minute, thirty-four and two-fifths seconds." Twenty years is considered a ripe old age, but many exceed that term by years, and a few have been known to live into their thirties.

Jargon of the track is extensive and baffling. A "high school horse" wins when the odds are high; he is suspected of being able to read the board. If a horse is "pitched up," he is running in better company than usual. A jockey who "hand-rides" makes a rousing finish without resorting to whip or spurs. A "grafter" is a pet kept in a racing stable. A Kentucky horseman is called a "boot"; a "chalk eater" plays favorites; a "throat-latcher" consistently finishes second and seldom wins; a "tumble-bug" is a horse that likes to roll in his stall.

Kentucky owners, like all American Thoroughbred breeders, are hoping for a repeal of the so-called Jersey Act, a rule set up in England in 1913, which declared some American Thoroughbreds "half-bred." Horses whose lineage cannot be traced in every line to horses already in the British Stud Book fall into this category. Since the blood of the illustrious Lexington (foaled in America) carries through a great many American Thoroughbreds, it automatically outlaws the strain. The rule was made to hamper our export trade with England at a time when racing reached a low ebb in the United States and owners were shipping their Thoroughbreds abroad. It has been suggested that a committee of experts select certain superior American horses and register them in the British Stud Book to redeem this country's Thoroughbreds from unfair discrimination.

Producing a Derby winner is the dream of every thoroughbred owner and trainer in Kentucky. When Colonel Bradley came to Kentucky to raise horses, he was told that it would take 15 years to breed a Derby winner; it took him just that long. The procedure starts several years before the Derby "in the imagination of some sportsman when he decides to match his knowledge of breeding and bloodlines against that of other horsemen." Joseph E. Widener knows the hazards that obstruct entrance into that exclusive society. In 1927 his colt, Osmand, was thought unbeatable, but he lost to Whiskery by a head. In 1935 one of his favorites, Chance Sun, broke down in training. In 1934 Peace Chance set a mile record before the Derby, but finished far behind Cavalcade. In 1936 Brevity, widely accepted as the favorite, lost to Bold Venture, a 20–1 shot.

The Derby is about the most popular sporting event in America. Since Matt Winn took over the management of Churchill Downs in 1902, the Derby has become a national fiesta with an economic importance that can hardly be estimated. In the dark spring of 1908 when Stonestreet and Sir Cleges seemed likely to languish in their stalls because of a ban against illegal betting, Colonel Winn dug down into the archives of Kentucky legislation and produced an old law permitting pari-mutuel betting. The day was won; the system became popular not only in Kentucky but also throughout the Nation. Winn encouraged bookmakers to open a winter book, which gave the Derby nationwide publicity. Land used for pasture rose in price—the value per acre is three times that of the best Burley tobacco land—the value of horses increased, and interest in breeding ran high. Winn's dream of attracting brilliant three-year-olds from all parts of the United States came true. Although there are older and larger stakes than the Derby, none attracts a more cosmopolitan crowd. It is the dramatic climax to the Kentucky legend, or, in the words of a well-known sports writer, " 'My Old Kentucky Home' acted out before your eyes."

All roads lead to Louisville where 70,000 people spend more than a million dollars. Sleeping quarters cost all the way from one dollar for a room to a thousand dollars for a large house over the weekend. Justice relents, and rash and noisy revelers are smilingly indulged. All the juleps served in Churchill Downs Club bar on Derby Day would make a long, long drink. Ambassadors, Governors, and screen stars enter the stands with collegians and stenographers from bordering States, and all suddenly wish they had been born in Kentucky. Occasionally julep-husky baritones of city "big shots" can be heard when the crowd stands to sing "the sun shines bright . . ." A million radios throughout the country are tuned to give the richest two-minute suspense of the year. A blanket of roses awaits another champion.

PRESS AND RADIO

IN MAY 1785 the second convention to discuss "separation from Virginia and the formation of a new state," in session at Danville, passed a resolution to establish a printing press in the western territory for the purpose of "giving publicity to the proceedings of the Convention."

A committee was appointed to negotiate with a printer and start a paper. But for some reason the West had not appealed to printers, and none could be found among the settlers in the territory. Finally a young surveyor and soldier of the Revolution, John Bradford of Fauquier County, Virginia—without any previous experience as a printer or editor, but a man of unusual common sense—approached the committee with the proposition that he would undertake the establishment of a newspaper if the convention would assure him of public patronage when the new State came into existence. His terms were met and the *Kentucky Gazette* was launched.

The citizens of Lexington were more generous in their support of the new movement than the citizens of Danville, and when the town council of Lexington granted Bradford lot number 43, free of cost as long as the press continued, Lexington became the birthplace of the first newspaper published in Kentucky.

An antiquated press, type, ink balls, and ink were secured in Philadelphia in the summer of 1787. This equipment was hauled over the mountains to Pittsburgh, loaded on a flatboat and transported to Maysville, then taken by pack horse to Lexington. Some of the type was set by Bradford's brother, Fielding Bradford, as they drifted down the river, but most of it was reduced to "pi" on the journey from Maysville to Lexington. Nevertheless, on August 11, 1787, Bradford issued the first edition with an editorial apology. It was a small sheet about 8 x 10½ inches, folded once, making a four-page paper of news collected by the Bradfords on their journey to and from Philadelphia. No copies of this first issue of about 180 papers are in existence. Local news was given little consideration in the early editions, but partisan editorials attacking political opponents of the idea of statehood filled its columns. About the only news preserved for posterity in the existing issues of the *Gazette* is what may be gleaned from paid advertisements and notices.

Bradford became one of Lexington's leading citizens. He served several terms in the town council, was for many years a trustee of Transylvania University, and at the time of his death was high sheriff of Fayette County. He not only published the *Gazette* but issued many books and pamphlets. In 1788 he published the first *Kentucky Almanac*, and later the first acts of the legislature and *Bradford's Laws*.

The second newspaper to appear was the *Kentucky Herald*, published in 1793, also at Lexington, by James H. Stewart. It had a short life, but was revived in 1797 at Paris and became the first newspaper of Bourbon County. The *Kentucky Mirror*, published at Washington under the editorship of William Hunter, appeared in the same year. Hunter was elected State printer in 1798 and moved the *Mirror* to Frankfort, where it was published by the *Kentucky Journal*, begun in 1795 by Benjamin J. Bradford. Hunter and Bradford established the *Palladium* in 1798, and the *Mirror* was discontinued in 1799. During the next thirty-five years dozens of newspapers sprang up in villages and towns throughout the State. Many of them lived for only a short time and were of no consequence. The only factual evidence that some of these papers actually existed is found in the proceedings of the early legislatures, which authorized the publication of State advertisements in them.

The first newspaper that can be considered a success was the *Advertiser*, established in Louisville in 1818 and edited by Shadrach Penn. In 1826 it became the first daily paper in the West. Politically it was Democratic and supported Andrew Jackson for the Presidency in 1828. Penn was an able and virile editor, feared by his enemies. But in 1830 he encountered his equal in George D. Prentice, a young New Englander, who had been sent to Kentucky by the Whigs to write a biography of Henry Clay for campaign purposes. Prentice attracted the attention of the Kentucky Whigs and was persuaded to accept the editorship of the newly established Whig organ, the Louisville *Journal*. An editorial battle began at once between the Democrats, represented by Penn in the *Advertiser*, and the Whigs, represented by Prentice in the *Journal*. Penn went down in defeat in 1841, discontinued the *Advertiser*, and moved to St. Louis.

The *Journal* from its beginning in November 1830 enjoyed a large circulation, and for more than forty years Prentice edited it and fought consistently and courageously for the Whig Party. He was indifferent to the institution of slavery, but bitterly opposed it when war threatened, since he was a strong advocate of the Union. Throughout the War between the States, Prentice stood steadfastly by the Union. In 1868 he sold his interest in the *Journal* and was succeeded by Henry W. Watterson.

The Louisville *Courier,* a successful newspaper more interested in news than editorials, was established in 1844 by Walter N. Haldeman. Although ordinarily without strong editorial convictions, it took sides against the North in the War between the States, and was suppressed by Union forces in 1861. For four years it was published in different places and under many names; in 1865 it was brought back to Louisville by the original owner and re-established.

A third important Louisville paper, the Louisville *Democrat,* sponsored by the Democratic leader of his time, James Guthrie, was also established in 1844. It was first edited by Phineas Kent, later by John H. Harney, and existed until 1868. In that year the *Journal, Courier,* and *Democrat* were merged into one paper, the *Courier-Journal,* under the able editorship of Henry Watterson. Under his editorial leadership the *Courier-Journal* became the outstanding newspaper of the State and one of the foremost of the South.

Henry Watterson (1840–1921) was born in Washington, D.C., the son of a Tennessee Congressman. He began his journalistic career on *Harper's Weekly,* the New York *Times,* and Horace Greeley's New York *Tribune.* When the storm of the War between the States began to gather, Watterson went back to Tennessee, his father's native State, to become associate editor of the Nashville *Banner.* During the war he served as a staff officer and as chief of scouts in the Confederate Army. He then spent a year in Europe, and returned to revive the *Banner.* His success in this undertaking attracted the attention of Prentice of the Louisville *Journal;* although they had supported opposite sides in the War between the States, Prentice chose the young man as his successor. Watterson soon became the dean of southern journalism, as Prentice had been before him.

Affectionately known as "Marse Henry," Watterson was active in Democratic party affairs, a pleasing and forceful public speaker, and progressive in thought and action. His literary style was polished and forceful, and his keen, sometimes caustic, pen roved from heated political diatribes to scholarly essays. One of his favorite topics was the authorship of Shakespeare's works, which he attempted to prove were written by Christopher Marlowe. Although opposed to the saloon, he did not think prohibition enforceable and considered it an infringement of the liberties of the American people. He favored a restriction rather than an extension of suffrage, believing that there already existed an excess of uninformed voters. Watterson won the Pulitzer Prize in 1917 for editorials celebrating the entrance of the United States into the World War. Although a staunch, at times militant, Democrat, Watterson opposed the League of Nations. On March 5, 1919, he wrote, "Government is a hard and fast and dry reality. At best statesmanship can only half do the things it would. Its aims are most assured when tending a little leeward; its footing safest on its native heath. We have plenty to do on our own continent without seeking to right things on other continents."

In 1884 Walter N. Haldeman established the Louisville *Times,* with Emmet Garvin Logán and E. Polk Johnson as editors. Logan's editorials were short and pithy, usually without headlines, and although not finished and well organized like the editorials of Watterson, they appealed to a large constituency. The *Times* succeeded, and it is now the only afternoon paper published in Louisville.

Judge Robert W. Bingham purchased the *Courier-Journal* and the *Times* in 1918. Watterson retired from the editorship of the *Courier-Journal* and was succeeded by Harrison Robertson. Arthur Krock, subsequently (1923) compiler of Watterson's *Editorials* and in 1935 and 1938 a Pulitzer award winner, became the editor of the *Times* and was later succeeded by Tom Wallace.

The *Courier-Journal* and the *Times* have aggressively supported the Democratic Party. In 1935 Judge Bingham was made Ambassador to the Court of St. James's, where he served until his death.

In Lexington the first successful newspaper was the *Kentucky Reporter,* established in 1807 by William Worsley and Samuel Overton. As its name implied, it stressed local news and was less concerned about foreign affairs than its predecessor, the *Gazette.* In 1832 the *Reporter* merged with the Lexington *Observer* and continued the policy of emphasizing local news. In politics it was Whig and supported Henry Clay. After the War between the States it became a staunch Democratic organ, edited by W. C. P. Breckinridge. Another Democratic paper emerged during the Reconstruction period,—the Lexington *Press,* that city's first daily, established by Colonel Hart Foster and Major Henry T. Duncan in 1870. It was later consolidated with the Lexington *Transcript* and was called the Lexington *Herald,* with Desha Breckinridge, son of W. C. P. Breckinridge, as editor from 1897 to 1935. The *Herald* became an outstanding and aggressive mouthpiece of the Democratic Party in the Bluegrass.

The Lexington *Leader* was founded in 1888 as a Republican daily by Samuel J. Roberts of Canton, Ohio. It was one of the pioneers in the field of specialized news and departments for family reading. In 1937 its owner purchased the *Herald* and published both papers from the same press without disturbing the political policy or integrity of either.

Many newspapers in Kentucky—such as the Owensboro *Messenger,* established by Urey Woodson in 1881, and the Frankfort *Daily and Weekly Commonwealth,* published by Albert Gallatin Hodges—have had brilliant careers editorially. In most instances the newspaper was the editor, and the editor was the newspaper. A Kentuckian, for example, can hardly think of the *Courier-Journal* without thinking of Henry Watterson. These editors were born writers without formal training in schools or colleges of journalism. They fought for ideas and issues with their pens, and seldom yielded any ground. They had no press associations where they exchanged views and contributed to each other's welfare.

This situation was characteristic of the Kentucky press until very recent years. The newspaper business, however, has become more and more complex and demands specialized training. In response to this demand, the University of Kentucky has developed its school of journalism and sponsors the well-organized Kentucky Press Association. In addition to its annual meetings, sectional gatherings, where editors and business managers discuss their mutual problems, are held in various parts of the State from time to time.

Radio

Anxious listeners in both America and Europe, hearing over the air waves the incessant plea "Send a boat" during the 1937 flood disaster, realized that radio, in that tragic hour, was an integral part of Kentucky life.

On Sunday, January 24, 1937, Louisville lay submerged, with only a skeleton telephone service, and in near darkness. The order had been issued that what remained of electric power must be rationed. Hospitals and broadcasting stations awaited from moment to moment the interruption of all power. Station WHAS must be kept on the air until a hook-up with WSM could be completed, and Nashville was ready to take up broadcasting with the least possible delay. Marooned people heard that an equipment truck from Nashville had gone astray, that power was failing rapidly; they listened to offers of aid from all over the country; at last came word that Nashville was standing by. A few moments before 1 A.M., in the middle of a sentence, the tired voice of Louisville's announcer halted. Nashville took up the call—"Send a boat."

During the emergency period Station WHAS never left the air, putting on approximately 115,000 broadcasts in 187½ hours of uninterrupted service. It served as nerve center of the volunteer network that carried official flood news. All relief work was directed through WHAS. The chain included WAVE of Louisville, WCKY at Covington, WPAD at Paducah, WLAP at Lexington, WOMI at Owensboro, and WCMI at Ashland, in addition to WSM at Nashville, Tennessee, and WFBM at Indianapolis, Indiana. Bulletins sent out calls for doctors, medical aid, food, and resources.

On January 25 a three-way telephone conversation among WHAS, Columbia Broadcasting System, and National Broadcasting Company, resulted in the formation of a network covering the United States and Canada. The British Broadcasting System and, later, other foreign networks were included. This tied in approximately 5,000 short-wave stations throughout the world, the largest network ever established in the history of radio. All directions emanated from Station WHAS. Volunteer sound equipment units went as near the flooded areas as possible to amplify directions to rescue workers through loud speakers. The resultant saving in life and property cannot be estimated.

The flood reached its crest on January 27. The waters receded; reconstruction work commenced; life resumed its normal course. On the second Saturday of May sports commentators at Churchill Downs were broadcasting the Kentucky Derby.

Radio experimentation in Kentucky began in the late nineteenth century. About 1892, in the little town of Murray, a wireless telephone was successfully demonstrated before an audience of 1,000 persons. The crude radio consisted of a rough box, some telephone equipment, rods, and a coil of wire, and was the invention of a farmer, Nathan B. Stubblefield.

In 1902 Stubblefield went by invitation to Washington, where he broadcast for a group of prominent scientists from the steam launch "Bartholdi." The same year he gave a demonstration in Philadelphia from Belmont mansion and from Fairmont Park, projecting his voice more than a mile by wireless.

The St. Louis *Post Dispatch,* in a full-page article on January 12, 1902, said: "However undeveloped his system may be, Nathan B. Stubblefield, the farmer inventor of Kentucky, has accurately discovered the principle of telephoning without wires."

Through an attorney, Rainey Wells, he secured patents in the United States, Canada, England, France, Spain, and Belgium. To raise capital for marketing his invention he had sold stock, in 1900, to a small group of friends. The end of Stubblefield's business career is shrouded in mystery. He advised his friends to withdraw such funds as they had invested, hinting darkly of the rascality of certain eastern associates. But to none of them did he give concrete information. An old trunk, in which he kept the invention and the documents concerning it, was not with him when he subsequently returned from the East, broken and embittered, to Murray. Whether it was a case of open theft, or whether he had been the dupe of unscrupulous manipulators, was never known. He continued his experiments with wireless in a two-room shack of his own construction. Cornshucks provided protection against rain and cold. Offers of neighborly aid were refused, an estranged family was spurned. On March 28, 1928, the body of Stubblefield was found in his shack; he had apparently been dead about forty-eight hours.

The State's present radio stations have all developed since 1922, when an amateur station was licensed as WLAP (now in Lexington), and WHAS, now part of the Columbia System, went on the air in Louisville. The National Broadcasting System is represented by WAVE, in Louisville. Station WCKY is in Covington, WPAD in Paducah, WOMI in Owensboro, and WCMI in Ashland. WGRC, the George Rogers Clark Station, has studios in Louisville, as well as in New Albany and Jeffersonville, Indiana.

Kentucky, because of its topography, offers unusual opportunities for radio experimentation. Although it was known by 1923 that the human voice, without the aid of wires, could encircle the earth, there remained doubt as to whether radio could penetrate the depths of the earth as well. Radio history was made on July 21, 1923, when a successful broadcast was sent out from Mammoth Cave at a depth of 378 feet. That morning a junior operator, with assistant and guide, entered the cave. The personnel of Station WHAS in Louisville was standing ready to send vocal signals at given hours. The first attempts were complete failures. The crust of century-old dust made it impracticable to drive the ground spike. Walls and ceilings dripping with moisture became natural conductors with a tendency to absorb the signals before they reached the aerial. At length a spot was found where walls were dry and the path slightly moist. By mid-afternoon WHAS came in with surprising volume and complete absence of static.

The mountains and remote country sections also provide territory for radio development. One of the most interesting experiments is that of the Mountain Listening Centers. Broadcasts arranged by the University of Kentucky and made possible by private contributors, with the co-operation of the National Youth Administration, supplement other forms of educational work among the Kentucky mountaineers.

On October 21, 1934, a series of Sunday morning broadcasts from the Jefferson County Jail was inaugurated by the Volunteers of America, with Major W. O. Ulrey in charge, and Lillian B. Ulrey as soloist. A tiny organ was used at first, but has since been replaced by a larger electric organ. These broadcasts are heard in jails and penal institutions in 101 Kentucky counties and in seven State prisons, including those in Ohio, Indiana, Tennessee, and Michigan. Thousands of prisoners, their friends, and relatives have written to the broadcasters who perform this service.

Interest in television was evident in Kentucky as early as 1929, when Station WHAS began experimentation, though it had at that time a power of only a fifth of its present 50,000 watts.

THE ARTS

The Theater

THE FIRST record of public amusement in Kentucky, was an advertisement of May 31, 1797, in the *Kentucky Gazette,* a Lexington paper. It announced that "a room for exhibition purposes" had been erected adjoining Coleman's Tavern for "an exhibition of tumbling, balancing on slack wire, slack rope walking and dancing. Admission to pit, 2 shillings, to gallery, 2 shillings, 2 pence. Doors open at sunset, performance beginning at dark."

Not until January 1, 1802, however, did theater items begin to appear in the *Gazette,* nor was the location of the building, corner of Spring and Vine Streets, given until June 25, 1811. The owner was Luke Usher, who was probably the first theatrical manager in central Kentucky; he also controlled houses at Frankfort and Louisville and sent his actors from one town to the other, as business justified. Noble Luke Usher, nephew of the theater owner and a Shakespearean actor of some standing, joined the company in 1812 with his wife, Harriet L'Estrange, an actress of unusual attainments and charm. Both were from the south of Ireland and had been members of a theatrical company which included the parents of Edgar Allan Poe. It may be that Poe's story, "Fall of the House of Usher," was based on some tradition of this family.

The theater of Kentucky was of little consequence until the coming of the Drake family and their company. The story opens in Albany, New York. In 1814 Noble Luke Usher arrived at the Albany Theater to recruit actors for his houses in Kentucky, then regarded as "the Far West." The adventure appealed to Samuel Drake, stage manager; he agreed to get a company together and start for Kentucky the following spring. But the task was difficult, for experienced actors hesitated to make the hazardous journey into "the unknown." However, members of Drake's own family, all actors, and young N. M. Ludlow, who had recently joined the company to play small parts, were eager for the adventure.

The party—including Samuel Drake; his sons, Samuel, Jr., Alexander, and James; his daughters, Martha and Julia; and Frances Ann Denny, N. M. Ludlow, Mr. and Mrs. Lewis, and Joe Tracy, a man of all work—set out in wagons from Canandaigua, New York, late in July 1815. They traveled across New York State, thence by boat to Pittsburgh where they played for some time. In November they started on their 400-mile journey in a flat-bottomed boat, known in that day as an "ark" or a "Kentucky broadhorn." Floating down the Ohio River to Limestone (Maysville), Kentucky, they made the remainder of the trip in wagons to Frankfort. Here, in December 1815, Kentucky's first real theatrical season opened with *The Mountaineer* by Coleman, followed by a farce, *The Poor Soldier*. The season was a good one and lasted until March. The players then proceeded by private conveyance to Louisville, a distance of 50 miles, making the trip in two days.

"On arriving in Louisville," wrote Samuel Drake, "we found the people on the tiptoe of expectation, and anxious for the opening of the season; but the theater was not in a position to be occupied; it was dark, dingy and dirty. The scenery was badly painted, the auditorium was done in the most dismal colors, and the house badly provided with means for lighting. In about two weeks the theater had been turned into passable condition for the opening, and we commenced our season with Coleman's comedy, *The Heir at Law*, and the comic opera, *Sprig of Laurel*. The performance went off with great applause, and the people appeared delighted with the company. This season of ours in Louisville, I understand, was the first that had been made by any theatrical company. It lasted ten or eleven weeks and was undoubtedly profitable to the management, for the house was well filled every night. The season closed with benefits for the company, all of them being well attended, and this in a town of less than 3,000 inhabitants. But these people were gay, prosperous and fond of theatrical entertainment."

Drake's company met with similar success in Lexington, where they opened with *Speed the Plough*. The old theater building, 80 feet long by 30 feet wide, had a lower floor with pit and boxes in the London style; the seats, built up the side of Spring Street hill and rising gradually from the stage, were covered with canvas and without backs. The interior was plain, the scenery limited and badly painted, judged by modern standards. The *Kentucky Gazette* in 1812 announced that "hereafter the smoking of segars" in the theater would be prohibited; but a coffee-room and bar "near the stage," offered consolation. The most popular actors were those who could "hold their liquor like gentlemen."

John Palmer, in *Travels in the United States in 1817,* mentions attending a performance at Limestone (Maysville), given by a company of strolling players from England. The plays, *Honeymoon* and *'Tis All a Farce,* were presented in a frame building "appropriate for theatrical purposes. . . . The scenery and performance were miserable," he reported, "but the buffoonery of the farce and the orchestra of Negroes, who performed two tunes with two fiddles and two triangles, kept the audience in good humor; segar smoking during the performance was practiced by most men."

Dr. H. McMurtrie, in his *Sketches of Louisville,* described the Louisville theater of 1819 as "a handsome brick building of three stories." Drake's playhouse, called the old City Theater, "was a very creditable one and had some features not excelled by its successors," wrote Colonel John T. Gray. "It had a row of private boxes occupying the whole front of what is now the dress circle, as in the French Opera House in New Orleans. They were closed in the rear, having doors for entrances, and open at the front. The second tier was open and corresponded to the latter day dress circle, while the third was low priced as now. The pit was not the choice place, as now, but was occupied by men, veteran theater-goers and critics. The theater was lighted with a grand chandelier swung from the dome, and with side lights, all of sperm candles, and there was never a dripping one."

Samuel Drake successfully managed theaters in Kentucky until 1830. (He then purchased a farm in Oldham County, where he died October 16, 1854, at the age of eighty-six.) His company remained together until about 1835 after which some returned East, while others joined N. M. Ludlow, author of *Dramatic Life as I Found It,* and head of a company which held a prominent place in the theatrical world of the Midwest until the 1850's. Ludlow's "Kentucky Comedians" played in Louisville, Lexington, Frankfort, Harrodsburg, Danville, Cincinnati and adjoining towns. They also ventured as far afield as Nashville, Natchez, St. Louis, Mobile and New Orleans.

The customary program of this period consisted of a three- to five-act drama, followed by a two-act farce or comedy; sometimes comic dialogue or musical solos were added for good measure. Most in demand, judging by advertising and requests for return performances, were: *The Soldier's Daughter, The Rivals, The Wheel of Fortune, Animal Magnetism, or the Doctor Outwitted, Matrimony, or the Happy Imprisonment, Love à la Mode, or Humors of the Turf,* and *Raising the Wind, or How to Live Cheap.* Romantic dramas such as *Blue Beard, or Female Curiosity, Abeallino, or the Venetian Outlaw, Rudolph, or Robbers of Calabria,* were enthusiastically received time and again. The tragedies most frequently advertised were *The Revenge, The Roman Father, Barbarossa, or Tyrant of Algiers,* and *Macbeth, Othello, Romeo and Juliet, Hamlet,* and *Richard III.*

Sol Smith, author of *Theatrical Management in the South and West,* and member of a traveling company which played in the villages throughout central Kentucky as early as 1829, calls attention to Drake's singular propensity for adding second titles to plays. "To the *Honeymoon* he would add, *or The Painter and His Three Daughters.* He always announced the *Hunter of the Alps* with this addition: *Or The Runaway Horse that Flung its Rider in the Forest of Savoy.*"

Benefits for the actors were given at the end of the season to provide funds for idle months ahead. On these nights, friends bought large blocks of tickets, and added to the success of the performance by applause. On February 6, 1850, Julia Dean, best remembered as Lucretia Borgia, took a benefit at the old City Theater in *The Wrecker's Daughter,* and *Faint Heart Never Won Fair Lady.* The crowd was tremendous; many were turned away and the occasion made theatrical history, setting a mark often referred to later. The *Daily Journal* went into raptures. "She is not a mere machine," said the critic, "moving first one arm and then another, uttering mechanical things, but a creature of fiery genius and passion, pouring forth her emotions from the depths of an unburdened heart." When Mrs. Kent took her benefit on April 11 of the same year in *Katherine and Petruchio,* an arrangement of Shakespeare's *Taming of the Shrew,* bouquets and baskets of flowers were thrown at her feet, with money hidden among the flowers.

The City Theater was destroyed by fire in May 1843, and Louisville remained without a theater until February 9, 1846, when the new Louisville Theater, built on the old site, opened. Douglas Jerrold's *Time Works Wonders* was presented, with Julia Dean, granddaughter of old Samuel Drake, playing Florentine; *The Widow's Victim* and *The Stagestruck Chambermaid* were played as after pieces. Until it was abandoned in 1873 the Louisville Theater housed the favorite actors and actresses of their day. Junius Brutus Booth appeared there in December 1848 in a number of his characterizations, his Richard III being spoken of as "full of genius, truth and nature." The great Macready played a week's engagement in April 1848 and was said to have drawn the largest audience ever seen in the theater. The 1860 season closed with Charlotte Cushman's performance in *The Stranger*. Laura Keene, the resourceful actress-manager, played here with her company for three weeks in 1863, presenting such plays as *She Stoops to Conquer, School for Scandal,* and *Our American Cousin,* in which the elder Sothern later rose to glory. James E. Murdock, James K. Hackett, John McCulloch, Mr. and Mrs. James Wallack, Frank Mayo, and Clara Morris appeared year after year. In 1872, when the prestige of the old house was already waning, Cooper and Pyne, Harrison, and the New Orleans English Opera Company presented a series of operas, and Strakosch's company with Christina Nilsson filled a short engagement.

The Louisville Theater was abandoned in 1873 when Barney Macauley, who had come to Louisville from Memphis, Tennessee, about the time of the War between the States, offered his first play in the new $200,000 theater which bore his name. An old "dodger" described the building as "constructed and finished in the highest style of modern art . . . and one of the most substantial and elegant theaters in the world." The opening performance on October 13, 1873, given before a fashionable crowd in the high hats and pompadours of the period, was the play *Extremes,* with Marie Bates starred as Lady Cosby. This marked the beginning of a series of notable productions that won for Macauley a national reputation.

Colonel John T. Macauley succeeded his brother Barney as manager in 1879 and retained the management until his death in 1916. Here on the night of November 27, 1875, Mary Anderson, Louisville's best beloved actress, made her first appearance as Juliet. Sarah Bernhardt came to Macauley's in 1880 during her first American tour. It was at Macauley's on December 7, 1883, that Helena Modjeska, talented Polish actress, appeared in Ibsen's *A Doll's House,* the first presentation of Ibsen in America. Given under the title of *Thora,* the name of the heroine, now known as Nora, the Ibsen ending was replaced by a "happy" one. The *Courier-Journal* critic reported a brilliant audience. The production, he observed, "was a novelty, curiosity to see Modjeska in a new role as well as admiration for the great actress" brought it together. He thought the tragic ending more consistent and predicted the play, which "lived through Modjeska," would never "be very popular." Joseph Jefferson, Edwin Booth, Lawrence Barrett, Fanny Davenport, Mrs. Fiske, Maggie Mitchell, Lotta, Ada Rehan, and such foreign celebrities as Bernhardt, Salvini and Langtry, appeared time after time at Macauley's until Louisville audiences knew them well and loved them all. The final chapter was written at the closing performance of the Malcolm Fassett stock season on August 25, 1925. Macauley's was then torn down to make way for the Starks office building; with its passing, Louisville lost one of its most colorful and glamorous historical landmarks.

Other theaters in Louisville came and went, but none ever attained the prestige of Macauley's. In the nineties Colonel Norton built a huge, sprawling auditorium on Fifth Street, where prize fights and Italian opera were housed indiscriminately. Mozart Hall, on Fourth Street near Liberty, renamed Woods in 1863, was an early amateur enterprise, one of the first theaters to inaugurate matinees. Later this theater became the Academy of Music, flourished briefly as the Theatre Comique, and then passed out of existence. Among the other houses were the Hopkins, the Masonic Temple, the Buckingham (now the Savoy) and the Gayety—a vaudeville house. The Brown Theater on Broadway took the place of Macauley's for a brief while.

The glamorous days of stock companies and road shows are over, and today Louisville has no legitimate theater. The few noted actors who still tour the country—such as Katharine Cornell, Helen Hayes and Walter Huston—play at the Memorial Auditorium.

The little theater movement, however, has had a phenomenal growth in Kentucky, dating from a performance by the University of Louisville Players in 1911. The initial production of this group was given in the old clinic of the medical school, with a stage measuring eight by twelve feet. The first regular season began in 1913. At the present time practically all the State colleges, the larger high schools, churches, and many independent organizations have active groups producing plays regularly. The Little Theater, of Louisville, the Guignol Theater Company, of Lexington, which owes much of its success to Carol Sax, and a club at Bowling Green, all give productions of real merit. The yearly productions at the Louisville Municipal College for Negroes encourage dramatic activity in Kentucky's Negro schools.

Boyd Martin, dramatic director of the University of Louisville for the last 25 years and dramatic critic of the *Courier-Journal,* is in great measure responsible for the activity of three groups of players in

Louisville: the University of Louisville Players, The Players Club, and the Alumni Players. These clubs have been recently combined as the Little Theater Company of Louisville. Five plays are presented each season at the Playhouse on Belknap Campus, University of Louisville. Dedicatory services for the Playhouse, a small Tudor Gothic building recently remodeled, were held November 12, 1925, the same year in which Macauley's Theater was razed. Here is housed the gallery of theatrical pictures formerly a feature of Macauley's lobby, a gift to the University from Macauley's heirs. The collection, begun when the old theater opened its doors, contains 3,000 pictures of famous actors and actresses, many of them autographed. The Guignol Theater in Lexington, under the direction of Frank Fowler, is sponsored by the University of Kentucky and offers five or six plays during the school term and usually one during the summer.

The newest and one of the most ambitious adventures in theatrical entertainment in the State is the open air theater in Iroquois Park, Louisville, built with the aid of the Works Progress Administration. Ground was broken on April 18, 1938, and the theater opened with a performance of *Naughty Marietta*. The seats are in the open and are placed on natural terraces with a garden wall across the back. The permanent structure consists of stage, dressing rooms, and offices. The Park Theatrical Association, a non-profit organization, accepts from the Park Board responsibility for providing attractions, underwriting the project against loss, and at the end of each season, turns over profits, if any, to the city for further improvement of the property. It is noteworthy that the initial season (1938) showed a profit of $900. The operas presented were: *Naughty Marietta, Rose Marie, The Mikado,* and *Rio Rita.*

Painting and Sculpture

The pioneers who penetrated the Appalachians could carry but little equipment; and when they settled on the land they were compelled to rely upon their manual skill for a home and its furnishings. During the early days handicrafts supplied almost all necessary articles. Furniture, utensils, brooms, rugs, quilts, coverings, cloth, baskets, were woven, spun or tooled by hand. The pioneer women picked, washed, carded, and spun wool and cotton, and colored them with dyes made from clays, roots, and bark.

Although utility is the primary aim of the crafts, they stimulate by their very nature the development of the arts of decoration. The homespun fabrics were woven according to both new and traditional designs. The carving of chairs, stools, tables, benches, and bedsteads produced in time an indigenous style. Coverlets and quilts, objects of special regard among pioneer women, were ornamented with colored flowers and stitching which often reached a high level of creative design.

The pioneer crafts declined with the advance of roads and machine-made goods, and by the end of the nineteenth century they had all but disappeared. A few "pockets" in the mountains and valleys of eastern Kentucky continued, however, to preserve the remnants of the old skills. Recently a broad movement, in which Berea College took the lead in 1893, has developed to revive and stimulate the local crafts. Schools and centers have been set up in many parts of the State to encourage their practice and to carry them forward in new directions. Besides furniture and textiles, ironwork, poppets (mountain dolls), dulcimers, toys, and whittled animals and figures are among the products of the "contemporary ancestors."

The early history of the State was not, however, solely one of frontier hazards. Some of the pioneers who settled in the soft lands of central Kentucky soon built fine homes, lived in comfort, and even with a degree of luxury, entertained visitors from the East, and fostered whatever fine arts were accessible. Here the collection of silverware was popular, and knives, spoons, forks, pitchers, ladles, and mint julep cups were fashioned from coin metal. Asa Blanchard and Samuel Ayres are among the silversmiths whose names have survived. A good deal of this early work is still to be found in Kentucky, including a teapot and pitcher made for Isaac Shelby, first Governor, and a service (dated 1819) for General Green Clay.

By 1825 Lexington, then the cultural center of the State and proud to be known as the "Athens of the West," ranked with New Orleans as a center for portrait painters. John Neagle, who came from Philadelphia in 1818, found himself in competition with a native Kentuckian already firmly established as one of the leading portrait painters of his day. This was Matthew H. Jouett (1787–1827), called "the best painter west of the Appalachians."

Jouett had been a student of Gilbert Stuart for several months, but was largely self-taught. Showing a keen sense of character, firm drawing and brush work, and a feeling for strong composition, his work set a standard for the Kentucky portraitists who followed. Though but fifteen years of his brief life were devoted to painting, he left hundreds of portraits, which today constitute a roll call of the notable figures of early-Republican Kentucky. The J. B. Speed Memorial Museum in Louisville includes in its collection ten Kentucky portraits by Jouett; Transylvania College in Lexington has his painting of Henry Clay; and the Kentucky State Historical Society has a number of his canvases, including a full-length portrait of the Marquis de Lafayette, painted as a memento of his visit to Kentucky in the spring of 1825.

A contemporary of Jouett, William Edward West (1788–1857), son of a Lexington inventor and silversmith, studied under Sully in Philadelphia, and later continued his education abroad, where he received attention for his portrait of Byron. West also made a sketch of Shelley, and was commissioned for portraits by many well-known figures of his day. In Paris he formed the acquaintance of Washington Irving and became his close friend, illustrating his *The Pride of the Village* and *Annette Delabre*. The career of West is a Kentucky example of the early tendency among American artists to seek education and a congenial life in the cities of Europe.

In sculpture Italy was the chief influence in the first half of the nineteenth century. Joel T. Hart (1810–1877), who was born in Winchester, spent many years in Florence. His *Triumph of Chastity* is typical in style and theme of the sculpture of the period. He is perhaps most popularly known for his statue of Henry Clay at Richmond, Virginia, a copy of which stands in the rotunda of the Jefferson County Courthouse in Louisville, Kentucky. Hart was associated with Gideon Shryock (1802–1880) in the building of the Old Capitol at Frankfort.

In contrast with these expatriate artists, John James Audubon (1779–1851) and Chester Harding (1792–1866) established wide reputations through their paintings of local subjects. Audubon lived at Henderson and at Louisville for several years, and gathered material on the Ohio River for his monumental *Birds of America*. The J. B. Speed Museum has five portraits by him, and there are numerous collections of Audubon's prints in Kentucky, the largest of which is housed in the Museum in Audubon Memorial Park at Henderson.

Chester Harding, who achieved a tremendous reputation during his lifetime, was born in Massachusetts, but spent much of his early life wandering in the newly settled territories. He arrived in Paris, Kentucky, about 1818 when portraits were much in demand. Later he went to Missouri and painted the picture of Daniel Boone, which hangs in the Filson Club in Louisville.

Other Kentucky painters of this epoch were Joseph H. Bush (1794–1865); John Grimes (1799–1837), a pupil of Jouett; Oliver Frazer (1808–1864); and E. F. Goddard, who settled in Georgetown about 1840. Edward Troye (1804–1874), a Swiss who arrived in America in 1828, achieved much renown as a painter of horses. James Reid Lambdin (1807–1889), famous for his portraits of American Presidents, moved to Louisville in 1832.

Frank Duveneck (1848–1919), outstanding American painter, sculptor, etcher, and teacher, was born in Covington. During a prolonged period of study at Munich, he absorbed the new brushwork technique of that school, and on his return to America became a leading influence of the latter half of the nineteenth century. In his later years he served as Dean of the Cincinnati Art School and made his home permanently in Covington. In St. Mary's Cathedral in Covington are some large murals by Duveneck, *Crucifixion, Christ at Emmaus,* and others painted about 1910.

Alfred L. Brennan (1853–1921), born in Louisville, was known for his illustrations. Charles Courtney Curran, winner of many prizes and medals both in America and abroad, was born in Hartford, Kentucky, in 1861. Charles Sneed Williams (b. 1882) is represented at the State Capitol, the Kentucky State Historical Society, and the Speed Memorial Museum. Enid Yandell (1870–1934), whose work in sculpture is well known, was a native of Louisville. Her *Daniel Boone,* a character study, first exhibited at the Chicago Fair in 1893, stands in Cherokee Park in Louisville. Near by is Hogan Fountain also designed and executed by her.

Paul Sawyier (d. 1917) painted views along the Kentucky and Dix Rivers above Frankfort. His water colors and oils are subjective interpretations, rich in atmosphere and feeling. Dean Cornwell, who has achieved a reputation as an illustrator and mural painter, was born in Louisville in 1892 and received his first instruction in art there; his work has been exhibited at the Speed Museum. Charles Warner Williams, an example of whose work is to be seen at Berea College, was born in Henderson in 1903.

In recent years a number of public monuments have been dedicated in the State. A. A. Weinman's (b. 1870) seated *Lincoln* is in the

public square at Hodgenville, and another *Lincoln,* in a standing pos-
ture, by the same artist, is in the rotunda of the State Capitol at Frankfort. A replica of George Gray Barnard's colossal *Lincoln* at Cincinnati, Ohio, stands in the grounds of Louisville's Public Library. The
statue of William Goebel in front of the Capitol grounds in Frankfort
is by Charles N. Niehaus (1855–1935), and one of James Kennedy
Patterson on the campus of the University of Kentucky is the work of
Augustus Lukeman (1871–1935). A bronze statue of Thomas Jefferson, a work of much imagination by Moses Jacob Ezekiel (1844–1917),
stands in front of the Jefferson County Courthouse in Louisville.
George Rogers Clark's departure from Fort Harrod on the expedition
that was to win the Northwest Territory is commemorated at Harrods-
burg, the site of Fort Harrod, by a high-relief done in granite by Ulric
Ellerhusen (b. 1879). Other Kentucky monuments are the statue of
John B. Castleman by Roland Huston Perry, a memorial to Governor
H. Clay Egbert by John Carlisle Meyenberg, and the Charles J.
Duncan Memorial by George Julian Zolnay—all in Louisville.

Of major interest is the current revival of mural painting. The
Marine Hospital in Louisville has a series of panels by Henrick M.
Mayer, executed under the section of painting and sculpture of the
Federal Treasury Department, dramatizing the Ohio River steamboat
trade of half a century ago. In the lobby of the Seelbach Hotel,
Louisville, is a series of murals by Arthur Thomas, depicting the pioneer life and history of Kentucky and Northwest Territories. In the
Federal Building at Louisville, the postal service and Kentucky industries are shown in a group of decorations by Frank Long, whose two
murals at the University of Kentucky Library are a vigorous interpre-
tation of rural and mountain life. In the foyer of the University's
Memorial Hall is a fresco by Ann Rice, the only example of this medium in the State. In Louisville two murals by Ferdinand G. Walker
are in St. Peter's Church, and the State Capitol at Frankfort has
murals by Gilbert White.

Several nationally known cartoonists and caricaturists—including
Fontaine Fox, Wyncie King, and Paul Plaschke—are from Kentucky.
In the field of "popular" art, paintings, prints, tombstones, and monu-
ments of horses are among Kentucky's interesting contributions. A
life-size bronze stands over the grave of Fair Play, great sire of the
Elmendorf Farm, the central Kentucky estate of Joseph Widener. At
Hamburg Place, the property of Ed Madden, is a graveyard enclosed
by a gray stone fence, horseshoe-shaped; here are buried many famous

Madden runners, including Nancy Hanks, champion trotting mare. At Colonel E. R. Bradley's place, near Lexington, a small bronze statue has been erected over the grave of North Star III.

The Federal Art Project, started in February 1936, has worked to promote the development of native talent. Besides its other activities, the project has made valuable reproductions of old furniture and designs with the aim of perpetuating the tradition and accomplishments of early Kentucky craftsmen.

Literature

Since Kentucky was admitted to the Union as early as 1792 it might be assumed that its literary development would, in a general way, parallel that of the new Nation, moving through a protean romanticism to an equally protean realism. And that, up to a certain point, and with modifications imposed by its sectional character, is precisely what Kentucky literature has done.

To a population whose booklovers had been reared pretty largely in the traditions of Walter Scott and Lord Byron, a love for historical fiction, for florid oratory, for the passionate expression of emotion, came without much effort. Its liking for the Gothic elements of narrative has not yet been wholly satisfied, and from Catharine A. Warfield's *The Romance of Beauseincourt* (1867) through Robert Burns Wilson's *Until the Day Break* (1900), down to the detective novels of the late Foxhall Daingerfield, Kentuckians have enjoyed the stock materials which arouse horror and mystery. This sensationalism, growing out of an essentially aristocratic attitude, is a minor trait of Kentucky literature, to be sure. The spread of democratic feeling in a State which was, despite any pretensions to the contrary, founded upon a midwestern democracy, was inevitable; by the middle of the nineteenth century, books which had the best chance to succeed in Kentucky were those which had not a little relation to actualities—books which preserved the homely manners, the homely humor, and the homely dialect of its people. Out of this regionalism—qualified, it is important to note, by a gentility which survived from the height of the romantic movement—came the impetus for the most noted of Kentucky's novelists.

The first of these, and the one that should be read first by the visitor to Kentucky, is James Lane Allen. Born near Lexington in 1849, he located the scenes for fifteen of his nineteen books in the Bluegrass of his native State. His second volume, *The Blue-grass Region of Kentucky* (1892), was an account of Kentucky landscapes, houses, people, and manners, with a nostalgic longing for a culture which had died during the War between the States. In his fiction Allen made the central plateau of Kentucky as familiar to the national public as any other section popularized by any author. If the name of Kentucky is today an alluring one, it is chiefly because of the legends and facts that cluster about the figure of Daniel Boone, because of the fading convention of resounding public speech, because of the genuine balladry of the mountains and the simulated balladry of Stephen Collins Foster, and because James Lane Allen wrote such novels as *A Kentucky Cardinal* (1895), *The Choir Invisible* (1897), and *The Reign of Law* (1900).

Allen began by following in the steps of the local colorists. Before the opening of the twentieth century he passed on into a realism inspired by his reading and by a maturing philosophy, a realism which eventually shocked and alienated his readers, especially his Kentucky readers. Disturbed by the antagonism and condemnation he had inspired, Allen turned back briefly to romance, then experimented with a realism deeply colored by symbolism, and ended with narratives which he intended to transcend all schools. Much of what he wrote is now forgotten; much will never have value save for the student and historian. But Allen did preserve, in a style which became progressively imposing and artificial, many scenes and people, and customs which anyone who wishes to know the Bluegrass must read. Note, for example, what tinges of romance his early "The White Cowl" and "Sister Dolorosa" add to the Trappist monastery of Gethsemane and the convent at Loretto. One should read *The Choir Invisible* for an unmatched re-creation of the idealism of the best Bluegrass blood of a former age. A reading of "King Solomon of Kentucky" and "Two Gentlemen of Kentucky" will add sentimental interest to any stay at Lexington. Allen's writing after 1910 failed to win critical or popular approval; today it is little known and probably on the way to oblivion. This decline was owing, as intimated, to the fact that he became the victim of his precious style, and to the additional fact that he was unwilling to throw off his mantle of gentility. Before he died in 1925 he had outlived both his fame and his once sizeable earnings.

Influenced at the outset by James Lane Allen, John Fox, Jr., managed to combine romance and realism more shrewdly, more palatably. Born near Paris in 1863, Fox later made his home in the highlands which meet on the borders of Virginia and Kentucky at Big Stone Gap. Here he found the material which put two of his novels among the best-selling American books of all time: *The Little Shepherd of Kingdom Come* (1903) and *The Trail of the Lonesome Pine* (1908). The material, of course, was the mountaineer and his manners. In narrative these novels, perhaps, surpass anything Allen wrote; indeed, *The Trail* builds a climax which most novelists would be glad to equal. A pupil of the regional writers, Fox met the demands of his generation by idealizations of character which now provoke skepticism. Commentators are likely to complain of the romanticism which made the primitive mountaineer a nobler individual than the inheritor of Bluegrass civilization. On the other hand, the mountain people protest that his representations of them are unfair and untrue, particularly as he emphasizes feuds, lawlessness, and moonshining. Like Allen, Fox found his literary reputation waning before he died in 1919. Authors who put their trust in regionalism are likely to find their material limited, their themes repetitious.

This is the peril confronting Elizabeth Madox Roberts, born near Perryville in 1885, who writes not of the mountaineers, as most eastern reviewers take for granted, but of the farmers southward from Louisville. Miss Roberts is at her best when most subjective; perhaps no living American writer has more truthfully explored the consciousness of the adolescent girl, of the lonely and poetic woman. Her first volume was verse, *Under the Tree* (1922), now very rare. She has also attempted the historical novel in *The Great Meadow* (1930), which introduces Boone and what is now Harrodsburg, and satire upon the contemporary scene in the obscure but not doctrinnaire *Jingling in the Wind* (1928) and *He Sent Forth a Raven* (1935). Her latest story, *Black is My Truelove's Hair* (1938), is a tragi-comedy of the Kentucky countryside. No well-read person will be unacquainted with her first novel, *The Time of Man* (1926), which in its universality has the earmark of a classic.

Irvin S. Cobb, also an offspring of the regionalists, will escape their fate by virtue of his humor and because he has created one of the most lovable heroes, the canny, benevolent Judge Priest. Cobb describes a still different section of Kentucky—the Purchase, whose capital is Paducah, where he was born in 1876. He captures and reveals with sometimes irrelevant details the era of steamboat traffic on the Ohio, of leisurely and kindly living in southern provinces. One of the best-paid of present-day story writers, he is usually represented in anthologies by "The Belled Buzzard" and "Words and Music," the latter perhaps his finest narrative so far.

Another Kentuckian to produce a book ranking among the best sellers of all time is Alice Hegan Rice, of Louisville, whose *Mrs. Wiggs of the Cabbage Patch* (1901) taught the favorite American gospel that poverty can be supported with courage and honor. The scene is laid in Louisville. Widely read, too, have been the "Emmy Lou" stories of Mrs. George Madden Martin and the "Little Colonel" series of Annie Fellows Johnston, both of Pewee Valley.

Kentucky regionalism found a virile, lyrical voice in 1935 when Jesse Stuart (1906–   ) surprised the literary world with his *Man with a Bull-Tongue Plow*, a prodigal book of more than 700 sonnets about "birds, cornfields, trees, wildflowers, log shacks, my own people, valleys and rivers and mists in the valleys." Often crude in form and mediocre in content, these musical sonnets have a refreshing spontaneity and a ringing sincerity. Stuart resorts to poetry to celebrate the beauties of nature and an ancestral way of life, that he finds good, but uses prose to tell about the people of the foothills of eastern Kentucky. Something of their angularity is portrayed in some of the casually grim or profanely humorous stories in *Head o' W-Hollow* (1936). In these stories, with their odd characters and episodes of frustration and tragedy, Stuart achieves a form of implicit criticism not often found in his poetry. His autobiography, *Beyond Dark Hills* (1938), first written while he was attending college, is an understanding account of the more representative folk of his region—the hill farmers who have wrestled with a tough, stingy soil for generations, and faced sickness, hardship, isolation and death with equanimity.

It is difficult to account for the absence of first-rate poets among a people fundamentally romantic. The explanation probably lies in the lack of critical guidance, in a hampering conservatism, and in the lack of local encouragement. Madison Cawein, for example, blinded by the magic of Keats and Spenser, could do no better with Kentucky than populate the woods near Louisville with fays, elves, pixies, oreads, and the like; in this process he was too prolific, too oblivious to things human. Sometimes called the greatest nature poet of his day, he died disappointed, convinced that his world of dreams had been shattered by pressing poverty and illness. A less melodious poet is Cale Young

Rice, of Louisville, who carries on the classical tradition of English verse and resents recent experiments in versification. It must be said of Kentucky poets, as of the prose writers, that they have failed, either through lack of vision or of courage, to give the State the epical treatment in literature which it deserves.

Architecture

Kentucky, like most of our western States, passed through a pioneering period—the period of the "clearing" in the timber, the stockade fort, and the Wilderness Road. Forests had to be cleared; land had to be broken; a new domain had to be brought under the hand of the plowman. The story of those early parties, of their settlements here, of grim days of privation and Indian peril, are eloquently recorded in the architecture of the old stockade forts like Fort Harrod, so admirably reconstructed at Harrodsburg.

As soon as the country had been made safe for settlement, Kentucky's virgin acres had to be made to produce, and produce abundantly, before anything like a real competence could be won from the soil. But the sturdy pioneers did conquer the soil and did establish in the wilderness the foundations of a commonwealth as early as the last quarter of the eighteenth century.

With the establishment of an agricultural economy there came a second architectural expression—the log cabin. These staunch and rugged four-square old houses, with rough-hewn walls and dirt floors, are emblematic of the type of life which was lived in them, and symbolic of the men and women who inhabited them. Good examples of the house of this period are the Marriage Place of Tom Lincoln and Nancy Hanks in Pioneer Park at Harrodsburg, and the old Creel Cabin *(see Tour 6)* on the Lincoln birthplace farm near Hodgenville.

Beginning with stockade forts and log cabins, architectural expression in Kentucky passed through successive phases, eventually culminating in the great porticoed brick mansions which lend so much charm to the countryside.

Thus Kentucky architecture parallels the course of architecture upon the Atlantic seaboard with this difference; a style or a fashion well known in the maritime States will often not make its appearance in Kentucky for from 10 to 30 years later. Once acclimated, however, such vogues are as likely to persist here as in other areas. It is, therefore, not feasible to set down the chronology for seaboard architecture and expect it completely to apply to the course of the art in Kentucky.

Chronologically it must be pointed out that the term "Colonial," so far as Kentucky architecture is concerned, can have no *historic* connotation and is employed only to refer to that variety of architecture which arose upon the Atlantic seaboard during the Colonial period and belatedly reached Kentucky. Because of this fact one should be careful in the use of the word. The term is generally very loosely applied to Kentucky architecture, being used to designate not only the true Colonial but also the porticoed house of the Greek Revival, so common in the State. "Liberty Hall" in Frankfort, "Federal Hill" (*see Tour 15*) near Bardstown, and the Benjamin Gratz House in Lexington are perfect examples of the Georgian phase of Kentucky Colonial and should not be confused with such Greek Revival examples as the Orlando Brown House in Frankfort, Beaumont Inn (Daughters' College) in Harrodsburg, or old Centre College at Danville, Morrison College of Transylvania, and the Old Statehouse at Frankfort.

After the advent of railways and the accompanying facility in the exchange of ideas and materials, the development of architecture in Kentucky, particularly in the towns and cities, more nearly paralleled that of the eastern part of the United States. This was especially true after the reconstruction period that followed the Civil War.

The first phase (the log cabin) of early Kentucky architecture dates from 1767 to 1786. Although Gabriel Arthur, of Virginia, appears to have traversed territory now within Kentucky as early as 1674, nothing that can even remotely be termed architecture was erected in the State for nearly a century. What purports to be the ruined chimney of the "first house in Kentucky," built by Dr. Thomas Walker (*see Tour 4A*) about 1750, is today preserved at the Walker State Park near Barbourville. The exact form of this house is not known, but a log cabin in the accepted style of the day has been erected to give the visitor some notion of Kentucky's "first home." At the time that Kentucky was being settled the log cabin built of horizontal logs had long since become the recognized type for the pioneer woodsman. These houses could be built of the timber taken from the lands which the settlers cleared for cultivation and were, when well "chinked" with mud or plaster, warm in winter and cool in summer. The simpler cabins usually consisted of one room, sometimes of two. Often two portions of a house were separated by an open passageway or "dogtrot" porch, as it was sometimes locally called. This passageway often served as a washroom, where extra wood for the kitchen fire and a bench with water pail and wash basin were kept.

Such cabins were usually constructed of round logs flattened upon two sides in order to make a better joint. These were halved into each other at the corners, the ends left to project about a foot. If a foundation was used, it was of stone and the massive fireplace was of the same material. Above the throat of the fireplace the chimney was constructed of "stocks" or logs carefully chinked, at first with clay but later with mortar. In time the "stock" chimneys, always in danger of burning, were replaced with stone. The roofs were at first covered with "shucks," later with bark "shingles," and finally with hand-split "shakes" held in place by long poles secured at the ends. Often the floors were of dirt, but these were in time replaced with "puncheons" or split logs, usually very uneven and sometimes full of splinters. Before glass was available windows were protected by skins or heavy shutters. Upon occasion oiled paper was used in lieu of glass, this being protected by wooden slats. Kentucky has a wealth of examples coming down from pioneer days, the old Creel cabin on the Lincoln Birthplace farm being a good example of the more elaborate type. Old Fort Harrod at Harrodsburg, reconstructed in 1926, forms an easily accessible exhibit of the pioneer stage of Kentucky architecture.

Succeeding the earliest cabins just described there appeared a more refined variety of log house. This was constructed of beautifully hewn squared logs carefully jointed and calked. Stone foundations and stone or brick chimneys were usual, and in general plan such houses resembled the more adequate types left behind by the settlers who came from the Atlantic seaboard. Many comfortable and respectable looking Kentucky houses of this type of construction are still standing, an excellent example being the Wilmore Garrett place not far from Lexington. It is a well proportioned two-story house of Georgian Colonial lines, resembling in general character the architecture of Tuckahoe in Virginia. The stairway ascends from a central hallway, the more important rooms flanking the entry. This house, like many another, was covered with clapboards and, with the addition of a classic portico, attained a real gentility. At the rear of this house a fine stone wing, the next step in the utilization of materials, is to be seen.

Stone, where it was readily available, early became a favorite material. As a matter of fact, stone as an architectural material really came into prominence before the cabin type went out of use. There are still extant many smaller stone houses, now long used for Negroes or servants, that were the habitations of the original landowners. More genteel and commendable examples of stone construction, however, are the fine old structures at Shakertown *(see Tour 15)*, the rear wing of the Garrett house above mentioned, and the old DuPuy farmhouse below Versailles in Woodford County. This latter house is of two stories with a central hall, a quaint front porch, and simple but dignified mantels. Built of cream-gray Kentucky "marble" with white wood trim and green shutters, this staunch old house has real distinction.

Georgian and Federal architecture in Kentucky prevailed from 1786 to 1825. In a sense the advent of brick as a structural material may be said to signalize the arrival of Georgian forms in Kentucky. The William Whitley House *(see Tour 3)* in Lincoln County, built in 1786, was one of the earliest of the Georgian types, and the "first brick house" in the State. In mass this structure is not unlike the simpler two-story houses of old Virginia and, as in these, the brick work is in Flemish bond with dark headers. It was followed by a brilliant company of noble houses, the general arrangement of which, following the models of Virginia, provided a broad central hall with a stairway up to a landing from which it returned to the second floor. Ceilings were high and windows double-hung with 12- or 16-paned sashes.

Often Palladian windows, an invention of the Italian Renaissance introduced through England to America, were used either over the principal portal, as at "Liberty Hall" in Frankfort, or for the regular opening, as at the old Muldrow farm *(see Tour 14)* near Milner, and at the Eliza Cleveland house in Versailles. Each important room had a beautiful mantel, while an arch, spanning the central hall and supported upon delicately fluted columns, often divided the hall into "front" and "back."

Perhaps no single example of Georgian architecture in Kentucky is better known than "Federal Hill" *(see Tour 15)* near Bardstown. Built in 1795 by John Rowan, this sedate but graceful home was constructed of native brick with stone foundations, the brick laid in Flemish bond but without the dark headers. The main house, consisting of two stories and a low attic, would present the typical Georgian plan were it not for the fact that what would ordinarily be a rear room, on the west side of the hall, is here replaced by a service court which intervenes between the dining room and the one-story detached kitchen wing. The house is nobly proportioned, both inside and out. The windows are of the generous 12-paned variety, while long side windows, fitted with double-hung six-paned sashes, flank the simple, classically enframed portal.

A broad central hall, spanned by a beautiful arch carried upon delicately fluted colonnettes, leads through the house. At the right, beyond the archway, the stairway ascends to a landing above the rear door, from which it returns on the left of the hall to the second floor. At the right as one enters is the dining room; at the left the parlor, behind which is a lower bedroom. Above, a similar arrangement provides three bedrooms with a library over the front hall. The parlor, dining room and bed chambers are provided with mantels, which connect with chimneys that go up through inside walls. Each of these mantels is a splendid example of the carver's art.

A Georgian house quite similar in plan to "Federal Hill" is "Liberty Hall" in Frankfort. In this notable house, built by the Honorable John Brown in 1796, the plan suggested in the remarks about "Federal Hill" is realized; that is, the central hall with spanning arch and stairway is flanked by two rooms on either side. Moreover, the kitchen wing, which at "Federal Hill" is upon a lower level, is here upon the same level and is better related to the house proper. "Liberty Hall" therefore represents the full-blown Georgian plan.

Here also the general mass of the house has received greater thought and presents, in its pediment-crowned frontal bay, a motif quite usual in the Pennsylvania and Virginia houses of its day. The portal is of noble lines and above it is the handsomest Palladian window in Kentucky. The interior woodwork, particularly the doors, windows, and wainscots, are chaste in proportion and classic in detail.

A charming Federal example is the fine old house in St. Matthews, now owned by Judge Churchill Humphrey (see *Tour 16*). This house has a well-designed central mass flanked by outlying wings connected by lower links. In massing, this structure recalls the Maryland plantation houses and bears a striking resemblance to "Homewood," the old Carroll mansion now on the campus of Johns Hopkins University at Baltimore. The beautiful tetrastyle portico, with its delicate attenuated columns, makes a splendid entrance to the spacious arched front hall, which leads into a cross corridor giving access to the wings. In the central mass just beyond the cross corridor are the high-ceilinged living room at the left and the dining room at the right. The woodwork throughout the house is as refined as the frontal portico, the whole constituting an excellent example of that simplicity, lightness, and delicacy in carving that characterizes the "Federal" era at its best. Lovely mantels grace each room.

Other outstanding examples of Georgian and Federal architecture are the Crittenden house in Frankfort, "Wickland" near Bardstown; the Eliza Cleveland and Lyle houses in Versailles; "Clay Hill" and the Vaught (Burford) house, in Harrodsburg; "Castlewood," "Woodlawn" (see Tour 4), and "Woodstock" at Richmond; "Rose Hill," "Eothan," the John W. Hunt house, "Loudoun," Bodley House, and the Benjamin Gratz house, in Lexington; Xalapa Farm near Paris; the "Grange" and the Clark farm on the Paris-Maysville Pike, various brick houses in Shakertown (see Tour 15); the Colonel Andrew Muldrow house (see Tour 14) near Milner; and various lesser, though often as interesting, structures throughout the State.

The Greek Revival was tardy in reaching Kentucky. By 1825, however, Greek details were beginning to make their appearance upon otherwise Georgian structures and by 1830, largely through the instrumentality of Gideon Shryock, the style was well established in Kentucky.

Shryock, who was born in Lexington where he learned the practical art of building from his father, Mathias Shryock (1774–1833), pursued the study of architecture with William Strickland of Philadelphia, who, in turn, had been trained by Latrobe. Perhaps Shryock's most notable work is the Old Capitol (now the State Historical Society Building) in Frankfort. This beautiful and well proportioned edifice, built of Kentucky "marble," immediately set a precedent for elegance and dignity in public buildings in the State, and did much to stimulate interest in classic design. Other important public structures, designed by Shryock, are Morrison College, Lexington, the old Bank on Main Street, the Blind Institute and the Jefferson County Court House, all in Louisville.

The Greek influence in Kentucky was first apparent in classical porches, mantels, and other details, which were used to adorn masses otherwise reminiscent of the past vogue in architecture. Soon, however, the masses themselves took on more and more of the Greek temple and all details—doors, windows, and stairways—became completely Hellenized. It was at this period that the stately columned porticoes, usually of the Doric or Ionic order, made their appearance. Gleaming white, these classic portals, seen across a bluegrass greensward or discovered at the end of a shady tree-lined drive, are among the most delightful sights in the older sections of the State.

One of the earliest true Greek Revival houses in Kentucky is the Orlando Brown House in Frankfort, built in 1835 by John Brown of "Liberty Hall" for his son. Gideon Shryock, architect of the Capitol, was called to execute this task and here showed himself as much a master at the design of private buildings as of public structures. The simple four-square mass of this brick structure is crowned by a low pediment fronting the street and pierced by a fanlight—reminiscent of the Georgian. A one-storied tetrastyle Ionic portico shelters a simple rectangular doorway and forms a "support" to a triple-membered unshuttered window in the upper hall, similar to the windows at "Mansfield" described below. The four other windows of the façade have six-paned Georgian sashes, flanked by slatted blinds.

A full-blown Greek Revival example is "Mansfield," the Thomas Hart Clay house, just east of the famous "Ashland" on the Richmond Pike in Lexington. Like the Churchill Humphrey house, it has a dignified central mass with low attic and ridge paralleling the street, flanked at either end by lower masses with gable ends. Still lower, links join the three masses and complete the ensemble. A feature of the central façade is a graceful tetrastyle Ionic portico sheltering a Greek pilastered entrance, which is capped with transom and entablature. The walls of the façade are relieved by pilasters in brick with membering at the corners and triple windows enframed in the same style as the doorway. These Greek windows are not shuttered. Throughout this house, inside and out, the chaste sobriety of the Greek Revival at its best is exemplified.

While the typical Greek Revival house is fronted by a two-storied portico of Doric or Ionic design, many examples in Kentucky exhibit variations therefrom as charming as they are unusual. An excellent and unique portico is that of the old Adam Childers House on the high school campus at Versailles, where a splendid effect has been obtained, not by the use of columns at all, but by the use of square piers simply molded and decorated by a necking embodying a simple Greek fretwork.

At "Diamond Point" in Harrodsburg a two-storied portico with Doric columns, set between square end piers, shelters a rich and elaborately carved doorway and a narrow lacy balcony that crosses the façade at the second story level.

Sometimes the use of a portico is dispensed with altogether and the façade is decorated with a two-storied recessed entrance, as in the Dr. Robert Alexander Johnston house in Danville. Here simple fluted Doric colonnades, set distyle in antis, form the entrance on the first floor, while a similar arrangement above, provided with a balcony rail, makes a small recessed porch. An important portal of this type, but under a portico, is to be seen at the Moberly house in Harrodsburg.

Windows enframed with simple Greek architraves often exhibit Greek anthemion and "honeysuckle" motifs as applied decoration. Good examples of these are seen at the Stephenson house in Harrodsburg.

The plan of the Greek house in the main followed Georgian lines, an arrangement which in the preceding period had been found admirably adapted to living in Kentucky. Often Georgian details were retained inside the house, an excellent example being the staircase, which seems to have remained steadfastly Georgian even in the late Greek house, as at "Scotland" on the Frankfort-Versailles Pike. But alongside the Georgian staircases one finds heavy Greek enframed interior doors and windows, mantels, and woodwork. Often Ionic and upon occasion Corinthian columns carried a cornice, which, at the wall, rested upon pilasters to form effectively trimmed openings between rooms. The Doctor Carrick residence in Lexington, "White Hall," and the Helm Place, south of Lexington, show good examples. At the latter, sliding doors, encased by recessed wing walls, made their appearance. Interior doors may have horizontal or vertical panels and may be enframed by a splayed casing with Greek "ears" at the top, or by a rectangular casing resting upon simple plinths and carved with fret or key designs and including recessed corner blocks at the top. A prominent interior feature of this period was the elaborate decorative plaster work in the form of deep cornices and central medallions in the ceilings. The latter were decorated with the Greek "water leaf," anthemion, acanthus, and other motifs executed exquisitely in plaster of Paris, and were tinted in delicate pastel colors; they formed the motif from which crystal chandeliers were suspended.

Fine old examples of Greek Revival architecture are the McClure, Barbee (Adams), and Chestnut houses in Danville; "Aspen Hall" and the Ben Lee Harden House in Harrodsburg; the Showalter, Brooker, and Shropshire houses at Georgetown *(see Tour 4);* the Colonel James Marshall Brown and Carrothers houses in Bardstown; the James Wier-Duncan (Dr. Carrick) home in Lexington; and Helm Place, south of that city. Certain of the buildings at the Kentucky School for the Deaf at Danville, old Centre College *(see Tour 5)* in the same city, Daughters' College (now the main hall of Beaumont Inn) at Harrodsburg.

A number of churches and residences in Kentucky are excellent examples of the Gothic Revival style (1835–1860). The First Presbyterian Church of Louisville (organized in 1816) erected a Gothic church edifice with a square English tower, while St. Paul's Episcopal Church in the same city built one of Gothic design with tower and spire. An interesting church of this era is the fine old First Presbyterian at Danville. Another very choice example is the little sexton's house in the abandoned Episcopal Cemetery in Lexington, designed just prior to the War between the States by John McMurtry, a prominent architect of the city. The Gothic continued to be the popular ecclesiastical style up to the war, and so strong was its momentum that it survived as "Victorian Gothic" in the post-war period.

There are five typical examples of the Gothic Revival residences left in Kentucky, four of brick and one of wood. Three of these—the Alexander-Alford house, "Ingleside" and "Loudoun," in Lexington— may be attributed to McMurtry, who made a trip to England to study the details of the Tudor Gothic style of that country. The date of the building of "Ingleside" is generally given as 1852. "Loudoun," on the Bryan Station Pike (Loudoun Avenue) at the northern limits of Lexington, now beautifully overgrown with English ivy, is a handsome Gothic Revival house. "Mound Cottage," in Danville, said to have been built in the late fifties, is another splendid example constructed of brick; while "Woodland Villa" on the Paris-Maysville Pike is an interesting example, built of wood.

The War between the States and the reconstruction period were generally very discouraging eras for architecture in America. The blight that settled over building in the Nation was, if anything, more pronounced in the border States than elsewhere. Kentucky was a part of the battleground, and many a fine ante bellum structure was pressed into wartime service. As a result a number of fine old buildings, like Bacon College at Harrodsburg and the "second" Medical Building of Transylvania University at Lexington, both in the Greek style, were burned during the war. Not until the expansive industrial period which followed reconstruction was there a revival of building activity in Kentucky, and by this time eclecticism, which has since characterized art in America, had begun its riotous career.

During the reconstruction period American architecture reached its depth of degradation. Indeed the country did not awaken to the ugliness of its art until the Centennial Exposition in Philadelphia in 1876 gave us some notion of the art of other nations. The period between this exposition and that of Chicago in 1893 was a backward one, but during this interim American students who had been studying architecture abroad, particularly at the *Ecole des Beaux Arts* in Paris, returned to give a new impetus to architectural design in America.

One of these students, Richard Morris Hunt, who had gone to Paris in 1843, had returned home just prior to the War between the States. During the seventies and eighties he was at the height of his professional career and, being a champion of the French Renaissance, generated a great vogue for this style through the example of his works. Following his precedent, buildings throughout the Union were conceived and erected in the mansard-roofed style, capitols, courthouses, city halls, post offices, and large residences in particular being adapted to this manner. The Louisville City Hall and the old Post Office (1886–1892), at the northeast corner of Fourth and Chestnut Streets, together with other buildings in the city and elsewhere in the State, were part of this movement.

Just at the close of the War between the States, Henry Hobson Richardson, a native of Louisiana, returned from his architectural studies in Paris. Soon he was in practice, and, although he died at the age of forty-eight, his influence upon American architecture was most pronounced. He espoused the Romanesque manner of the south of France and the north of Spain, and designed many buildings throughout the Union in a manner so highly personalized that it has since been called the Richardsonian Romanesque. This vogue, although highly eclectic, so captivated the American people that Montgomery Schuyler, an architectural critic and writer of the time, hailed it as the "American National style." Trinity Church in Boston is, perhaps, Richardson's most beautiful building. Kentucky, in common with other States, exhibited considerable enthusiasm for the Romanesque and within the State there are a number of examples in this manner, among them the post offices at Lexington (1886–89), Owensboro (1888–89), Paducah (1881–83), and Richmond (1893–97); the Lexington City Hall; and the Central Christian Church in the same city; the Christian Church in Cynthiana, and the State Street Methodist Church in Bowling Green. Essentially a style adapted to construction in stone or brick, the Romanesque is still popular in some sections for hospitals, schools, and churches.

Once eclecticism had set in, the architect felt free to examine Old World styles and to adopt any that seemed appropriate to the task at hand. This led to an infusion into American architecture of Italian, English, French, and Spanish ideas and motifs, and most cities show the personal predilections of the architects who designed their structures. Not finding a better style than the Gothic for church buildings, architects generally reverted to this manner for ecclesiastical work. Certainly the influence of Ralph Adams Cram and his associates in the East has helped to fix upon America the Gothic as a church style; upon occasion, other structures have been built in this manner. A good example is the old post office in Covington (1875–79), which is an American adaptation of the Italian Gothic popular at the time it was built. In a sense the continuity of the Gothic Revival has never been broken, except for the interlude of the War between the States, when most architectural activity ceased. Thus by 1872 Cincinnatus Shryock, brother of Gideon, was constructing the First Presbyterian Church in Lexington of brick in Gothic style. St. Rose Church at St. Rose, Kentucky, and the church of Gethsemane Abbey *(see Tour 6)* belong also to this continuation of the Gothic Revival, which we generally call Neo-Gothic. Kentucky is well supplied with churches of this type, many of them, like the Chapel of the Good Shepherd in Lexington, being of very excellent design.

American architecture, with the exception of the Romanesque and Gothic infiltrations, has derived its inspiration largely from the Classic. Therefore, when the Chicago World's Fair of 1893 blossomed forth in forms almost exclusively classic, the country was very ready to accept them; and, as a result, American architecture for the past forty years has remained decidedly classic in flavor. This classicism has been attained at times through the adoption of the Greek or Roman forms, at other times through a skillful rendition of American utilities in the spirit of the Italian Renaissance, as in the new State Capitol at Frankfort. An interesting example of the adaptation of Italian Renaissance architecture was the famous Galt House, on Main Street in Louisville, which showed unmistakable inspiration from the Palazzo Farnese in Rome.

Henry Whitestone was the architect of a great number of commendable structures in the city of Louisville, which, in general, may be said to be of classic design. In addition to structures with a decidedly antique flavor, like the new Post Office in Louisville and the Lincoln Memorial *(see Tour 6)*, on the Lincoln Farm at Hodgenville, there has been a recent tendency to revive another style of classic derivation, the American Georgian. The Christian Church in Harrodsburg, the new Baptist Theological Seminary in Louisville, and many residences throughout the State indicate a growing regard for indigenous American types.

Part II
Cities and Towns

ASHLAND

Railroad Stations: Carter Ave. and 12th St., for Chesapeake & Ohio Ry.; N. end Interstate Bridge, for Norfolk & Western R.R.; Kenova, W. Va. *6 m.* E. for Baltimore & Ohio, and Norfolk & Western R.R's.
Bus Station: Union Depot, 13th St., near Winchester Ave., for Greyhound and Sparks Bros. Lines.
Local Buses: Local, interurban, and jitney buses; fare 5¢ and 10¢.
Airport: L. from Winchester Ave. on 34th St.; no scheduled service.
Taxis: 25¢ minimum.
Toll Bridge: Kentucky-Ohio Interstate Bridge: autos, 25¢; pedestrians, 5¢.
Traffic Regulations: No U-turns or left-turns on business street intersections.

Accommodations: Two hotels; rooming houses and private homes cater to tourists.

Information Service: Eastern Kentucky Auto Assn., Henry Clay Hotel.

Radio Station: WCMI (1310 kc.).
Motion Picture Houses: Four.
Swimming: South Side Pool, off Blackburn Ave., E., 10¢ and 25¢.
Golf: Hillendale Club, Division St.; 18 holes, greens fee 50¢ and $1.

ASHLAND (555 alt., 29,074 pop.), largest and most important city in Eastern Kentucky, is concentrated on a rather high and wide flood plain of the Ohio River. The river makes a great bend around the southernmost tip of Ohio, receives the waters of the Big Sandy at the border between West Virginia and Kentucky, and then sweeps northwest with slow, easy curves past the long waterfront of Ashland. The city stretches up the river to Catlettsburg at the mouth of the Big Sandy, and down to the rolling mill plant, a distance of seven miles, widening and narrowing with the contour of the river bluffs overlooking the town.

Ashland is the chief Kentucky unit of an industrial area that includes Huntington, Ceredo, and Kenova, West Virginia; and Coalgrove, Ironton, and Portsmouth, Ohio. The river bank at Ashland is uncommonly high, acting as a wall against all but the superfloods that ravage most river towns year after year. This protected river front is, however, strictly utilitarian. Along it are strung the steel and iron mills, the sawmills, the coke plants, and brickyards. In front of the city fleets of barges pass, pushed by stern-wheeled tugboats, carrying thousands of tons of freight—far more than in the heyday of river boats. In the decade before the turn of the century the Ohio River peak was 12 million tons, whereas in 1936 it was in excess of 24 millions of tons. The *Gordon Greene,* last of the packets making the run up-river to Pittsburgh, periodically sweeps by with the old grace.

Down near the river front, too, are many of the warehouses, wholesale houses, packing houses, the livestock market, and a few of the retail stores. But this part of the city is caught by high floods, and the modern business district has centered along Winchester Avenue and intersecting streets, three blocks inland on a higher plain. Here are the banks, hotels, modern office buildings, churches, and department stores, and, immediately adjoining them, the downtown residential section, all showing the marks of the boom in the 1920's. On a third and still higher terrace, from Carter Avenue to the hill, and well above even the 1937 flood level, is the chief residential area, with the 52-acre Central Park, only five minutes' walk from the shopping district. Near the park are the fine houses of Bath Avenue, built by the iron masters, the lumber men, and the "wholesale" families. To the south the town has spread, up the river bluffs and over the irregular, wooded plateau where the new, winding streets follow the contour lines, and buses and jitney service connect the residents with downtown business and industry. These terraces provide natural zoning for the city and account in part for the unusual attractiveness of Ashland. It is a steel, coal, iron, and railroad center, free of the appalling grime and ugliness that disfigure so many American steel towns.

The population of the city is divided into four rather distinct groups. The first of these is made up of the old families that have been here for three or four generations—the people who made their money from iron, clay, coal, and lumber, and the professional people. Next to them are the workers of the older generation who used to live in a kind of feudal relationship to the owners of the mills and factories. In the last three decades, as Ashland doubled its population and the small mills grew large and were absorbed by outside interests, two new elements were added—the clerks, managers, technicians, and white collar workers who poured into town, and the hill people who came down to find work. There are very few foreign-born, and the rather small Negro settlement has its own educational plants and community life.

Eighty percent of the homes are owned by those who live in them. Small business and "corner groceries" thrive in the newly incorporated neighborhoods. Education and the schools are the object of a zeal that is almost a crusade. In the last few years new elementary school buildings like the Hager and the Hatcher, and junior high school buildings like the recently completed Putnam, have sprung up in the downtown area and the suburban hills, and a city library has been erected in Central Park. Churches are well attended and play a large part in the spiritual and social life of the community.

From the very beginning the rich natural heritage of the region has been the dominant factor in its growth. Natural resources determined where white men first would settle in this eastern section of Kentucky, and then dictated the types of industrial enterprise in which they would engage.

Even the Indians placed a special premium on this section and were extremely loath to give it up. Of all the choice hunting grounds in this area, the red men held on to the timbered valley of the Big Sandy and the neighboring banks of the Ohio long after white settlers had forced them out of surrounding territory. While the local deposits of coal, iron ore, fire clay, sandstone, limestone, oil, and gas meant little or nothing to the Indians, they did value highly the fine hardwood timber, the convenient watering places, and the abundance of wild game. Also, they favored the high bench on the site of Ashland as a convenient place to bury their dead, as evidenced by the number of burial mounds that remain in the heart of the city.

Eastern Kentucky did not beckon to white pioneers until the Indian power north of the Ohio was broken at the Battle of Tippecanoe in 1811. The first pioneers to come to the high flood plain and establish the forerunner of Ashland brought with them a fixed determination, and a willingness to fight—an attribute that quickly found expression in disputes over land claims growing out of inaccurate surveys. These disagreements cluttered the local courts and some of the disputants "lawed" each other for years, settlement in many cases coming long after the original contestants had died. True to the early feudist's code, a number of the belligerents chose a more expeditious method of settling arguments and disposed of their opponents in the orthodox frontier fashion.

When three Poages—George, Robert, and Robert, Jr.—came from Virginia in 1815 to settle in the fertile lands now occupied by Ashland, they chose a spot that is included in the present downtown section, and there established "Poage Settlement." As other pioneers moved in from the East and erected log cabins, the settlers' attention was focused on the industrial potentialities of the fine forests and the transportation facilities of nearby streams. The great stretches of timber already had made the Big Sandy Valley the scene of much activity, and Catlettsburg, five miles up the Ohio, was becoming widely known as a lumber town.

Naturally, therefore, lumbering was the first and most important industry of the new village which developed from Poage Settlement. Soon, however, with the discovery of iron ore and other mineral deposits, much of the hardwood in the vicinity of Ashland was being converted into charcoal for use in the production of iron. The Bellefonte furnace, first in Ashland and Boyd County, was set up in 1826; it consumed millions of feet of Kentucky's best timber, but produced thousands of tons of iron. By the time Ashland was formally laid out in 1850, most of its inhabitants had been attracted by the promise of the vicinity's valuable mineral deposits and hardwood timber. The village took its name from Henry Clay's home, "Ashland," in Lexington.

Industrial development came rapidly. The new village was only one year old when the State legislature authorized incorporation of the community's first railroad, now the Kentucky division of the Chesapeake & Ohio. Ashland welcomed its first bank in 1856 and immediately assumed a more important commercial standing when the bank established a branch in Shelbyville. The first railroad was completed in 1857, and the next year Ashland became an incorporated village.

During the War between the States, Ashland's iron production increased. However, it was not until after the conflict, when iron became a vital factor in reconstruction, that the community gained the dominant Kentucky position in the industry. With the basic requisites, coal, limestone, and iron ore, immediately at hand in the hills just south of the town—territory that now is included in the city—it was only a short time until many furnaces were erected, and Ashland and its environs vied with the iron-producing towns of Hanging Rock and Ironton on the Ohio side of the river. Notable among the new plants was the Star Iron Works, which was built along the river front in 1868. This plant, in 1870—the year in which Ashland became an incorporated city—was taken over by the Ashland Furnace Company, owned by the Ashland Coal & Iron Company Railroad. From March 1871 through June 1874 the furnace produced an average of more than 1,000 tons of pig iron per month, or a gross of 40,527 tons, a record that was not broken until 1916.

The Norton Iron & Nail Works, established in 1873, built a blast furnace, a rolling mill, and a nail mill; and in the same year "Big Etna," at that time the largest blast furnace in the West, added to Ashland's prestige as an iron center. Of all its iron family, Ashland's Bellefonte furnace probably had the most colorful history, although later ones outstripped it in production. In the days before the Ohio was alive with big steamboats, the Bellefonte's products were shipped down the river in barges. In the same manner, coal was brought down the Big Sandy to the furnace, and the fire clay and ore were taken from the hills at what was then Ashland's back door.

As iron and steel forged to the front in Ashland, the community began to mine the clays of Boyd County. Brick- and tile-making became an important industry, and when, within a few years, nearby oil and natural gas deposits were developed, Ashland embarked upon a well-rounded, modern industrial era. Although the source of iron ore supply soon shifted to the head of the Great Lakes, relegating Kentucky ores to the background, the vast supply of other crude essentials and the advantageous transportation facilities of the Ashland area enabled the town to improve its position as a steel center. With the opening of the Ashland Steel Company's Bessemer mill in 1891, the town definitely assumed its modern industrial role; the climax came with erection of a big plant of the American Rolling Mill Company in 1920. Ashland still looks to its own community for the major part of its basic industrial materials, and the hills of the immediate region are the great storehouses from which its rolling mills, coke ovens, fire-brickworks, and lumber mills draw their supplies.

The comparatively high plain on which the town sits saved it from a most disastrous experience during the Ohio River floods in 1937. Although the flood waters went to an unprecedented high mark, inundating the lower streets, and reaching Winchester Avenue in the modern business section, actual losses in Ashland were slight in comparison with those in river towns less fortunately situated. During the flood period, 2,200 residents were evacuated; and property loss, resulting largely from damage to industrial plants, wholesale and retail establishments, and to household furnishings, was estimated by local officials at less than $1,500,000. Ashland cared for 600 refugees from other flood areas until they could be rehabilitated. The city's recovery from the river's onslaught was so rapid that within six months few marks of the flood's ravages remained and Ashland resumed its role of a busy industrial spot where substantial homes, excellent educational institutions, and a culture befitting a sizeable community provide an even balance with steel, coke, brick, and lumber.

POINTS OF INTEREST

1. AMERICAN ROLLING MILL *("ARMCO") PLANT (open on special occasions or by appointment)*, Winchester Ave., West, was begun in 1920, when the city had a population of 14,000. Five years later, due chiefly to the growth of this plant and its associated activities, the population had doubled, and Armco was employing a force of 3,200. Its present monthly payroll approximates $400,000. Here are seen the processes by which the major raw materials entering into the steel industry—iron ore, coal, and limestone—become, by reduction and intricate chemical processes employing less well known but essential metals, the specialized steels used in modern manufacture. These raw materials enter at one end of the works, go through the conversion process en route, and emerge at the other end in the forms of steel adapted to the factory requirements of automobile and other manufacturers.

The floor space of the Armco plant, which extends to the west of the business section along the Ohio River, exceeds 1,600,000 square feet. Twenty-two miles of standard-gauge side track serve this shop area. Two steam and five oil-electric locomotives, more than 30 freight cars, 60 electric cranes and 15 tractors are employed in shifting materials in and about the plant.

2. NORTH AMERICAN REFRACTORIES PLANT *(open)*, 701 Winchester Ave., a branch of the nationwide concern with offices in Cleveland, Ohio, manufactures locomotive fire boxes, furnace linings, gas retorts, and similar articles capable of withstanding intense and long continued heat. Eastern Kentucky, especially the vicinity of Ashland, is rich in non-plastic clays that possess the unusual quality of resistance to temperatures up to 3,000 degrees F. The plant was built in 1886, and gives employment to an average of 200 men.

3. CENTRAL PARK, Central Ave. and 17th St., is a 52-acre native woodland area in the heart of the city. Within the park are six Indian mounds, conical in shape, where the red men buried their dead.

On the north side of the park entrance, head of 17th St., is the CITY LIBRARY *(open 9–9 weekdays)*. The building, completed in

1937, was erected with government funds. It is a one-story-and-basement, T-shaped structure of Georgian Colonial design, built of dressed local sandstone. The reading room is furnished simply and supplied with current magazines. The stack room provides adequate space for the development of a fiction, reference, and general purpose library. In the basement are conference rooms and an auditorium provided with a small stage and picture screen. The exterior is dominated by a Classic Revival portico of restrained proportions and a belfry tower surmounting the roof.

4. LAWRENCE LEATHER BELTING PLANT *(open)*, Central Ave. and 25th St., manufactures leather belting of all kinds. Hides are transformed by intricate processes into the continuous belting that drives a threshing machine or the fly-wheel of a great power plant, and the plant extends its search for materials into the hide markets of the world.

5. SCRAP IRON YARDS. Skirting the N. side of Winchester Ave., E. of the downtown business section, are great yards where old iron gathered from the farms, back yards, and refuse heaps of a wide region throughout Kentucky, Ohio, and West Virginia is concentrated preliminary to its movement to the steel mills. The "old iron" is stripped of everything undesirable, sheared into workable sizes, and then caught up by electro-magnets and loaded into cars for transfer to local or perhaps far-distant steel furnaces. At the furnace it becomes an important part of the white-hot mixture that is drawn off into huge mechanically controlled ladles from which is poured the ingot steel that, under the tremendous pressure of huge rollers, is flattened out into whatever rough form may be required by the manufacturer.

6. ASHLAND LIVESTOCK MARKET *(open Mon.)*, 36th St. and Winchester Ave., is the scene of an activity of considerable interest to visitors. The hilly region adjacent to Ashland is not generally adapted to field crop production, but the field and wood pastures of the area feed a very considerable quantity of livestock, principally cattle and hogs. These are concentrated for sale and shipment on Mondays at the livestock yards. Picturesque in garb and speech, drovers from the hills come in with their offerings, to barter and haggle. After the sale the stock goes by rail to the great midwest packing houses.

7. SEMET-SOLVAY COKE PLANT *(not open to the public)*, 40th St. and the river front, presents a spectacular sight by night when the flames from the ovens light up the whole countryside. Coke making is an adaptation, applied to coal, of the long known process of burning wood under conditions that allow insufficient oxygen, with the result that a high-efficiency fuel remains after the moisture and gases are driven off. In similar fashion certain grades of coal are "baked" in great ovens. After the volatile materials are driven off and captured (later to be employed in industry), the residue forms the ordinary coke of commerce. Coke has a thermal efficiency, ton for ton, approximately equal to the best anthracite, and is widely employed both in industry and in the heating of dwellings.

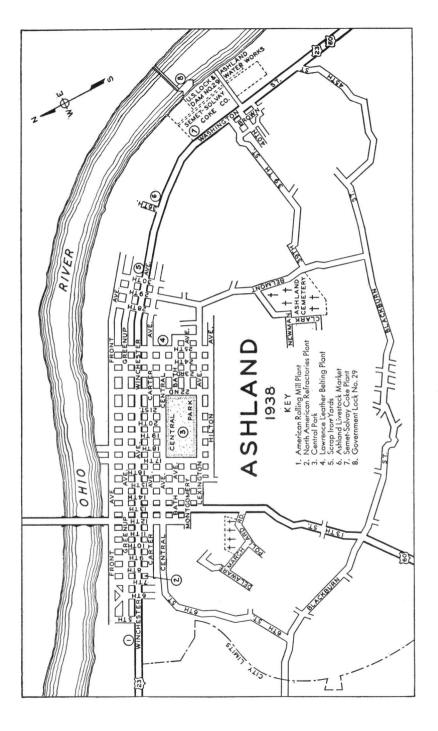

ASHLAND
1938

KEY

1. American Rolling Mill Plant
2. North American Refractories Plant
3. Central Park
4. Lawrence Leather Belting Plant
5. Scrap Iron Yards
6. Ashland Livestock Market
7. Semet-Solvay Coke Plant
8. Government Lock No. 29

8. GOVERNMENT LOCK NO. 29, Riverside, opposite Clyffeside (E. end), includes one of the dams that control the low-water stage in the Ohio River at a minimum navigation depth of nine feet, the draft necessary for barges. The location of these dams, designed to provide for navigation rather than power, is determined by the slope of the stream bed. They divide the river, from Pittsburgh to Cairo, Illinois, into "pools" that can retain sufficient water for navigation purposes at all times. The Ashland dam illustrates the entire river-control system, and the manner in which barges and their tows are passed through the locks. Government dredges remove the silt that accumulates, and the maintenance of a nine-foot minimum stage provides, for Ashland and for all cities along the Ohio, a low cost route for the movement of iron, coal, limestone, oil, timber, and other basic commodities, as well as for the finished manufactured products in transit to key distribution points.

COVINGTON

Railroad Station: Union Depot, Pike and Russell Sts., for Louisville & Nashville R.R., and Chesapeake & Ohio Ry.
Bus Station: 6th St. between Scott Blvd. and Madison Ave., for Greyhound, Fleenor, and Blue Ribbon Lines.
Airport: Lunken Field, *6.5 m.*, via Cincinnati on US 50 (River Road), for American Air Lines.
Taxis: 15¢ and upward according to distance and number of passengers.
Toll Bridges: Suspension, N. end of Court Ave., passenger autos 10¢ and 15¢, pedestrians free; Covington-Newport, E. end of 4th St., passenger autos 10¢ and 15¢, pedestrians 2¢.
Traffic Regulations: Right turn on red light only at intersection of Starrett St. and Madison Ave. Watch signs for parking limitations.

Accommodations: Nearest hotels in Cincinnati; private homes cater to tourists.

Information Service: Chamber of Commerce, SW. corner Pike St. and Madison Ave.; Kentucky Motor Club, 417 Scott St.

Radio Station: WCKY (1490 kc.).
Motion Picture Houses: Seven.
Swimming: Rosedale Park, entrance Carroll St., near 45th St.; Y.M.C.A., Pike St. and Madison Ave.
Golf: Devou Park, entrance on Western Ave. between 6th and 7th Sts., 9 holes, greens fee 50¢, 75¢ and $1; Twin Oaks Country Club, E. end of Baltimore St., 18 holes, greens fee 75¢ and $1.
Tennis: Dixie Court, Madison Ave. and 2d St., 20¢ per hour; Goebel Park, 5th and Philadelphia Sts., free; South Covington Court, W. end of 45th St., 50¢ per day.
Riding: Sunny Side Riding Club, Park Hills, 75¢ and $1 per hour; Pleasure Isle, $1 per hour.
Racing: Latonia Race Track, S. and Latonia Ave. car line; spring and fall meetings (pari-mutuel betting). See local papers for schedules.

Annual Events: Egg Fight, Easter Sunday, Devou Park.

COVINGTON (513 alt., 65,252 pop.), second largest city in Kentucky, lies on a flood plain of the Ohio River at the foot of suburban hills that reach back to a high plain of the Bluegrass. Highways from Louisville and the hills of central Kentucky sweep rather suddenly into position for a fine view of the city. To the east the Licking River separates old Covington residences from Newport; to the west the Ohio River bends away past scattered suburbs and the long Cincinnati waterfront; and to the north most of Covington's business houses, factories, churches, parks, and homes are clustered against a magnificent backdrop, where five bridges cross the Ohio to Cincinnati on the opposite side of the river.

In this setting Covington looks like a city on the Rhine. The impression is heightened by the spires of many churches—Covington has more than threescore—that taper up from among compact business and factory buildings and the plain brick structures put up by German immigrants of the mid-nineteenth century.

Though the Germans have stamped the pattern of the city indelibly, other influences have been almost equally strong. The early settlers came mainly from the South, and they brought slaves and plantation culture with them. They built the walled- and fenced-in homes lining the streets that criss-cross the angle formed by the intersection of the Licking with the Ohio. When the Negroes were freed, they went to live in what were then the outskirts of the city, farther up the Licking and beneath the bluffs toward which the industrial areas were expanding. The neglected homes of the Negroes in Covington are small, but the Negro's contribution to the city, especially in the way of education, is large. Through the good work of their public and parochial schools, Covington's Negroes have reduced the more than 90 percent illiteracy of the 1860's to almost zero. In 1930 only 501 Covington residents (and many of these white) were illiterate.

Covington does not have skyscrapers, huge photoplay palaces, gigantic department stores, or bulky hotels, because it has geared its economic and social life to that of Cincinnati, only a bridge toll away. Each weekday morning Covington empties motorcars and little green trolleys full of people into Cincinnati; each weekday afternoon Cincinnati sends the steady, noisy stream of traffic back to Covington. In the evening Covingtonians generally relax in their homes or recross the river for entertainment, while their city plays host to many Cincinnatians who find Kentucky less restricting than Ohio.

On St. Valentine's Day in 1780, George Muse, a soldier of Virginia in the French and Indian War, swapped for a keg of whisky his scrip for 200 acres of land allotted him for military service. The new owner of the land traded it for a quarter of buffalo that Gen. James Taylor offered him. Taylor dickered it off to Col. Stephen Trigg, who got rid of it to John Todd, Jr., who unloaded it onto James Welch. Welch kept the land long enough to get it surveyed, and in 1801 sold it to Thomas Kennedy for $750. Kennedy erected a huge stone house overlooking the Licking near what is now the approach to the Suspension Bridge, and lived there as a tavern-keeper and ferry-man until 1814. Then he sold 150 acres of his property to John S. Gano, Richard M. Gano, and Thomas Carneal. In the following year, the three men chartered a town and named it for Gen. Leonard Covington of Maryland, a hero of the War of 1812 who died of wounds received during the Battle of Chrystler's Field.

Covington's growth was negligible during the years of national depression following 1819, but in 1830, with a population of only 715, the town had a log church, several inns, and a schoolhouse which was also a meeting place for a light infantry troop, the town trustees, and the Social Polemic Society. A few streets were paved; those running east and west were numbered, those north and south were named for notables. The town also had a fire brigade, a steam ferry, and the store of Benjamin J. Leathers, who issued so much scrip in hard times that "paid in Leathers" became Covington argot.

Beginning with the 1830's, as settlers headed West over Kentucky land routes and the Ohio River, Covington became a trade center for livestock, grain, and other products of the countryside. An influx of people from over the Appalachians (principally Pennsylvania, Maryland, and Virginia) was succeeded by the large German immigration of 1840–1860.

By 1847 there were two leading educational institutions in Covington—the Western Baptist Theological College and Dr. Orr's Female Seminary. The seminary stressed good manners and deportment. One teacher, a Miss Robb, dismissed her class one by one, and exacted from each girl a Victorian curtsy—the spreading of the skirt and making a low bow, not one of the "silly bobs" as of later days.

In the 1850's the Kentucky Central Railroad was begun from Covington to Lexington, a high school opened, the seat of a Roman Catholic bishopric established, a local Turnverein organized, and gas first used for lighting. In 1860 the first hospital, St. Elizabeth's, was established. Covington people made furniture, farm tools, rope, and cloth, and brewed beer, packed meat, and participated in the growing river commerce.

Covington commuted to Cincinnati by ferry. But service was interrupted during flood times, and it sometimes took a whole day to make a business trip to Cincinnati and back. The State of Kentucky had already bought the macadamized highway coming up from Lexington over an old Indian trail. Elimination of road tolls drew Covington and interior Kentucky together, but the city was more closely associated with its big neighbor to the north, and it needed better means of getting across the Ohio. In 1846 the State legislature authorized the building of a bridge over to Cincinnati, but work on the structure was postponed periodically. When actual construction finally began, along came the panic of 1857, followed by the War between the States four years later, and work was stopped.

Although Kentucky wanted to be neutral in the war, neutrality was impossible. The State became a battleground, and Covington an armed camp, half its citizens Northern, half Southern, in sympathy and enlistment. Actual warfare, however, came only as close to Covington as Morgan's and Kirby Smith's raids in north-central Kentucky.

One threatened raid, however, had beneficial after-effects. When a detachment of Kirby Smith's men was detailed to terrorize the Cincinnati region, Gen. Lew Wallace declared martial law in Cincinnati, Newport, and Covington, and laid a pontoon of coal barges across the Ohio so Cincinnati troops could hurry over to Covington and help build earthworks on the southern border of the town. The Confederates skirmished with a few pickets, and then withdrew.

The pontoon bridge, however, had proved its value. After the War, work on the Suspension Bridge was resumed, and this solid symbol of commercial and political union between North and South was completed in 1866. During the years that followed, new industries, such as brewing, yeast making, and distilling were established and old ones, such as the manufacture of tobacco products, were enlarged. Real estate boomed phenomenally. In 1870, although the taxable value of the city's property was 700 percent greater than it had been 30 years before, suburbs were laid out rapidly and many newcomers settled in new homes. All this growth was stunted, however, by the panic of 1873.

Covington aroused itself quickly following the panic years. By the end of the decade the present Federal Building was completed. During the next few years the Maysville and Big Sandy Railroad came through from Ashland, and in 1888 a bridge was built across the Ohio River. In 1899 the city waterworks (in Fort Thomas) was completed. In the 1890's the chamber of commerce was organized; an electric power and light plant built; and the streetcar system, acquired by Cleveland capitalists, fitted with single-trolley electric cars.

During this long middle period, characterized industrially by the establishment of "one man" shops, the genius of Covington flowered. John G. Carlisle and William Goebel grew to national stature politically; Archbishop Maes inaugurated the construction of huge St. Mary's Cathedral; and Frank Duveneck painted murals in Covington homes. When the twentieth century arrived, Dan Beard, raised in Covington on the banks of the Licking, began his program of young character building by helping to found the Boy Scouts of America.

As the Nation emerged from the depression-ridden 1890's, Covington industry expanded. The "one man" businesses grew into small but substantial industrial concerns. The outstanding Covington example of this change is the firm that supplies X-ray equipment to hospitals and to private manufacturing industries. Another company that grew up within the last 40 years, makes the machinery that wraps razor blades and other goods into small packages. Still another builds cell blocks for prisons. Many more produce specialties such as signs, ornamental fences, locks and safes, and a host of other things not subject to mass production. In addition, several packing houses, milling establishments, distilleries and breweries, brick and tile works, tobacco warehouses, and rope-making plants are in the city.

From time to time the Ohio and the Licking Rivers have overrun their banks and pillaged Covington. The flood of 1832 taught a lesson that was not well learned, for the floods of 1883 and 1884 brought great ruin—and that of January 1937 was even worse. Two-thirds of the business section was submerged. Lights and power were shut off, transportation was at a standstill, and schools were closed. Hospitals were badly damaged, but their staffs worked on heroically. Property loss ran into the millions. By summer of 1937, however, debris had been cleared away and buildings repaired, and the city was back to normal. Immediate help was given by the American Red Cross, and Covington citizens quickly rehabilitated their homes and business places.

POINTS OF INTEREST

1. SUSPENSION BRIDGE (tolls 10¢ and 15¢; pedestrians 2¢) across the Ohio River, N. end of Court Ave., connects Covington with Cincinnati. Designed and built by John A. Roebling of New York, and completed at a cost of $1,871,000 in 1866, this is the first of America's great suspension bridges. It is 36 feet wide and 2,252 feet long, and its towers are 100 feet high.

2. GEORGE ROGERS CLARK MEMORIAL PARK, Garrard St. and Riverside Drive, is a small square of landscaped ground on the Ohio River bank, from which the Cincinnati waterfront seems but a stone's throw away. Near the alleyway that runs behind the park is the SITE OF THE THOMAS KENNEDY HOUSE, marked by a boulder and inscribed plaque. Kennedy operated a ferry across the river and was a congenial host in the stone tavern, called Kennedy's Ferry, which he erected here in 1801.

3. The CARNEAL HOUSE, now the ROTHIER HOME (private), 405 E. 2nd St., was built in 1815 by Thomas D. Carneal, of Covington and Ludlow. The two-story mansion, set above the street level, is designed in the late Georgian Colonial manner, with such Italian Renaissance detail as the loggias that break the wide front of the structure on the first and second stories. The main doorway is a fine example of the Georgian Colonial style, but the door itself is of a later date. Tradition says that Carneal aided Negroes to escape by giving them asylum in his home and helping them to cross the Ohio into free territory. Eliza, heroine of *Uncle Tom's Cabin*, is said to have been aided in this way.

4. DAN CARTER BEARD BOYHOOD HOME (private), 322 E. 3rd St., a comfortable two-story brick residence dating from the mid-nineteenth century, bears a plaque on the side facing Licking River stating that here lived, in his boyhood, the founder of the Boy Scouts of America. As a boy Beard (b. 1850) consorted with the soldiers at Newport Barracks. Later he became well acquainted with stories and legends of Kentucky pioneer life, and formed a band called the Sons of Daniel Boone. The youngsters took oath and named themselves for Boone, Kenton, and other noted pioneers. They became adept at making dugout canoes, brush shelters, and other woodcraft necessities. When Sir Robert Baden-Powell formed the Boy Scouts of England in 1908, he made use of Beard's plan of organization. In 1910, when the Boy Scouts of America was incorporated, Beard merged the Sons of Daniel Boone with the Boy Scouts. Today (1939) the American branch of the world-wide organization, of which Beard is still an active member, has an enrollment of about a million and a half.

5. The JOHN W. STEVENSON HOME (private), 318–320 Garrard St., built about 1820, is a two-story brick structure fronted by a portico of white fluted columns. The large windows have the original

mullioned panes. The house is connected by a large brick tunnel with a private home at Seventh and Garrard Streets. According to local tradition, a second tunnel once ran from a mansion on Second Street up along the river bank into the backyard of the Stevenson home. Beneath the house and in the yard are huge subterranean cellars, with thick brick walls, said to have been used for concealing slaves during the War between the States. Stevenson was Governor of Kentucky from 1867 to 1871.

6. The CLAYTON HOUSE *(private)*, 528 Greenup St., a story-and-a-half white frame structure built of ship's timbers, was put up in 1839 by John W. Clayton, and is now the residence of his grand-daughter. During the War between the States it housed a private school, kept by Clayton's daughter, among whose pupils was Frederick D. Grant, son of Gen. U. S. Grant.

7. The BAKER HUNT FOUNDATION and the WILLIAMS' NATURAL HISTORY MUSEUM *(open 1–3 weekdays, 1–6 Sun.)*, 620 Greenup St., are housed in simple brick buildings adapted to educational work. The dual organization is the result of two gifts to the city of Covington. Margaretta W. Hunt provided in her will for the establishment of the foundation (1931), and Archie J. Williams gave the rare insects he collected in the course of wide travels and research. The foundation offers after-school classes in the arts and crafts for adults and children.

The Natural History Museum, which includes the Williams' collection and later accessions, has about 200,000 insect specimens and more than 5,000 natural history volumes, including what is said to be the largest collection of books on insects. Kentucky plant and animal life is particularly well represented.

8. COVINGTON PUBLIC LIBRARY *(open 9–9 weekdays)*, SE. corner Robbins St. and Scott Blvd., established through an act of the Kentucky legislature in 1898, was inadequately housed in a room on Seventh Street until a gift by Andrew Carnegie made possible the present two-story concrete building (1901). The library has about 50,000 volumes for adults and 15,000 for children, and a great deal of miscellaneous Kentuckiana. In the building is an auditorium seating 750 persons.

9. ST. MARY'S ROMAN CATHOLIC CATHEDRAL, Madison Ave. between 11th and 12th Sts., is the seat of the Diocese of Covington. The plan of the nave, transept, and apse, designed by Leon Coquard, begun in 1895 and finished in 1900, follows that of the Abbey of St. Denis, France; while the façade, designed by David Davis in 1908 and completed two years later, is patterned after that of the Cathedral of Notre Dame in Paris. The bas-relief above the main portal is Clement J. Barnhorn's portrayal of the *Ascension of the Blessed Virgin*. The two front towers (now 128 feet high, eventually to be 180) are surmounted by gargoyles.

Within the massive hand-tooled doors tall graceful columns line the

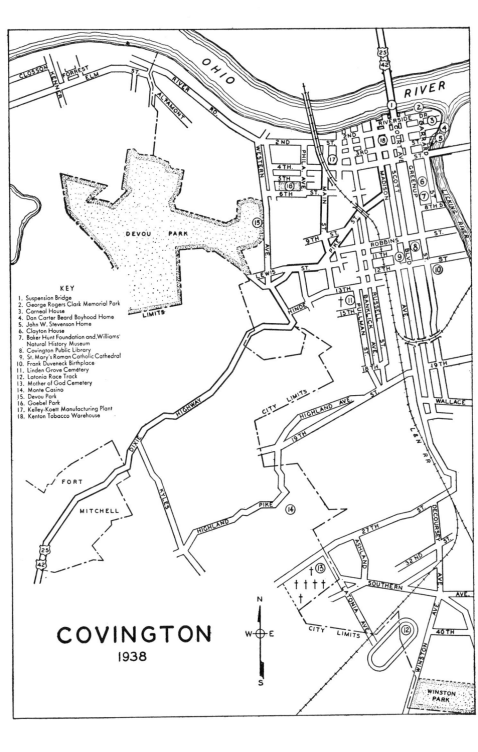

KEY

1. Suspension Bridge
2. George Rogers Clark Memorial Park
3. Carneal House
4. Dan Carter Beard Boyhood Home
5. John W. Stevenson Home
6. Clayton House
7. Baker Hunt Foundation and Williams Natural History Museum
8. Covington Public Library
9. St. Mary's Roman Catholic Cathedral
10. Frank Duveneck Birthplace
11. Linden Grove Cemetery
12. Latonia Race Track
13. Mother of God Cemetery
14. Monte Casino
15. Devou Park
16. Goebel Park
17. Kelley-Koett Manufacturing Plant
18. Kenton Tobacco Warehouse

COVINGTON
1938

aisles. Among the high windows of the nave and apse, that in the north wall, 24 by 67 feet, depicts the *Coronation of the Virgin*, the *Council of Ephesus*, and the *Fathers of the Church*, in stained and leaded glass.

The mosaics on the Stations of the Cross are the work of Italian artisans. The pulpit, altar, and other wooden fixtures were hand-tooled by Swiss craftsmen. In the right end of the transept is the Chapel of the Blessed Sacrament, on the walls of which are three frescoes by Frank Duveneck, Covington-born artist. Divided into three parts like the medieval triptych, these frescoes have as their central theme Christ's sacrifice on Calvary, and on either side are shown priests of the Old and the New Law.

10. The FRANK DUVENECK BIRTHPLACE *(private)*, 1226 Greenup St., is a simple frame house marked by a plaque. Duveneck (1848–1919) worked for several local church decorators and later studied art in Munich. In 1875 he exhibited a group of sensational paintings in Boston, and became famous in this country overnight. After his wife died at Florence, Italy, in 1888, Duveneck came to Cincinnati to teach at the Art Academy, and became the dean of Ohio Valley artists. As teacher and exemplar, Duveneck was one of the pioneers of modern American art. He executed the murals in St. Mary's Cathedral as a gift in memory of his mother. Some of his paintings are on the walls of the State Historical Museum (Old Capitol) in Frankfort. The best collection is in the Cincinnati Art Museum, to which Duveneck donated a large group of his works in 1915.

11. LINDEN GROVE CEMETERY, Holman St. between 13th and 15th Sts., one of Covington's oldest burial grounds, contains graves of men who fought in the Revolution and in all wars of the United States. Toward the rear of the main driveway (R), a simple stone marks the GRAVE OF JOHN GRIFFIN CARLISLE, Secretary of the Treasury under Cleveland. Carlisle, who was born in Kenton County in 1835, distinguished himself as a lawyer, State legislator, Lieutenant Governor, Congressman, and Speaker of the House of Representatives. In 1893 Cleveland selected him as a member of his cabinet, and his efforts to avert the panic of that year won him wide acclaim.

12. LATONIA RACE TRACK *(gate open the year around)*, S. end Latonia Ave., opened in 1883 by the Latonia Agricultural Association, is one of the great running tracks of America, second in Kentucky only to Churchill Downs, home of the Kentucky Derby. The spring-summer racing season follows the May meet at Churchill Downs with a 31-day schedule. A similar late fall schedule succeeds the autumn season at Churchill Downs. The Latonia Oaks, Latonia Cup, and Latonia Championship stakes are among the regular events, but the greatest attraction is the Latonia Derby, a mile-and-a-quarter event carrying an added purse of $15,000. Latonia has been dubbed "Death Valley" by some Kentucky "hard boots" (chronic backers of Kentucky horses) because they believe the best of horses are beaten here.

13. MOTHER OF GOD CEMETERY, 27th St. and Latonia Ave., is the resting place of many who have brought fame to Covington. The GRAVE OF FRANK DUVENECK, marked by a rose-colored granite tomb, is to the right of the driveway, near the center of the grounds.

14. MONTE CASINO *(open all hours),* off Highland Pike (entered over a twisting road), is a two-story gray brick building, constructed about 1850, on a farm owned and rented out by the Benedictine Fathers of St. Vincent Archabbey, Latrobe, Pa. The building was a family residence before the War between the States. The estate once contained a vineyard yielding grapes for the sacramental Benedictine and Red Rose wines produced by Brothers of the Order of St. Benedict. Wine making by the brothers and their hired help was begun soon after this property was bought, and continued until Prohibition in 1919. The brothers then returned to Latrobe.

About 1878 Brother Albert Soltis, for his private devotions, erected what is widely referred to as the TINIEST CHAPEL IN THE WORLD (accommodating only three persons), in front of the home atop the cliff. Except for the wood in the door, window casing, and sash, and the glass in the one small leaded window, it is entirely of native limestone. The interior is decorated with religious emblems.

15. DEVOU PARK, entrance Western Ave. between 6th and 7th Sts., donated to the city in 1910, is a 550-acre rolling wooded park that looks down from the Knobs directly upon Covington, Ludlow, and the Ohio River. Thirty miles of bridle path, athletic and picnic grounds, and a lake, public golf course, target range, and natural amphitheater are distributed among the hills and valleys. From LOOKOUT POINT Cincinnati's western and northern hills and its downtown office buildings appear above the smoke and fog that often hang over this populous section of the Ohio Valley.

16. GOEBEL PARK, SW. corner 5th and Philadelphia Sts., is a 14-acre civic recreation center purchased about 1906 from the late Gov. William Goebel. It has swimming pools, baseball and football grounds, and a shelter house. Band concerts, furnished by the city throughout the summer, are attended weekly by thousands.

17. KELLEY-KOETT MANUFACTURING PLANT *(open by permission),* 212 W. 4th St., is one of the world's largest producers of X-ray equipment. During the years when Roentgen was developing the X-ray, a Virginia boy, John Robert Kelley, was experimenting with methods for its use. He came to Covington and became acquainted with Albert B. Koett, who backed him financially. This partnership was the basis for a concern (1903) that supplies X-ray apparatus to industrial and clinical laboratories throughout the world.

18. KENTON TOBACCO WAREHOUSE *(open during winter sales season, Dec.-Feb.),* SW. corner 2nd St. and Scott Blvd., one of the largest loose-leaf tobacco warehouses in northern Kentucky, covers more than a city block. It is a typical one-story brick structure

equipped to handle the tobacco that the growers haul here to be sold. Sales begin on or about the first of December and continue through February.

POINTS OF INTEREST IN ENVIRONS

Fort Thomas Military Reservation, *5 m. (see Tour 3).*

FRANKFORT

Railroad Station: Union Station, Ann St. and Broadway, for Louisville & Nashville R.R., Chesapeake & Ohio Ry., Frankfort & Cincinnati Ry.
Bus Station: Ann and Main Sts. for Greyhound and Nunelly Lines.
Local Buses: Fare 10¢. Service from downtown to all residential districts, inclusive of New Capitol.
Taxis: 25¢ to any point in city; $1 an hour with a 10-mile maximum distance.
Traffic Regulations: No right turn on red lights. Restricted parking areas so marked. Two hours parking on unmarked streets.

Accommodations: Three hotels. Convenient, reasonably priced rooming houses open to tourists.

Information Service: Chamber of Commerce, Capital Hotel.
Motion Picture Houses: Four.
Fishing: Forks of Elkhorn *(see Tour 9),* 4 *m.,* for bass.
Baseball: Hoge-Montgomery Park, State 37, *1 m.* N.

FRANKFORT (504 alt., 11,626 pop.), capital of Kentucky, lies within the S-loops of the Kentucky River as it thrusts first against the eastern and then against the western bluffs that border its deep and narrow valley. Upon the alluvial plain, through which meanders the navigable stream, stands the city, separated by the river into north and south sides which are connected by three bridges.

The north side embraces the older residential section of the city, the Old Capitol, and the downtown business section. The south side, chiefly residential, is expanding southward to and beyond the New Capitol, that lifts its dome high above the roofs and spires of the town. To the eastward, beyond the city limits, where US 60 traverses the rolling Bluegrass highland, an addition is steadily extending the urban area, which, inclusive of the overflow of population beyond the borders of the city proper, covers approximately four square miles.

Along Main Street and the intersecting business streets, old buildings of brick and stone, having the impression of earlier generations, are interspersed with substantial and imposing modern structures. Loungers and passers-by represent a cross-section of every phase of Kentucky life.

For a portion of each year politics dominates the scene, and Frankfort is then the gathering place of legislators and of others materially interested in legislation. Year in and year out the city is the home of a fluctuating group of officeholders and State employees.

Workers, white and Negro, from the factories within the city and from the distilleries in its environs, throng the streets on holidays or when the work of the day is over, and farmers from the rich agricultural lands in the vicinity come in, especially on Saturdays, to do their trading. At such times the city assumes the air of an old-fashioned country town, its streets filled with a leisurely moving crowd, colorful, chattering, parcel-laden. Daily, among all these, move men and women whose traditions root deeply in the past, who live on quiet streets, in old houses rich in history.

It is probable that Christopher Gist was the first white man to view the lovely valley in which Frankfort lies; his journal tells of being in this region in 1751. More than twenty years later, in 1773, Governor Dunmore of Virginia sent a survey party into the West to look into the land; Robert McAfee and his group surveyed and claimed some 600 acres, including the site of the present Capitol. In the following year land-hungry adventurers accepted the opportunity, and "squatted" in miserable shelters on the land, seeking thus to get by the law which required "settlement and improvement." The Indians were not slow to sense the menace. Shawnee, Miami, Delaware and Wyandotte went on the warpath, murdering and burning at large. So grave was the situation that Virginia was compelled to send militia and "Regulars" to restore peace and protect the settlers, Lord Dunmore himself heading one regiment.

In 1773 Hancock Taylor had surveyed, in behalf of Robert McAfee, lands that are now within the downtown section of the north side. The following year it was discovered that the McAfee claim, always shadowy, had lapsed, and Humphrey Marshall, while working as attorney for the estate of Francis McConnell, secured a grant from the Province of Virginia. The McConnell heirs considered this a breach of trust and a lawsuit resulted, which the court settled by giving the heirs half the profits Marshall had realized from his title to the land. Prior to the settlement of this suit, known as Patrick *vs.* Marshall, Gen. James Wilkinson, friend of Washington and one time commander of American armies in the West, later involved in the Burr conspiracy, purchased the lands from Marshall for the present-day equivalent of $433. This purchase, made in 1786, gave Wilkinson a not-too-clear title to the major portion of that part of Frankfort lying north of the river—the downtown district.

Wilkinson immediately set about organizing the new town. He secured passage of an act of the Virginia Legislature (1786) which set aside 100 acres as a town site, provided a ferry and fixed its rates. When he found the Kentucky River flooding parts of the city as planned, he put in a drainage system. The town as platted extended from the present site of the New Capital Hotel westward to the river, and from Fort Hill, the height that overlooks the north end of the city, to the old bridge connecting the downtown district with the south side. The name Frankfort was chosen by Wilkinson in memory of a pioneer who, some years earlier, had been shot by Indians, and whose surname, Frank, had already been given to a ford within the area chosen as the town site. By a slight change the name "Frank's Ford" became "Frankfort." Within this tract streets were laid out and named in honor of the general and his friends. Ann Street, running north and south on the west side of the New Capital Hotel was named for his wife, and Mero Street for the Spanish Governor General of the Province of Louisiana who was involved with Wilkinson and others in the historic Burr conspiracy. The name of Wapping Street, on which the post office is now, was suggested by a visiting Englishman, for a street in London famous in that day but now only a memory recorded in song. Other streets bear names familiar in early American history.

Wilkinson visioned Frankfort as a port of the Bluegrass country, connected directly with the rising towns on the Ohio—also with New Orleans, with the West Indies and with the Atlantic Coast. The advent of steamboating encouraged these early ambitions, but the Lexington and Ohio railroad entered Frankfort in 1835, concentrating transfer and wholesale business at Ohio River points. Nevertheless the town prospered; tobacco, salt pork, skins, and hemp gave place in business importance to livestock and lumbering. About the middle of the nineteenth century Frankfort again became an important primary tobacco market but today the last tobacco-floor has disappeared. The vast timberlands of the upper Kentucky River and its tributaries made Frankfort a leading sawmill town during the period 1865–1900. The industry also has vanished, but furniture and shoe manufacturing, once incidental to lumbering and local Bluegrass livestock slaughtering, still survive. The accessibility and quality of the crystalline limestone of the adjacent bluffs, known as "Kentucky marble," not only provided the material out of which the statehouse was built in 1827–1830 *(see Point of Interest No. 2)*, but for many of the earliest business buildings and homes. The bluffs still furnish building stone for the more enduring structures, and materials for extensive road-building about Frankfort.

June 1, 1792, Kentucky became the fifteenth State of the Union, and the first west of the Alleghenies. The first session of the legislature convened in Lexington on November 5, "to fix on a place for the permanent seat of government." Five commissioners were appointed to consider applications from various points that included Ledgerwood's Bend, Delaney's Ferry, Petersburg, Louisville, Lexington, Danville and Leestown. The commissioners demanded a free site and the expense of erecting necessary buildings. December 5, Frankfort was adjudged to be "the most proper place" and on December 22 the legislature adjourned "to hold its next session in the house of Andrew Holmes, at Frankfort, on the Kentucky River." Holmes, in behalf of Frankfort, agreed to convey to the government:

(a) For seven years, the house and tenement lately occupied by Gen. James Wilkinson; (b) Absolutely, the lots marked Public Ground, Nos. 58, 59, 68, 74, 75, 79, 83, and 84; (c) Choice of 30 lots yet unsold, *or* alternate-choice of half of all the unsold lots, and if more space is requisite will lay off into half-acre lots 50 acres more and convey one-half of them; (d) The rents of the warehouse for 7 years; (e) 10 boxes 10 x 12 window glass, 1,500 lbs. nails, £50 worth of locks and hinges, stone and scantling for building to an equivalent value, all delivered upon the Public Ground—Or, in place of the latter, stone that will build 1,590 perches of wall in any part of Frankfort, and the use of Holmes's sawmill, carriage, wagon, and two good horses until a sufficiency of scantling for a statehouse is procured, and the privilege of timber from any part of his tract; 2d, The bond, dated Aug. 9, 1792, of 8 citizens of Frankfort—Harry Innes, Nat Sanders, Bennett Pemberton, Benj. Craig, Jere Craig, Wm. Haydon, Daniel James, and Giles Samuel— to pay to the commissioners $3,000 in specie (gold or silver).

The choice of the little village on the Kentucky River midway between the two, settled amicably, if not to their individual satisfaction, the claims of Lexington and Louisville, chief contenders for the Capitol site. The fact of its central location satisfied the remainder of the State—for the time only, however. Twice the Capitol burned, 1815 and 1824, and each time Frankfort's availability was challenged before the structure was rebuilt.

Perhaps, when "Jim" Mulligan told in his ballad how politics were "the damnedest in Kentucky" he was thinking of Frankfort and the General Assembly. There, just the same, leaders have been developed and history made. As far back as 1811, a European traveler passing through Frankfort heard that the legislature was in session and thought he would drop in and look it over. "Backswoodsmen," he supposed, were less competent at such a game than their Eastern rivals. Thus he reports: "There was a silver-tongued orator speaking. . . . 'Gentlemen, we must have war with Great Britain— War will ruin her commerce— Commerce is the apple of Britain's eye— There we must gouge her!' " He was convinced of his error.

Since 1825, when Lafayette was entertained here, the presence of the State Capitol has flavored the social life of Frankfort throughout the years. From all parts of Kentucky have come men and women to live beside its quiet streets and bring distinction to the city by their part in the shaping of State policies and development. The effect has been to develop a distinguished political and social atmosphere. Henry Clay, John J. Crittenden, Ninian Edwards, John G. Carlisle, John M. Harlan and many others have trained in Frankfort for the national scene. The social tone is quiet and somewhat reserved; a typically southern city where what one *is* takes precedence over what one *has*.

The early settlers of Kentucky, notably those who left western Pennsylvania about the time of the "Whisky Rebellion" (1791–1794), were acquainted with the methods employed in the British Isles in the distilling of whisky. The low price of corn and wheat on western markets favored their conversion into whisky, a product that improved with age, and that was readily transportable. Out of this economic situation developed "corn liquor" for which Kentucky is famous. From the Civil War era, Frankfort began the commercial development of its distilleries at points near the city where flowing springs furnish limestone water, a prerequisite to a first-class product. During the prohibition era the distilleries about Frankfort, with one exception, were closed; they resumed operation on repeal (1933) of the Prohibition Amendment.

Only once, in 1862, has war invaded the peace of Frankfort. Bragg's Confederate forces swept northward out of Tennessee, seized the city, and set up a Confederate State Government. Before the ceremonies of installation had ended, the guns of the North were hammering from the crest of the bluffs west of town. The Confederates withdrew, and the new Governor, Richard J. Hawes, hastily retired to Lexington.

The years of reconstruction and those that have followed have witnessed the modernization of the city, the development of its schools, the upbuilding of the newer section of the city adjacent to the New Capitol; but the city as a whole retains the quiet charm of its earlier years. The Capital Bridge is the most recent of many civic improvements that include a modern system of public schools, an excellent hospital, playgrounds, and churches.

The Ohio Valley Flood of 1937 brought great property loss to Frankfort. The swollen Ohio formed a dam at the mouth of the Kentucky, causing that river to rise out of its banks; then torrential rains within the valley inundated the city, cut it in two parts, flooded cellars, interrupted light, gas, and water service, and swirled through the lower streets, carrying smaller homes and business houses off their foundations. The damage to properties, personal and civic, was estimated at $5,000,000. Within the State Reformatory, one of the oldest penal institutions in the Nation, the water rose to a depth of six feet, and the inmates were evacuated to the heights on the east side of town. Later, steps were taken for the abandonment of the old stone-walled enclosure for a less restricted and more healthful site near LaGrange.

POINTS OF INTEREST

1. The NEW CAPITOL (open 9-5 weekdays), S. end of Capitol Ave., encircled by a broad drive, stands within an extensive grassy plot on a gentle slope overlooking the Kentucky River. The main, or north, entrance is approached from Capitol Avenue by a walk and flights of steps that accentuate the elevation of the building above the surrounding area. The superstructure, gleaming white in the sun, is of Bedford stone on a high granite base. Surrounding the lower story is a broad paved terrace with balustrade. Designed with majestic symmetry, the exterior is adorned with Ionic colonnades, entablature and crowning balustrade; its simple rectangular lines are broken only by the massive pedimented central section and smaller end pavilions. The dominant feature of the exterior is the high central dome, raised on a graceful Ionic peristyle, or drum, and crowned with a slender lantern cupola.

The designer of the richly sculptured pediment, above the north entrance, was Charles Henry Niehaus, of New York. It was executed by Peter Rossack, of Austria. Frank M. Andrews was the architect of the building completed in 1909 at a cost of $1,820,000.

Beyond the vestibule, where visitors register and guides are provided, is the central corridor. The floors are of Tennessee marble, the wainscoting and pilasters of Georgia marble; monolithic Vermont granite columns, 36 in number, ornament the interior. Among the paintings that adorn the interior are the LUNETTES in the east and west ends of the corridor. These murals, executed by T. Gilbert White, of Michigan, portray events in the early history of Kentucky.

On the first floor, directly beyond the vestibule and beneath the massive dome, is the HALL OF FAME, where stand four memorials to noted Kentuckians. In the center is a bronze figure of Abraham Lincoln by A. A. Weinmann. Nearby is the statue of Jefferson Davis, President of the Confederacy, the work of Frank Hibbard, and a plaster facsimile of C. H. Niehaus' marble statue of Henry Clay, the conciliator. A marble statue of Dr. Ephraim McDowell, by Niehaus, honors the great pioneer in the field of abdominal surgery.

The chambers of the senate and the house of representatives are on the third floor. Visitors are admitted to the galleries when the legislature is in session.

On the grounds of the Capitol, and overlooking the Kentucky River, is the EXECUTIVE MANSION, residence of Kentucky's Governors. It harmonizes in architectural detail with the Capitol.

2. OLD CAPITOL *(open 9–12, 1–4:30 weekdays)*, St. Clair St. and Broadway. Twice, in the early days of statehood, the Capitol burned. The edifice, now known as the "Old Capitol," is an excellent example of the Greek Revival style of architecture, and first of the many notable buildings designed by Kentucky's early-day architect, Gideon Shryock. It was built (1827–1830) out of the native rock of the bluffs of the Kentucky River. This rock, a durable white limestone, was sawn at nearby quarries, and the timbers were hewn out of the native forest. The entire cost of this statehouse that served the State for eight decades was $95,000.

Set into the concrete walk to the portico is a bronze tablet that marks the spot where, in 1900, William Goebel, contender for the governorship, fell, shot by an assassin whose identity never has been divulged. Three days later Goebel died, after having been proclaimed Governor by the legislature then in session. He was succeeded in office by Lieutenant-Governor J. C. W. Beckham. At once a number of suspects were apprehended and put on trial. One turned State's evidence whereat three were convicted; Secretary of State Caleb Powers was given the death penalty. In course of time all were pardoned and Powers was later sent to Congress.

The front façade of the building is dominated by a hexastyle portico of the Ionic order. The columns, each four feet in diameter and 33 feet high, carry the weight of the massive, severely plain pediment. The walls and stone window casings are also unadorned. Above the copper roof rises the cupola, a pedestal 25 feet square, on which stands a circular lantern 22 feet in diameter, surmounted by a dome. Inside the great double doors are floors of "Kentucky marble," polished and mellowed in color by more than a century of use. A broad corridor extends back to the rotunda beneath the dome, where a transverse cor-

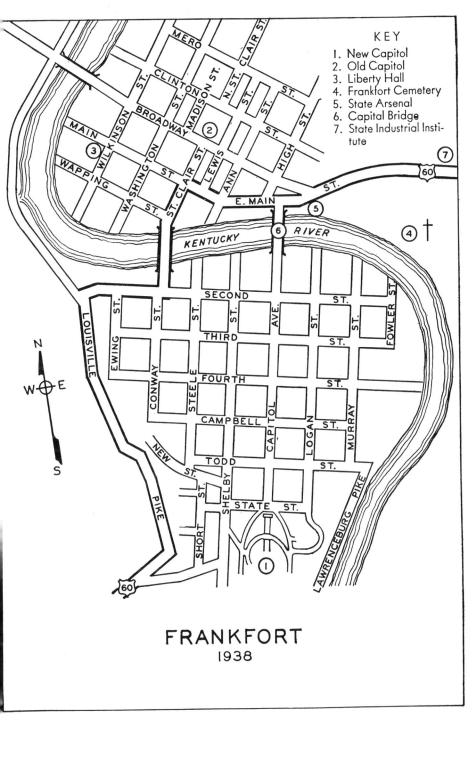

KEY
1. New Capitol
2. Old Capitol
3. Liberty Hall
4. Frankfort Cemetery
5. State Arsenal
6. Capital Bridge
7. State Industrial Institute

FRANKFORT
1938

ridor leads to exits on either side of the building. On the right of the entrance are the offices of the STATE HISTORICAL SOCIETY *(open 9–12, 1–4:30 weekdays)*, custodian of a rich collection of Kentuckiana. Left is the LIBRARY *(open 9–12, 1–4:30 weekdays)*, a treasure-house of Kentucky history.

From the main floor to the balcony rises the beautifully executed double stairway of self-supporting stones designed by Shryock. In its construction the architect made free use of the principles that govern the construction and support of the Roman arch.

On the second floor are the large, simply-designed rooms where the houses of the legislature met. These two rooms have collections of historic value. On the walls of the building hang paintings that recall the history of the State from earliest days. Among these is Oliver Frazer's copy of Stuart's *Washington*, the Historical Society's most valued possession.

3. LIBERTY HALL *(open 9–5 weekdays, adm. 25¢)*, 218 Wilkinson St., was originally the home of John Brown, first United States Senator from Kentucky, who, with his family, occupied it in 1796. Since that time until 1937, when it was taken over by the State, it remained in possession of his heirs. It stands in the corner of a large lawn and garden that extends back to the river. Late Georgian Colonial in architecture, it is simple and dignified in its lines. A short walk leads from the street to an entrance above which rises a fine Palladian window. Within the entrance a broad hall opens on either side into spacious, high-ceilinged rooms, heated by huge fireplaces. Mantels and other interior woodwork are hand-carved.

At the rear of the main hall a stairway rises to the second floor where in early days a large ballroom was the scene of many entertainments. The remainder of this story was originally divided into guest rooms and sleeping rooms for the family; it is now somewhat altered. In the attic and in the great basement, other rooms provided space for the liberal entertainment that was part of the family scheme of living. Monroe, Lafayette, William Henry Harrison, Jackson, Taylor, "Teddy" Roosevelt, among others, were entertained in this home. The furnishings are the former personal possessions of the Brown family. A portrait, by Gilbert Stuart, of one of the members of the family hangs on a downstairs wall. The piano and some music that belonged to Margaretta, wife of the builder, remain.

The area bounded by Wapping, Wilkinson, Washington and Main Streets is known as the CORNER OF CELEBRITIES. Brown owned the entire block on which Liberty Hall stands. For his son Orlando he built the house that stands on the opposite corner. Around this nucleus developed a remarkable neighborhood. During the five generations since the Browns first made their home in Frankfort, the little neighborhood has been the birthplace, or the later home, of two Justices of the Supreme Court, nine United States Senators, six Representatives, seven Ambassadors, and three Admirals of the United States Navy.

Two other residents—Marshall M. Bibb and John J. Crittenden—served in the Federal Cabinet.

4. FRANKFORT CEMETERY, E. Main St., lies along the edge of the bluff that overlooks Frankfort from the east. Within its rolling acres are the graves of distinguished Kentuckians. Near the entrance (R) is the GOEBEL MONUMENT, where is buried the man who in 1900 was assassinated on the steps of the Old Capitol.

At a point where the drive closely skirts the edge of the bluff (R), is the BOONE MEMORIAL. A footpath winds downward from the drive to the single grave beneath the trees where lie Daniel Boone and Rebecca Boone, first of the pioneers. The monolithic limestone memorial that stands above their grave was quarried from the Kentucky River cliffs at Boonesboro, where in 1775 Daniel helped establish the first seat of government in the West. On the four sides of the monolith are inset panels of Italian marble, representing scenes from the life of the frontiersman.

After the settlement of Kentucky began in earnest Boone, unfortunate in his business enterprises, moved his family into the wilderness west of the Mississippi which was then a Spanish possession. In 1820 he died at the home of his son Nathan Boone, in the southern section of St. Charles County, Mo. In 1845 the Legislature of Kentucky brought his remains to Frankfort and erected the memorial.

From the center of an oval plot, known as STATE CEMETERY, rises the tall Carrara marble shaft of the monument, dedicated by the State in 1850 to the memory of Kentuckians who fell in foreign wars. Surmounting the shaft is the figure of *Victory* designed by Robert E. Launitz of New York. He also executed the monument. The *Victory* and the four eagles seen at its feet were made in Italy from detail designs by Launitz. Inscriptions on the four sides of the shaft tell the part that Kentucky has played in the wars of the Nation. Encircling the base are the graves of soldiers whose remains were brought here from the battlefields of the Mexican War.

Within the oval, just outside the circle of soldier dead, is the TOMB OF THEODORE O'HARA, citizen of Frankfort, editor, soldier of the Mexican War and of the War between the States. Engraved upon his tomb are verses from his ode, the *Bivouac of the Dead,* memorializing his comrades of the Mexican War.

Beyond the O'Hara tomb, at the southern tip of the oval and screened by heavy foliage, is the COL. RICHARD M. JOHNSON TOMB. Johnson led the Kentucky troops who in 1813, at the Battle of the Thames, helped break the Indian power north of the Ohio. He is credited with killing Tecumseh, the Indian leader, in this battle.

5. STATE ARSENAL *(not open to public),* E. Main St., at foot of hill, attracts attention by its commanding position, rather than from its size or style of architecture, which with its ornamental battlements and turrets is suggestive of the Tudor. It was erected in 1850 as a storagehouse for equipment and materials belonging to the State Militia and it still serves that purpose.

6. CAPITAL BRIDGE, E. Main St. and Capitol Ave., is dedicated to the memory of those who fell in the World War. It unites north and south Frankfort, crossing the Kentucky River at a level that assures uninterrupted highway communication in the event of a flood similar to that of 1937, when all highway travel by way of Frankfort was suspended.

The area between Capital Bridge and the intersection of East Main and Ann Streets (L) is one of the oldest business blocks in the west. The STONE HOUSE, the first abutting the street on the left, was built by John Hampton, an early settler. A few doors beyond an old building reveals itself as a clapboarded LOG HOUSE, one of the first in the growing village. First built as a home, it has served several uses since. The largest building in the row, formerly a livery stable, is used as a garage. The buildings between the old barn and the Ann Street corner are of the same early period. The great hewn timbers, doorways, windows, worn thresholds, chimneys, weathered siding between the buildings all attest their age. At the southeast corner of Main and Ann Streets, a BRONZE MARKER attached to the Ann Street wall of the building tells that a few feet from the corner, and toward the river at a jog in the building line abutting the street, the first stake was driven of the original survey of the town site.

7. STATE INDUSTRIAL INSTITUTE (Kentucky Negro College), E. Main St. and City Limits, is a teachers' training school for Negroes. The plant is on a 35-acre campus overlooking the northwestern section of Frankfort and consists of six modern, well-equipped school buildings, together with dormitories provided for students and faculty. A farm of 265 acres, owned and operated by the school, lies immediately south of the highway and serves as an out-of-doors laboratory for students in agriculture. It is equipped with barns, a silo, cattle and hog sheds, and a poultry building. Training for steam and electrical engineering, manual training, dressmaking and domestic science is stressed. Students also may receive a thorough training in teaching, for which purpose there are maintained elementary courses that any Negro child may attend. The institution possesses the finest library of Negro literature in Kentucky.

Under the laws of Kentucky white and Negro children are separately educated. Negro children receive training under Negro teachers. An impartial pro-rata division of school funds assures to children of both races their full share of school equipment and of teacher-service. To meet the demand so created with trained men and women, the State Industrial Institute was founded by an act of the legislature in 1886. The Negro illiteracy, estimated at 96 percent in the late 1860's, now averages 5 percent for the State as a whole.

POINTS OF INTEREST IN ENVIRONS

8. US LOCK 4, N. end of Kentucky Ave. *(open),* part of the engineering improvement by which the Kentucky River is made navigable.

9. HEMP MILLS (Kentucky River Mills), Wilkinson St. extended, N. of City Limits.

10. O.F.C. *(Frank Stagg)* DISTILLERY *(open weekdays on application),* Leestown Pike (Wilkinson St. extended), where Bourbon (corn) whisky is manufactured.

HARRODSBURG

Railroad Station: Depot and Office Sts., for Southern Ry.
Bus Station: Main and Lexington Sts., adjoining post office, for Greyhound and Fleenor Lines.
Taxis: 25¢ within city limits; 10¢ per mile outside city.
Accommodations: One hotel; inns, and tourist homes.
Information Service: Chamber of Commerce, in Hotel Harrod.
Motion Picture Houses: Two.
Annual Events: Historical pageant, usually June 16; Mercer County Fair, last week in July; Fox Hound Show, second day of fair.

HARRODSBURG (824 alt., 4,585 pop.), first permanent white settlement in Kentucky, is on a hill of the Bluegrass just west of the upper Kentucky River.

Set on a lawn facing the main street, the Mercer County Courthouse lifts a white clock tower and cupola high over the countryside. Around it hurries the vigorous life of this tourist city. Along College Street old families live in homes designed in early nineteenth century styles.

Around the city in all directions cluster horse farms, tobacco farms, and chicken farms with their distinctive houses in the southern plantation manner.

Harrodsburg's fine homes and mineral springs are less cherished than the historic shrines assembled here in Pioneer Memorial State Park. Kentucky looks to Harrodsburg for reminders of long struggles during surveying and settlement; and great deeds of men like James Harrod and George Rogers Clark are commemorated here.

Early in 1773 Governor Dunmore of Virginia sent surveyors into Kentucky to survey public land, to be used in paying off veterans of the French and Indian War. One of these surveying parties, led by Thomas Bullitt and James Harrod, left Fort Pitt in the spring of 1773 and descended the Ohio River to the mouth of the Kanawha. Here the party met the McAfee brothers—Robert, William, James, and George—who had left Virginia on a similar mission. The two parties joined forces and continued down the Ohio River to Big Bone Lick, where they camped July 4 and 5. On July 7 they separated. Bullitt and his followers went to the Falls of the Ohio where they laid out the site of Louisville. Harrod accompanied the McAfees up the Kentucky River beyond the present site of Frankfort, where they crossed over into the valley of the Salt River. At its headwaters they located two proposed settlements, one by James Harrod where Harrodsburg now stands, the other by the McAfees a few miles north. They then returned to Pennsylvania and Virginia to plan for a migration in the following spring.

Early in 1774 James Harrod and 31 other men returned to the site of Harrodsburg. On June 16, 1774, a settlement called Harrodstown was laid out near Boiling Springs, three miles east of the later Harrod's Fort. A half-acre town lot and a 10-acre out-lot were assigned to each man. All the men took shares, but only five or six cabins were built that summer.

On July 20, 1774, while resting near a spring, four Harrodstown men were fired on from the underbrush. One was killed. Two fled through the woods to the Ohio River; they went down the Mississippi to New Orleans, and took ship for Philadelphia. The fourth ran to the settlement and told of the attack.

The Indians were on the warpath! Early that summer they attacked surveyors and settlers north of the Ohio River, and Lord Dunmore sent Daniel Boone and Michael Stoner to order the return of Kentucky surveyors until the Indian war was over. By the end of 1774 the cabins at Harrodstown were deserted and few white men remained in Kentucky.

While Daniel Boone, in the employ of the Transylvania Company, was blazing the trail across the mountains to the site of Boonesboro, James Harrod and 30 men in March 1775 occupied cabins built the previous year. On higher ground they constructed a palisaded village. It was a defensive arsenal and fortified town, the residents serving as a garrison ready to protect settlers living on the outside. Women and children arrived in September 1775.

Late in the summer of that year, James Ray, a boy of 16, was hunting near the fort. He had just killed and roasted a blue-winged duck when a "soldierly looking" man stepped from the forest. The boy offered to share his duck. "The man seemed starved and ate all of it," Ray said later. The stranger asked a great many questions about the settlement, and Ray offered to lead him to the fort. In this way, according to old accounts, George Rogers Clark introduced himself to Harrodstown (later Harrodsburg), and became its leader.

Besides the usual pioneer troubles, Harrodstown settlers soon faced the problem of proving title to their land. The Transylvania Company claimed a large tract of Kentucky land through purchase from the Cherokee. The company attempted to exert authority over the territory settled by Harrod and others. Clark called a meeting of the settlers in June 1776. The settlers authorized Clark and Gabriel Jones to go to Virginia to re-establish their claims.

The two men set out over the Wilderness Trail, but in the Cumberland foothills were halted by an acute case of "scaldfeet." They were delayed just long enough to prevent their arrival at Williamsburg, Virginia, before adjournment of the assembly. Clark went to Governor Henry, who gave him a letter of approval to the council of state. The council offered to lend him 500 pounds of powder if he would defend and settle the country across the mountains. Clark refused, saying that a country not worth claiming is not worth protecting. Clark was then given the powder, with the assurance that Virginia would back him.

As Clark returned to Kentucky he was hotly pursued by Indians along the Kentucky River and was forced to land at Limestone (now Maysville) to hide the powder. On the way to Harrodsburg he met a group of surveyors. They returned to the powder cache, recovered the explosive, and took it to Harrodsburg. Clark evidently conceived the idea of attacking the British in the northern territory either before or while he was at Harrodsburg, for he obtained permission from Gov. Patrick Henry to attack wherever he thought advisable.

Throughout the Revolutionary War, Harrodsburg was the seat of Kentucky County, which was organized in December 1776. According to the census, the town had a population of 198 persons, of whom 81 were eligible for military duty. The first court held in Kentucky convened January 16, 1781, in the blockhouse at Harrodsburg. One of the first cases tried was that of Hugh McGary, charged with playing the races. He was found guilty as charged, and the court proclaimed him "an infamous gambler . . . not [to] be eligible to any office of trust or honor within the State."

Harrodsburg people were industrious and thrifty. In 1775 John Harman raised the first corn in Kentucky in a field at the east end of Harrodsburg. The first woolen mill and the first gristmill in the West were operated here, and pottery, plows, flour, and textiles were manufactured.

The first school in the State was conducted within the fort in 1778. The teacher had no textbooks, and the children used smooth boards for paper and juice of ox galls for ink. They learned to write and read, and studied the Bible and hymnals.

By 1800 the community was prosperous. Rich farm lands surrounding the town encouraged cultivation of flax, hemp, tobacco, and other money crops. Harrodsburg's industries thrived. Then the development of roads to other Kentucky settlements and the coming of the steamboat in 1811 shifted Kentucky's major trade routes. Harrodsburg fell back on agriculture, and developed a tourist trade—at first because of its sulphur springs, later because of its historic interest. Harrodsburg was the summer resort of plantation owners in the Deep South, and Graham Springs alone is said to have had more than a thousand guests at one time.

Despite its industrial collapse Harrodsburg so profited from tourist business and marketing that the period 1820–1860 was one of steady growth. Log cabins gave way to more genteel houses modeled after the mansions on the Potomac and James Rivers. Bacon College was removed from Georgetown to Harrodsburg in 1839, and remained here until destroyed by fire in 1864, when it was merged with Transylvania College at Lexington. Greenville Female College, later known as Daughters' College, now Beaumont Inn, began in 1840. In 1847 there were two female academies: one, under the management of the Christian Church, enrolled 60 to 70 students; the other, under the care of the Presbyterian Church, 100 to 120 students.

During this period many men of distinction were born or lived in Harrodsburg. Gabriel Slaughter (1818–20), John Adair (1821–24) *(see History)*, and Beriah Magoffin (1859–62) became Governors of Kentucky; George S. Houston took the same high office in Georgia. John B. Thompson was a United States Senator (1853–59). William Marcus Linney (1835–87) was a pioneer Kentucky botanist and geologist.

This era of prosperity was seriously interrupted by the War between the States. Nearly all nearby farmers were slave owners. Their slaves were liberated, their fields laid bare, their livestock and horses taken, and their estates impoverished. Property built up through three generations passed into other hands. The family ownership of practically all the old homes of Harrodsburg can be traced back no further than 1870, when the population was 2,200.

In the decades that followed, rehabilitation and growth were slow. Competition from imported sisal and jute, because of practically no tariff protection, caused the hemp industry to fail. Prices of grain were uncertain, and tobacco gradually became the chief money crop. Little by little, farms restocked sheep and beef cattle, and by 1900 Harrodsburg had regained some of its prosperity.

During the last 30 years Harrodsburg has become the trade center of a farming region producing exceptional trotting horses, poultry, and white burley tobacco; its few industries operate on power furnished by the Dix Dam hydro-electric plant. Its tourist and resort trade is enormous. Throughout the warm season beginning in May, a number of people come from all parts of the country to "take the water" at its sulphur springs and visit its historic shrines.

POINTS OF INTEREST

PIONEER MEMORIAL STATE PARK, Lexington and Warwick Sts., is a tract that occupies the site of Old Fort Harrod and its immediate environs. Before 1923 only a neglected graveyard marked the place and quarrying operations threatened the site. One of America's historic landmarks was going to ruin, and Kentucky citizens undertook to restore the fort and beautify the grounds. The old Taylor Mansion was acquired for a museum; Congress provided funds for the erection of the Clark Memorial; the Thomas Lincoln Marriage Cabin was set up in a building especially erected to house it; the palisades and fort buildings were reconstructed as nearly as possible like the originals. On November 16, 1934, President Franklin D. Roosevelt and Gov. Ruby Lafoon joined in dedicating the park. It is fenced by a brick wall on Warwick Street, and a gateway opens on a wide road running through a bluegrass lawn to a parking space at the foot of the memorial, the fort (directly in front), and the cemetery.

OLD FORT HARROD *(open 8–6 in summer; 8:30–6 in winter; adm. adults 25¢, children 10¢, including adm.* to *Mansion Museum),* end of drive in the park, is a reconstruction of the original fort that occupied this site. It is 64 feet shorter than the 264-feet-square original. Blockhouses at the southeast and southwest corners are connected by cabins with roofs sloping inward. The remainder of the enclosure is a palisade of upright logs 12 feet high. The outside chimneys are of clay-chinked logs set on stone foundations. In former times each cabin had a pole to push over the chimney in case it caught fire. The spring, still flowing, furnished sufficient water for the inhabitants.

Within the cabins and blockhouses are pioneer relics—homemade wooden utensils, hand-made furniture, crude agricultural tools, lanterns, dishes, spinning wheels, copper kettles, pioneer beds, and many other items preserved by descendants of early settlers.

Within the fort is a reproduction of the FIRST SCHOOLHOUSE, where Mrs. William Coomes taught reading and writing to the children of the settlement.

In this fort Ann McGirty operated the first spinning wheel in the West; John Lythe preached the Gospel; Squire Boone, brother of Daniel, walked about with a Bible in his hand; the first white child in Kentucky was born; and George Rogers Clark prepared to march into the Old Northwest.

LINCOLN MARRIAGE TEMPLE, R. at Warwick St. entrance, is a red brick building, cruciform in plan, its 12 angles representing the 12 Apostles. In the central tower is the bell, rung twice each year—on the marriage anniversary of Thomas and Nancy Hanks Lincoln, and on the anniversary of Abraham Lincoln's death. The floor plan of the temple was suggested by an old Baptist church in the neighborhood where the pulpit was in the center of the church. The LINCOLN MARRIAGE CABIN stands where the pulpit would be ordinarily. It was removed from its original site in the Beech Fork Settlement, where Thomas Lincoln and Nancy Hanks were married June 12, 1806. The cabin resembles the one in which Lincoln was born *(see Tour 6).*

PIONEER CEMETERY, N. side of the park, oldest in the West, is the burial place of more than 500 early settlers and soldiers. Few names appear on the gravestones. A coffin-shaped stone, near the middle of the cemetery, marks the grave of the first white child who died in the settlement.

GEORGE ROGERS CLARK MEMORIAL, SE. of entrance to the fort, is a heroic granite bas-relief, the money for which was appropriated by Congress. The central section shows Gen. George Rogers Clark standing beside his horse. To the right is a young pioneer and an old one; to the left, a frontier soldier bids wife and child good-by. The memorial was designed and executed by Ulric Ellerhusen, sculptor, and Francis Keally, architect. In a granite stone, lying flat before the sculptured figures, is chiseled an illustrated map of the Northwest Territory.

The MANSION MUSEUM *(open 8–6 in summer; 8:30–6 in winter)*, Warwick and Poplar Sts., built by Maj. James Taylor in 1830, is a post-Colonial two-story brick house built close to the sidewalk. It was acquired by the Harrodsburg Pioneer Memorial Park Association in 1925.

Portraits are hung around the front hallway. The Lincoln Room contains Lincolniana. The Confederate Room has battlefield relics and paintings and prints of many Southern leaders. The George Rogers Clark Room preserves prints and papers about Clark and his conquest. There is a collection of firearms in a room on the second floor. Next to it in the music room are many old instruments, some of them rare. In another room are old costumes, Indian relics, and historic books.

The DOCTOR SHOP, Warwick St. S. of the main entrance, was dedicated in June 1924 by the Kentucky State Medical Association in memory of pioneer physicians. This small one-story brick building contains a museum of early medical books, surgical instruments, and pictures pertaining to the medical profession.

GRAHAM SPRINGS *(open)*, in the extreme SW. section of the city *(roadway marked)*, is a mineral spring in a grove once occupied by a famous resort. The SPRING SHELTER is near the site of the old resort building burned during the War between the States. Wealthy Kentuckians and planters from the Deep South, accompanied by their slaves, menservants and maids, came here in great numbers during the years before the war.

At the FAIRGROUNDS *(adm. to fair 50¢)*, adjoining Graham Springs, the Mercer County Fair Association holds its annual exhibits and meetings. The fair has agricultural and industrial displays common to rural fairs, but emphasizes its horse shows, and has stables for 300 show horses. The annual Fox Hound Show is held on the second day of the fair.

MORGAN ROW *(private)*, Chiles St. opposite Courthouse Square, is a compact series of four two-story brick buildings set flush with the street, constructed between 1807 and 1836. They are separated by fire walls that extend some distance above the roof level. Seven doors in the houses open on limestone steps leading down to the original brick sidewalk. At the north end of the row is a post-Colonial structure built by John Chiles, an innkeeper and stagecoach operator of the 1830's. The buildings were operated by Chiles as an inn and as a rendezvous for gamblers. One of the doors still has the peephole used by the suspicious doorman.

DIAMOND POINT *(private)*, Price Ave. and College St., is a two-story Greek Revival brick home built in 1840. The deep Doric portico, with two central columns and corner pilasters, protects the long French windows and the richly carved doorway. Across the façade extends an iron balcony with diamond-shaped tracery, one of the first of its kind in the State.

BURFORD HILL *(private)*, W. of cemetery at N. city line, is a one-and-a-half-story late Georgian Colonial house built in 1820. The original west wing was destroyed by lightning. The bricks, burned locally, are laid in Flemish bond. The arched, fanlighted doorway is protected by a small Doric portico topped with a steep pediment. The gable roof is broken by small dormers.

AVALON INN, Main, Maxwell, and Chiles Sts., was originally the home of a Presbyterian academy for girls. In the Main Street façade four massive Doric columns rise two stories to support an entablature and cornice which carry out the Greek Revival design even to the dentils, triglyphs, and simple metopes. The doorway, with rectangular side lights and transom, is severely plain.

CLAY HILL *(private)*, Beaumont Ave., late Georgian Colonial in style, was built in 1812 by Beriah Magoffin, father of the Kentucky Governor (1859–62) of the same name. This two-story brick structure with one-story wings is noted for its handsome carved mantels and the loggia in the rear.

BEAUMONT INN *(open)*, Danville St. near the city line, is a Greek Revival brick building erected by John Augustus Williams in 1845, and was for some years the home of Daughters' College. Six tapering Ionic columns of the impressive entrance portico support a plain entablature.

POINTS OF INTEREST IN ENVIRONS

McAfee Station, *8 m. (see Tour 5)*. Old Mud Meeting House, *3 m.;* Shakertown, *8 m.;* Herrington Lake, *11 m.;* Perryville Battlefield, *12.4 m.;* High Bridge, *16.4 m. (see Tour 15)*.

LOUISVILLE

Railroad Stations: Union Station, Broadway and 10th St., for Louisville & Nashville R.R., Pennsylvania R.R., and Chicago, Indianapolis & Louisville R.R. (Monon Route). Central Station, N. 7th St. and Ohio River, for Baltimore & Ohio R.R., Chesapeake & Ohio R.R., New York Central R.R., Illinois Central R.R., and Southern Ry.
City Ticket Offices: Starks Bldg. Arcade, 4th and Walnut Sts., for all railroads.
Bus Stations: Union Bus Depot, 5th and Broadway, for Greyhound, Blue and White, Chaudoin (Carrollton division), Meadors & Allen Lines; 403 S. 3rd St. for Blue Motor Coach Lines; 240 W. Jefferson St. for Chaudoin Bus Lines, all divisions; 502 S. 3rd St., Interstate Bridge Transit Co. (inter-city) for Jeffersonville, Ind.
Airport: Bowman Field (Municipal), Taylorsville Rd. E. of Bon Air Ave., *5 m.* from business section, for American and Eastern Air Lines. (Ticket office, Kentucky Hotel.)
Taxis: Separate systems for white and Negro patrons, 15¢ for the first ⅘ m., 5¢ for each additional ⅖ m.; maximum capacity for a single cab 4 passengers.
Streetcars and Buses: Fare 10¢ or three tokens for 25¢; transfers interchangeable.
Toll Bridges: Kentucky and Indiana Terminal R.R. Bridge (Louisville to New Albany, Ind.), 31st St. and Western Parkway (US 31 W and US 150, Ind. 63, and Ind. 64), toll 25¢ for vehicles and all passengers; 5¢ for each pedestrian; Municipal Bridge (Louisville to Jeffersonville, Ind.), 2nd and Main Sts. (US 31 E and US 150, Ind. 60 and Ind. 62), toll 25¢ for vehicle and all passengers, 5¢ for each pedestrian.
Traffic Regulations: Strictly enforced. Right turns against a red light may be made from curb lane after a full stop anywhere outside the area between S. 1st and S. 6th Sts., from Broadway to the river. Left turns in the downtown area only at intersections indicated by large signs painted on the street. U-turns prohibited at intersections and boulevards, on through streets, and in central traffic district. Hand signals required. Pedestrians observe traffic lights.
Street Order and Numbering: Main St. divides the city's N. and S. street numbering, and 1st St. the E. and W. numbering.

Accommodations: Forty-one hotels (three for Negroes); many boarding houses and tourist homes. During week of Kentucky Derby rates are much higher.

Information Service: Louisville Board of Trade, Lincoln Bank Bldg., 421 W. Market St., Louisville Automobile Club (AAA), 800 S. 3rd St.

Radio Stations: WHAS (820 kc.); WAVE (940 kc.); WGRC (1370 kc.).
Theaters and Motion Picture Houses: Five first-run motion picture houses downtown, 25 second-run and community houses (two for Negroes). Road attractions and local musical and dramatic productions occasionally at Memorial Auditorium, S. 4th and Kentucky Sts.; Columbia Hall Auditorium, 820 S. 4th St.; Playhouse, Belknap Campus, S. 3rd and Shipp Sts.; Jefferson County Armory, Liberty St. between Armory Place and S. 6th St.; and the Woman's Club Auditorium, 1320 S. 4th St.
Baseball: Parkway Field, Eastern Parkway and Brook St., for Louisville and American Assn. teams.
Swimming: Public outdoor pools: Reservoir Park, Frankfort Ave. and Grinstead Dr., 25¢; Shelby Park, Oak St. between Hancock and Shelby Sts., 25¢; Shepard Park (for Negroes), 16th and Magazine Sts., 25¢. Indoor public pools: Y. M. C. A., Broadway and S. 3rd St., 25¢; Y. W. C. A (medical examination

required before entering pool), Broadway and S. 2nd St., 25¢; Henry Clay Hotel, S. 3rd and Chestnut Sts., 25¢.

Golf: Public courses in Shawnee Park, W. end of River Park Dr., 18 holes, greens fee 50¢; Crescent Hill Golf Course, Brownsboro Rd. and Lucile Ave., 9 holes, 35¢; Seneca Park, Taylorsville Rd., E. of Bon Air Ave., 18 holes, 50¢.

Tennis: All major public parks, free. Reservations required.

Steamer Excursions: Up Ohio River at least once daily during summer.

Annual Events: Kentucky Derby 1st or 2nd Sat. in May. Kentucky State Fair, 2nd or 3rd week of Sept.

LOUISVILLE (Loo-i-vil, 463 alt., 307,745 pop.), noted for its fine whisky, beautiful women, and the Kentucky Derby, lies across the Ohio River from New Albany and Jeffersonville, Indiana, on a low, level plain that curves for eight miles along the river. Midway in the adjoining river are the Falls of the Ohio, which determined the location of the original settlement and provided it with a name (Falls of the Ohio) until, as a gesture of gratitude for the aid given by Louis XVI and the French Nation to the American Revolution, the name was changed to Louisville. It is the largest and most important city, commercially and industrially, in the State.

The main portion of Louisville is built on a flood plain, about 60 feet above the Ohio River, surrounded by the river on the north and west and by low hills on the south and east. The residential area spreads into the Highlands. Northeast of the city the Ohio stretches in a bent swath nearly a mile wide and six miles long, forming one of the finest harbors in the whole course of the river. Passenger steamers, ferries, and tugs fill the harbor. An excursion boat, which periodically plies the tree-banked stream, plays its steam calliope. Across the river the low skylines of New Albany and Jeffersonville bespeak a more rural existence than that of their metropolitan neighbor.

The business section extends east and west from Fourth Street, which runs from the Ohio River southward into the Highlands. Like a giant chessboard, the taller buildings along this street stand like castles, knights, and bishops, while the lower business buildings and dwellings in the downtown area are pawns in the background.

In general, the city has the form of a letter T with the top approximately three miles wide, extending from the Highlands about nine miles westward along the south shore of the Ohio River. A southward projection of this urban area, forming the stem of the T, extends about seven and one-half miles from the river into the Highlands. Near the river front are tobacco warehouses, mills, livestock yards, distilleries, and the wholesale district that make Louisville one of the South's great distributing centers.

In the downtown area old homes suggest the social prestige of their owners, and indicate that the city was important even at an early date. On the highways leading into the city are mansions of plantation days, reminders that this early prosperity depended largely upon agriculture.

Between Jefferson Street and the Ohio River are a number of brick homes in the Greek Revival style sandwiched between business properties. Conspicuous among them are the three-or-four-room brick cottages with pretentious classic façades. Substantial homes of French and Italian Renaissance and Georgian design, built after 1835, are set far back from the street on spacious grounds south of Walnut Street between Floyd and Sixth Streets. With southward expansion of the city, continued until the middle 1870's, came the houses of gingerbread Victorian styles, many of which are still standing.

Louisville's parks ring the city in a loose half-circle. Shawnee Park, on the west, is formally arranged on flat land near the Ohio River. Iroquois and Cherokee Parks, thickly planted with trees, climb the hills that skirt the city on the south and east. Thirty-two miles of boulevard wind through the parks.

Louisville is a border metropolis that blends the commerce and industry of a Northern city with a Southern city's enjoyment of living. The result is an attractive compromise. Louisville is too busy making and selling things to have the languor of a town in the Deep South; but it does have its special graces. Its people are friendly and hospitable. The phalanx of clothing shops on Fourth Street north of Broadway contributes to the reputation of Louisville women for being well-dressed. Bourbon and water or a cocktail after work is popular; amusement and relaxation are nearly as important as work. Downtown theaters, restaurants, and hotel lobbies are invariably crowded; and it is still a favorite custom to drive or walk "in Fourth Street" of an evening.

Horse racing is by all odds Louisville's most exciting sport. The *Racing Form* is sold on the downtown streets like a newspaper. At nearby Churchill Downs 29 days of each year are given over to races. The spring and fall meets provide something to see, and add an extra fillip to conversation. During Derby Week in May, Louisville is the most feverish city in the Nation. Highways entering the city carry a steadily increasing number of automobiles and buses into the downtown area, hotels are "all out," and the streets teem with thousands of happy, hysterical townsmen and visitors. "A Kentucky girl," Irvin S. Cobb has said, "does not consider that she has been properly launched into society until she has seen a Derby run off." Seventy thousand people pack the stands, bleachers, and infield at Churchill Downs to see, in slightly more than two minutes, the start and finish of America's most celebrated horse race.

When the Kentucky State Fair is held in early September, Louisville again plays host to Kentuckians and out-of-Staters. The horse show and the livestock exhibit are outstanding attractions.

Many early planters who later became associated with the life of the city were large slaveowners, and the residents of Louisville kept house servants who, after the manner of the time, assumed the family name. This transplanted Negro stock is the foundation of the city's present Negro life and culture. Despite his background of decades of slavery, the Negro in Louisville has adapted himself remarkably to the environment of freedom. Illiteracy among Negroes has dropped from about 96 percent in 1865 to a percentage level only slightly above that of the whites. Illiterates, white and Negro, reported by the U.S. Census of 1930 reached a low of 2.2 percent. The first free public library for Negroes with Negro attendants was opened at Louisville in 1905 as a branch of the city Free Public Library. Louisville is the only city in the State that has two Carnegie branch buildings for Negro readers. Local Negroes have a complete system of primary and secondary schools in addition to the Louisville Municipal College—part of the University of Louisville—which, in October 1937, had an enrollment of 224 students working toward the A.B. degree. Opened in 1931, it is the only institution of its kind in the Nation.

Negro neighborhoods have their own stores, hotels, restaurants, newspaper publishing houses, and theaters. The 1930 census figures record 45.6 percent of all Negro families as homeowners. This slightly exceeds the white ownership percentage, but because of the low economic status of the Negro the individual value of these homes is still sub-standard. The voting power of the city's 47,354 Negroes is a factor in the progress of the race in Louisville.

The Ohio River—commonplace enough today—played a vital part in the development of Louisville and the surrounding country. The French were the first to explore the river they called "La Belle Rivière" *(the beautiful river)*. During the next hundred years a long line of adventurers, explorers, traders, and surveyors saw the Falls of the Ohio, stopped here for a time, and passed on.

In 1773, after England had won the Ohio Valley from France, the first permanent settlement was attempted at the falls. In the summer of that year Capt. Thomas Bullitt, commissioned by Lord Dunmore, Governor of Virginia, to locate land warrants granted to Virginia soldiers of the French and Indian War, camped on the Ohio River shore near the present interstate bridge. He surveyed 2,000 acres of land, for which Dr. John Connolly, a native of Pennsylvania who had served in the war, received a patent from the British Crown. Col. John Campbell became joint owner of the land with Dr. Connolly, and they issued proposals for the sale of lots. Before they could establish settlers here, Connolly was charged with being a Tory and his land was confiscated by Virginia.

In May 1778 young George Rogers Clark, with 150 volunteer soldiers and about 20 families, left the Redstone settlement (now Brownsville, Pennsylvania) on the Monongahela and came down the Ohio. His purpose was to establish a military base along the lower Ohio before starting his campaign for the conquest of the Old Northwest, then held by the British. When the party reached the falls they landed on an island, long since swept away by floods, where they built blockhouses and planted corn; Clark and his raw recruits then pushed on into the wilderness to capture the British posts at Kaskaskia, Cahokia, and Vincennes. In the fall, Clark sent some of his men back to the settlement to establish a fort on the mainland. This fort, built during the winter 1778–79, near the present junction of Twelfth Street with the river opposite Corn Island, became the nucleus of the settlement and headquarters of General Clark until Fort Nelson was completed in 1782. The falls, which interrupted navigation except in periods of high water, determined the site of the settlement. Downstream boats had to be piloted, and upstream boats towed by men familiar with the dangerous rapids.

That winter was a hard one, with food and wild game scarce; but great preparations were made for the first Christmas party. The men brought in venison. The women made "hoecakes, hominy, and other frontier fancies." Old Cato, a Negro fiddler, was distressed because he had only one string for his fiddle. On Christmas Eve a canoe landed, and in it was a Frenchman with a fiddle. Old Cato traded him coonskins for new fiddle strings, and gave him an extra skin to say nothing about the trade, because he wanted to surprise his white folks. To Cato's chagrin the Frenchman was asked to play for the dancing. He tried to teach some of the dances of his own country, but they were too complicated. He gave it up in disgust, and yielded the honors to Old Cato and the Virginia Reel.

News of Clark's victories in the Northwest lured many settlers to this region. Three hundred arrived in the spring of 1780, and in May, Col. George Slaughter and 150 soldiers came from Virginia to protect the fledgling community. In the same month the legislature of Virginia passed an "Act for establishing the town of Louisville at the Fall of the Ohio."

The appearance of the little town was not inviting. A large fort, and a number of log cabins, occupied by several score families who had cleared and cultivated garden plots, stood not far back from the river front. The roar of the falls was sometimes broken by the howl of wolves and the yell of savages. Indians sometimes attacked the fort, and usually made their escape across the river. In 1781 such an attack occurred, and the whites, thinking that the Indians had fled across the river, started in canoes to pursue them. They were fired upon from the Kentucky side, and nine were killed. The Indians often fired at the flatboats of the whites as they plied the river.

The first court convened here on March 7, 1781, and one of its first official acts was to fix the charges for the "necessities of life." These included whisky, which could not be sold for more than $15 a half-pint, and shelled corn, not to sell for more than $10 a gallon. A man might object if a hotel keeper charged him more than $18 a day for board or more than $6 a night for a feather bed; the stabling of his horse was not to exceed $4 a night. These prices were computed in terms of the depreciated Continental currency.

In 1781–82, Fort Nelson, named in honor of Governor Nelson of Virginia, was erected north of Main Street between Seventh and Ninth Streets, covering an acre of ground along the Ohio shore. General Clark had his headquarters here and the fort served as courthouse and jail.

With the westward expansion Louisville assumed the character of a commercial city. At the opening of the new century, it had 600 people, and soon it had sanitary laws and police and fire protection.

The New Madrid earthquake of 1811–12, which shook the greater part of the continent, and formed Reelfoot Lake *(see Tour 10)*, rocked Louisville. The first shock, lasting four minutes, was felt here on December 16, 1811, at 2 P.M. It was accompanied by thunder and was followed by "complete darkness and saturation of the atmosphere with sulphuric vapor." Eighty-seven shocks occurred during the following week and temblors continued through part of 1812. One very frightened and penitent person rushed in on a group of card players, exclaiming, "Gentlemen, how can you be engaged in this way when the world is so near its end?" The party rushed into the street, where, from the rocking of the earth, the stars seemed to be falling. A member of the group was constrained to remark, "What a pity that so beautiful a world should be thus destroyed." Public morals improved noticeably during this period.

The steamboat *New Orleans*, first successful steamer on the Ohio and Mississippi Rivers, stopped at Louisville on its way to Natchez in October 1811. Latrobe describes the occasion in his *Rambler in America:*

Late at night on the fourth day after quitting Pittsburgh, they arrived in safety at Louisville, having been but 70 hours in descending upwards of 700 miles . . . and it is related that on the unexpected arrival of the boat before Louisville, in the course of a fine, still, moonlight night, the extraordinary sound which filled the air, as the pent-up steam was suffered to escape from the valves on rounding to, produced a general alarm, and multitudes rose from their beds to ascertain the cause. I have heard that the general impression among the Kentuckians was that a comet had fallen into the Ohio.

This trip inaugurated the steamboat era, which vitally affected Louisville. In 1815 the *Enterprise* steamed upriver from New Orleans to Louisville in 12 days, less than half the time it took broadhorns and keel-boats to make the journey downstream. Talk revived about building a canal around the falls in front of Louisville.

From 1820 to 1870 this river town's prosperity was measured by its boat traffic. During the first three decades of the nineteenth century portaging cargoes around the Falls of the Ohio was Louisville's chief concern. Shipments were unloaded, carted overland to Towhead Island above the falls, and put on boats for the upriver journey. Except in periods of high water, when the falls were navigable, the same transfer of goods took place in moving cargoes downstream.

In 1825 a private company was organized to construct the long-deferred canal project, and in December 1830, the *Uncas* passed through the locks of the completed Portland Canal, which ran laterally across Louisville's river front. The canal opened through navigation on the Ohio from Pittsburgh to its mouth. The movement of commerce picked up. Less than a decade after it was completed, 1,500 steamers and 500 flatboats and keel-boats entered the canal annually, bearing 300,000 tons of produce for Southern markets. Today, along Fourth and Fifth Streets, near the river, are many landmarks of the gilded days when river trade brought Louisville its first prosperity; and to the foot of Fourth Street occasionally comes the *Gordon Greene*, the only packet now making the journey upriver to Pittsburgh.

Meanwhile, in 1828, Louisville was incorporated and received its first city charter. The makeshift village government was superseded by a mayor and a board of aldermen elected by the voters. The loss of the portage business following the opening of the Portland Canal brought on a temporary local depression, made more acute by the cholera epidemic of 1831.

By the middle 1830's Louisville had two noted hostelries—the Louisville Hotel, still standing at Main and Sixth Streets, and the Galt House. The spacious architectural design of the Louisville Hotel, built in 1832 of native limestone, was for many years a model for hotel building throughout the South and Middle West. The Galt House, razed in 1920, for 75 years had a reputation for fine Southern cooking and service. Charles Dickens was a visitor in 1842: "We slept at the Galt House, a splendid hotel, and were as handsomely lodged as though we had been in Paris, rather than hundreds of miles beyond the Alleghenies."

Caleb Atwater, in *Remarks Made on a Tour to Prairie Du Chien,* written in 1831, said of Louisville:

Main St., for the distance of about one mile, presents a proud display of wealth and grandeur. Houses of two and three lofty stories in height, standing upon solid stone foundations, exceed anything of the kind in the Western States. The stores filled with commodities and manufactures of every clime and every art, dazzle the eye . . . the ringing of the bells and the roaring of the guns, belonging to the numerous steamboats in the harbor, the cracking of the coachman's whip, and the sound of the stage driver's horn salute the ear. The motley crowd of citizens, all well dressed, hurrying to and fro—the numerous strangers from all parts of the world almost, visiting the place to sell or to buy goods—the deeply loaded dray cart, and the numerous pleasure carriages rolling to and fro, arrest and rivet the attention of a mere traveler like myself. . . . There are at this time about 1,200 dwelling houses in the town, mostly built of brick. Many are equal to any in the Atlantic cities. . . . There are probably more ease and affluence in this place than in any western town—their houses are splendid, substantial, and richly furnished.

Louisville in its early years drew its population mostly from Virginia, Maryland, and the Carolinas. Louisville early became an important outstation in the expanding New Orleans commercial empire. Men of wealth, character, and influence came up from that city, entered the Louisville scene, and left the imprint of their early training and social environment.

By way of Pittsburgh and down the Ohio came another, larger stream of men seeking their fortunes in the expanding West. Among them were New Englanders and people from the Middle Atlantic States. This group added materially to the business caution of the roaring river town and much to its diversity of opinion. Their active participation in political life explains the fact that Louisville, a Southern city, was vocally Northern during the War between the States.

During these first few decades, Louisville was influenced by a number of French *emigrés*. Michel Lacassagne, the first postmaster, reproduced a French garden at his home on the river front; Tarascon built mills and utilized the water of the falls; Audubon painted birds and taught drawing; the young Duke of Orleans, afterwards Louis Philippe, King of France, was among the first musicians in the city; the Barbaroux brought mercantile and manufacturing skill; the Berthouds and Honorés, like Tardiveau, were pioneers in navigation and commerce. Some traces remain of their architectural contributions. Tradition remembers their graceful living and dancing feet.

The 1840's started off with a fire that burned a large part of the business district. It was rebuilt, and the town continued to grow. In this decade many Germans came to Louisville. They brought little of tangible wealth but much practical education and industrial skill. They founded stores and industries, and in time exercised a definite influence upon the social and commercial life of the community. Some of the firms they established are still doing business under the German names of the founders.

By 1850 Louisville had a population of 43,194. A new charter, granted March 24, 1851, provided for election of all city officers.

On election day, August 6, 1855, the Know Nothing Party precipitated a riot in Louisville. A mob with a cannon went fighting and burning through the streets. Several lives were lost and a number of houses were burned. The day is known as "Bloody Monday."

The 1850's were years of general prosperity, and Louisville inaugurated street railways and witnessed the completion in 1851 of the Louisville, Frankfort & Lexington Railroad. The Louisville & Nashville Railroad, actively promoted by Louisville, was completed to Nashville in 1859.

Louis Kossuth, Hungarian exile, visited Louisville. A member of his entourage wrote: "We were astonished at the expanse of Louisville which, we were told, twenty-four years ago was but an insignificant town. The streets are broad, the houses substantial, with neat front and back gardens; carriages are numerous; Negro footmen wear livery; everything looks more aristocratical than economical."

The outbreak of the War between the States brought a bitter division of opinion in Louisville. The predominant Union sentiment within the city vied with the pro-Confederate temper of the adjoining rural section. Many residents with Southern sympathies were compelled to espouse the cause of the Union as a matter of self-preservation. Louisville was military headquarters and supply depot for the Armies of the North throughout the war.

The end of the conflict found the South's traditional plantation economy bankrupt. Louisville, one of the most important distributing centers for the Southern States, had to adjust to changed conditions. It pressed new merchandising methods and established railroad connections with Memphis, New Orleans, Mobile, Atlanta, and other Southern cities. Louisville merchants sent salesmen in two-horse rigs to all parts of the South with instructions to get orders at any cost. For two decades Louisville and Cincinnati waged an intense struggle for Southern trade. Eventually it was divided between them.

Louisville's third charter was approved March 3, 1870. Local population reached 100,753, an increase of 41 percent in 10 years. The decade from 1870 to 1880 was marked by the completion of a railroad bridge across the Ohio and the erection of a new city hall.

In the spring of 1890 a devastating wind swept through the western part of the city, causing the loss of 106 lives and extensive property damage. In 1893 Louisville again approved a new charter, with changes to conform to the State constitution adopted the previous year. A system of bureaus was created, which took charge of business details previously administered by the city council.

The census of 1900 showed Louisville with a population of 204,731. Since the World War a new sewerage system has been installed at an outlay of $8,000,000; the municipally owned water company has spent $5,000,000 in expansion and improvements; and the elimination of grade crossings within the city limits (to cost $21,000,000) has been undertaken.

Louisville boomed through the 1920's. The downtown skyscrapers that give Fourth Street and Broadway an elevated skyline have all been built since 1920. In 1925 the Falls of the Ohio were harnessed for the production of electricity. The depression did not affect it as severely as many other American cities because of the diverse character and wide distribution of its industries. Through the lean years its tobacco trading and manufacturing maintained most of their normal prosperity, and the revocation of the eighteenth amendment set in motion the long-idle distilling business. In spite of these material advantages, unemployment became a pressing problem in an industrial city, and municipal officials, co-operating with the Federal Government, began construction and improvement of parks and parkways, the building of model homes for whites and Negroes, the extension of street paving, and the construction of a municipal boat harbor.

The city was carrying increased expenditure, with good promise of lessening its relief load, when in January-February of 1937 the Ohio swept out of bounds in the greatest flood ever recorded for this river. Boats patrolled Broadway from the Highlands to Shawnee Park. Except for a small downtown district, the entire lowland area was inundated. Transportation of all kinds came to a standstill. Basements were flooded. Heating plants shut down. The city was placed under emergency control. Thousands were evacuated to the Highlands and neighboring cities. For a month and more the ordinary processes of living ceased to function, but by rigid enforcement of sanitary regulations and because of warm weather, an epidemic was avoided. By April daily life over the major part of the city had returned to normal. Losses within the city amounted to more than $52,000,000, and necessitated costly renovation and replacement of goods. With the assistance of rehabilitation loans and Red Cross aid the city by mid-summer of 1937 had resumed its usual way of life.

Throughout its history, Louisville has contributed to the intellectual and cultural life of the Nation. Its press has voiced the sentiments of the early West, the Middle West, and the renewed South. The first newspaper was the *Farmer's Library,* which appeared in 1801 as a four-page, 11- by 19-inch sheet having little more than foreign news and advertisements. The *Public Advertiser* was established in 1818 by Shadrach Penn; it began as a weekly, but on April 24, 1826, it became the first daily published in the West. The Louisville *Journal,* edited by George D. Prentice, began in 1830. In 1868 it merged with the Louisville *Morning Courier and American Democrat,* started in 1844 but suppressed by the Federal Government in 1861. Henry Watterson (1840–1921), the South's most noted editor of the last century, edited the newspaper for the next fifty years, and made the *Courier-Journal* influential in Southern and national affairs through its vigorous editorials *(see Press and Radio).*

John James Audubon (1785–1851), the naturalist, lived here from 1808 to 1812. Mary Anderson, born in California in 1859, was Louisville's contribution to the stage, and Enid Yandell (1870–1934) was the city's most notable sculptor. Madison Cawein (1865–1914), Cale Young Rice (b. 1872), and David Morton (b. 1886) are leading Louisville poets. Alice Hegan Rice (b. 1870) has refreshed readers everywhere with *Mrs. Wiggs of the Cabbage Patch* and other stories. (Mrs.) George Madden Martin (b. 1866), dean of Louisville writers, is best known for her delightful chronicles of *Emmy Lou.* Ellen Churchill Semple (1863–1932) attained international prestige with *American History and Its Geographic Condition* and other scientific works. Josephine McGill added to Kentucky's published treasure of ballad material with her *Folk Songs of the Kentucky Mountains* (1917). Louisville was also the birthplace (1856) of Louis Dembitz Brandeis, a member of the U.S. Supreme Court (1916–1939) and the author of several important books *(see Literature).*

Since the War between the States, industrial development has centered about the manufacture of farm implements, tobacco products, meat-packing products, leather goods, flour, and whisky. Tobacco is the leading cash crop in the neighboring area. Prior to about 1918 the burley tobacco sold here was packed in great hogsheads, each containing about a thousand pounds. These containers were broken open for inspection, and a handful of tobacco determined the grade of the entire hogshead. From this custom originated the name "Breaks" for tobacco market floors. Louisville is still the leading "hogshead market." Principal marketing activities run from about Thanksgiving to Easter. Approximately one-fifth of the Nation's cigarettes are manufactured here.

Two-thirds of Kentucky's wealth from manufactures is concentrated in Louisville and Jefferson County. Livestock receipts and the meat-packing industry are vital factors in the city's business. Since repeal the old distilleries on Main Street have awakened to new life and made the city once more one of the Nation's ranking distributing centers for liquor, especially Bourbon whisky. Plumber's supplies, sanitary equipment, and mill and factory supplies are extensively produced; and Louisville is outstanding in the manufacture of reed organs, baseball bats, boxes, mahogany veneering, nicotine products, hickory handles, minnow buckets, wagons, and the milling of soft winter wheat.

Local deposits of alluvial sands and glacial gravels, with clays and some sandstone, have provided the materials for many of Louisville's residences and business buildings. Underneath this downtown area once ran the channel of the Ohio River. Long since silted up with sand and gravel, this channel provides an unlimited supply of cold sanitary water used in air-conditioning hotels, theaters, factories, and office buildings, and to some extent in manufacturing processes, particularly distilling.

POINTS OF INTEREST

1. ROMAN CATHOLIC CATHEDRAL OF THE ASSUMPTION *(open daily)*, 435 S. 5th St., was consecrated in 1852, the year of its completion. Constructed of brick trimmed with limestone, in Gothic Revival style, the building is the work of William Kelly. The spire with its 24-foot cross rises to a height of 287 feet. Within the lofty tower is a 4,500-pound bell, given to the cathedral by the Right Reverend Monsignor LaBastida, an Archbishop of Mexico. The tower clock was made in Paris by Messieurs Blin. Among the treasures of the cathedral is an old painting that depicts St. Bernard with the Sacred Host. In its bold conception, brilliant coloring, and general composition, the painting recalls the work of Rubens and Van Dyck.

2. The GRAYSON HOUSE *(private)*, 432 S. 6th St., a broad, nearly square structure of one-and-a-half stories with outer walls 17 inches thick, is the oldest brick house in the city. It was built not later than 1810 by John Gwathmey, a Virginian, on an Indian burial mound. The brick, laid in Flemish bond, was brought from the East and shipped down the Ohio in keel-boats. The house has 17 rooms and a large central hall. Slave quarters and a kitchen formerly occupied the basement level. The earthquakes of 1811–12 and the tornado of 1890 did no serious damage to this robust house.

3. COLLEGE SQUARE, W. Chestnut St. between S. 8th and S. 9th Sts., was set aside by the city in 1837 as the site for a college. The Medical Institute, from which the University of Louisville ultimately developed, opened here in the year 1839. In 1838 Gideon Shryock, Lexington architect, designed and built the Greek Revival building on the corner of Eighth and Chestnut Streets. With the exception of the inner two, the Corinthian columns supporting the severely plain pediment are square in design. Shryock also designed

the building at the corner of Ninth and Chestnut Streets. A third structure, midway between the others, and like them in plan, has been added in recent years. In 1852 a fire gutted the original building at the corner of Eighth and Chestnut Streets, and subsequent alterations of the reconstructed building left little of the interior plan. However, the façade and exterior, which emerged whole from the flames, are designed in the best Shryock manner. The property is occupied by the Central Colored High School, which emphasizes training in the manual arts.

4. FORT NELSON MONUMENT, NW. corner N. 7th and W. Main Sts., is an irregular slab of Georgia granite bearing a bronze tablet; it commemorates a fort, built in 1782, which extended from this point west approximately two blocks along what is now Main Street, and north to the river shore. Fort Nelson was a Revolutionary fort built by George Rogers Clark as a military base and as a refuge for Louisville's first settlers. The monument, presented to the city by the Colonial Dames of America, was dedicated in 1912.

5. JEFFERSON COUNTY COURTHOUSE, W. Jefferson St., between S. 5th and S. 6th Sts., designed in the Greek Revival style with an impressive Doric portico, is a characteristic work of Gideon Shryock, designer of the Old Capitol at Frankfort and of the Bank of Louisville building. The limestone structure was begun in 1838–39, but was not completed and occupied until 1850. In the center of the rotunda is a life-size white marble STATUE OF HENRY CLAY by Joel T. Hart, unveiled in 1867. It is a replica of the original at Richmond, Virginia. In front of the courthouse is a THOMAS JEFFERSON STATUE by Moses Ezekiel, the gift of I. W. and B. Bernheim.

6. OLD BANK OF LOUISVILLE BUILDING *(open 9–5 weekdays)*, 320 W. Main St., occupied by the Louisville Credit Men's Association, is popular with artists who come to sketch the stately façade. The structure was designed in the Greek Revival style by Gideon, Shryock and erected in 1837. The façade is of dressed limestone and incorporates a portico with a pediment supported by two Ionic columns and, at either end, a tapered pylon. Within, an elliptical dome and skylight, supported by four classic columns, forms the major part of the building.

The WHARF AND WATERFRONT, N. end of N. 3rd St., are closely associated with the history of Louisville. Visible (L) along the water's edge is the upstream end of the LOUISVILLE AND PORTLAND CANAL, rebuilt in 1927 to provide a nine-foot navigation stage. The original canal, dug by slave labor in 1830 at a cost of $740,000, opened a new era in inland navigation. The canal was twice rebuilt before the present locks and dam were completed. U.S. GOVERNMENT DAM 41 floods the rapids and eases a drop of 37 feet in the river level. The dam, largest on the Ohio River, is constructed of reinforced concrete and was completed in 1928. Backwater from the dam floods Corn Island, site of the original settlement of Louisville. In the im-

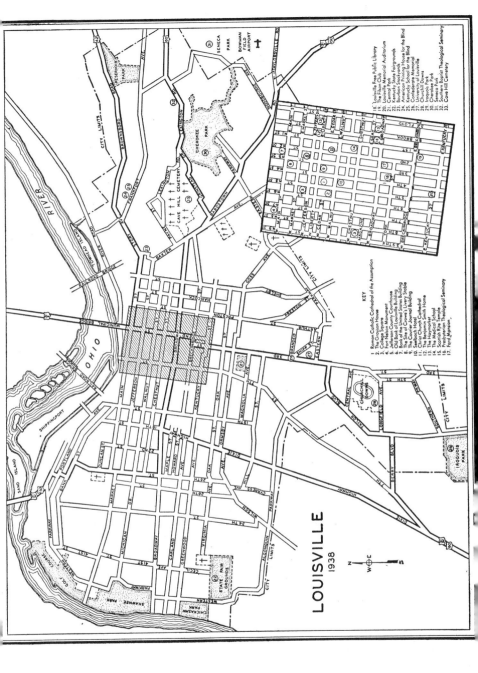

LOUISVILLE
1938

KEY

1. Roman Catholic Cathedral of the Assumption
2. The Grayson House
3. College Square
4. Fort Nelson Monument
5. Jefferson County Courthouse
6. Old Bank of Louisville Building
7. Bank of the United States Building
8. The Site of Crow's Livery Stable
9. The Courier-Journal Building
10. Seelbach Hotel
11. Christ Church Cathedral
12. The Benjamin Smith Home
13. The Harmony
14. The Medical School
15. Scottish Rite Temple
16. Presbyterian Theological Seminary
17. Ford Mansion

18. Louisville Free Public Library
19. The Filson Club
20. Louisville Memorial Auditorium
21. Central Park
22. Kentucky State Fairgrounds
23. Bourbon Stockyards
24. American Printing House for the Blind
25. Kentucky School for the Blind
26. Confederate Memorial
27. University of Louisville
28. Churchill Downs
29. Iroquois Park
30. Cherokee Park
31. Seneca Park
32. Southern Baptist Theological Seminary
33. Cave Hill Cemetery

mediate foreground, at the water's edge, is the only inland U.S. COAST GUARD STATION, established in 1881 to protect life at the Falls of the Ohio. Up to 1937 more than 9,000 persons had been rescued from drowning. Directly across the river is the Jeffersonville, Indiana, plant of the Colgate Company, bearing a great illuminated clock that tells time for people in Louisville. To the right is Towhead Island, so named because, prior to the building of the canal, it provided the up-harbor on the river between it and Shippingport harbor below the falls. Goods were transferred overland and boats were towed, except when periods of high water permitted navigation of the river channel.

Four bridges span the Ohio River at Louisville; one of them, generally known as the K. & I. (Kentucky and Indiana) bridge, is just over the falls and connects New Albany, Indiana, with Louisville, near North Thirty-second Street. It is a combined highway, trolley, and railroad bridge. The Pennsylvania Railroad bridge, built in 1870, is exclusively for railroad purposes. The Big Four Railroad bridge was rebuilt in 1928 to accommodate railroad and trolley traffic to Jeffersonville, Indiana. The MUNICIPAL BRIDGE, a giant steel structure 5,750 feet long, built in 1930 for highway traffic, runs from North Second Street to Jeffersonville. At the Kentucky end of the bridge tall stone pylons are surmounted by large wrought-iron lamps. In front of each of these fluted pylons is a lower pylon bearing in bas-relief the seal of Kentucky surmounted by an eagle. They were designed by Paul Cret of Philadelphia, who planned the Folger Shakespeare Library in Washington, D.C. A marker, erected in 1935 by the Colonial Dames of America on the Kentucky approach to the bridge, records La Salle's alleged discovery of the Ohio River in 1669.

7. BANK OF THE UNITED STATES BUILDING, 231 W. Main St., was built by the Government in 1832 to house the Louisville branch of the Bank of the United States. It is a brick structure two stories high, chiefly Greek Revival in design, now used as an office building.

8. The SITE OF CROWE'S LIVERY STABLE, 224 S. 3rd St., is occupied by a deserted brick building. About 1825 Thomas Crowe, a retired stagecoach driver, operated a livery on this plot, near which was the stage entrance to the old City Theater on Jefferson Street. Crowe had several slaves who were stable hands, among them one called Jim Crow. Jim was a jovial, elderly Negro, much deformed, with a high right shoulder and a stiff left leg as bowed as a new moon, which gave him an odd limp. One day in the spring of 1828 when the Drake Stock Company was playing at the City Theater, Thomas D. Rice, a member of the company, was standing at the theater entrance watching the old Negro and listening to him singing at work. At the end of each verse Jim gave a queer little jump, and when he came down, he set his "heel a rockin'."

The words of the refrain were:

Wheel about, turn about,
Do jes so;

An' every time I wheel about
I jump Jim Crow.

Rice was cast as a Kentucky cornfield slave in *The Rifle,* then playing at the theater. Drake reluctantly consented to let Rice insert the Jim Crow song. Rice made himself up like Jim Crow, sang his song, and did his queer little dance. The audience went wild. It is said that he was recalled 20 times the first night. The play ran for many nights to crowded houses. After that Thomas Rice was nicknamed "Jim Crow" Rice, and even as late as the forties he was still playing Jim Crow and other Negro impersonations. Jim Crow terminology, with its many variations dealing with the Negro, has developed from this character.

9. The COURIER-JOURNAL BUILDING, SW. corner S. 3rd and W. Liberty Sts., is a plain four-story dressed limestone structure built in 1858 by the U.S. Government as a post office and Federal building. It later became the home of the *Courier-Journal,* established in 1868 by a merger of the *Daily Journal* with the *Courier,* and Henry Watterson was made editor-in-chief *(see Press and Radio).* In August 1918 R. W. Bingham purchased the *Courier-Journal* and *Times* from the heirs of W. N. Haldeman. As editor emeritus, Henry Watterson continued to direct its policy until his death in 1921.

Robert Worth Bingham (1871–1937) was born in Orange County, N.C., and was graduated from the University of North Carolina in 1888. In his early twenties he became a resident of Louisville, where he was admitted to the bar, and received his degree in law from the University of Louisville in 1897. In Kentucky, Judge Bingham was best known as a publisher, though he served as mayor, chancellor of Jefferson Circuit Court, and county attorney before acquiring the two newspapers associated with his name. He was appointed U.S. Ambassador to Great Britain in 1933.

10. SEELBACH HOTEL, SW. corner S. 4th and W. Walnut Sts., has murals in the main lobby depicting the pioneer life and history of Kentucky and the Northwest Territory. This work was completed in 1904 by Arthur Thomas. The central panel shows Colonel Henderson calling to order the first legislature of Kentucky. Adjoining panels portray scenes in the life of Daniel Boone and Gen. George Rogers Clark in the march on Vincennes. Smaller panels of a pioneer distiller, a tobacco field slave, a pioneer farmer, and an Indian chief complete the series.

11. CHRIST CHURCH CATHEDRAL (Episcopal), 419 S. 2nd St., oldest church in the city, was built in 1822 after plans by Graham and Ferguson. It was originally a two-story building, almost square, with two tiers of windows. In 1872 the front wall was removed and the building extended west to Second Street. Two towers, one topped with a spire and cross, were included in the later Gothic Revival façade. Although the diocese of Kentucky was established in 1829, Christ Church was not consecrated until 1894.

12. The BENJAMIN SMITH HOME *(open 10–5 daily)*, 114 E. Jefferson St., now headquarters of the Union Gospel Mission, was built in 1827 by a retired Southern planter. It is a three-story house of Classical Revival design. Its massive walls are of brick with rusticated limestone trim. The façade is also of limestone and the four fluted monolithic columns of the portico were carved by hand. The rear and side walls are plastered and marked off to simulate stone. The original hand-wrought ironwork and light standards at the entrance are still in use. The rooms are finished in solid mahogany woodwork, Italian marble mantels, and finely etched glass. An oval spiral stairway winds from the first floor to the third.

13. The HAYMARKET *(open day and night throughout the year)*, E. Jefferson St. between S. Brook and S. Floyd Sts., in the 1880's was an abandoned railroad yard where farmers congregated to sell their hay and other produce. In order to protect the market place against intrusion by city buildings, the farmers formed a stock company in 1891, which today owns and administers the property. Stalls are rented to actual producers who, under the charter, pay no license to the city. No discrimination is made between near and distant producers so long as they can certify that the produce offered for sale is of their own raising. The market sells vegetables, fruits, honey, and other home-grown products.

14. The MEDICAL SCHOOL *(open 9–5 weekdays)*, 101 W. Chestnut St., is a three-story stone structure of Renaissance design, erected in 1893 for the Louisville Medical College. In 1909 it became the home of the original unit of the University of Louisville. Behind the older building is a modern four-story brick addition, built in 1935.

15. SCOTTISH RITE TEMPLE, 200 E. Gray St., neo-classic in design, is a huge building constructed of dressed Bedford stone. The pediment of the portico is supported by six thick Doric columns. The interior contains an auditorium seating 500 and a room paneled with cedar of Lebanon. The cedar, pronounced genuine by the Smithsonian Institution, was obtained from the estate of a French officer, who had taken it from the ruins of an ancient Syrian building.

16. PRESBYTERIAN THEOLOGICAL SEMINARY *(open 9–4 weekdays)*, 109 E. Broadway, forms an open quadrangle fronting on Broadway. It consists of several contiguous Tudor-Gothic style halls, the general mass resembling that of Balliol College, Oxford, England. The battlemented walls are faced with machine-tooled Bowling Green limestone, and the traceried windows are designed in the English perpendicular style. The seminary owns the Palestinian Archeological Collection of antiquarian articles from Palestine. In 1938 the institution had an enrollment of 62 students.

17. FORD MANSION, SW. corner W. Broadway and S. 2nd Sts., now occupied by the Y. W. C. A., was built in 1858 for James Ford, a retired Mississippi planter. The building was designed by the Louisville architect, Henry Whitestone, in a modified Italian Renaissance

style. Additions have been made, but the beauty of the original dressed stone façade is unchanged. Spaciousness and excellent decorative detail, carried out in finely carved rare wood, marble, and plaster, characterize the interior.

18. LOUISVILLE FREE PUBLIC LIBRARY *(open 9–9 weekdays, 2–6 Sun.)*, W. York St. between S. 3rd and S. 4th Sts., was designed by Tilscher and Tachau and opened to the public in 1908. The two-story building, French Renaissance in style, is T-shaped in plan and has a full basement. A wing to the right of the entrance is used as a reference room and that to the left for open bookshelves and general reading. Directly opposite the entrance is the circulation room decorated in the Louis XVI style. Its walls are finished in ivory and embellished with murals symbolizing the advance of civilization. Two stairways lead from this room to the balcony above, at one end of which is the original of Canova's *Hebe,* and at the other, Joel T. Hart's copy of the *Venus de Medici.* On the balcony is a room housing Henry Watterson's private library, which he bequeathed to the city. Adjoining it is the Civics Room, where files of the leading Kentucky, national, and foreign papers are on racks open to the public. In the basement is the MUNICIPAL MUSEUM, which contains collections of minerals, birds, butterflies, and fossils. On the grounds facing Fourth Street stands Barnard's heroic LINCOLN STATUE, and immediately in front of the building is Bouly's PRENTICE STATUE.

19. The FILSON CLUB *(open 9–5 weekdays)*, 118 W. Breckinridge St., a square, three-story red brick structure, has served since 1929 as the home of the historical society, which collects Kentuckiana. The eleventh volume of its magazine, *The Filson Club History Quarterly,* was completed in 1937. The *Quarterly* publishes current findings of society members and staff workers. The club was founded in 1884 and named for John Filson, first historian (1784) of the State of Kentucky. The library contains a large collection of books and manuscripts pertaining to the State.

In the MUSEUM on the second floor, which exhibits pioneer relics, are mementos of James D. (Jim) Porter, the Kentucky Giant, including his rifle, 7 feet 10 inches long, and his leather boot, 14½ inches long. Other Porter relics are preserved by descendants living in Shippingport.

Porter, the second tallest man in the world at the time he lived, was born in Portsmouth, Ohio, in 1810. A year later his parents moved to Shippingport where he remained the rest of his life. His phenomenal growth began at about the age of 17 and, as he said, while he was growing his mother had to sew an extra foot of cloth on his pantaloons every night. It was a favorite pastime of local people to measure Big Jim. An inch a week was his greatest record, and at the age of 24 he had achieved his full stature of 7 feet 9 inches, or "6 feet 21 inches" as he expressed it. Apprenticed to a cooperage, he outgrew his task of making barrels, then that of making hogsheads, and for a time he tried hack driving. Annoyed by the curious public, he gave that up to go into business as keeper of the Lone Star Tavern. After two years as a tavern proprietor, Porter built an 18-room house with doors, ceilings, and furniture on a scale to accommodate his stature. Charles Dickens, who visited him in 1842, described Porter "among men of six feet high and upwards, like a lighthouse walking among lamp-posts." Big Jim, a "powerful drinker," was joined in his sprees by little Elisha Reynolds, 5 feet 4 inches tall, his partner in the Tavern, which they ran until Porter's death in 1859. He was buried in Cave Hill Cemetery, Louisville.

20. LOUISVILLE MEMORIAL AUDITORIUM *(open by permission)*, NW. corner S. 4th and W. Kentucky Sts., is a massive neo-classic building of Bedford stone opened in 1929 as a memorial to Jefferson County soldiers, sailors, and marines who died in the World War. Ten fluted Doric columns support the entablature of the broad, shallow front portico; behind them are four huge entrance doorways. Above the colonnade is a high attic, adorned with classic bas-reliefs and surmounted with decorative tripods at the corners. Beneath the skylighted dome is the auditorium, seating 3,151. The interior is decorated in soft shades of blue and gray. Spanish marble surfaces the lower walls. Lectures, dramas, and occasional operas are presented on the stage. On the second floor is the Trophy Room where flags of the Allied and Associated Nations are displayed. Another memorial of the World War, set within a bit of the soil of France, is a weathered wooden cross that was erected above an American killed in battle and buried as a *Soldat Français Inconnue*. When the "unknown soldier's" nationality was determined by some trinket, he was returned to his native land, and with him came this graying cross.

21. CENTRAL PARK, S. 4th St. and Magnolia Ave., a 17-acre tract, contains several huge specimens of tulip poplar, survivors of the virgin forest. The natural amphitheater here is the scene of occasional pageants and civic gatherings. West of Central Park, extending along the railroad tracks for several blocks, is the locale of Alice Hegan Rice's *Mrs. Wiggs of the Cabbage Patch*. The land was originally used as a cabbage field. Then a sub-division was laid out, but the lots did not sell. Squatters came in and built shacks of materials salvaged from the nearby city dump. Comfortable homes now fill the area.

22. KENTUCKY STATE FAIRGROUNDS *(open throughout the year)*, 1400 Cecil Ave., were acquired in 1908, when the State Fair became a permanent institution, and the $100,000 livestock pavilion was built. The MERCHANTS AND MANUFACTURING BUILDING, erected in 1921, is devoted to industrial and commercial exhibitions. A LOG HOUSE, built and furnished in pioneer style, memorializes the pioneer home. In front of the grandstand is a half-mile track on which saddle racing is held daily during the State Fair in September. The feature of the fair is the Kentucky Horse Show, where native and foreign horses vie for honors. The standards of excellence include the breeding and quality of the horses and the showmanship of the trainers.

23. BOURBON STOCKYARDS *(open 9–2)*, SE. corner Main and

Johnson Sts., received its name because it is on the SITE OF BOURBON HOUSE, a drover's tavern of the early days where, according to tradition, Louis Philippe, later King of France, stayed for a time. Spring lamb marketing is one of the stockyards' most important activities.

24. AMERICAN PRINTING HOUSE FOR THE BLIND *(open 9–4:30 weekdays)*, 1839 Frankfort Ave., one of the largest and oldest establishments of its kind, prints Braille books for the blind. It was established in 1858, and was supported by individual subscription and by the State until Congress in 1879 made an annual appropriation of $10,000. In 1919 this grant was increased to $50,000. This publishing house, occupying a three-story brick building, supplies books for the blind in the United States and abroad. Its catalogue of published works lists more than 5,000 volumes, including standard works on the arts, sciences, history, travel, fiction, poetry, and general information.

25. KENTUCKY SCHOOL FOR THE BLIND *(open 9–4:30 weekdays)*, 1867 Frankfort Ave., designed in 1855 by F. Costigan, is Greek Revival in design. All outer walls are of stuccoed brick with stone trim, except the first story of the main building on the south elevation, which is of dressed stone, and is dominated by a graceful Ionic portico. Its three domes are visible from many points in the city.

TOUR 1

The tour—*26 m.*—begins at Third Street and Broadway in downtown Louisville, covers a portion of the boulevard system that practically encircles the city, passes through the older residential section, and into the more recently developed Highlands. It includes three of the city's finest parks and Cave Hill Cemetery, burial place of many distinguished former residents of the city.

S. from Broadway on S. 3rd St.

26. CONFEDERATE MEMORIAL, S. 3rd and Shipp Sts., is a large, tapering, Georgia granite shaft erected by the Kentucky Women's Confederate Monument Association in honor of Confederate soldiers. Cavalry and artillery groups are on two sides of the shaft. A medallion in the center depicts a mounted cavalryman. At the top is a square decorated with palm leaves, wreath, and crossed swords, on which stands a sentinel-like figure facing the North. His knapsack, canteen, and long rifle are characteristic of the Confederate infantry. This memorial, unveiled in 1895, was designed by the Louisville-born sculptress, Enid Yandell.

27. UNIVERSITY OF LOUISVILLE, on 55-acre Belknap Campus, S. 3rd and Shipp Sts., running to Eastern Parkway, is the oldest municipally owned university in America. The 1937 enrollment exceeded 3,500 students. The university started in 1837 as the Louisville Medical Institute. In 1846 the Institute and Louisville College were merged as the University of Louisville, and a law school was added. For half a century law and medicine were the only courses offered by the university. In 1907 the College of Liberal Arts was established

through a private fund. Since 1910 appropriations have been made by the city. In 1911 five medical schools amalgamated as the Medical School of the university. The School of Dentistry was added in 1918. In 1922 co-operation was arranged between the City Hospital and the university, and in the same year summer terms were initiated. In 1925 the present main campus was purchased and the Speed Scientific School established, and two years later the College of Music was organized.

On the left of the entrance is SPEED MEMORIAL MUSEUM *(open 10–5 Tues.-Sat., 2–5 Sun.)*, an Indiana limestone structure erected in memory of James B. Speed, prominent Louisville resident. The building contains a collection of pottery and porcelain by English, German, and Austrian artisans. Miniatures by English, American, French, Swedish, Russian, Austrian, and Persian artists of the past three centuries are also on display, among them *Lord Byron*, by C. Q. A. Bourgeois. Paintings of more than 100 artists include *The Arrival at the Inn*, by Vincent Augustus Tack, and portraits by Peale, Sully, Healy, and Matthew Harris Jouett.

Immediately beyond the Museum is a group of buildings housing many of the activities of the university proper. The Schools of Medicine and Dentistry and the Louisville Municipal College for Negroes are in downtown Louisville.

R. from S. 3rd St. on Central Ave.; L. on S. 6th St.

28. CHURCHILL DOWNS *(open)*, S. 7th St. and Central Ave., the 180-acre park-like tract of the Kentucky Jockey Club, provides one of the fastest tracks in the world for the 19-day spring and 10-day fall race meets and the Kentucky Derby, usually run the first or second Saturday in May. The green-trimmed white clubhouse and grandstands and the landscaped grounds have changed little in appearance since the course was opened in 1875. It was a 1½ mile track until 1896, when it was shortened to 1¼ miles. Under the main grandstand are pari-mutuel betting machines, pay-off windows, offices, and the café. To the right is the clubhouse, and to the left the Negro grandstand. Directly in front of the grandstand, the bluegrass lawn of the infield, broken by beds of flowers, shrubs, and low-growing trees, is enclosed by the white guard-rail of the mile oval. Beyond and facing the oval is a group of one-story green and white horse barns against a background of forest trees.

The Kentucky Derby, America's supreme racing event, open to the three-year-olds, was inaugurated in 1875 and has continued without a break. In 1912 Sotemia established a world's running record at Churchill Downs by doing 4 miles in 7:10⅘, and in 1931 Gallant Knight clipped another world's record for 6½ furlongs in 1:16⅕. Famous winners of the Derby include Bubbling Over (1926, time 2:03⅗) and War Admiral (1937, time 2:03⅕). The largest Derby purse was $55,375, won by Reigh Count in 1928. Lawrin was the first "winter horse" to win the Derby, being first over the line in 1938.

Retrace S. 6th; R. on S. 3rd, which at Kenton St. becomes Southern Parkway.

29. IROQUOIS PARK, Southern Parkway and Taylor Blvd., contains 676 acres of heavily wooded land acquired by the city in 1890 as the nucleus of the present park system. A roadway and footpaths wind from the base of Burnt Knob, center of the park, to its summit, from which the countryside can be seen for miles. Point Lookout has an elevation of 720 feet and looks down on Louisville, the Ohio River, and the Indiana hills to the north.

Retrace Southern Parkway; R. on Eastern Parkway to Cherokee Rd.

30. CHEROKEE PARK, Eastern Parkway at Cherokee Rd., is a rolling tract of 409 acres in the eastern section of the city. The Middle Fork of Beargrass Creek, winding through the area, is fed by springs from limestone cliffs above. The BIRD OBSERVATORY houses a large collection of mounted native Kentucky birds. In a wild spot is Enid Yandell's DANIEL BOONE STATUE, placed so that Boone, clad in his traditional hunting garb, seems to be stepping out of a thicket. The statue was presented to the city by C. C. Bickel.

Follow Cherokee Park Trail beside headwaters of Middle Fork of Beargrass Creek, past Big Rock to entrance of Seneca Park, just beyond the city limits.

31. SENECA PARK is a continuation of the city's park system. The trail climbs from the valley of Middle Fork and passes through a region of rolling green hills.

L. from Cherokee Trail on Beal's Branch Rd.; R. on Garden Dr.; L. on Lexington Rd.

32. SOUTHERN BAPTIST THEOLOGICAL SEMINARY (*open 9–4:30 weekdays*), 2825 Lexington Rd., a group of Georgian Colonial buildings of red faced brick with dressed Bowling Green stone trim, is situated in a 55-acre grove of huge beech trees. NORTON HALL, three stories high, contains administration offices, museum, and library.

The MUSEUM (*open by appointment*) has exhibits of the Departments of History, Religion, and Missions. An eleventh century Greek parchment of the Four Gospels and a reprint of the 1587 "Breeches Bible" are among the rare items. The seminary was first opened in Greenville, S.C., in 1859. It closed during the War between the States, re-opened in 1865, and in 1877 was moved to Louisville, where it operated in its own buildings on Fifth Street and Broadway until 1926, when it was moved to the present location. The 1937–38 attendance was more than 400.

L. from Lexington Rd. on Grinstead Dr.; R. opposite head of Ray Ave., through rear entrance to Cave Hill Cemetery.

33. CAVE HILL CEMETERY, main entrance at Baxter Ave. and E. Broadway, is a 291-acre burying ground containing the graves of famous men and women, among them Gen. George Rogers Clark and George Keats, brother of the English poet. Six miles of driveway, planted with trees, shrubbery, and flowers, wind through park-like grounds that overlook downtown Louisville. Near the main entrance stands a lofty campanile, its clock tower surmounted by a life-size white marble copy of Thorwaldsen's *Angel*. Lower, in a niche, is a copy of the same sculptor's *Christ*.

POINTS OF INTEREST IN ENVIRONS

Fort Knox, *32 m. (see Tour 7)*. Monument and Tomb of Zachary Taylor, *7.2 m. (see Tour 12)*. My Old Kentucky Home, *39.6 m. (see Tour 15)*.

LEXINGTON

Railroad Stations: Union Station, Viaduct and E. Main St., for Louisville & Nashville R.R., and Chesapeake & Ohio Ry.; S. Broadway and Angliana Ave. for Southern Ry.

Bus Station: Union Station, 244 E. Main St. for Greyhound, Fleenor, Nunnelly, Phillips and Cooper Lines.

Airport: Municipal, *6 m.* N. on Newtown Pike; chartered planes, no scheduled service.

Buses: Fare 5¢.

Accommodations: Five hotels.

Information Service: Lafayette Hotel, E. Main St. at Union Station Viaduct; Phoenix Hotel, Main and Limestone Sts.; Board of Commerce, Main and Upper Sts.; Bluegrass Auto Club, Esplanade.

Radio Station: WLAP (1420 kc.).

Theaters and Motion Picture Houses: Little Theater, Transylvania College and Guignol Theater, University of Kentucky, monthly civic talent plays; six motion picture houses.

Swimming: Municipal Pool, Castlewood City Park, 25¢; Clay's Ferry, *15 m.* on US 25; Valley View, *15 m.* S. on Tates Creek Rd.; Boonesboro, *25 m.* S. via US 25; Joyland Park, *3 m.* N. on US 27; Johnson's Mill, *12 m.* N. on Newtown Rd.

Golf: Picadome, S. Broadway extended, 18 holes, greens fee 50¢ Mon.-Fri., 75¢ Sat. and Sun.

Tennis: Woodland Park, Woodland and High Sts., free; Duncan Park, Limestone and 5th Sts., free; University of Kentucky, Rose St., 10¢ per hour; Castlewood Park, Bryan Station Rd. and Castlewood Drive, free.

Riding: 123rd Kentucky Cavalry Club, Henry Clay Blvd., 75¢ per hour. Lexington Riding School, Tates Creek Pike, 75¢.

Racing: Keeneland, *5 m.* W. on US 60, running races (mutuel betting), April and October.

Trots: Kentucky Trotting Horse Breeders' Association, S. Broadway extended, June and September.

Polo: Iroquois Hunt and Polo Grounds, *6 m.* E. on US 60, June through September.

Annual Events: Blessing of Hounds, beginning of hunt season, November, Iroquois Hunt Club; May Day Festivals, University of Kentucky and Transylvania College; Junior League Horse Show (Saddle Horses), latter part of July; Tobacco Carnival; Farm and Home Convention, University of Kentucky, November.

> For further information regarding this city, see LEXINGTON AND THE BLUEGRASS COUNTRY, another of the American Guide Series, published April 1938 by the city of Lexington, Ky.

LEXINGTON (957 alt., 45,736 pop.), third largest city in Kentucky, lies on a rolling plateau in the heart of the Bluegrass Country. The golden stallion weathervane on the Fayette County Courthouse symbolizes an aristocracy of horses. An early law passed in this county just after the Revolution was designed to keep the blood of race horses pure. The law was superfluous. The city has few industries except those that have to do with tobacco and horses; and it preserves and advances education and culture.

Lexington draws shoppers and sightseers from the farms and small cities of the Bluegrass, and from the more distant hills. It is unusually busy on Saturday nights when farmers and horse breeders and Negro farm hands come to town. In early fall about 4,000 students of the University of Kentucky and of Transylvania College pour into the city.

In December, January, and February, the tobacco auctions are held. By wagon, bus, and truck, a-horse and in limousine, on shanks' mare and thoroughbred, come tobacco growers, buyers, auctioneers, warehousemen and officials of billion-dollar cigarette companies, all bound for the 26 huge tobacco warehouses. Often $40,000,000 is exchanged over the baskets of sorted tobacco leaves in this important looseleaf light burley tobacco mart. During this season Lexington's Main Street (the Dixie Highway through the city) is a particularly active shopping thoroughfare. Stores in old and new buildings are concentrated on Main Street between Broadway and Rose, and on intersecting side streets. There are few modern buildings—most of them date from the War between the States, and they bear their age with dignity.

Just north of Main Street are the churches, the public buildings, the old Georgian Colonial houses with gleaming white doorways, highly polished door knockers, and ivy-clad walls. Just south of Main Street are the railroad tracks flanked by livestock, wool, bluegrass seed, and grain warehouses and markets, and a rooming house, pawnshop, and saloon district.

The University of Kentucky is only a few blocks farther south on Limestone Street, and the university boys and girls overflow into Main Street, where comfortable and well-dressed Bluegrass folk stroll, rubbing elbows with hill people in less fancy clothes, city business men, tobacco men, horse breeders and horse buyers.

Scattered through all the better sections of town are some of the big old homes, set back among trees and shrubs and well-kept lawns. Local industry has never driven the old families out of their early homes.

The Negroes make up more than a third of the population, and live in their own sections in the northeast and the southwest. Partly because they are integrated in Lexington life, their place is fixed and fairly secure; they are cooks, horse trainers, farm hands, servants, and local laborers. They have their churches and burying societies, their choirs and their parties, and they have made substantial progress in education and home ownership.

The city was named after the Battle of Lexington by Robert Patterson, Simon Kenton, and others who in June 1775 were camped nearly opposite the present Lexington Cemetery while on their way to build a fort near the Kentucky River. Four years later the town was founded when a blockhouse was put up at Main and Mill Streets and in 1782 the General Assembly of Virginia granted it a charter.

In 1784 Gen. James A. Wilkinson, friend of Washington, entered his checkered western career by opening a store in the village. The next year the first tavern hung out its hospitable sign on West Main Street: "Entertainment for man and beast, by James Bray." In 1787 Transylvania Seminary was removed here from Danville. The first issue of John Bradford's *Kentucky Gazette* appeared in the same year.

Merchants brought wares from Philadelphia and Baltimore, accepting in payment ginseng, homespun linens, and cured meats. Hemp, a fine cash crop, and lumber, tobacco, and whisky were exported. Money was scarce, barter common. Change was made by cutting coins into halves, quarters, and eighths.

Raw materials were made into shoes, hats, woolen goods, ducking, white lead, and other commodities. Most important of all was the making of hemp rope for ships' rigging. Lexington was the chief industrial city of Kentucky until about 1820 when the paddlewheeler began industrializing the Ohio Valley and attracting inland industrial plants to the river bank.

One early industry that the Ohio River had nothing to do with was the breeding of light horses—thoroughbreds, trotters, and saddle horses. "They may race 'the ponies' at Louisville, Santa Anita, Paris, France, or Timbuctoo," says the staunch booster of Lexington, "but they breed them, and they rear them, and they train them at Lexington." It was a horse named Lexington, foaled in 1850 at The Meadows, an estate nearby, that founded the family of Fair Play, Man o' War, and War Admiral, and men say there are others here as good.

The men from Virginia and Maryland who settled the city rode their best horses over the mountains, or floated them on flatboats down the Kentucky River. The first impromptu Lexington races were held in 1787, and the first jockey club was organized 10 years later. In the early years of the next century breeding stallions were imported from England and Arabia. From these came the modern race horse *(see Kentucky Horses)*.

By 1800 schools of medicine and law had been added to Transylvania, making the town one of the most important academic centers in the West. Notables came to the town and college: Henry Clay led a group of men who for fifty years spread the fame of the college and Lexington across the Nation.

In 1830 Lexington started to build the Lexington and Ohio Railroad, which was finished in 1832 to a point six miles west of the town. That year the town became a city.

Despite a cholera epidemic that swept the Bluegrass in 1833, killing 500 in the city alone, the young metropolis at the end of the decade was riding high on increased farming and light horse and livestock breeding. The richest money crop of those days was hemp, which went into the rigging of Yankee clippers. The soil was also fine for tobacco, which became much more important to the city.

The nation-wide panic of 1837 stifled Lexington business. Then, as the city was getting back on its feet, North and South came to blows. Although it gave a cavalry general, John Hunt Morgan, to the South, and Jefferson Davis went to school here, Lexington also spilled its blood for the Union.

The War between the States, however, established the cigarette market. Before the war, men were content to chew tobacco or smoke an occasional cigar; but soldiers began "rolling their own" with bits of tobacco, and unconsciously started one of America's biggest industries. When the war was over they carried a craving for cigarettes to all corners of an expanding Nation. It was a good thing for Lexington, because steam was driving the clipper from the seas, and Lexington's hemp lay unsold.

Lexington after the war, however, concentrated primarily on horses. In the 1870's, when the bookmakers appeared and betting became an industry, racing again revived—and with it Lexington's favorite work of breeding, rearing, and training thoroughbreds. The great horse farms began to revive; wealthy easterners, attracted to the Bluegrass, started to buy land, build estates, and raise horses. Neighborly dash races were held, and stallion shows were feature events just outside of town.

During the war, the State-supported University of Kentucky was started in the city. It took over much of Transylvania's work, whose faculty and students were scattered by the war. Transylvania later affiliated with the College of the Bible and specialized in religious teachings. Growing swiftly after 1900, the university was modernized and expanded, and today it ranks high among State educational institutions.

The World War boomed the cigarette industry. Tobacco sales and prices went so high that Lexington did not suffer much when prohibition came and closed the distilleries. With record crops and soaring prices, tobacco money became plentiful in the Bluegrass and its capital. When Lexington celebrated its sesquicentennial with a round of speech-making and pageantry in 1925, it was a wealthy and going city.

The 1929 crash hit the city hard for a while. Poverty-stricken farmers in other States and in Kentucky all began to grow tobacco. Prices held up until excess production cut them sharply in 1932. They lay at rock bottom until the great drought in the middle thirties, and then began to rise gradually. In 1937 Lexington markets, which open before any others in the Burley Belt, cashed in on a record crop which sold at the high average of $22.45 a hundredweight.

The University of Kentucky is one of the most important sources of business in the town. Each year thousands of school children, farmers, ministers, and others flock into Lexington to attend conferences and athletic contests conducted under the auspices of the university. Hundreds of research people come annually to the town to use the rare materials contained in the two university libraries and the Lexington public library. The combined facilities of these libraries constitute a notable collection of Americana, especially that relating to the Ohio Valley.

POINTS OF INTEREST

1. ASHLAND *(private)*, SE. corner Sycamore and Richmond Rds., was the home of Henry Clay (1777–1852). The present house, reconstructed by Maj. T. Lewinski, Lexington architect, dates from 1857 and although it follows the same plan as the original designed by Latrobe and built for Clay in 1806, the architectural detail is greatly changed. Set back from the street among trees planted by Clay, the two-story central mass of this great brick house is flanked by one-story wings. The main entrance projects in the form of a bay; the simple doorway has a half-circle fanlight and plain molded architrave and cornice. The Palladian window above is accentuated by a small eave pediment that relieves the straight cornice line of the roof.

Beside the house is a thick pine grove, and the path Clay liked to pace as he composed his speeches. Mrs. Clay's garden, laid out by L'Enfant, is behind the house. Beyond the south lawn were the slave quarters and barns, with the great estate, on which Clay bred fine cattle and horses, spreading away to the south.

Clay lived here from 1797 until his death in 1852. Becoming a United States Senator at 29, he formulated and championed the "American System" based on a protective tariff. He advocated aggression in the War of 1812 and was one of the commissioners who concluded the peace. Clay was Speaker of the House of Representatives, Senator, and Secretary of State, but he failed in his life's ambition—to reach the Presidency.

2. CHURCH OF THE GOOD SHEPHERD (Episcopal), E. Main St. and Bell Court, neo-Gothic in style, dedicated in 1926, is known as the "Horseman's Church" because Bluegrass horsemen gave generously toward its building. In the interior are carvings by Gustav Lang, brother of Anton Lang, famous Christus in the *Passion Play* of Oberammergau.

3. The SENATOR POPE HOME *(open by appointment)*, 326 Grosvenor Ave., a two-story red brick structure built soon after the War of 1812, is now an apartment house. The balcony above the deeply recessed, arched entrance is part of the original design, but the porches that flank it are of later date.

John Pope, for whom the house was built, was United States Senator from Kentucky, 1807–13. At this house on July 3–4, 1819, he entertained President Monroe, Gen. Andrew Jackson, Gov. Isaac Shelby, and others.

One-armed Senator John Pope was a strong political opponent of Henry Clay. During one of their races for Congress, Clay approached an Irishman and asked him why he was going to vote for his opponent. The Irishman replied, "Och, Misther Clay, I have concluded to vote for the man who has but one arm to sthrust into the sthreasury."

4. The JOSEPH FICKLIN HOUSE *(private)*, SW. corner High and S. Limestone Sts., is a plain red brick late Georgian Colonial house. Here in the 1820's lived Lexington's postmaster, Joseph Ficklin, and with him Jefferson Davis during the three years (1821–24) that he was a student at Transylvania University.

5. BOTHERUM *(private)*, 341 Madison Pl., was designed and built in the 1850's for Maj. Madison C. Johnson by architect John McMurtry. The trees on the lawn and a profusion of vines veil the Greek Revival one-story stone mansion. Massive stone steps lead up to the four entrances, one to a side. White Corinthian columns support low porticos on each façade. A deep-sunken brick walk leads out from the north façade to the property line, beyond which stands a giant ginkgo tree, sent from Japan to Henry Clay, who gave it to his friend. Major Johnson is said to have been the prototype for Col. Romulus Fields in James Lane Allen's story, *Two Gentlemen of Kentucky*.

6. LEXINGTON CEMETERY, W. Main St. at city limits, is the burial place of many of Lexington's illustrious men, including James Lane Allen, John C. Breckinridge, John Hunt Morgan, and Henry Clay. The HENRY CLAY MEMORIAL (1857) has a large square base from which rises a lone Corinthian column supporting a statue of Clay. The original, designed by Joel T. Hart and cast by John Hailey of Frankfort, was destroyed by lightning in 1903. The statue now in place, copied from the Hart design, is the work of Charles J. Mulligan. Within the base of the monument are the sarcophagi of Clay and his wife.

7. GLENDOWER or PRESTON PLACE *(private)*, W. 2nd St. between Jefferson and Georgetown Sts., now a nurses' dormitory connected with St. Joseph's Hospital, was built early in the nineteenth century. Here Robert Wickliffe, Col. John Todd's son-in-law, entertained lavishly. After William Preston, aide on the staff of Confederate Gen. Albert Sidney Johnston, and son-in-law of Wickliffe, became owner of the property, its reputation for hospitality was equaled only by that of Col. David Meade's La Chaumière.

8. The MARY TODD LINCOLN HOME *(open by appointment)*, 574 W. Main St., is the Georgian Colonial red brick house where Mary Todd lived as a child and at the time she married Abraham Lincoln. It is now a rooming house, and a grocery store occupies half of the first floor.

Mary Todd was born December 13, 1818, on West Short Street where the Roman Catholic parish house now stands. Her mother died when Mary was seven years old. An older sister, Elizabeth, married the son and namesake of Gov. Ninian Wirt Edwards, and moved to Springfield, Illinois. Completing her education in the private schools of Lexington, Mary went to live with Elizabeth, at whose home she met a young lawyer named Abraham Lincoln. They kept company, quarreled to the breaking point in 1840, married in 1842, and made Springfield their home. From Springfield Mary went to the White

1. Ashland
2. Church of the Good Shepherd
3. The Senator Pope Home
4. The Joseph Ficklin House
5. Botherum
6. Lexington Cemetery
7. Glendower or Preston Place
8. The Mary Todd Lincoln Home
9. First Presbyterian Church
10. The Thomas Hart Home
11. Hopemont
12. The Benjamin Gratz Home
13. Transylvania College
14. Lexington Public Library
15. The Bodley House
16. Christ Church
17. Courthouse Square
18. The Tobacco Markets
19. The Trotting Track
20. University of Kentucky
21. "Lexington's Westminster Abbey"
22. The William Morton Home

23. Loudoun
24. Sayre College
25. Whitehall
26. Rose Hill
27. Phoenix Hotel

LEXINGTON
1938

House. After Lincoln's assassination, she traveled about, and then sought sanctuary at the home of her sister Elizabeth, where she died in 1882. She was buried beside her husband in Springfield.

9. FIRST PRESBYTERIAN CHURCH, 174 N. Mill St., designed by Cincinnatus Shryock and completed in 1872, is the home of a church congregation organized in the late eighteenth century.

10. The THOMAS HART HOME *(private)*, 193 N. Mill St., a two-story Georgian Colonial brick house, was built in 1794 for Thomas Hart, whose daughter, Lucretia, married Henry Clay here. The young couple lived in the attached house on North Hill Street until Ashland was ready for them. In this building lived John Bradford, editor of the *Kentucky Gazette,* John Hunt Morgan, Confederate leader (who also was married here), and Cassius M. Clay, the emancipationist.

11. HOPEMONT *(open 10–5 weekdays; adm. 25¢),* 201 N. Mill St., the John Hunt Morgan home, is a post-Colonial white-painted brick mansion built in 1811 by John Wesley Hunt, grandfather of John Hunt Morgan. House and grounds are about as they were on the day in 1861 when grandson Morgan rode away at the head of the Lexington Rifles to join the Confederate Army. An extensive Confederate museum has been installed in the home, filled with treasures of five generations of Hunts and Morgans.

The house is entered through a doorway capped with an elliptical fanlight and flanked by traceried side lights. Immediately within is the reception hall and the room that John H. Morgan used as a business office, which contains many of his personal belongings. To the rear of the reception hall is the dining room, off which a long living room looks out upon the flower garden.

Above stairs and below are Morgan family portraits and prints. In the basement are the kitchens, storerooms, and servants' quarters of slavery days, and in the rear of the main structure is a wing with additional living quarters for the household. Behind this wing are the carriage house and the stable where Morgan's Black Bess was kept.

John Hunt Morgan (1825–1864), born in Huntsville, Alabama, grew up in Lexington. He saw service as a first lieutenant in the Mexican War, and in the War between the States became a Confederate general with a roving commission to hamper the southward advance of the Union Armies. Early in July 1863 he raided Indiana and Ohio, and on July 26 was captured near New Lisbon, Ohio. On November 27 he escaped from the penitentiary at Columbus, Ohio, rejoined the Armies of the South, took command in the department of southwestern Virginia, and later at Jonesboro, Georgia. On September 4, 1864, he was killed in Greeneville, Tennessee. His grave is in Lexington Cemetery.

12. The BENJAMIN GRATZ HOME *(private),* 231 N. Mill St., is an excellent example of the late Georgian Colonial style. The exterior is distinguished by a fine hand-wrought iron railing on the entrance stoop and a wide arched doorway with paneled door, flanked by side lights, and surmounted by an elliptical fanlight of leaded glass. This

house was built for Mrs. Mary G. Maton in 1806. In 1824 Benjamin Gratz, brother of Rebecca, came to Lexington from Philadelphia and bought the property. Members of the Gratz family have lived in this house continuously since that date. In the rear, abutting a side street, stands what is said to be the OLDEST BRICK BUILDING in Lexington, used as a laundry for the household.

13. TRANSYLVANIA COLLEGE, W. 3rd St. between Upper St. and Broadway, with an enrollment of 500 students, is maintained by the Christian Church (Disciples of Christ). Its several red brick ivy-covered buildings and Greek Revival Morrison College are distributed over a small campus.

Transylvania College, oldest educational institution west of the Alleghenies, grew out of an act of the Virginia Legislature of 1780 setting aside 8,000 acres of confiscated Tory land in Kentucky for the development of higher education. Twelve thousand acres were added in 1783, and in 1785 Transylvania Seminary was opened in the home of "Old Father Rice," near Danville. Three years later this seminary was removed to Lexington, where the first building was erected in 1794. Following a dispute over doctrinal matters, Presbyterians on the board seceded and set up a school known as Kentucky Academy at Pisgah, 11 miles west of Lexington. In 1798 Transylvania Academy and Kentucky Academy were merged as Transylvania University.

Transylvania took high rank among early educational institutions. In its Law College, where Henry Clay was a professor (1805–07), were trained many of the early leaders of the legal and political life of the West. Dr. Samuel Brown, pioneer in smallpox vaccination, founded the College of Medicine (1799), which in its first 60 years graduated more than 2,000 physicians. Affiliated with Transylvania is the College of the Bible, a post-graduate theological school.

MORRISON COLLEGE is a Greek Revival brick building designed by the Lexington architect Gideon Shryock and completed in 1833. The three-story structure has a massive two-story Doric portico with fluted columns, approached by a broad flight of steps. In one of the vaults flanking the steps are the remains of Constantine Rafinesque. Born in Turkey, of French and German descent, Rafinesque settled in America in 1815. He was one of the strangest and most brilliant figures of the middle frontier, an authority on natural history, especially botany, shells, fishes, banking and political history. At Transylvania he was professor of modern languages, practically founding that subject in America, and was possibly the first to give illustrated lectures. In 1824 he published *Ancient History: or Annals of Kentucky*, and his later works on American flora were authoritative for their day. Traversing the wilderness hunting specimens, bearded and oddly clad, with a pack on his back, he was often taken by the natives for an itinerant peddler, and many pranks were played on him by John James Audubon and other wilderness men. The LIBRARY *(open 8–4 Mon.-Fri., 8–12:15 Sat.)* was long rated one of the best in the United States. Its collection of medical books is especially notable. RUSH MUSEUM *(open by appointment)* has good collections of bird specimens and classroom apparatus used a century ago in natural science classes.

14. LEXINGTON PUBLIC LIBRARY *(open 8:30–9 weekdays; 2–6 Sun.)*, W. 2nd St. between Market and N. Mill Sts., was organized in 1795 as a pay library endowed by annual subscriptions, and is the oldest circulating library west of the Alleghenies. In 1903 Andrew Carnegie gave $60,000 toward the construction of the present building. The library has numerous volumes on the history of Lexington and the Bluegrass, and a file of rare newspapers, including issues of the old *Kentucky Gazette*.

On the second floor, at the head of the stairs, is a case containing a collection of coins, State money, "shinplasters," and other early curios; and in another is a collection of stuffed Bluegrass song birds, among them the Kentucky cardinal, "redbird" of the South.

15. The BODLEY HOUSE *(private)*, 200 Market St., an old post-Colonial house once the property of Col. Thomas Bodley, War of 1812 veteran, was built soon after that war. During the War between the States this home was a headquarters for Union troops, and Dr. Benjamin Winslow Dudley, surgeon and Transylvania professor, owned it for a time.

16. CHRIST CHURCH (Episcopal), NE. corner Church and Market Sts., a Victorian Gothic structure designed by Maj. T. Lewinski, stands on a site occupied by Episcopal churches since 1796. The cornerstone of the present brick building was laid in 1847. The chimes in the tower were given by Mrs. Rosa Johnson Rhett in memory of her mother, Rose Vertner Jeffrey, Bluegrass poetess.

17. COURTHOUSE SQUARE, W. Main St. between Upper St. and Cheapside, is in the center of downtown Lexington. Within the park-like area stands FAYETTE COUNTY COURTHOUSE, a massive three-story stone building designed in the Romanesque style, surmounted by a dome above which swings the golden stallion weather vane.

On the east lawn of the square is the equestrian STATUE OF JOHN HUNT MORGAN, showing him sitting in full uniform upon his charger. Among the names on the plaque of the SOLDIER'S MEMORIAL, World War monument before the Main Street entrance, is that of a woman, Curry Desha Brickinridge, Red Cross nurse. On the west side of the square in CHEAPSIDE PARK is the BRECKINRIDGE STATUE, erected by the State of Kentucky in memory of John Cabell Breckinridge (1821–1875), Lexington lawyer who at 30 was elected U.S. Representative, and at 35, Vice President of the United States. At the Baltimore Convention of 1860 he was nominated for the Presidency by pro-slavery seceders from the convention. With the outbreak of the War between the States, Breckinridge joined the Confederate army, was put in command of the Kentucky Brigade under Gen. Albert Sidney Johnston, and in January 1865 became Confederate Secretary of War.

Throughout the years Cheapside has been an open-air forum where men with causes, or no causes at all, air their opinions. Statesmen and office seekers harangue the passing crowd. The strolling ballad singer finds a sympathetic audience. An occasional group of worshipers gather about the fountains for prayer and praise. Perched on the base of the Breckinridge Memorial, a lanky religious exhorter sometimes tells his little circle of listeners about death and judgment to come.

18. The TOBACCO MARKETS *(open from first Mon. in Dec. until about March 1)* are held in southwestern Lexington, in the heart of the tobacco warehousing district. Here, in 26 handling houses, called "sales floors," the "brown gold" crop of the Bluegrass is sold. Several times during each winter these sales floors are cleared, filled with new deliveries from the farms, and cleared again, until the last of the crop has moved on to processors.

The tobacco, known to the farmer and the tobacco merchant simply as "white burley," comes to the sales floor cured and graded by the farmer. His entire crop is arranged, according to quality, in baskets upon each of which an agent of the warehouse has placed a starting bid. Down the narrow aisle between the high-piled baskets pass auctioneer, bidders, and gallery. The auctioneer, sing-songing a sales jargon, unintelligible to the visitor, tries to drum up the bid. The jew's-harp chant goes on continually, interrupted only by a nod, a wink, or a word spoken by competing buyers. An unsatisfactory bid can be rejected by the owner, whose lot is then held for a subsequent sale.

Close on the heels of the main actors shuffles the gallery, straining forward to catch every shift in the action, for upon these sales depends the good or ill fortune of the year.

19. The TROTTING TRACK (1873), S. on Broadway in the rear of Tattersall's Sales Stables, is the mile oval of the Kentucky Trotting Horse Breeders' Association. Spring and fall meets on the Grand Circuit are held here on what horsemen believe to be the fastest trotting strip in the world. Twenty American trotting and pacing records have been made on this track. In 1937, Alma Sheppard, 11 years old, drove Dean Hanover over the track in 1:58½. This horse was given to the girl by her father, when no one else seemed to be able to do anything with him. She trained him herself, entered him in the race, and set one of the track records, only 2½ seconds from the world's record. Other records made on this track include the fastest three heats, by Rosaline in 1937; trotting record with mate against time, Uhlan (1:54½) 1913; trotting record by team, Uhlan and Louis Forest, 1912. One of the two world records broken in 1938 was the mile pacing time of Dan Patch in 1905, shattered by Billy Direct (1:55).

20. UNIVERSITY OF KENTUCKY *(buildings open daily except Sun. and holidays)*, S. Limestone St. and Euclid Ave., was established in 1866 as a land-grant college (following the passage of the Morrill Act in 1862) and became part of Kentucky University, formerly Transylvania University. The Agricultural and Mechanical divisions were located on the Henry Clay farm, Ashland, but due to unfavorable financial arrangements the Agricultural and Mechanical college was transferred to its present location, and completely separated from Kentucky

University. The university has been on its present 94-acre campus since 1878.

The plant, excluding the experimental farm, consists of forty-eight buildings located somewhat at random on the campus. On the left of the north gate entrance is the NEW STUDENT UNION BUILDING, which houses all the offices of the student activities, the ball and assembly rooms, the cafeteria and other shops. Beyond and immediately to the left is FRAZEE HALL in which are the departments of Sociology, Philosophy, History, and University Extension.

The oldest classroom building now in use is the classic revival ADMINISTRATION BUILDING, at the top of the hill facing the parade ground and Limestone Street, which houses the administrative offices. East of the Administration Building are the Archeological Museum (Old Library), the Faculty Club (Patterson home), Lafferty Hall, and the Library. The Faculty Club building is typical of the homes built in Kentucky during the latter part of the nineteenth century. Lafferty Hall is modern in design and typifies the plan of the buildings which have been constructed since 1935. The LIBRARY, the first unit of which has been completed, was constructed in 1931 and is Georgian in design. It houses the university's collection of approximately 270,000 books and pamphlets. This is the largest and most complete library collection in the State.

East of the Library is MAXWELL PLACE, the home of the President of the university. The house, Italian Renaissance in design, was formerly the home of James Hilary Mulligan.

West of the library is a hall which houses the State department of Mines and Geology, and the university department of Botany. To the south beyond the library are the Physics and Chemistry buildings. Across the open court to the south is McVey Hall, a classroom building. At the end of the quadrangle is the new 1939 Biological Science Building.

West of McVey Hall in the center of the large commons is the MEMORIAL HALL, of Greek Revival design with a Christopher Wren tower. The building was erected by public subscription as a memorial to Kentucky's World War dead. On the left and right of the foyer are memorial plaques and on the wall facing the entrance is a large mural depicting the growth of the State. The auditorium seats eleven hundred. Immediately west of Memorial Hall is the College of Agriculture Building.

North of Memorial Hall is the Engineering College quadrangle. Directly west of the quadrangle is Neville Hall and farther west, facing the front circular drive, is the building which houses the university dispensary and the classrooms of the department of Hygiene.

To the north and rear of Neville Hall is the Natural Science Building, which houses the geological library and exhibits. West of the Administration Building, across Limestone and Upper Streets, is the College of Education and Associated Schools, a Greek Revival building of three units. East on Euclid from its intersection with Limestone are other buildings of the university.

Across Graham Avenue to the south are some of the experimental buildings of the College of Agriculture, and at Graham Avenue and Limestone Street is the Agricultural Experiment Station with its laboratories and offices. The UNIVERSITY FARM of 620 acres is on the east side of Rose Street beginning at Graham Avenue.

The university is composed of seven colleges, the Experiment Station, and the Department of University Extension. The enrollment is approximately 3,700 and about 2,000 students attend the summer sessions.

The Experiment Station has associated with it the sub-station of 15,000 acres at Quicksand, and the sub-station of 600 acres at Princeton.

21. "LEXINGTON'S WESTMINSTER ABBEY," E. 3rd St. between Walnut and Deweese Sts., is a local name for several old cemeteries dating from the years immediately after the 1833 cholera epidemic. Within this area lie members of the Bradford family; John Grimes, the artist whose portrait by Jouett hangs in the Metropolitan Art Museum; John Postlethwait, early innkeeper; and many other old-time residents. The SEXTON'S COTTAGE, designed by John McMurtry, is an excellent example of a Tudor cottage. The little GREEK TEMPLE was erected by Gideon Shryock as a memorial to his parents.

22. The WILLIAM MORTON HOME (Duncan Park Day Nursery), NE. corner N. Limestone and 5th Sts., was built and furnished on a lavish scale in 1810 by William ("Lord") Morton, younger son of a titled English family. After the death of "Lord" Morton in 1836, the place became the home of Cassius M. Clay.

23. LOUDOUN (*open 8:30–5:30 weekdays*), Bryan Ave. and Castlewood Dr., now the city's Castlewood Community Center, was erected in 1850 by Francis K. Hunt, son of a pioneer Lexington industrialist. Architect John McMurtry designed the building in the Gothic Revival style, and embellished it with pointed-arch windows, a battlemented turret, hand-carved woodwork, and Jacobean chimneys.

24. SAYRE COLLEGE (*open weekdays on request, during school year*), 194 N. Limestone St., preparatory school dating from 1854, was among the first schools in America to offer women a full college curriculum. It is housed in three red brick buildings, each three stories high.

In the basement of Sayre is BARLOW PLANETARIUM, invented in 1844 by Thomas Harris Barlow of Lexington. Designed to illustrate the activity of the solar system, this invention so simplified the teaching of astronomy that 300 like it were manufactured and sold to the United States Government, public institutions, and colleges throughout the world. Only a few are still in use.

25. WHITEHALL (*private*), NE. corner Limestone and Barr Sts., a two-story white brick structure in the Greek Revival style, designed by Gideon Shryock and built 1834–36 for the Wear family, stands well back from Limestone Street. Here in the 1850's lived Thomas Marshall, a descendant of Chief Justice John Marshall.

26. ROSE HILL *(private)*, 461 N. Limestone St., a low, rambling Georgian Colonial structure, was built in 1818 by John Brand, hemp manufacturer. The entrance is copied after that of the Temple of Minerva in the Maison Carrée of Nîmes, France.

27. PHOENIX HOTEL, 120 E. Main St., stands on the SITE OF POSTLETHWAIT'S TAVERN. In the lobby hang pictures of great Kentucky thoroughbreds. The dining room behind the lobby is finished in early English tavern style. The coffee shop displays medallions of prominent Kentuckians.

In 1790 Capt. John Postlethwait, Revolutionary officer, came to Lexington and for 43 years put his finger into every Lexington pie. He was trader, merchant, innkeeper, and generous citizen. His first tavern was built in 1797. He gathered the horsemen of his time about the huge fireplace of his tavern, and talked up the breeding of light horses. The tavern caught fire twice, and thenceforward the name Phoenix was attached to the hotel. The old section of the present structure dates from the third fire, which occurred during a race in 1879.

HORSE FARM TOUR 1

Lexington to Lexington, *22.5 m.;* US 60 (Winchester Pike), Hume Rd., Bryan Station Pike, Johnston Rd., US 27–68 (Paris Pike), Ironworks Pike, Newtown Pike.
Hard-surfaced throughout.
Horse Farms on this route open to public; permission to visit stables must be obtained at farm offices. Visitors are required to refrain from smoking and to shut all gates that they open. Many of the gates are of the patent type that can be opened and shut from motor cars. Numbers in parentheses correspond with numbers on Horse Farm Tour map.

East on US 60 from the Zero Milestone, at the corner of Main St. and Union Station Viaduct on Walnut St., to Midland St.; L. on Midland St. to 3rd St., here called Winchester Pike.

The entrance to (28) PATCHEN WILKES STOCK FARM (L), is at *3.2 m. (open 9–4 on request).* This once busy horse place, now devoted to the raising of cattle and sheep, was owned a century and more ago by Capt. Benjamin Warfield on land granted to the Warfield family by the colony of Virginia before the Revolution. Prior to 1825 he built the one-story brick house with rooms opening on a porch enclosing three sides of a flower-bordered rear court. The white house, sheltered by a grove of trees, the large barn and other buildings are in a striking position on the brow and crest of two sweeping slopes half a mile from the highway. For years the horse farm was operated by W. E. D. Stokes, of New York.

The farm was named for the blooded sire, Patchen Wilkes. Peter the Great, purchased as a nine-year-old stallion with a track record of 2:07½, having stood here for more than a decade, sold at the age of 21 for $50,000.

At *3.6 m.* is the entrance to (29) HAMBURG PLACE (R), acquired

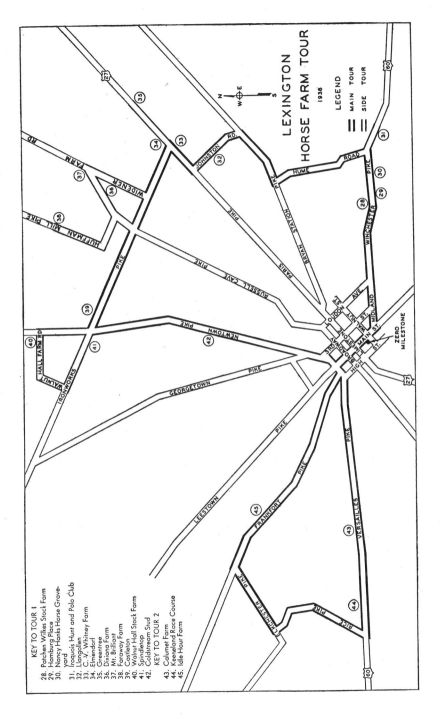

LEXINGTON
HORSE FARM TOUR
1936

LEGEND

══ MAIN TOUR
═ SIDE TOUR

KEY TO TOUR I

28. Patchen Wilkes Stock Farm
29. Hamburg Place
30. Nancy Hanks Horse Grave-
    yard
31. Iroquois Hunt and Polo Club
32. Llangollen
33. C.-V. Whitney Farm
34. Elmendorf
35. Greentree
36. Dixiana Farm
37. Mt. Brilliant
38. Faraway Farm
39. Castleton
40. Walnut Hall Stock Farm
41. Spindletop
42. Coldstream Stud

KEY TO TOUR 2

43. Calumet Farm
44. Keeneland Race Course
45. Idle Hour Farm

in 1897 by John E. Madden, and since owned and operated by his son J. E. Madden, Jr. The estate, consisting of approximately 2,700 acres and extending several miles along the highway, was named for Hamburg, a great thoroughbred, which, after being successfully campaigned 30 years ago, stood after his retirement with pronounced success. Since 1929 Hamburg Place has been important for the breeding of polo ponies.

At Hamburg Place have been foaled and bred six Kentucky Derby winners—the largest number to come from any one nursery. Plaudit, the first of these, won the Kentucky Derby of 1898 *(1¼ m.)* in what was then the creditable time of 2:09.

Behind the unpretentious green-trimmed white frame residence is the old-fashioned barn in which were foaled and bred the other five Kentucky Derby winners. Old Rosebud, the second Madden Derby winner, after establishing a reputation when a two-year-old, went to the post in the 1914 Derby as a favorite and ran the distance handily in 2:03⅖, a new track record. Old Rosebud was a frequent winner in high class company after taking the purse at Churchill Downs, until, as an aged horse, patched up and returned to the turf following a breakdown, he met with a fatal accident during a race in the East. Sir Barton, winner of the Kentucky Derby in 1919, was the last of the great Star Shoots and the only maiden performer ever to win this stake. Although Sir Barton's time was slow (2:09⅘) due to an off track, he demonstrated his class later in the month by winning the Preakness in Maryland. Paul Jones, a fine mudder, won the Kentucky Derby in 1920 over a heavy track (2:09). Zev, the fifth Derby winner, was by the successful Madden sire, The Finn, from the good race mare, Miss Kearney. Zev, possessed of a high flight of speed, was also a superior mud runner. For the Derby of 1923 he turned in the fair time of 2:05⅖. Zev defeated the great English colt, Papyrus, in their $100,000 match race in the East in 1924, and In Memoriam at Churchill Downs later. Flying Ebony, another son of The Finn also ridden to victory by the much-publicized jockey, Earle Sande, won the Kentucky Derby of 1925 over a sloppy track in 2:07⅗.

The stables of Hamburg Place are empty except in winter when polo ponies are quartered here.

NANCY HANKS HORSE GRAVEYARD (30) *4.1 m.* (R), surrounded by a horseshoe-shaped field-stone fence, is the burial ground of a dozen horses that made John E. Madden famous as a breeder. Nancy Hanks, considered one of the greatest trotters that ever lived, is buried in the center of the plot. A stone monument, topped with a miniature statue of the great mare, stands over her grave. Eleven other noted harness horses and thoroughbreds are buried in a semicircle around the Nancy Hanks monument. Of these Plaudit is perhaps the best remembered. The others are Hamburg Belle, noted trotting mare, Ida Pickwick, Imp. Star Shoot, famed mostly as a successful sire of brood mares, Lady Starling, Ogden, Major Delmar, Siliko, Silikon, and Imp.

At *4.5 m.* is the junction with Hume Rd. The main route of the tour turns L. here.

Right (straight ahead) on US 60, *0.6 m.* to (31) the IROQUOIS HUNT AND POLO CLUB *(open May or June to September 1)* entered (R) through iron gates bearing silhouetted figures of polo players. The landscaped grounds of the club include four polo fields—one for exhibition matches, another as a practice field for men, a third for women, and the fourth field for children.

Polo ponies are drawn from the best blooded and mixed stock obtainable, using sires and dams of all three light horse breeds. Nimble, intelligent native mares, bred to thoroughbred, trotter, or saddle horse sires, produce a high proportion of colts having the desired qualities, and Western ponies have been crossed upon thoroughbreds. Polo ponies range in weight up to 1,400 pounds, and the qualities demanded are good bone, intelligence, quick action, and sure-footedness. Matches, open to the public, are frequently played here.

Left on Hume Rd., at *7 m.* is the junction with Bryan Station Pike; R. on Bryan Station Pike to the junction with Johnston Rd., *9.3 m.;* L. on Johnston Rd.

On Johnston Rd. is (32) (L) LLANGOLLEN (Welsh, pronounced Thlangothlen), *10.3 m.,* which has a color motif of white trimmed in black. This 273-acre farm, owned by John Hay Whitney, is one of the three Whitney horse farms in the Bluegrass. At the head of this stud for seven years was Imp. Royal Minstrel, a gray, many of whose get are of that color. This horse, returned to England in the latter part of 1938, was campaigned in America and is said to have won more for his American owner than his purchase price of $75,000. His victories on English courses include the Eclipse, Craven, Cork and Orrery Stakes, and the Victoria Cup. Here also is standing the Bonnie Scotland thoroughbred, The Porter. This horse, a small chestnut and a superior performer in "sloppy" going, was owned when in training and for some time after his retirement by E. B. McLean of Washington. Somewhat like Ferdinand the Bull, The Porter, a dignified old gentleman, is fascinated by butterflies, but despises dogs, cats, and roosters. It is estimated that his get have won more than $1,350,000. The Porter sired Toro, a bay from Imp. Brocatelle, in 1925, who as a three-year-old was just about the shiftiest of his age. Although Toro's turf career was short his winnings amounted to $142,530.

Johnston Rd. runs to a dead end at its junction, *10.8 m.,* with US 27–68, which is here called the Paris Pike. Right on US 27–68.

The C. V. WHITNEY FARM (33) *11.4 m. (open 11–4, February-June 20: no specific hours at other times),* its yellow buildings (R) forming a striking contrast with the green landscaped grounds, is entered from the Paris Pike. The 900-acre estate has 11 well-built and ventilated barns including three for stallions (one of them floored with cork), a two-story frame cottage, and a two-story stone farm office building (L), and a one-mile training course. About a mile from the entrance, in a wooded area near one of the stallion barns, is the cemetery where Broomstick, Peter Pan, Whiskbroom II, Prudery, Regret—only filly ever to win the Kentucky Derby—Pennant, and the great Equipoise (d. 1938) are buried.

Broomstick, favorite stock horse of James (Jimmy) Rowe, head trainer for so many years for Harry Payne Whitney, was a consistent winner regardless of the fields in which he competed. Through his sire, Ben Brush, he came of the hardy Bonnie Scotland line. Broomstick headed the stud founded by William C. Whitney, and, among a goodly number of superior performers, he sired Regret, Dam, Jersey Lightning, by Hamburg. In the Kentucky Derby, over a track thought to have been fully a second and a half on the slow side, he won easily by two open lengths over Pebbles in 2:05⅗. Whiskbroom II, a chestnut foaled in 1907 by Broomstick-Audience, could run fast and far, even under high imposts. Among the successful performers sired by him is the Kentucky Derby winner, Whiskery. Prudery, a filly rated good enough to be started in the Kentucky Derby (1921), finished third to the Bradley pair, Behave Yourself and Black Servant. Prudery, by Peter Pan-Polly Flinders, was a fine race mare, and in the stud she produced Victorian and Whiskery, winners respectively of $253,425 and $103,565. Peter Pan, by Commando-Imp. Cinderella, was owned and raced by James R. Keene. A son of one of America's truly great horses, Peter Pan, a fine performer and a stock horse of more than usual merit, won above $100,000, and among his get were Pennant, sire of Equipoise, outstanding performer of recent years, and the noted race and brood mare, Prudery. Pennant, best remembered as the sire of Equipoise, was a good thoroughbred race horse.

Equipoise, by Pennant-Swinging, one of those thoroughbreds that breeders, large and small, live from year to year in the hope of producing, was one of the outstanding performers of all time. Campaigned by C. V. Whitney, he was retired in 1937 and put at stud after winning stakes and purses of $300,000 or more. Only Sun Beau, W. S. Kilmer's champion handicapper, with winnings of $338,610, has exceeded those of Equipoise. A brown chunk of a horse, on the small side, Equipoise completed his two-year season by finishing an eyelash behind Twenty Grand in the Kentucky Jockey Club Stakes at one mile, in time that broke the record for horses of his age at the distance, under scale weight. He was handicapped by a bad hoof, and failed to train for the Kentucky Derby of 1931. He died unexpectedly from an intestinal ailment after standing little more than a year.

Chicle, of fashionable blood line (Spearmint-Lady Hamburg) foaled in 1913, has sired horses that have won more than a million dollars. At stud here are such excellent performers during their days on the turf as Peace Chance, one of the fastest running horses America has produced, Halcyon, Whichone, and Firethorn, a good thoroughbred race horse (by Imp. Sun-Briar-Baton Rouge) campaigned actively since 1935.

Peace Chance, a bay by Chance Shot-Peace, was foaled in 1931. Although his career was shortened by a leg ailment, his winnings amounted to almost $50,000. Possessed of blinding speed and a stout heart, this young stallion promises to be a successful stock horse. Halcyon, a bay foaled in 1928, is by Broomstick, from Prudery, both of which are dead. Halcyon, a shifty performer in good company and now at stud on the C. V. Whitney farm, has the making of an excellent stock horse, and choice mares are being sent to his court. Whichone, one of the fastest two-year-olds of record, is a bay horse, by Chick-Flying Witch, foaled in 1927. Although he went amiss early and was retired, his winnings amounted to $192,705, most of it earned during his first season on the turf.

At *11.5 m.* is the junction with the Ironworks Pike. The main tour route turns left on Ironworks Pike.

Right (straight ahead) on US 27–68, *0.2 m.* to (34) ELMENDORF (L) *(open 8–4 weekdays),* owned by Joseph E. Widener. This 1,300-acre estate, through which North Elkhorn meanders, has a natural beauty enhanced by landscaping. Four Corinthian columns and two marble lions on a hilltop are all that remain of the marble palace built in 1897–1900 by James B. Haggin, copper magnate, for his bride. The house was razed in 1929 to avoid payment of taxes on so costly a building. Mr. Haggin built up an estate of 13,000 acres from the original 564 acres, which he acquired in 1891.

Among the many barns at Elmendorf the red brick Norman French barn (L) is the most striking, its slate roof decorated with models of animals and birds. Above it rises a two-story tower with a clock from Normandy and a bell that strikes every half-hour. Another barn is in two parts with the 30 stalls facing an enclosed oval tanbark track. Among the thoroughbreds housed here are Brevity, Chance Shot, son of Fair Play, dam, Imp. Quelle Chance, Imp. Sickle, and Haste.

Brevity, a bay by Chance Shot, or Imp. Sickle, dam, Imp. Ormando, was the best of the 1935 two-year-olds, and his brilliant performances at that age were followed by an equally impressive race or two at Miami the following winter. He came north to fulfill his engagement in the Kentucky Derby of 1936, the odds-on favorite in a smart field. Knocked to his knees at the start, he got away tenth in a field of fourteen, and worked his way up to finish a head behind Bold Venture, the winner. He went amiss in his three-year-old season, and has since been at stud. Chance Shot, a bay foaled in 1924, has been a consistent sire of winners, among them no less a performer than Peace Chance, turf winner of $142,277. Imp. Sickle, an English thoroughbred by Phalaris-Selene, she by Chaucer, is a brown foaled in 1924 and imported for breeding purposes. A prolific sire, he has sent to the races such performers as Brevity, Stagehand, Reaping Reward, and others of stakes caliber. Haste, a bay thoroughbred by Imp. Maintenant-Miss Malaprop, foaled in 1923, was an excellent performer and has sired a number of good horses, usually with high flight of speed and ability to excel over muddy going. As a two-year-old he won the Saratoga Special and the Grand Winner Hotel Stakes, and at three years old the Withers and Fairmount Derby.

In the Elmendorf cemetery is a large bronze statue of Fair Play which, even as an aged stallion in 1919, brought $100,000. Fair Play, by Hastings-Fairy Gold, sired Man o' War. In front of the statue are the graves of Fair Play and of Mahubah, dam of Man o' War, with huge gravestones bearing wreaths. Mahubah, by Imp. Rock Sand, was the dam of Fair Play's greatest sons, the peerless Man o' War, often called a super-horse, and of My Play, a pronounced success on the turf and at stud.

The Paris Pike (US 27–68) continues to (35) GREENTREE (R), *0.6 m.,* a 750-acre breeding farm owned by Mrs. Payne Whitney. The Whitney colors, white and black, are used on buildings that dot the estate and on fences that divide the farm into fields and paddocks.

Mrs. Whitney's Imp. St. Germains, a French horse foaled in 1921, spends the sunset of his life in a pasture all his own with his companions, Lum and Abner, two bewhiskered goats. St. Germans is the sire of Twenty Grand, holder of the record (2:01⅘) for the Kentucky Derby (1931) and the Churchill Downs three-year-old record for that distance. Twenty Grand in 1930 also set the record (1:36½) of the Kentucky Jockey Club Stakes, a one-mile race for two-year-olds run in the fall. St. Germans also sired St. Brideaux, and Bold Venture, winner (1936) of the Kentucky Derby (2:03⅗) and of (1936) the Preakness (1:59). Also at stud here is Questionnaire, by King-Miss Puzzle, foaled in 1927.

Left from US 27–68 on Ironworks Pike, now the main route. At *13.4 m.* is the junction with the George Widener farm road.

Right on the Widener road; at *0.1 m.* is back entrance (L) of (36) DIXIANA FARM, one of the showplaces of the Bluegrass, owned by Charles T. Fisher, manufacturer of motor car "bodies by Fisher," who acquired it after the death of James Cox Brady (1882–1928) of New York. The 1,100-acre estate is a prominent Kentucky nursery, known at a much earlier date as the Hamilton Stud, and was once part of the 13,000-acre estate of James B. Haggin. Maj. B. G. Thomas, who once owned it, named the place Dixiana in 1877 in honor of his favorite brood mare. Mr. Fisher has a fine stable of running horses. In addition to numerous modern barns, the farm has an excellent one-mile training track.

Sweep All, Peter Hastings (sold), and High Time (dead) lived in the small barn (R) near the office. The stable hands insist that when any performer sired by High Time was winning a race, he sensed it and kicked and "raised sand." Sweep All, Peter Hastings, and High Time were all excellent performers on the turf but their fame rests chiefly upon their value at stud. High Time was for years a steady producer of winners, among them the great gelding, Sarazon, one of the fastest thoroughbreds that ever came up, and the American which defeated Epinard, leading French performer of his day. Mata Hari, a filly adjudged smart enough to be sent in the Kentucky Derby of her year (1934) is one of the leading brood mares at Dixiana. Near by are the large barns where 24 American Standard Bred horses, each a familiar figure among the winners of its class in the show rings, lived until 1938, when the stables were broken up.

At *1.2 m.* is the junction with Russell Cave Pike; L. on this road.

On Russell Cave Pike opposite the Junction is (37) MT. BRILLIANT *(private)*, a two-story brick mansion built in 1792, home of Louis Lee Haggin. The wide veranda is noteworthy for its four massive Doric columns.

Left from the Dixiana front entrance on Russell Cave Pike to a junction with Huffman Mill Pike, *1.8 m.* Right on Huffman Mill Pike *3.3 m.* to (38) FAR-AWAY FARM (R) *(open 7:30–4:00)*, owned by Samuel Riddle. This is the home of Man o' War (1917–   ), greatest thoroughbred race horse of his day and by some authorities ranked the greatest native performer of all time in this country. Man o' War was by Fair Play, dam Mahubah. Bred by August Belmont, he was put for sale as a yearling at the annual Saratoga auction and bid in by Mr. Riddle for $5,000. As a performer, he was started 21 times and won 19 stakes and purses and the match race at Windsor, Ontario, in 1920 against Sir Barton. Man o' War is a strapping fellow, in color a dark chestnut. He was not raced after completion of his season as a three-year-old. Insured for $500,000, he was put at stud on Mr. Riddle's estate, where he is constantly under guard. Man o' War has sired 236 horses (November 1938) and of these 176 have been winners. Around $2,500,000 has been won by his get, and the great sire took approximately $250,000 on the turf, in only two seasons at a time when purses were not so large as today.

American Flag, at stud here, is one of the several high class thoroughbred race horses sired by Man o' War. He was campaigned in the East, where he won a substantial sum in stakes and purses. War Admiral, foaled and bred here, is, per-haps, the greatest son of Man o' War. Lightly campaigned and running not a little green as a two-year-old, he became the recognized champion of the three-year-olds (1937), when he joined the select circle whose few members have won in succession the Kentucky Derby, the Preakness, and the Belmont. In winning the Belmont, he shaded his sire's time. War Admiral, a five-year-old in 1939, was retired after fulfilling a final engagement in November 1938.

Russell Cave Pike continues southward from its junction with Huffman Mill Rd. to the junction with the Ironworks Pike, *2.4 m.*

The Ironworks Pike continues northwestward (straight ahead) from the junction with the Widener farm road, crossing Russell Cave Pike, at *13.4 m.*, the junction with the side tour to the home of Man o' War. Northwest of the junction with Russell Cave Pike, the Ironworks Pike passes the entrance (R), *15.2 m.*, to (39) CASTLETON, 1,132 acres, owned by David M. Look. This was once the estate of the Castleman family, which earlier was known as Cabell's Dale, home of John Breckinridge (1760–1806), sponsor of the Kentucky Resolutions of 1798–99, and U.S. Senator from Kentucky, 1801–05. Breckinridge left the Senate to become Attorney General of the United States and died in office.

Beyond the two-story, green-shuttered, white brick house, built in 1806, is a large yellow barn occupied by Standard Bred horses, and in a building near by are the stables of Castleton's stallions: Guy Castleton, Spencer, Rutherford, Schuyler, Lee Tide, and Moran. Among the great winners foaled and bred at Castleton were Colin, Domino, Commando, Peter Pan, Pennant, and numerous others. Colin, a brown by Commando-Imp. Postorella foaled in 1905, raced in the colors of James R. Keene, and, although there were some shifty horses in his day, none ever got near him. He was retired, an unbeaten winner of $181,610. At stud Colin failed to measure up to expectations. Domino, also a brown, by Himyar-Mannie Gray, was foaled in 1891. During his brief career on the turf, his winnings totaled $193,550. The Negro who proudly exhibits the horses to visitors sometimes sleeps in the barn. He is roused promptly at 4 A.M. by a disturbing clatter. The culprit is a spotted pony, rattling his empty bucket until breakfast is served.

At *15.8 m.* on Ironworks Pike is a junction with the Newtown Pike.

Right on Newtown Pike to (40) the WALNUT HALL STOCK FARM (L), *0.9 m.;* L. through the farm. This estate of 3,500 acres, having the appearance of a large well-kept park, is one of the world's foremost trotting horse nurseries. The farm, established in 1892 by Lamon V. Harkness of Pittsburgh, is owned by Dr. Ogden M. Edwards. Near the large Colonial-style yellow brick residence (Walnut Hall) stands the main barn. Peter Volo, which died in 1937 at the ripe age of 25, was at stud here. His son Protector, sold for $1,200 and later repurchased for $25,000, heads the stud. Volomite and Guy Abbey are also on this farm. On the morning of a race, when the stable routine is changed, the horses, like those in other racing stables, become very restless. In the cemetery, where 11 famous horses are buried, is a life-size statue of Guy Axworthy.

The Walnut Hall Farm road turns L. and reaches a junction with the Ironworks Pike, *3.4 m.* Left on Ironworks Pike.

At *4.3 m.* is (41) SPINDLETOP (R), owned by Mrs. M. F. Yount, with 826 acres of almost treeless land. The palatial residence was built in 1936. The stable houses some beautiful American saddle horses, among them Beau Peavine and Chief of Spindletop. The latter was one of the winners of the $10,000 award annually offered by the Kentucky State Fair for championship form in the three- and five-gaited classes. These two sires are Standard Bred American Saddle Horses, perhaps the most notable breed of its kind of purely American origin. These horses are bred for gaits and action from beautiful and enduring foundation stock.

Southeast of the entrance to Spindletop, Ironworks Pike reaches its junction, *5.2 m.*, with Newtown Pike, the point at which the loop to Walnut Hall Farm and Spindletop started.

The main route turns L. from Ironworks Pike on Newtown Pike.

On the Newtown Pike is COLDSTREAM STUD (42), *18.5 m.*, bordered by a limestone wall four miles long. The 1,855-acre estate (R) has been owned since 1915 by C. B. Shaffer. The main barn remodeled from a dairy, contains 32 stalls for thoroughbreds, including Bull Dog, sire of many winning performers. There is a tradition that Price McGrath, the first owner, hid a fortune in the walls of the barn, but search has not revealed it.

Newtown Pike continues south to a junction with Main St. in Lexington; L. on Main St. to the Zero Milestone, *22.5 m.*

HORSE FARM TOUR 2

Lexington to Lexington, *18 m.;* US 60, Rice Pike, Elkchester Pike, Old Frankfort Pike.

Four-lane concrete highway to Rice Pike; asphalt roads from Rice Pike into Lexington.

West on US 60 from Zero Milestone (Main and Walnut Sts. at the Union Station Viaduct) on Main St. to Jefferson St.; L. on Jefferson St. over Viaduct to W. High St.; R. on W. High St., which becomes Versailles Pike (US 60).

On US 60 is (R) CALUMET FARM (43), *4.7 m. (visiting hours 9–4 throughout year)*, originally known as Fairland when owned by Joseph W. Bailey, Senator from Texas. Calumet Farm was the home of W. M. Wright, whose fortune was made in Calumet baking powder. It is now (1939) owned by his son, Warren Wright of Chicago. Calumet is important as a stud, with such successful younger sires as Hadagal, Bostonian, and Chance Play. Hadagal, a bay by Imp. Sir Galahad III—out of Imp. Erne, foaled in 1931—was a stakes winner at two, and as a three-year-old broke the track record to win the Governor Green handicap at 1⅛ miles. Bostonian, a black by Broomstick-Yankee Maid, was foaled in 1924. He was raced only two seasons, yet won a number of stakes, including the Preakness. Chance Play, a chestnut horse by Fair Play-Imp. Quelle Chance and a half brother to Man o' War, was foaled in 1923. His winnings totaled nearly $138,000 and among his get are such sterling performers as At Play, Grand Slam, Good Gamble, and Psychic Bid. Galsum, a gelding, Nellie Flag, a filly, and Nellie Morse, dam of Nellie Flag and Count Morse, are also housed at Calumet. Nellie Morse, filly winner of the Preakness, was campaigned by Bud Fisher, creator of Mutt and Jeff. The 1,000-acre

Calumet Farm, its color motif white and red, was purchased by the senior Wright in 1924 in the hope of breeding a winner of the Hambletonian—the most desired stake in the harness horse field. He won this stake in 1931. The air-conditioned stallion barn with classic portico and turret has a cork floor and handsome woodwork. Behind the barn is an outdoor track. There is an estate house, 18 barns, and cottages for employees. In November 1938, there were three stallions, 65 mares, and 30 weanlings in the stables.

KEENELAND RACE COURSE (44), on US 60 at *6.4 m.* (R), held its inaugural meeting in 1936. This track, which supplants Lexington's century-old Association Course, is patterned after the great English race courses where the chief considerations are the sport of racing and the improvement of thoroughbred stock. The grandstand seats 2,500 people. The $1\frac{1}{16}$-mile oval track here is considered one of the fastest in America. In the three-story stone clubhouse are photographic murals by the best photographers of the Bluegrass, in the stag-room, on the second floor, are Currier and Ives lithographs of events on the tracks. The offices and facilities of Keeneland, including pari-mutuel wagering, a restaurant, bars, and private dining rooms, are all in the clubhouse.

There is a Currier lithograph of Lexington, the great thoroughbred stallion of the Bluegrass which held the running record of four miles at $7:19\frac{3}{4}$. As a performer Lexington was matchless, and for about a quarter of a century the turf's most tempting prizes fell largely to members of his family. He was light bay of 15 hands, 3 inches, by Boston, himself the greatest performer of his day; dam, Alice Carneal, she by Imp. Sharpedon. He was bred by Dr. Elisha Warfield, master of the meadows near Lexington, and was named Darley. Richard Ten Broeck acquired and renamed him Lexington. A horse of stout heart, superb muscular development and action, Lexington never broke down, but shortly after his last race, in which he defeated Lecompte, his eyes failed, and Mr. Ten Broeck sent him to Kentucky, where he made his first season at W. F. Harper's place, near Midway. His get won nearly $1,000,000, despite the War between the States during his day at stud. For 14 consecutive years, and in all 16, he led American thoroughbred sires in earnings of their get, a record never equaled. Lexington's health was excellent until his death in 1875. Buried in his paddock, his bones were later placed in the Smithsonian Institution, Washington, D.C.

The Keeneland Race Course occupies about 150 acres of the old Keene Place, founded on a tract of approximately 8,000 acres granted by Patrick Henry, then Governor of Virginia, to his kinsman, Francis Keene.

West of the race course is the junction with Rice Pike, *7.1 m.;* R. from US 60 on Rice Pike to a junction with Van Meter Pike, *8.7 m.;* L. on Van Meter Pike to a junction with Elkchester Pike, *9.9 m.;* R. on Elkchester Pike to a junction with the Old Frankfort Pike, *11.7 m.;* R. on the Old Frankfort Pike.

IDLE HOUR FARM (45), *12.5 m. (open 9* A.M.*–3:30* P.M.*),* owned by Col. E. R. Bradley, covers 1,300 acres on both sides of the Old Frankfort Pike. Miles of white fences divide the farm into paddocks and pastures. An underground passageway connects the paddocks on each side of the pike. White and green, the racing colors of Bradley's horses, give the many buildings a neat and striking appearance. The private race course was the scene of an annual Charity Day program for the benefit of Kentucky's orphans. The farm has a tiny Catholic chapel, a solarium for yearlings, a large brick residence, and numerous barns. Colonel Bradley had four Kentucky Derby winners—Behave Yourself, 1921 (2:04⅕); Bubbling Over, 1926 (2:03⅘); Burgoo King, 1932 (2:05⅕); and Broker's Tip, 1933 (2:06⅘).

Behave Yourself, a big gangling colt, was a surprise winner. Colonel Bradley sent Behave Yourself and his crack colt, Black Servant, his chief dependence, to the post. Black Servant took the track and led until, half way down the home stretch, Behave Yourself came along to challenge and finally to nose out his stable mate in a whipping finish. As a green two-year-old Bubbling Over scored in his maiden effort at nearly 50–1, by coming from behind down the home stretch. Burgoo King, whose total winnings are well above $100,000, was by Bubbling Over. Broker's Tip, by Black Toney, won the Derby by a nose over Head Play.

To the left of the residence are the stables where Burgoo King and Bubbling Over are kept, together with such racers as Blue Larkspur, Balladier, and Black Servant. Blue Larkspur, a bay by Black Servant-Blossom Time, foaled in 1926, won $272,000 in the short time he stood training. Now at stud, he is sending some fine performers to the races. Black Servant, Black Toney's best son, dam Imp. Padula, was foaled in 1918. He was an excellent thoroughbred race horse in fast company, and has now replaced his sire at stud. Black Toney, foaled in 1911 and head of the stud for so many years, died in 1938. He was a thoroughbred by Peter Pan and was himself a great race horse. Black Toney sent winner after winner to the races, among them Black Gold, winner of the Kentucky Derby in 1924, Black Maria, Black Servant and Miss Jemima.

It is said of Colonel Bradley, who purchased the estate in 1906, that the name of any employee who dies in his service is never removed from the payroll as long as there is a surviving dependent. Since most of the thoroughbreds bearing the Bradley colors were named with words starting with "B," his string is known everywhere as the "B" stables.

The Old Frankfort Pike continues eastward into Lexington over the viaduct to Jefferson St.; L. on Jefferson St. to Main St.; R. on Main St. to the Zero Milestone, *18 m.*

PADUCAH

Railroad Station: Union Depot, Brown and Caldwell Aves., *2 m.* from downtown section, for Illinois Central R.R.; Chicago, Burlington and Quincy R.R.; Gulf, Mobile and Northern R.R.; Nashville, Chattanooga and St. Louis R.R.; Paducah and Illinois R.R.

Bus Stations: 220 S. 5th St. for Greyhound, C. Ray, and Ohio Lines; Broadway and 2nd St. for Cardinal and Mohawk Lines; Arcade Bldg., 5th and Broadway, for Southern Limited Line; 4th St. and Kentucky Ave., for Chaudoin Bus Lines.

Airport: Cairo Rd. *4 m.* W.; no scheduled service.

Street Buses: Fare 5¢.

Taxis: 25¢ and upward; $2 per hour.

Traffic Regulations: Right turn on red light. Parking restrictions indicated by signs.

Accommodations: Eight hotels, three for Negroes; tourist camps *4 m.* south on US 68 and *5 m.* W. on US 60.

Information Service: Irvin Cobb Hotel, Broadway and 6th St.

Radio Station: WPAD (1420 kc.).

Motion Picture Houses: Three.

Swimming: Noble Park, Park Ave. and 28th St., adm. to pool 25¢.

Golf: Noble Park Municipal course, Park Ave. and 28th St., 9 holes, greens fee 15¢; Lakeview Country Club, *4 m.* S. on Lovelaceville Rd., 18 holes, greens fee 50¢.

Tennis: Municipal courts in Noble Park, entrance 28th St. and Park Ave.

Annual Events: Strawberry Festival, movable date varying with crop season, usually early in June.

PADUCAH (326 alt., 33,541 pop.) is the seat of McCracken County, and the most consequential port and distributing center for the extreme western section of Kentucky. It lies on the flood plain of the Ohio River at the point where the Tennessee, pouring down from the Southern Highlands, joins the larger stream before it goes on fifty miles to the Mississippi. Cypress and sycamore trees thrive in the low, moist land, giving Paducah the appearance of an Old World town surrounded by rivers and trees.

The city is laid out in a rectangular plan, its streets running parallel to and at right angles with shorelines of the Ohio and Tennessee Rivers. Numbered streets, parallel with the river, begin at the waterfront with 1st Street. Except for Broadway and three streets named for Kentucky and neighboring States, the rest, for the most part, honor Presidents and statesmen.

Paducah seems on first sight to be peaceful and unhurried; actually it is a rather busy place. The waterfront, built up for utility rather than beauty, is still active in a modest way. Paducah pioneers discovered very early that in winter the mouth of the Tennessee River was usually free of ice because of its warm waters from the south, and that it offered a winter haven for Ohio River boats. Today the left shore of the Tennessee, sheltered by a low-lying island that separates it from the Ohio, is lined with boatyards, fuel storage tanks, and warehouses, remnants or expansions of the once lively river traffic; and Paducah is still the center of boatbuilding and boat repairing for the Ohio Valley.

Farther down the Ohio and extending through much of the older section of the city are the various factories, the extensive railroad shops—five lines serve Paducah—and the vast tobacco warehouses which have grown up in this principal dark-tobacco market of the country. Four blocks inland from the river is the business center of brick structures, largely dating from the last century, packed into a few blocks along Broadway and 4th Street. Commerce has invaded the old residential section in the downtown areas, leaving the homes and lawns looking bedraggled and forlorn.

The newer homes have reached out over the flood plain into higher ground back of the river, from which the eastern foothills of the Ozarks in Illinois, lying low beyond the bend in the Ohio, are visible on clear days. Playgrounds and parks are scattered over Paducah's nine square miles, and to the south are small farms devoted to livestock, tobacco, dairying, and berry culture. Peach and apple orchards front the many State and Federal highways that lead into the city.

The Negroes represent about 20 percent of the population of Paducah. They have their own schools, churches, and social life. Friendly co-operation between the races is maintained in all business and labor relations. The older generation of Negroes engages in the unskilled labor of various Paducah industries. Among the younger generation are many skilled mechanics and tradesmen who enjoy the better economic conditions given by industrial training, and the Negro students of Paducah are taught by members of their own race, in Negro public schools and the West Kentucky Industrial College for Negroes. The more than 90 percent Negro illiteracy of 1865 dwindled to less than 4 percent in 1930.

In 1778, when George Rogers Clark advanced upon the British military posts in the Old Northwest, his last base before striking into the wilderness was at the mouth of the Tennessee River. In 1795 the State of Virginia gave Clark, in compensation for his services, 72,962 acres of land along the southern shore of the Ohio between the Tennessee and Mississippi Rivers. Though claimed by Virginia under its Colonial Charter from the British Crown, this area was not included in the agreements by which the rights of the Indians to the balance of Kentucky had been upheld, and Clark derived no benefit from the grant; it was still the property of the Chickasaw Indians. On October 19, 1818, a special commission headed by Gen. Andrew Jackson and Gov. Isaac Shelby negotiated a settlement known as the Jackson Purchase, following which the Chickasaw evacuated the region and moved into northern Mississippi.

News of the impending purchase spread, and in 1817 a migration to the area began. Settlers poured in by flatboat and wagon from North Carolina, Virginia, Tennessee, Pennsylvania, and Kentucky settlements already established for some years. James and William Pore built the first log cabin in Paducah (then known as Pekin) at the foot of Broadway. James Davis who came with his family down the Licking River from Harrison County, Kentucky, to Cincinnati, then by way of the Ohio to Paducah, built a hut at the northwest corner of First and Broadway, and later erected a house where Riverside Hospital now stands.

When George Rogers Clark died in 1818, his claim passed into the hands of his brother William, of the famous Lewis-Clark expedition along the Missouri and Columbia Rivers. William Clark, who was made Superintendent of Indian Affairs for Missouri (1822–1836), revived his brother's claim and in 1827 laid out the town site, and named it for his Chickasaw friend, Chief Paduke. Paducah was incorporated as a village in 1830, and as a city in 1856.

The growth of Paducah has been slow, continuous, and at no time spectacular. In early steamboating days its proximity to four great navigable rivers made it convenient for the transshipping of goods and passengers. This fact lured merchants and business men to the new town. The first store, in which furs were used for money, was erected in 1826 at the northeast corner of what is now First and Broadway. Opposite this store Albert Hays in the same year built the first frame house. Although it was not a hotel, the three rooms, considered elaborate in that day, often housed traders overnight.

When the logs began to come down from the Tennessee and Cumberland Valleys during the mid-nineteenth century, there arose a thriving lumber industry, with its attendant mills and factories. As this industry declined, its place was taken by the handling and transshipment of agricultural products down the river to the seaports, and of goods from the Atlantic Coast and from Europe destined for the interior towns and cities of the Cumberland and Tennessee Valleys.

Because of its location Paducah was a strategic point during the War between the States. For a brief time in the earlier months of the war, Kentucky, striving to be neutral, served as a no man's land between North and South. Both sides rushed their armies into this area, for mastery over it would give the victor control of western Kentucky, Tennessee, and a good-sized portion of Alabama. In September 1861, General Grant took military possession of Paducah. Thereafter, until the close of military operations in the West, the city was one of the important depots of supply that linked the farms and storehouses of the North with the Union Armies in the field.

During this occupation by Federal troops, Gen. Lew Wallace, later the author of *Ben Hur*, for a time commanded the garrison. In 1864, after the main theater of action had been moved southward, Gen. Nathan Forrest, Confederate cavalry leader, trying desperately to turn back the Northern invasion by destroying Union Army bases, struck savagely at Fort Anderson, which controlled the Ohio River from its position at the west end of 5th Street. The attack, known as the Battle of Paducah, was from the south along Lovelaceville Road and down Broadway toward the river. After burning Union supplies stored along the river front, Forrest retired. In his report to President Jefferson Davis, he explained that he withdrew because of an epidemic of small-pox in the city, rather than because of the formidable nature of the Union entrenchments. This raid ended operations in western Kentucky for the remainder of the war.

After the war the city resumed its customary place in river transportation. The great steamboating era that continued in its prime to about 1880 gave life to its shipbuilding and ship repair industries, and those depending upon lumbering and farming adjusted themselves to the dwindling of the lumber trade and the expansion of agriculture. Southward extension of rail lines connecting the Great Lakes region with the Gulf Coast, which took place shortly after the conclusion of the War between the States, made Paducah an important river-and-rail junction point, and the Illinois Central Railway located its locomotive rebuilding and repair shops in the city. Revival of river transportation since 1920 has brought about the establishment, on the ice-free Paducah shore of the Tennessee, of a Government plant for the building and repair of boats, barges, and other river equipment used by the Inland Waterways Corporation. Other important industries that have survived from early days or have developed since the War between the States are the manufacture of textile machinery and textiles, garments, hosiery, leather goods, furniture, barrels, and sundry other products depending on a plentiful supply of workable timber. The volume of Paducah industry is indicated by bank clearings that average about $80,000,000 a year.

Paducah is the center of dark tobacco growing. The tobacco in "the Purchase," known to the trade as "dark fire-cured," is brought to the loose-leaf floors, where it is auctioned off chiefly for the export market. A steady movement of livestock from the Jackson Purchase country to Middle West packing houses goes through the local yards, and the shipping of fruit—apples, peaches, and strawberries—is lucrative in Paducah. The localized cultivation and co-operative shipping of a strawberry known as Dixie Aroma is the basis for the Strawberry Festival, held usually in June. Business men and farmers alike join in the festivities, that usually include a street parade.

Like other river towns, Paducah has had its battles with floods. The most damaging was the Ohio River flood of January 1937, which swept with full fury over low-lying Paducah. The flood crest of the Mississippi River, reached before that of the Ohio, acted as a dam to retard and spread out the waters of the Ohio, which backed over the low grounds in the vicinity of Union Station, and ran through the entire downtown area. Water rose into the elevated first floor of the City Hall. Government barges steamed up Broadway and rescued refugees from the second story of the Irvin Cobb Hotel. Stocks of goods, transferred to supposedly safe altitudes, were soaked by oily waters. Ninety-three percent of the buildings in the city were made untenable. Paducah's damage bill totaled $30,000,000. Prompt relief work, however, reduced disease to a minimum, and by midsummer of 1937 few visible effects of the disaster remained.

Irvin S. Cobb was born at Paducah in 1876, and up to the age of 17 was a shorthand reporter, a contributor to comic weeklies, and a reporter on a local paper. At 19 he edited the Paducah *Daily News.* He was in the town off and on, and from 1901 to 1904 served as managing editor of the Paducah *News Democrat.* The first collection of his Judge Priest stories, *Old Judge Priest,* was published in 1915; the last volume, *Judge Priest Turns Detective,* in 1936. The list of his writings is too long for mention, but in 1922 he won the O. Henry Award for the best short story of that year; has been starred and featured in movies; wrote and collaborated in plays; and is a Chevalier of the Legion of Honor (France, 1918).

The New York *Times,* reporting a movement in August 1938 to name a bridge across the Ohio River for Cobb, printed the following characteristic comment:

There is a brass marker in the sidewalk before the house where he was born sixty-two years ago. A cigar has been named for him, a beauty shop, a barber shop. Even a Kentucky mint julep honors Irvin S. Cobb.

This son of Paducah has sometimes been cited as an authority on different kinds of alcoholic beverages. To the Distillers Code Authority, back in the NRA days, he gave this description of corn liquor: "It smells like gangrene starting in a mildewed silo; it tastes like the wrath to come, and when you absorb a deep swig of it you have all the sensations of having swallowed a lighted kerosene lamp. A sudden violent jolt of it has been known to stop the victim's watch, snap both his suspenders and crack his glass eye right across—all in the same motion."

POINTS OF INTEREST

Much of Paducah's early history was made within an area of four or five squares in either direction from the Ohio river front. Poorly made, poorly placed markers and crumbling old buildings do not tell a great deal about the city's past, and sites are not always definite. The best-informed people therefore usually say "about here," and point with a moving finger to places where great events happened.

1. The SITE OF CLARK'S LANDING, Ohio River shore and Kentucky Ave., is recorded by a sidewalk marker. Local tradition has fixed this as the point where Gen. George Rogers Clark, after leaving his base at the Falls of the Ohio (Louisville), paused to reorganize his forces for their successful campaign in the Illinois wilderness. Clark's journal, however, seems to indicate encampment on Tennessee Island, visible offshore.

2. The GRANT MARKER, 1st St. and Broadway, designates the place where Gen. U. S. Grant landed his Union forces in the fall of

1861 and proclaimed martial law. Paducah then became the base for extensive Union operations.

3. The CONFEDERATE FLAG MARKER, 3rd St. between Broadway and Kentucky Ave., is a sidewalk slab telling that here, early in the summer of 1861, was unfurled the first Confederate flag publicly shown in Paducah.

4. FORT ANDERSON SITE, Trimble St. between 4th and 5th Sts., is the place where the fort's Union guns commanded the Ohio River, and Confederate soldiers stormed the breastworks *(see History)*.

5. The SOUTHERN HOTEL, NW. corner 1st St. and Broadway, a three-story brick building, was one of the leading Western hotels in the 1850's. This old structure, which shows plainly the marks of time and recurring floods, is used by temporary occupants for various commercial purposes. It stands upon the SITE OF THE FIRST INN, a log building erected by John Field in 1830 on a lot costing $12.

6. MARINE WAYS *(open by permission)*, 101 Washington St., is a shipyard where river craft are built or reconditioned. Boats to be overhauled are floated into a "cradle" resting on inclined tracks that run down from the Tennessee River bank into the water. Resting sidewise, boats to be repaired are carried ashore on these tracks, and vessels built ashore are launched down them from the cradles. Here are boats ranging from the old "floating palace" to the newest self-propelled barge boats.

7. INLAND WATERWAYS CORPORATION SHIPYARDS *(open by permission)*, Meyers St. between Island Creek and E. City Limits, build and repair power barges, tow barges, dredges, and tenders.

8. The OLD BRAZELTON HOME *(private)*, NW. corner 6th and Clark Sts., erected in 1858, was originally a comfortable two-story frame structure designed to house a large family. During the War between the States its ten rooms served as headquarters for Gen. Lew Wallace, for a time commandant of the Union forces quartered in the city. In it Wallace entertained Grant when the Union chief of staff came to Paducah on one of his wartime visits.

9. The McCRACKEN COUNTY COURTHOUSE, 6th St. between Clark and Washington Sts., extending to 7th St., is a two-story gray brick building erected in 1857. Judge Bishop, prototype of the Judge Priest in Irvin Cobb's stories, sat on the bench in its courtroom.

10. The FEDERAL BUILDING, NW. corner Broadway and 5th St., is a modern building which replaced the old post office structure (1883). The present building houses not only the post office, but also the Federal District Court and Government offices.

11. IRVIN COBB HOTEL, Broadway and 6th St., opened in 1929 with Paducah-born Irvin S. Cobb as the first registered guest. The façade is a combination of stone, brick, half-timbers, stucco, turrets and broken parapets characteristic of medieval English castles. The romantic feeling of Old English architecture is carried out more fully in the interior by the elaborate paneling and decorative balconies in the main lobby.

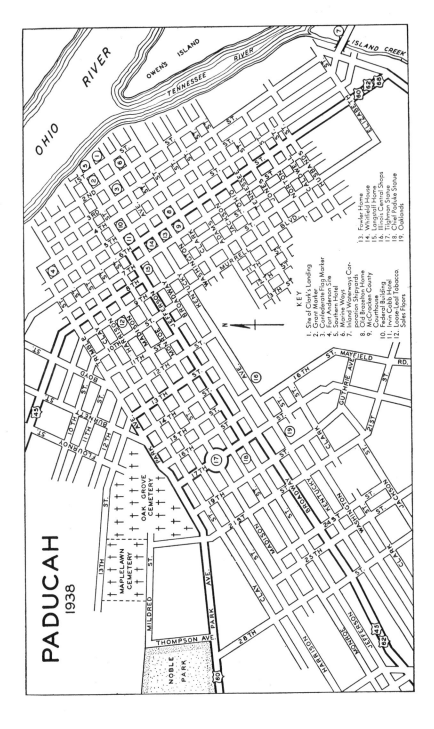

PADUCAH
1938

KEY

1. Site of Clark's Landing
2. Grant Marker
3. Confederate Flag Marker
4. Fort Anderson Site
5. Southern Hotel
6. Marine Ways
7. Inland Waterways Corporation Shipyards
8. Old Brazelton Home
9. McCracken County Courthouse
10. Federal Building
11. Irvin Cobb Hotel
12. Loose-Leaf Tobacco Sales Floors
13. Fowler Home
14. Whitfield House
15. Langstaff Home
16. Illinois Central Shops
17. Tilghman Statue
18. Chief Paduke Statue
19. Oaklands

12. LOOSE-LEAF TOBACCO SALES FLOORS *(open, sales daily during marketing season)*, between Madison and Harrison Sts., and extending from 8th to 10th Sts., is the center of intense activity during the marketing season, which begins in mid-December and lasts until May. The tobacco crop from "the Purchase," prepared for sale on the farm by a process known as "fire-curing," is offered on the floors, and sold at auction to the highest bidder. The yield varies widely, depending upon the season and the prospective market demand at the time of planting.

13. The FOWLER HOME *(private)*, 619 Kentucky Ave., a two-story house with 15 rooms, built by R. C. Woolfork about 1830, has been the home of the Fowler family for five generations. During the War between the States it served as headquarters for Col. S. G. Hicks, of the Union Army.

14. The WHITFIELD HOUSE *(private)*, corner 7th St. and Kentucky Ave., built in 1857, was the home of Gen. Lloyd Tilghman, Confederate leader. Later it was occupied by Sgt. William G. Whitfield, said to be the model for the Sergeant Jimmy Bagby of Irvin Cobb's *Back Home Stories*.

15. The LANGSTAFF HOME *(private)*, 800 Broadway, is a Victorian Gothic structure erected in the 1850's. It has an ornamental iron porch across the front, and a railing runs around the roof. The main façade is broken by the straight lines of the entrances, projecting several feet in bays. Its otherwise plain wall surfaces are relieved by broad, shuttered windows with dog-eared trim. In the rear of this home is a BOMBPROOF SHELTER built by residents of the neighborhood in the 1860's.

16. The ILLINOIS CENTRAL SHOPS *(open by permission)*, Kentucky Ave. and 15th St., are mainly engaged in rebuilding engines. The 38 separate units, covering 21 acres, take care of all the repair work on the Illinois Central Railroad south of the Ohio River. The shops, one of the four largest industrial plants in Kentucky, represent an investment of $11,000,000 and sometimes employ as many as 2,500 men.

17. The TILGHMAN STATUE, 17th and Madison Sts., unveiled in 1909, was erected by members of the Tilghman family and by Daughters of the Confederacy to honor Gen. Lloyd Tilghman, C.S.A., who served with distinction through the Mexican War and later helped build the Baltimore & Ohio Railroad and other important lines through the South. At the time of the War between the States, Tilghman organized the Third Kentucky Regiment, C.S.A., and was assigned to the defense of the Tennessee and Cumberland Rivers. In 1863 he was killed during the Battle of Champions' Hill. The statue, by Henry Kitson, of Boston, shows him standing in field uniform.

18. CHIEF PADUKE STATUE, 18th and Jefferson Sts., by Lorado Taft, was given in 1909 to the city by the Paducah chapter of the D.A.R. The statue shows the Indian chieftain sitting, staring into distance.

19. OAKLANDS *(private)*, 1710 Kentucky Ave., is a two-story yellow brick structure erected in 1833. A spacious porch of much later construction almost conceals the simple lines of the original dwelling. This was the home of Linn Boyd, Speaker of the House of Representatives (1851–1855). Mrs. Boyd (nee Anna L. Rhey) was the cousin of President Millard Fillmore.

POINTS OF INTEREST IN ENVIRONS

Fort Massac State Park (Illinois), *10 m.* N. on US 45 *(see ILLINOIS GUIDE)*. Ballard Lakes, *29 m.;* Buried City, a prehistoric Indian center, *33 m. (see Tour 2)*.

Part III

Highways and Byways

Tour 1

(Portsmouth, Ohio)—South Portsmouth—Ashland—Catlettsburg—
Paintsville—Prestonsburg—Pikeville—(Norton, Va.); US 23, the Mayo
Trail.
Ohio Line to Virginia Line, 194.6 *m.*

Hard-surfaced roadbed in most places; remainder graveled.
Chesapeake & Ohio Ry. parallels route throughout.
Accommodations chiefly in towns.

This route follows the low bluffs along the curving Ohio River; the
Big Sandy Valley, and the Levisa Fork, a tributary of the Big Sandy
River. In the southern section it passes between a cordon of small
hills that increase in height toward the south until, at the Kentucky-
Tennessee border, they are stopped by the great purple and green wall
of the Cumberland Mountains. Veined by the river and its tributary
creeks and locked on three sides by hills and mountains, the Big Sandy
country was the last part of Kentucky to be surrendered to the white
man by Indians. Game abounded here and salt licks were plentiful;
until 1795 this common hunting ground was regularly visited by Creeks,
Choctaws, and Cherokees from the South, and by Shawnees, Miamis,
Delawares, Wyandottes, and Illinois from the North.

The rest of Kentucky had already been cleared before this section
was settled, and in the 1820's population in the Big Sandy Valley aver-
aged only about six inhabitants to the square mile. But hardy, independent men continued to come into the valley by way of the four gaps
through the Cumberlands and along the Indian trails, or down the Ohio
and up the Big Sandy Rivers to the dark hills beyond. These men
established farms in open hollows; the loggers arrived later, to "bring
daylight in the swamp" and send millions of logs floating down the Big
Sandy; little towns arose in some of the more accessible pockets of the
region; and to the long-sounding toot of the packets that plied the river
was added, in the 1870's, the clear sharp whistle of locomotives announcing the coming industrialism. The hills were tapped for their mineral resources and coal mining became a major industry in the valley;
in some of the larger towns small factories developed. Today the Big
Sandy Valley has hard-surfaced roads, modern hotels, schools, and
churches. As seen from US 23, it has a settled appearance. Just across
the hills from the river, however, the isolation still continues. Side
roads leading off from the highway are few; in the remote hollows, or
on the steep slopes of countless hills, are lonely little cabins where the
spinning wheel is kept busy and the wagon carries the family to
"buryin's," "meetin's" or "foot-washin's." This is Jesse Stuart's coun-

try *(see Literature)* and the locale of Jean Thomas' stories about the hill people of the Big Sandy region.

US 23 crosses the Ohio Line 0 *m.* at Portsmouth, Ohio *(see Ohio Tour 21)*, by way of a bridge *(autos 25¢, pedestrians 5¢)* over the Ohio River.

SOUTH PORTSMOUTH, 0.4 *m.* (660 alt., 500 pop.) *(see Tour 11)*, is at the junction with State 10 *(see Tour 11)*.

Between FULLERTON, 2.4 *m.* (1,239 pop.), and Greenup the highway closely parallels a long right-angle bend of the near-by Ohio and crosses fertile bottoms behind the dark, squat bluffs that border the river. Fruit growing is the chief activity in this level region.

GREENUP, 18.7 *m.* (478 alt., 1,125 pop.), seat of Greenup County, was named for Christopher Greenup, Governor of Kentucky (1804–1808). The town was known as Greenupsburg until 1872 when the name was changed to avoid confusion with Greensburg in Green County. The old brick GREENUP COUNTY COURTHOUSE was erected in 1811 to replace an earlier one built of logs with puncheon floor and benches.

Greenup is no longer an important river port, and only a few farmers use the old ferry between this point and Haverhill. But the town still attracts the hill folk so colorfully pictured in the autobiography and short stories of Jesse Stuart. Greenup was almost obliterated by the disastrous flood of 1937 when the entire population was suddenly marooned, and desperate efforts had to be made to prevent destruction.

During his later years Daniel Boone *(see Tour 17A)* is said to have made his home on the Kentucky side of the Ohio River near Greenup. About 1799 he removed from Kentucky to West Virginia by going up the Ohio in a canoe made of the trunk of a tree.

Right from Greenup on State 2, an improved road, to RACCOON IRON FURNACE (R), 6.5 *m.,* not operated since 1872. The final charge of ore has never been removed.

East of Greenup as US 23 passes through some of the best eastern Kentucky bottom lands, there are occasionally fine views of the sweeping Ohio River.

RACELAND, 26.2 *m.* (1,088 pop.), has a track that is the center for horse racing in eastern Kentucky.

RUSSELL, 28.1 *m.* (549 alt., 2,084 pop.), named for John Russell of Ashland, one of the region's former ironmasters, lies directly opposite Ironton, Ohio, with which it is connected by a highway bridge *(autos 20¢, pedestrians 5¢)*. The town has grown up around the large railroad yards, containing 147 miles of track, owned and operated by the Chesapeake & Ohio Ry. Company. A modern car shop with a capacity for rebuilding 45 cars daily is also here.

In the vicinity of Russell are a few ivy-mantled ruins of old blast furnaces that are the sole reminders of the iron industry that flourished here and on the opposite side of the Ohio from about 1812 until the closing decades of the nineteenth century. These silent and ghostly structures sprang up as enterprising capitalists began exploiting the rich iron, coal, clay, stone, and timber resources of the region. The pioneer furnaces were called "salts" because the iron they produced was cast in 40-inch pots used for evaporating salt. The Ohio River offered convenient transportation; shortly pots and pans, fireplace implements, waffle irons, trivets, and the like were being made here and sold up and down the Ohio and Mississippi. With the coming of the industrial period and the building of railroads, dozens of furnaces in the iron fields bordering both sides of the river roared with activity. Plumes of pale blue smoke curled skyward and then films of wood ash settled on the hillsides as the tapped furnaces surrendered the molten metal that was to become cannon and rails and plowshares and machines. A special class of men arose, the ironmasters, mostly Scots and Englishmen, who gave flavor and excitement to the entire region as they compelled their men and their furnaces to produce more and better iron and large personal fortunes for themselves. They were the lords of the country living in regal mansions in the larger towns and visiting Maysville or Cincinnati for week-end jollities, yet they mingled freely with their workers and cared for them paternally in hard times.

The opening of a new furnace meant a holiday celebration attended by the ironmaster, his family, and all his workers. Old songs were sung, and after the sun was up (there was a superstition about this) a lady, often the betrothed of the ironmaster's son, lighted the first fire in the furnace. At noon a prodigious feast was served, consisting of quarters of barbecued beef, sweet potatoes, large loaves of bread, and burgoo—large pieces of prime steer, vegetables, and imported spices boiled in a large kettle. The blast was applied and the ironmaster, certain that he had another successful furnace, mingled with the crowd and received their congratulations. Young couples stood upon the runners and pressed their initials in the pig iron mold; if the initials of a young man and woman were broken off in the same piece of iron from the first cast, they would be married and the bonds of matrimony would be as strong as bands of iron. When night came, square dances were performed in the spacious commissary until a horn blast ended the festivities as the next shift came on duty at the furnace.

The furnaces had their greatest activity about the time of the War between the States. The discovery of superior metal in the Upper Great Lakes region and the depletion of the local ores caused iron making to decline in this area; the rise of the Youngstown-Pittsburgh region brought it to an end. The furnaces still standing have been cold and silent for decades, and the steel mills at Ashland look elsewhere for their iron.

Through Ashland and southeast of it, the highway continues for 10 miles through the concentrated industrial area of eastern Kentucky.

ASHLAND, 33.4 m. (552 alt., 29,074 pop.) (see Ashland).

Points of Interest: American Rolling Mills, Ashland Coke Company Plant, Central Park.

Between Ashland and CATLETTSBURG, 39.3 *m.* (552 alt., 5,025 pop.) *(see Tour 16),* US 23 and US 60 *(see Tour 16)* are united.

Between Catlettsburg and Louisa US 23 abruptly leaves the Ohio and Big Sandy Rivers (the latter flows into the Ohio just east of the town), and makes a short cut back through the hill country with its frame houses in the good bottoms, log cabins up narrow hollows, small patches of tobacco, one-room schoolhouses, and an indefinable sense of isolation.

At **51.6** *m.* is the junction with an unmarked graveled road.

Right on this road to the TRAIPSIN' WOMAN'S CABIN *(open by request),* **1.6** *m.,* owned by Jean Thomas, founder of the American Folk Song Festival *(adm. free).* On the second Sunday of June each year a large audience gathers here to hear the ballads and see the folk dances presented by the mountain people. The songs and dances are performed with strict attention to appropriate costuming, steps, and music. Women in linsey-woolsey, slat bonnets, and homespun shawls dance to the tunes of "Chimney Sweeper" and "Prince Charley." Mrs. Thomas, whose home is in Ashland, Ky., was born of mountain folk and early became interested in the folk customs of her people. Traveling through the mountains, sometimes in a jolt wagon, sometimes on foot, she made a study of the legends, ballads, and dances of the Kentucky mountaineer. Her works include *Devil's Ditties,* a collection of songs, and the *Traipsin' Woman,* an account of her experience in the Cumberland Mountains.

Mrs. Thomas' log cabin is a reproduction of the type occupied by the more prosperous settlers of 100 years ago. It is on an eminence among wooded hills. Jilson Setters, the left-handed fiddler from Lost Hope Hollow, who journeyed to London to sing for the English Folk Song Society, sings ballads of his own creation about his travels. He helped Mrs. Thomas found the folk pageant. It was the mountain people who first called Mrs. Thomas the "traipsin' woman," for they described her journeyings from county to county as "considerable spells of traipsin'."

LOUISA, 75.7 *m.* (526 alt., 1,961 pop.), seat of Lawrence County, was named for Louisa, Duchess of Cumberland. It is a pleasant old town, dating from the flatboat era, and is in a region of considerable natural beauty at the head of navigation on the Big Sandy River. During the Napoleonic wars thousands of bearskins were collected along the Big Sandy and Kanawha Rivers and sent from Louisa down river to the Ohio, then down river to New Orleans, and thence to Europe, where they were made into headpieces for Napoleon's grenadiers. Big Sandy has been used for transportation for more than a century. Packets and barges superseded the crude early flatboats; down Tug and Levisa Forks came millions of logs from the forests of the upper valley, bound for Louisa and the sawmills along the Ohio River; the Chesapeake & Ohio Ry. built a terminus here decades ago. Today an occasional steamboat continues to carry traffic between this point and Catlettsburg.

At the northern end of Louisa along US 23 is the BIG SANDY DAM (L), the first movable needle-type dam built in the United States. This dam was erected in 1896 at a cost of $396,305.

The old FREESE HOUSE *(private),* at the end of Sycamore St. overlooking the Big Sandy, is the only old Georgian Colonial home in Louisa. This two-story brick structure, with walls 13 inches thick, was built about 1840. A front porch and a rear ell have been added, and the house has been painted red with white trim. The original yellow poplar woodwork, all of it hand-whipsawed, is still in place. This was first the home of Capt. Milton Freese, who operated packets on the Big Sandy and Ohio Rivers for 50 years.

According to a tradition, believed by many, George Washington, before the Revolution, had a tract of 2,084 acres surveyed on both sides of the Big Sandy River, including the present town site of Louisa. The story is supported by the fact that a cornerstone on this survey bears the initials "G.W."

Another tradition concerning the selection of the Kentucky-Virginia boundary relates that three commissioners, selected by the Governors of the two States, arrived late one evening in October 1799 at the point where Louisa now stands. Rains had been falling and the waters of both forks of the Big Sandy were rising. After the commissioners had enjoyed the refreshments and conviviality of pioneers, it was decided that the boundary should follow the larger fork of the Big Sandy. The next morning the Tug Fork, which had been rising steadily during the night, appeared to be much larger than the Levisa Fork and forthwith became the boundary. The commissioners departed before the slowly rising waters of the Levisa, normally the larger of the two, reached the junction of the forks. Satisfaction with the result was widespread; many years later it was realized that, had the Levisa Fork been selected, the rich bottom lands and extensive mineral resources of the Big Sandy Valley would have remained a part of Virginia.

There is a story that in 1760 John Swift left Alexandria, Va., with a party and came through the mountains to some place in Kentucky where they knew of a silver mine. They worked the mine that summer and returned to Virginia in the fall; a program they repeated each year until 1769. A manuscript of their travels and operations gives the dates of the various trips and the names of Swift's companions. It asserts that they also had some interests in piratical enterprises along the Atlantic Coast, and gives an account of money coined and treasures of thousands of dollars hidden when either Indians or the weather made it difficult to get the money out. Although the journal seems to point to the region around Paint Creek in Johnson County as the place where Swift's party camped and worked and the Mine Fork of Paint Creek was so named for their mine, nearly every county in eastern Kentucky has a tradition linking it with this romantic story; searching for the lost treasure has long been a favorite pastime in Kentucky, Virginia, North Carolina, and Tennessee.

Left from Louisa on State 37, a paved road, to the center of the FORT GAY BRIDGE (toll 15¢ for auto and driver, 15¢ each additional passenger), 0.5 m., over the point where the Levisa and Tug Rivers converge to form the Big Sandy. This bridge connects two States (West Virginia and Kentucky), two counties, two towns, crosses two rivers, charges two tolls, and has three approaches. There is an excellent view here of the Big Sandy River.

Right on State 3, from the center of the bridge, a short distance to the so-called "Point" section, between the forks of the Big Sandy. The first settlement in Lawrence County, consisting of three cabins connected by palisades, was founded here in 1789 by Charles Vancouver of London, England, who had received a grant of land from King George III in 1772; the patents were issued by Governor Randolph of Virginia in 1768. William M. Fulkerson, an attorney of Louisa, has in his possession this old parchment document with the official seal of the Lord Mayor of London.

South of Louisa the highway (now graveled) follows Levisa Fork through mountain farm lands typical of the Big Sandy Valley. There are a few small villages, but most of the region appears to be uninhabited as the hills near the highway conceal more distant hills in the hollows and bottoms of which are the cabins and farms of the mountaineer. Hard put though he is to scrape a living from his steep and sometimes unfertile patches, the mountaineer has a deep attachment for his farm and his home; he would not think of forsaking them (as long as they are his) to go out to "the level land" beyond the mountains. Proud and sensitive, he is quick to resent the flouts of outsiders, and contemptuous of any of his own kind who "git above their raisin'." He is unfailingly kind and hospitable because he holds individuality in high esteem; his cabin often has a place set at the table for a chance visitor, he is "mighty proud" to meet someone he likes, and his traditional invitation is, "Drag up a cheer and sit a spell."

In these hollows bearing such names as Lonesome, Troublesome, and Peevish, the traditions, songs, customs, and handicrafts of the original settlers still survive among their descendants who continue to live in the same way and often in the same places as their great-grandsires. The pattern of life is simple but tenacious. The typical mountaineer owns a cow, a couple of mules, hogs, chickens, geese, turkeys, and ducks. His house is usually a log cabin. He raises corn and tobacco for a "money crop," an acre of cane for sorghum, and potatoes, turnips, and sometimes pumpkins and apples for winter use. Wild berries, game, and fish in the mountain streams also provide him with food. The material with which he clothes his family is still woven on hand looms and he needs money chiefly for taxes; many of his possessions he acquires by barter. Paths and old creek beds join hollow to hollow and serve in lieu of roads. The ham a traveler eats at one of the town hotels in this region quite likely comes from a Chicago packing house because the mountaineer cannot bring in his hogs from his farm four miles away.

Music is second only to religion in the hearts of the mountain people; and while the women have preserved the handicrafts of their ancestors, it is the mountain men chiefly who have cherished their songs. The fiddle, the dulcimer, the banjo, and the guitar are met with at infares (weddings), dances, frolics, and impromptu gatherings; and to this day there is found in the mountains of Kentucky the wandering minstrel who trudges along quiet creeks and into lonely hollows to bring cheer with his "sure-enough fiddle" (as contrasted with the children's gourd fiddle) and his songs. Religious extremists call these lively jigs or sweet romantic ballads "devil ditties." But it delights most of the mountain people, from the "leastuns" (youngest children) to the grandsires, to gather about the minstrel who can sing and play these old, sometimes Elizabethan, songs that their ancestors knew in the shires of England or the highlands of Scotland; a "right ditty singer" means as much in their lives as a "mighty knowin'" doctor or a good preacher. Some of the more famous mountain minstrels are said to be able to carry on for days without repeating themselves. Old favorites include "Lord Lovell," "The Dying Knight's Farewell," "Lady Isabel and the Elf Knight," "Barbara Allen," "Thread the Needle," "Rickett's Hornpipe," "Give the Fiddler a Dram," "Lord Dannel," "Pa's Done Et the Shotgun," and "My Gal is Billy-be-Damned."

The mountaineer's life is hard but self-contained, and the sense of independence is his most prized trait. His psychology is still that of the frontier; he is suspicious of outsiders, takes strong measures against real or fancied wrongs, yet withal is extremely sociable. He describes his neighbors as sometimes "contrarious," sometimes "witchy" (claiming power to bewitch people); others are "flighty" and some are "drinlin" (frail). He respects "larnin'," even though he may not be able to read or write himself, so long as it does not make the possessor flout the ways of his people. Rooted to the soil and ancestral traditions, the mountaineer's concern with elemental things gives him a strength of character and a basic permanence that is not found elsewhere in the United States; to find his like, one must look to the English yeoman.

At 106.5 *m.* is the junction with State 40 *(see Tour 17);* between this point and Paintsville, US 23 and State 40 are united.

PAINTSVILLE, 108.3 *m.* (620 alt., 2,411 pop.), seat of Johnson County, was named for PAINT CREEK which flows through the town, and along which early settlers found many of the large trees stripped of their bark and embellished with drawings of birds and animals, painted in red and black on the smooth undertrunk of the trees. There were found also odd figures of buffalo and deer painted in red and black on the clifflike sandstones of the creek gorge. Various undecipherable hieroglyphs were once visible near the drawings, but these have become obliterated by the weather during the last 40 or 50 years.

The town is on the SITE OF PAINT LICK STATION, an old trading post. Indian traditions cling to this part of the valley, which was apparently a favorite burial ground of the Indians. On the hills surrounding Paintsville many graves and burial mounds have been found; and artifacts, such as pipes, tomahawks, pottery, and beads, have been taken from them. The ROCK HOUSE, a natural rock formation with a circular opening cut to provide entrance, stands on a hill facing the river just north of Concord Baptist Church. Such shelters, bearing evidence of Indian occupation, replaced wigwams in times of danger.

Paintsville is at the junction with State 40 *(see Tour 17).*

EAST POINT, 114.5 *m.* (627 alt., 265 pop.), lies directly across the Levisa Fork of the Big Sandy River from Blockhouse Bottom, the SITE OF HARMON'S STATION. This, the first fort in the Big Sandy Valley, was founded in 1787 by Matthias Harmon and a party of settlers from Draper's Meadow. Attacked by Indians in 1788, the station was abandoned and burned, but a year later rebuilt.

In the fall of 1787, while practically all the men from Harmon's Station were on a hunting trip in the Big Sandy Valley, a band of Cherokee and Shawnee attacked the home of Jennie Wiley at the settlement of Walker's Creek. With Mrs. Wiley were her 15-year-old brother and her four children. Realizing from the actions of the two leaders that they had mistaken her home for that of Matthias Harmon, who had defeated the Indians a few days before, Mrs. Wiley tried to fight them off only to see three of the children and her brother tomahawked and scalped. After setting fire to the cabin, the Indians, with Mrs. Wiley and her 15-month-old baby as captives, left the settlement. During the 11 months in which she was held, Jennie Wiley saw them kill her baby by dashing its brains out against a tree.

During the winter the Indians camped near the head of Cherokee Creek. While they were on one of their hunting trips, Mrs. Wiley, bound with rawhide thongs, crawled to the corner of the cabin; she allowed the rain to drip through the roof and to fall on the leather until it stretched. Then she freed herself and escaped down Little Mud Lick Creek and up another small stream, which the settlers later named Jennie's Creek in honor of this brave pioneer woman. At East Point she crossed the river on a log and reached Harmon's Station just before the Indians who were pursuing her appeared on the opposite side.

The Bottoms between East Point and Prestonsburg were used as camping grounds during the War between the States by Union forces under Gen. James A. Garfield.

PRESTONSBURG, 121.2 *m.* (643 alt., 2,105 pop.), between the river and the hills, was first known as Preston Station, named for Col. John Preston, a surveyor from Augusta County, Virginia, who camped here in 1791. The erection of John Spurlock's house on this site in 1791 distinguishes Prestonsburg as the oldest settlement in the Big Sandy Valley. The building stood here for many years as a landmark.

On Second Ave., north of Court St., is the house used as COLONEL GARFIELD'S HEADQUARTERS (*open by request*) during his Big Sandy campaign. The building, facing the river, is a rambling two-story frame structure with brick end chimneys and a two-story veranda across the front. Soldiers camped 300 yards north of the house.

During the War between the States the Big Sandy Valley was the scene of an important military campaign. The Battle of Middle Creek, fought on January 10, 1862, within three miles of Prestonsburg, determined the control of eastern Kentucky and drove a Union salient into the broken Confederate line that cut across southern Kentucky. Col. James A. Garfield, who commanded a brigade of Ohio and Kentucky troops under General Buell, planned and executed the campaign. In a month he succeeded in driving the Confederate forces under Gen. Humphrey Marshall from the Big Sandy Valley, causing them to retreat into southeastern Virginia, thereby preventing them from descending the Ohio River to Cincinnati. The Battle of Middle Creek was the first substantial victory for the Union cause. It was the success of Garfield's campaign in the Big Sandy that gave him the general's star and started him on the road leading to the Presidency.

A story is told that illustrates some of the difficulties of the campaign. The Big Sandy was in flood, the roads deep in mud, and the brigade in need of supplies. Garfield, with one other soldier, descended in a skiff from Pikeville to Catlettsburg where they found the steamer *Sandy Valley*. He loaded the boat with supplies and commanded the captain and crew to pilot him back to Pikeville. The captain refused, so Garfield took the wheel himself, and after a perilous trip reached Pikeville.

Between Prestonsburg and Pikeville the highway winds along the east side of Levisa Fork, much of the distance in plain sight of the river.

At 130.5 *m.* is the junction with State 80 *(see Tour 18)*.

US 23 passes through several little towns whose men work irregularly in the numerous hillside coal mines of the area *(see Tour 19)*. Since the highway has opened this region to products from the South, the farmers, living a mile or two back from the road, are no longer able to sell the garden products with which they formerly paid their taxes; their situation is desperate. In this region dwell many relatives and descendants of the Hatfield and McCoy families, whose feuds were notorious for several generations *(see Tour 19)*.

Back from the highway are isolated little graveyards usually perched on hilltops under a cluster of oak trees. Many of them have "grave houses"—rude log and clapboard shelters—that the mountaineers customarily erect over and around the graves of their relatives.

PIKEVILLE, 152.2 *m.* (680 alt., 3,376 pop.), with its long narrow streets, is surrounded by thickly timbered countryside that ranges from the hilly to the mountainous; neighboring roads reveal scenes of wild, almost breathtaking, beauty. Although the Levisa, which flows through the town, no longer carries its once heavy burden of logs and other freight, Pikeville is still a lumbering and coal mining center. It is also the administration office of the Pikeville terminus of the Chesapeake & Ohio Ry. It was named for Zebulon M. Pike, the explorer, and was developed chiefly by the younger sons of the Rees family of Virginia who took up thousands of acres here.

The HOTEL JAMES HATCHER, Main St., completed in 1931, has an odd assortment of relics on display in its lobby—ox-yokes, hoop skirts, cannon balls, ox-shoes, chain dogs, cant hooks, bootjacks, spinning wheels, looms, and flintlock rifles. On the walls are popular bits of rural humor: "To live a long life, reside in Pikeville—the only city on the map where an undertaker ever failed in business"; "There is a noticeable increase in population in these mountain counties. Why?

True mountaineers obey the commandments and never allow a twin bed in their homes"; "Visiting Pikeville is like making love to an old maid. You'll have to do it all over again"; and "We serve free beer if you are over 95 years old and accompanied by your parent."

Pikeville is at the junction with US 119 *(see Tour 19)*; between Pikeville and JENKINS, 191.5 *m.* (1,527 alt., 8,465 pop.) *(see Tour 19)*, US 23 and US 119 are united *(see Tour 19)*.

South of Jenkins the route leads over continuous elevations to the crest of Pine Mountain, thence through historic POUND GAP, 194.6 *m.* (2,366 alt.), a mountain pass that connects the South with the Big Sandy Valley. It is called a wind gap because water no longer flows through it. Pound Gap, like many mountain passes, has been a high-road of adventure and romance. The Kentucky, the Cumberland, and the Big Sandy head near it; Indian trails passed through it; pioneers eventually utilized it. At first called Sounding Gap because the rocky formation seemed to give back a hollow sound, the name was corrupted to Pound Gap.

A marker on the Kentucky side of the gap lists important dates in the early history of the State and of this pass.

Pound Gap is on the Virginia Line, 20.5 miles west of Norton, Va. *(see Virginia Tour 15)*.

Tour 2

Winchester—Stanton—Jackson—Hazard—Junction with US 119; 161.9 *m.* State 15.

Hard-surfaced roadbed.
Louisville & Nashville R.R. roughly parallels entire route.
All types of accommodations in larger towns; limited elsewhere.

This route, between Winchester and the junction with US 119, passes from the fertile fields and spacious farmhouses of the Bluegrass region, along Indian and pioneer trails and winding streams, to the wooded hills of the mist-hung Appalachians.

WINCHESTER, 0 *m.* (981 alt., 8,233 pop.) *(see Tour 16)*, is at the junctions with US 60 *(see Tour 16)* and US 227 *(see Tour 17A)*.

Southeast of Winchester State 15 winds through rolling country to INDIAN OLD FIELDS (R), 11 *m.*, the SITE OF ESKIPPAKITHIKI, an Indian village that was here from about 1718 to 1754, and is believed to have been the last one in Kentucky. Early Scottish traders, referred to the Piqua, a band of Shawnee who lived here, as Picts, and their

village as Little Pict Town.   The first white settlers found remnants
of Indian cornfields, cabins, and a palisade here.
At 12 *m.* is the junction with an unimproved road.

Left on this road to OIL SPRINGS, 0.5 *m.*, a once popular resort marked by
an abandoned hotel and a few servants' quarters.   There are both sulphur and
chalybeate springs here.   Like others in the vicinity, they contain traces of
petroleum.
The overflow from the springs forms LULBEGRUD CREEK, beside which
John Finley, Daniel Boone, and several others camped in 1769.   They had been
reading *Gulliver's Travels* at night by the campfire, when one evening one of the
men returned to camp and reported that he, like Gulliver, had been to Lorbrulgrud,
capital of Brobdingnag, and had killed two of the inhabitants.   He had in reality
been to near-by Oil Springs and had killed two buffaloes.   The name, twisted into
Lulbegrud, is still applied to the creek.
Left 4 *m.* from Oil Springs on a trail, passable in good weather, to PILOT
KNOB, 800 feet above the plains.   The superb view from this point includes
the towns of Winchester and Mount Sterling, 20 miles distant.   From this summit
John Finley and Daniel Boone *(see Tour 17A)* first glimpsed the Bluegrass uplands in 1769.   Pilot Knob had been a landmark to Indians passing up and down
the great Warriors' Trace many years before the first pioneers arrived in Kentucky.

CLAY CITY, 19.5 *m.* (628 alt., 528 pop.), is the site of the once
prosperous Red River Iron Works, known as early as 1802 for the
superior quality of the nails, stoves, plowshares, cannon balls, and
other products manufactured in its blast furnace and forge.   Tradition
states that many of the cannon balls used in the War of 1812 were
made here.
STANTON, 24.3 *m.* (562 alt., 423 pop.), seat of Powell County, is
on the flood plain of Red River.   Stanton, first called Beaver Pond
for a small lake created by a beaver dam in the swampy lowlands just
east of the town, was renamed in 1852 to honor Richard H. Stanton
of Maysville, Representative in Congress from 1849 to 1855.   Hunting
is a popular sport during the fall season in the extensive woodlands
of the mountainous region surrounding Stanton, where small game, including fox, raccoon, opossum, rabbit, and squirrel are plentiful.
SLADE, 36.4 *m.* (890 alt., 418 pop.), is a hamlet lying in rugged
uplands.

Right from Slade on graveled State 11 to NATURAL BRIDGE STATE PARK,
2.6 *m. (adm. adults 10¢, children 5¢; overnight parking, 25¢; lodge, shelter houses,
hotel and cabins; boating and bathing facilities).*   NATURAL BRIDGE, a reddish
rock-span of the Paleozoic era, forms a dividing ridge between Wolfe and Powell
Counties.   Contrary to the popular impression, it was not carved by stream
erosion but by the disintegrating action of wind, mist, rain, and frost on the
softer conglomerate limestone under the hard capstone.   This vast arch has a
clearance of 92 feet, a width between abutments of 76 feet, and a roadway breadth
of 24 feet.   Trails lead to the top of the bridge, from which there is a magnificent
view of the surrounding countryside.   In the park's 1,127 wooded, hilly acres
are cliffs and huge balanced rocks, as well as a profusion of wild flowers, rhododendron, and mountain laurel.

Between Slade and Jackson the route is through a deep gap in Holly Ridge, the mountain on the south side of which the highway follows a small ravine which is cool even in the hottest weather. The surrounding hills are covered with shrubs and vines and in the spring and early summer they fairly glow with mountain laurel and rhododendron. At intervals the waters of mountain streams can be heard plunging against rocks.

South of this peaceful valley the highway winds in and out, making sweeping curves and sharp turns to the top of FROZEN MOUNTAIN (1,500 alt.). From this point is a panorama of jagged cliffs rising above wide expanses of woodland. In late fall the varicolored foliage of the deciduous trees—chiefly scrub oak—contrasts pleasingly with the green of the conifers. South of Frozen Mountain the highway follows the devious course of the North Fork of the Kentucky River.

JACKSON, 77.9 m. (790 alt., 2,109 pop.), the seat of Breathitt County, straggles over a hillside around which the North Fork curves. Houses in this town face a narrow valley through which the river flows toward a towering mountain. Jackson, named by admirers of Andrew Jackson, was formerly so isolated that its inhabitants retained for many years the customs and peculiarities of speech of their pioneer English ancestors. Since 1890, when the railroad was extended from Lexington, Jackson has become a distributing point of merchandise for the remoter mountain regions and its residents have abandoned not only the feuds (see Tour 19) which caused the county to be called Bloody Breathitt but also most of their distinctive mountain customs and occupations. One of the latter, "senging," or the gathering of ginseng, was an important source of income of the early settlers. The roots of this herb were dried, baled, and shipped to China where they are valued for their medicinal properties. The hillspeople—especially the womenfolk—used to troop into the mountains at dawn with sacks and small hoes. There they worked busily all day filling their bags with roots which they dragged wearily home at twilight. At the end of each week all of the dried ginseng was exchanged at the country store for "factory" gingham and calico, salt, soda, coffee, and other necessities that could not be produced on the little hillside farms. There was keen competition among "sengers" for the award given to the digger who had brought in the greatest quantity by the end of the season. The prize, often a pair of coarse shoes or only a bright ribbon, was eagerly coveted, and the winner was lauded throughout the county.

LEE'S JUNIOR COLLEGE, at Jackson, established in 1864, is maintained by the Presbyterian Church of Kentucky. The school is co-educational and has an enrollment of approximately 100 students.

In QUICKSAND, 82 m. (673 alt., 90 pop.), is a substation of the forestry division of University of Kentucky College of Agriculture. A tract of 15,000 acres here is devoted to experiments in reforestation. On the top of a ridge in Quicksand overlooking the river is a large MOUND of unknown origin and purpose. It consists of an immense

VI. IN THE BLUEGRASS

ARISTOCRAT

CHURCHILL DOWNS, LOUISVILLE

WAR ADMIRAL, WINNER OF THE 1937 KENTUCKY DERBY

MAN O' WAR

COMING OUT OF PADDOCK, CHURCHILL DOWNS

BLUE GRASS TROTTERS IN ACTION

ON DIXIANA FARM

STABLES AT ELMENDORF

IDLE HOUR STABLE

SPRING IN THE BLUEGRASS

BLESSING OF THE HOUNDS CEREMONY BY IROQUOIS HUNT CLUB

GRIME'S MILL HOUSE, HEADQUARTERS OF IROQUOIS HUNT CLUB

ROAD THROUGH THE BLUE GRASS COUNTRY

A KENTUCKY PIKE

heap of stones, many of which are believed to have been brought from a considerable distance. In a neighboring valley is an Indian village site that has yielded some artifacts.

Quicksand is the scene of the annual Robinson Harvest Festival *(last Thurs. and Fri. of Sept.)*, during which products of the fireside industries of the mountain people are displayed and sold, and contests in folk singing and dancing are held.

RIVERSIDE INSTITUTE in LOST CREEK, 89 *m.* (40 pop.), is described as a "small Berea" *(see Tour 4)*. Here about 70 mountain boys and girls are given vocational training. The school is conducted by the United Brethren in Christ. This Protestant sect was founded in the United States by Philip W. Otterbein (1726–1813).

Between DWARF, 114.3 *m.* (900 alt., 118 pop.) *(see Tour 18)* and 120 *m.*, State 15 and State 80 *(see Tour 18)* are united.

HAZARD, 121.6 *m.* (833 alt., 7,021 pop.), seat of Perry County, was named by men who served under Oliver Hazard Perry in the Battle of Lake Erie, September 10, 1813. Shortly after the close of the War between the States, natural gas was discovered in this region, and in 1917 oil was found. In 1910 Hazard had only 537 inhabitants, but after the Louisville & Nashville R.R. tracks had been extended from Jackson into the Perry County coal fields—one of the finest in the State —Hazard grew steadily. Because of the ready accessibility of fuel, a large steel mill has been erected in the town. Large quantities of timber are still available in this vicinity and numerous sawmills are in operation.

The French-Eversole feud, which began in 1882, was principally confined to Perry County. The worst conflict occurred in Hazard (1888) where members of one faction barricaded themselves in the courthouse and the other faction occupied nearby dwellings and stores. Twelve men were killed and several were wounded in this battle.

Between Hazard and Whitesburg the highway leads through rugged hills and short fertile valleys. Lonely little cabins with their small patches of corn perch on the ridges or nestle in the coves. This is the region of Chaucerian English, old ballads, and the dulcimer *(see Tours 1, 18, and 19)*.

WHITESBURG, 160.2 *m.* (1,146 alt., 1,804 pop.), seat of Letcher County, is named for C. White, a member of the legislature when the county was formed. Before the coming of the railroad in 1912, Whitesburg with a population of 300, was the only town in Letcher County, and lumber milling was the chief industry. Between 1880 and 1890 great quantities of timber from the vast forests along the headwaters of the Kentucky and Cumberland Rivers were floated downstream to the mills here from which lumber was shipped to many parts of the world.

At 161.9 *m.* is the junction with US 119 *(see Tour 19)*.

Tour 3

(Cincinnati, Ohio)—Newport—Cynthiana—Paris—Lexington—Nicholasville—Lancaster—Somerset—(Chattanooga, Tenn.); US 27.
Ohio Line to Tennessee Line, 221.4 m.

Hard-surfaced roadbed.
Cincinnati, New Orleans, and Texas Pacific R.R. parallels route between Eubank
and Tennessee Line.
All types of accommodations in larger towns; limited elsewhere.

This route crosses rolling hills, fertile Bluegrass lands, and the foothills and mountains of southeastern Kentucky. US 27, bordered by
white rail fences or old stone walls, passes fine farms in central Kentucky with their stately old mansions; great stables kept with the tidi-
ness of a Dutch kitchen; sleek horses, purebred cattle, and sheep brows-
ing in blue-tinted fields; and broad acres of waving grain, tobacco, and
hemp.

Section a. OHIO LINE *to* LEXINGTON; *98.3 m. US 27*

US 27, the Lookout Mountain Airline, crosses the Ohio Line, 0 *m.,*
at Cincinnati, Ohio *(see Ohio Tour 26),* on the Central Bridge *(toll
10¢ to 75¢)* over the Ohio River.

NEWPORT, 1 *m.* (512 alt., 29,744 pop.), directly above the confluence of the Licking and Ohio Rivers, is within the Cincinnati metropolitan area. Seen from a distance on winter days when the city
is blanketed with Cincinnati's smoke, Newport seems to be a gray
lake buoying up church spires and chimneys. Most of the buildings,
erected in the days of chimney pots, coal stoves, and open fires, are of
brick and are utilitarian in workmanship and design. The town is
quiet on weekdays, when so many of its citizens have gone over the
river to work in Cincinnati, but on Saturdays farmers from the nearby
fertile farm lands come to do their trading or discuss crops and politics.

A young soldier by the name of Hubbard Taylor came here in 1790
with the Kentucky troops from Lexington, on their way to join St.
Clair at Fort Washington. When young Taylor saw the lush vegetation here, he went no farther. Acting as agent for his father in Virginia, he bought holdings and roughly planned the town, naming it
Newport in honor of Christopher Newport who had come to America
in 1607 as commander of the first ship to reach Jamestown.

There is no record of what became of Hubbard; two years later
when his brother James came to visit the family holdings, he found

little except the name and the fine land. James returned to Virginia and the following spring came back to Newport with Robert Christy, an Englishman. He also brought his wife, two slaves, a pair of blooded horses, and farming and household equipment.

During the first two years the place continued to be little better than a clearing in the wilderness, though in 1796, a year after its incorporation as a village, Newport became the county seat. In 1798 William Kennedy and other prominent citizens of northern Kentucky established Newport Academy, a school that soon became famous throughout the region. In spite of early steps in education and the building of churches, more than one citizen protested through the Cincinnati papers against the practice of staining Newport's riverbanks with gore from frequent duels. Others spoke against the custom of burning useless flatboats on the riverbanks; still others complained of disturbances made by inebriates.

By 1835 Newport had again been incorporated, this time as a city. The mayor and the trustees seem to have been men of dignified manners and strict morals, judging from the laws they passed. Hallooing was declared illegal, day or night; swearing was likely to cost five dollars; swimming was prohibited within the town limits between 4 A.M. and 9 P.M.; and four trustees had to give permission for the interment of any body within the public burying ground.

Like other Kentucky towns, Newport was caught between the North and the South during the War between the States. A mob of Southern sympathizers in 1856 destroyed the office and equipment of the *True South*, an abolitionist newspaper. Many secessionists were arrested; prominent men were found hiding from Union sympathizers in the cellars of their homes; female Southern sympathizers insulted Union soldiers.

By the eighties and nineties, Newport was enjoying a mild boom— the only one in its history. The coming of Germans in large numbers, the completion of bridges over the Ohio to Cincinnati, and the growth of the county agricultural population, were all contributing factors. The many small industries gave place to a few large ones such as breweries and a steel mill; while quick, cheap transportation tempted more and more of its citizens to go over the river for work. In 1921 steel workers in Newport began a strike that lasted for seven years (*see Labor*).

Newport has grown little within the past 40 years. Many who might settle here prefer the higher elevation at Fort Thomas; others who must work in Cincinnati move there in order to save time and carfare.

THE SOUTHGATE HOUSE (*visit by appointment*), 24 E. 3rd St., now a clubhouse, was built by Col. Wright Southgate about 1821. This 20-room brick mansion later passed into the hands of the Talliaferro family. The house is Southern Colonial in design and has a winding staircase of mahogany and a small observation tower with four windows, each less than one foot square.

The JAMES TAYLOR MANSION *(visit by appointment)*, 3rd and Overton Sts., is now a funeral home. It occupies the site of the frame building erected in 1812 by James Taylor. A discontented slave burned the first home in 1837, and soon after, Taylor built this four-story brick and frame mansion. The pillared veranda originally faced the river, and a winding driveway formed a semicircle through the shade trees surrounding the house, but in 1888 the house was remodeled so that the back became the front. The name Taylor is still legible on the front door, while his love of horses is shown by the figure of a brown horse standing on the spread wings of an eagle above the motto "Ready and Faithful."

The interior of the house has wide halls, a winding stairway, and spacious rooms with ceilings 16 feet high that are supported by wooden columns of Corinthinian design. The basement, which was used to house the slaves, has stone walls that are two feet thick, low ceilings, and small windows heavily barred. The basement dining room still contains the plank dining tables, scarred by countless jackknife blades of restless slaves. Many notables were served by these slaves; among them Lafayette.

The TAYLOR METHODIST EPISCOPAL CHURCH, 123 E. 3rd St., is a simple red brick building with plastered walls, cherry pulpit, and hand-made wooden pews. It was erected in 1831. In the deed to the lot appears the name of Henry Ward Beecher, then a student at Lane Theological Seminary in Cincinnati.

From the NEWPORT CITY PARK, a six-acre wooden tract on the point between the mouth of the Licking River and the Ohio, is a view of downtown Cincinnati. The U.S. Government acquired part of this area in 1803 by gift and purchase from James Taylor. Between 1806 and 1884 this was the site of Newport Barracks, the headquarters in 1812 of the 5,000 militia under Col. Isaac Shelby *(see Tour 5)* that later marched to reinforce General Harrison against the British. The drills, parades, and Sunday band concerts grew to be a colorful part of the town life, and on summer Sundays attracted barge-loads of Cincinnatians. After the great Ohio River flood of 1884 had inundated the barracks, the post was moved to what is now Fort Thomas, and all that remains today are a part of the brick wall and a bronze cannon captured from the Spanish at the battle of San Juan Hill.

At the NATIONAL BAND AND TAG COMPANY PLANT *(no admission)*, 720 Orchard St., are manufactured metal and celluloid identification bands for poultry, game, and livestock. Since each band must bear the name and address of the animal's owner, all work is done to order and a large percentage of the business is carried on by mail, orders being secured through advertisements in national farm papers and magazines.

The CAMPBELL COUNTY COURTHOUSE, SW. cor. 4th and York Sts., a brick structure of Tudor design with stone trim, stands on the plot of ground deeded to the city by James Taylor for one shilling in 1795. The first log courthouse built here the following year was replaced in

1815 by a brick building called the Palace of Peace. The present building, erected in 1884, has a large window of colored glass, a rotunda, and a clock tower. On the elm-shaded grounds are two cannon.

About 3,000 men are employed at the ANDREWS STEEL COMPANY PLANT *(no admission)*, 9th and Lowell Sts. There are about 30 buildings in which are manufactured such varied steel products as refrigerators and truck bodies, and heavily galvanized sheet metal for South American ranchers who use them to protect their crops against hordes of grasshoppers.

Between Newport and Cynthiana, US 27 traverses the outer Bluegrass. The land is quite hilly in some places, gently rolling in others. Valleys and creek beds are cut deeply into the limestone; there are occasional stands of second- or third-growth timber, and in spring the wild plum, dogwood, and redbud are much in evidence. Outside the towns the homes are usually modest farmhouses, frequently backed by tobacco or cattle barns.

FORT THOMAS, 4.3 *m.* (852 alt., 10,008 pop.), is an attractive residential city of secluded streets and landscaped lawns and gardens on a rolling ridge that rises between the Ohio and Licking Rivers. Most of its people are connected with the business and industrial life of the metropolitan area.

In the COVINGTON WATERWORKS, occupying an extensive area in Fort Thomas, water drawn from the Ohio River is filtered and pumped through supply mains to reservoirs. The reciprocal agreement by which Fort Thomas draws its water supply from the Covington reservoirs in return for the space occupied by the waterworks has been in effect for many years.

A 90-foot water tower, of rough-hewn Kentucky limestone, South Fort Thomas Ave. at the entrance to Fort Thomas Military Reservation, was presented by citizens of Covington, Cincinnati, and Newport as a SPANISH-AMERICAN WAR MEMORIAL. It commemorates members of the U.S. Infantry who lost their lives in that war and Brig. Gen. Harry Clay Egbert, colonel of the 6th Infantry during the Cuban campaign, who was killed in action in the Philippines. The two cannon near the tower, excellent specimens of the workmanship of Spanish gunsmiths of the eighteenth century, are trophies of the Cuban campaign.

The FORT THOMAS MILITARY RESERVATION *(open with restrictions)* was named for Gen. George H. Thomas, the "Rock of Chickamauga." The site was selected in 1887 by Gen. Philip H. Sheridan, and the first building, the commanding officer's quarters, was completed in 1888. The present development of the fort represents an investment of nearly $4,000,000. The post has been garrisoned continuously since its establishment, except for a period in 1911 and 1912. The 10th U.S. Infantry *(drills daily at 8:00 and 11:45* A.M.; *parades Tues. and Thurs. at 4:30* P.M.*)* is now stationed here, and this is the headquarters of the eastern Kentucky district of the CCC, which consists of approximately 5,000 men. From the driveway as it circles the parade ground and drill field is a wide-spreading view of the Ohio River Valley.

ALEXANDRIA, 14.2 *m.* (845 alt., 424 pop.), in a rich agricultural area, is an old village with sturdy brick homes and many trees. On the highest promontory of the county, in the heart of the village, is the old brick CAMPBELL COUNTY COURTHOUSE, whose clock tower and dome are visible for miles. Many valuable old records are housed here. When Kenton County was formed from the western half of Campbell County, the seat of government was transferred from Visalia to Alexandria. Through the years this little town has clung tenaciously to the honor of being the county seat, though Newport has its own courthouse and criminal and chancery courts, and keeps the records relating to northern Campbell County.

Alexandria is at the junction with State 10 *(see Tour 11)*.

In GRANT'S LICK, 22.4 *m.* (1,293 pop.), a village originally settled by the Grant family, relatives of Daniel Boone, salt was manufactured at the old salt lick as early as 1793.

The old COVERED BRIDGE, 30 *m.*, across the Licking River, is 500 feet in length, one of the longest wooden bridges in existence.

The Licking River is a narrow, deep-flowing stream whose canal-like lower course is now the scene of commercial activity. Barges from the Ohio enter it and discharge their cargoes at private landings along its banks. The Licking rises near the Virginia border and flows in a northwesterly course across the State, traversing the "big bend" region and forming the dividing line between Kenton and Campbell Counties. Long before the white man came, it was the route by which the Indians who lived north of the Ohio River entered the Bluegrass region abounding in deer and buffalo. On August 19, 1782, on the banks of the Licking occurred the fierce Battle of Blue Licks *(see Tour 15)*, and from the spot where the Licking joins the Ohio, George Rogers Clark launched his avenging drive against the Indians on the Little Miami. Again, at the outbreak of the War of 1812, it was from the mouth of the Licking that the soldiers of Kentucky marched against the allied British and Indians. When the war with Mexico broke out, Newport Barracks was a rallying point of volunteers who helped form the conquering armies that crossed the Rio Grande. In a later day, when the Union was torn by the struggle between North and South, the banks of the Licking, at this point, were again a center of military activity.

At 36 *m.* is the junction with State 22 *(see Tour 13)*; between this point and Falmouth, State 22 and US 27 are united.

FALMOUTH, 39.3 *m.* (525 alt., 1,876 pop.), known as the Island City, is at the confluence of the Main and South Licking Rivers. Its tree-shaded streets and well-kept old houses create an atmosphere of hospitality. First settled in 1776, the town was established in 1799 by Virginians who named it for Falmouth, Virginia. Until 1854, when the railroad was extended to this point, Falmouth was a village of "mud roads, tin lanterns, and tallow dips." All merchandise had to be hauled in covered wagons from Foster's Landing, 13 miles distant, on the Ohio River. The stores were "swapping posts," where feathers, rags, tallow, hides, furs, beeswax, ginseng, ax handles, and whisky were exchanged for calico, sugar, coffee, gunpowder, and lead.

One of the earliest sawmills in the State, established at "Fallsmouth" (Falmouth) in 1793, was advertised in 1794 in the Cincinnati *Centinel of the North-Western Territory:*

Plank and scantling of every kind, delivered at the mill or in Cincinnati, on the shortest notice. Orders will be thankfully received and pointedly attended to.
                                                              JOHN WALLERE.
Fallsmouth, Forks of Licking, Dec. 15, 1794.

N.B. The subscriber will be down with a quantity of planks as soon as the water of Licking will admit.

In June 1780 Captain Bird of the British Army, with a Canadian and Indian force of 600 men, ascended the Licking River to the confluence of its forks at Falmouth. Here he landed his cannon and concentrated his forces. From this point he proceeded on his march to the attack of Ruddle's Station, about seven miles north of the present town of Paris; his trail can be distinguished in many places by the blazes that still mark the trees.

Pendleton County, of which Falmouth is the seat, is sometimes called "the county that came back." At one time a third of its population moved away because of the decreasing productivity of its land. Eventually the remaining residents adopted new methods of cultivation and planted clover and other soil-enriching crops on the barren wastes. Today beekeeping is an extensive business, annual shipments of honey approximating 2,000,000 pounds. A queen-rearing plant is in operation in the region in which 4,000 queen bees are bred and shipped to various parts of the State.

Falmouth is at the junction with State 22 *(see Tour 13)*.

CYNTHIANA, 64.7 *m.* (718 alt., 4,386 pop.), lying in the outer Bluegrass region, on the banks of the South Fork of Licking River, is a residential town with a leisurely social life, and a background of tradition, culture, and wealth. Established in 1793 and incorporated in 1806, Cynthiana was named for Cynthia and Anna, two daughters of the first settler, Robert Harrison. The stately old red-brick HARRISON COUNTY COURTHOUSE, Main St., was built in 1851 in Greek Revival style, with an octagonal clock tower. Preserved in this building are valuable county records, many of them bearing the handwriting of prominent statesmen, including Henry Clay who in 1801 was admitted to the bar of the Quarter Sessions Court at Cynthiana.

Directly back of the courthouse square is an old log house, built in 1790 and used successively as a courthouse, law office, printing office, photograph gallery, and residence. In this house Bishop H. H. Kavanaugh and Ambrose Dudley Mann, later special commissioner of the United States Government to the German States (1846), special agent to Hungary (1849), and to Switzerland (1850), served as apprentices. The *Guardian of Liberty,* Cynthiana's first newspaper, was also published in this old building. A left wing, also built of logs, has been added recently.

The JUDGE BOYD PLACE, on Pike St. R. from Main St., faces the river. This mansion, built in 1807 and designed in the late Georgian Colonial manner, is still in excellent condition. On the outskirts of town, on N. Main St., is a BURYING GROUND established in 1793; it contains many old gravestones.

Cynthiana was the scene of a severe battle during the War between the States. On July 17, 1862, Gen. John H. Morgan, with about 800 men, captured the town which was defended by a Federal force under Col. John J. Landrum. Much of the fighting was around the old covered bridge over the Licking River.

Again in 1864 General Morgan, with 1,200 men, captured the town after two days' fighting. Federal forces, under the command of Gen. E. H. Hobson, surrendered. On Sunday morning, June 12, 1864, the day after the battle, General Morgan's troops, fatigued from the fighting, were suddenly attacked by Gen. Stephen G. Burbridge and a force of 5,000 fresh troops. This surprise attack resulted in the retreat of General Morgan's troops. Most of the business section of Cynthiana was destroyed by fire during the fighting and the loss of life on both sides was unusually heavy.

Cynthiana is at the junction with US 62 *(see Tour 14).*

Left from Cynthiana on Millersburg Rd. to BATTLE GROVE CEMETERY, 1 *m.,* the site of the second day's battle on June 12, 1864. A Confederate monument, erected in 1869, memorializes the spot. A monument here to the memory of Harrison County soldiers who lost their lives in the Mexican War was erected in 1848 on the Courthouse Square, but was moved to Battle Grove in 1868.

Between Cynthiana and Stanford the route, bordered with old stone walls and shaded by rows of honeylocust trees, goes through the inner Bluegrass, one of the most fertile agricultural regions in the country. It was a landowner in this region who, upon hearing one night from a guest that there was a weed in one of his 10-acre pastures, got up and went hunting with lights and lanterns until he found it. Judging from the neatness of the pastures, the story might well be true; barns and stables in the Bluegrass are clean as can be, the old elms and beech trees in the pastures show signs of careful pruning, and the stone walls are neatly and strongly built, some having stood for more than 150 years with no help from cement. In many places the mansion with its attendant barns, trainers' and laborers' quarters, stables, and paddocks has the look of a small prim village.

In the early days, settlers on this fertile land used it to produce almost all of their needs—corn, wheat, hogs, sheep, cows, horses, bluegrass for pasture, clover for hay, and oats for feed. Hemp and tobacco were grown to be sold, and from the beginning the horse was an important product. But as the western corn and wheat lands were opened to settlement, the functions of the Bluegrass farms decreased in number. Cultivation of tobacco and the breeding of horses are predominant now, the Bluegrass farmer often finding it cheaper to buy his oats and corn than to use precious tobacco land and pasturage for their cultivation.

PEAVINE'S HIGHLAND CHIEF STUD, the well-known saddle horse farm (L), at 68.1 *m.*, is typical of many in the Bluegrass region. Harrison Chief, the prize winner admired by all lovers of the Kentucky saddle horse, was bred here; his stall is still preserved.

Across the Licking River from the tiny settlement of LAIR, 69.2 *m.*, is the LEWIS HUNTER DISTILLERY *(open)*, still producing the same brand of whisky it made in the 1860's.

The EWALT HOUSE *(open)*, 75.2 *m.*, was built (R) in 1794 by Henry Ewalt, a soldier in the Revolutionary War. On a 200-acre tract, for which he paid 110 pounds sterling, he erected a two-story frame house with a stone chimney, seven feet wide and three feet deep at the base, at each end. About 1808 a stone ell of four rooms was added to the house; its walls are 22 inches thick. The interior walls are paneled in ash and walnut and decorated with hand-carved moldings. This site has belonged to the Ewalt family since 1788. In the old burying ground near the house are graves of several members of the Ewalt family.

At 78.8 *m.* is the junction with State 40 *(see Tour 17)*; between this point and PARIS, 80.3 *m.* (826 alt., 6,204 pop.) *(see Tour 15)*, US 27 and State 40 are united. Paris is also at the junction with US 68 *(see Tour 15)* and US 227 *(see Tour 17A)*.

Between Paris and Lexington, US 27 and US 68 are one route *(see Tour 15)*.

LEXINGTON, 98.3 *m.* (957 alt., 45,736 pop.) *(see Lexington)*.

Points of Interest: Homes of Henry Clay, Gen. John Hunt Morgan, Mary Todd Lincoln, and John Bradford; Transylvania College, University of Kentucky, loose-leaf tobacco market.

Lexington is at the junction with US 60 *(see Tour 16)*, US 25 *(see Tour 4)*, and US 68 *(see Tour 15)*.

Section b. LEXINGTON *to* TENNESSEE LINE; *123.1 m. US 27*

South of Lexington, 0 *m.*, US 27 passes through several towns of the Bluegrass, towns that draw their life from the surrounding country rather than from industrial establishments. They are centers of market for tobacco and stock, and distributing points for farmers' needs. Many wealthy farmers live in town, and rent their two or three farms to others. Busy days in spring or a good spell of tobacco-stripping weather find the towns almost deserted, for the farmers do not have time to loiter on the courthouse lawn. On Saturdays the streets are crowded with farm folk and gay with Negro laborers who have come in from their jobs of stock tending or field work. The tobacco season comes in late fall and early winter; it is then that the town is crowded with sellers and buyers whose trucks and wagons, canvas-covered, creak along the country lanes and highways under loads of cured, stripped, and tightly pressed white burley.

ALLEGHAN HALL (R), 2.7 *m.*, with its massive Ionic columns and fine proportions, is a good example of the Greek Revival type of architecture in Kentucky. A stone fence covered with honeysuckle and roses encloses the tree-shaded lawn, and iron gates guard the circular driveway. This site was part of a 2,000-acre tract that formerly belonged to John Campbell of Louisville. Ownership of the land changed several times before William Pettit bought it and built Alleghan, just before the outbreak of the War between the States. During the war Pettit was driven out of the State, and his home was occupied by Federal forces. There is a story that upon the outbreak of hostilities Pettit drove to Lexington, withdrew his money from the bank in gold, and buried it on his place. He died shortly after his return from his wartime exile, and in his last hours is said to have made repeated but futile attempts to reveal the hiding place of the treasure.

NICHOLASVILLE, 12.5 *m.* (947 alt., 3,128 pop.), seat of Jessamine County, resembles a Kentucky town of earlier days. Many old houses border its quiet, tree-shaded streets. It was first settled in 1798 and named for Col. George Nicholas, a native of Williamsburg, Virginia, and a member of the convention that met in Danville in 1792 to frame a State constitution. A geography, written by Jedidiah Morse and published in 1789 at Elizabethtown, New Jersey, contains the following description of this region:

"Elkhorn River, a branch of the Kentucky, from the southeast, waters a country fine beyond description. Indeed, the country east and south of this, including the headwaters of Licking River, Hickman's and Jessamine Creeks, and the remarkable bend in Kentucky River, may be called an extensive garden . . . The banks, or rather precipices, of the Kentucky and Dick's (Dix) Rivers are to be reckoned among the natural curiosities of this country. Here the astonished eye beholds 300 or 400 feet of solid perpendicular rocks—in some parts of the limestone kind and in others of fine white marble, curiously checkered with strata of astonishing regularity. These rivers have the appearance of deep artificial canals. Their high rocky banks are covered with red cedar groves."

Right from Nicholasville on the Old Frankfort Pike to the JOSEPH DRAKE HOUSE, 5 *m.*, which, according to legend, was built prior to 1770 by Joe Drake, described as a descendant and heir of Sir Francis Drake, the English admiral. The red brick house contains seven rooms with beams and sills of hand-hewn logs and massive walnut mantels and cabinets. Parts of the house are joined by large crude iron spikes, instead of the wooden pegs found elsewhere. The use of brick and iron makes its alleged age questionable. Across the road on land belonging to the estate is an old burying ground in the midst of a clump of trees. In the center stands a reproduction of the original gravestone, bearing this inscription:

JOSEPH DRAKE
of
Buckland, Monaghorum England
Born 1694
Died 1777
Beloved Husband of Rebecca Hamble of
Bodwin Cornwall, England.

In a primitive setting is GLASS'S MILL, 6 *m.*, erected in 1782, and said to have been the first gristmill in Kentucky. It later became a paper mill, and in 1849 was converted into a distillery which is no longer in use.

South of Nicholasville the highway descends gradually along the banks of Hickman Creek to the Kentucky River.

The CAMP NELSON UNITED STATES MILITARY CEMETERY (L), 19.8 *m.*, contains the graves of more than 500 soldiers who lost their lives at the Battles of Perryville and Richmond during the War between the States.

FORMER CAMP NELSON (L) 21.3 *m.*, is at the mouth of Hickman Creek; this was one of the leading concentration camps for Federal troops and munitions during the War between the States. It was also the main camp in the State for the enlistment of Negro troops and a refuge for Negro slaves. Established in 1863 and named for Gen. William Nelson, it remained a military camp until the close of the war.

The highway crosses the new concrete bridge over the Kentucky River. Nearby are the stone abutments of an old covered bridge recently torn down. It was considered an engineering triumph at the time of its construction in 1838, being then one of the longest wooden bridges in the United States. The length was 240 feet and no metal was used in the construction.

At 24.9 *m.* is the junction with State 152.

Right on this road to the junction with an unmarked graveled road, 2.6 *m.* Right on this road to CHIMNEY ROCK, 5 *m.*, a remarkable formation 125 feet high, carved by slow erosion from the limestone of the Kentucky River cliffs.

At 7 *m.* is HERRINGTON LAKE *(fishing, swimming; motorboats, $1 an hour or $3 a day; furnished cabins)*. This lake was formed in 1925 when the Kentucky Utilities Company completed the construction of a dam across Dix River near its confluence with the Kentucky River *(see Tour 15)*. Herrington Lake, 35 miles in length, covering 3,600 acres and ranging in depth to 250 feet, has a picturesque setting amid cliffs, rolling hills, upland farms, and forests.

In BRYANTSVILLE, 26.2 *m.* (150 pop.), is (R) BURNT TAVERN *(open)*, a popular roadhouse in stagecoach days; it was so named because it was twice destroyed by fire. One wing, which was saved, is now (1939) more than 100 years old. The porch across the front of the present two-story brick building is a later addition. This tavern was the birthplace of Henry Smith, Provisional Governor of Texas (1824 and again in 1837–38), who was a son of the original owner, Edward Smith of Virginia.

CAMP DICK ROBINSON, 28.4 *m.*, established in 1861 over the protest of Beriah Magoffin, then Governor of Kentucky, was the first Federal

Recruiting station south of the Ohio River. Gen. William Nelson, who was in command of the camp, had his headquarters in (L) the old DICK ROBINSON HOUSE *(open)*, a very long two-story frame building. In the central third, which is recessed, is a two-story galleried porch, topped with a gabled pediment.

Right from Camp Dick Robinson on State 34 to a junction, 1 *m.*, with an unmarked road; right on this road to the BIRTHPLACE OF CARRY NATION *(open)*, 4 *m.*, at Pope's Landing on Herrington Lake. The long one-story house of logs, now clapboarded, has outside end chimneys and rear additions. The house has a pedimented Doric portico of Greek Revival design.

Carry Amelia Moore Nation, the temperance agitator, was born here November 25, 1846. George Moore, her father, was a prosperous stock dealer and her mother a descendant of Alexander Campbell, founder of the Christian Church. About 1853 the family moved to Glen Artney in Woodford County *(see Tour 14)* and two years later to Cass County, Mo., where for a few years Carry attended a boarding school. She was married in 1867, but because of her husband's excessive drinking the marriage proved to be an exceptionally unhappy one and was of short duration. In 1877 she was married to David Nation, a lawyer, minister of the Christian Church, and editor of the Warrensburg *Journal.* After 25 years of married life, he divorced her in a spasm of revolt against her saloon-smashing activities. Between 1900 and 1910 Carry, an ardent member of the Woman's Christian Temperance Union, became internationally known for her hatchet-wielding against saloons, in which she indulged until a short time before her death in 1911.

BURDETT'S KNOB (1,090 alt.) 28.9 *m.*, is (L) a monadnock—a hill of resistant rock projecting from a plain that has been greatly reduced by erosion. It was used in pioneer times by settlers as a lookout.

The FORK CHURCH, 29.2 *m.*, is (L) a small brick structure, on the site of the log church, built in 1782 by Lewis Craig and other Baptist pioneers.

LANCASTER, 35.6 *m.* (1,032 alt., 1,630 pop.), seat of Garrard County, like many southern towns, is built around a public square in the center of which is a small park. On one corner is the red-brick GARRARD COUNTY COURTHOUSE designed in the Greek Revival style. The business section encircles the park, from which the tree-shaded streets radiate. The home demonstration agents of the Department of Agriculture have been reviving the art of rug-hooking in the county and some of the women are now placing their products on sale. *(Apply Home Demonstration office in courthouse for Information.)* The returns from this home industry are very low but the housewives are willing to work at it for the sake of bringing in even a small amount of cash. The town was settled in 1798 by pioneers from Lancaster, Pennsylvania, who designed and named it for their native city. When the town founders met to choose a site, Capt. William Buford persuaded them to build on his land at the crossroads, promising to donate land for a public square and courthouse, and to provide water for all those attending court during his life. The numerous public wells that surrounded the square until a few years ago were the result of this promise. The first courthouse, built in the center of the square in 1798 by

Stephen Giles Letcher and Benjamin Letcher for the sum of 410 pounds sterling, was torn down in 1868 and the present courthouse erected.

The BRADLEY HOUSE (L), on a spacious lawn on Main St., opposite the high school, is a red brick Gothic-style structure with seven gables. This was formerly the home of William O. Bradley, Governor of Kentucky (1895–99).

The old LETCHER HOUSE *(open)*, on Maple Ave., is (R) a one-and-one-half story clapboarded structure remodeled from a double log house that was erected in 1789 by John Boyle, who later served as Chief Justice of the Kentucky Court of Appeals (1810–26) and U.S. Representative (1803–09). When Boyle vacated his log cabin home here, Samuel McKee, who succeeded Boyle in Congress (1809–17), moved in with his bride. George Robertson, elected to the U.S. Congress in 1817 and Chief Justice of Kentucky from 1829 to 1843, later brought his bride to this little house. Robert P. Letcher, a young lawyer of Garrard County, moved in when Robertson left for Washington. Letcher served as a Member of Congress from 1823 to 1833 and Governor of Kentucky from 1840 to 1844; in 1850 he was appointed Ambassador to Mexico by President Zachary Taylor.

1. Left from Lancaster on State 52, an improved road, to the junction with the Walker Pike, 8.4 *m.;* R. 1 *m.* on this road to the SITE OF THE KENNEDY HOUSE. So many parts of the building have been carried away by antique dealers and souvenir hunters that only the foundation remains. Harriet Beecher Stowe is said to have visited this place when she was in Kentucky gathering material for *Uncle Tom's Cabin,* which was published (1851–52) first as a serial in *The National Era.* Her trips to Kentucky were made while she was a resident of Cincinnati (1832–50). Gen. Thomas Kennedy owned 200 slaves and 15,000 acres of land, one of the largest plantations in the South. General Kennedy's daughter, Nancy Kennedy Letcher, who lived in this house and reared a family of 10 children, is said to have been the inspiration for the little Eva of the story. Lewis Clark, a Negro slave owned by General Kennedy, was the George Harper of the story. After the death of General Kennedy, Clark, who feared that he would be sold on the New Orleans slave market, fled to Cambridge, Mass., where he lived for many years in the family of Mrs. Stowe's sister; his descriptions of old slaves are said to have suggested to Mrs. Stowe the character of Uncle Tom.

At 11.6 *m.* on State 52 is PAINT LICK (250 pop.), a hamlet near the site of Paint Lick Station, which was established in 1782 and so named because the first settlers found Indian symbols painted in bright colors on trees and stones along the creek and around the near-by salt lick.

PAINT CREEK PRESBYTERIAN CHURCH, designed in the Gothic manner, was erected in 1872 to replace the second church on this site. The original meeting house was built of hewn logs in 1782, immediately after the pioneers had reached Kentucky. Among the prominent clergymen of the period who occupied the pulpit of this little meeting house were James Blythe and the Rev. David Rice, a minister of the Presbyterian Church. A communion cup with gold markings, easily mistaken for a shaving mug, and a grease lamp belonging to the first church are kept in the present building. The BURIAL GROUND adjoins the church. In the shade of its maple trees are the graves of several veterans of the Revolution, including the GRAVE OF GEN. THOMAS KENNEDY.

2. Left from Lancaster on State 39, an improved road, to the SITE OF GILBERT'S CREEK MEETING HOUSE, 2.8 *m.*, erected by members of the Traveling Baptist Church. In 1781 about 600 people left Spotsylvania County, Virginia, under the leadership of Capt. William Ellis and Lewis Craig, a devout young minister

who had long chafed against what he considered the injustice of the church laws of Virginia. On reaching the Gilbert's Creek settlement, the company organized their church and erected the little log meeting house that became the first Baptist Church in the State. The building was loopholed and the settlers brought their rifles with them when they came to worship. When they bowed in prayer two of the men stood armed at the door to guard against surprise attacks by Indians. This building was used by various denominations. Alexander Campbell, founder of the Disciples of Christ or Christian Church, and the Reverend David Rice, a pioneer Presbyterian minister, both preached here.

In 1783 Lewis Craig and a part of his congregation moved to South Elkhorn, about five miles southeast of Lexington, where they established the first Baptist church in central Kentucky. The church at Gilbert's Creek declined and by 1865 the brick building that had succeeded the little log church had become a ruin. The foundation of the church and its adjoining graveyard, with a few stately old walnut and cedar trees standing watch, are all that remain on the hill overlooking Gilbert's Creek.

The WILLIAM OWSLEY HOUSE (R), 36.5 *m.*, was built in 1813 on an eminence overlooking the Wilderness Road. The house is a two-and-one-half story brick structure of Georgian Colonial design with a two-story portico. William Owsley, Governor of Kentucky (1844–48), lived here until 1843 when he moved to Boyle County. This house was also the home of Robert P. Letcher for a few years.

STANFORD, 44.6 *m.* (1,032 alt., 1,544 pop.), an attractive residential town with a leisurely life, has many old houses bordering its quiet tree-shaded streets. It is the seat of Lincoln County, one of the three original counties of the Kentucky District of Virginia formed in 1780. The red brick LINCOLN COUNTY COURTHOUSE, Main St., built about 1915 to replace an earlier structure, has Ionic porticoes on the front and sides and a tall clock tower which dominates the town. The courthouse contains sheepskin documents dating back to the pioneer era of the State.

Stanford, founded by act of the Virginia Legislature in 1786, is near the SITE OF ST. ASAPH or Logan's Fort, established by Col. Benjamin Logan in 1775. When their efforts to capture it proved unsuccessful, Indians named the settlement Standing Fort, which was later contracted to Stanford. On the morning of May 20, 1777, when the women of the fort were outside of the gate milking the cows, and the men were acting as a guard, they were fired upon by more than a hundred Indians who had concealed themselves in the thick canebrake. One man was killed and two were wounded; the remainder made their escape into the fort and closed the gate. Harrison, one of the wounded men, ran a few paces and fell. Colonel Logan, ignoring the danger, dashed out of the gate to the spot where the wounded man lay, threw him on his shoulders and, amidst a shower of rifle balls, made a safe retreat into the fort which was now vigorously assaulted by the Indians. When the scarcity of powder and balls made additional supplies essential, Logan and two companions, under cover of darkness, slipped through the Indian lines and with almost incredible rapidity made the journey over the mountains and through the valley to the Holston River settlements, returning on the tenth day with the ammunition.

A few days later Colonel Bowman with a party of men arrived at St. Asaph's and compelled the Indians to retire.

1. Right from Stanford on US 150, an improved road, to BRIGHT'S INN *(open on request)*, 1.5 *m.*, a two-story brick and stone building (R). The brick ell was added in 1916 to replace a log house built in 1816 and was operated as a tavern by Capt. John Bright, son of a Revolutionary soldier. Captain Bright's business flourished; in 1820 he added the stone building that still stands. On the premises he built a blacksmith shop, stables, slave cabins, coach house, and a horse-powered gristmill. A cave served as a cooling plant.

The stone section of Bright's Inn has a central hall 10 feet wide and 100 feet long, with 10 rooms on each side. This hall, with its huge fireplace, was a favorite gathering place and re-echoed to the dance music of several generations. The cuisine of the old days was famous for its corn pone baked in a Dutch oven, and roasts of venison, pork, and beef cooked on the spit. Meals were 25¢ with whisky thrown in, or metheglin, a drink made of honey and vinegar, for the temperate. Captain Bright, the jovial host, weighed 340 pounds, but in spite of his size often rode horseback, and insisted that his horse, Nigger, was the fastest in Kentucky considering the weight it carried.

2. Left from Stanford on US 150 to the WHITLEY HOUSE *(open)* 10 *m.*, standing (R) well back from the highway. This structure, built about 1783 by Col. William Whitley, is said to have been the first brick house in Kentucky; it is now (1939) being restored and is to be included within a State park.

This tall two-story structure, with walls laid in Flemish bond and with small windows placed high above the floor, is an interesting example of pioneer architecture. Restoration of the house has included removal of a comparatively enor-. mous two-story pedimented Doric portico that was probably added after the family had prospered. Over the simple entrance door are the initials of Colonel Whitley in brick; the initials of his wife are over the rear door. The interior exhibits much more elegance than the exterior. Over the mantel in the parlor are 13 small panels symbolizing the Thirteen Colonies, and one entire side of the room has elaborately carved paneling. The handrail of the stairway balustrade is curved downward and outward to form the newel. Other unusual features of the house include the high placement of the first floor windows to prevent the Indians from seeing the occupants and a third floor ballroom, once furnished as a courtroom, which contained a secret hiding place for women and children. Records show that Whitley paid for the bricks and masonry with one farm, for the liquor furnished to the laborers with another, and for the carving (done by a man named Swope) with still another tract.

William Whitley, born in Amherst County, Va., August 15, 1749, was a skilled Indian fighter. In this home, a favorite with the important persons of his day, George Rogers Clark and Gov. Isaac Shelby were guests. Theodore Roosevelt, in his book, the *Winning of the West*, describes this house as the center of the religious, political, and social life of the Transylvania region, and the aristocratic home of the Wilderness Road *(see Tour 4A)*. Though he was more than 60 years old when the War of 1812 broke out, Colonel Whitley, disregarding his previous service and rank, enlisted as a private and was killed in the Battle of the River Thames in 1813.

At 11.8 *m.* on US 150 is CRAB ORCHARD (919 alt., 576 pop.), on the old Wilderness Road *(see Tour 4A)*, early noted as a watering place because of the number, variety, and excellence of its mineral springs. The friendliness, hospitality, and old-fashioned manners in this quiet resort are in keeping with its old buildings. Crab Orchard Salts, a highly valued medicinal remedy, were produced here by evaporation.

3. Left from Stanford on the Ottenheim Pike, a graveled road, to the village of OTTENHEIM, 6 *m.*, a tiny settlement established in 1885 by Jacob Ottenheim, steamboat and railroad passenger agent. The community, composed of the de-

scendants of Swiss, Austrians, and Germans—the latter predominating—has been noted for the production of wine and Swiss cheese.

South of Stanford, US 27 again penetrates the outer Bluegrass, though the terrain differs from the outer Bluegrass to the north in that it is flatter and has low abrupt knobs instead of shaggy hills. There are fewer horses and more sheep here than in the inner Bluegrass; and the fields are not so fine. Violets, wild roses, and daisies bloom in spring and early summer; the yellow-white of honeysuckle and scarlet of trumpet vine are frequently seen on the fences, and in the fields bloom Queen Anne's Lace, wild aster, and goldenrod.

Through HALL'S GAP, **51.5** *m.* (1,200 alt.), on the dividing line between the Bluegrass area and the mountains, an important road has run since pioneer times. An observation tower (L), 1,000 feet from the highway, affords a view on a clear day of five counties. The view embraces mile upon mile of bluegrass rolling away to the north, and toward the south and east the first foothills of the mountains are outlined against the sky.

EUBANK, **65.9** *m.* (1,172 alt., 334 pop.), is in an agricultural region noted for the quantity of buckwheat grown.

SOMERSET, **80.1** *m.* (879 alt., 5,506 pop.), a growing railroad town, was named for the Duke of Somerset and made the seat of Pulaski County by court order in 1801. Built on the sunny side of a sloping ridge, where surrounding terrain embraces characteristics of both knobs and mountain areas, Somerset is known as the Gateway to the Mountains. Along its main street are small shops, motion-picture houses, and a $250,000 hotel, opened in 1930. MEMORIAL SQUARE, Main St., is dedicated to Somerset's distinguished citizens, one of them was Edwin P. Morrow, Governor of Kentucky (1919–23). Somerset has one of the outstanding school plants of the State; the group of buildings, which include CARNEGIE LIBRARY, SOMERSET HIGH SCHOOL, and SOMERSET GRADE SCHOOL, form an imposing block in this secluded mountain town. Cyrenius Wait is credited with producing in Somerset, about 1840, the first raw silk in Kentucky.

Somerset is at the junction with State 80 *(see Tour 18)*.

PISGAH PRESBYTERIAN CHURCH, **86** *m.*, on an eminence about 200 yards R. of the highway, is one of the State's oldest churches. The small brick structure is rectangular in shape, with a low square bell tower. A well-kept cemetery adjoining the church is the resting place of pioneers.

US 27 crosses the Cumberland River, **89.5** *m.*, on a bridge *(toll 30¢)*.

BURNSIDE, **89.6** *m.* (705 alt., 914 pop.), straggling along the banks of the Cumberland River and its confluent South Fork, clings to the steep slope of a hill. The business section of the town lies at the hill's base. Here the route crosses the old corduroy road, built and used by Federal troops during the War between the States. Originally known as Point Isabel, the town was renamed for the Union general who made this his headquarters. GENERAL BURNSIDE'S HEADQUARTERS (R) is a rambling two-story frame building with a two-story porch.

Burnside is at the junction with State 90 (see Tour 20).

The highway, following a ridge that rises at times to an altitude of 1,300 feet, leads through rugged, wooded hills and along winding streams.

PARKER'S LAKE, 104.3 m. (1,256 alt., 200 pop.), is at the junction with State 90 (see Tour 4B).

WHITLEY CITY, 112.2 m. (1,322 alt., 1,200 pop.), seat of McCreary County, is one of the highest county seats in the State. Until the formation of the county in 1912, this was one of Kentucky's most isolated regions; the people, dwelling in log cabins, led a primitive life in their small self-sufficing communities. Hostilities frequently developed, and feuds (see Tour 19) were common. With the building of US 27, Whitley City developed rapidly into a progressive community with modern schools, churches, and a new fireproof brick courthouse.

STEARNS, 114.9 m. (2,176 pop.), is the center of a thriving lumber industry and a shipping point for both the coal and timber of the region.

PINE KNOT, 118.4 m. (1,410 alt., 500 pop.), until 1913 the seat of McCreary County, lies in the foothills of the Cumberland Mountains. There is little arable land in the surrounding region except that along the creek bottoms and on top of the level plateaus.

US 27 crosses the Tennessee Line, 123.1 m., at a point 146 miles north of Chattanooga, Tenn. (see Tenn. Tour 6).

Tour 4

(Cincinnati, Ohio)—Covington—Georgetown—Lexington—Richmond —Corbin—Williamsburg—(Jellico, Tenn.); US 25 and 25W Ohio Line to Tennessee Line, 223.7 m.

Hard-surfaced roadbed throughout.
Cincinnati, New Orleans & Texas-Pacific R.R. roughly parallels route between Cincinnati and Lexington, and Louisville & Nashville R.R. between Richmond and Jellico.
All types of accommodations in cities; limited elsewhere.

US 25, locally called the Eastern Dixie Highway, reveals a typical cross-section of Kentucky. It crosses the low wooded hills of the Ohio River, passes rolling orchard land and prosperous country estates with waving bluegrass meadows, and between the great gorge cut by the Kentucky River and the rugged foothills of the Appalachians, follows Daniel Boone's Wilderness Road.

Section a. OHIO LINE *to* LEXINGTON; *84.1 m.*

US 25–42 crosses the Ohio Line, 0 *m.*, on the southern outskirts of Cincinnati *(see Ohio Tour 22)*, on the OHIO RIVER SUSPENSION BRIDGE *(toll 15¢)*. This bridge with its 1,057-foot middle span was built in 1867 by John A. Roebling, who also designed New York's Brooklyn Bridge.

COVINGTON, 0.5 *m.* (513 alt., 65,252 pop.) *(see Covington)*.

Points of Interest: Carneal House, Devou Park, Monte Casino Chapel, St. Mary's Cathedral, Latonia Race Track, Baker-Hunt Foundation, and William's Natural History Collection.

Covington is at the junction with US 42 *(see Tour 12)*.

Right from Covington on Main St. to the junction with State 20, 0.2 *m.;* L. on State 20 to LUDLOW, 2.3 *m.* (6,485 pop.), overlooking part of Cincinnati's industrial waterfront from its slightly elevated position before the high Kentucky hills that press it against the Ohio River. Ludlow had a few settlers in the 1790's, but was not chartered as a village until 1864. Today it is an industrial city that manufactures furniture, compressing machines, and brass and electrical apparatus; the shops of the Southern Railway are also here.

MASONIC LODGE HALL *(open to Masons)*, on Closson St., Greek Revival in style, was built in 1832 by Simon Kenner of Baton Rouge, La., as a summer residence. The story-and-a-half brick structure has a central hall, 44 feet long, flanked on either side by spacious rooms, trimmed in fine woodwork. In 1885 this property was bought by A. B. Closson, from whom the Unity Lodge of Freemasons purchased it in 1924.

ELMWOOD HALL *(open weekdays, 8–6)*, 244 Forrest Ave., is a low, compact, stuccoed building, built of stone and brick in 1819 by Thomas Carneal. Its hip roof is topped with an observation deck 16 feet square. The building, now occupied by the Eda E. Thomas Candy Company, originally faced the narrow driveway that leads from the street. The façade, with its recessed Doric portico and its small-paned windows, is still handsome. (The original portal, with fanlights and side lights, is gone.) The central room on the north side was formerly a reception hall. Most of the fireplaces, with brick hearths, marble borders, and mantelpieces, remain.

In its early days Elmwood Hall estate, stretching down-river for 2.5 miles, was densely covered with beech, oak, walnut, and elm trees; it became a vast park and bird sanctuary, and tame deer, bison, and elk grazed on its 1,000 acres. Brilliant parties and receptions took place here. In 1827 William Bullock, owner of the Piccadilly Museum in London, bought the place as a site for a dream city, which he wanted to call Hygeia. Bullock went back to England for awhile and wrote a book about his American travels that featured an account of the model city—it was to have "cultural" gardens along the river, streets with imposing names, inns, theaters, baths, and even a brewery. He then returned to Elmwood Hall and gave a long series of balls and gatherings, in honor of such personages as Mrs. Frances Trollope, Henry Clay, New York Governor De Witt Clinton, and President James K. Polk. When his model town idea died, Bullock sold Elmwood to Israel J. Ludlow, son of one of the three founders of Cincinnati, who continued to uphold Elmwood's tradition of hospitality.

BROMLEY, 3.6 *m.* (489 pop.), a Ludlow suburb of small workers' cottages, is squeezed tightly against the river by the dark hills behind it. Garden patches are strung along the river opposite the few steamers usually offshore on the Cincinnati side, where houses and some industries fill the bottom land. In Bromley, houses clamber, stairstep fashion, up the steep, rugged heights. On a slight rise sloping down to State 20 (L) is the LANDMARK, a two-story house that, tradition relates, was built in 1765—it was probably built later. About 2,000 pieces of stone went into the construction of this dwelling whose walls are almost two feet thick. White pine was used for the flooring; ash trees, split in half and still showing their woodland bark, made the cellar rafters; and black walnut was used for door sills and other purposes. Hand-wrought nails and wooden pins hold the structure together. A keystone on the east wall of the house bears the head of an Indian in stone. The present owner has installed hardwood floors on the first story, modernized the large open hearths and the old narrow, enclosed stairways, and built a frame addition. The small, one-story frame structure east of the house formerly stood to its rear and was a slaves' quarters.

The route continues westward over a narrow shelf of land continually flanked by dark hills and the broad quiet sweep of the Ohio. Plain little frame houses having garden patches, cornfields, and some livestock around them stand by the road or near the river; an occasional summer house of the lodge type is seen. The Cincinnati suburbs are in view across the river. On State 20 is CONSTANCE, 7.4 *m.* (87 pop.), a river village whose old FERRY HOUSE (R), a large and substantial structure, did a bustling trade before the turn of the present century. The little steam ferry operated for many decades by the Anderson family still plies back and forth on the Ohio River at this point and a few shantyboats sometimes tie up here; but Constance's real river life is gone. Fleets of long, low, steel barges pushed by blunt-nosed stern-wheelers commonly called towboats sweep by with never a pause, bound for the big industrial cities up or down the Ohio. Steamers pass by once in awhile, and occasionally the *Gordon Greene,* last of the packets making the trip up-river to Pittsburgh, is seen, a graceful white creation.

Between Covington and Florence US 25 and US 42 are one route, traversing the hilly orchard land of the Ohio River's north bend, with a fine view of Cincinnati and the winding river.

FORT MITCHELL, 4.4 *m.* (359 pop.), is a residential suburb. During the War between the States, when Confederate forces, in 1862, were threatening an invasion of the North, Gen. Lew Wallace—the author of *Ben Hur* and the commander of the Union forces assigned to the defense of Cincinnati—led 15,000 men across the Ohio River on a hastily constructed pontoon bridge formed of coal barges. He erected a series of defensive earthworks reaching from the Ohio River at Bromley on the west to the banks of Licking, then to the Ohio near Fort Thomas. These temporary defenses were under the direction of Professor Ormsby Mitchell, and were called by his name. The FORT MITCHELL COUNTRY CLUB, Mitchell Ave., has a nine-hole golf course and is the local center of social life.

ERLANGER, 8.4 *m.* (905 alt., 1,854 pop.), is a residential town of the Cincinnati-Covington metropolitan area.

FLORENCE, 9.8 *m.* (935 alt., 450 pop.), provides the locale for one of John Uri Lloyd's best-known stories, *Stringtown on the Pike.* Here US 42 turns R. *(see Tour 12),* leaving US 25.

Right from Florence on State 18, an improved road, to BURLINGTON, 6 *m.* (848 alt., 600 pop.), seat of Boone County, incorporated in 1824. Burlington is a prosperous farm trade center. Cereals and a fine grade of white burley tobacco are the main agricultural products of the surrounding countryside.

In CRITTENDEN, 26.3 *m.* (908 alt., 265 pop.), is (R) the LLOYD RESERVATION, founded in 1918 by Curtis Lloyd, professor of botany at the University of Cincinnati, for the preservation of native plant life; it covers more than 400 acres. The Wild Flower Preserve, in a woodland on the reservation, contains every known species of this region. On the preserve is a community house, built by Professor Lloyd, and a log cabin containing fine old furniture.

Near the southern limits of Crittenden on US 25 is (R) the SHERMAN TAVERN, a one-story frame structure, 26.7 *m.*, once the most popular inn on the stagecoach route between Cincinnati and Lexington. It had the first plastered interior walls in this section of the country, one of the first pianos in the State, and its proprietor dispensed free bourbon to guests. The bar still occupies a room in the rear of the house. Lafayette is said to have spent a night here in 1825, while traveling by stage from Cincinnati to Lexington, Kentucky.

DRY RIDGE, 33.4 *m.* (929 alt., 97 pop.), first called Campbell's Station, was settled before 1792 near a mineral spring later valued for its medicinal qualities. Between Dry Ridge and Williamstown, US 25 and State 22 *(see Tour 13)* are united.

WILLIAMSTOWN, 36.5 *m.* (943 alt., 917 pop.), a lively town and the seat of Grant County, is in the fertile agricultural region. It was named for William Arnold, who in 1820 gave the land for the public buildings, and free timber to all who purchased lots from him.

South of Williamstown the gently rolling highway is flanked by fields of tobacco and corn, and pastures in which cattle browse.

CARDOME *(open by permission)*, 70.2 *m.*, was built (R) in 1821 by Maj. Benjamin Stuart Chambers, an officer in the War of 1812. After having passed through the hands of various owners, this fine old estate, first called Acacia Grove, became a Catholic school for girls. In 1896 a four-story brick building with a tall square bell tower above the entrance was added to the original mansion.

GEORGETOWN, 70.4 *m.* (866 alt., 4,229 pop.), with its many large trees and old houses, is a college town and the seat of Scott County. Incorporated by the Virginia Legislature in 1790, and named for George Washington, the town grew up around and still obtains its water supply from ROYAL SPRING (R), one block from the highway on Water St. The spring was discovered and named, in 1774, by Col. John Floyd, a pioneer adventurer and surveyor, who was impressed by the volume and crystal clearness of its water and by the beauty of its setting.

In 1775, John McClelland, a landowner residing near Pittsburgh, accompanied by his family and several frontiersmen, floated down the Ohio River in flatboats to Salt Lick Creek, now in Mason County. Here they were joined by Simon Kenton *(see Tour 15)* and Thomas Williams. When they reached the Royal Spring in 1776 they built here. This became an outpost of civilization in the wilderness where pioneers, passing to and from the larger settlements south of the Kentucky River, found refuge and shelter. McClelland's Station suffered from frequent Indian attacks; one of these, in December 1776, was led by the famous Mingo chief, Pluggy, who was killed during the fight. After the Indians had been driven off, Pluggy was buried on the bluff that overhangs the spring. For many years superstitious inhabitants of the settlement believed that the echo in the spring was the death cry of the Indian chief.

On College St. is GEORGETOWN COLLEGE (L), a Baptist institution, established in 1829; it has a campus of 20 acres, an enrollment of approximately 600 students, and awards the bachelor of arts degree.

GIDDINGS HALL, the oldest building on the campus, was erected in 1839 as a monument to Dr. Rockwood Giddings, a former president of the college. This structure was designed by Dr. Giddings and erected entirely by student and faculty labor. The bricks, burned and laid by the students, are of clay dug from a corner of the campus. It is said that a quart of bourbon reposes under each of the six Ionic columns of the portico. This stately building is one of the most notable examples of Greek Revival architecture in the State. The one-story red brick gymnasium has an Ionic portico between the wings.

An old one-story house at 140 E. Washington St., now in poor condition, has a fine Palladian doorway with carved frame and a well-modeled cornice, and stands on a stone-paved terrace.

The SHROPSHIRE HOUSE on Main St., has a Greek Revival portico and an elliptical-fanlighted doorway with side lights. The window openings on the first story, with long narrow side lights and hinged panels below the sashes, open on the terrace. Within, a graceful arch supported by Ionic columns ornaments the hall.

The charming SHOWALTER HOUSE, on W. Hamilton St., of brick painted white, is designed in the Greek Revival style with four Ionic columns supporting the pediment of the two-story portico. The house is on the site of a slave market whose auction block still stands in the yard.

Georgetown is at the junction with US 62 *(see Tour 14)* and State 40 *(see Tour 17)*.

Between Georgetown and Lexington US 25 crosses the Bluegrass—the world's finest pasture for the rearing of blooded horses, as is demonstrated by the large number of notable breeders who maintain farms in it. The highway passes one estate after the other with trim white fences or old stone walls covered by vines, with large well-kept farm buildings—particularly stables—and with tree-shaded country houses, some of which belong to ante bellum days.

HURRICANE HALL (R), 76.8 *m.*, is an old Georgian Colonial style house of whitewashed brick, built prior to 1801; it stands at the head of an avenue of locusts and wild cherry trees, with an aged, vine-covered end turned to the highway. The wallpaper of the hall and the parlor was hung in 1817. The old parlor paper, depicting the ruins of Rome and scenes along the Tiber, was hand-blocked. Roger Quarles, who built the house, brought his family, slaves, and furnishings in wagons from Virginia.

The house of EOTHAN (L), 81.8 *m.*, was built in 1798 by the Reverend James Moore, organizer and first rector of Christ Church Episcopal parish, later president of Transylvania University. From the gate a road winds through a meadow to the house which is concealed from the road by trees and a hedge of syringa and roses. The one-story brick structure, painted white, of Georgian Colonial design, has a fine paneled door and fanlight. On both sides of the doorway is an arched window. This was the home of the music master, described by James Lane Allen in his story, *Flute and Violin*. It was long the home of Miss Fanny Frazer Redd, granddaughter of Oliver Frazer, the lovable artist, who purchased the place during the War between the States. Many portraits painted by him, as well as those by his teacher, Matthew Jouett, adorn the walls.

LEXINGTON, 84.1 *m.* (957 alt., 45,736 pop.) *(see Lexington).*

Points of Interest: Homes of Henry Clay, Gen. John Hunt Morgan, Mary Todd Lincoln, and John Bradford; Transylvania College, University of Kentucky, Looseleaf Tobacco Market.

Lexington is at the junction with US 60 *(see Tour 16)*, US 27 *(see Tour 3)*, and US 68 *(see Tour 15).*

Section b. LEXINGTON *to* TENNESSEE LINE, *139.6 m.*

South of Lexington, 0 *m.*, US 25 passes through the Kentucky River gorge, widely known for its scenic beauty, and crosses the KENTUCKY RIVER on a bridge at Clay's Ferry. From a parking space near the top of the bluff is a splendid view of the palisades and the winding river.

Between Clay's Ferry and Richmond is a fertile, undulating upland plain where farming and stock raising are the outstanding occupations and fox hunting a favorite sport. Hunters in pink mounted on thoroughbreds, and those in overalls on farm horses and mules, mingle and ride to hounds side by side. Young and old, rich and poor, gather at dawn on a frosty morning at the casting grounds. The master calls the roll and each handler answers to the number that has been assigned to his hounds. After the master has instructed the judges, he gives the word to turn the hounds loose. Without a sound they trot out of sight.

When the strike is made, the hounds advance in full cry—a crescendo of deep and high shrill tones. Suddenly the beautiful little quarry is seen in the open, loping speedily and easily over the ground with the full pack following, each hound baying with every bound. In a flash, fox, hounds, and hunters are gone—the sound grows fainter and dies away. Kentuckians have inherited a love of this sport from their English forebears. It is said that when "Pidgeontail" Bedford, an inveterate follower of the hounds, married and took his bride home, the house he had built for her had been completed except for the hanging of the front door. After carrying her over the threshold in the traditional manner, he set out on his horse to borrow a pair of hinges from a neighbor. In the snow he saw the track of a fox, and, forgetting his errand, he and his hound gave chase. It is said that three days elapsed before he returned with the brush as a present for his bride.

One of the most notable fox hunters of the State, and one of the most picturesque characters of his time, was Gen. George Washington Maupin (1807–1868) of Madison County. He is described as having been primarily a fox hunter, secondarily a trader in Negroes and mules, and last a planter. With his high peaked cap, flowered waistcoat, and garish scarf, he was conspicuous at every hunt. The noted Maupin-Walker foxhound traces its pedigree to his dogs. Foxhounds bred in this section of Kentucky are shipped to many parts of the world and many of the field trials of the National Foxhunters Association are held in this area.

At 22 *m.* is the junction with Whitehall Lane.

Right on this road to WHITEHALL *(open on request),* the home of Gen. Cassius M. Clay, noted abolitionist and, in 1861, Minister to Russia. The tall two-and-one-half-story building, designed in 1864 in the General Grant manner by T. Lewinski, a Pole living in Lexington, contains 22 rooms and three wide hallways. It was built about the original mansion, said to have been the first brick house erected in Madison County, constructed in 1787 by Brig. Gen. Green Clay, who represented Madison County, Ky., in the Virginia convention called in 1788 to ratify the Federal Constitution. It was he who unsuccessfully attempted to raise the siege of Fort Meigs by the British and Indians in 1812.

RICHMOND, 26.8 *m.* (926 alt., 6,495 pop.), named for Richmond, Virginia, and referred to in early writings as "a manufacturing little log village," is an old town with majestic trees bordering the streets and many dignified old houses. The first settlement was made in 1784 by Col. John Miller, who served at Yorktown. When Richmond was made the seat of county government in 1798, the first court was held in Colonel Miller's barn. The beautiful MADISON COUNTY COURT-HOUSE (L), on Main St., is on the site of the Miller barn. The building, completed in 1849, has a pedimented Doric portico surmounted with a clock tower having two octagonal stages. The flanking wings are lower than the central unit.

From the spring of 1861, when Federal forces took control of Madison County, to the end of the War between the States, Richmond was a scene of conflict. Many of its buildings bear the scars of the engagement between Gen. William Nelson's Union forces and Gen. Kirby Smith's Confederates that took place August 29–31, 1862. The battle, which began six miles south of Richmond at Mount Zion Church, and developed into a sharply contested retreat through Richmond and along the highway north toward Lexington, resulted in the first Confederate victory in Kentucky.

In Richmond is the EASTERN KENTUCKY STATE TEACHERS' COLLEGE, which in 1906 took over the buildings and campus of old Central University, established in 1874 and united with Centre College at Danville *(see Tour 5)* in 1901. Among magnificent trees is UNIVERSITY HALL, built in 1874, a three-story brick structure with a Greek Revival portico. Memorial Hall, built in 1883 to commemorate the 100th anniversary of the founding of the Presbyterian Church in Kentucky, is a men's dormitory. Outstanding among new buildings is the Coates Administration Building, designed in the Renaissance style. It contains the Hiram Brock Auditorium which has a seating capacity of 1,760. The library of John Wilson Townsend, historian and author of *Kentucky in American Letters,* was purchased by the school in 1930. This includes one of the largest and best collections of books and pamphlets written by Kentuckians about Kentucky. Many of the works are autographed first editions, accompanied by letters relating to the contents.

In the Courthouse Square is the PIONEER MEMORIAL FOUNTAIN, erected 1906. Surmounting the tapering shaft is a bronze bust of a pioneer wearing the traditional coonskin cap. The fountain was the gift of David R. Francis, Governor of Missouri (1889–1893), a native of Richmond.

In the RICHMOND CEMETERY (R), on US 25, is the GRAVE OF GEN. GREEN CLAY, that of his son, Cassius Marcellus, and of his grandson, Brutus J. The Irvine Monument marks the GRAVE OF CAPT. CHRISTOPHER IRVINE, the Indian fighter, and the GRAVE OF COL. WILLIAM IRVINE, his brother who was the hero of Estill's Defeat, 1782. The Miller Monument stands at the GRAVE OF COL. JOHN MILLER, donor of the site of Richmond.

IRVINETON *(open),* Lancaster Ave., was built in 1820 by Dr. A. Q. Rollins and came into the possession of the Irvine family in 1829. Mrs. Elizabeth Susan Irvine, at her death in 1918, left the house to the Medical Society of Kentucky which, in conjunction with the U.S. Public Health Service, uses it as a hospital for the treatment of trachoma. Old paintings and heirlooms of the Irvine family remain in the building, whose bay windows and other alterations belie its age.

Crowning a wooded hill at 27.9 *m.* is WOODLAWN (R), a brick house of Georgian Colonial design built in 1822 by Gen. Green Clay for his daughter, the wife of Col. William Rodes. A small one-story balustrated porch is flanked by four Palladian windows, two on each side. The doorway, with fanlight and side lights, opens into a wide hall. A carved arch, supported by twin columns, spans the hall, and the chair rail, carved in flowers, still shows old colors—faded rose and gray. The semicircular headings of the cupboards on each side of the mantel in the back parlor are exquisitely carved. The cut glass doorknobs resemble old bridle buttons. John Fox, Jr., wrote a description of this house in his novel *Crittenden.* Woodlawn was occupied by both Federals and Confederates during the War between the States.

Richmond is at the junction with US 227 *(see Tour 17A).*

Left from Richmond on State 52 to the WACO AND BYBEE POTTERIES, 8 *m. (open to public),* established almost a century ago by John Corneilson to supply his neighbors with brick, tile, and earthenware; the enterprise continues to employ old-fashioned methods of production. The present owner, Webb Corneilson, specializes in the production of blue earthenware of his own design and coloring. The local clay used for this pottery is mixed by mule power, fashioned by hand on the potter's wheel, and then "fixed"—a process taking in all about a week.

CASTLEWOOD (L), 30.1 *m.,* was designed and erected in 1820 by Gideon Shryock, Kentucky architect, for James Estill, Jr., on a part of the 15,000-acre tract surveyed and owned by Capt. James Estill, a Revolutionary soldier and pioneer. This two-story house of modified Georgian Colonial design and built of brick, contains some of the finest hand-carved woodwork in Kentucky; the mantels, especially, illustrate the skill of the pioneer craftsman.

On US 25 at 31.1 *m.,* is the point where Boone's Trace *(see Tour 4A)* from North Carolina turned to follow Otter Creek to the south bank of the Kentucky River, where Fort Boonesboro *(see Tour 17A)* was built. The trail entered Madison County over the crest of Big Hill, the landmark on the Jackson County line, and went down the hills to the headwaters of Otter Creek.

MOUNT ZION CHURCH (R), 32.7 *m.,* is a small rectangular brick building erected in 1852. It has two small entrances and lacks ornamentation but its simplicity is attractive. The Battle of Richmond in 1862 began at this point.

BEREA, 41.6 *m.* (943 alt., 1,827 pop.), in the foothills of the Southern Highlands, is the seat of BEREA COLLEGE *(student guides at Boone Tavern),* founded in 1853; this is the oldest and largest of the mountain schools in Kentucky. The 85 well-equipped brick and stone buildings of the college, and its unusually beautiful campus of about 300 acres, comprise a large part of the village. The FEE MEMORIAL CHURCH, of Greek Revival design, stands almost in the center of the campus. People of 23 denominations worship together in this church. The BEREA COLLEGE CHAPEL, a red brick building with Greek Revival features, was presented to the college in 1904 by an anonymous donor on condition that it be erected by student labor. In the chapel tower are the WILLIAM GOODELL FROST MEMORIAL CHIMES, which honor a former president of the college, and were presented in 1917 by the same benefactor. John G. Lee, Cassius M. Clay, and John A. R. Rogers, cofounders of Berea, were opposed to slavery, and the college admitted both white and Negro students till 1904, when the State enacted prohibitive legislation. The school's endowment was then divided; Lincoln Institute *(see Tour 16),* near Louisville, was provided for Negro students and Berea became a co-educational school for white students. Berea's purpose is to contribute "to the spiritual and material welfare of the mountain region of the South, affording to young people of character and promise a thorough Christian education, elementary, industrial, secondary, normal, and collegiate, with opportunities for manual labor as an assistant in self-support." Berea, now (1939) under the leadership of Dr. William James Hutchins, had an enrollment of 1,692 in 1937.

While the college entrance requirements are high, lack of pre-college training is no barrier to the ambitious student. Both boys and girls live under a dormitory system that provides comfortable living conditions at the minimum cost. All students pay at least part of their expenses by labor in some of the schools. Varied activities include weaving, spinning, the manufacture of furniture, and the operation of a broom factory, a college laundry, a bakery, a store, a printing shop, a farm, and a hotel.

On the outskirts of Berea are (L) the CHURCHILL WEAVERS *(loom house and display room open to public)*. Since 1922, when it was founded, this institution has grown to be one of the largest of its kind in the country, operating more than 40 looms. After D. C. Churchill, the founder, graduated from the Massachusetts Institute of Technology as an engineer, he spent some time in India, where he studied the art of weaving. He designed a loom and took first prize for both speed and quality of cloth in an all-India competition. He came to Berea, at the invitation of President Hutchins, to take the chair of physics and motor mechanics. Three looms, including one he had designed for his wife—who soon displayed unusual ability in combining and blending colors—and a hastily constructed loom-house were the first plant of the present Churchill Weavers, now working in well-equipped, well-lighted buildings. The looms are all of Churchill's design and were made in the plant shop. Many of the designs used follow the patterns traditional among the Kentucky mountaineers.

Left from Berea on State 21, an improved road, to INDIAN FORT MOUN-TAIN, 3 *m.*, a prehistoric stronghold with more than 200 acres inside its defenses. Seventeen stone walls and barricades defend the summit. Caves and rock houses contain the graves of warriors who once held this mountain.

Left 0.5 *m.* from Indian Fort Mountain to BASIN MOUNTAIN, another pre-historic fortification on a smaller flat-topped knob. Two stone walls guard the summit, which is 18 acres in extent. This mountain is named for the two basins that were hollowed out on its crest to hold water for the defenders of the fort. Both fortifications are in a strategic position near the Warriors Path *(see Tour 4A)*, which passed through Boone's Gap, three miles south of the present site of Berea.

A marker (L), **45.1** *m.*, commemorates Daniel Boone's Trail (Boone's Trace) which was blazed from North Carolina into Kentucky in 1775 *(see Tour 4A)*.

MOUNT VERNON, **59.6** *m.* (1,150 alt., 939 pop.), seat of Rock-castle County, was incorporated in 1817 and is in the foothills of the Cumberland Mountains, a region in which isolated knobs and ridge tops rise to a height of 1,500 to 2,500 feet.

Immediately back of the courthouse is the old LANGFORD HOUSE *(open)*, built in 1790 as a blockhouse for defense against the Indians. Although the front of the building has been weatherboarded, and windows have been cut where there were formerly only loopholes, the interior is little changed. This house became a hotel in stagecoach days, and later was a station on the Underground Railroad.

On court day, which is observed regularly in Mount Vernon, country-folk from the surrounding region come in wagons and on horseback to trade, talk, and drink a little.

Fox, coon, and 'possum hunting are favorite sports in this region where most farmers own three or four hounds apiece. Each hunter bets on his own dogs, and the hunt usually lasts from one to three days. According to a local sportsman, when the dogs announce by loud barks that a coon has been "treed," the hunters gather under the tree to wait till morning when they "either chop the tree down or shoot the coon out."

At **65.7** *m.* is the junction with a dirt road.

Left on this road to the GREAT SALTPETER CAVES, **4** *m.*, which were mined extensively for material to manufacture gunpowder during the War between the States.

LIVINGSTON, **69.7** *m.* (858 alt., 912 pop.), on Rockcastle River, is a weather-beaten hamlet in a setting of natural beauty. It was formerly a shipping center for coal mined in the surrounding region.

South of Livingston is a rugged, hilly area, where the scenery is particularly attractive.

US 25 crosses Rockcastle River, **77.4** *m.*, so named because of its characteristic large rocks and cliffs. In the NARROWS extending for half a mile near the mouth of the river the water is 10 to 100 feet deep and so blocked with enormous rocks that in many places a canoe cannot pass. This river is a favorite hunting and fishing ground, and has long been celebrated for the wild, romantic character of its surroundings. Mineral springs, for which therapeutic value was claimed, occur near the lower waters of Rockcastle.

LONDON, **92.4** *m.* (1,209 alt., 1,950 pop.), in a mountain valley, is the seat of Laurel County and the shopping center for owners of small mines and for corn and tobacco farmers, many of whom still live as did their ancestors in eighteenth century England *(see Tours 1, 18, and 19)*. It has a five-block business street, a Federal building where court is held, a Methodist college, hotels, and a motion picture house.

County court day here is the second Monday of each month, and at this time every man in the county who can comes in to "Jockey Lot" to talk and trade. Near election time politicians are everywhere. Guns, watches, knives, harness, wagons, horses, mules, dogs—anything and everything that can be "swapped" or sold is "fetched in." One can trade extensively on court day without a cent of money; the best currency is a young filly or a foxhound. The story is told of a penniless young farmer who arrived afoot one court day, leading a pair of well-matched foxhounds. Late in the evening he returned home in state, riding a frisky two-year-old, with sugar and coffee for his family in the saddlebags. In explaining the situation to his admiring neighbors, he exclaimed, "You see hit's all erlong ov my bein' sich er doggoned good jedge uv er anermule." In small Kentucky county seats women seldom appear on the crowded streets on court day, though occasionally a farm-wife comes to exchange her butter and eggs for coal oil and calico, and, if she dares, to keep an eye on "pa." The farmer tells his wife, "Court day hain't no fit'n time f'r women folk to be draggin' roun' town nohow."

SUE BENNET COLLEGE *(co-educational)*, within the corporate limits of London, was established in 1896 by the Methodist Episcopal Church, South. It has six modern red brick buildings on a 26-acre campus and is accredited by the Southern Association of Colleges.

In the FEDERAL BUILDING is the office of the district Forest Ranger who is in charge of Sublimity Farms.

London is at the junction with State 80 *(see Tour 18)*.

Right from London on a hard-surfaced road to the Forest Service's SUBLIMITY FARMS, 2.1 *m.*, a 583-acre area divided into 52 part-time and 14 full-time farm units, a community pasture, and a community woodlot. Designed as a demonstration in proper land use, this project contains 59 new houses and 7 renovated houses—all with modern plumbing and electricity, root cellars, barns, and coal sheds. These units are rented by the Government under contracts which encourage the homesteaders to follow the scientific farming and home managing plans worked out for them by an agronomist and a home economist whose headquarters are in London. The adjacent Cumberland National Forest supplies employment for those living on the part-time farms.

The entrance (L) to LEVI JACKSON WILDERNESS ROAD STATE PARK *(adm. 10¢, overnight camping 25¢; fishing and swimming, 25¢ each)*, is at **95.6** *m.* In 1784, 40 pioneers, traveling over the Boone Trail, stopped for the night here on the Little Laurel River. They were attacked by Indians in what has been called the Defeated Camp Massacre, and all but three of the company were slain or taken captive; two of the survivors hid in a hollow tree. The grandchildren of Levi Jackson, Revolutionary soldier who received land here for war services, gave the State more than 300 acres of this site to commemorate the slain pioneers. Improvements made by the National Park Service, utilizing CCC labor, include water, sewerage and lighting systems; roads, foot and bridle trails; a reproduction of a pioneer's two-story log dwelling housing a museum; shelter houses; picnic facilities; a lookout tower; a bridge across the Laurel River; and the planting of several thousand trees and shrubs.

At **105.8** *m.* is the junction with US 25W, now the route, and with US 25E *(see Tour 4A)*.

CORBIN, **107.5** *m.* (1,046 alt., 8,026 pop.), a busy railroad center in a level part of the Cumberland Plateau, is surrounded by a generally mountainous area with large tracts of timber. Coal mining is the chief occupation with farming and stock raising second in importance. In 1775, when Daniel Boone cut his trace, which later became a part of the Wilderness Road *(see Tour 4A)*, into Kentucky, he turned north at this place. The land on which the town stands was granted to Alex McClardy, one of Boone's associates, in 1798, but remained little more than a wilderness until 1883 when the main line of the L. & N. R.R. was built. It is now one of the three major supply points of the system and furnishes such materials as coal and timber.

Corbin is the junction with State 90 *(see Tour 4B)*.

The GATLIFFE FISH HATCHERY (R), **124.6** *m.*, was built in 1929, and operated by the Kentucky State Fish and Game Commission.

Eleven of the plant's 30 acres are in ponds supplied with water from Watts Creek by means of a levee. Largemouthed, smallmouthed, and Kentucky bass are raised here at the rate of 1,000,000 a year for distribution into streams throughout the State.

Approaching Williamsburg from the north the highway winds down cliffs in a succession of curves that reveal fine views of the town.

WILLIAMSBURG, 209.1 *m.* (975 alt., 1,826 pop.), as well as Whitley County, of which it is the seat, is named for Col. William Whitley, a pioneer renowned as an Indian fighter. Surrounded by a coal-mining and agricultural region it is on a low spur merging into the flood plain of a wide meander of the Cumberland River, and is walled in by steep winding ridges that rise to a height of 1,900 feet. To the southwest, uplands adjacent to Pine Mountain rise to an elevation of 2,500 feet. In this region, which is on the Indians' great southern trail, scientists have found numerous remains of towns and mounds. The artifacts include unusually fine specimens of flints, commonly known as "chunkee stones."

Williamsburg's site was selected at the county's first term of court held in 1817 at the house of Samuel Cox, who agreed to give the county half the proceeds from the sale of lots for the town, if a site on his land —which included a fine spring—were chosen for the county seat. The records of this offer and its acceptance are stored in the old brick WHITLEY COUNTY COURTHOUSE in the center of the public square.

CUMBERLAND COLLEGE, founded in 1889 by the Baptist Church, has an endowment of $500,000. It is a co-educational junior college offering vocational and preprofessional courses. The school owns a 15-acre campus with nine buildings, including a library, and has an enrollment of 500 students.

KING'S MILL, on the Cumberland River, 300 yards from the courthouse, has been in use for more than 100 years. Its dam is a popular fishing hole.

Participants in the annual community "sing" *(1st Sun. in July)* bring basket dinners and spend the whole day at the gathering. Local and visiting choral groups contribute to the program of hymns and spirituals.

South of Williamsburg US 25W winds near the towering JELLICO MOUNTAINS (R) and through quiet river valleys.

In JELLICO, 139.6 *m.* (937 alt., 405 pop.), US 25W crosses the Tennessee Line, 67 miles north of Knoxville, Tenn. *(see Tenn. Tour 5).*

Tour 4A

Junction with US 25—Pineville—Middlesboro—Cumberland Gap—
(Tazewell, Tenn.); US 25E.
Junction with US 25 to Tennessee Line, 54.4 m.

Hard-surfaced roadbed.
Louisville & Nashville R.R. parallels route throughout.
All types of accommodations in towns; limited elsewhere.

Through Cumberland Gap at the southern end of US 25E, and over
the route now followed in part by US 25E, came the first western surge
of Kentucky pioneers, singly or in small groups, attracted by tales of
fertile land yet unclaimed, of springs and brooks and rivers, of plentiful
game and endless adventure.

Daniel Boone and his companions, sponsored by Col. Richard
Henderson, became the advance guard for this westward movement,
when in 1775 they marked the way to the site of what was to become
Fort Boonesboro (see Tour 17A). Boone's Trace was not a new trail
through the wilderness; it was a combination of paths long used by the
buffalo and Indians, and later by French hunters and trappers. North
of Cumberland Gap, for about 50 miles, Boone followed the Warriors
Path—which extended from the Shawnee villages on the Ohio and
Scioto Rivers to the Cherokee country of the south—then selected a
buffalo trace that took him westward to Rockcastle River, up Round-
stone Creek, through the gap in Big Hill, and down Otter Creek to
the Kentucky River.

In the same year Benjamin Logan marked and improved a trail to
the site of St. Asaph (see Tour 3), a track that branched westward
from Boone's Trace at Rockcastle River, extended to the site of present
Crab Orchard, and on to the Falls of the Ohio (Louisville). Logan's
trail, which became more important than Boone's Trace, was referred
to as "the road through the great wilderness," and finally the Wilderness Road. As early as 1779 the Virginia Assembly passed an act
providing for improvement of the Wilderness Road. Similar acts were
passed by the Kentucky Legislature in 1795 and 1797, but it remained
little more than a pack road until 1818, when definite steps were taken
to widen it and to improve the fords.

The southern section of the Wilderness Road (paved US 25E) still
passes through a land of mountains veined with mineral deposits, of
rivers and ravines, of woods and flowers. But generations of white
men have cleared and cultivated much of its fertile land and mined its

VII. ALONG THE HIGHWAY I

GOLD DEPOSITORY, CAMP KNOX

FORT KNOX

INDIAN BURIAL GROUND, WICKLIFFE

BRYAN STATION SPRING, LEXINGTON

FORT HARROD, HARRODSBURG

FLOOD WATERS REACH STATUE OF CHIEF PADUKE, PADUCAH (1937)

COVERED BRIDGE, CYNTHIANA

OLD CANE RIDGE MEETING HOUSE (1792), NEAR PARIS

WOOLRIDGE MONUMENTS, MAYFIELD

MT. LEBANON, NEAR PARIS

MINING TOWN

THE FAITH HEALER

MINER'S HOME

CUMBERLAND FALLS LODGE

ELKHORN CREEK, NEAR LEXINGTON

ore. Their rail fences trail along the highway, enclosing cornfields that interspace the timber; cabins are perched on the hillsides; and busy manufacturing cities or drab mining towns deface the mountains and valleys.

US 25E branches southeast from its junction with US 25 *(see Tour 4)*, 0 *m.*, on the northern outskirts of CORBIN (1,046 alt., 8,026 pop.) *(see Tour 4)*, and, passing between rugged cliffs and towering mountains, traverses an area in which coal mining is the chief industry.

At 16 *m.* is the junction with old US 25E.

Right on old US 25E to BARBOURVILLE, 1.4 *m.* (975 alt., 2,375 pop.), seat of Knox County, in a broad valley of the winding Cumberland River. It is surrounded by thickly forested ridges that rise in the southern part of the county to a height of 2,000 feet. The soil, a sandy loam and clay, is productive and well adapted to agriculture. When Knox County was created in 1799, it included 5,000 acres belonging to Richard Barbour, a Virginian. By 1800 the land had passed into the possession of James Barbour, a kinsman, who gave this town site to the county and persuaded it to donate half the proceeds from the sale of lots to a fund for erecting public buildings. The town was named in his honor.

UNION COLLEGE *(co-educational),* a Methodist institution housed in plain red brick buildings, was founded in 1879. It is accredited by the Southern Association of Colleges, and has an enrollment of 400 students. The college library contains approximately 11,000 volumes. Dahlia growers from a wide area participate in a Dahlia Show, held each October in the Union College Gymnasium.

The GEORGE OWENS COLLECTION *(open on request),* Knox St., contains arrowheads, pipes, tomahawks, beads, bone objects, fossil remains, pottery, and other Indian relics and objects of archeological interest.

In an old frame building *(open)* on Liberty St. (R), built in 1846, were the LAW OFFICES OF SAMUEL F. MILLER and SILAS WOODSON. Miller (1816–1890) was Associate Justice of the U.S. Supreme Court (1862–1890). Woodson was Governor of Missouri (1873–1875). This small, one-story building has never been altered and is (1939) in need of repair.

Joseph Eve, a circuit judge and the only American minister sent to the Republic of Texas (1841), lived in Barbourville.

Right 0.1 *m.* from Barbourville on State 6 to junction with State 11; L. 4.6 *m.* on State 11 (Thomas Walker Memorial Highway) to the 12-acre DR. THOMAS WALKER STATE PARK. A REPRODUCTION OF DR. WALKER'S LOG CABIN marks the site of the dwelling built in 1750 by Dr. Walker, a surveyor and physician, who was born in Virginia in 1715. He and several companions had been sent on an exploration into Kentucky by the Loyal Land Company of London. They cleared the land near the site of Barbourville and built a cabin here on this rolling hill that overlooks the river named by Dr. Walker for the Duke of Cumberland, son of George II. The park acreage was acquired and the memorial cabin built by the Barbourville Post of the American Legion. The reproduction of the old one-room cabin is built of round logs with wide chinked joints and a small end chimney, curiously "framed in" at the base with notched logs.

On State 6 is DISHMAN SPRINGS HOTEL (R), 6 *m.*, a summer resort on a mountain lake in the foothills of Cumberland Mountains. *(Golf, tennis, fishing, swimming, canoeing for hotel guests; small fee to others.)*

At 2.7 *m.* on old US 25E is the junction with 25E.

At 18.5 *m.* on the new US 25E is the junction with State 225.

Right on this road to (L) the MINTON HICKORY FARM AND STABLES *(open on request),* 0.4 *m.*, where the Minton Hickory saddle horses are trained. From this stable have come such champions as the Feudist, Vendetta, Mountain Echo, Etta Kett, Mountain Laurel, Fiery Crags, and Maiden Blush.

The MINTON HICKORY MILL (R), 1.1 *m.*, manufactures golf shafts, broom handles, and canes. Hickory grown in the Kentucky Mountains is a standard material for golf clubs. This factory, which has become widely known, has a yearly output of 1,500,000 shafts.

FLAT LICK, 27.9 *m.* (986 alt., 500 pop.), straggling along the road, was one of the old salt licks and a center of life in pioneer times.

PINEVILLE, 36.9 *m.* (1,025 alt., 4,000 pop.), a growing mining town and the seat of Bell County, lies within a bend of the Cumberland River at a gap in Pine Mountain called the Narrows. In 1797 the Kentucky Legislature appropriated 500 pounds sterling for the repair of the Wilderness Road and for the erection of a tollgate at the Narrows. This tollgate, around which early Pineville developed, was the first ever established in the State and the first to be abandoned (1830). The newer part of the town is built around CUMBERLAND FORD (L), where the trail crossed the Cumberland River.

The Indians who visited this region and camped here for long seasons left many remains. Near Cumberland Ford is an INDIAN MOUND, 10 to 15 feet in height and 100 feet in circumference, which was a prehistoric burying ground.

An Indian effigy carved out of yellow pine was found on a cliff near Pineville in 1869. This, believed to be the only thoroughly preserved wooden prehistoric image found in Kentucky, is now in the Museum of the American Indian, Heye Foundation, New York City.

Pineville is now a shipping point for lumber and for four large coal fields that are within a short distance of the town.

Schools, bands, and bugle corps, representing a large section of country around Pineville, meet here for the annual Cumberland Valley Music Festival (May). Contests as well as concerts feature the programs.

A winding foot path leads from Pineville to one of the best-preserved INDIAN ROCK SHELTERS in Kentucky. This enormous structure, traditionally an ancient habitation, is near the top of the mountain (R) overlooking the town.

At 37.3 *m.* is the junction with US 119 (*see Tour 19*).

At 38.2 *m.* is the entrance (R) to 4,000-acre PINE MOUNTAIN STATE PARK (*adm., 10¢; overnight camping, 25¢; lodge; picnic facilities, boating and swimming*). Established in 1928, this was the first State park in Kentucky. Within the park the PINNACLE OF PINE MOUNTAIN (2,200 alt.) is accessible by a road. The plant life is characteristic of the Cumberland Range; on the uplands are holly, spruce, pine, wahoo, dogwood, scarlet chestnut, oak, red maple, spicebush, wintergreen, mountain laurel, rhododendron, azaleas, and many varieties of wild flowers and ferns. Black willows, river birch, blue beech, and giant sycamores grow along the banks of Clear Creek, which winds through about 60 acres of the lowlands. Chimney Rock, Sharktooth Rock, and Candlestick Rock are among the most interesting of the park's geologic formations.

Near the center of the reserve is LAUREL COVE, a natural amphitheater in which the Mountain Laurel Festival is held annually *(two days in May or June)*. A stone cliff is the backdrop of the stage constructed of local stone and banked on each side with laurel and rhododendron bushes and giant wahoo trees. Mountain ballads are played and sung, original plays presented, and folk dances performed by the mountain people. A queen selected from the college girls of the State is crowned with mountain laurel by the Governor of Kentucky. With the exception of the Kentucky Derby, this festival is the most important annual event in the State.

At 38.6 *m.* is the junction with State 190.

Right on this road to CLEAR CREEK SPRINGS 2 *m.*, a recreational center and religious resort within Pine Mountain Park. It was established by members of the Baptist churches of Pineville and Middlesboro who hold encampments and schools here during the summer months.

MIDDLESBORO, 50.9 *m.* (1,150 alt., 10,350 pop.), trading center and largest town of southeastern Kentucky, was named for the iron city of the English Midlands. Though the first settlers had entered Kentucky through near-by Cumberland Gap, they were seeking fertile lands easy to cultivate, and this deep circular valley, surrounded by mountains seamed with coal, limestone, and deposits of iron, was ignored for nearly a century. In 1885 Col. Alexander Allen Arthur, a Scottish-Canadian mining engineer, surveyed the region and realized its industrial possibilities.

British investors supplied the capital, a large tract was bought, and, in 1889, settlers began to arrive. Within a year 6,000 people were leveling forests and clearing fields, and two railroads, the Louisville & Nashville, and the Southern, were being built to the new city whose wide streets bore the names of English shires. By 1890 Middlesboro had 10,000 inhabitants. Hotels, stores, and churches had been completed as well as an artificial lake and one of the first golf courses in the United States.

But with the fall of the great London banking house of Baring Brothers and Company, in 1893, Middlesboro, as well as its other projects, was abandoned. At the same time money was tight in this country and the banks nearly paralyzed. Middlesboro's streets were deserted, its hotels and stores empty. Recovery was slow, but eventually the coal mines brought about prosperity. Today there are modern schools, fine homes, handsome churches, theaters, clubs, and banks. The importance of coal in the development of Middlesboro is publicized by the COAL HOUSE *(open)*, on Cumberland Ave., the office of the Middlesboro Chamber of Commerce, built of solid blocks of local coal.

BARTLETT-RHODES PARK (R), near the southern outskirts of the town, has a recreation hall, a swimming pool, and tennis courts.

FERN LAKE *(boating and fishing $1)*, 20th St. extended, approximately one mile south of the business center of Middlesboro, is the source of the city's water supply. The lake is surrounded by mountains whose gentle slopes, rising from the water's edge, are covered with a dense growth of hardwood trees and shrubs, interspersed with pine, spruce, and hemlock. Ferns grow in great profusion along the banks which are gay in the spring with the snowy white, deep rose, and lilac blooms. The winding lake is two and one-half miles long and is fed by mountain springs and streams issuing from massive sandstone ledges, along a seven-mile watershed. It has been converted into a wild-game sanctuary.

The MIDDLESBORO COUNTRY CLUB *(open for a small fee)*, at the western outskirts of the city, has an unusually sporty golf course that is kept in excellent condition. The view from the veranda of the club-house is unsurpassed in this section.

Right from Middlesboro on State 74, hard-surfaced, to a junction with an improved road, 12 *m.;* R. here to HENDERSON SETTLEMENT SCHOOL, 20 *m.*, founded by H. M. Frakes. This school has transformed the surrounding isolated region from one notable for lawlessness to a quiet, peace-abiding community. Here both boys and girls from an inaccessible mountain region receive training, part of which they earn by manual labor. Activities include cooking, farming, dairying, weaving, spinning, woodwork, and allied crafts and occupations.

CUMBERLAND GAP, 53.8 *m.*, on the dividing line of Virginia and Kentucky on the north, and Tennessee on the south, is a trough between hills thickly covered with laurel and rhododendron. It was through this pass in the Appalachians, called by the Indians Quasioto (pronounced Wah-see-o-to; *the mountains where deer are plenty)* that Dr. Thomas Walker entered Kentucky in 1750. Hunters, explorers, and pioneers followed Dr. Walker, and in 1769 John Finley led Daniel Boone into this uninhabited western region. Two years later Boone, in his own words, "returned to my family, being determined to reside in Kentucky which I esteemed a second paradise." He returned in 1775, and behind him, through Cumberland Gap and over the brow of Pinnacle Mountain, came pioneers from the settled East with toiling oxteams and horses laden with household goods for their new homes in the wilderness. It is recorded that as many as 20,000 passed through in one season.

About 1850 Henry Clay, riding from his home near Lexington to speak to the mountain people, halted at the gap. Someone asked him why he lingered. "I am listening," he said, "to the tread of the coming millions."

In the gap is the junction with the Skyland Highway.

Left on Skyland Highway *(adm. 40¢ each person; 40¢ each car)*, which reveals alluring vistas at every turn as it gradually ascends to the PEAK OF PINNACLE MOUNTAIN (2,860 alt.), 2 *m.* From this point on clear days is a view extending for 50 miles over a sea of blue-crested timbered ridges, jagged cliffs, ravines, and Fern Lake. Here also are the RUINS OF FORT LYON. During the War between the States this was one of the strategic points held in turn by the contending Confederate and Union Armies, and, as the tides of battle moved eastward, abandoned by both.

Left from the saddle of the gap on a trail that leads to SOLDIERS' CAVE *(permission to visit obtained at L.M.U., at Harrogate, Tenn., 2 m. S. of Cumberland Gap)*, 0.5 *m.*, now owned by Lincoln Memorial University. Soldiers' Cave, said to have been discovered by Confederate soldiers while digging a rifle pit, has war reminiscences cut on the walls and into the stones.

KING SOLOMON'S CAVE *(permission to visit obtained at L.M.U.)*, 3 *m.*, has a series of apartments or smaller caves that follow the contour of the mountain in a horizontal direction. Within, a river rushes over a cataract 20 to 30 feet high.

Among the many smaller caves in this section are LEWIS CAVE, WELL HOLE, and SALTPETER CAVE where early inhabitants obtained saltpeter for making gunpowder.

At **54.4** *m.* US 25E crosses the Tennessee Line, 14 miles north of Tazewell, Tenn. *(see Tenn. Tour 3)*.

Tour 4B

Corbin—Cumberland Falls State Park—Parker's Lake; **30.2** *m.* State 90.

Hard-surfaced roadbed.
Good accommodations at Cumberland Falls State Park.

State 90 branches west from US 25 *(see Tour 4)* at CORBIN, 0 *m.*, (1,046 alt., 8,026 pop.) *(see Tour 4)*, and passes through a primitive sparsely settled region of great natural beauty. The road, winding over low hills, offers far-reaching views of purple and blue-green mountains and short fertile valleys.

From LOOKOUT POINT (R), **15.6** *m.*, an elevation surrounded by walls of natural stone, is a wide view of row upon row of distant blue peaks and deep, thickly wooded gorges.

CUMBERLAND FALLS STATE PARK, **18.6** *m. (open May 15-Oct. 1; adm. 10¢; hotel accommodations, $1.50 and up; furnished cabins, $1 a day; overnight camping 25¢; bathhouses, picnic facilities)*.

This park, covering 500 acres of virgin forest, was the gift in 1930 of T. Coleman duPont, a Kentuckian. It is rough mountainous country cut by the Cumberland River, which threads its way over a rocky course through the rugged hills.

CUMBERLAND FALLS, 68 feet high and 125 feet broad, has an average flow of 3,600 cubic feet of water a second. Immediately behind the falling sheet of water is a recess in the rock wall, which makes it possible to go almost across the river through the arch formed on one side by the rock and on the other by the flashing waters. Below the falls are many whirlpools and rapids in the river as it flows for seven miles through a boulder-strewn gorge, whose cliffs are 300 to 400 feet high.

A winding trail leads from the falls, half a mile down the river to LITTLE EAGLE FALLS, small but picturesque, surrounded by heavily wooded hills. It is said that this spot was regarded as a sacred place by the Indians who guarded it day and night and even fought a battle (the Indian Battle of Shiloh) in its defense. On the south side of the river is a CLIFF WALK, a narrow ledge high above the water, which winds around the shoulders of the hill until it reaches a shelter house at the top.

A fine growth of yellow pine crowns the ridges, while on the steep slopes and ravines leading down to the river is a mixed forest growth of hemlock, tulip, magnolia, oak, sweetgum, dogwood, and holly, the latter especially abundant and of large size. Azalea, rhododendron, spicebush, Stewartia, blueberry, St.-John's-wort, and strawberry bush are among the many plants.

The old MOONBOW INN, on a ledge above the falls, is so named because in the full of the moon Cumberland Falls has a moonbow, a spectrum formed in the mist—one of the few to be seen on this continent. Moonbow Inn is a rambling two-story frame structure, erected in the 1860's, and later restored. The main building forms an ell that faces the falls. A two-story porch extends entirely across the façade next to the river.

DUPONT LODGE, named in honor of T. Coleman du Pont, stands on a ridge overlooking the Cumberland River, one mile from the falls. It is built of wood and stone.

The 900,000-acre CUMBERLAND NATIONAL FOREST, encircling Cumberland Falls State Park, contains thousands of acres of virgin timber and a variety of wild game including deer, black bear, and smaller fur-bearing animals, as well as wild turkey, quail, and waterfowl.

A thickly wooded region of hills lies between the Cumberland River, crossed by a ferry *(free)*, and PARKER'S LAKE, 30.2 *m.* (1,256 alt., 200 pop.), which is at the junction with US 27 *(see Tour 3)*.

Tour 5

Warsaw—Frankfort—Lawrenceburg—Harrodsburg—Danville—Jamestown—Albany—(Chattanooga, Tenn.); State 35.
Warsaw to Tennessee Line, 187.7 *m.*

Hard-surfaced roadbed between Warsaw and Liberty, graveled between Liberty and Jamestown, and graded between Jamestown and Tennessee Line.
Southern Ry. parallels route between Lawrenceburg and Danville.
All types of accommodations in larger towns; limited elsewhere.

This route runs through a sparsely settled hilly area, fine stock farms of the Bluegrass, many small old towns, and the wooded foothills of the Cumberland Mountains.

WARSAW, 0 *m.* (459 alt., 800 pop.) *(see Tour 12)*, is at the junction with US 42 *(see Tour 12)*.

South of Warsaw State 35 winds across the outer Knobs area, which borders the Ohio Valley. Small farms lie in the fertile bottom lands, and along the hillsides flocks of sheep graze on the abundant grass and clover. The wool produced in this region is of fine quality.

On almost every farm are patches of burley tobacco, usually two acres or larger. The cultivation of tobacco requires such a large amount of hand labor that acreage is limited by the amount of help obtainable. The average tobacco field, cared for by one man and his family, rarely exceeds 10 or 12 acres. Cultivation begins as early as February with the burning over of the seedbed to destroy parasites and weeds. In March and April the seeds are planted in cold frames and protected from wind, hail, and sudden changes in temperature by thin white muslin stretched above the beds. In May or June the young plants are set in rows in ground that has been fertilized and brought into good tilth by plowing and harrowing. The planting is usually done with a horse-drawn transplanter that opens a furrow, releases water at set intervals, and covers up the roots of the young plants, which a man drops into the ground. While the crop is growing it is sometimes dusted (though there is danger of the poison remaining on the leaves), the worms are removed, and tops and suckers are broken off by hand. When the crop is ready for harvesting in August or September, the tobacco plants are cut by hand and placed six on a stick either by splitting the stalk almost to the base and inverting it over the stick or by piercing the stalk near the base. To protect the leaves from bruises, the tobacco plants are carried to the barn on trucks or wagons equipped with frames that hold the sticks horizontally so the stalks hang in a vertical position several inches apart. In the barns it is hung up to dry, without the aid of artificial heat. After curing, the tobacco is stripped and graded into "hands," the term used for a marketable unit. The hands are sorted, according to grade, into baskets, each of which is sold separately on the tobacco sales floor. Droning monotonously in a jargon that is understood by only the initiate, the auctioneer walks between the rows of baskets. Buyers stand among the crowd of spectators and when ready to buy give a sign to the auctioneer who promptly announces, "Sold!" Prices vary widely according to grade and general demand. The yield may exceed $500 an acre, or may not even compensate the farmer for his labor. After the auction the purchaser packs the tobacco in hogsheads and stores it for aging, a process that sometimes requires two years. The aged tobacco is again carefully graded to meet the standards required by various brands and purposes.

In SPARTA, 9 *m.* (500 pop.), are nurseries specializing in evergreen trees and shrubs. Here, too, are the remains of old EAGLE CREEK COVERED BRIDGE.

At 15.5 *m.* is the junction (R) with US 227 *(see Tour 12A)*. Between this point and Owenton, State 35 and US 227 are united.

OWENTON, 22.8 *m.* (1,000 alt., 975 pop.) *(see Tour 12A)*, is at the junction with US 227 *(see Tour 12A)* and State 22 *(see Tour 13)*.

Between Owenton and 23.4 *m.* State 35 and US 227 are united.

South of Owenton the highway winds down steep hills and around sharp curves to the valley of the Kentucky River, frequently affording wide views of blue-green hills and deep waters.

MONTEREY, 32.9 *m.* (203 pop.), nestled at the foot of the hills in a valley between towering green palisades, is at the confluence of the Kentucky River and Eagle Creek *(fishing; camp sites)*. Near Monterey is POND BRANCH, where the water, rising from springs, flows through an old channel of the Kentucky River.

At 45.9 *m.* is the junction with a private roadway.

Left on this road 5 *m.* to the old INNES HOUSE, on the farm of Joe D. Bradburn, Jr. *(inquire at farmhouse for permission to visit)*. This two-story hewn-log house, on a stone foundation, was built by Harry Innes during the last quarter of the eighteenth century. Innes subsequently became first U.S. District Judge of Kentucky.

The house, now dilapidated, stands on a ridge between two dry forks of Elkhorn Creek—a vantage point from which the approach of Indians could easily be observed. Shortly after its completion, Indians went on the warpath in this region and the settlers gathered at Innes' Station, as the house was then called, for protection. The house was besieged for several hours but its occupants withstood the attack without loss of life. Loopholes are plainly visible between the logs of the second floor.

CEDAR COVE SPRING, 51 *m.* (R), was the source for the first public water-supply system in Kentucky, established in 1804. The water was transported to Frankfort and the penitentiary in wooden pipes laid by Richard Throckmorton.

FRANKFORT, 52.6 *m.* (512 alt., 11,626 pop.) *(see Frankfort)*.

Points of Interest: Old State Capitol, State Cemetery, Liberty Hall, and others.

Frankfort is at the junction with US 60 *(see Tour 16)*.

South of Frankfort State 35 ascends a hill from which is an excellent view (L) of the town lying in the Kentucky River Valley, the new State Capitol, and the Governor's mansion.

The STEWART HOME TRAINING SCHOOL *(open)*, 56 *m.*, is (L) a private institution for the education of backward children. Its main buildings, surrounded by a spacious lawn and landscaped gardens, are set in 500 acres of bluegrass and forest.

ALTON, 62.3 *m.* (112 pop.), was originally named Rough and Ready in honor of Zachary Taylor.

LAWRENCEBURG, 66.7 *m.* (788 alt., 1,763 pop.) *(see Tour 14)*, is at the junction with US 62 *(see Tour 14)*.

At **69.2** *m.* is the junction with the McBrayer Rd.

Right on this road to BOND'S MILL COVERED BRIDGE, **2.5** *m.*, over the Salt River. This is one of the few century-old covered bridges in the State.

In SALVISA, **75.2** *m.* (500 pop.), is (R) the SAMUEL MCAFEE HOUSE *(private)*, built in 1790 by Samuel McAfee. The house, now called the Gabe Hall Place, stands on a spacious lawn through which a little creek flows. The clapboarded log structure has a deep two-story portico and vine-covered end chimneys.

The NEW PROVIDENCE PRESBYTERIAN CHURCH (L), **78.5** *m.*, is a rectangular brick structure with gabled roof, the gable end being pierced by a half moon "sentinel" window that is now boarded up. The long rectangular windows and high pilasters accentuate the severe lines. This structure, whose construction was begun in 1861 and completed in 1864, is the fourth occupied by the congregation since it was founded in 1784 by the Reverend David (Father) Rice, a circuit rider, who for many years conducted services here at intervals. The McAfee brothers, Scotch Presbyterians, contributed the site and erected the first church, a log structure, which they opened in 1785, as an offering to Providence for saving them in the Indian attack of 1781.

McAFEE, **79.7** *m.* (100 pop.), was named for the adventurous McAfee brothers.

Right from McAfee on the Talmadge Pike to the JAMES MCAFEE HOUSE *(open by request)*, **1.2** *m.* (R), built in 1790 by James McAfee, oldest of the brothers. It is a two-story gable-roofed house, said to have been modeled after the builder's home in Armagh, Ireland. The walls of the house are built of partly dressed field stone in random sizes and are 30 inches thick. The interior woodwork is hand-carved. Some of the strap hinges, badly worn, appear to be those on which the doors originally swung.

On the façade of the McAfee house is a bronze marker erected in tribute to the founders of McAfee Station—James, George, and Robert McAfee, and James Mc-Coun, James Pawling, and Samuel Adams. These pioneers came in July 1773 from Botetourt County, Virginia, and surveyed land in Kentucky. Indian wars kept them in Virginia during the succeeding year, but 1775 found them again among the canebrakes, where they cleared the ground and planted an orchard along Salt River, returning the same year to Virginia because of Indian hostilities.

In 1779 the McAfees returned with their families to Kentucky and built a fortified hamlet on Salt River. The stockade, on the south side, was little more than a barricade, and there were but 13 men in the garrison. On May 4, 1781, ignoring the uneasiness of the dogs and cattle—domestic animals reacted to the smell of an Indian as they did to that of a wild beast—the stock was turned loose, and four of the men went out to work. Two of them with a horse started towards the corncrib. About a quarter of a mile from the stockade their path dipped into a hollow; here they suddenly came on Indians. At the first fire one of the men was killed; and the other who had started running toward home, was intercepted by an Indian who leaped into the path directly ahead of him. Though both fired at once, the Indian's gun missed and he was killed. The survivor reached the fort in safety.

When the other two men, who had gone to work in the turnip patch, heard the shooting they seized their guns and ran toward the sound but were alarmed by the number of Indians and turned back to the fort, trying to drive the frightened stock in as they went. One of the men reached the gate safely; the other, being cut off, took a roundabout route through the woods. He outdistanced all but one of his pursuers, a Shawnee chief whom he finally killed after jumping a fence in the cleared ground around the fort and crouching in the weeds till the Indian peered over the fence and thus exposed himself to the settlers' fire.

Those inside the stockade had closed the gate and grasped their rifles the moment the first shots were heard. One man who hid under a bed was found by his wife, dragged out, and made to run bullets with the women and children. When the Indians rushed the fort, they were driven off at once, one of their number being killed and several badly wounded, while but one of the defenders was slightly injured. In a short time 45 horsemen, headed by Captain McGarry, galloped up from Harrodsburg where they had heard the firing. The Indians retreated immediately. McGarry halted long enough to allow the McAfee men to bridle their horses, then began pursuit. In the fight that followed, the white men dismounted, and both sides took shelter behind tree trunks. After two more Indians had been killed, the others scattered.

HARRODSBURG, 86.5 *m.* (871 alt., 4,029 pop.) *(see Harrodsburg), is at the junction with US 68 *(see Tour 15).*

Between Harrodsburg and Danville the gently rolling highway traverses a fertile agricultural region containing many fine old homes.

It is in this region that the male elite of the villages once gathered in the fall of the year, after a few heavy frosts, to enjoy 'possum or coon suppers—a long-established Kentucky institution. The preparation of these dishes was an especial achievement of the old-time black mammy who boasted that she could make anybody eat 'possum or coon and like it.

FAIR OAKS (R), 87.6 *m.,* was built about 1845 by Dr. Guilford D. Runyon, a Shaker who renounced his vows of celibacy and erected the house in anticipation of his marriage to Miss Kate Ferrel, who died before the house was completed. Doctor Runyon remained a bachelor until his death in 1873. The house, of Georgian Colonial design, is a two-story brick structure, with two-story porches on each side. The ends of the porches are sheltered by screens; those of the second floor are beautifully carved with a willow leaf and tendril motif. A six-room wing at the rear and a Greek Revival portico with four massive Ionic columns have been added. The doorway is flanked by columns of similar order and the façade is embellished with elaborately carved lintels. The two-room brick cottage, still standing, served as the kitchen and dining room for the "big house" during the life of Doctor Runyon.

The CALDWELL HOUSE (R), 93.4 *m.,* erected in 1823 by Jeremiah Clemens for his daughter, Elizabeth Caldwell, is constructed of local limestone. A spacious front porch with massive Ionic columns is formed by recessing the central portion of the façade. Some years after completion the outer walls were stuccoed and painted white.

DANVILLE, 96.4 *m.* (955 alt., 6,279 pop.), on the southern edge of the Bluegrass region, is the seat of Centre College and of the State school for the deaf. It has wide tree-shaded streets and fine old homes, built in the Greek Revival style. It was founded in 1775. Ten years later the Supreme Court of Virginia made it the seat of government west of the Alleghenies and ordered court buildings erected here. At Danville were held the nine conventions preceding the admission of the State into the Union. The most noted of Kentucky's pioneers served as delegates. A center of culture in pioneer days, Danville dropped from political leadership upon the removal of the seat of government, June 4, 1792—the day on which Isaac Shelby was inaugurated as first Governor of Kentucky—but regained a small measure of prestige by the establishment of a district court that operated here from 1796 until 1803. From the latter date the town was without a court until Boyle County was formed from parts of Mercer and Lincoln in 1842. During the years of political eclipse, the citizens of Danville turned to educational affairs, and early in the nineteenth century established the institutions for which it is now noteworthy.

CENTRE COLLEGE, in the western part of town, a liberal arts school endowed for more than $1,000,000, was chartered in 1819, and is under the joint management of the northern and southern synods of the Presbyterian Church. The administration building of the college (L) on Main St. is a striking example of Greek Revival architecture. Among the graduates of Centre are some of Kentucky's illustrious sons, including Beriah Magoffin, Governor of Kentucky, class of 1834; Maj. Gen. John C. Breckinridge, Vice President of the United States (1856), and defeated by Lincoln for the Presidency, class of 1839; Robert C. Wickliffe, Governor of Louisiana, class of 1840; and George A. Vest, Senator from Missouri, class of 1848. The Centre College football team, known as the "Praying Colonels," astonished the sports world in 1920 when it defeated some of the strongest teams in the country. The students' annual year-end festival arouses State-wide interest because of the age and prestige of the institution and the elaborate character of the celebration. The crowning of a carnival king and queen is accompanied by a number of allied events covering several days. Although Centre College is not co-educational, its president and board of trustees also direct in the eastern section of the town a school for women formerly called Caldwell College.

The old DANVILLE COURT SQUARE (R), on Main St. between 1st and 2d Sts., was once Virginia's western capitol.

In the McDOWELL HOUSE, 123 S. 2d St., on December 25, 1809, before the discovery of methods of anesthesia, Dr. Ephraim McDowell performed the first successful ovariotomy.

Doctor McDowell, of Scotch-Irish ancestry, was born in Augusta County, Virginia, November 11, 1771. His father, Samuel McDowell, one of the judges of the first Kentucky court in 1783 and president of the convention that framed the first constitution of Kentucky, took his family to Danville when Ephraim was 12 years old. Ephraim studied anatomy and surgery with Dr. Alex Humphreys of Staunton, Virginia, and in 1793–94 attended the University of Edinburgh, where he was for a time the private pupil of Dr. John Bell. He left the university without his degree, and returned to Danville, where he began the practice of medicine. In December 1809, called to treat Mrs. Jane Todd

Crawford of Greensburg, Doctor McDowell told his patient an examination had convinced him that her only chance for relief was a dangerous internal operation that he had never before performed, but was ready to undertake if she would come to his home in Danville. Mrs. Crawford, frantic from pain, set out immediately and made the journey of 60 miles on horseback in a few days.

The doctor improvised an operating room in his home. The patient was placed on a long wooden table covered with a blanket. She was fully dressed and perfectly conscious of every movement of the surgeon and his assistants. To restrain her involuntary muscles, and permit the surgeon to work, men held down her arms and legs with force. During the operation Mrs. Crawford repeated the Psalms. Later Doctor McDowell reported, "In five days I visited her, and much to my astonishment found her engaged in making her bed. I gave her particular caution for the future and she returned home as she came, in good health, which she continues to enjoy." Mrs. Crawford was 47 at the time of the operation and died at the age of 78. This operation, the first ovariotomy performed in this country, was not considered important by McDowell himself. However, after seven years, he was persuaded to publish in the *Eclectic Repertory and Analytical Review,* Volume VII, an account of this operation and of several others of similar nature which he had performed later. The announcement met with indifference, incredulity, and even ridicule, and many years passed before his work began to receive recognition. Doctor McDowell continued to practice medicine until his death, June 20, 1830. The residence, a simple two-story clapboarded structure with its 24-paned windows and transomed doorway, and the adjoining one-story brick apothecary shop, have been restored with the aid of Federal funds. The house and grounds were given to the State by the Kentucky Medical Association to be administered through the State Park Commission as a memorial to Doctor McDowell and to Jane Todd Crawford, his patient.

McDOWELL PARK, 5th St., between Main and Market Sts., contains a monument to Doctor McDowell and one to Jane Todd Crawford.

The KENTUCKY DEAF INSTITUTE was founded in 1823. Many trades are taught here, including printing and domestic science, as well as academic subjects.

The PHILLIP YEISER HOUSE, 135 Lexington Ave., designed in the Classic Revival style and built early in the nineteenth century, is constructed of brick covered with plaster. The house is on a wide, shady lawn that is slightly above the street level. The older central unit of two stories is flanked by high one-story wings, which have balustraded roofs. There is a pedimented portico.

Central Kentucky's FIRST POST OFFICE, established in 1798, occupied the corner of a room in the old house at 310 W. Walnut St. This building, now used as a dwelling, has been weatherboarded and has an addition of a one-story wing. Originally built of hewn logs, the structure was rectangular in plan and a story and a half high. The dormers seem to be part of the original plan. Gen. Thomas Barbee was the first postmaster.

Left from Danville on State 34, an improved road, to PARKSVILLE, 8 m. (228 pop.), is one of the most important berry-growing sections of the State. Here the residents of the village and neighboring farms follow an ancient Indian custom of holding a religious ceremony early in the spring to pray for bountiful crops. The ceremonial as revived by the Berry Growers' Association, includes music, prayer, and scripture reading. The extent to which raspberries are grown in this region is a result of several years' effort on the part of the county farm agents, who recognized that the hilly, rocky land, on which many of the farmers were attempting to make a living, was not suited to the crops they were trying to grow.

WARRENWOOD (R), 99.3 m., was built approximately in 1847 on part of a tract of land owned by Capt. William Warren, who came from Virginia in 1776. The two-story house, of brick burned on the grounds, is of the Gothic Revival type. Practically all the work was done by the slaves of John F. Warren; he and his brother, Samuel Warren, were the first owners and builders.

JUNCTION CITY, 101.4 m. (731 pop.), is a railroad crossing.

Left from Junction City on the Stanford Pike, an improved road, to the SITE OF TRAVELER'S REST, 3 m., home of Isaac Shelby, first Governor of Kentucky (1792–96) who served again in 1812–16. The old house, constructed of stone by Thomas Metcalf in 1786, was destroyed by fire a number of years ago and has been replaced. The graveyard, in which Shelby and members of his family were buried, is near by.

HUSTONVILLE, 110.1 m. (504 pop.), an old town lying in a rich agricultural section, was first called New Store, later renamed Huston's Villa, and then Hustonville.

LIBERTY, 125.1 m. (549 pop.), seat of Casey County, is at the headwaters of the Green River in the eastern section of the Pennyrile and on the southern edge of the Knobs belt. Liberty was named by veterans of the Revolutionary War who came to this section from Virginia in 1791. Col. William Casey, a pioneer in whose honor the county was named, established a station near Green River for protection during the Indian wars. Associated with Colonel Casey was Christopher Riffe, who in 1793 bought from the grandfather of Abraham Lincoln 800 acres of land in what is now Casey County.

RUSSELL SPRINGS, 147 m. (1,080 alt., 500 pop.), a resort long known as Big Boiling Springs, was for many years operated by members of the family of Sam Patterson, first settler. When the spring was found to have a high iron and sulphur content, a dozen log cabins, called Long Row, were built for the accommodation of visitors. In 1898 Long Row was replaced by a frame hotel that is still in operation. The old cylindrical sandstone capping of the spring has been replaced with concrete.

Russell Springs is at the junction with State 80 *(see Tour 18)*.

JAMESTOWN, 154.1 m. (950 alt., 410 pop.), seat of Russell County, was first called Jacksonville in honor of Andrew Jackson. By

1826 the Whigs came into power and, resenting the tribute to their opponent, changed the name to Jamestown, honoring James Wooldridge who had donated 110 acres for a town site. Along Water and Main Sts. in Jamestown are numerous old clapboarded log houses. Outstanding among these are the J. R. McFARLAND HOUSE and the OTHA WELLS HOUSE, the oldest structures in the town. An annual community singing contest is held in the courthouse on the last Sunday in August.

1. Right from Jamestown on the Greasy Creek Rd., unimproved, to the GREASY CREEK WOOLEN MILL, 1 m., an old water-power mill that manufactures cloth and knitting yarns. Many farmers bring their fleeces to be processed here, paying for the work with a part of the raw wool. Near by is the KARNES GRISTMILL, one of four in operation in the county. The mills here were established before the War between the States.

2. Left from Jamestown on the Somerset Rd., unimproved, to INDIAN CAVE, 3 m., in a bluff 75 feet high. Its entrance pierces the mountain side to a depth of about 20 feet in a straight line and then continues in a meandering path for more than 300 feet. Several large chambers branch from the main passageway. A stream near the cave pours into the Narrows, a gorge that is only two feet wide at some points. Near by is the SHINBONE, a peculiarly shaped hill that is about 100 feet high and averages 30 feet in width at its base. Its rocky sides are covered with low-growing bushes. Big and Little Lily Creeks meet about 300 yards above the Narrows through which Lily Creek cascades to the Shinbone, which it encircles.

South of Jamestown the route continues through a hilly region, crossing Cumberland River by way of a free ferry.

The name of SEVENTY-SIX FALLS (L), 178.1 m., indicates the number of feet down which Indian Creek drops perpendicularly. Near the basin into which the creek plunges it sinks into the earth but emerges again after a subterranean flow of about one-half mile, only to fall another 10 feet into a watermill pond, the dam of which adds an additional 15-foot drop.

The route passes SEWELL MOUNTAIN (1,720 alt.), a spur (L) of the Cumberland Mountains.

ALBANY, 181.9 m. (964 alt., 852 pop.) (see Tour 20), is at the junction with State 90 (see Tour 20).

South of Albany JENNY'S KNOB (L) is visible for miles along the highway.

State 35 crosses the Tennessee Line, 187.7 m.

Tour 6

(Indianapolis, Ind.)—Louisville—Bardstown—Hodgenville—Glasgow —Scottsville—(Nashville, Tenn.); US 31E.
Indiana Line to Tennessee Line, 147.8 m.

Hard-surfaced roadbed.
Louisville & Nashville R.R. parallels route between Louisville and Bardstown, and between Scottsville and the Tennessee Line.
All types of accommodations in cities; limited elsewhere.

US 31E, the Jackson Highway, winds over the central part of the State, which is rolling or hilly for the most part. Towns of any size are far apart, and except for some truck gardening near Louisville, the farms along this highway hold to the typical Kentuckian pattern in that they chiefly produce corn and tobacco, or are given over to the raising of livestock. The winter scene is flat in tone except for the evergreens and the orange of sage grass; but in April and May, the woods are gay with the bloom of redbud and dogwood, and brilliant through the fall with the contrasting colors of the frosted leaves.

US 31E crosses the Indiana Line, 0 *m.*, the north bank of the Ohio River, and crosses the river itself on a toll bridge *(toll 25¢)*, eight miles south of Sellersburg, Indiana *(see Ind. Tour 13)*.

LOUISVILLE, 0.8 *m.* (525 alt., 307,745 pop.) *(see Louisville)*.

Points of Interest: Speed Museum, Memorial Auditorium, Presbyterian Theological Seminary, Churchill Downs, Cave Hill Cemetery, Cherokee Park.

Louisville is at the junction with US 31W *(see Tour 7)*, US 60 *(see Tour 16)*, and US 42 *(see Tour 12)*.

The flat country immediately south of Louisville is bare and brown in winter, but green with potato plants and other truck-farming vegetables in summer. Farther south the land is rolling and clumps of evergreens, fields of corn, and grass pastures appear by the roadside; then, at 17.4 *m.*, a series of rounded hills, darkened by a notched plume of evergreens, appear on both sides of the highway. These are the Knobs that rim the Bluegrass plains. Red cedars and old oak or gum trees, the latter often entwined with mistletoe, are common along this route.

FARMINGTON (L), 5.2 *m.*, is the house built in 1810 by John Speed who came with his father over the Wilderness Road from Virginia to Kentucky in 1782. A long avenue bordered with trees leads to the one-and-one-half-story house of brick. The wide recessed entrance provides additional space under the portico which has an elliptical window in the pediment. The doorway is ornamented on each side with four reeded pilasters, side lights, and it has a segmental arched fanlight above, all beautifully executed. The wide central hallway opens into two large front rooms and into two octagonal rooms behind them. The ceilings of the first floor are 15 feet high, the windows have nine-paned sashes and in the octagonal rooms are hand-carved wooden mantels identical in design and ornamentation, one of the features of which is a gleaming metal eagle. A short distance from the house stand the brick smokehouse, the remains of an old stone stable, and a stone spring house. James Speed, one of the sons of John Speed, was Attorney General under Abraham Lincoln and Joshua, another son, was Lincoln's intimate friend at Springfield, Illinois. In 1841,

Lincoln, after an early love affair turned out unhappily, spent most of the summer and fall here.

MOUNT WASHINGTON, 20.9 *m*. (686 alt., 350 pop.), was a flourishing community on the stage turnpike from Louisville to Nashville as early as 1800. The settlement was first known as The Crossroads, then as Mount Vernon; finally, by order of postal authorities, as Mount Washington.

The two-story BRIDWELL HOUSE (R), built in 1797 of rough hewn poplar logs, has been little altered since it was constructed.

In the vicinity of the Salt River, 26.1 *m*., US 31E suddenly comes alongside of a great bottom land (L) far below the highway. The bottom is zoned out like a model city into neat, flat fields of corn and soil-building crops. In the center are two small stands of second-growth timber, rivulets cross the entire area, and here and there are a few farmhouses and barns. An ornamental stone wall by the roadside forms a parking space for those who wish to enjoy the view.

COX'S CREEK, 32.5 *m*. (40 pop.), was named for Col. Isaac Cox, who, with a small band of settlers, built a fort here in 1775.

At 37.4 *m*. is the junction with a road.

Right on this road to the entrance, 0.3 *m*., to NAZARETH JUNIOR COLLEGE AND ACADEMY (R), a Roman Catholic school established in 1814. The administration building, with its imposing portico, is approached by an avenue shaded with oaks and maples. The school has a library of more than 15,000 volumes, including several rare ones; a museum with an extensive collection of geological specimens; and a number of old paintings, one, ADORATION OF THE MAGI, is a copy of the one in Madrid by Peter Paul Rubens and may have been made in his workshop.

BARDSTOWN, 39.8 *m*. (637 alt., 1,767 pop.) *(see Tour 15)*, is at the junction with US 62 *(see Tour 14)* and at the northern junction with US 68 *(see Tour 15)*. US 31E and US 68 are united for 58.5 miles.

The route passes the TOM MOORE DISTILLERY, 40.4 *m*. *(permission necessary to view plant)*, whose large, silver-painted warehouses range along the road (R). As US 31E climbs a plateau, the land levels back from the highway in wide, treeless spaces distantly edged with timber; and miles away the dim hills throw a straight dark line against the sky. The road then spirals down through a low, attractive group of hills green with stands of cedar, sycamore and pine, and passes more knobs pointing their cones to the sky.

NEW HAVEN, 53.7 *m*. (444 alt., 445 pop.), a quiet, tree-shaded town founded in 1820, was first called Pottinger's Landing. Harrod's company had established a station on Pottinger Creek in 1781 and Col. Samuel Pottinger, one of its members, envisaging this as an important shipping point, built a large landing and warehouse here for the storage of whisky and other products that were to be shipped on flatboats down the Rolling Fork, Salt, Ohio, and Mississippi Rivers to New Orleans. Pottinger renamed his town, it is said, because he admired New Haven, Conn. While this village never achieved the position its founder had hoped for, large quantities of whisky, cured meat, and timber were shipped from the area. The production of whisky remains its foremost industrial activity.

Left from New Haven on State 52, an improved road, to the ABBEY OF OUR LADY OF GETHSEMANE *(open to men only, adm. free),* 4 *m.* This Trappist monastery was founded in 1848, when the chapter of the monastery of Melleray, France, fearful of the revolution of that year, determined to find a home in America for a part of their crowded community. The Trappists are Cistercians of an order that came into existence in 1664 after a housecleaning by Armand J. le B. de Rance at the abbey of La Trappe. The Cistercians themselves were founded after a reform in the Benedictine order, the oldest of the Roman Catholic Church. Various independent congregations of Trappists arose after 1664 but all were united in the Reformed Order of Strict Observance in 1892. This order fasts continually and accepts the discipline of silence. The vow of perpetual silence holds except during conference with superiors, when in choir, or on other very special occasions. They greet each other in silence, with a bow, and use sign language for any necessary communication. One monk, as host to the many who visit the abbey, is released from this vow.

Through the efforts of the Rt. Rev. Joseph Flaget, first bishop of Louisville, a 1,400-acre tract of land, subsequently enlarged, was purchased, and 40 members under the leadership of Dom Proust crossed the Atlantic and began the difficult work of clearing land and building a home for the order.

The abbey, a rambling white stuccoed structure of Gothic design, was completed and consecrated in 1866. The buildings form an immense quadrangle, one side of which is the church, also of Gothic design; this building, 226 feet long, has a white spire rising 166 feet. Within, sharply pointed, cross-ribbed vaults are supported by octagonal columns with delicately molded and foliated Gothic caps.

The porter's building has a wide arched entrance. Within this long low structure are a small museum, a post office, and a dressing room for the only women ever admitted—the wife of the President of the United States and the wife of Kentucky's Governor. Two walls connect this building with the abbey proper and enclose a quadrangular garden.

Behind the guest house is the cloister garden, containing many rare shrubs and plants. In its center is a statue of Our Lady of Gethsemane above a circular roofed shelter.

The library consists of more than 60,000 volumes, including ancient manuscripts and rare old liturgical writings. More than 40,000 of its volumes were donated in 1901 by Monsignor Batz of the archdiocese of Milwaukee. In the abbot's office, adjoining his cell, is a small collection of handwritten and illuminated books.

The monks are divided into two groups, lay brothers who wear brown cassocks and choir religieuse who wear white. Morning devotions begin at 2 A.M. and last until 6 o'clock, when there is an hour for meditation, followed by a one-hour mass. From 8 until 11:30 the monks do manual labor. Then the one meal of the day is served, the food consisting usually of vegetables and milk. The afternoon program includes both labor and devotions, and the day is brought to a close by vespers at 6. At 7 P.M. the brothers retire to their cells. The lay brothers devote eight hours a day to physical labor, the choir religieuse but four. In addition to the monastery's market, there are a blacksmith shop, a wheelwright shop, a carpenter shop, a tinsmith shop, and a steam sawmill.

This community is described in James Lane Allen's *White Cowl.* In 1933 there were 44 choir religieuse and novices, 40 lay brothers and oblates.

Also on State 52, in the part of Kentucky that early became a field of Roman Catholic immigration to the West, is LORETTO CONVENT AND ACADEMY *(open),* 13 *m.,* the outgrowth of a little school opened on Hardin's Creek, Marion County, by Anne Rhodes early in 1812. She, with four other women who soon joined her, became the nucleus of the Sisters of Loretto, founded by the Reverend Charles Nerincx. The first home of the order, about six miles from the present mother house, was a log cabin furnished with a table and wooden benches. Sister Anne Rhodes became the first mother superior; by 1816 the Sisterhood had grown to 26 members. In 1824 the convent was moved to St. Stephen's Farm, former home of the Reverend Theodore Badin, cofounder with Father Nerincx of Roman Catholicism in Kentucky. In 1888 the institution completely outgrew its quarters, so new buildings were erected, quite in contrast with the original log houses of pioneer days. Brick buildings at the mother house stand in the midst of a large farm, with orchard, gardens, and fields for raising grain and other food products. The Sisterhood has numerous branches throughout the South and West. Teachers for these are provided by a normal school at Loretto. This convent is the locale for James Lane Allen's "Sister Dolorosa," contained in his book, *Flute and Violin and Other Kentucky Stories.*

South of the Rolling Fork of Salt River, 56 *m.*, the terrain is considerably broken, though there are many areas of good farm land.

On the SITE OF THE KNOB CREEK FARM *(open)*, 57 *m.*, where the Lincoln family lived between Abraham's fourth and eighth years, is a REPRODUCTION OF LINCOLN'S BIRTHPLACE; the original log cabin is now at Lincoln Memorial National Park.

In 1813 Thomas Lincoln and his family moved from the barren Sinking Spring farm to this region, where fish and game were plentiful and the soil unusually fertile. In a letter written in 1860 to Samuel Haycraft, Abraham Lincoln said: "My earliest recollections are of the Knob Creek place." For approximately three months of the sojourn here Abraham Lincoln trudged to school with his sister, Sarah, but his teachers were inadequately qualified and the schooling was of little practical value. At other times the boy helped his father with the farming (sometimes carrying corn seven miles to Hodgen's mill to be ground), hunted rabbits, fished, and climbed the rugged hillsides with his companions.

HODGENVILLE, 65.1 *m.* (720 alt., 1,104 pop.), seat of Larue County, is one-half mile below the confluence of the three branches of Nolin River. In 1789 Robert Hodgen erected a mill on his land. In addition to operating his mill and farm, he conducted a tavern or "ordinary," in which many notables were entertained, including the French botanist Michaux, in January 1797, and the royal travelers, Louis Philippe and his brothers, in April 1797. Hodgen died in 1810, and soon afterward the settlement that had sprung up near his tavern was named for him. In the public square is a bronze STATUE OF ABRAHAM LINCOLN by Adolph A. Weiman, erected in 1909 through National and State appropriations.

The LINCOLN MEMORIAL NATIONAL PARK, 67.9 *m.*, is on the old Sinking Spring Farm (R), the birthplace of Abraham Lincoln.

Crowning an eminence within the park is the LINCOLN MEMORIAL, an austere square structure approached from a plaza by a long flight of steps, 30 feet wide, flanked by hedges and trees. SINKING SPRING, its waters still sweet and clear, is protected by stone walls and flagging at the foot of the knoll.

The memorial, designed by John Russell Pope, is built of Connecticut pink granite and Tennessee marble. Across the front are six granite Doric columns; similar columns frame three grilled openings on each side. Over the entrance is carved "With Malice Toward None with Charity for All." On the rear inside wall are inscribed the life stories of Thomas Lincoln and Nancy Hanks.

Marble tablets bear quotations from Maurice Thompson and Edwin Markham and Lincoln's simple one-paragraph autobiography.

In the center of the building stands the log cabin that is believed to have been the BIRTHPLACE OF ABRAHAM LINCOLN. When the cabin was restored and placed within the walls of the Memorial Building, its size was reduced slightly. It is now 12 feet wide and 17 feet long and its walls are 11 logs high. The spaces between the logs are chinked with clay, and a clay-lined log chimney stands at one end. A small window gives the only light, and the doorway is so low that a man of average height must stoop when entering.

Abraham Lincoln, the grandfather, came to Kentucky from Virginia between 1782 and 1784 (see Tour 16). His son, Thomas Lincoln, and Nancy Hanks were married at Beechland in Washington County in 1806 (see Tour 15 and Harrodsburg), and set up housekeeping at Elizabethtown (see Tour 7).

In December 1808 Thomas Lincoln purchased this farm on the South Fork of Nolin River, and came here with his wife and daughter. In the short time he lived on it, he farmed a few acres, hunted, and did carpentry work for other farmers. Hardin County tax records show that he was taxed for possession of a few horses. On February 12, 1809, Abraham Lincoln was born, and in 1811 another son, Thomas, was born and died. In 1813, possibly because of a dispute over title to the land, the Lincoln family moved to a Knob Creek farm where they lived until they moved to Indiana.

In 1894 Alfred Denett of New York purchased 110½ acres of land, including the site of the log cabin in which Abraham Lincoln is believed to have been born. This was all but 10 acres of the Lincoln tract. The log cabin was moved from place to place for exhibition purposes; it was shown at the Tennessee Centennial Exposition at Nashville, in New York City's Central Park, and at the Pan-American Exposition in Buffalo. About 1904 it was stored in the basement of the Poffenhaufen mansion at College Point on Long Island.

These exhibitions aroused widespread interest, and, as a result, the Reverend Jenkin Lloyd Jones of Chicago proposed that the Federal Government buy the farm. His son, Richard Lloyd Jones, who was managing editor of Collier's Weekly, interested Robert Collier, the publisher, in the proposal, and other publications took up the cause. The Lincoln Farm Association was organized to raise money for buying both the farm and the cabin and to erect a memorial to Lincoln. By 1905 the organization had obtained sufficient contributions, mostly in small amounts, to purchase the farm and cabin. The cornerstone of the memorial was laid by former President Theodore Roosevelt on February 12, 1909, the centenary of Lincoln's birth, and the completed structure, containing the log cabin, was dedicated by former President Taft on November 9, 1911.

A company, including former President Woodrow Wilson, gathered here on September 14, 1916, when the property, together with an endowment fund of $50,000, was received by the Secretary of War, Newton D. Baker, on the part of the United States, as a gift to the Nation. In 1933 the property was transferred to the control of the Department of the Interior.

South of Knob Creek Farm for about 15 miles, the land is roughly level or mildly rolling, with occasional stands of timber by the roadside and fields of corn or tobacco between large pastures. Sage grass makes a green or orange ripple (depending on the season) across the open fields and hillsides. A few small frame shacks are passed, and some old log cabins. The road then winds through and around some high hills well covered with woods, and crosses, at 86.2 m., the Green River whose deep emerald waters are bordered by low corn bottoms and large sycamores.

The Green River country, of the subsistence farming type, is often poor or depleted, and a Kentuckian who is trying to describe an angular woman will say, "She's as bony as the hips of a Green River cow." Natives add to their income through the sale of handicraft articles. Along US 31E in the vicinity of Green River are roadside displays of baskets, colored pottery, quilts, bedspreads, and embroidered cushions. The quilts and bedspreads have designs in bright colors.

South of the Green River, US 31E winds through hills overlooking small valleys, meets several small trading centers where blue-shirted, overalled school boys play along the highway, and then enters open rolling country. This is a cave region and sinkholes—called "goose nests" by the natives—small caves, and sinking streams are prevalent.

At 98.3 m. is the southern junction with US 68 (see Tour 15).

ADAIRLAND (R), 104.7 m., is a large stock farm whose rolling pastures spread back from the highway for a considerable distance, latticed at regular intervals by the white fences enclosing a dozen or more grass fields. A long, white-fenced lane leads straight to a two-story frame house, also painted gleaming white, with a high portico. Large white barns stand nearby. The red roofs of the house and the barns contrast pleasantly with the green of the pastures and the white of the buildings and paddocks; landscape and architecture combine to form a scene of geometrical orderliness and beauty. Adairland is more suggestive of the Lexington horse farm area than any other farm along this route.

GLASGOW, 112.1 m. (780 alt., 5,042 pop.), a lively, bustling town, is the business center of a petroleum-producing field. It was named for Glasgow, Virginia, in 1799. This area was settled by Virginians who, after the Bluegrass section of Kentucky had been filled, moved farther west into the Barrens, then an almost treeless plateau. Long before the advent of the white man, the forests of this region had been burned; the abundance of grass on this prairie provided an excellent grazing ground for big game. The trees of the area are younger and therefore smaller than those of the eastern section of the State. Maj. John Gorin, a soldier of the Revolutionary War, was the first to settle here on a land grant awarded for Revolutionary services. A good spring was the deciding factor in his selection of a site for his homestead. Soon other settlers, most of them veterans of the Revolutionary War, came to take up land grants. After the formation of the county Major Gorin gave a 50-acre tract, including the spring, as a town site and the settlement grew up about the courthouse square. Early in 1800 the Kentucky Legislature authorized a State road between Lexington and Nashville, Tennessee, passing through Glasgow. The first stage traversed this road in 1836.

Among early settlers from Virginia was Alexander E. Spottswood, a general in the Revolutionary Army and the first lawyer to live here. He was the grandson of a Colonial Governor of Virginia who married Elizabeth Lewis, niece of Martha Washington. In addition to the land grant that General Spottswood received for his war services, he purchased land in Glasgow, where he built (L) the SPOTTSWOOD HOUSE, N. Race St., two blocks from the courthouse. It was said to have been the town's first brick building; it is Georgian Colonial in style, has 28-inch walls, and contains eight rooms and a basement that was used as slave quarters. During the War of 1812 much saltpeter was produced in Barren County. In 1813 a powder mill was erected on Coon Creek and the manufactured product was transported by wagon through Lexington to Philadelphia. An old battery, erected during the War between the States, is on the western edge of the town.

Glasgow is at the junction with State 90 *(see Tour 20)* and State 80 *(see Tour 18)*.

South of Glasgow, US 31E continues through a countryside that is rolling to hilly. Many excellent farms skirt the highway. In this section much land is devoted to the culture of berries and other fruit for northern markets. Cotton has been grown successfully.

After crossing Peters Creek, 124.7 *m.*, with its old frame mill and dam (L), the highway passes a file of sycamores (R) and then crosses Barren River, 126.7 *m.*, flush with a low corn bottom. As Scottsville is approached, gray, dilapidated two- or three-room board shacks of poor farmers are seen by the roadside.

SCOTTSVILLE, 137.3 *m.* (750 alt., 1,867 pop.), seat of Allen County, looks like many other county seat towns in southern Kentucky. It is spread over a central hill surrounded by other hills. The old red brick courthouse stands in the center of a round public square encircled by the highway; on its outside bulletin board are pasted numerous legal notices. Dozens of overalled farmers or workingmen mill about the place, exchanging small talk or laying down their opinions. Scottsville was named for Gen. Charles Scott, fourth Governor of Kentucky; the county's name was selected as a tribute to Col. John Allen, who fell in the Battle of the River Raisin. Scottsville was raided by guerrillas in December 1863.

Opie Read, lecturer and writer, was once editor-owner of the Scotts-ville *Argus* (*see Literature*).

US 31E crosses the Tennessee Line, 147.8 *m.*, 51 miles north of Nashville, Tennessee (*see Tenn. Tour 7*).

Tour 7

(New Albany, Ind.)—Louisville—Elizabethtown—Munfordville—Horse Cave—Bowling Green—Franklin—(Nashville, Tenn.); US 31W, the Dixie Highway.
Indiana Line to Tennessee Line, 150.9 *m.*

Hard-surfaced roadbed.
Louisville & Nashville R.R. parallels route throughout.
Accommodations chiefly in cities.

Taking a course through west central Kentucky, US 31W runs near the river for a time, approaches it, and then goes up the Salt River Valley. It enters the Knobs region where the countryside lumps up into small round hills streaked with ravines. Near the south-central part of the State the route makes a great elbow curve through the cavernous limestone region containing Mammoth Cave and many other subterranean wonders, then, below Bowling Green, runs through the Pennyrile. Few cities or towns line this highway. Corn, tobacco, and livestock production is the chief interest of the countryside.

The route follows the general course of the old Louisville-Nashville stagecoach road. Prior to the completion (1859) of the Louisville & Nashville R.R., travel over this road was greater than over any other road in Kentucky. Stephen McMurtry, a Vine Grove farmer who lived within sight of the pike, often had as many as 25 freight wagons, stagecoaches, and other vehicles rolling by in view at the same time. In 1825 Bayard Taylor made a journey over this road to Mammoth Cave, admired the scenery at the mouth of the Salt River, and picked up an explanation of the phrase, "going up Salt River." The story he got was that in earlier days, when the saltmakers up Salt River were the terror of the countryside, the steamboat captains subdued unruly members of their crew by threatening to send them up Salt River among the rowdy saltmakers. According to other sources, the phrase originated in 1832 when Henry Clay, who had an engagement to speak in Louisville during his campaign against Andrew Jackson, was per-suaded by a Jackson man to take a packet trip up Salt River. While the boatman was delaying the excursion so that Clay could not arrive in Louisville until the day after the rally, Jackson apologists for Clay's absence were explaining to the crowd at Louisville that he had gone up Salt River and had been unavoidably detained. After Clay had been beaten by Jackson in the election, defeated candidates were said to have gone "up Salt River."

US 31W crosses the Indiana Line, 0 *m.*, eight miles south of Sellersburg, Indiana *(see Ind. Tour 13)*, by way of a bridge *(toll 25¢)* over the Ohio River.

LOUISVILLE, 2 *m.* (525 alt., 307,745 pop.) *(see Louisville)*.

Points of Interest: Speed Museum, Memorial Auditorium, Presbyterian Theological Seminary, Churchill Downs, and others.

Louisville is at the junction with US 60 *(see Tour 16)*, US 31E *(see Tour 6)*, and US 42 *(see Tour 12)*.

Between Louisville and TIP TOP, 30.6 *m.* (793 alt., 50 pop.), US 31W and US 60 are united *(see Tour 16)*. US 31W branches southwest from the junction at Tip Top.

FORT KNOX, 34 *m.* (760 alt., 500 pop.), is a 33,000-acre military reservation on both sides of US 31W. The tract, including the town of Stithton, was purchased by the U.S. Government in 1917 for a World War training camp and named for Henry Knox, an artillery commander during the Revolutionary War. In 1932 the War Department designated the camp a permanent military post and changed the name to Fort Knox. In 1933 the 1st U.S. Cavalry, mechanized, was stationed at the post, and two years later work on the first permanent structures was completed. Subsequently the 13th Cavalry, mechanized, has been stationed here, the two regiments forming the 7th Cavalry Brigade, mechanized.

In 1936 the Treasury Department built the GOLD BULLION DEPOSITORY (R) in which to store about nine million pounds of the Federal gold reserve. The treasure house, 100 feet square, is of bombproof construction; its walls and roof are faced with huge granite blocks. Atop each corner of the building are machine-gun turrets where guards keep vigil against intruders who might attempt the risk of scaling the high iron fence. Interlaced steel coils with openings too small to admit a man's hand are set in the concrete of the walls as an added protection. Constant inspection of the interior of the two-story vault, which is 60 feet long and 40 feet wide, is maintained by means of an open space under the floor and one over the ceiling; mirrors and brilliant lights make every corner visible. Supersensitive microphones in the vault are connected with the central guardroom. In addition to the vault, the building contains offices and dormitories.

Bird-dog field trials are held in the vicinity of Fort Knox semiannually on varying dates in March and November. The trials last three days, usually at a week end; the spring meets are generally more popular than those held in the fall.

South of Fort Knox, US 31W lopes off among tall, ragged cliffs and gorges. It winds through countryside splotched with stands of cedar, pin oak, and scrub pine. Daisies line the roadside, and gentian and trumpet vine break the pattern of the near-by fields. This is good country for hunting rabbit, squirrel, and quail.

At 41 *m.* is the junction with an unimproved road.

Left on this road to MILL CREEK CEMETERY, 7 *m.*, in which are the LINCOLN FAMILY GRAVES; here lies the dust of Bersheba Lincoln, Abraham's paternal grandmother, and of Mary Lincoln Crume and Nancy Lincoln Brumfield, his aunts.

At 52 *m.* is the junction with an unmarked road.

Left on this road to a PREHISTORIC MOUND, 10 *m.*, which has never been excavated. Near by in a line of cliffs along Rough Creek are two ROCK SHELTERS (R) on the Hugh Yates farm. The dirt-and-pebble floors of these shelters have yielded 15 human skeletons and hundreds of artifacts—arrowheads, tomahawks, beads, pottery, and utensils. Most of these objects are in the Museum of Archeology of the University of Kentucky *(see Lexington).*

ELIZABETHTOWN, 52.5 *m.* (708 alt., 2,590 pop.), is a county seat laid out in wheel pattern. The hub is a red brick courthouse that looks like a modern rural school building. Around it runs a narrow, traffic-packed street broken at four places by the highways that enter the town amidst the two-story shops that surround the circle. Beyond this central business section the radiating streets pass neat, well-spaced dwellings with spreading old trees on the roomy lawns.

Elizabethtown is a busy trading center for a rather large rural area in which livestock, tobacco, and grain are produced. On county court days, if the Hardin County farmer has caught up with his chores, he generally comes to town to listen in during the court sessions. On Saturdays he puts the family into the old car, or the jolt wagon, along with farm products he wants to trade, and they all come to town and spend the day selling their wares, buying groceries and dry goods, and wandering around with their neighbors.

In the fall of 1780 Capt. Thomas Helm, Col. Andrew Hynes, and Samuel Haycraft arrived from Virginia and built three stockades a mile apart at the points of a triangle. In 1793 Colonel Hynes had a town plat made of his land, and named it in honor of his wife.

A familiar figure on the streets of Elizabethtown in its early days was "Old General Braddock," a Negro belonging to the Vanmeter family. Soon after their arrival, a band of Indians began to snipe at the settlement. The slave took down a rifle and killed nine of them. His good aim discouraged the other Indians, who fled. The Vanmeters were so grateful that they gave him his freedom.

During the War between the States several skirmishes took place here and on December 26, 1862, the town was shelled by the Confederate cavalry leader, Gen. John Hunt Morgan. The town was strongly garrisoned with a regiment of Illinois troops, and its defenses, brick warehouses with loopholes, seemed adequate; but Morgan took Elizabethtown without much trouble.

According to local tradition, Thomas Lincoln lived here as early as

1796. However that may be, county records show that in 1804–05 he served on juries here, guarded prisoners, and was assessed for a horse. He found time to court Sarah, daughter of Christopher Bush, but she preferred Daniel Johnston to Thomas Lincoln. So in 1806 he married Nancy Hanks *(see Tour 15 and Harrodsburg)*, and they set up housekeeping in a log cabin and here their first child, Sarah, was born. In 1808 Lincoln bought Sinking Spring Farm *(see Tour 6)* and moved his family there. Following the death of Nancy Hanks in 1818, Lincoln came back to Elizabethtown to see whether his former love, Sarah, now a widow, would reconsider her refusal of him. The widow Johnston accepted the widower Lincoln, and, according to records in the Hardin County Courthouse, they were married on December 2, 1819. Sarah Lincoln was a kind and devoted stepmother to Thomas Lincoln's children, and Abraham cared for her lovingly after his father's death.

There is a story that in 1813, when Thomas Lincoln was living on his Knob Creek farm, 20 miles away, a man destined to precede his son Abe in the Presidency stayed awhile in Elizabethtown. James Buchanan, Sr., had a lawsuit pending in the local courthouse, and he sent for his son, James, Jr., a vigorous young lawyer practicing in Pennsylvania, to come West and assist him. James, Jr., represented his father through several months of litigation. It was the younger Buchanan who became fifteenth President of the United States.

As early as 1806 Elizabethtown, with 22 lawyers, had a reputation as a legal center. Of the 22, Felix Grundy later became a United States Senator from Tennessee (1829–38); Thomas Buck Reed, United States Senator from Mississippi; John Rowan, United States Senator from Kentucky (1824–30); Ninian Edwards, Territorial Governor of Illinois (1809–18); and W. P. Duvall, Territorial Governor of Florida (1822–34).

Duff Green, later of Andrew Jackson's Kitchen Cabinet, arrived here from Fairfax County, Virginia, and became the merchant-partner of Maj. Ben Helm, son of Capt. Thomas Helm. As a child, Abraham Lincoln often helped his stepmother do her shopping in the Green-Helm store. They were served by John B. Helm, a nephew of Ben Helm who was to become a Hannibal, Missouri, judge. When Lincoln visited Hannibal in 1860 he searched out Judge Helm. After remarking about the changes 40 years had made, Lincoln introduced Judge Helm to his companions simply as "the first man I ever knew who wore store clothes all the week . . . who fed me on maple sugar, when as a small boy I sat upon a nail keg in his uncle's store."

Another member of the local Helm family, John L. Helm, was Governor of Kentucky (1850–51, re-elected in 1867). Gen. Ben Hardin Helm commanded the 1st Kentucky Cavalry, dubbed the "Orphan Brigade" of the Confederate Army because so many of its officers were killed in action. General Helm became Abraham Lincoln's brother-in-law by marrying Mary Todd's sister, Emily. At the outbreak of the

War between the States, Lincoln offered to appoint General Helm Paymaster of the U.S. Army, but Helm declined, and became instead a brigadier-general in the Confederate Army. He was killed at the Battle of Chickamauga, September 20, 1863, while leading an infantry brigade in Gen. J. C. Breckinridge's division.

Elizabethtown's last contribution to the list of successful sons was John Young Brown, Kentucky Governor from 1891 to 1895.

The city has two outstanding private collections of Indian artifacts found in Kentucky; one is owned by Bell Smoot, on Public Square, and the other by Ben Ailes, of Poplar Street. These collectors also have about 3,000 old firearms.

In the HARDIN COUNTY COURTHOUSE is a room *(adm. free)* housing Lincolniana. These records escaped the fire of 1932 which partly destroyed the old courthouse. After the structure was rebuilt in 1936, they were collated and placed in the new building by WPA workers.

In the SMITH HOTEL, formerly the old Eagle House, erected early in the nineteenth century, Jenny Lind appeared on April 5, 1851. The crowd that gathered to hear her sing was so large that gracious Jenny went to Aunt Beck Hill's Inn, now the Brown-Pusey Community House, where she sang to the townspeople from the stone steps.

The BROWN-PUSEY COMMUNITY HOUSE *(open)*, cor. N. Main and Poplar Sts., was presented to the city by Drs. W. A. Pusey and Brown Pusey of Chicago. It was a stagecoach inn and called the Hill House; Aunt Beck Hill, great-aunt of the community house donors, was the proprietor. The simple two-story brick building, erected in 1818, has a low-pitched gable roof and inside end-chimneys. The lower two-story ell in the rear borders the side street. The front of the building has long 18-light windows in the first story with segmental arch headings, a deeply recessed paneled entrance door with square transom and simple frame, and a small entrance stoop with twin transverse flight of steps and a simple wrought iron railing. The interior of the house has been little changed and many of the furnishings have been restored. The garden behind the house is planted in flowers particularly popular in pioneer days.

Gen. George Custer lived next door to the community house (1871–73) while writing *My Life on the Plains*. His stay was comparatively quiet but in memory he was having a stirring time. As his biographer remarked, "All rifles were trusty to Custer, all comrades gallant, and a horse was always a noble steed."

Elizabethtown is at the junction with US 62 *(see Tour 14)*.

South of Elizabethtown the road winds between the knobs; some of these lumpy outcroppings are denuded of everything except grass, others have small stands of timber near their crowns. In summertime the light green of tall cornstalks blends with the darker green of the tiny tobacco patches and rough fields; but with fall's coming, dun-colored wigwams of shocks stretch across the fields of stubble, the truncated tobacco plants make a dark brown stain upon the clay, and large plots of broom sage ripple over the fields and hillsides.

South of the Nolin River 62.5 *m.*, is a small area of livestock farming with substantial houses and multiple fodder ricks bunched in the fields that are separated from the highway by dense clusters of honeysuckle.

The thick, dark shadow of a sizable evergreen woods falls across US 31W as it winds up and around hills to UPTON, 69.8 *m.* (402 pop.), a trading center that looks to the Louisville & Nashville R.R. for its life. Some quarrying is carried on in the vicinity.

Just south of Upton a few ramshackle frame houses appear—one-story affairs with one or two rooms, feebly lit through small-paned windows. They suggest a farm's outbuildings rather than dwelling places. The small plots surrounding these places are littered with sundry articles, and the hand plow is sometimes seen in use. Here live poor white families who eke out a borderline existence. They are not representative of the region, and their number is small.

The highway dips up and down as it penetrates a cheerless country with jumbled contours, veined by steady erosion. Cornfields and pasture lands are plotted irregularly over the terrain; here and there a bared stretch of dark red soil stands on a drab hillside. The railroad tracks along the road (R) seem like an intruder in this nearly primitive landscape where the dwellings are log cabins and big, black mules take the place of horses.

At 73 *m.* is the junction with Ridge Rd., unimproved.

Right on this road to WILLIAM CAVE FARM (L), 13 *m.*, on which are many rocks pitted with holes, several feet deep, made when the Indians used them as mortars in grinding corn. In the vicinity are beds of flint fragments splintered off during the making of weapons and implements.

BONNIEVILLE, 77 *m.* (846 alt., 27 pop.), consists of a few old frame houses, on whose porches are displayed the split white oak, hickory and willow baskets often found on sale in the South.

South of Bonnieville the road occasionally moves close to the hills, where rocks jut forward like crude gargoyles. In other places struggling corn patches waver over the rolling land; a tangled thicket spreads along a section of the route; and the roadside embankments, stripped of grass, are red clay. The road passes log cabins and frame shacks, peopled by families who till their poor acres for all they will yield. They also make excellent baskets and chairs from split white oak; for several miles south of Bonnieville, all kinds of basketry are displayed by the road or on the little porches of the houses. Near Munfordville, Negroes are seen strolling up or down the road. They live in the raffish cabins and box-like houses near the highway.

At 82 *m.* is the junction with an unimproved road.

Left on this road to GLEN LILY *(visitors welcome)* 9 *m.*, the birthplace of Simon Bolivar Buckner (1823–1914), standing solitary in the woods alongside Green River. The crude two-story rectangular house is of hewn logs, with a tin roof and a narrow gallery extending along three sides. The front façade is broken at the center by a clapboarded section—probably a closed-in breezeway, or dog-trot. It stands on what was formerly a farm of 1,000 acres. Near by on the riverbank are the moss-covered ruins of the old IRON FOUNDRY built by General Buckner's father in 1823. For two years after his graduation from West Point, in 1844, Simon Buckner served as an instructor at the institution. He resigned to take part in the Mexican War; when the War between the States broke out, he was made commander of the Kentucky Militia and soon espoused the Confederate cause, rising to the rank of lieutenant general. After the Battle of Fort Donelson he surrendered to General Grant, who had been his friend for many years before the war. During Grant's last illness General Buckner visited him, and he was a pallbearer at Grant's funeral. Buckner was a Governor of Kentucky (1887–91) and a candidate for the Vice-Presidency in 1896.

MUNFORDVILLE, 83.8 *m.* (571 alt., 649 pop.), named for Richard I. Munford, member of the House of Representatives in 1820, 1822, and 1827, is high on the northern bank of Green River. It is the seat of Hart County, named for Capt. Nathaniel G. T. Hart, a Revolutionary officer. The courthouse, of the familiar red brick schoolhouse type, is on one of the knolls that crop up on the rough ground that is the town site.

The major event in the history of the town was the so-called Battle of Munfordville. The Union fort here and 4,000 men under Colonel Wilder, together with supplies, artillery, and ammunition, were captured by Confederate General Bragg on September 17, 1863, three days after an abortive attempt to take the town. Bragg succeeded in reaching Munfordville in advance of Union General Buell, who was racing towards Louisville to protect it from the advancing Confederates. Having captured Munfordville, Bragg was in a position either to fight the oncoming Union forces or to march into Louisville ahead of them. He did neither; instead he marched away to the east, leaving Buell free passage to Louisville. The withdrawal from Munfordville, and the indecision shown by Bragg from that time until his final retreat into Tennessee, were strongly condemned by the Southern press and public.

OLD FORTIFICATIONS (R) are visible from the highway. The MUNFORD INN, Main St., is a two-story frame structure erected in 1806 along an old buffalo trace that had become a highway.

1. Right from Munfordville on State 88, a partly improved road, to CUB RUN, 14 *m.* (760 alt., 89 pop.). Left from Cub Run 1 *m.* on an unimproved road to the CASTLE, a curiously shaped rock shelter. The presence of a hominy hole, kitchen midden, arrowheads, flint chips, and flint and bone tools attest Indian occupancies. Practically all of these relics are in the Museum of Archeology of the University of Kentucky.

Right from State 88 at the Castle, 4 *m.*, on a road that leads to the GEORGE WADDLE FARM, near which is a row of 15 ROCK SHELTERS, high above the valley of Little Dog Creek. The dirt floors have yielded flint chips, arrowheads, scrapers, and human bones.

In a line of cliffs on the W. A. Bracher farm, across the road, similar relics were uncovered. The arrowheads from this site have serrated edges and unusually broad shoulders. A sandstone hominy hole rock weighing two tons was moved from here to the University of Kentucky.

2. Left from Munfordville on State 88 to CUB RUN CAVE, 2 *m.*, in which lay three human skeletons. One was that of a child about 10 years old.

The highway runs on a long trestle, 84.1 *m.*, high above a broad corn bottom before crossing Green River. Floored with rough, loose planks that rattle loudly every foot of the way, and weakly guarded along the sides by low wire fencing, this rickety structure calls for slow driving.

At **85.9** *m.* is the junction with State 335, an improved road.

Left on this road is MAMMOTH ONYX CAVE *(adm. $2)*, **3** *m.*, containing some of the most beautiful formations in the cave area. The entrance is practically on a level with the surrounding terrain, and the floor slopes almost imperceptibly. Among the many huge high-ceiled chambers is Paradise Garden, in which are onyx trees, flowers, human figures, and porticos. A giant Tree of Life, in onyx of many hues, translucent and fine-grained, covers one whole wall of another chamber.

At **4** *m.* in the corner of a lonely pasture is a lone, unmarked GRAVE OF AN UN-KNOWN CONFEDERATE, a 16-year-old Mississippi boy who served under General Bragg. While marching to Munfordville to reinforce the main body of Bragg's troops, a detachment of Confederates stopped for a drink of water at a cool spring near by. Worn out by the pressed march, a young soldier scarcely of shaving age sat down to await his turn at the water. By accident he kicked the trigger of his gun, shooting himself.

A wide, saw-toothed sweep of hills rims the horizon at **88.8** *m.* Trees scallop their crests above small cultivated fields.

HORSE CAVE, **91.4** *m.* (603 alt., 1,259 pop.), most of which is scattered away from the road and from a curious L-shaped business section, is said to have been so named because Cherokee used a near-by cave as a corral for stolen horses. Another story is that the cave gained its name when a horse fell into it. A part of the town is built over HIDDEN RIVER CAVE *(adm. $2)*, which has a continuously flowing underground river with pearly white "eyeless" fish, and the largest known domes in the area. Its entrance is more than 250 feet wide and 450 feet long. Hidden River Cave has never been extensively explored.

Between Horse Cave and Bowling Green US 31W and US 68 *(see Tour 15)* unite.

A dozen or more WIGWAMS (R), **94.7** *m.*, arranged in an oval, offer a novel variation from the usual tourist cabins.

CAVE CITY, **95.5** *m.* (613 alt., 775 pop.), is at the junction with State 70, leading to Mammoth Cave *(see Tour 7A)*.

Between Cave City and Bowling Green, US 31W bears west-south-west with the hills (R), a third of a mile away, a series of humps. As the route progresses southward, the hills (R) are darkly green with thick masses of evergreens, striped in summer by the lighter green of oak trees—brownish in the winter. The land gradually levels out for a long stretch with hills furrowing the skyline (R).

Scores of signs, arrows, and billboards southwest of Cave City in-sist that it is only so many miles to this or that cave. This is cave country, and dozens of cave-owners, in spite of the near-by Mammoth Cave, do a good business. Roadside stands sell large and small rock formations from the caves.

Though the land may seem poor to out-of-Staters, farming is the occupation of most of the people in this region. Corn, tobacco, and livestock are the principal products. There is a cornfield every few hundred yards, on a low, level stretch when possible, but otherwise on rolling swells. Every farm has its tobacco patch of one to six or eight acres. While maturing in summer, the oblong leaves of the plant make a green spread across the fields; after harvest, the stalks, left in the ground, remain upright, richly brown through the winter. Large pastures hold grazing cattle, a few horses, mules, and sometimes sheep in large numbers. Each farmer usually raises a few hogs for home consumption. Most farms have a water pond near the road, 15 to 50 or more feet in diameter, where the animals drink, and several low hay stacks, with an exposed center pole, where they can chew when the pasturage is poor. A farmer in this region may own 400 or 500 acres of land, but timber stands and unproductive sections prevent the cultivation of a good part of it. Barns, seldom painted, take on a gray, weather-worn appearance, that deepens with the years. Most of them are substantial enough, but here and there a barn along the way is a good subject for a woodcut romanticizing decay, and the narrow dirt lanes that sometimes spiral their way across a hilly farm make good backgrounds. Farming, however, is relatively prosperous, and the houses are the typical two-story frame structures.

GLASGOW JUNCTION, 101.8 *m.* (623 alt., 374 pop.), another town whose chief concern is the tourist and his interest in caves, was first called Three Forks, then Bell's Tavern. The second name came from an inn built in the 1820's and operated by Col. William Bell of Virginia.

Within sight of the highway, near the railroad station, stand the RUINS OF BELL'S TAVERN (L). The first structure, a rambling wooden affair, built in the 1820's and added to from time to time as patronage grew, was noted for the hospitality dispensed by its owner, Col. William Bell, a Revolutionary officer from Virginia. The service was lavish and the fare testified to the epicurean taste of the owner. Colonel Bell himself prepared his favorite appetizer, peach brandy and honey, a beverage of exhilarating potency, and he was generous in dispensing it. Coffee was served from a silver coffeepot that was carried from table to table by Shad, the "blackest little Negro with the whitest teeth anyone had ever seen." Shad is buried under an apple tree in the old orchard.

Bell's Tavern was a favorite meeting place for the leading politicians of the day. Henry Clay, the Marshalls, the Humphreys, Judge Rowan, and Aaron Harding were among the frequent guests. Nathaniel Silsbee, Senator from Massachusetts (1826–35), wrote to a friend who contemplated the journey to Nashville:

"Stop for a day or two at the famous Bell's Tavern. Should you arrive late at night and find the yard filled in with rough carts and wagons, with perhaps uncouth men or maybe Indians stretched upon

VIII. ALONG THE HIGHWAY II

TROUBLESOME CREEK DAM

IN THE LICKING RIVER VALLEY

SHEEP GRAZING

MOUNTAIN ROAD

THE PASTURE

CUTTING BURLEY TOBACCO

TOBACCO CURING

GRINDING SORGHUM CANE

BOILING SORGHUM

MOUNTAIN CABIN

HOME IN CUMBERLAND MOUNTAINS

HELL-FER-SARTAIN CREEK

HOME

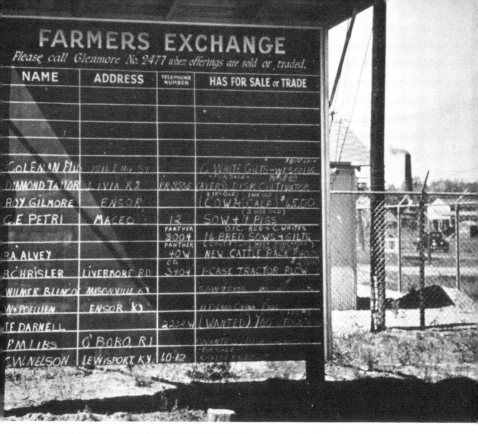

BULLETIN BOARD OF FARMERS EXCHANGE, OWENSBORO

porch and hall floors, keep up good heart; there will be a comfortable bed for you, and at breakfast—such a breakfast as you have seldom sat to—you will have for company men, learned men, not unlikely a prince or a potentate, a world famous actor or a prima donna; it may be all of these. But mark you, should none of these fall to your share you will find in your host a cultivated, charming gentleman who can keep up his end of the conversation with even you. There is no other hostelry of its like upon the length of the continent."

After the death of Colonel Bell, his son's widow, Mrs. Robert Slaughter Bell, maintained the tavern's reputation until it was destroyed by fire about 1858. Mrs. Bell planned to build a magnificent stone structure, whose proportions and appointments would be worthy of the tavern's reputation, and she began construction though friends warned her of the gathering war clouds. The building, which was never completed, was to be 105 feet in length and about 60 feet wide. The massive walls of dressed stone had reached a height of 15 feet or so before the work was stopped. The vine-covered walls, arched windows, and moss-grown steps attest the magnificence of Mrs. Bell's plans.

Right from Glasgow Junction on a graveled road to DIAMOND CAVERNS *(adm. $1 to $2 including guide service)*, 2 *m.*, one of the smaller caves of the area but one of the most beautiful. It is illuminated with floodlights and the trip through it requires from one to two hours.

At 107.3 *m.* is the junction with State 65.

Right on this road, across which scamper many animals from the near-by Mammoth Cave National Park Game Refuge, is BROWNSVILLE, 11 *m.* (537 alt., 359 pop.), seat of Edmonson County, on the left bank of Green River in an area of mediocre farm lands where nature has lived untouched and its wild-life flourishes. Brownsville's old homes stand beneath magnificent trees, and in almost every yard are beds of hollyhocks, larkspur, and asters. The town still lives along the grooves of the 1850's. Everybody hereabouts is a good story teller. Barn-raisings, quilting parties, bran-hullings, apple peelings, logrollings, and singing parties are a major part of its social life. Square dances are as common as the tales of "hants" in Edmonson County, which is rich in folklore. Brownsville is so quiet that the tinkle of the cow bells going to pasture in the morning and coming back to the barn in the evening is as significant to its residents as reveille and taps are to soldiers.

In Brownsville is the CARMICHAEL COLLECTION OF PREHISTORIC RELICS *(free; by appointment)*. Practically all of the specimens were found within the county.

At Brownsville is the junction with Indian Hill Road.

Right on this road to INDIAN HILL (628 alt.), 1 *m.*, below which slide the waters of Green River, Indian Creek, and Nolin River. Indian Hill continues to yield flint artifacts.

At 111.4 *m.* is the junction with State 101.

Left on this road to SMITH'S GROVE, 4 *m.* (607 alt., 718 pop.), where a Government emergency landing field is maintained. In the Smith's Grove Cemetery is the GRAVE OF SUSAN MADISON, sister of Patrick Henry and wife of Thomas Madison, a brother of George Madison former Governor of Kentucky.

At 118.7 *m.* is the junction with State 80 *(see Tour 18)*.

BOWLING GREEN, 125.4 *m.* (469 alt., 12,348 pop.), seat of Warren County, rides the uplands along the Barren River. The city rises, in a series of narrow streets, up to a central square with a thinly planted park as its core; it rises farther to the top of a hill on which, occupying a fort site, is the Western State Teachers' College. On another hill is a reservoir. From these elevations it is seen that the city is speckled with quite large and ornate houses among the trees and shrubs that tone down the industrial color of Bowling Green.

The city has taken full advantage of surrounding natural resources. Asphalt rock from along Barren River is brought here by barge, crushed, and reshipped to various points for road building. Near-by oil pools, in the decade after the World War, gave Bowling Green its one boom era; although these pools still produce, the output has dropped off appreciably. Tobacco, both dark and burley, is a cash crop that contributes much to the prosperity of the city; the tobacco warehouses are the most interesting places in town during the auction sales in the late fall and early winter. Strawberries are prominent among the products produced for the market; Bowling Green was formerly the foremost strawberry market in the State, and still attracts numbers of pickers during berry season. Men, women, and children arrive on freight trains, in mule-drawn buggies, in model-T Fords, in jolt wagons, and afoot, to tent in the strawberry fields for a fortnight or so, and then move northward to continue the work in other berry-growing areas.

In 1780 Robert and George Moore, with some associates from Virginia, established a settlement here in the Barrens, a treeless plain. The town site was chosen because of its proximity to an excellent spring, and the navigability of the Barren River up to this point.

The Moore brothers provided land for the first log courthouse. Until its erection in 1797, the county court had held its sessions in the home of Robert Moore. The visiting lawyers and court officials long used the yard about Moore's house as a green for playing bowls, as did many people in the town. From this custom Bowling Green derived its name. The growth of the town was gradual and constant until the War between the States. Immediately after the outbreak of the war, the town became a center of attention because of its importance as a railroad center and river shipping point, and because of its position on the chief western wagon road between the North and the South. Further hardship was faced by the city because of the divided sympathy of its people—a large part of whom favored the Union.

In November 1861 Gen. Simon Bolivar Buckner, in command of a body of Kentuckians from Camp Boone in Tennessee, occupied the town. He was followed by a division of the Confederate Army led by Gen. Albert Sidney Johnston, the Confederate commander in the West, who immediately commenced to fortify the place as a permanent headquarters from which to operate in Kentucky. These plans were shattered by the reduction of forts Henry and Donelson in 1862. The

Confederates evacuated the city and Federal soldiers moved in and completed the fortifications.

The WESTERN KENTUCKY STATE TEACHERS' COLLEGE, 5th St., is on the eminence occupied by the fort. Earthworks and some of the equipment are preserved on the campus. In 1813 the General Assembly established Warren Seminary in Bowling Green. Six years later legislative approval was given for the establishment here of the Southern Normal School, a private institution. A few years later Potter College for young ladies was opened. These schools were highly successful until the War between the States; afterwards Warren Seminary became Warren College, and was later renamed Ogden College. In 1928 Ogden College leased its property to the Western Kentucky State Teachers' College—which had developed from the Southern Normal School—and ceased to function.

On the campus of the college, which covers 60 acres, are cottage dormitories, a model rural school, and athletic fields. Honeysuckle Lane, a broad flagstone walk, winds through what was the fort. All buildings of major importance are on College Heights from which there is an excellent view of the beautiful Barren River Valley with hills behind it to the north and west. The Administration Building is constructed of red face brick with limestone trim. The Cedar House Club, a broad one-story structure of cedar logs, is the center of social life on the campus.

The Kentucky Building, faced with brick and trimmed with limestone, is of Georgian Colonial design. In it is the KENTUCKY LIBRARY OF FOLKLORE *(open)* and a museum containing Indian and early Kentucky relics and collections of old furniture, papers, documents, and oddities of natural science.

An Italian Garden, on the old Ogden Campus, contains a group of Florentine statuary and a heroic statue of *Apollo*. Near by is the Experimental Farm of 149 acres, used for demonstration.

BOWLING GREEN BUSINESS UNIVERSITY, College St., a privately owned institution, is an accredited senior college that offers a four-year course in business, administration, finance, and commerce. Its gray brick building contains an auditorium, classrooms, and offices. The library, a frame structure immediately back of the main building, contains about 16,000 volumes.

Bowling Green is the home of Mrs. Eliza Calvert Hall Obenchain (1856–   ), author of *Aunt Jane of Kentucky,* and *Sally Ann's Experience.*

Bowling Green is at the junction with US 68 *(see Tour 15).*

Right from Bowling Green on State 67 to the junction with a dirt road, 3 *m.;* R. on this road to the C. A. SMITH FARM, 4 *m.,* where large beds of flint fragments and numerous artifacts have been found. The quantities of kitchen midden near by on the same farm indicate that this was long an Indian village site.

At 128.4 *m.* is (L) LOST RIVER CAVE *(adm. 10¢),* a large rock chamber whose ceiling forms a natural bridge on which the highway runs. The cave was so named because of the short, deep stream that starts 350 feet above the mouth of the chamber, tumbles in a waterfall at its entrance, then disappears entirely. A gristmill was operated here prior to the organization of Warren County in 1796. On the levels now used as dance floors Indian skeletons and relics have been found, indicating that this place was once an Indian burial ground. Soldiers camped here during the War between the States, and John Morgan hid in the cave while Federals were looking for him when he burned the depot at Shakertown. The notorious James boys are said to have made their hideout here in 1868 after they had robbed the Russellville bank. The cave has been developed as a night club and picnicking spot, with tourist cabins available near the entrance. Between Lost River Cave and Franklin, the land levels out into broad fields used for pasturage and the production of corn, tobacco, strawberries, and livestock. Ponds are by the roadside, and broom sage waves greenly across the fields until frost turns it russet. All through this region, fine Georgian Colonial homes with gracious porticos alternate with ordinary frame farmhouses and gray, weathered shacks; jolt wagons drawn by plodding mules share the road with automobiles.

FRANKLIN, 145.8 *m.* (717 alt., 3,058 pop.), tightly hugs a central courthouse square rimmed with low brick buildings, each of which has a hitching post. It was founded in 1820, named for Benjamin Franklin, and is the seat of Simpson County, which was named in honor of Capt. John Simpson, whose company of riflemen joined the first Kentucky troops that marched to reinforce General Hull at Detroit during the War of 1812. Captain Simpson was killed in the Battle of the River Raisin.

The ONE-SUCKER TOBACCO MARKET here is unusually large. The growing plant is trimmed of all except a single sucker on the main stem, thus producing a superior quality of tobacco. A municipally owned MINERAL WELL in the public square has water of a high sulphur content.

The people in this remote hilly region have songs, superstitions, and customs that belong to eighteenth-century England *(see Tours 1, 18, and 19)*. Children are admonished never to pluck mistletoe from an oak. Though it is believed to attach itself naturally to any other tree, it is supposed to be held in place on an oak by the druids, and to break their hold would bring calamity upon the "hull relation." An expression often heard here, "as thick as fiddlers in hell," undoubtedly sprang from the mouths of early reformers.

South of Franklin is rolling farm country, where the highway passes orchards and fields of corn. Honeysuckle and brier mesh the fences.

A favorite legend of GEDDES, 149.3 *m.* (688 alt.), a roadside community, is a variant of the popular Barbara Frietchie story. It is said that when Gen. John Hunt Morgan crossed the Tennessee Line near by, a few days before Christmas in 1862, his command encountered a Union flag flying over the farmhouse of an aged widow. A member of the advance guard started to climb to the roof to haul down the colors, to the ire of the old lady who soundly berated him, telling him that she loved the flag and would rather die than see it in the hands of "rebels." Morgan had ridden up during the altercation, ordered the man to come down, and told the woman to take the flag down; he allowed her to keep it. This courtesy from the much dreaded "raider" so impressed the Union sympathizer that she offered to serve all the food she could "rake and scrape" and all the "parched corn coffee they could hold." But Morgan declined, saying that his men would feast at Christmas on the pigs and turkeys held by the Union commissaries, which they were going to capture.

At 150.9 *m.* US 31W crosses the Tennessee Line, 37 miles north of Nashville.

Tour 7A

Cave City—Mammoth Cave National Park—Mammoth Cave; 9.6 *m.,* State 70.

Accommodations at Mammoth Cave National Park: Open day and night throughout year; guides compulsory; adm. (includes any chosen route through the old cave) adults, $2; for each route thereafter, $1; children, 8–12 yrs., $1; children under 8 yrs., no charge. De Luxe Route, adults, $4, children 8–12 yrs., $2; Star Chamber and Mummy Combination Route, $3; children $1.50; lunch in Snowball Dining Room, 60¢. Two modern hotels, rates from $1; horseback riding, boating, hiking, tennis, croquet, and dancing.

State 70 branches west from US 31W *(see Tour 7)* at CAVE CITY, 0 *m.* (613 alt., 773 pop.) *(see Tour 7).*

MAMMOTH CAVE NATIONAL PARK ENTRANCE, 9.6 *m.,* introduces the visitor to a 49,000-acre area of forested rolling hills, deep valleys, and streams, with Mammoth Cave as the chief attraction. The profusion of local flora is well illustrated by the fact that here are more than 180 varieties of plant life, of which 109 are shrubs and trees. A project now under way (1939) will make this park part of a scenic loop route embracing the Great Smoky Mountain National Park of North Carolina and Tennessee and the Shenandoah National Park of Virginia.

Mammoth Cave is a product of geologic action and of erosion, a process that began many million years ago. In the ancient period a shallow sea covered the region that is now central Kentucky. Within these waters coral shellfish and other forms of marine life grew in profusion. The sea floor gradually sank, and as it sank reefs, built up in the same manner as those off the coast of Florida, grew to a thickness at this point of more than 325 feet. Then the subsidence stopped.

Sand was deposited over the marine sediments. Finally the waters receded and Green River began cutting its present valley, a process that took millions of years. Underground water, coming in contact with the limestone strata, acted physically, as an erosive agent, and chemically, as a solvent, and over periods of time inconceivable to the mind of man, carved out the giant tunnel.

The rock mass, within which the cave has been carved, is now above the stream level of Green River, into which the subterranean waters of the cave flow. The cave itself, with its five levels, covers an area approximately 10 miles in circumference. Its explored passageways, 325 of which have been mapped, extend to an estimated length of 150 miles. These passageways lead visitors to three rivers, a lake, and numerous rooms and domes.

The principal attractions are reached over six routes, some of them electrically lighted and all free of danger. A natural phenomenon is the "in-breathing" or movement of air from the outside when the surface temperature is below the cave's constant temperature of 54° F., and the "out-breathing" when the surface temperature is above that of the cave.

The cave has six entrances, two natural, the other four man-made. The natural entrance, called the Historic Entrance, is 194 feet above the level of the valley and 118 feet below the crest of the overhanging bluff. The other principal entrance has a man-made stairway descending to the level of Frozen Niagara.

Mammoth Cave was first discovered by white men about 1800; claims have been made for 1794, 1802, and 1809. Since 1811, when the nitrate deposits in the cave were first mined, explorations, some planned and some accidental, have broadened knowledge of the cave to its present but still incomplete extent. During the second war with Great Britain, two men, one named Wilkins and another Benjamin Gratz, were owners of the property. The latter was prominent in early Kentucky history (see Lexington). They sent Archibald Miller from Philadelphia to take charge of the saltpeter works. After the conclusion of the war the property was sold to James Moore of Philadelphia. Later a man named Gatewood, who had previously owned the property, came into possession of it again and he opened it to the general public as a commercial attraction. In 1837 Frank Gorin purchased the land surrounding the single natural entrance and began development of the cave as a tourist attraction. Stephen Bishop, the first guide, and Matt Bransford, who, upon Bishop's death in 1859, succeeded him as chief guide, spent their lives exploring the passages and caverns. Both were slaves and men of unusual daring. Their knowledge of the cave has been transmitted in direct line to the guides who now conduct visitors through the underground wonders.

The fame of Mammoth Cave early spread to Europe where a young physician of Louisville, Dr. John Croghan, was traveling. In 1839, when he returned to America, he purchased the property and 10 years later it passed to his heirs, the sons and daughters of Col. George Croghan and Gen. T. S. Jesup.

ROUTE 1

The Historic Entrance is the natural opening through which the cave was first found. It is reached by a path that leads from the summit of the bluff. Stone steps lead to the vestibule.

The Saltpeter Vats are relics of the operations carried on during the War of 1812, when saltpeter was in great demand for the manufacture of gunpowder. The cave is rich in this mineral. The material was placed in these vats, hopper-like structures similar to the vats used in early days for the leaching of ashes to make the potash used in soap making. Water was poured over the material and the solution containing saltpeter in suspension was filtered into containers. It was boiled and again leached, this time through wood ashes. The saltpeter in crystalline form was shipped, by boat and wagon, overland to powder factories.

The Corkscrew Exit is a short and narrow but rough and winding passage to the surface discovered in 1870 by William Garvin, the guide. It makes unnecessary the physical difficulties of a return journey through the 18-inch passageway known as Fat Man's Misery. Garvin noticed the bats inhabiting the cave disappear, and by following them he reached the surface of the earth.

Gorin's Dome is over the spot where an exciting adventure of F. J. Stephenson, an English visitor, ended in 1863. Accompanied by Nick Bransford, he descended to the water level where today, filled with sand, lies the flatboat they used on their journey. They descended the sluggish stream to a point where Stephenson left the guide and boat and went on alone. Records say that when he was attempting to catch some "eyeless fish," his lamp went out, his matches became wet, and he was left in utter darkness. Despite that fact, he returned safely three hours later. The next day, his appetite for exploration still strong, Stephenson again descended the stream with Nick. Again Stephenson left the guide and went exploring alone, and again he returned safely.

The Bottomless Pit, discovered a century or more ago, was long believed to deserve its name. Actually it is about 200 feet deep. Above it, rising 140 feet, is Shelby's Dome, named for the first Governor of Kentucky.

The Bridge of Sighs is a stone arch so named because of a fancied resemblance to the Bridge of Sighs in Venice, Italy.

Fat Man's Misery is a 200-foot passage that narrows in places to 18 inches. It is the only way by which the visitor can go farther into the cave.

River Hall, believed to extend for miles underground, is the place where the waters from various caverns and galleries gather. The Dead Sea is a still pool beneath a 60-foot cliff.

The River Styx was named for the mythical Greek river across whose dark waters Charon transported the spirits of the dead.

Echo River, first crossed in 1837 by the guide and cave explorer, Stephen Bishop, flows at the lowest cave level, 360 feet below the earth's surface, on its way to near-by Green River. Here are facilities for a subterranean water journey on a stream like Coleridge's, which flowed "through caverns measureless to man, down to a sunless sea." Along this underground stream sounds are echoed with an unusual lengthening and blending. Echo River contains a translucent blind fish—best known of the Amblyopsidae family—interesting illustrations of evolution under unusual conditions of life. This underground fish, mistakenly spoken of as "eyeless," has vestigial eyes, but is totally blind.

Nathaniel P. Willis (1806–67), the journalist, described one of these fish: "In size, he was like the larger size of what boys call a 'minim'—say an inch and a half long—but very different in construction and color. His body was quite white, translucent, and wholly without intestinal canal. His stomach (what there was of it) was directly behind the brain (if brain there was) and all the organs of the system were forward of the gills, the head alone having blood or other discoloration. Under the chin he disposed of what was superfluous in his nourishment. He was curiously corespondent indeed in the poetized character of the place—like was a fish in process of becoming a fish in spiritland. Nothing could be more purely beautiful and graceful than the pearly and spotless body which had 'heavenlified' first, leaving the head to follow." These fish apparently derive all nourishment from the chemical content of water. In the course of an experiment a captive blind fish lived a year in a bowl of water without food. When a few crumbs were introduced the fish died within 24 hours.

ROUTE 2

The FROZEN NIAGARA ENTRANCE is a man-made opening cut in 1924, at a point about 3.5 miles southeast of the main entrance.

RAINBOW DOME has a wide range of color in its walls and ceilings. To the left is the huge stalactite called Onyx Pyramid.

CRYSTAL LAKE *(boats)*, a body of clear water, is 2 to 38 feet deep. The boat landing is called Plymouth Rock. A stairway leads to a higher level affording a view of the lake.

The RADIO ROOM has had a radio since 1925. No aerial is used and the reception is unusually good.

FROZEN NIAGARA, 75 feet high, is a deposit of onyx bearing a striking resemblance to a waterfall. Indirect lighting creates a spectacular effect. Fancy has vested its immediate surroundings with names. One formation is thought to resemble a tobacco leaf, others are the Golden Fleece, the Arizona Giant Cactus, the Chinese Idol, and the Chinese Family.

From the ceiling of THANKSGIVING HALL hang stalactites that are supposed to resemble turkeys and other viands that grace the Thanksgiving board.

ROUTE 3

The ROTUNDA, a vast hall about 1 mile from the Historic Entrance, is beyond the iron gates that exclude unguided visitors. Flares are employed to demonstrate the extent of this underground chamber.

AUDUBON AVENUE recalls the memory of John James Audubon, noted Kentucky ornithologist to whose life clings the legend that he was in reality the son of Louis XVI, the Lost Dauphin of France, who disappeared during the Reign of Terror.

The METHODIST CHURCH, with its resemblance to a chancel, at one end of which is a formation resembling a rostrum and pulpit, was occasionally used in early days by itinerant ministers—or so the legend runs.

BOOTH'S THEATER is a natural auditorium from the stage of which it is recorded that Edwin Booth once recited his favorite "To be, or not to be," from *Hamlet*.

Someone believed that the PILLARS OF HERCULES resembled the rocky headlands that face each other across the Strait of Gibraltar.

The BRIDAL ALTAR, bearing a striking resemblance to a small temple, was formed by the union of four pairs of stalactites and stalagmites. Numerous marriage ceremonies have been performed here.

ELBOW CREVICE is a water-fluted dome from which the musical murmuring of unseen waters is heard.

The GIANT'S COFFIN is a block of stone, 40 feet long, beside the trail.

The CONSUMPTIVES' CABINS recall a tragic delusion of medical science during the 1840's. Some doctors believed that conditions within the cave were favorable to recovery from "consumption," as pulmonary tuberculosis was then called. In this belief, these stone cabins were built, and for a considerable time a group of tubercular people lived here in a vain quest for health.

The STAR CHAMBER is a vast room in the ceiling of which are crystals of black oxide of manganese that under artificial light look like stars. For the diversion of visitors, the guides extinguish all lights. The intense darkness is broken as the stars appear one by one. As an added touch, the twittering of birds is reproduced.

The MARTHA WASHINGTON STATUE, apparently a female figure in silhouette, is created in part by the use of lights.

ROUTE 4

This tour begins at FROZEN NIAGARA *(see Route 2).*

The large ROOSEVELT DOME, named in honor of former President Theodore Roosevelt, is 130 feet from apex to base.

GRAND CENTRAL STATION is so called because of the many routes that intersect here.

The NEW YORK HIPPODROME, a room 200 feet long, 100 feet wide, and 68 feet high, is said to be directly below Frozen Niagara Hotel.

FAIRY CEILING, 100 feet long, is notable because of its smooth surface.

COLLEGE HEIGHTS AVENUE is named in honor of Western State Teachers' College in Bowling Green, Ky.

Thanksgiving Hall, September Morn, Crystal Lake, Onyx Colonnade, and Rainbow Dome *(see Route 2)* are also included in this tour.

ROUTE 5

This route combines Routes 1 and 2, the chief points of Route 3, as well as the following:

OLE BULL'S CONCERT HALL named for the Norwegian-born violinist who played in it.

The PASS OF EL GHOR marks the point from which three early-day cave explorers, Charles and Abraham Merideth and F. M. De Monbrum, made their way into a vast cavern that no one has since been able to re-discover.

MARY'S VINEYARD has a stalactite that winds from ceiling to floor and resembles a grapevine. Nodules of limestone coated with black oxide of iron heighten the resemblance to a vine loaded with grapes.

The SNOWBALL DINING ROOM, 267 feet below the surface, is a lunch room for cave visitors. Its ceiling is festooned with "snowballs" of gypsum.

BOONE AVENUE is a rough pass, noted for the coloring of its walls.

The MAMMOTH GYPSUM WALL, bordering Kentucky Ave., contains formations resembling celery stalks and flowers.

The GRAND CANYON, a large water-eroded channel, was so named because of a fancied resemblance—in miniature—to the great gorge of the Colorado River.

The remainder of the route is Route 2.

ROUTE 6

This route is Route 2, with the addition of the following:

PROCTOR'S ARCADE is an enlargement of the main cave that, in early days, was coupled with the avenue known as Kynney's Arena. It has passages with high ceilings and well-proportioned arches.

The INDIAN RELICS—torches made out of bundles of reeds, wooden bowls, woven sandals, and the ashes of fires—were found in a room of the cave and attest to the presence of the natives long before the white man discovered these wonders. Archeologists agree that these relics are those of a race that preceded the Indians living in Kentucky when the earliest whites appeared.

WRIGHT'S ROTUNDA was the name first given to Chief City. It is now applied to this T-shaped hall, and honors Dr. C. A. Wright, a Louisianian who published one of the earliest histories of the cave.

CHIEF CITY, a single room two acres in extent, is awe-inspiring. Its ceiling, unsupported by pillars, is smooth. In this room were found a large number of relics of prehistoric man. Archeologists believe that both the Indian of historic times and his predecessor used this room for special purposes, as a tribal gathering place, or as a place for religious ceremonies.

The CATARACTS is a cascade where waters seeping through the porous rocks gather into a stream that plunges downward over a cliff. Following heavy rains, or the melting of deep snows, the cascade becomes a noisy torrent.

WALDACH'S DOME commemorates Charles Waldach of Cincinnati, Ohio, an early photographer whose pictures gave the cave wide publicity.

The BODY OF PREHISTORIC MINER, near Waldach's Dome, is preserved in a glass case where it was found in 1935. The so-called miner had been caught beneath a slab of stone.

On MUMMY LEDGE was found the mummified body of a woman about five feet ten inches tall, who was killed by a stab beneath the heart. The body was discovered by the miners of 1812. According to legend, her skin was dark and her close-cropped hair had a reddish tint; she was dressed in clothing woven from linden (basswood) fibers and a robe of deerskin bearing traces of formal designs. Feather headdresses, one for each day in the week, were found beside her body, and a tiny musical instrument resembling a flute lay in her hand. Small beads and a necklace made of fawn's hooves, together with the claws of an eagle, adorned her. The exceptional care with which the body had been prepared for burial indicates that the woman had been a person of importance. This find, which has disappeared, passed into the possession of a Bostonian, who, according to the tale, gave it to a museum. No museum has reported such a possession.

HAINES' DOME was named in honor of Ben Haines, an early photographer of New Albany, Indiana, who devoted much of his time and effort to exploration of the cave and to photographing its features.

In the SNOW ROOM deposits of Epsom salts hang like hoarfrost from the walls and ceiling. The slightest vibration of the air will cause a shower of this snowlike substance to fall. Early settlers collected the salts for medicinal purposes.

ULTIMA THULE was named before the beginning of the twentieth century, when it was supposed to be the end of the cave.

VIOLET CITY was discovered in 1918 by Max Kaemper, a German scientist, who with Edwin Bishop, a guide, found the "crawl-way" connecting Ultima Thule with Kaemper's Hall and all that part of the cave now called Violet City. Kaemper's Hall is 160 feet long, 120 feet wide and 60 feet high. ELIZABETH'S DOME was named, according to local legend, for Kaemper's sweetheart. GRAND PORTAL, 60 feet wide and 50 feet high, is reached by an imposing stairway. The MARBLE TEMPLE, its wall studded with many-colored onyx, glows under electric lights. The CHIMES are slender reeds made in the meeting of hollow stalactites and stalagmites, and resemble organ pipes. When struck, they emit musical tones.

The man-made exit at this point is 3.5 miles southeast of the Historic Entrance.

At Mammoth Cave archway is the junction with a graveled road.

Right on this road to GREAT ONYX CAVE *(adm. $2, combination route $3, guides; hotel, rates from $1)*; **3 m.**, one of the principal caves in this region. Great Onyx Cave contains miles of avenues leading into corridors and spacious chambers with great fluted columns of onyx, draperies of translucent alabaster, and a gleaming garden of lilies, daisies and chrysanthemums reproduced from snow white gypsum.

Near the entrance to the cave a winding pathway bordered with ferns and flowers leads among stately trees to the shores of Green River, an ideal place for swimming, boating, and fishing.

At **4.3 m.** is FLOYD COLLINS CRYSTAL CAVE *(adm. $2)*, within the Mammoth Cave National Park. This cave, one of the largest in the area and only partly explored, was discovered in December 1917 by Floyd Collins while making a round of the traps on his father's farm; it has two well-defined routes. In them is a dazzling display of delicate formations of gypsum, crystal, and onyx, resembling lilies, chrysanthemums, peonies, and asters—white, gold, pale yellow, and pink. Many of the rare bush-like helectite formations, as yet of undetermined origin, ornament small alcoves on each side of a passage more than a mile long. GRAND CANYON AVENUE, an imposing chamber 200 feet high, 110 feet wide, and 700 feet long, contains the tomb of Floyd Collins, who lost his life in 1925 in an effort to discover a new entrance to Crystal Cave from the highway at Sand Cave. During the period when searchers were frantically trying to find the lost man, the whole Nation waited for daily reports.

Tour 8

(Evansville, Ind.)—Henderson—Madisonville—Hopkinsville—Guthrie —(Nashville, Tenn.); US 41 and 41E, Dixie B-Line.
Indiana Line to Tennessee Line, 114.5 *m.*

Hard-surfaced roadbed throughout.
Louisville & Nashville R.R. roughly parallels US 41 throughout.
All types of accommodations in larger towns; limited elsewhere.

This route follows an old Indian trail that ran between the Great Lakes and the Gulf of Mexico. It was first made by the great herds of buffalo in their seasonal migrations from South to North and back again. Their trails, always following the least difficult routes, have become main roads throughout the State. Meriwether Lewis, while Governor of Upper Louisiana Territory, once had occasion to traverse this trace and recorded that he and his companions were so engrossed with its rugged beauty as to relax from their eternal lookout for lurking Shawnee and Wyandotte.

Between Henderson and Nashville this route was long a post road, called the Buttermilk Road, because farmers along the route set aside crocks of buttermilk and dippers, from which travelers might freely drink.

In Kentucky, US 41 passes throughout the entire Pennyrile, a region whose name was derived from pennyroyal, a herb of the mint family. The Pennyrile has rather vague boundaries but extends from the low wooded hills of the Ohio River on the north to the rich coal fields of southwestern Kentucky, a pastoral land cut through by deep winding streams.

US 41 crosses the Indiana Line, 0 *m.*, 2 miles south of Evansville, Ind. *(see Ind. Tour 16).*

DADE PARK (L), 1 *m.*, was built by James Ellis in 1922, on the part of Henderson County that was cut off on the north when the Ohio River changed its course. Races are held here for a period of 28 days, usually in August.

The highway crosses the Ohio River on the Henderson-Evansville (Audubon Highway) Bridge, 2 *m. (toll 30¢).*

AUDUBON MEMORIAL STATE PARK (L), 4.1 *m.*, is a 400-acre tract donated by citizens of Henderson County in memory of John James Audubon (1785–1851), the ornithologist, who roamed through Kentucky from 1808 to 1826. It includes one of his favorite haunts, Wolf Hill, where he hunted, studied the birds, and sometimes cut his name on trees. Here, too, though the exact spot is unknown, is the GRAVE OF LUCY AUDUBON, his little daughter. Shelters, roads, sanitary facilities, and offices have been built; trails have been developed, some of them following old trails probably used by Audubon.

A reproduction of a FRENCH NORMAN INN, with a cobbled courtyard for tables, serves as a gatehouse just off the 100-foot road that traverses the park. It contains, in addition to a lunchroom, a banquet hall, dormitories for hikers, and quarters for the caretaker. In the FRENCH GARDEN is a small stone pavilion; also two bird baths formed from the old millstones found on the site of Audubon's "infernal mill" on the Ohio at Henderson. These millstones, called French burr, were brought from France.

The AUDUBON MUSEUM houses a collection of Audubon prints. On the second floor is a collection of stuffed birds, books, and portraits. Also on the first floor is a Kentucky Room holding relics of Daniel Boone and other pioneers, and a Transylvania Room. The French Norman style of architecture was chosen for this building because of Audubon's French ancestry, and because it permitted the round tower that contains holes in the masonry for nesting birds.

At *5.2 m.* is the junction with US 60 *(see Tour 16)*, which is united with US 41 between this point and HENDERSON, 6.6 *m.* (382 alt., 11,686 pop.) *(see Tour 16)*.

Between Henderson and Dixon the road passes through rolling lands covered with orchards and tobacco fields.

The highway passes HARPE'S HEAD ROAD (R), 29.6 *m.*, so named because Big Harpe, a notorious outlaw of early days, was slain here July 22, 1806, and his head placed on a pole near an oak tree by the roadside. The initials, H. H. (Harpe's Head) cut into the bark of the tree, were legible for more than 60 years.

The Harpes—Micajah (Big Harpe) and Wiley (Little Harpe)— traveled with three women, two of whom were described as the wives of Big Harpe. The gang is believed to have come into Kentucky from North Carolina in 1802. Their appearance was first noted near Stanford in Lincoln County. A few days later came the first of the crimes with which they blazed their way to the Green River country. In the Rockcastle hills along the Wilderness Road a young Virginian named Langford disappeared. A posse caught the Harpes near by and carried them into Stanford; in their possession were the Virginian's fine shirts, one of them bullet-pierced and stained with blood. After the bandits had been transferred to Danville for trial, they broke jail and escaped. Rumors of atrocities flew thick and fast through the settlements, and when the small son of Captain Trabue disappeared in Adair County the parents and neighbors blamed the gang; many years later the bones of a small child were found in a sinkhole near which the child was last seen. Terror mounted, however, and all the murders and robberies that were common at the time on the frontier, were laid to the Harpes.

One night the Harpes arrived at the home of a man named Stigall; they said they were Methodist preachers and asked for a night's shelter. Another traveler was already there but Mrs. Stigall felt no fear in her husband's absence and, with the usual frontier hospitality, took them in. The next morning Stigall returned to find his home in ashes; in the ruins were the bodies of his wife and children and that of a stranger, all showing evidence of murder. Stigall ran to the home of his neighbor, Capt. John Leeper, who immediately called out other men to help find the Harpes, who were suspected of being in the vicinity. It was agreed that Leeper should have the honor of killing Big Harpe and Stigall should shoot Little Harpe. The party soon found the women who traveled with the Harpes; the men had left them behind when they fled. The Kentuckians continued the chase and at length caught up with the bandits at this place. Leeper fired at his chosen target, who was on horseback. Both man and horse went down, the horse on top. Harpe screamed for release and mercy, but Leeper waited until Stigall arrived, then shot Big Harpe, cut off his head, and placed the trophy on a tree as a warning to other outlaws.

Little Harpe escaped and when next heard of had joined two land-pirates, Mason and Mays, who were terrorizing travelers on the Natchez Trace. A price had been set on Mason's head; one day when Mason was dividing a particularly large amount of loot, Little Harpe and Mays shot him, cut off his head, carried it into Natchez, and attempted to claim the reward. They were recognized and arrested but managed to escape. They were again captured at old Greenville and hanged; their heads were placed on poles along the trace, one at each end of town.

There is the usual legend in the neighborhood of Harpe's Head Road that large sums of "treasure" were buried here by bandits; none has ever been found.

DIXON, 31.8 m. (544 alt., 650 pop.), seat of Webster County, is a quiet town named for Archibald Dixon, Lieutenant Governor of Kentucky 1844–48, and member of the United States Senate 1852–55, when he filled the unexpired term of Henry Clay after Clay's death.

Many large Revolutionary War bonus-grants lay in this vicinity. Robert Morris, the financier of the Revolution who speculated so disastrously in soldiers' grants, held a tract of several thousand acres between Dixon and the Tradewater River. These grants were allowed to lapse, and some years later the land was regranted to settlers. The town of Dixon was laid out on the land of Ambrose Mooney, who gave the land on which the courthouse stands.

What is left of what was the HALFWAY HOUSE, on Dixon St., once a stagecoach inn, has been weatherboarded and is now a filling station. In 1794 William Jenkins, the town's earliest promoter, constructed the log hostelry within the stockade "for the shelter of those who may become residents of this rich and beautiful land, and for the rest and comfort of travelers passing over the main trail leading from the great trading posts of the North to Natchez Trace, far to the South." Soon after its erection, Jenkins was captured by a band of Cherokee who came to like him and kept him for several years. They were so fearful of losing him that they plucked his hair out to keep a neighboring tribe from scalping him. When Jenkins at last returned, he enlarged the inn, in 1816 built the first frame house here, and yet later established a cotton gin. The rates of the Halfway House appear in an old day book: "Meals, 4.s each; bed, 4.s, for each person; whisky, 1.s the drink. Exchange 1 bu. corn for 1 gal. whisky." The menu was game, corn pone, pork, and hominy. Shuck mattresses were used on the beds, and the rule of the inn was that not more than four persons might occupy one bed. The only guest who did not sleep on a shuck mattress was Meriwether Lewis. The Governor, in spite of his military and exploring experiences, liked his feather bed and deep pillows; so, when he arrived, the slaves went scurrying about the village to borrow these comforts.

Alfred Townes, eccentric friend of Audubon, was the first to mine and use coal in Webster County. This coal was an outcropping on a hillside at the edge of town, just off the old Indian Trail. During his development of the coal industry, Townes made an attempt to build a railroad into the section. In the enterprise he utilized the labor of his slaves and spent $125,000 of his own money but he failed because his financial backers withdrew their support. Audubon described it as a "fine dream that will some day be true."

On the court square is the SITE OF THE PRISON PEN where Confederate prisoners were confined after the skirmishes of Slaughters (1862) and Providence (1864). As the story goes, after the Providence skirmish 30 Confederate prisoners, who happened to be clad in unusually good uniforms, were stripped of their garments, clothed in odds and ends, and placed in this log pen, from which they promptly escaped. At the close of the war, when the survivors of the group marched through Dixon on their way home, and saw their uniforms on the home guards, they were so amazed that they not only took the uniforms but compelled the guards to carry the logs from the pen to the county jail, where several Confederates were still held. The prisoners were freed and the logs were used to set the jail on fire.

The RICE HOUSE, on Main St., at the southwestern end of town, is the birthplace (1872) of Cale Young Rice, the Kentucky poet. In 1934 the Webster County Historical Society planted a FRIENDSHIP GARDEN around the house. Each tree, shrub, and flower bed is a tribute from some Kentucky admirer.

Between Dixon and Madisonville US 41 passes through farming and mining country.

MADISONVILLE, 55.6 *m.* (470 alt., 6,908 pop.), named for James Madison, is in the center of the plateau between the Pond and Tradewater Rivers, a region of hills, rivers, and creek bottoms, where it is said "anything grown in the temperate zone will grow." Tobacco is the money-crop, this town being one of the principal loose-leaf tobacco markets in western Kentucky. Large quantities of hardwood timber are also shipped from here.

In this section a great many Indian artifacts and relics have been found along the creeks and rivers. It is believed that in the group of HOMINY HOLES near Government Schoolhouse, milling was carried on by mechanical means. As archeologists have decided, six of these round holes in the hard sandstone, which are 30 to 40 inches in diameter and 10 to 14 inches deep, were used to hold corn that was crushed by large stone pestles, operated by spring poles and counterweights.

The DANIEL MCGARY HOUSE, built of brick in 1817, is a one-story structure with a gabled roof and an ell. Facing the street and occupying a large part of the angle of the ell is a vine-hidden porch, added in recent years.

South of Madisonville US 41 traverses coal fields.

EARLINGTON, 59.7 *m.* (422 alt., 3,309 pop.), a railroad junction, is the heart of the coal fields. On Saturday the streets are filled with miners and their families from near-by settlements. On the southern outskirts of the town is the ATKINSON ARBORETUM *(open)*, containing a variety of trees and shrubs.

EARLINGTON LAKE, 60.7 *m.* *(open to public)*, offers excellent boating, swimming, and fishing.

In MORTON'S GAP, 63.4 *m.* (451 alt., 1,068 pop.), is the THOMAS MORTON HOUSE, built by the town's founder in 1804. It is a rectangular, two-story, gable-roofed structure with two rooms on each floor; various additions, including a porch, now give it a rambling appearance. The different colors of the brick, which range from light yellow to deep red, are the result of the differences in the amount of heat used in the process of burning. The crack between the front windows was made by the earthquake in 1811.

At NORTONVILLE, 66.7 *m.* (429 alt., 829 pop.) *(see Tour 14)*, is the junction with US 62 *(see Tour 14)*.

South of the coal fields of Hopkins County the highway passes through stretches of level pasture lands and rugged picturesque hills.

HOPKINSVILLE, 91.4 *m.* (541 alt., 10,746 pop.), one of the leading dark-fire tobacco markets of the country, gives evidence of long prosperity in its large comfortable old houses on wide lawns and in its tree-shaded streets and many stores. In 1797 Bartholomew Wood gave some of his land to the county to bring the county seat to the settlement here; court opened in November in a log house 20 feet square—quite large enough for the business of the very thinly settled region. The town was incorporated in 1804, about the time the rush of settlers from Virginia and North Carolina began. The settlement, renamed to honor Gen. Samuel Hopkins, a hero of the War of 1812, grew slowly but steadily, serving the people of a wide section of the southern Pennyrile. In the early days, a visit to Hopkinsville was a visit to a great city for those who lived on the scattered farms and in the hills.

The town is still the center of business and culture in the region. On Saturday the downtown streets are filled with dusty cars and slow-moving streams of shoppers—or those who make shopping an excuse to visit the movies and to see crowds. During November, December, and January, however, farmers are seen on the streets every day of the week. It is then that the trucks and wagons bring in dark-fire and burley tobacco to the 21 large warehouses, and stand in long lines as the farmers wait their turns to unload. After the unloading the trucks stand empty along the streets for hours as their owners celebrate their relief after the months of toil, exchange gossip and surmises on prices, pay their accumulated bills, and buy the necessities whose purchase has been deferred for want of cash.

Hopkinsville is the headquarters of the Farm Security Administration's Christian-Trigg Farms, a project covering more than 8,000 acres in Christian, Trigg, and Todd Counties. It was designed to provide small farms—they average 67 acres—for a selected group of tenants and sharecroppers in these counties as well as families removed from near-by areas that were submarginal for farming. Each unit includes a house, barn, smokehouse, and poultry house. Forty-eight of the 103 farms planned were occupied in October 1938 and the homesteaders, advised by Federal agents, had worked out a diversified crop plan by which the families raise the major portion of their food and the feed for their stock (chickens, hogs, and milk cows), plant legumes to enrich the soil, and produce tobacco and cotton for cash crops.

The KNIGHT HOUSE, 1810 S. Main St., is a one-story brick house of the Classic Revival style built about 1832 on a high basement. The structure has had numerous alterations and additions that have changed its original lines. When first built it was apparently a one-story dwelling with a recessed entrance in the front gable end. The sill of the old entrance is now several feet above the floor of the simple pedimented portico, which has five square columns and a rectangular window in its pediment. A new entrance has been built in one corner of the façade at a much lower level than the old one. On one side is a frame wing and on the other a porch entered from the higher floor level and set on tall brick pillars.

The STITES HOUSE, 714 E. 7th St., is a spacious two-story low-roofed frame structure built about 1850. Its two-story pedimented central portico of modified Greek Revival style has only two square columns. The corners of the structure are pilastered and the enframement of the windows and side-lighted entrance has a restrained elegance.

The ROSS DILLARD HOUSE, corner of Main and 14th Sts., built about 1856, is known as the "steamboat house" because of its resemblance to the river craft of the mid-nineteenth century, left high and dry. It is of frame construction, two stories high. At the corners of the low façade heavy white pilasters rise to a classic frieze. A long, shallow, one-story semicircular porch, its floor only slightly above ground level, has a paneled balustrade around its deck roof, which is supported by five round tapering columns on high square bases. Two large windows in the low second-story opening onto this deck give the illusion of a pilot house. The low sloping roof is pierced by two stack-like chimneys some distance from the low gable ends.

Tradition is that prior to the War between the States, Dillard, a farmer, was so impressed by the steamboat in which he traveled to New Orleans that on his return he had an architect build this house for him, a memorial to the floating palace. During the War between the States this home became for a time military headquarters of the Federal forces of occupation.

The WALTER DOWNES HOUSE, 15th and Main Sts., is a large two-story brick structure built in the 1840's. It has brackets under the eaves and tall chimney pots—possibly later additions—but the details of the trim and the four tall, fluted, Ionic columns of the broad pedimented portico have a Greek Revival refinement. An unusual feature is the paneled balustrade of the small balcony over the side-lighted entrance doorway.

The main building of BETHEL WOMEN'S JUNIOR COLLEGE, a Baptist institution founded in 1854, is three stories high, built in brick in the Greek Revival style.

The STATE ARMORY, corner Main and 5th Sts., is owned jointly by the State, county, and city.

Hopkinsville is at the junction with US 68 (see Tour 15).

1. Right from Hopkinsville on State 107 to SWALLOW SPRING, 5 m. (open to public), an ordinary-looking sinkhole in a field by the side of the road, surrounded by fertile land. At intervals, sometimes several years apart, this sinkhole becomes a boiling spring that fills the valley with a lake several acres in extent. After remaining for months, the water eventually subsides, often leaving a large number of fish. The roadway has been raised at this point to avoid the overflowing waters.

2. Right from Hopkinsville on US 41W to EDGETON, 16.7 m., on the Tennessee Line, 59 miles north of Nashville, Tenn. (see Tenn. Tour 8A).

South of Hopkinsville US 41E, now the route, crosses many meandering streams as it traverses a region with great stretches of level pasture lands, spacious homesteads surrounded by orchards, gardens, and groves of beech, walnut, and oak.

GUTHRIE, 114 m. (1,272 pop.), is a railroad center named for James Guthrie, president of the Louisville & Nashville R.R. in 1867, when the town was incorporated. The LOUISVILLE & NASHVILLE TIE-TREATING PLANT is here.

US 41E crosses the Tennessee Line, 114.5 m., 52 miles north of Nashville, Tenn. (see Tenn. Tours 8 and 9).

Tour 9

(Metropolis, Ill.)—Paducah—Mayfield—Fulton—(Martin, Tenn.);
US 45. Illinois Line to Tennessee Line, 53.4 *m.*

Hard-surfaced roadbed.
Illinois Central R.R. parallels route throughout.
All types of accommodations in towns, limited elsewhere.

This route crosses the western section of the State, which is called
the Jackson Purchase because the United States, on October 19, 1818,
through its commissioners, Gen. Andrew Jackson and Gov. Isaac Shelby,
purchased from the Chickasaw Indians, for the sum of $300,000, 8,500
square miles of desolate wilderness, west of the Tennessee River. Today
that territory comprises eight counties in the westernmost section of
Kentucky and 20 counties in Tennessee, and is among the most fertile
sections in both of these States. The surface of the region is gently
undulating with a few ridges along the highway. The area yields such
a quantity of fruits and vegetables that huge trucks loaded with strawberries, dewberries, apples, peaches, and tomatoes, lumber over the highways day and night during the growing season. Tobacco and corn are
also raised in quantities and, in the southernmost section, cotton is
grown. In the southwestern part are still many fine stands of poplar,
hickory, and oak. Near the Tennessee Line trees and shrubs border the
road.

US 45 crosses the Illinois Line, 0 *m.,* 13 miles southeast of Metropolis,
Ill. *(see Ill. Tour 3),* on the Brookport-Paducah Bridge *(toll 50¢)* over
the Ohio River.

PADUCAH, 4.5 *m.* (341 alt., 33,541 pop.) *(see Paducah).*

Points of Interest: Paduke Statue, Tilghman Memorial, Irvin Cobb Hotel, Mc-
Cracken County Courthouse, Nobel Park, and others.

Paducah is at the junction with US 60 *(see Tour 16),* US 62 *(see
Tour 14),* and US 68 *(see Tour 15).*

MAYFIELD, 30 *m.* (421 alt., 8,177 pop.), seat of Graves County,
like many other Southern cities, is built around the courthouse which
is in the center of a block known as Court Square.

A man named Mayfield, according to local legend, journeyed from
Mississippi to Mills Point (now Hickman) in 1817 to attend the races.
There he was captured by a band of ruffians who carried him to the
banks of a near-by creek to rob him. After carving his name on a tree
near the stream, Mayfield attempted to escape by crossing the creek

on a log, but was shot and fell into the water. Afterward the creek was called Mayfield, and when this town was organized in 1823 the name was applied to the town.

In MAPLEWOOD CEMETERY (L), within sight of US 45 in the northern outskirts of the city, are the WOOLRIDGE MONUMENTS. These memorials were erected by Henry C. Woolridge, who accumulated a large fortune in Mayfield as a horse trader and breeder. All facing toward the east and surrounding the vault, where the body of Woolridge now lies, are the life-sized stone statues. The standing figure of Woolridge was carved in Italy of marble. Those of his mother, his brothers, two girls who were friends of his youth, his favorite dogs, a deer that heads this procession, a fox, and a sculpture of Woolridge mounted on his favorite horse, Pop, are the work of a stonecutter from Paducah. At the rear of the lot are figures of his sisters made by a third sculptor.

Near the northern limits of Mayfield is (L) the PET MILK COMPANY PLANT *(open)*, which employs 50 men, and pays to farmers an average of $37,000 monthly for milk. The MERIT CLOTHING COMPANY FACTORY *(open)* and the CURLEE CLOTHING COMPANY FACTORY *(open)* together employ 1,800 men and women in the manufacture of men's and boys' suits and overcoats.

On Mule Day *(3rd Mon. in Feb.)* mules are brought to the city in droves or by truck and offered for sale in the "swapping ring," a reserved portion of the street around the public square. The ring presents a lively scene, thronged with mules and buyers, traffickers, and speculators who dicker for anything from a mule to a pocketknife.

Mayfield is in the center of a large area that produces dark fire-cured tobacco. During the loose-leaf sales season *(Dec.-May)* from 15 to 20 million pounds of tobacco are sold from the sales floors here *(see Tour 5)*. Representatives of manufacturing and exporting firms from many parts of the country attend these sales.

Thousands of tons of clay are dug annually between Mayfield and the Tennessee Line—an area noted for the variety of its clays—and sent from Mayfield to other parts of the country for utilization in the manufacture of ceramic ware. The largest of these mines, the KENTUCKY-TENNESSEE CLAY COMPANY MINE *(open)*, 32 *m.* (L), has been continuously worked for more than 40 years, and produces ball clays of high type. The production of ball clays in the United States began in 1891, when a deposit of exceptional quality was revealed near this mine by the digging of a water well.

At 44 *m.* is the junction with a graveled road.

Left on this road to a monument, 1 *m.*, marking the SITE OF CAMP BEAUREGARD, named in honor of Gen. P. G. T. Beauregard, commander of the western department of the Confederate Army. This camp was established in August 1861 as a recruiting station and assignment base for the Confederate troops. In November 1861, 6,000 Alabama, Georgia, Tennessee, Louisiana, and Mississippi troops arrived here; inclement weather and lack of accommodations brought on an epidemic of measles, meningitis, typhoid, and pneumonia. During the month over 1,500 burials were made, and the survivors were removed. Camp Beauregard continued to be used as an assignment base until January 7, 1862, when it was captured by Gen. C. F. Smith and his Union forces.

WATER VALLEY, 46.3 *m.* (351 pop.), contains a canning plant that furnishes employment to a large number of people during the season.

Between Water Valley and the Tennessee Line is the northern border of the South's cotton-growing region.

FULTON, 52.5 *m.* (357 alt., 3,503 pop.), named for Robert Fulton, consists really of two towns, being on the border line between Kentucky and Tennessee. The Tennessee section, with a population of 2,000, is called South Fulton. Each has its own city government and school system, but the single post office is on the Kentucky side. Three lines of the Illinois Central System converge at Fulton, attracting numbers of people from the North as well as the South. The average monthly payroll of employees in the railroad yards is approximately $40,000. Poultry and milk plants belonging to Swift & Company also provide employment. The city also has a COTTON GIN.

Fulton is at the junction with US 51 *(see Tour 10).*

US 45–51 crosses the Tennessee Line, 53.4 *m.*, 10.8 miles north of Martin, Tenn. *(US 45, see Tenn. Tour 10)* and 10.9 miles north of Union City, Tenn. *(US 51, see Tenn. Tour 11).*

Tour 10

(Cairo, Ill.) — Wickliffe — Bardwell — Clinton — Fulton — (Memphis, Tenn.); US 51.
Illinois Line to Tennessee Line, 45 *m.*

Illinois Central R.R. parallels the route.
Hard-surfaced roadbed.
All types of accommodations in towns; limited elsewhere.

US 51, in crossing the westernmost tip of Kentucky, passes through an area rich in agricultural products and replete with historical associations. Along the roadside are level fields of grassland interspersed with tobacco, corn, and, in the southern extremity, cotton. Back from the highway, extending from the Ohio River to Tennessee, is a chain of attractive small lakes fringed with cypress. Along the high bluffs overlooking the Mississippi River are ancient barrows, remains of stone forts, fortified towns, and a paved canal, last traces of the prehistoric people who preceded the Indians in this region.

US 51 crosses the Illinois Line, 0 *m.*, on the west bank of the Ohio River, almost a mile south of Cairo, Ill. *(see Ill. Tour 4),* on a bridge *(toll, 75¢; combination toll for this and Mississippi River bridge, $1)* over the Ohio River.

Between this point and Wickliffe, US 51 and US 60 are one route *(see Tour 16)*.

WICKLIFFE, 5.1 *m.* (332 alt., 1,108 pop.) *(see Tour 16)*, is at the junction with US 60 *(see Tour 16)*.

The SITE OF OLD FORT JEFFERSON (R), 5.9 *m.*, is on a hill overlooking the Mississippi River. In 1780 Gen. George Rogers Clark, under orders of Thomas Jefferson, then Governor of Virginia, constructed a stockade at this point. It was later abandoned because of its isolated position.

BARDWELL, 14 *m.* (390 alt., 1,139 pop.), seat of Carlisle County, last established county of the Jackson Purchase, derived its name from a bored well here, which supplied trains with water. The town is a retail center.

Right from Bardwell on State 123, an improved road, to COLUMBUS, 11.5 *m.* (513 pop.), first seat of Hickman County, and COLUMBUS-BELMONT MEMORIAL STATE PARK *(adm. 10¢, picnic grounds, shelter houses)*, 12.1 *m.*, on the bank of the Mississippi River at the old town site of Columbus.

The site was named Iron Banks by early French explorers, who discovered the iron deposits that made the great bluffs rust-colored at this point. In 1784 when Virginia, in order to pay off its soldiers in the Revolutionary Army, issued warrants for lands along the Mississippi River, a group of Gen. George Rogers Clark's veterans took up land in this area. A military post was here in 1804, when Federal troops were rushed to this place at the time of the Burr conspiracy. A settlement grew up and a courthouse and jail, the first in the Purchase, were built in 1823. The purchase of Louisiana from France in 1803 and the burning of the Capitol at Washington in 1814 caused real estate speculators to proclaim this place as the approximate center of the Nation and to start propaganda to remove the seat of the national government to this less vulnerable spot. Engineers laid out plans for a city to be named Columbus. The promoters were unsuccessful, but the name remained. The plan of the development is among the early records in the courthouse.

During the War between the States, Columbus again sprang into the national picture. The Northern program for conquest of the South involved, as its major Western feature, the opening of the Mississippi. To checkmate that strategy Gen. Leonidas Polk, C.S.A., seized and heavily fortified the bluff at the point known as Iron Banks. Although this act was the first official violation of Kentucky's avowed neutrality, both sides had been recruiting and propagandizing in the State from the very beginning of the war. General Polk's move was dictated by the fear that Union troops might forestall them in seizing this strategic position. A great chain more than a mile long was stretched across the river to prevent further passage southward of the Union gunboats. Its links weighed 15 pounds each; the chain was attached on the Kentucky shore to a six-ton anchor bedded deep in the side of the bluff. One hundred and forty guns, so placed as to sweep the river, were arranged at four elevations—40, 85, and 97 feet above water, and crowning the 200-foot top of the bluff. This formidable array of artillery was protected by massive earthworks against the gunfire of the fleet, and, by an intricate system of trenches, parapets, redoubts, and abatis, against attack by land. The Missouri bank of the river at Belmont was also held by a small Confederate force.

In November 1861 Gen. U. S. Grant moved south from Cairo and landed his army on the Missouri side of the river. He overwhelmed the Confederate forces, and burned the Confederate camp at Belmont. General Polk sent troops across the river that struck at the Union force, driving it back to its transports, and a

Union disaster was narrowly averted. Realizing that Columbus was impregnable, Grant swung eastward, captured the Confederate position at Fort Henry, forced the surrender of General Buckner at Fort Donelson, fought the bitter battle of Pittsburg Landing, or Shiloh, and by this surrounding movement forced the evacuation of Columbus. Some of the guns were spiked and thrown into the river; others were taken to the next Confederate defensive position at Island Number 10. The battle of Belmont was the beginning of the great Western struggle that continued without interruption until Vicksburg had fallen, and the armies of the North swept eastward to the sea.

When, in 1927, the high water of that year forced the citizens of Columbus to abandon their homes, the American Red Cross built a new town on the higher land to the east. All persons securing home sites in the new town, conveyed their former lands back to the city, which in turn deeded these lands, together with the streets and alleys, to the Commonwealth of Kentucky. Other lands were acquired by purchase and a total of 331 acres was made available as a site for the present State park, built since July 1934 by CCC labor, to commemorate the struggle that took place here between Union and Confederate forces.

The restored FORTIFICATIONS AND TRENCHES approach, in their completeness of detail, those built during the World War. The great SEA ANCHOR with links of the huge chain are among the show pieces of the park. A blockhouse, similar to the one erected in 1780 by Gen. George Rogers Clark, houses many of the smaller relics gathered from the trenches. Roads and a lookout tower afford views of the winding river and fortressed hill.

CLINTON, 29.2 *m.* (389 alt., 1,204 pop.), seat of Hickman County since 1829, and retail trade center for a fertile agricultural region, is an attractive small town with beautiful homes and spacious lawns. The town was platted in 1826 by James Gibson and incorporated in 1831 after the seat of county government had been moved here from Columbus. Cotton growing and cotton ginning—early occupations—have steadily grown in importance. An article by Don Singletary, M.D., gives an excellent picture of Clinton in the early nineteenth century:

"When I first saw Clinton it was a very small crossroad village. . . . Professors George and Marion Ray had built Clinton Academy and had filled it with pupils from four or more States. Up to 1850 our county was mostly wooded where grew great oaks, whose acorns fed and fattened our hogs, and we lived on hog and hominy—the fat of the land. Cattle kept fat in the woods all summer and early fall, and even did fairly well by nosing under great beds of dry leaves and getting dry green grass and acorns in winter. We lived well: Milk and butter, chickens and eggs were abundant. Eggs were sold at 5 and 6 cents a dozen, and large fat hens at 25 cents each. Money was scarce, but we did not need much. Our clothes grew by special hand work. I remember well our cotton and flax patches, and sheepfold. We picked and de-seeded our cotton by hand and carded and spun our thread for sewing, and wove our own cloth. We cut, fitted and made beautiful clothes. Women folks were also experts in cloth dyeing. Walnut, oak, and hickory bark and elder berries made a variety of lovely colors. The spinning wheel and the old loom come back in memory. I see the shuttle fly and hear the wheel hum right now. We also treated our wool in like manner. We were warmly dressed in winter, and also had blankets galore. Our shoes grew up at home and were home-made, after a year's tanning."

Along the entire course of Bayou De Chien Creek, which runs through Hickman County and a corner of Fulton County, is a series of mounds, camp sites, and burial fields that have yielded unusual and beautiful artifacts covering a wide range of subjects and designs.

At 39 *m.* is the junction with State 94, a paved road.

Right on this road to the CASEY JONES MONUMENT, **6.9** *m.*, a limestone slab that bears a bronze tablet showing a bas-relief of the *Cannon Ball*—the engine Jones was driving at the time of his death. John Luther Jones, later known to fame as "Cayce" or "Casey" Jones, was born March 14, 1864, at Jordan, Kentucky, the son of a schoolteacher. At the age of 17 he grew restless, walked the ties to Cayce and there got his first job. Promotion came rapidly: before he was 30 Jones had passed successively from helper for a Mobile & Ohio telegraph operator through all the steps to passenger engineer on the Illinois Central, an important job in those days.

He settled in Jackson, Tennessee, while still with the Mobile & Ohio, and his proud boast was that he always got his train through on time. Casey had been given the crack assignment, Old 382, the *Cannon Ball,* in the early morning of April 30, 1900, and while driving through a thick fog near Vaughn, Mississippi, he saw a freight train a few feet ahead on his track. He ordered his Negro fireman to jump, stuck to his cab, and though he was unable to prevent a crash, kept his load on the rails, and saved the passengers in the 12 coaches. His scalded body was removed from the tangled wreckage and buried at Jackson, Tennessee. It became the custom for engineers to salute his grave with a whistle as they passed the cemetery. Before long doggerel celebrating the engineer was being recited and sung. It is believed that a Negro worker in Memphis first gave the ballad wide popularity. Eddie Newton scored it and had it published. Every singer felt free to add a verse or two, some of which were none too complimentary to Casey's widow who at length appealed to law to restrain public performers from singing the slanderous additions.

CAYCE, **7.3** *m.* (131 pop.), was the boyhood home of "Casey" Jones.

At **14.3** *m.* on State 94 is the junction with a graveled road.

Right on this road, 2 *m.*, to the junction with an unimproved dirt road beside an Indian fortification, on a high bluff known locally as Indian Hill, and to archeologists as O'Byam's Fort. It is believed to be one of the most ancient mounds in the Mississippi Valley. This site, from which many artifacts have been taken, has been partially obliterated by cultivation and by the grading of a road.

Right 4 *m.* from the Indian fortification on the unimproved dirt road, which follows Bayou De Chien Creek, to the FORT BAYOU DE CHIEN MOUNDS, locally known as the Roberts Mounds and believed to be very old. The seven large mounds that form the group average 15 to 20 feet in height, 50 to 100 feet in diameter, are grouped rather closely together in an area of about five acres, and are built upon an elevated artificial plateau rising 10 to 15 feet above the surrounding plain. The largest three mounds are quadrangular, while the others are circular. One high mound stands like a sentinel dominating the entire scene.

A short distance from the mound group a PREHISTORIC CANAL, locally known as Lake Slough, connects Bayou De Chien Creek with Obion Creek, at the northern end of which is another group of mounds representing a prehistoric village site locally known as McLeod's Bluffs Mounds. The canal, approximately five miles in length, is believed to be entirely artificial and to have been used as a waterway, for the passage of canoes between the two ancient cities that were separated by an almost impenetrable jungle. The ancient Bayou De Chien, unlike the present stream whose course was changed by the earthquake of 1811–12, found its way to the Mississippi by way of Reelfoot Lake at a point southwest of the lake. Canoes making the river trip had to make a dangerous 100-mile voyage in order to reach a point five miles away. Within a primeval forest here are unexplored mounds and fortifications which, according to scientists, present the richest opportunity for archeological research in southwestern Kentucky. This site was mentioned by Rafinesque in his *Ancient History of Kentucky,* written in 1824.

In HICKMAN, 15.9 *m.* on State 94 (306 alt., 2,321 pop.), is one of the two seats of Fulton County, a river town that serves the surrounding agricultural region as a shipping point. In the town are some small manufacturing plants including several cotton gins. Hickman is built on three levels of a great bluff overlooking the Mississippi River; the bottoms contain the business section; on top of the bluff, 200 feet above the second level of the town, is the main residential section with churches, schools, a library, and a courthouse, from which there is an exceptionally fine view. In his *Life on the Mississippi,* Samuel L. Clemens mentioned Hickman as one of the most beautiful towns along the river. A concrete sea wall, erected by the U.S. Government in 1934 to protect the low-lying business district, withstood the flood of 1937. This site, known first as Mills Point, was settled in 1819 by James Mills whose cabin home became a shipping point for the Mississippi River trade. Long ox trains rolled laboriously over the roads to Mills Point bearing the produce of farms to be shipped to the markets. Returning, they carried merchandise to the inland towns and supplies to the settlers. To Mills Point pioneers came in their covered wagons and ferried over the Mississippi to settle Missouri and Arkansas. In the days of the great Ohio and Mississippi river packets, this was the metropolis of an extensive area. In 1834 a large part of the area was purchased by a Tennessee settler who named it Hickman in honor of his wife's family. Early accounts of the village reprinted in the Hickman *Courier* in 1885 record that in 1840, when the town's population was only 500, its exports included 50,000 bushels of wheat, 200,000 bushels of corn, 3,000 hogsheads of tobacco, 2,000 bales of cotton, and 30,000 dozen turkeys and chickens.

Fulton County, especially the rich flat alluvial land south and west of Hickman, raises much of the cotton grown in Kentucky. The land in this region is held mostly in large tracts, still called plantations, and is worked mainly by Negro tenants and sharecroppers *(see Labor).* The landowners live in town and drive to their plantations each day. Groups of pickaninnies play about the doors of the tiny cabins scattered along the roadside and in the fields of cotton, corn, and alfalfa. During the cotton-picking season, in September, the snowy fields are full of Negro men, women, and children, often dressed in bright colors; they pick the fleecy bolls, which are dropped into long canvas bags that are dragged behind them across the hot fields. The picking is often done to the drone of the traditional songs.

The northern end of REELFOOT LAKE *(hunting and fishing)* is on State 94 at 29 *m.* This lake, most of which is in Tennessee, was created by sudden inundation by the Mississippi River during the New Madrid earthquake of 1811–12. Twenty miles in length, and varying from one to five miles in width, the lake covers a submerged forest that lifts skeleton arms above the surface of the water. Wild game, ducks, geese, and other waterfowl inhabit the region, and the deep pools abound with game fish. In Tennessee the lake is a part of a State preserve.

FULTON, 44.1 *m.* (357 alt., 3,503 pop.) *(see Tour 9),* is at the junction with US 45 *(see Tour 9).*

At 45 *m.* US 51–45 crosses the Tennessee Line, 10.8 miles north of Martin, Tenn. *(US 45, see Tenn. Tour 10)* and 10.9 miles north of Union City, Tenn. *(US 51, see Tenn. Tour 11).*

Tour 11

South Portsmouth—Vanceburg—Maysville—Alexandria; **109.7** *m.*
State 10.

Hard-surfaced roadbed throughout.
Chesapeake and Ohio R.R. roughly parallels this route.
Hotels chiefly in cities.

State 10, called the Mary Inglis (or Ingles) Trail, runs along the
Ohio River most of the way between South Portsmouth and Vanceburg,
makes a detour to the outer Knobs plateau, comes back to the river at
Maysville, and then relegates itself again to the back country, though
at several places it is fairly close to the Ohio in point of miles.

At one time the slopes of the billowing plateau that rears up beside
the Ohio were densely wooded. Besides the common maples and sycamores, this region had a good deal of poplar and some scrub pine.
Then, in the early nineteenth century, lumbering took away the best
timber, leaving the land scraggly and subject to erosion. All the top-
soil was soon carried off down the river. Attempts to till the badly
wornout land have almost completely ruined it, and today it climbs
bare to a meager tree line.

Except for Vanceburg and Maysville, the communities along the
route are tiny, and cluster beside the highway or along the railroad
tracks. The road is seldom out of sight of habitation, which is usually
a frame house that has somehow managed to remain erect. The people
eke out a slender existence by farming and have a few mangy dogs,
cattle, and horses, but they go out hunting 'possum and rabbits during
the fall season and at all times seem less unhappy than the stranger
expects them to be.

Life along the route is closely tied up with the river and the road;
the traveler is conscious of one or both throughout his journey. From
1780 to 1815, the period when the wave of Western settlement crossed
the Alleghenies and penetrated the Ohio River region, the river brought
boatloads of restless immigrants down to Limestone (now Maysville),
then picked them up again and took them westward. Some people remained in Limestone and along the Kentucky shoreline. Except at
Limestone, Vanceburg, and Augusta, the succeeding era of great river
traffic brought little prosperity to the immigrants scattered along the
river and among the near-by knobs.

When the Maysville & Big Sandy R.R. rushed up to compete with
the steamers in the early 1880's, the towns became sprightly and hope-
ful. But the C. & O. R.R. bought the Maysville & Big Sandy in 1888,

and made it merely a coal-bearing branch of the main road terminating at Russell, Ky. When the development of the steel industry in northeastern Ohio shifted importance to roads cut through eastern Kentucky to the coal fields, Russell became a great freight terminal and Ashland a steel center; the rest of the Kentucky side of the river languished.

SOUTH PORTSMOUTH, 0 *m.* (660 alt., 500 pop.), a scattering of frame houses looking at Portsmouth on the Ohio side of the river at the mouth of the Scioto, is on THE SITE OF LOWER TOWN, the first white village in Kentucky. The group of log cabins was established by French traders with the help and protection of Shawnee many years prior to the French and Indian War (1753). An entry in Christopher Gist's journal of 1751 tells of his visiting the French traders who lived in the Shawnee town built on both sides of the Ohio at the mouth of the Scioto River. In July 1765 Col. George Croghan, then an agent of the British Government, also visited the place and noted in his journal:

"On the Ohio, just below the mouth of the Scioto, on a high bank, near forty feet, formerly stood the Shawneese town called Lower Town —which was all carried away, except three or four houses, by a great flood. I was in the town at the time. Although the banks of the Ohio were so high, yet the water was nine feet over the top, which obliged the whole town to take to their canoes and move with their effects to the hills. They returned to the south bank of the Ohio, but abandoned the settlement because of fear of the Virginians during the French and Indian War."

South Portsmouth is at the junction with US 23 *(see Tour 1).*

Between South Portsmouth and Vanceburg the road crawls along at the foot of the Kentucky hills, usually not far from the river and the railroad. Sometimes the river is lost beneath an intervening terrace, but it always comes in sight again, its muddy waters spreading toward the Ohio shore. For most of the distance the traveler sees more of Ohio than of Kentucky, because the Kentucky hills crowd the road.

In the summer, back from the river a short distance, the wild strawberry shines like red tufts on a new green carpet; the wild blackberry grows in great, thorny tangles; the pawpaw is plentiful in hillside thickets; and the persimmon bears fruit for the coon and 'possum, which boys hunt at night.

The road passes houses scattered in the hills and "hollers" and along the railroad tracks. The farms are ravined and water-cut, and the farmyards littered with discarded objects for which the farmer still hopes to find some use. A few scraggly cornfields labor up the slopes.

The people back in the hills here still prefer the square dance, play the fiddle, and sing songs such as:

> There was an old nig in Kentuck brake,
> He made the woods all 'round him shake,
> And this was the song he used for to sing,
> 'Ree, raw, my Dinah gal,
> Can't you git along, my darlin'?

The highway closely follows the trail taken by Mary Inglis in her escape from Indians in 1756. During that year a war party of Mingos living on the north side of the Kanawha attacked a settlement within the present limits of Westmoreland County, Virginia. Mrs. Inglis, two of her children, and a sister-in-law were captured and taken to the Mingo villages. Her children were taken away, and her sister-in-law was forced to run the gauntlet, but Mrs. Inglis, because of her skill in cooking, won the respectful interest of the natives. When a band of the Indians set out for Big Bone Lick *(see Tour 12)* to make salt, they took with them Mrs. Inglis and an old Dutch woman—also a prisoner— who thus became the first white women to step into what is now the State of Kentucky.

At Big Bone Lick, the two women escaped from the Indians, traveled through what is now Kenton County to the southern shore of the Ohio, and finally reached Big Sandy River. They crossed this stream on a floating log and continued up the Ohio until they reached the Kanawha, which they followed toward Mrs. Inglis' home in the mountains. Before reaching civilization, the Dutch woman, crazed by her privations, attempted to kill Mrs. Inglis, who swam the Kanawha and escaped. Finally, after 40 days of wilderness travel, Mrs. Inglis reached her friends in the frontier settlement.

At 19 *m.* the road leaves the river and cuts into the hills. The scene changes swiftly; tall hills rise suddenly with great topsy-turvy stretches of slope etched haphazardly by trees and hillside fences. Then again the route comes out to the river, affording a sweeping view up and down stream.

VANCEBURG, 22.4 *m.* (523 alt., 1,388 pop.), stretches finger-like along the river beneath a barrier of steep hills. The town presses tightly against the road, which passes rickety frame houses, then more substantial dwellings before reaching a compact business section along one side of which is a line of similar two-story brick buildings connected with the curb by a porch roof supported by hitching posts. Old wooden signs, nearly all white lettered on black, announce the wares—hardware, furniture, dry goods, clothing, shoes, groceries. The store selling sodas, powders, and patent medicine has no sign. On the opposite side of the street are a bank; the office of the county agricultural agent, with a dentist's office above; a barber shop; a feed, grain, and farm tools establishment; a garage; a restaurant; and a poolroom. Just across the rail tracks is a hotel. Here in a capsule is the economic center of the average small Kentucky town, in an area small enough to be photographed in a single picture.

Vanceburg was a port of entry in pioneer days for hunters from Pennsylvania and the East who came down the Ohio in search of game in the wild hills and well-watered valleys to the south. Later, as the packets plied the Ohio River, Vanceburg started to take on the proportions of a town. Since it was never an important steamboat stop, the community saw a good deal more of the sad aspects of river life than of the gay. For example, on June 2, 1832, it saw the paddlewheeler *Hornet*, captained by a man named Sullivan, struck broadside by a southwest gale. When it capsized, 20 passengers drowned. The overturned boat was pulled ashore by the *Guyandotte*.

Vanceburg took on life in 1865, when a legislative act made it the seat of Lewis County and lawyers, adventurers, and business opportunists arrived.

Left from Vanceburg, on State 59, a graveled road, to KINNICONNICK *(furnished camps, $10 per week)*, 6 *m.*, where there is excellent fishing, swimming, and boating. Kinniconnick Creek, whose clear waters are well stocked with bass, winds for many miles past old mill sites and through quiet green valleys.

At Vanceburg, the road cuts back into the hills again, to ride the ridges, coast down into hollows, and make whiplash turns; when snow and ice cover it in winter, the road is as dangerous as a toboggan slide. Small, unpainted houses are visible on the hills and in the valley notches, and here and there a high catwalk over a creek gives access to a remote farmhouse. The soil is fairly good for pasturage, and multiple hay stacks, nosed by cattle and sheep, squat in the fields.

HUNTER HOUSE, 25 *m.*, a small log structure now weatherboarded, was built by W. B. Parker for use on his annual hunting expeditions in the early nineteenth century.

Tips of far-off hills make a hedgerow on the horizon as the route twists through several villages bent by the road. The complete lack of filling stations and roadside advertisements is conspicuous.

At 36.8 *m.* is CABIN CREEK, spanned by an old covered bridge. From the mouth of the creek, marauding Indians once forded across the Ohio River. Leading out from the creek mouth to the Upper Blue Licks were a lower war road and an upper war road, along which the trees were marked with crude drawings of wild animals, the sun, and the moon.

MAYSVILLE, 52.1 *m.* (448 alt., 6,557 pop.) *(see Tour 15)*, is at the junction with US 68 *(see Tour 15)* and US 62 *(see Tour 14)*.

Above Maysville, State 10 rises to a point offering a fine view of the river, its boats, the lanky new steel bridge connecting Maysville with Aberdeen, Ohio, and flat bottomland along the Ohio shore. Most of the Ohio River is under Kentucky jurisdiction. When the Northwest Territory was carved out by the United States, the low-water mark was its southern limit. After Kentucky and West Virginia were split from Virginia, the Ohio River bordering Kentucky was included in its territory.

This stretch of the river was at one time crowded with river craft *(see Tour 12)*. In those days a river steamer was a floating palace, glistening with white paint and gilding. It had thick carpets, tiny white beds, glittering chandeliers, fine music, and an elegant table, set with all the delicacies of the season in lavish profusion. Eating went on all day. At the bar, mint juleps and planters' punch were mixed by wizards with shiny black faces and white aprons. Always lolling near by was the cardsharp.

Defective boilers and a mania for speed often ripped open the boat hulls, set them afire, and took many lives. The races between the *Handy* and the *Phaeton* led up to such calamity. On June 28, 1881, as both boats were running side by side for Brook's Bar near the Maysville bend of the river, the boiler of the *Phaeton* blew up, tore off the pilot house and smokestacks of the *Handy,* threw the pilot onto the Ohio shore, and killed several deckhands. A few years later one of the through mail packets, the *Bostonia,* took fire while discharging cargo at the Maysville wharf. Its cargo of cattle stampeded. Cut loose, the boat drifted to a near-by bank and burned to the water's edge. These mishaps sometimes had comic relief. Some panicky passengers even took life-belts to bed with them. After a false alarm one buxom lady in a white nightgown constrained by a deflated belt, burst breathlessly from the ladies' cabin. "Blow me up," she shrieked. "For God's sake, won't somebody blow me up!"

At **56.9** *m.* is the junction with State 8, a graveled road.

Right on this road to MINERVA (127 pop.). In an old cemetery here is the GRAVE OF LEWIS CRAIG (1737–1825), pioneer Baptist minister, who brought the Traveling Church from Spotsylvania County, Virginia, to Kentucky in 1781 *(see Tour 3).* The BRACKEN CHURCH at Minerva was built by Craig, who was a stonemason as well as a preacher. Craig was the pastor of this church from 1793 through 1807.

The FRAZEE HOUSE *(open on request),* **64.8** *m.,* is a one-and-a-half story gray-painted brick house (R) with outside chimneys and a long veranda built in 1795 by Samuel Frazee, Indian fighter and scout under Gen. George Rogers Clark. The land upon which the building stands was said to have been bought from the Indians for several hundred bushels of salt.

GERMANTOWN, **65.2** *m.* (490 alt., 283 pop.), is a sizable town drawn out along several sharp turns in the highway. It was laid out by Whitfield Craig in 1784, called Buchanan Station, and later settled by Pennsylvania Germans. The Germantown Fair and Horse Show has been held annually since 1854 during the last week in August. Livestock, horses, poultry, and many kinds of farm products and handicrafts are exhibited, and prizes awarded to the winners.

Between Germantown and Brooksville the road runs through open hilly terrain punctuated by tree clumps. Most of this is pasture land, but a few frugal fields of tobacco vary the monotony of the agricultural pattern.

BROOKSVILLE, **72** *m.* (925 alt., 615 pop.), seat of Bracken County since 1832, centers about a small row of shops with hitching post porches, a larger row strung along a sidewalk several feet high, and a huge open space on which stands the yellow brick courthouse with its clock tower. The region about Brooksville, first known as Woodward's Crossroad, chiefly produces burley tobacco.

Right from Brooksville on State 19, a paved road, to AUGUSTA, **9.5** *m.* (444 alt., 1,675 pop.), beautifully situated on a high bank of the Ohio River. It has an excellent harbor and is an important shipping point for tobacco. Augusta College, one of the first Methodist schools, was here as early as 1799. When the large forest trees were cleared for the village site in 1792, numerous skeletons and arti-facts were found, indicating that this was a prehistoric burial ground.

During the War between the States, Augusta was the scene of a battle between Morgan's cavalry, led by Gen. Basil W. Duke, and Federal Home Guards under Col. Joshua T. Bradford. Many of the Home Guards were Southern sympathizers who had been impressed for service by Colonel Bradford. Since the Home Guards were using the brick houses of the town as garrisons, the fighting took place in the streets. General Duke had to burn many of the buildings to dislodge the Federal troops, who finally surrendered. Two gunboats had been stationed at the landing for the protection of the town, but as soon as General Duke's guns were turned on them, they steamed off upriver. This was a Pyrrhic victory for Duke: the heavy loss in officers and men defeated his original purpose—to ford the Ohio River below Augusta and march toward Cincinnati.

POWERSVILLE, 75.4 *m.* (103 pop.), a mere sprinkling of houses, was settled about 1783 by Capt. Philip Buckner, soldier of the Revolutionary War. The GRAVE OF CAPTAIN BUCKNER, near the western limits of the town, has been enclosed with an iron fence.

At WILLOW, 76.1 *m.* (500 alt., 12 pop.), is a junction with State 22 *(see Tour 13)*.

The route wanders about among hills that fall into gullies; the land stretches away in endless wrinkles to a far horizon.

As the highway goes north, it touches the outer Bluegrass, and at 105.5 *m.* leads down between hills flanked everywhere by spare, softly molded hills with long slopes. Clumps of trees decorate a landscape green in summer, bleak and brown in winter.

ALEXANDRIA, 109.7 *m.* (513 alt., 424 pop.) *(see Tour 3)*, is at the junction with US 27 *(see Tour 3)*.

Tour 12

(Cincinnati, Ohio)—Covington—Warsaw—Carrollton—Louisville; US 42. Ohio Line to Louisville, 106.9 *m.*

Hard-surfaced roadbed throughout.
Accommodations of all kinds available; hotels chiefly in cities.

US 42, the down-river route between Cincinnati and Louisville, swings cross-country at Covington and does not meet the Ohio River again until Warsaw is neared. In most places between this point and a short distance beyond Carrollton, highway and river run side by side accompanied by the rolling Kentucky hills with their masses of foliage and, across the river, by the low bottomlands and low hills of Indiana.

The route once more strays away from the river, though closely parallels it all the way to Louisville.

Numerous villages and a few small county seats lie along the route. But pastures, corn fields, patches of tobacco, livestock, and grass- or tree-covered hills are seen more frequently.

US 42 and US 25 *(see Ohio Tours 16 and 22)* are united as they cross the Ohio Line, 0 *m.*, at the north side of the Ohio River, by way of the Suspension Bridge *(toll 15¢)*.

COVINGTON, 0.5 *m.* (513 alt., 65,252 pop.) *(see Covington)*.

Points of Interest: Carneal House, Monte Casino, Devou Park, Birthplace of Frank Duveneck, Latonia Race Track, and others.

Covington is at the junction with US 25 *(see Tour 4)*.

Between Covington and FLORENCE, 9.8 *m.* (935 alt., 450 pop.), US 42 is united with US 25 *(see Tour 4)*.

The highway crosses a countryside with low, sloping hills tumbling back on both sides of the road. Cornfields alternate with clumps of elms, maples, and oaks.

At 20.4 *m.* is the junction with a graveled road.

Right on this road to BIG BONE LICK, 3 *m.* (20 pop.), whose few scattered houses, a church, a deserted hotel, and a somewhat bedraggled lake in a 100-acre valley, is one of the Nation's outstanding prehistoric boneyards. Long ago the sulphur springs and salt formations of this valley attracted hordes of mastodons and other gigantic mammals. Many of them mired in the soft soil of this area, or died otherwise, and their bones were preserved through millenniums. Later, Indians from as far north as Lake Erie came here to kill the deer, buffalo, and other game that habitually visited the lick in large numbers; the place was apparently a neutral hunting ground for many tribes, as no relics of Indian battles have ever been found here. In 1739 the French-Canadian explorer, Charles de Langueil, arrived at the lick, probably led by Indian guides. Celeron de Blainville is thought to have stopped here in 1749, while engaged in his mission of burying lead plates at various points along the Ohio River, claiming the Ohio Valley for France. It was from Big Bone Lick that Mary Inglis and an old Dutch woman made their successful escape from the Indians in 1756 *(see Tour 11)*. When Col. George Croghan made a trip here in 1765, he wrote in his *Journal* of the large quantities of bones scattered about the springs. James Douglas, a Virginian, who visited here with a party in 1773, found the valley covered with the bones of huge animals, some of them half buried in the bog, others lying in a heap where they had fallen. The visitors used mastodon ribs for tent poles, and vertebrae for seats. When they left they carried with them mastodon teeth weighing 10 pounds each, tusks 11 feet long, and four- and five-foot thigh bones.

As the fame of the great bones spread, more and more expeditions came here to collect them. In 1805 Thomas Jefferson, as an official of the American Philosophical Society, had a party gather one of the most complete collections ever taken from the lick (an ignorant servant later caused the entire collection to be ground into fertilizer). A Dr. William Goforth of Cincinnati, at his own expense, dug up a number of notable specimens, among them the bones of an enormous three-toed sloth. In 1840 it was estimated that the bones of 100 mastodons, 20 Arctic elephants, and numerous other mammals had been removed. Specimens were still plentiful two years later when the English geologist, Lyell, came here; but the hunt for bones went on until they were all gone. Museums in Europe and America now exhibit some of Big Bone's ancient visitors.

In the period preceding the War between the States, Big Bone Lick became a fashionable watering place for young ladies who had gone into "declines" and for men and women who ate too much and exercised too little. A hotel was built to accommodate those who came here to drink sulphur water. Other fads and more fashionable resorts caused the local spa to disappear; the abandoned hotel is its only relic today.

US 42 now runs a course between high hills whose long slopes have cornfields staggering up to their tops. Here and there phalanxes of young, slim trees march down from the hillcrest to the road. For a mile the route crosses the top of the plateau, then sinks down between the hills once more. At 30.6 m. the road moves to the bank of the Ohio River, which makes a big bend at this point. The Kentucky hills bare occasional rock outcroppings above the highway. With a few brief interruptions, road and river move side by side, paced by low, broad bottomlands on the Indiana side that run back to a continuous chain of far hills.

WARSAW, 35.6 m. (459 alt., 800 pop.), on a level terrace overlooking the Ohio River, was once a prominent river port. A little coal is brought here by boats, and a side-wheel ferry makes cross-river trips to the Indiana shore; but the Warsaw of today depends upon its position as a trading center and county seat for its life. The town boasts that poverty is unknown in it and that its county jail is seldom occupied. The JAIL (L), on the second floor of a small brick building, with thick vertical bars of stone across the front, is sufficiently forbidding to discourage the most obstinate wrong-doers.

In the center of the public square is the dun-colored, two-story GALLATIN COUNTY COURTHOUSE, erected in 1838, with a bell tower. It was remodeled in 1938–39. PAYNE MANOR, at the western end of town (R), overlooking the river, is a brick Greek Revival structure of two stories, painted white, that was built in 1850 by the son of Gen. John Payne, an officer of the Revolutionary War. Four Corinthian columns ornament the small portico, and a balcony is below the front upper story windows. In the hall hangs a painting of the steamer, *Jacob Strader,* which plied the Ohio in the fifties.

Warsaw is at the junction with State 35 *(see Tour 5).*

At 36.1 m. is (L) an EMERGENCY LANDING FIELD for airplanes. The broad, level grass plot runs back from the road to the rim of hills.

Between Warsaw and Carrollton US 42 twists and turns with the Ohio, sometimes dipping out of sight of it for a brief period; the hills are always near.

The towns along the way—Warsaw, Ghent, and Carrollton—are called river towns because they once depended on the Ohio for their existence. Today steamers and barges loaded with steel, sand, or stone pass them but do not stop; dredges sometimes pause to clean the river channel of its silt and debris, then move on; even the shanty boats make a brief stay. Main St. is now the paved highway back from the river front several blocks, and only some old houses along Front or River St. remain to show the once-intimate relationship of town and river.

These old houses, or their predecessors along the banks, saw the pageantry of river traffic in all its mutations: the canoe used by the Indians, trappers, and explorers; the flatboat or Kentucky "broadhorn," carrier of cargo and settlers downriver for fifty years; the keel-boat that could go up-stream as well as down; after 1811 the steamboat, which became more magnificent with each new decade. Individual steamers acquired distinct personalities up-river and down, based on their speed, showiness, captain, crew, cuisine, musicians, the splendor of the ballroom, and the gaiety of the entertainment. There were also floating stores, stocked with groceries, dry goods, and endless bric-a-brac, tieing up at cobblestoned levees to be met by a bevy of excited women. And by the river bank was the wharf boat, which served as a wharf, freight house, exchange, and gathering place for the lusty roustabouts. When the showboats came, life along the river reached its height.

Before the railroads finally took over the river's commerce, towns like Warsaw, Ghent, and Carrollton each had landing places, warehouses, creaking drays, odorous drinking taverns. All the river towns received their foodstuffs, clothing, furniture, raw materials, from the boats, and by them shipped out their farm and garden produce, livestock, lumber, and whatever products they manufactured. They became so identified with the river that they took on some of the color and light-heartedness characteristic of the rough men who manned the boats and rousted the freight. A small cannon was fired when a steamer, often racing with another boat beside it, was approaching a town. On his deck would be the captain, preening himself in a fancy suit. In half-an-hour or an hour the freight would be taken care of and the boat would be off, hellbent for the next stopping place. Not until their boat put up somewhere could the rivermen resume their boasting, their drinking of whisky that was like greased lightning, and settle old scores with wrestling and gouging matches.

Mike Fink was one of them. "I can hit like fourth-proof lightnin' an' every lick I make in the woods lets in an acre o' sunshine. I can out-run, out-jump, out-shoot, out-brag, out-drink, an' out-fight—rough-an'-tumble; no holts barred—ary man on both sides the river from Pittsburgh to New Orleans an' back ag'in to St. Louie," Mike said. The river encouraged boasting. Every boatman liked to think that his was the fastest boat, under the finest captain, manned by the best crew. The boats were so light in draft that, as one captain said, "we can pass over a heavy mountain dew." The shallowness of the river in places was the reason.

GHENT, 44.9 *m.* (389 pop.), lies below a rim of hills on a small plain looking down at the river. Its houses reflect its age and settled ways of life. Ghent was founded in 1809 by 13 families from the Rappahannock River region of Virginia, and named in 1814 by Henry Clay for the Belgian city where the peace treaty between the United States and Great Britain was signed.

The BAPTIST CHURCH (L), erected in 1843, is the fifth church the congregation has had since its organization in 1800 as a result of the great revival at the mouth of the Kentucky River. The red brick, story-and-a-half structure is Greek Revival in style and has curved brick columns on its portico. When subscriptions were being taken to erect the present church, the donations included sheepskins, bags of wool, bales of hay, and several barrels of whisky. It is said that in the early years of the church, whenever the preacher "went for dinner," the whisky bottle was always set on the table. The FOURTH BAPTIST CHURCH, now a residence, is on Sanders Pike (L), opposite the cemetery. It is a small story-and-a-half brick structure, painted white.

John Taylor who attended the revival meeting at the mouth of the Kentucky River was constrained to write:

"From the dull feelings of my heart, I took the text which suited my own state—'Lord, help me." I continued but a short time, for I felt myself very worthless. After which they continued on, in prayer, praise, and exhortation, with much noise, at times, till late at night. Some were rejoicing, having lately obtained deliverance; others groaning in tears, under a pensive load of guilt. My own heart was so barren and hard, that I wished myself out of sight, or lying under the seats where the people sat, or trodden under their feet. Many of the people tarried all night."

At the western limits of the village is (L) a three-story brick building with tall, narrow windows, the FORMER GHENT COLLEGE, once a well-known institution. An elementary school is here now.

RIVERVIEW (L), 48.6 m., is a two-story Greek Revival house overlooking the river from a hill. Built in 1805 from brick burned on the place, the handsome white structure has Ionic columns in front of its small recessed portico.

In 1781, when Benjamin Craig I came from Virginia with his brother Lewis and members of the congregation who formed the Traveling Baptist Church (see Tour 3), he brought with him his wife and three small children. In the journey across the mountains some of the men usually traveled ahead to clear the trail and scout for Indians. The older children drove the cattle and tried to prevent them from straying off the trail. Next came the women on horseback; the children and bedding were strapped with willows in panniers on the sides of the horses.

One morning Mrs. Craig laid the baby on a bed of leaves while helping to make ready for the day's journey. After she had mounted her horse, her four-year-old daughter asked if the baby might ride in the basket with her. This the mother granted and went on her way. After an hour's journey through the forest, Mrs. Craig looked back and saw only two children in the panniers. She quickly gave the alarm, and the baby's father with several of the men hurriedly rode back in search of the baby. After several hours, the child was found sleeping on the bed of leaves. This child was Benjamin Craig II, for whom Riverview was built.

The GEORGE CRAIG HOUSE, directly across the Ohio River in Indiana, and plainly visible from the highway, was built in 1807 by the brother of Benjamin Craig II.

At 51.6 *m.* is the junction with US 227 *(see Tour 12A).*

CARROLLTON, 52.6 *m.* (484 alt., 2,409 pop.), stretching along the river bank, is a quiet old town of tree-shaded streets and old houses of considerable charm. The town was incorporated in 1794 under the name of Port William. In 1838 it was renamed in honor of Charles Carroll of Carrollton, Maryland, signer of the Declaration of Independence. The town was platted by Benjamin Craig I, who donated the land upon which the courthouse was built. The tiny stone CARROLLTON JAIL (R), with a high iron fence around it and vertical stone bars across its front, looks like something out of Dumas.

High on a slope (R) overlooking Highland Ave. (US 42) is the BUTLER HOUSE, a one-story Georgian Colonial structure of brown brick with a foundation of Kentucky marble. Front and side entrances have gracious fanlighted doorways with side lights. A large central hall leads back to a spacious library with windows overlooking a court from which there is a fine view of the river. The house was built in 1825 by Charles Stringfellow for Maj. Gen. William Orlando Butler *(see Tour 12A),* who, with other members of the Butler family, is buried in the Butler Memorial State Park *(see Tour 12A).*

On Highland Ave. (L), standing close to the sidewalk, is the DARLING HOUSE, erected prior to 1850. Pilasters ornament the façade of this gray-painted brick house.

The road crosses the KENTUCKY RIVER at 53 *m.,* near its confluence with the Ohio, on a high-arched bridge. An advertisement from the Cincinnati *Centinel of the North-West Territory* tells of the opening of business on the Kentucky River:

Notice—the subscriber informs the gentlemen, merchants, and emigrants to Kentucky, that he will be at the mouth of the Kentucky River on the first day of February next, with a sufficient number of boats to transport all goods, etc., which they may think proper to entrust him with, up the river. He will also keep a store-house for the reception of any goods which may be left with him. Carriage of goods to Frankfort 50 cents per hundred, to Sluke's warehouse 75 cents, to Warwick 100 cents, Dick's River 125 cents.

Mouth of Kentucky, Jan. 15, 1795.   ELIJAH CRAIG, JR.

At 54.2 *m.* is the junction with State 36, a paved road.

Left on this road, which follows the course of the Ohio River, to the HOAGLAND HOUSE, 6.9 *m.,* a one-story structure, Georgian Colonial in style, erected in Hunter's Bottom in 1838. This time-mellowed house contains many old furnishings.

MILTON, 11 *m.* (450 alt., 347 pop.), was established in 1789 by the Virginia Legislature, three years before Kentucky became a State. Milton is opposite Madison, Indiana, with which it is connected by a bridge *(toll 20¢).*

Right from Milton, 5 *m.*, on Peck's Pike, an unimproved road, to the PRESTON HOUSE, a Greek Revival structure built by Col. John Preston. This structure, among fine old trees, faces the river; it is of brick, later plastered and weather-boarded, and contains 15 rooms. A spiral stairway leads to the second floor. The woodwork is embellished with a narrow stripe of gold leaf, which still glistens with its former luster. On the walls are the original painted decorations. The SMOKE-HOUSE, in the yard, is a tall brick building with four tiers of poles, designed to hold 100 hogs. In the center of the dirt floor is a pit where hickory logs were kept burning until the meat was satisfactorily cured. NORFOLK SCHOOL, the brick build-ing now a tenant house, was built by Mrs. Preston as a chapel and school.

Left from Milton on State 37, which becomes the main side route, to LOOKOUT POINT on MILTON HILL, 12 *m.*, which affords a sweeping view of the Ohio River, Hunter's Bottom, and of Madison, Indiana.

At 23.2 *m.* on State 37 is Bedford.

West of Carrollton US 42 breaks away from the river and winds be-tween high hills, close to the highway, that are dotted with sparse clus-ters of trees. This is farming country and cattle and sheep are seen on hillside pastures. The road climbs up to a plateau, a rolling highland presenting spacious vistas of fields, farmhouses, and ravines with ever-greens.

BEDFORD, 65.1 *m.* (892 alt., 286 pop.), seat of Trimble County, was incorporated in 1816. The town is surrounded by valley farms producing tobacco, grain, and livestock.

Bedford is at the junction with State 37.

Still crossing the plateau that reveals tiers of hills rising to a wide, tree-hazed horizon (L), the highway makes a sweeping curve and passes (L) KENTUCKY TAVERN, 70.1 *m.*, a long, low story-and-a-half structure that was an important stopping place in stagecoach days. Half frame and half brick, the white building has dormers.

SLIGO (10 pop.) is met at 73.8 *m.;* then tourist cabins soon appear along the way, some of them of whitewashed logs. The route continues over high, choppy terrain, passing farmsteads, pastures, little log pig pens, and clumps of oak, evergreen, and sycamore.

US 42 descends into PROSPECT, 93.9 *m.* (484 alt., 30 pop.), in the Louisville metropolitan area. The place was settled in 1783 by people from Virginia. It is said to have received its name about 60 years ago, when the narrow gauge railroad, which was being built along the river, seemed a long time in reaching the community.

Between Prospect and Louisville, a four-lane highway runs through a well-to-do metropolitan area with many new houses.

The TOMB OF ZACHARY TAYLOR, 99.7 *m.*, is in a parklike area (R), once part of the Taylor farm and now in the custody of the Federal Government. Adjoining the park is (R) the TAYLOR HOUSE *(private)*, where the twelfth President of the United States grew to manhood. The two-and-a-half-story house, built of brick, is on ample grounds extending along the west side of the TAYLOR MEMORIAL CEMETERY, where members of the Taylor family are buried. A driveway, bordered with shrubbery and century-old pine, maple, and walnut trees, leads around the house to the entrance. Across the front and sides of the building are wide porches, evidently later additions. Two paneled doors give entrance to a wide central hall with two rooms on each side. A winding stairway leads to four bedrooms on the second floor. The original four-inch ash flooring is still in good condition.

In 1785 Col. Richard Taylor, a native of Virginia and soldier of the Revolution, brought his family to this place, where he built a log house. Several years later the present building, designed in Virginia, was built and the log cabin was moved to the rear to house slaves. This building, painted white, still stands.

Zachary Taylor (1784–1850), born in Virginia, was nine months old when the family came here. As a boy he roamed the fields near by and hunted along Beargrass Creek. He went to school in a little log schoolhouse near his home before entering William and Mary College. In 1808 he was appointed a first lieutenant in the 7th Regiment of the United States Infantry. Except when he was away on military duty and in the White House, the farm here was always his home. General Taylor's daughter, Knoxie, much against her father's wishes, became the wife of Jefferson Davis, later President of the Confederacy.

LOUISVILLE, 106.9 *m.* (525 alt., 307,745 pop.) *(see Louisville).*

Points of Interest: Speed Museum, Memorial Auditorium, Presbyterian Theological Seminary, Churchill Downs, Cave Hill Cemetery, Cherokee Park, and others.

Louisville is at the junction with US 31E *(see Tour 6)*, US 31W *(see Tour 7)*, and US 60 *(see Tour 16)*.

Tour 12A

Junction with US 42—Butler Memorial State Park—Owenton—Junction with State 40; 61.1 *m.* US 227.

Hard-surfaced roadbed throughout.
Branch of Louisville & Nashville R.R. parallels route between Carrollton and Worthville.
All types of accommodations in towns; limited elsewhere.

This route runs between the Ohio River and the Bluegrass region, traversing hilly farm lands and fertile green valleys.

US 227 branches southeast from its junction with US 42, 0 *m.* *(see Tour 12)*, 0.5 miles east of Carrollton.

BUTLER MEMORIAL STATE PARK *(adm. 10¢, boating, fishing, overnight camping 25¢ each; furnished cabins, couple, $2)*, 2 *m.*, 350 acres of hills and valleys on both sides of the road, was named for

William Orlando Butler (1791–1808). A native of Carrollton, Butler served as a captain in the War of 1812 and was breveted a major for distinguished service in the Battle of New Orleans. He later practiced law at Carrollton, and was a member of the Kentucky House of Representatives, 1817–18, and a Representative in Congress 1839–43. In June 1846 he was appointed major general of volunteers raised to support General Taylor in his invasion of Mexico. In 1848 he succeeded General Scott in the chief command of the United States forces in Mexico. He was an unsuccessful candidate for Vice President of the Democratic Party in 1848, and in 1855 declined appointment as Governor of Nebraska Territory.

The work of developing the park, begun in 1934, has been carried on by the Civilian Conservation Corps. A 30-acre lake has been created by construction of a dam in the upper stretches of the valley. There are two lodges of stone for the caretakers, shelter houses, cabins, and many winding roads and trails. The majority of the one- and two-room cabins are of stone; a few are of logs with stone chimneys.

LOOKOUT POINT, a rough stone tower built in irregular terraces, commands a sweeping view of the Ohio River. Within the park is the THOMAS BUTLER HOUSE *(adm. 25¢)*, now a museum. It is a two-and-one-half-story brick structure shaded by tall elms and surrounded by a terraced wall of stone. The house was designed in the Georgian Colonial style with wide central halls upstairs and down, flanked on each side by two large square rooms. A winding stairway leads to the upper floor. The kitchen wing is separated from the rest of the house by a dog-trot. The house is furnished in the style of the 1860's. It was originally the home of Thomas L. Butler (1789–1879), the eldest son of Percival Butler, and aide to General Jackson at the Battle of New Orleans.

In the little BUTLER CEMETERY near the house are the graves of members of the Butler family. Thomas Butler, born in Kilkenny, Ireland, April 8, 1720, had five sons, all of whom attained eminence in America. The five brothers and their immediate descendants saw military service in all of the contemporary wars of this country. General Lafayette said of the family, "When I wanted a thing well done, I ordered a Butler to do it." Among others is the GRAVE OF GEN. PERCIVAL BUTLER, one of the five sons of Thomas Butler and the father of William Orlando and of Thomas L. Butler.

South of the park, the road passes through an undulating, well-watered region whose limestone soil is well suited to stock raising. Pastures with grazing sheep and cattle alternate with fields of tobacco, buckwheat, corn, and barley.

From the top of the hill at 13 *m.* is a widespreading view of the countryside and of the Kentucky River valley.

NEW LIBERTY, 19.7 *m.* (190 pop.), once an important trading center for a productive farming area, has been decreasing in population for many years because of the impoverishment of the soil in the region.

The BAPTIST CHURCH (L) was established here in 1801, 18 years before the county was formed. The old bell in the tower has been in constant use since 1841.

At **23.1** *m.* is the junction with State 35 *(see Tour 5)*; US 227 and State 35 are united for 7.9 miles.

OWENTON, **30.4** *m.* (1,000 alt., 975 pop.), and Owen County, of which it is the seat, are named for Col. Abraham Owen, an early settler who was prominent in the War of 1812. He was killed in the Battle of Tippecanoe. The stately old OWEN COUNTY COURTHOUSE, built of brick in the Greek Revival style in 1850, was occupied by Federal troops during the War between the States.

Owenton is at the junction with State 22 *(see Tour 13)* and State 35 *(see Tour 5)*. State 35 and US 227 are united for 2.1 miles south of Owenton.

1. Right from Owenton on an unmarked road to the THOMAS LAKE FISHING CLUB *(open)*, **2** *m.* The clubhouse, of logs taken from another building, has an appearance of age. The lake and the building, erected as a PWA project, are municipally owned.

2. Left from Owenton on an improved road to LUSBY'S MILL, **10** *m.* (30 pop.), on Eagle Creek. A FISHING CAMP *(open)* provides fishing, swimming, and tennis. During the War between the States a recruiting station was established at this place by Gen. Humprey Marshall.

At **31** *m.* State 35 *(see Tour 5)* leaves US 227, and at **32.4** *m.* State 22 *(see Tour 13)* leaves US 227.

In BEECHWOOD, **43** *m.* (540 alt., 32 pop.), are mineral springs of asserted therapeutic value, from which water is bottled and shipped. The hotel that formerly stood on the grounds was burned down several years ago and has never been rebuilt.

STAMPING GROUND, **55.6** *m.* (341 pop.), was so named because the herds of buffalo that came here for salt water, tramped or stamped down the soil for a great distance around the lick. Lindsey's stockade was built here in 1790. BUFFALO SPRINGS (R), a new modern distillery, has been built on the site of the old spring, again bringing prosperity to the little town.

At **58** *m.* is the junction with a dirt road.

Right on this road to BLUE SPRING, **0.5** *m.*, named for Blue Spring Creek, and formerly the estate of Col. Richard M. Johnson (1781–1850), distinguished statesman and soldier in the War of 1812. Colonel Johnson was a Representative in Congress from 1807 to 1819, United States Senator for two terms beginning in 1819, and was elected Vice President of the United States in 1836. Blue Spring is the SITE OF A CHOCTAW INDIAN SCHOOL, established by Johnson in 1825 and operated by the Federal Government for 40 years. Several of the old buildings still stand.

GREAT CROSSINGS, **60.6** *m.* (80 pop.), was named for the buffalo trace from the interior of Kentucky to the confluence of the Ohio River and Elkhorn Creek. Johnson's Fort was built here in 1783 by Robert

Johnson, an early Kentucky statesman. Crossings Church belongs to a Baptist congregation organized here May 28, 1785; this was the mother church from which sprang the religious organizations at McConnell's Run (later Stamping Ground), Dry Run, and Georgetown.

At 61.1 *m.* is the junction with State 40 *(see Tour 17)*, 2.6 miles west of Georgetown.

Tour 13

Willow—Falmouth—Owenton—New Castle—Junction with US 60; 116.4 *m.* State 22.

Hard-surfaced roadbed throughout.
Accommodations limited.

The route, following roughly the base of a triangle, two sides of which are formed by the Ohio River, passes through a rolling-to-hilly region that frequently affords superb views of the hills and river valleys. Tobacco of especially fine quality is produced in this area.

State 22 branches west from State 10 *(see Tour 11)* at WILLOW, 0 *m.*, and at 12.1 *m.* passes the forks of the Licking River.

FALMOUTH, 12.4 *m.* (525 alt., 1,876 pop.) *(see Tour 3)*, is at the junction with US 27 *(see Tour 3)*.

Between Falmouth and 15.5 *m.* State 22 and US 27 are united.

WILLIAMSTOWN, 29.3 *m.* (943 alt., 917 pop.) *(see Tour 4)*, is at the junction with US 25 *(see Tour 4)*.

Between Williamstown and DRY RIDGE, 33.2 *m.* (929 alt., 500 pop.) *(see Tour 4)*, State 22 and US 25 are united.

At 52.3 *m.* is the junction with US 227 *(see Tour 12A)*; between this point and OWENTON, 54.4 *m.* (1,000 alt., 975 pop.) *(see Tour 12A)*, State 22 and US 227 are united. Owenton is also at the junction with State 35 *(see Tour 5)*.

GRATZ, 63.5 *m.* (139 pop.), a deserted river town on the western bank of the Kentucky River, was once a bustling and important shipping point. For more than 50 years steamers stopped at this landing to load and unload produce and receive passengers for Louisville or Cincinnati. A Sulphur Well (R), near the river, is 1,200 feet deep.

Right from Gratz on a dirt road to an old Lead Mine, 1 *m.*, which has not been worked for many years.

At 64 *m.* on State 22 is the junction with State 83, an improved highway.

Right **0.4** *m.* on this road to a lane leading to CASA BIANCA (Ital., *white house),* the home of Adjt. Gen. Charles E. Marshall, great-grandson of Chief Justice John Marshall. The one-and-a-half-story house, of Greek Revival style, is on a 1,000-acre farm and commands a wide view of the Kentucky River and adjacent valleys.

At **6.8** *m.* on State 83 is DRENNON SPRINGS, 7 *m.,* in the center of an amphitheater of hills. Indians and buffalo had worn paths from every direction to the lick many years prior to July 1773, when Jacob Drennon and Matthew Bracken, directed by an old Delaware Indian, reached this place. Drennon gave his name to the creek and the spring, but neither he nor Bracken ever attempted to secure title to the property. In 1779, George Rogers Clark obtained a deed to a 400-acre tract that included the spring. In the closing years of the eighteenth century, salt was made here in large quantities, but the crude, slow process of boiling the water in huge iron kettles over wood fires lasted only as long as the price of salt (20 shillings a bushel) made the manufacture profitable. The reputed medicinal quality of the water began to attract invalids, and by 1840 a popular summer resort, a few crude log cabins, had been established; a large hotel known as the North and South House was later erected, with cottages adjoining. The resort was honored by the attendance of 13 State Governors at one notable social function. In the 1850's the Western Military Academy was established here; James G. Blaine was one of the instructors in this school. During the War between the States the buildings were used as a recruiting station for the Federal Army. In 1864 all of the buildings were destroyed by fire and never replaced.

West of the Kentucky River Valley the highway follows an undulating upland plateau.

At **78.8** *m.* is the junction with State 146, an improved road.

Left on this road to EMINENCE, 2.6 *m.* (1,323 pop.), an enterprising town known for the registered breeding stock produced on neighboring farms. Many of the Hereford cattle in this country can be traced to sires owned within a few miles of Eminence. Beau Donald, Perfection, Prince Rupert, Beau Roland, Britisher, and Acrobat, names familiar to stockmen throughout America, were raised here, and today their progeny are being shipped to South and Central America, Cuba, and the Hawaiian Islands.

The ODD FELLOWS AND DAUGHTERS OF REBEKAH HOUSE, on the outskirts of Eminence, is a spacious, two-story brick structure erected in 1916. It cares for the aged and infirm members of the two orders. The entrance to the farm is through a tree-banked stone gateway.

At Eminence is the GRAVE OF ZACH F. SMITH, educator and historian, born in Henry County in 1827. He served as president of Henry Female College, New Castle, and was State superintendent of public instruction and curator of Transylvania University for 50 years.

Left from Eminence on State 55, an improved road, to the HAYS HOUSE, 5 *m.,* a two-story frame structure, erected early in the nineteenth century by John F. Hagan for Squire Helm. The eight-room house, designed in the Greek Revival style, has hand-carved woodwork and a paneled stairway. The doors have the original brass knobs and locks, and the floors are of white ash.

The POLLARD HOUSE (R), 79.4 *m.,* erected about 1790, is built of brick and is a story and a half high. The long slope of its roof is pierced by dormers, and in recent years a front porch has been added. Originally the structure had two-story wings, but these have been razed as have the stone barns that once stood behind the house. This section of State 22 was once a part of the old Frankfort-Milton Post Road, and at that time the house with its spacious wings was a tavern. James G. Blaine was a frequent guest here while he taught at the Western Military Academy (1850–51) in Drennon Springs.

On the night of December 1, 1863, Pollard, the owner, admitted two strangers who appeared to be cattle buyers. One of the men saw on the table a copy of the Cincinnati *Enquirer*, considered a "Copperhead" publication, that bore headlines announcing the escape of Gen. John H. Morgan and other Confederate officers from the Ohio Penitentiary at Columbus. Pollard's possession of this paper revealed his sympathy for the Confederacy and prompted the younger of the two guests to mention his having heard that General Morgan and Captain Hines were on their way south through Kentucky. "And you are Captain Hines?" Pollard asked. Hines admitted his identity and introduced General Morgan. The two officers spent the night there, and after breakfast the following day, Pollard arranged to take them to Judge W. S. Pryor of New Castle for assistance.

NEW CASTLE, 83.5 *m.* (825 alt., 447 pop.), is the third oldest incorporated town in the State. Many old houses border the quiet streets radiating from the public square.

Confederate Gen. Kirby Smith conducted a military school in a house here, still standing, built in 1800. The Henry County Male and Female College, a popular school for several decades, attracted students from many southern States.

Near the center of New Castle is the THOMAS SMITH HOUSE (L), a two-story structure of red brick. Designed in the Georgian Colonial style, it has a fanlighted doorway and a wide entrance hall with a winding stairway of cherry. All of the woodwork is hand-carved, and the walls of the hall are decorated with murals. The house was built in 1818 by Thomas Smith, who made his money in Henry County in the produce business. Smith is said to have owned 40 percent of all the land in Henry and Shelby Counties and was one of the builders of the Louisville & Nashville R.R. in 1830–35. When he died in 1850, at the age of 51 years, he left an estate valued at more than a million dollars.

The PRYOR HOUSE, a two-story brick building, is Georgian Colonial in style. Its interior trim of cherry and white pine is elaborately carved. Ornate plasterwork lends much to the charm of the first floor rooms, which are high, with 10-foot doors. Judge W. S. Pryor, who built this house in 1859 and lived in it until his death in 1914, was an ardent Confederate. During the War between the States the Union soldiers who came to New Castle to buy cattle and hogs and stayed overnight in the town's hotel were invariably tormented or frightened by the pranks of Judge Pryor's slaves, acting under his instructions. Pryor, made chief justice of the Kentucky Court of Appeals on September 6, 1871, was the first Confederate named to the court after the War between the States.

On Main St., standing flush with the sidewalk, is an old gray brick house (R) known as BUCKLEY TAVERN, which was a popular place in stagecoach days.

Reuben T. Durrett, Kentucky historian and eminent lawyer of Louisville, was born near New Castle in 1824. From 1857 to 1859 he was editor of the Louisville *Courier* and he founded the Filson Club of Louisville and the Louisville Public Library.

On the outskirts of New Castle is the one-and-a-half-story GRAVES HOUSE, built of gray brick in 1820. A fanlighted doorway gives entrance to a wide hall in which is a circular stairway with balustrade of cherry. William Jordan Graves was a Member of Congress from 1835 to 1841, and a prominent lawyer of Louisville. On February 24, 1838, he fought a duel at Bladensburg, Maryland, with Jonathan Cilley, a Member of Congress from Maine. The weapons were rifles, and the distance was 80 yards. Cilley was killed at the third shot. The duel, which created a Nation-wide sensation, was the last in which men of prominence were involved, and was partly responsible for the outlawing of this custom. Cilley had risen in Congress to denounce an anonymous gossip article accusing a colleague of immorality; he had blamed the article on a Member of Congress from Virginia. Graves had challenged him in defense of the Virginian.

LA GRANGE, 96.5 *m.* (850 alt., 1,121 pop.), seat of Oldham County, was named for the French estate of General Lafayette.

The ROBERT MORRIS HOUSE *(open)*, 110 Washington St., a simple two-story frame house (L), is preserved as a memorial to the man who established the order of the Eastern Star in 1850. Born in Massachusetts in 1818, Morris became a traveler and writer often referred to as the "Poet Laureate of Free Masonry." He died here in 1888.

The D. W. GRIFFITH HOUSE (L), cor. 4th and Madison Sts., is a spacious, two-story frame house built by the motion-picture producer. David Wark Griffith, son of Confederate Lt. Col. Jacob Wark Griffith, was born in this town on January 16, 1880. He was educated in the local public school and in time became a reporter on the Louisville *Courier-Journal.* He left this position to join the Louisville Stock Company. After a succession of theatrical engagements, he went to work in a foundry at Tonawanda, New York. In 1908 he was engaged by the Biograph Company of New York City to write scenarios and that same year directed the highly successful picture, *The Adventures of Dollie.* As a producer Griffith has been notable for the spectacular and sentimental character of his films; his most popular pictures are *The Birth of a Nation* and *Hearts of the World.*

The new MEDIUM SECURITY PRISON (R), 98.3 *m.,* is being erected (1939) on a 200-acre tract to replace the antiquated prison at the State capital *(see Frankfort).* When completed this prison will comprise a hospital, gymnasium, library, industrial buildings, and dormitories, erected according to modern standards of penology, with emphasis on corrective treatment.

CRESTWOOD, 105.3 *m.* (300 pop.), is a residential village.

1. Left from Crestwood on an improved road to FLOYDSBURG, 1 *m.* (200 pop.), named for Col. John Floyd, who was sent out in 1774 by Patrick Henry

and other prominent Virginians to hunt choice lands in this vicinity. In the cemetery is the DUNCAN MEMORIAL CHAPEL, erected in 1937 by a former resident, Alexander Edward Duncan, a banker of Baltimore, Maryland, in memory of his wife,
Flora Ross Duncan. The chapel, at the entrance to the Duncan family burial
ground, now a public cemetery, is of stone with white oak interior trim; it is
Gothic in style and has an unusually slender central spire. The stone, gray from
age, came from old buildings and fences in the neighboring countryside. An ell-
shaped extension at the rear, connected with the chapel by a loggia, contains living
quarters for the caretaker. The interior of the building is lined with cut Indiana
limestone. The altar carving, suggested by Da Vinci's *The Last Supper*, was executed by F. Pescosta, formerly of Oberammergau, Germany. A grapevine motif
is carved on the pews, lectern, pulpit, and around the altar. The stained-glass windows are outstanding examples of modern work; the two lower medallions over the
altar were designed by Henry Lee Willett of Philadelphia, Pennsylvania, and were
exhibited in the 1937 Paris Exposition. The electrically operated chimes play every
half-hour during the afternoon on Sunday and holidays. Around this chapel, which
is non-sectarian and for the use of the community, are old tombstones, trees, and
a landscaped garden with a lake, carefully tended walks, and rose beds.

2. Right from Crestwood on an improved road to the CLORE HOUSE, 1 *m.*, built
by Richard Clore and his wife, Narcissa, early in the nineteenth century. The old
one-and-a-half-story house, of brick burned on the place by slave labor, is on the
site of the cabin that was the first Kentucky home of Richard Clore. The slave
quarters stand in the yard.

PEWEE VALLEY, 106.6 *m.* (582 pop.), is a quiet suburban village
with attractive old homes on spacious lawns. The streets are tree-
shaded. In 1852 this was Smith's Station; the name was changed to
Pewee Valley because of the great number of phoebes or pewees in
the region.

The BEECHES *(open on request)*, a large two-story white frame structure (R) with a wide porch across the front, was the home of Annie
Fellows Johnston (1863–1931), author of the *Little Colonel* stories for
children; it is now occupied by the author's daughter, Mary Lee Johnston. Annie Fellows Johnston acquired this property in 1911 on the
death of the widow of Gen. Henry W. Lawton, captor of the Apache,
Geronimo, and division commander at El Caney in the Spanish-American War. After General Lawton's death in the Philippine campaign,
this house had been purchased by Nation-wide subscription and given
to Mrs. Lawton. Practically all of Mrs. Johnston's writing was done
here, and many of her characters were neighbors. Hattie Cochran,
granddaughter of the Confederate Col. George Weissinger, was the
Little Colonel, and Craig and Billy Culbertson were the *Two Little
Knights of Kentucky.*

The CRAIG HOUSE (L), directly opposite the Beeches, is a two-story
gray brick structure built in 1861 by Walter N. Haldeman (1821–
1902), founder of the Louisville *Courier* and *Times.* This house is the
locale of *Two Little Knights of Kentucky.*

The JENNIE CASSEDAY REST COTTAGE (R), 107.1 *m.*, a vacation
home for young working women, was established in 1897 by Jennie
Casseday of Louisville. The rambling plantation-type house is of wood,
painted white, and has an ell with broad porches and several bays; it

is surrounded by a large shady lawn, part of the 56-acre tract owned by the institution. Miss Casseday, who inherited a considerable fortune from her father, was an invalid for more than 40 years. She provided a small legacy for Rest Cottage, the maintenance of which was then undertaken by the King's Daughters. It is now under Community Chest supervision. The 40 young women who can be accommodated at the cottage are allowed to stay two weeks, at a total cost of $5. There is a large recreation room, a library, and equipment for volleyball, tennis, ping pong, croquet, and other games. -

In the 1860's Rest Cottage was the home of Catherine A. Warfield, best known as the author of *Ferne Fleming* and its sequel, *Cardinal's Daughter*.

ANCHORAGE, 111.5 *m.* (564 pop.), with beautiful estates and winding lanes, shaded by giant trees, is a residential suburb of Louisville. It was first called Hobb's Station in honor of E. D. Hobbs, president of the Louisville & Lexington R.R. When the town was incorporated, in 1876, it was renamed for the estate of Capt. J. W. Goslee, a steamboat pilot, who, when he retired and built his home at Hobb's Station, said he wished "to anchor there for life." An ANCHOR (R) on the lawn of the Louisville & Nashville R.R. station is said to have been presented to the town by Captain Goslee. The anchor, surmounted with a gilded eagle, was used for many years as a fire alarm. The alarm was sounded by striking the anchor with an iron instrument. The CAPTAIN GOSLEE HOUSE, Evergreen Ave., is a two-story, red brick structure with a steep gable roof, built before the War between the States. The slave quarters remain in the yard.

In 1916 the offices of the Southern Pacific R.R. were moved to Anchorage, and the little village suddenly found itself the home office of a corporation controlling 13,000 miles of track, not one foot of which was near Kentucky. When corporation laws in the State were made more stringent, the railway offices moved away.

In LAKELAND (R), 112.2 *m.*, is the CENTRAL KENTUCKY STATE HOSPITAL, founded in 1870, largest State institution for the insane. Two farms are maintained. One here, comprising 900 acres, is worked in part by patients. The other, a 375-acre farm at Pine Bluff, Shelby County, includes a large dairy and is operated by about 40 patients who live there on a cottage plan. An average of 2,000 patients are cared for here.

The hospital was erected here because of the water supply, the lake for which the place is named being fed by a spring.

The HITE HOUSE, adjacent to the institution, now a dormitory for employees of the hospital, was erected about 1800 by Jacob Hite. The house, built of local brick, has walls 18 inches thick and carved woodwork. An old brick walk near the house leads down to a cave, which contains a spring and was formerly used for cold storage.

ORMSBY VILLAGE (L), 113.1 *m.*, the Louisville and Jefferson County Children's Home, is a model institution built and conducted on the cottage plan. The wards of the village are committed to its care in cases of neglect, ill treatment, delinquency, or undesirable home conditions. The home has evolved from the old House of Refuge, later the Industrial School of Reform, which was established in 1865 at Third and Shipp Sts. in Louisville on what is now the campus of the University of Louisville. The institution was moved to this place in 1925.

The KENTUCKY CHILDREN'S HOME (R), 114.2 *m.*, is conducted by a society founded in 1895 by Judge R. H. Thompson of Louisville. The work began in a modest frame house in Louisville. By 1922, through State, county, and municipal aid as well as private gifts, the society was able to erect this $500,000 plant. Approximately 8,000 children have been sheltered here and many of them have been placed in homes in the State under supervision of the society. An average of 350 children are cared for in the home at one time.

KENTUCKY MILITARY INSTITUTE (R), 114.3 *m.*, a private military academy, was founded in 1845 by Robert T. P. Allen, graduate of West Point and veteran of the Seminole War. A broad macadamized driveway, bordered on both sides by maple trees and bluegrass meadows, leads to the entrance, a massive arch, supported by ivy-covered columns of limestone. Along the driveway is a lake (L), fed by springs, which is used for recreational purposes. The campus is noted for its fine old trees, thick hedges, and grassy lawns. Facing a drive-encircled oval of grass, trees, shrubbery, and flowers, is the Administration Building, once the home of Stephen Ormsby (1765–1846), brilliant Kentucky statesman. This stately two-story building is of stuccoed brick, in the Greek Revival style. The pediment of its broad portico is supported by four massive columns of the Ionic order. Edison Science Building, named for Thomas A. Edison, is a two-story rectangular brick building with gable roof. The two are of Georgian Colonial design. Railed porches extend the entire length of each floor. The gymnasium, also of Georgian Colonial design, erected in 1928, is of white brick veneered over a reinforced concrete wall. The junior school is in Fowler Hall, a white one-story hipped-roof structure, forming an open quadrangle at the rear of the campus.

During the War between the States the institute furnished both the Federal and Confederate Armies with officers. After the Christmas holidays the entire cadet corps goes into the institute's winter quarters at Venice, Florida. Student enrollment during 1936–37 was 225.

LYNDON, 115.2 *m.* (250 pop.), is a small suburban village.

Right from Lyndon on Herr Lane to the junction with Wesport Rd., 1 *m.* Here is the HERR HOUSE (L), built in 1789 by Captain Edwards, and sold in 1814 to John Herr, a settler from Lancaster, Pennsylvania. The house, one of the earliest built of brick in the State, is shown on the map of John Filson, published in 1784. The bricks were burned on the place and laid in Flemish bond; the walls are 24 inches thick. The ash and walnut used in the construction came from the estate. The Herr homestead became a center of social life in the old German settlement; quilting parties and corn huskings were frequently held here. John Herr is said to have been the best shot and the best corn shucker in the community. This home also played an important part in early religious life, for it was here that Alexander Campbell and Elder John Smith ("Raccoon John") conducted some of the first meetings of the Christian Church *(see Tour 15)*.

At 116.4 *m.* is the junction with US 60 *(see Tour 16)*, 8 miles east of Louisville.

Tour 14

(Aberdeen, Ohio)—Maysville—Georgetown—Versailles—Bardstown—Elizabethtown—Central City—Paducah; US 62.
Ohio Line to Paducah, 358.9 *m.*

Hard-surfaced roadbed throughout.
Illinois Central R.R. roughly parallels route between Elizabethtown and Paducah; Southern Ry. between Georgetown and Versailles.
All types of accommodations in larger towns; limited elsewhere.

This route, a pleasant alternate to the more congested and commercialized highways across the State, traverses the steep hills along the Ohio River, the rich bottomlands of the Licking River Valley, and the rolling pasture lands of the Bluegrass. Between Springfield and Leitchfield it winds through the Knobs area; between Leitchfield and the Cumberland River it skirts undulating farm lands of the Pennyrile —local variant of pennyroyal, a pungent, aromatic plant of the mint family that grows in abundance along the banks of the streams. Between the Cumberland River and Smithland the route passes through a semibarren region that forms a watershed between the Cumberland and Ohio Rivers. These diverse physical features have produced a corresponding diversity of modes and conditions of life.

Section a. OHIO LINE *to* ELIZABETHTOWN; *170 m. US 62*

US 62 crosses the Ohio Line, 0 *m.*, on the north bank of the Ohio River; the river is crossed on a toll bridge *(toll 25¢)*, at Aberdeen, Ohio *(see Ohio Tour 3)*.
MAYSVILLE, 0.5 *m.* (448 alt., 6,557 pop.) *(see Tour 15)*, is at the junction with US 68 *(see Tour 15)* and State 10 *(see Tour 11)*.
Between Maysville and WASHINGTON, 4.6 *m.* (500 pop.) *(see Tour 15)*, US 62 and US 68 are one route *(see Tour 15)*.
Southwest of Washington US 62, extending along one of the high, rolling ridges that jut northward from the Bluegrass plateau, affords frequent far-reaching views of quiet green valleys and wooded hills, deep blue in the distance. The road winds through a sparsely settled

agricultural area, where tobacco and fruit are the principal crops and stock raising is a leading occupation.

The SITE OF McKINLEY'S BLOCKHOUSE (L) is at 7 *m.* The first wheat in Mason County was grown on the McKinley farm. It is said that half the men of the station stood guard to ward off Indian attacks while the remainder harvested the wheat.

The SHANNON METHODIST CHURCH (R), 9 *m.*, a small rectangular brick structure, belongs to a congregation formed in 1801. The burying ground contains many headstones with old-fashioned inscriptions, some bearing dates as early as 1824, and a large Indian burial mound. The size of the two tall pine trees growing on this mound indicate that its origin was in prehistoric times.

In MOUNT OLIVET, 23.8 *m.* (419 pop.), a quiet village, is the ROBERTSON COUNTY COURTHOUSE, erected in 1867. This was, until recently, the only brick building in the county. At the old tobacco house in Pinhook, an early settlement in Robertson County, originated the term "pinhooker," which is applied to the tobacco brokers who refuse to buy until the prices are low and the farmers are at their mercy, then resell to the warehouse for a higher price.

KENTONTOWN, 29.7 *m.* (100 pop.), established in 1795, was named in honor of Simon Kenton *(see Tour 15),* one of the first to explore and hold land in this region.

Right from Kentontown on an unimproved road to two METCALF HOUSES, 1 *m.,* built prior to 1829 by Thomas Metcalf—one for himself and one for his son *(see Forest Retreat, Tour 15).* These story-and-a-half houses, still in good condition, are of stone; they are basically Georgian Colonial in design, though they lack many of the Georgian details.

CLAYSVILLE, 35.7 *m.* (75 pop.), on the Licking River at the mouth of Beaver Creek, was laid out by Alex Curran about 1800. In its early years it was a flourishing commercial village and shipping point, but since the building of the railroad the population and commercial activity have steadily declined. A COVERED BRIDGE just outside the town spans Middle Fork of Licking River. Built in 1874, it is still in excellent condition.

CYNTHIANA, 50.6 *m.* (718 alt., 4,386 pop.) *(see Tour 3),* is at the junction with US 27 *(see Tour 3).*

An OLD COVERED BRIDGE, 50 *m.*, over the South Fork of Licking River, is 275 feet long. Erected about 1837, it has been in constant use ever since. The piers are of stone, the timbers oak and poplar, held together with hand-wrought spikes. The original wood shingles of the roof were made by hand. An old county court order book in the courthouse at Cynthiana records that:

"In January 1837 Samuel McMillain, James Finley, Wm. Stephenson, Wm. Moore and Josephus Perrin were appointed commissioners to draft a plan for a Bridge across South Fork of Licking, opposite the Town of Cynthiana, to fix on the eligible place for said bridge to cross said fork, for the materials of which it shall be made, and to open subscriptions to raise money to defray a part or the whole of the expense of erecting said Bridge."

In July 1837 a report was made showing subscriptions amounting to $500. Bids for building the bridge were "advertised in the *Palladium* and such other places as seemed proper," the "undertaker" being required to keep the bridge in repair for seven years after completion. The structure, built at a cost of $1,594, was ready for the passage of wagons in December 1837. This bridge played an important part in General Morgan's raid on Cynthiana during the War between the States.

At 71.4 *m.* is the junction with State 40 *(see Tour 17);* between this point and Georgetown, US 62 and State 40 are united.

GEORGETOWN, 72.5 *m.* (866 alt., 4,229 pop.) *(see Tour 4),* is at the junction with US 25 *(see Tour 4)* and State 40 *(see Tour 17).*

Between Georgetown and a point at 73.6 *m.* US 62 and State 40 are united.

Between Georgetown and Versailles are undulating fields, covered with either bluegrass or tobacco; in season wild roses and trumpet vines hide the old stone fences, and in many places rows of honey locusts form an arch over the roadway.

PAYNES DEPOT, 76 *m.* (50 pop.), is a railroad junction and shipping point.

MIDWAY, 83.7 *m.* (830 alt., 808 pop.), with its tree-shaded streets, old houses, and well-kept lawns and flower gardens, gives an impression of gracious living. The name refers to General Francisco's log house built here in 1795, midway between Lexington and Frankfort. Chief Justice John Marshall referred to Midway as "the asparagus bed of the garden spot of Kentucky," and the sobriquet has survived. According to tradition this place furnished local color for Mary J. Holmes' *Tempest and Sunshine.*

NUGENTS' CROSSROADS, 87.7 *m.,* is named for members of the Nugent family who operate the general store (L) on the corner. Opposite stands (R) an OLD TAVERN *(unoccupied)* built of red brick; in stagecoach days this was one of the important stopping places for rest and refreshment on the journey between Cincinnati and Louisville.

STONE WALL (L), 88.7 *m.,* is the stock farm of the Viley family. The wall that suggested the name of the farm was built in 1863 of field stone without mortar, like many of the older walls throughout the Bluegrass region. During the reconstruction period (1865–75) the grove of walnut trees, near the house, was the scene of political meetings and barbecues, attended by such men as James D. Beck and J. C. S. Blackburn, who was United States Senator from Kentucky, 1885–97 and 1901–07. After service in the Senate, Blackburn was made Isthmian Canal Commissioner.

The old-fashioned barbecue was attended by people from the entire countryside, who gathered to hear fiery political speeches and consume quantities of burgoo. This delectable concoction is still regarded as a requisite to every large gathering in Kentucky; no political campaign can be launched or thoroughbred sale conducted without this as the main dish. Burgoo is a rich, thick soup or broth made with beef, chicken, and vegetables. Huge caldrons containing the highly seasoned mixture are fitted snugly over ditches in which wood fires have been built. Burgoo must be stirred continuously, and the process of making it requires 24 hours.

There is a tradition that Gus Jaubert, a French member of Gen. John Morgan's cavalry, originated burgoo at a time when food was so scarce that all men but the officers had to eat blackbirds. He prepared a mixture with blackbirds as the main ingredient, and the story is that the officers, upon sampling the dish, liked it so much that very little was left for the troopers.

The secret of the seasoning of burgoo was passed on by Jaubert to J. T. Looney, named the Burgoo King by Col. E. R. Bradley *(see Lexington)*. Looney always prepared the burgoo served at Col. Bradley's annual Charity Day race meet, held for the benefit of Kentucky orphans. To honor Looney, Colonel Bradley gave this name to a colt that won the Kentucky Derby in 1932.

GLEN ARTNEY (R), opposite Stone Wall, was for a time the home of Carry Moore (1846–1911), who, as Mrs. Carry Nation, became a notable prohibition crusader *(see Tour 3)*. Her father, George Moore, owned the farm, called Lota Wana at the time.

At 90.4 *m.* is the junction with US 60 *(see Tour 16);* between this point and VERSAILLES, 91.7 *m.* (923 alt., 200 pop.) *(see Tour 16),* US 62 and US 60 are united.

At 91.9 *m.* is the junction with the McCoun's Ferry-Soards Ferry Turnpike.

Right on this road to the SCOTT HOUSE, 7.1 *m.,* built of logs in 1784 and now weatherboarded. This was the home of Gen. Charles Scott, Revolutionary soldier, commander of Kentucky troops in the War of 1812, and Governor of Kentucky (1808–12). The house was built on Kentucky River and was known as Scott's Landing.

At 95.7 *m.* is the junction with the Shryock's Ferry Rd., hard-surfaced.

Left on this road to Grier's Creek, 2 *m.,* from which an unimproved road and a footpath wind up a high hill to the MULDROW HOUSE *(open on request).* This late Georgian Colonial style house, which has been much admired by architects, was built in 1817 by Col. Andrew Muldrow, a leading citizen of his day, who was by turns a miller, distiller, legislator, and churchman. Colonel Muldrow served in the Kentucky Legislature (1822–29).

The graceful arched portico is reached by seven semicircular steps. The front door is flanked by side lights and topped with a fan transom of frosted glass in scroll design. There are handsome Palladian windows on each side of the portico and in each end of the second story. The house is two rooms in depth with a central hall 20 feet wide; a kitchen is connected with the main house by an open passage. The carved woodwork of the interior, notably the chair rails, the mantels in the two front rooms, and the arch that divides the hall with its twin reed columns and pilasters, are of unusually fine craftsmanship. The caps of the columns and pilasters are lightened by pierced work in graceful design; the trim of the arch, embellished with a classic egg-and-dart motif, stars, and dentils, is crowned with a reeded keystone.

JOE BLACKBURN BRIDGE *(toll 50¢)*, 97.7 *m.*, spanning the Kentucky River, is a concrete structure 175 feet in height. The approaches are curved, giving it the appearance of a huge S. The bridge was dedicated in June 1932 and the name honors J. C. S. Blackburn, United States Senator (1885–97, 1901–07). It affords an exceptionally fine view of the river and palisades.

The center of YOUNG'S HIGH BRIDGE (L), visible from the Joe Blackburn Bridge, is 265 feet above low water; the bridge is 1,665 feet long and carries railroad tracks.

TYRONE, 98.7 *m.* (120 pop.), named for County Tyrone in Ireland, is primarily dependent on the T. B. RIPY DISTILLERY (L).

LAWRENCEBURG, 101.8 *m.* (788 alt., 1,763 pop.), seat of Anderson County, was named in honor of Capt. James Lawrence, commander of the *Chesapeake*, whose last words were "Don't give up the ship." It has wide, tree-shaded streets and comfortable homes with well-kept lawns. The ANDERSON COUNTY COURTHOUSE (L), with its tall clock tower, is constructed of local limestone and designed in the French Renaissance style. The first settler of Lawrenceburg was a Dutchman named Coffman, who arrived in 1776 with his family from western Pennsylvania. He built a double log house, which later served as a stopping point between Harrodsburg and Frankfort and became known as Coffman's Station. Lawrenceburg, incorporated in 1820, prospered early, chiefly by the production of fine whisky.

The song "Oh, Mr. Johnson, Turn Me Loose" was written by Ben Harney while he was a prisoner in the Lawrenceburg jail. Harney's plea was meant for Jesse M. Johnson, the mayor.

Lawrenceburg is at the junction with State 35 *(see Tour 5).*

WALNUT GROVE FARM *(open on request)*, 104 *m.*, is a stock farm widely known for its saddle horses.

SINAI, 111.6 *m.* (45 pop.), is the post office for the little settlement of Shiloh, called Dogwalk in pioneer days. The little community was renamed to commemorate the Battle of Shiloh.

BLOOMFIELD, 132 *m.* (455 pop.), on Simpson Creek, was founded in 1799 by Dr. John Bemiss of Rochester, N.Y., but was not incorporated until 1819. The section of the town lying on the western side of the dividing creek was known as Gandertown because in early days the young men in this region indulged in gander pulling. A post set in the ground had a revolving crossbar from which a gander with a soaped neck was suspended by the feet. The men, mounted on horseback, rode at full speed past the post, attempting to seize the gander's neck as they went by. The prize was awarded to the contestant who succeeded in jerking off the head.

The D. Y. DAVIS HOUSE (L), on Main St., built of brick and designed in the Georgian Colonial style, has a recessed doorway with hand-carved woodwork and silver doorknob. The MINOR HOUSE (R), on Main St., an unusual Georgian Colonial house with a recessed two-story portico, stands on an eminence overlooking Simpson Creek. The house, of brick painted white, was built in 1813.

WICKLAND *(small fee)*, 142.5 *m.*, known as the "Home of Three Governors," (R) stands among stately trees. The estate once belonged to Dr. Walter Brashear, the Bardstown and Lexington surgeon who performed the first successful hip-joint amputation of record. On moving to Lexington in 1813, Dr. Brashear sold the property to Charles A. Wickliffe, who at once built the present house on the designs of the architects John Marshall Brown and John Rogers, to whose skill Kentucky owes many of its fine old homes.

The two-and-a-half-story house, has a low two-story ell and contains 14 rooms. The foundation is of limestone and the walls are of locally burned brick. Especially noteworthy are the fine doorways with side lights and large fanlights, the hand-carved woodwork, and the carved mantels, showing in their decoration the Adam influence. A graceful stairway rises from the well-proportioned entrance hall. A wide window on the stairs offers an excellent vista of the rolling landscape.

Charles A. Wickliffe, Governor of Kentucky (1830–40), was first of three Governors to reside here. The second was Robert Charles Wickliffe, Governor of Louisiana in 1855, and one of the leading criminal lawyers of the South. The third Governor was John Cripps Wickliffe Beckham, grandson of Charles A. Wickliffe; he was born here, and was the chief executive of his State (1900–07).

At **143.8** *m.* is the junction with US 68 *(see Tour 15)*, which unites with US 62 between this point and Bardstown.

BARDSTOWN, 144.1 *m.* (637 alt., 1,767 pop.) *(see Tour 15)*, is at the junction with US 68 *(see Tour 15)* and US 31E *(see Tour 6)*.

West of Bardstown, US 62 proceeds gradually into the Knobs belt, a region of rounded hills.

ELIZABETHTOWN, 170 *m.* (708 alt., 2,590 pop.) *(see Tour 7)*, is at the junction with US 31W *(see Tour 7)*.

Section b. ELIZABETHTOWN *to* PADUCAH; *188.9 m., US 62*

US 62 turns (R) at the courthouse in ELIZABETHTOWN, 0 *m.*, and runs southwest through the Knobs.

CLARKSON, 25.9 *m.* (356 pop.), is at the junction with State 88.

Left from Clarkson on State 88 to GRAYSON SPRINGS, 2 *m.*, a collection of numerous white sulphur springs that vary in temperature.

LEITCHFIELD, 30.4 *m.* (635 alt., 950 pop.), was named for Maj. David Leitch, who owned the land on which this county seat was settled. Leitch's land was adjacent to a 5,000-acre tract claimed by George Washington.

West of Leitchfield the land is much dissected by the tributaries of

Rough and Nolin Rivers, the most crooked waterways in the State. The general course of the highway is over the watershed between these two streams. Along the roadside are coal mine workings.

At 66.3 *m.* is the junction with State 71.

Right on State 71 to HARTFORD, 4 *m.* (425 alt., 1,106 pop.), seat of Ohio County, on the bank of Rough River, surrounded by hills that rise 650 to 700 feet. At the time of its founding in 1790, Hartford was called Deer Crossing, from which "hart-ford" was evolved. The COMMERCIAL HOTEL in Hartford, established in 1797, was first known as the Lyon Inn.

BEAVER DAM, 67.2 *m.* (1,036 pop.), is an important mining center of the western Kentucky coal fields. Excellent strawberries are grown in this region, and in early June at the close of the picking season Beaver Dam is the scene of an annual strawberry festival.

A ferry *(toll 50¢)* crosses the GREEN RIVER at 77 *m. (good muskellunge fishing)*, the narrowest stream in the State that can be navigated for any distance by steamboats; six locks and dams provide a constant five-foot channel. Its stillness, deep color, and closely overhanging trees produce a peaceful effect. It is believed that Green River was once a subterranean stream, and that through the ages the ceiling above wore away and caved in, bringing the stream to the surface. In this region have been found numerous shell mounds of a type exceedingly rare in Kentucky.

At 77.4 *m.* is the junction with Paradise Rd., unimproved.

Left on this road to the SITE OF AIRDRIE, 4 *m.*, a ghost town. On the narrow strip of land between Green River and the hill upon which Airdrie was built, is a vine-covered furnace stack among the cedars and sycamores. More than 50 feet in height, the stone stack has a cylindrical section on a square base. Near by is the old fortlike, three-story machinery house of dressed sandstone, now without floors, roof, or window frames. On the wall is a stone bearing the legend, "Airdrie, 1855." Shaded by trees and covered with Virginia creeper are 60 stone steps on the SITE OF THE ALEXANDER HOUSE, destroyed by fire in 1907.

Robert Alexander, founder of Airdrie, was born in Frankfort in 1819. He was educated in Scotland and, upon the death of his uncle, Sir William Alexander, succeeded him to the title. Several years later Alexander came back to Kentucky and bought about 17,000 acres of land along this section of Green River, where a deposit of ore had been discovered. Here he built an iron furnace, a mill, a large stone house, a hotel, and a number of houses for the iron workers that he had brought from Scotland. He called the place Airdrie, for his Scotch home. The venture was unprofitable, and, in 1857, Alexander abandoned the furnace and retired to his estate near Lexington.

In 1866 Gen. Don Carlos Buell bought 1,000 acres of land, including the Airdrie furnace, to prospect for oil. He found more coal and iron than oil, however, and began to work those deposits. But freight rates on Green River, his only outlet, were so high that he also abandoned the works. Buell lived here until his death in 1898.

West of the junction with Paradise Rd., US 62 continues through a comparatively desolate broken area, much dissected by the many small tributaries of Green River.

CENTRAL CITY, 85.6 *m.* (462 alt., 4,321 pop.), a mining town in a basin among the hills, has an air of industrialism because of the smoke and noise from its railroad yards. The community was long known as Morehead's Horse Mill, having been built on land once owned by C. S. Morehead, who operated a gristmill propelled by horse power. After the building of the Illinois Central R.R. in 1870, the name was changed.

At Central City is the junction with State 81.

Right on State 81, which passes through a region where large amounts of coal are produced. The ruins of many old furnaces are evidence that mining and the smelting of iron ore was formerly a flourishing industry here.

BREMEN, 9 *m.* (255 pop.), is a community settled by German immigrants, who named it for the German seaport.

In 1861 SACRAMENTO, 14 *m.* (327 pop.), was the scene of an engagement between Confederate troops under Col. Nathan B. Forrest, and a company of Federals under Capt. Robert G. Bacon. The Confederates were victorious.

RUMSEY, 25 *m.* (392 alt., 262 pop.), mainly a residential village, is connected with Calhoun by the JAMES BETHEL GRESHAM MEMORIAL BRIDGE *(toll 25¢)*, which spans Green River and was named in honor of one of the first three American soldiers to fall in the World War. Gresham, a corporal in the 16th Infantry, was killed at Batelmont, France, on November 3, 1917.

CALHOUN, 26 *m.* (392 alt., 683 pop.), seat of McLean County, on the north bank of Green River, was known as Fort Vienna in 1788, when it was founded by Solomon Rhoades. A granite marker (L) commemorates the SITE OF FORT VIENNA and indicates the hillside where the early settlers dug caves for refuge during Indian attacks.

John Calhoun, for whom the town was named, was the first circuit judge of old Fort Vienna, and United States Congressman for one term (1835–39).

Right 8 *m.* from Calhoun on State 138 to LIVERMORE (1,573 pop.), on the north bank of Green River. Logs are rafted down to Livermore for use by two chair factories. The industry exists also on a home production basis, and new rattan-bottom chairs are displayed on porches and in the yards of many dwellings.

South of Central City, US 62 traverses a country of scrub timber, denuded hillsides, and areas heavily brush-grown. There are many small coal mines along the highway; one of them, now abandoned, is the Dovey Mine. To it in the summer of 1881 came a stranger, apparently in search of employment. He casually inquired as to when the railroad pay train was due in Central City, was informed that it had passed through the morning before, and that William Dovey, who had gone for the money, would return some time during the night. The next morning three strangers appeared at the Dovey store. Two of them stood outside as guards; the third, with cocked pistol, entered the building and demanded the contents of the safe. Their holdup was successful, but because William Dovey had been delayed in bringing back the pay-roll money, the only loot was $13 in cash and a gold watch engraved with John Dovey's name. When Jesse James was killed a year later, the Dovey watch was among the things found in James' possession and was returned to its owner.

GREENVILLE, 93.1 *m.* (538 alt., 2,451 pop.), is the seat of Muhlenberg County, named for Gen. John Peter Gabriel Muhlenberg (1746–

1807), a Lutheran minister of Virginia, who left his pulpit at the beginning of the Revolutionary War to become a military officer. Although General Muhlenberg made two trips to Kentucky in 1784, he never visited the section that bears his name. Greenville is the unofficial capital of the Black Belt, an area that produces a large quantity of coal and most of the State's output of dark tobacco. Substantial dwellings with wide verandas and spacious, shady lawns reflect the leisure of the retired farmers who live here.

The WEIR HOUSE, 206 Main St., a two-story brick structure, built in the early 1840's, incorporates many Georgian Colonial features. Its entrance has an especially fine fanlight and side lights containing the greenish glass that was in common use when this house was built. The HENRY C. LEWIS HOUSE, a two-story Georgian Colonial style structure, was erected for the Presbyterian Academy in 1852 and used by it until 1873. In 1856 this school was placed under the supervision of Dr. James K. Patterson, who subsequently became president of the University of Kentucky. The Greenville school district now owns and uses the two large brick buildings that formerly housed Greenville College, a school that flourished from 1875 to 1890.

At 93.6 *m.* is the junction with State 107.

Left on this road to the RUINS OF BUCKNER FURNACE, 5 *m.*, erected in 1837 by Aylette H. Buckner, father of Gen. Simon B. Buckner *(see Tour 7)*, to refine the surface iron ore of southern Muhlenberg County. A pile of dressed rock in a thicket is all that remains of the stack, which stood intact until 1907, when it was dynamited by people seeking the iron that remained in it. The stack, a conical tower 80 feet high, 40 feet wide at the base, and 25 feet across the top, had a double wall of sandstone, hooped with six iron bands. To the north of the stack were the cabins of Buckner's miners and wood choppers, but all traces of these have now disappeared.

The three large stone chimneys about 300 yards east of the stack are the ruins of the two-story log house used by Buckner as a residence, office, and store. It is said that it took three yoke of oxen to haul Buckner's private library from Glen Lily *(see Tour 7)* in Hart County to this place. Opposite the southern end of the house in the hillside was the stone milk house over a spring. The spring still flows from under the crumbling walls.

West of Greenville there is a gradual improvement in the quality of the farm lands and the character of farm buildings.

On the bank of POND RIVER (R), 104.5 *m.*, near the highway bridge, is a ledge of rock bearing the imprint of horses' hoofs. Sections of this rock have been taken to the St. Louis Museum.

NORTONVILLE, 111.5 *m.* (429 alt., 829 pop.), a coal-mining community, is on the site (R) of a prehistoric village from which many artifacts have been recovered. These have been widely scattered, but good specimens are preserved in the museum of the University of Kentucky *(see Lexington)*.

Nortonville is at the junction with US 41 *(see Tour 8)*.

DAWSON SPRINGS, 125.7 *m.* (436 alt., 2,311 pop.), on the western edge of the coal fields, has noted mineral springs and resort hotels.

At the southern edge of Dawson Springs is a fine view of the meandering Tradewater River.

Left from Dawson Springs on State 109 to DAWSON SPRINGS STATE PARK, 3 *m.* This 500-acre tract, which has been reforested, includes a custodian's lodge, water system, trails, bridges, shelter houses, picnic areas, and improved roads.

In OUTWOOD, 4 *m.*, is the UNITED STATES VETERANS HOSPITAL *(open daily 9–4)*, in a densely wooded reservation of 5,000 acres. The 27 modern buildings, chiefly of brick, stone trimmed, occupy a landscaped plot of about 20 acres. These were erected at a cost of approximately $2,250,000. Reforestation and the reclamation of eroded tracts has been carried on.

West of Dawson Springs US 62 crosses the Tradewater River.

PRINCETON, 137.8 *m.* (484 alt., 4,764 pop.), an industrial and retail center and the seat of Caldwell County, is widely known for its beautiful tree-shaded streets and well-kept old homes. Fluor-spar mining is carried on in the vicinity. Underneath the town flows a subterranean stream that is the town's water supply. At BIG SPRING BOTTOMS, two blocks from the courthouse, the stream comes to the surface, and here the first settlers built their rude log cabins.

On county court day *(see Tour 4)*, held the third Monday of each month, the streets are filled with county folk visiting and trading. A farmer was once heard to remark that in "his best trading days" he had often taken a horse or mule to Jockey Street, "swapped around a spell," and at evening had gone home with the same animal and $100.

West of Princeton, tobacco fields dominate a countryside in which are some coal mines and old workings.

The old FLOURNOY HOUSE (R), 138.1 *m.*, a two-story frame dwelling of eight or nine rooms, has been unoccupied for nearly 20 years, but is kept in excellent condition. It was built early in the nineteenth century by the first of the Flournoys to settle here. Though weird stories of ghosts in the house began to circulate in 1890, the site and the splendid construction of the building attracted buyers who scoffed at "hants" but never remained long. Several groups of the most skeptical persons in the community each determinedly spent a night in the house but never cared to repeat the experience. Some asserted that they had heard the rattling of chains and soft footfalls that approached and passed; others insisted that they had heard the slow music of a funeral march. Verses were written in blue crayon on the walls by unseen hands. The verses were always about battles of the War between the States, the Spanish-American War, and the assassination of Gov. William Goebel. During the gubernatorial election of 1899 *(see History)* William Goebel, Democratic contestant, had been shot by an assassin whose identity was never learned. Among the doggerel that appeared on the walls was:

> Remember the Maine
> Goebel the same,
> A humble man of moral ways,

Lies murdered in his greatest days.
As long as they stand these walls proclaim
The glory of his shining name.
Who disturbs these lines shall find
The bounty of this curse in rhyme . . .
Chains shall bind thee, bats shall tear
Out your eyes, nest in your hair:
Oh guard thee well these thoughts of mine,
Ye haunts that lived in Goebel's time.

EDDYVILLE, 150.7 *m.* (436 alt., 1,990 pop.), seat of Lyon County, on the bank of the Cumberland River, was so named because of eddies in the river above and below the city.

The STATE PENITENTIARY *(visited by application 9–3 daily)*, often referred to by prisoners as the Castle on the Cumberland, has a grim, feudal appearance accentuated by the central entrance tower and the stone wall that encloses 12 of the 37 acres in the prison tract. The old stone structure received its first prisoners in 1885. Since then several wings have been added, including two cell blocks, a mess hall, and in 1938 a recreational center. Between 1911 to 1935, 84 prisoners were electrocuted here. In May 1938 the prison held 1,473 convicts.

KUTTAWA, 153.4 *m.* (436 alt., 833 pop.), is chiefly remembered for the beautiful trees that border the highway.

Right from Kuttawa on State 93 to the ruins of KELLY'S IRON FURNACE, 1 *m.*, where William Kelly (1811–88) invented the air-boiling process, later known as the Bessemer process of making steel. Kelly was born in Pennsylvania and about 1846 settled in Eddyville where he engaged in the iron business; here he accidentally discovered the revolutionary process of converting pig and cast iron into steel, but because of insufficient blast pressure he was only partly successful in making steel. From 1851 to 1856 he built experimental converters and worked secretly; through his tests he learned that when an air blast blew directly on the molten iron a greater heat was produced as a result of the more rapid decarbonization of the cast iron. Although his family and friends feared he was losing his mind, and attempted to persuade him to abandon his work, two Englishmen, whom Kelly had hired to assist in the experiments, greatly encouraged him. He therefore concealed nothing from them. When both Englishmen, who were familiar with his processes, disappeared one night, Kelly traced them to Pennsylvania, then to New York, where he learned that they had taken passage to England. In 1856 Sir Henry Bessemer of England was granted a United States patent on the perfected process. Upon hearing this, Kelly also applied for a patent and convinced patent officials of the priority of his process. On June 23, 1857, he was granted the patent and declared the original inventor. Fourteen years later Kelly's patent was renewed for seven years, while Bessemer was refused a renewal.

The contest between Kelly and Bessemer was settled by the formation of a corporation that united an ironworks company near Detroit, which manufactured iron under Kelly's process, with another in Troy, New York, which used Bessemer's patents. Kelly retired soon afterward, and only Bessemer's name became identified with the process.

KUTTAWA MINERAL SPRINGS PARK *(amusement charges 5¢ to 25¢),* 2 *m.,* is a well-shaded tract of 165 acres. Kuttawa's seven springs produce crystal-clear tasteless mineral water. Within the park are a hotel, cafe, cabins, open-air auditorium, tennis courts, ballground, and a swimming pool that is supplied with water from the spring at the rate of 150,000 gallons a day. A D.A.R. monument near the hotel commemorates Cobb's Battery, an artillery organization prominent in the War between the States.

At IUKA, 160.9 *m.* (381 alt., 55 pop.), US 62 crosses the Cumberland River by ferry *(toll 50¢)* and passes through the narrow hilly strip of land that forms a watershed between the Cumberland and Ohio Rivers. Here tobacco and corn are the chief products.

Between SMITHLAND, 172.8 *m.* (286 alt., 519 pop.) *(see Tour 16)*, and Paducah, US 62 and US 60 are one route *(see Tour 16b)*.

PADUCAH, 188.9 *m.* (341 alt., 33,541 pop.) *(see Paducah)*.

Points of Interest: Paduke Statue, Tilghman Memorial, Irvin Cobb Hotel, McCracken County Courthouse, Noble Park, Marine Ways, Brazelton House, Illinois Central House.

Paducah is at the junction with US 60 *(see Tour 16)*, US 68 *(see Tour 15)*, and US 45 *(see Tour 9)*.

Tour 15

(Aberdeen, Ohio)—Maysville—Lexington—Harrodsburg—Bardstown—Hodgenville—Cave City—Bowling Green—Paducah; US 68.
Ohio Line to Paducah, 381.8 *m.*

Louisville & Nashville R.R. parallels this route between Maysville and Lexington and between Cave City and Paducah.
Hard-surfaced roadbed throughout.
Accommodations chiefly in towns.

Section a. OHIO LINE *to* LEXINGTON; *63.8 m. US 68*

Between the Ohio and the Licking Rivers, US 68 follows an old buffalo trail that was used by Simon Kenton and other early travelers. It was known as Smith's Wagon Road, because in the summer of 1783 a Lexington man named Smith took a wagon over it for the first time. The route by 1816 was a part of a national post road between Zanesville, Ohio, and Florence, Ala.

New scenes unfold along the way at almost every turn. From the hills along the Ohio River there is a gradual transition to the rolling bluegrass meadows, where the farms are larger and the houses, standing back from the road at the end of avenues bordered with fine old trees, are more spacious. Along the roadside are stone fences, sometimes old and crumbling but usually, in the Bluegrass region, trim and smooth. Behind them splendid stallions or complacent mares with their long-legged colts graze under tall oaks. Stretching for miles along the highway in the vicinity of Lexington, the Bluegrass capital, are broad estates with stately pillared mansions—the property of some of the leading horse breeders and racers of America.

US 68 crosses the Ohio Line, 0 *m.*, at the edge of Aberdeen, Ohio *(see Ohio Tour 23)*, passing over the Ohio River on a bridge *(toll 25¢)*.

MAYSVILLE, 0.2 *m.* (448 alt., 6,557 pop.), as seen from the Ohio side of the river, resembles an Italian hill town, having been built on the steep slope of the riverbank, terrace on terrace, with gray walls and red roofs against a green background. The town, at the mouth of Limestone Creek, on a narrow flood plain, is leisurely and mellow, preserving the atmosphere of the old river days. Many of the handsome well-kept homes, on the sides of the bluffs, command a wide view of the sweeping bends of the river and the green hills and fields of southern Ohio. The town, first known as Limestone, was established by the Virginia Legislature in 1787, and by 1792, had become the leading port of entry of the State—"well laid out and flourishing." Maysville's wealth was not in its land-property, but in the steamers on the river and the traffic they brought to it; and its industrial activity was entirely confined to shipping and ship building. In those days merchandise came down the Ohio on barges to Maysville and most of it was hauled into central Kentucky, where the settlements were. The town changed its name from Limestone to Maysville to honor John May of Virginia, on whose land it had grown up.

At one time, probably in the spring of 1786, Daniel Boone and his wife opened a tavern here. They remained for three years, Mrs. Boone conducting the hostelry, while Daniel hunted and trapped as usual, and traded up and down the Ohio.

Maysville has been the seat of Mason County since 1848, when the growth of river traffic caused it to forge ahead of Washington, the first county seat.

The MASON COUNTY COURTHOUSE, Court and 3d Sts., is an imposing building, erected in 1838. It was built as a city hall and served as such until 1848, when the seat of county government was moved to this place. The clock in the tower of the building, made by a blacksmith of Flemingsburg, Kentucky, in 1850, was constructed almost entirely of wood and is still in good condition.

The small one-story brick building at the corner of 2d and Wall Sts. was the FIRST MAYSVILLE THEATER. John Palmer, in *Travels in the United States in 1817*, said that the building was adequate but "the scenery and performance were miserable." Junius Booth and many other important actors trod its boards.

The PUBLIC LIBRARY, Sutton St., contains a curio room in which are kept many relics of early settlers. Back of the library is the town's first graveyard.

As a boy, Ulysses S. Grant attended the Rand and Richardson School here for one year. The library has a minute book of the school debating society bearing his name. In his memoirs he speaks of making frequent trips to this place during his youth from his home at Georgetown, Ohio, 17 miles away.

The COCHRAN HOUSE, 16 W. 3d St., the home of Federal Judge A. M. J. Cochran, was built in 1838 by Judge Cochran's grandfather, Andrew McConnell. The two-story building is constructed of brick with stepped gable ends and a small Doric portico.

On top of a hill overlooking the Ohio stands the REED HOUSE, the summer home of Supreme Court Justice Stanley F. Reed (1938). Erected prior to the War between the States, this spacious two-story building, constructed of logs and stone, with great stone chimneys, was formerly a tavern.

Maysville is at the junction with US 62 *(see Tour 14)* and State 10 *(see Tour 11)*. US 68 and US 62 are united between this point and Washington.

Left from Maysville on State 11, which winds and twists around the tops of the river bluffs with widespread views of fertile creek bottoms and distant blue-green hills. Along the roadside are scattered small farms, with fields of corn, wheat, and tobacco, and hillside apple orchards. The soil is generally rich and productive but much of it is used for grazing, because the wool of the sheep raised here brings a good price.

FLEMINGSBURG, 18 *m.* (850 alt., 1,265 pop.), is a quiet, secluded village in the Knobs area. Flemingsburg and Fleming County, of which it is the seat, were named for John Fleming, a Virginian, who, with his half-brother, George Stockton, came down the Ohio in a canoe to Maysville in 1787. Both built stations in Fleming County, Stockton here and Fleming five miles to the west. Fleming died here in 1794, as the result of a wound received in a skirmish with Indians at Battle Run.

As an infant, Stockton, also a native of Virginia, had been taken captive by Indians. His years among the natives had given him a liking for the wilderness and when he left the tribe he determined to come to Kentucky. In 1790 Stockton and a companion, Beacham Rhodes, left the station Stockton had established here for a hunting trip along Fox Creek, where game was abundant. One night, when both men were asleep, two Indians happened on their camp, killed Stockton, and wounded his companion in the leg. Fiercely attacked by the dogs, the Indians jumped upon the hunters' horses—the main objects of the attack—and fled. Beacham, who was unable to walk, crawled back to the fort, a distance of 14 miles, to warn the occupants of danger. Friends found Stockton's body, guarded by his dog who had worn a path around it in an effort to keep wild animals away, and they buried it where it lay. A cairn, which still remains, was placed above the spot.

The spring (R) from which settlers obtained their water, and the old graveyard (L), opposite the spring, are at the northern end of town.

The STUCCOED COURTHOUSE, on an eminence at the head of Main St., is believed to be the oldest in constant use in the State. Its clock tower, which is surmounted with an octagonal cupola and low spire, dominates the town; except for the tower the structure looks like a house with a high veranda. The red-brick WILLIAM FLEMING HOUSE (L), on W. Water St., was built by slaves. The woodwork is hand-carved and the rafters are of cherry.

In Fleming County were born four Governors—Alvin Saunders (1817–99), the last Territorial Governor of Nebraska (1861–67); Claiborne F. Jackson (1807–62), Governor of Missouri in 1861; Willis A. Gorman (1814–76), second Territorial Governor of Minnesota (1853–57); and Richard M. Bishop (1812–93), Governor of Ohio (1878–80).

1. Left from Flemingsburg 10 *m.* on the Wallingford Rd., improved, to FOX SPRING, formerly a well-known summer resort that became popular about 1840. In the valley below the springs is PARK LAKE, a summer resort. The lake, which covers 20 acres, is well stocked with fish.

2. Left from Flemingsburg 5 *m.* on an unmarked, improved road, to BLUE-BANKS, where the road passes through a bowl-shaped depression in the earth, 100 yards in diameter. The sides of the bowl, 16 to 18 feet in height, are composed of a blue clay.

3. Left from Flemingsburg 8 *m.* on the Hillsboro Rd., improved, to a group of unusual STONE BOWLS, locally called Indian kettles. These formations, in sandstone and having definite rims, are 6 feet in diameter and 9 to 12 inches in depth. Near the bowls are sandstone discs, 6 feet in diameter and 5 inches thick, resembling covers. Their purpose and origin are entirely conjectural. Kitchen middens and an abundance of artifacts, found in the immediate vicinity, indicate that this was the site of an Indian village. The surrounding region has yielded additional artifacts and well-preserved skeletons.

South of Maysville the highway rises steeply in curves from the river to the rolling Bluegrass downs.

The MAYSVILLE COUNTRY CLUB *(open to public)*, 1.8 *m.*, on top of a high hill (R), overlooks the Ohio River and has a nine-hole golf course *(greens fee, $1)*.

A granite marker (R), 2.5 *m.*, erected in 1925 by the Washington Study Club, commemorates KENTON'S STATION, a stockaded trading post built by Simon Kenton.

Simon Kenton (1755–1836) ranks with Jim Bridger of the later West as a typical frontiersman. When he was 16 he believed he had killed a rival in a fist fight and fled into the wilderness. Managing to survive without supplies or weapons, he was soon beyond the country of law and order. When he next bobbed up at a frontier post he called himself Samuel Butler and, before long, had joined George Yeager and John Strader on a hunting expedition down the Ohio, which ended when they were attacked by Indians. He made another trip or so down the Ohio and then in 1774 entered the service of Lord Dunmore as a spy. In 1775 he was once more down the Ohio hunting for the cane lands of Kain-tuck-ee, of which he had heard from the Indians. On this trip he met Daniel Boone on the Limestone and for a time joined the little settlement at Boonesboro, where he was very useful during the Indian attack. But, like the trappers of the later West, domesticity irked him, so in 1778 he joined the expedition led by George Rogers Clark against Kaskaskia and Vincennes. When that expedition ended he joined Boone in the attack on Chillicothe. Then for a period he was in continual trouble with the Indians; he was captured, saved by a white renegade, condemned and then reprieved through the interference of a Mingo chief and a Canadian trapper. But his troubles were not over; the British held him a prisoner at Detroit until he escaped. Still unable to keep away from danger, in 1780 he joined a company of volunteers from Harrod's Station for the attack on the Indians that ended at Piqua. About this time he learned that the man he believed he had killed was still alive, so he went back to Virginia to visit his parents.

His stories of the fertility of Kentucky soil persuaded them to come West with him. But the arrival of his family did not hold him here; in 1787 he joined another expedition against the Indians, and in 1793 yet another. In 1799 he settled—as much as he was able to—in Ohio, where he was soon in the militia. In the War of 1812 he was again fighting with Kentuckians. Like everyone else of his day, he dreamed of holding vast quantities of land—and no one had a better chance than he to discover the best. But, like Boone and most other trappers and scouts, he was never able to master the game of making his claims stick; he died in poverty at the age of 81. Before his death his prowess had assumed almost legendary proportions and numerous people of importance liked to boast of their acquaintance with him.

Town and counties carry the name of Kenton; the Ohio and the Kentucky Legislatures voted money for monuments and quarreled over his body, which was finally reinterred at Urbana, Ohio. There in 1884 a monument, designed by John Quincy Adams Ward, was erected to his memory.

WASHINGTON, 4.1 *m.* (500 pop.), a charming village with slow-moving tempo, was once a "center of fashion and education," and the second largest town in the ·State. Created a municipality by the Virginia Legislature in 1786, the town was laid out on a well-selected section of the 700-acre tract of cane land belonging to Simon Kenton. Among the streets of Washington, which retain their early names, is one called Kenton's Line.

Washington came into existence because the hill at Maysville was so long and difficult that it required an entire day sometimes to bring heavily loaded wagons to the top. Travelers and teamsters usually spent the night at the crest of the hill or at least stopped there for refreshments. Until 1793, when Indian raids in Kentucky ceased, the place had been a rendezvous for volunteers led by Kenton to forestall attacks by the Indians, who often crossed the Ohio at this point. The town grew rapidly during the early years of its existence, when it was the principal place of trade for a wide area. The *Mirror,* third newspaper in Kentucky, was established here in 1797.

The first county court in Mason County met in the house of Robert Rankin, May 26, 1789. Among other acts, it adopted the following rates for tavern keepers:

	s.d.
A warm dinner	1 3
A cold dinner	1 3
A warm breakfast, with tea or coffee, etc.	1 3
A cold breakfast, with tea or coffee, etc.	1 0
Lodging, with clean sheets	0 9
Stablage and hay, per night	1 3

s.d.

Pasturage, per night 0 6
Corn, per gallon 0 8
Whisky, per half pint 0 9
West India Rum, per half pint 1 0
Continent Rum, per half pint 0 9
Apple or Peach Brandy per half pint 0 9
Madeira Wine, per qt. 0 9

(A Kentucky shilling was 12⅔ cents.)

The first courthouse, a massive stone building erected in 1794 by Louis Craig *(see Tour 3)*, the Virginia minister who brought the Traveling Baptist Church to Kentucky, was destroyed by fire in 1909. It had not been used as a courthouse since 1848, when the county seat was moved to Maysville. On Main St. is (L) the clapboarded log building that was the FIRST KENTUCKY POST OFFICE, the distributing point for mail for Kentucky and the Northwest Territory (now the States of Ohio, Indiana, Illinois, Michigan, and Wisconsin). Near by is the old building (R) that was the BRANCH BANK OF KENTUCKY, first bank in northern Kentucky. Gen. Henry Lee, farmer and surveyor from Virginia, was its first president.

The MARSHALL KEY PLACE *(open on request)*, a two-story brick house (L), has a recessed entrance at one side of the front and a beautiful old stairway. During a visit here, Harriet Beecher (later Mrs. Stowe), who was a schoolmate of Key's daughter in Cincinnati, witnessed sales on the SLAVE BLOCK that still stands on the courthouse green.

CEDAR HILL, a two-story house with wide veranda across the front, was built in 1807 by John Chambers, who was appointed Territorial Governor of Iowa (1841–45) by President William Henry Harrison. It stands among tall cedars on a hill overlooking Washington. Chambers (1780–1852) was brought to Washington from Lexington by his family when he was 14 years old. He later studied law, was admitted to the bar, and began practice in this town. In the War of 1812 he was aide-de-camp to General Harrison. He served in Congress as a Whig from 1828 to 1829, and from 1835 to 1839. He is buried in the family burial ground near his old home.

Another dignified house, THE HILL *(open)*, was built in 1800 by Thomas Marshall, Jr., brother of Chief Justice John Marshall. In 1785 Col. Thomas Marshall, who had become Surveyor General of Kentucky in 1780, came down the Ohio River in a flatboat "with a numerous family" and established a home in these cane lands. The two-story brick house, Georgian in style, has a pedimented central bay and a simple one-story central porch. In the family burial grounds near by is the GRAVE OF THOMAS MARSHALL, SR., and that of his wife. The inscription on the tombstone marking the GRAVE OF MARY MARSHALL, mother of the Chief Justice, reads: "Mary Randolph Keith b. 1737.

She was good, not brilliant, useful, not ornamental, and the mother of 15 children."

The JOHNSTON HOUSE (L), a two-story clapboarded structure with lean-to porch at one side, was the birthplace of Albert Sidney Johnston (1802–62), Confederate leader whose father, Dr. John Johnston, came from Cincinnati in 1785 and was the first physician in the town.

Albert Sidney Johnston was graduated from West Point in 1826. He served in the Black Hawk War, later enlisted in the service of Texas, and was made commander in chief of its forces. In 1839 he became Secretary of War of the Republic of Texas.

When the war between the United States and Mexico broke out in 1846, Johnston was engaged in cotton growing in Texas. He at once organized the 1st Regiment of Texas Infantry, and was soon afterward made inspector general of Butler's division. In 1849 Johnston was appointed paymaster of the United States Army on the Texas border, and in 1854 became colonel of the 2d United States Cavalry, with Robert E. Lee as lieutenant colonel, commanding the Department of Texas.

In 1858 Johnston commanded the United States expedition into Utah, which spent an unpleasant winter near Fort Bridger before making peace terms with the Mormons. Johnston was then assigned to the command of the Department of California. In 1861 he resigned from the U.S. Army to join the Confederate Army.

General Johnston was placed in charge of the Confederate Army of the West in 1861 and the following year was killed at the Battle of Shiloh while leading a charge against the "Hornets' nest."

On Duke of York St. was the old Franklin Academy, no longer in existence; it was established soon after Transylvania. Another early school, which taught young ladies "all the arts suited to their sex," was conducted here by Carolyn Warburton Fitz-Herbert Keats, whose husband was a cousin of John Keats, the English poet. The vine-covered two-story brick McMURDY SCHOOL (L) was attended not only by Kentuckians but also by girls from other States.

COVERED WELLS at regular intervals in the center of the sidewalks of Washington are remnants of the "first waterworks west of the Alleghenies." Early in the history of the town the legislature voted the sum of $1,000 for "adequate water protection" for the rapidly growing town, and 22 wells were dug, some of which have been restored by the Washington Study Club.

Washington is at the southern junction with US 62 (see Tour 14).

MAYS LICK, 12.1 m. (327 pop.), was named for John May, a Virginian who was first surveyor of Kenton County, and claimed land here, as well as a salt lick near by. The place was first called May's Spring, because of the large spring on what became a noted camping ground in early days and "one of the finest places on the north side of the Licking," according to an old chronicler. It numbered among its early settlers some whose families were later among the most influential of the State.

South of Mays Lick the road winds down to the valley of the Licking River on which, after spring freshets, logs are still floated down from the mountains.

BLUE LICKS BATTLEFIELD STATE PARK (R), 23.3 *m.*, is the site of the bloody battle of August 19, 1782, that ended the Revolutionary War in the West. A granite shaft bears the names of those who fell in this battle; the PIONEER MUSEUM *(adults 15¢, children 5¢)* houses many relics, including the Hunter Collection of prehistoric remains unearthed at the licks. An improved road and trails wind through the park.

In the spring of 1782 the British Capt. William Caldwell collected nearly 1,000 Indians and about 50 whites in southern Ohio for a raid upon the comparatively unprotected and weak settlements in the Bluegrass region of central Kentucky. Quarrels broke out among the Indians and numbers deserted, but Captain Caldwell, with the notorious renegade, Girty, were still supported by the whites and several hundred Indians. Moving swiftly, this force crossed the Ohio and on August 16, 1782, struck the feeble little frontier outpost of Bryan Station about six miles northeast of Lexington. Caldwell and his allies met stout opposition. Two days—time sufficient to arouse the settlers on farms and villages to the southward—were lost in a fruitless effort to storm the little stockaded fort, where men, women, and children determinedly fought on, waiting for the help they knew was coming. Aware that further penetration into the Bluegrass country would lead only to disaster, Caldwell's army retreated toward the Ohio. The garrison of Bryan Station, reinforced by volunteers to a total of nearly 200 mounted men, followed the retreating enemy. Within 24 hours this pursuing force, under command of Major Todd, overtook the invaders at this place.

A council of war was held by the pioneers at the ford; Boone advised that they delay the attack and wait for reinforcements. Todd, Trigg, and most of the other leaders agreed with him; but it is said that the hot-headed Maj. Hugh McGary, who possessed little military training, dared the young men to follow him and spurred his horse into the river. The younger men followed, leaving the leaders of the band no choice but to accompany them. The Kentuckians, outnumbered three to one, were ambushed and cut down. In a fierce battle, lasting but 15 minutes, 60 of the 176 combatants were killed and 7 were taken prisoners; the rest escaped. Todd, Trigg, and Boone's son, Israel, were among those killed; Boone escaped by swimming the river. But it was a bootless victory for the invaders. Volunteers from all the Bluegrass settlements were racing northward. Before the pioneers could strike, Caldwell and Girty fled across the Ohio, and Kentucky soil was clear of the invaders. George Rogers Clark's seasoned veterans, who had been massed at the Falls of the Ohio, took up the uncompleted work of the militia. With 1,100 Kentuckians he swept up the Miami Valley, burning Indian villages, laying waste their cornfields, clearing out the natives to make way for the white invaders who soon arrived to settle the north bank of the Ohio.

Near by is (R) the SITE OF BLUE LICKS SPRINGS TAVERN, once a popular stop on the stagecoach route between Maysville and Lexington as well as a resort. People journeyed to this place from the North and the South in order to drink the health-giving waters. In April 1862 the main building, which could accommodate from 400 to 600 guests, was destroyed by fire. Later it was replaced by a smaller structure, but the prestige of the old resort died with the passing of the stage-coach era.

The old BLUE LICK CHURCH (R), 23.8 *m.*, built in 1864, is a rectangular frame structure with twin doors in the façade. It is surrounded by pine trees.

FOREST RETREAT (R), 31.7 *m.*, was the home, during his later years, of Thomas Metcalfe (1780–1855), tenth Governor of Kentucky (1829–33). He had been a captain in the War of 1812, a Representative in Congress from 1819 to 1828, and United States Senator from 1848 to 1849. Metcalfe earned his sobriquet, "Old Stone Hammer," because of his vehemence as an orator and his skill as a stonemason; he erected stone buildings throughout the State, including the courthouse at Greensburg, which is still standing, and the Governor's mansion at Frankfort. THOMAS METCALFE'S GRAVE is in the family burial ground here.

Forest Retreat is old, though the actual date of erection is not known. It is a low, gabled, story-and-a-half dwelling of stone with gabled front dormers and small wings. Its center hall plan is typical of the southern Colonial architecture of the seaboard States. The shallow pedimented portico on the front, with its slender turned posts, is of a later date than the house. Many noted visitors stopped here, glad to accept the hospitality of the genial host in those days when inns were not always comfortable along this single road between the Ohio River and central Kentucky. Andrew Jackson, who visited here in 1829 while on his way to Washington for his first inauguration, remarked that Metcalfe fed him better than anyone he had ever met. Gen. William Henry Harrison also stayed at Forest Retreat for some time in 1840, while campaigning for the Presidency, and Henry Clay often stopped for "refreshments"—from the barrel of old bourbon, kept under the stairway for convenience. When James G. Blaine, an unsuccessful candidate for the Presidency in 1884, was teaching at the military school at Lower Blue Licks Spring, Forest Retreat was his home.

In MILLERSBURG, 37.6 *m.* (770 pop.), tree-shaded streets are lined with comfortable houses on large lawns. Established in 1817, the town was named for the Reverend John Miller, founder of Millersburg Female Seminary. The MILLERSBURG MILITARY INSTITUTE (R) is a privately owned secondary school.

South of Millersburg is the heart of the Bluegrass, with gently undulating surface and fertile soil.

The GRANGE (L), 42 *m.*, built in 1818, is a one-and-a-half-story house having a Doric portico, handsome dormers, and a deep-set doorway with fan- and side-lights. An unusual feature is the slightly curved front walls of the pavilions, pierced by Palladian windows with fluted frames and with shutters designed to cover side lights as well as the central window. The stairway has delicate balusters, newel post, and handrail. This house was built for Ned Stone, a slave dealer, who was slain during a mutiny aboard a slave ship bound for New Orleans. A short distance from the house is the old brick house used for slaves. Beneath its central hall is a dungeon with walls of solid stone, in which unruly captives were kept.

At 44.7 *m.* is the junction with State 40 *(see Tour 17)*.

The highway crosses STONER CREEK, 45.7 *m.*, a tributary of Licking River, named in honor of Michael Stoner (1748–1812), a companion of Daniel Boone. The first bridge over this creek was built in 1795.

PARIS, 45.9 *m.* (826 alt., 6,204 pop.), is the seat of Bourbon County, an unusually fertile agricultural area. The town, known as Hopewell when it was established in 1789, was later called Paris in appreciation of French aid during the Revolutionary War. The first court was held in May 1786 in the old rock house, Fairfield. In the same year a courthouse was erected with a jail 16 feet square. Among the old records, preserved in the courthouse, are those of several suits for debts against Daniel Boone, then a resident of Maysville, and against Simon Kenton, a resident of Washington. At that time both of these were in Bourbon County.

At Paris in 1790 Jacob Spears and others from Pennsylvania erected one of the State's earliest distilleries. The whisky made here was called bourbon for the county. Later the name bourbon was applied to any whisky made of corn according to this distillery's formula which produced a heavy-bodied, mellow liquor of a deep amber color. In the crude early distilleries all the work except grinding was done by hand. These plants were always near a good spring, and the use of limestone water contributed to the distinctive flavor of Kentucky whisky. Only the five general steps—grinding grain, mashing, fermenting, distilling, and aging—were commonly known. The actual formulas were guarded carefully and bequeathed by their owners to their heirs. Many Kentucky distillers continue to employ the hand processes, believing the unusual flavor and bouquet would be lost if they should adopt modern methods.

Paris, a leading bluegrass-seed market, has four seed-cleaning plants. A yearly average of 700,000 bushels of bluegrass-seed are bought, cleaned, and sold, much of it being exported.

A granite shaft marks DOYLES SPRING (R), on 2d St., about which the little log-cabin settlement that was to become Paris developed, as wagoners, traveling with supplies between Maysville and Lexington, stopped here for the pure water and pasturage. The expression of the drivers, "Hope we'll get there before night," is said to explain the first name of the settlement, Hopewell.

The Indian Queen, first hotel in Paris, was erected in 1804, and served travelers on the Maysville-Lexington stagecoach route. It has been incorporated in the WINDSOR HOTEL (L), on Main St.

The BURR HOUSE (R) on High St. was the birthplace of Joseph Duncan, Governor of Illinois (1834–38). The roof of this stone two-and-a-half-story building is pierced by two dormers; a front gable has a half-moon window. For a time the house was an inn conducted by the Widow Burr. Here in the long dining room the youth of Hopewell gathered to dance the Virginia reel, and here the first dramatic performances of the town were given in 1807.

William Holmes McGuffey (1800–73), compiler of the famous readers, taught school in Paris about 1822.

Paris is at the junction with US 27 *(see Tour 3)*, State 40 *(see Tour 17)*, and US 227 *(see Tour 17A)*. Between Paris and Lexington US 68 and US 27 are united.

1. Right from Paris on the Peacock Rd. to MOUNT LEBANON (L), 3 *m.*, surrounded by century-old cedar trees, is the home of Gov. James Garrard (1796–1804); it was built in 1786. The exterior walls of the tall, angular structure are of stone. The S-shaped anchor heads on the front wall mark the reinforcing timbers embedded by Governor Garrard after the house had been damaged by the earthquake of 1811. Much of the framework is hand-hewn and held together by wooden pegs; all the woodwork is of ash, and in excellent condition.

Across Stoner Creek on the same tract is the old rock house, FAIRFIELD, the first house built by Garrard. In it the first court in Bourbon County was held. Garrard and his wife and daughter are buried in the family burial ground here.

2. Left from Paris on the Cane Ridge Pike, an improved road, to the BREST TAVERN *(open)*, 4 *m.*, built (L) early in the nineteenth century. The story is told that Brest kept his accounts written on his whitewashed walls and when on one occasion his wife, while spring-cleaning, applied a fresh coat of whitewash, he regarded himself as ruined until his patrons voluntarily paid their debts.

CANE RIDGE MEETING HOUSE *(open)*, 6 *m.*, though built in 1791 by Presbyterians from North Carolina, is the parent church of the Christian denomination in Kentucky, otherwise known as the Disciples of Christ. After the major part of the congregation and their pastor, the Reverend Robert W. Finley, had migrated to Chillicothe, Ohio, in 1796, the Reverend Barton W. Stone became pastor of the Cane Ridge Meeting House. This was about the time that the "profound awakening" or religious revival swept Kentucky. The movement first took root in western Kentucky, centering in Logan County where Stone went, in the spring of 1800, to attend a meeting conducted by the McGhee brothers, one a Presbyterian and the other a Methodist. This joint occupancy of the same pulpit by two ministers with differing denominational views attracted such large crowds that the services had to be held out of doors. In August 1801 the Cane Ridge Meeting led by Stone held a revival that was described as the "most remarkable religious assemblage ever known on the continent." The congregation, numbering between twenty and thirty thousand, met outside the church in the flickering light of torches, to chant hymns, pray, and listen to five or more men preach simultaneously. During the impassioned exhortations the people sobbed, shrieked, and shouted until the whole throng reached a hysterical pitch of fervor and excitement.

Many were seized by spasms that caused them to fall to the ground, where they lay as if dead. Others jerked, danced, barked, laughed, or sang. After the converts had revived, they shouted joyously that they had been saved.

The established churches did not welcome these converts graciously, and as a consequence churches were often split or new congregations were formed. Barton W. Stone found himself involved in a controversy with the presbytery of which he was a member. In 1804 he and his congregation at Cane Ridge withdrew from the Presbyterian fellowship and organized an independent church to which they gave the name Christian. Similar splits and the organization of other independent churches followed all over the State. Thus a new Protestant sect, now ranking fifth in membership in the State, was born in Kentucky.

A similar movement later took place in Pennsylvania under the leadership of the Reverend Thomas Campbell and his son, Alexander, who came to Kentucky and organized churches to which he gave the name Disciples of Christ. Stone and Campbell found themselves in essential agreement and finally merged their organizations in 1832, but the Kentucky churches that entered the merger retained the name Christian, though they are officially affiliated with the denomination known as the Disciples of Christ.

The Cane Ridge building is constructed of ash logs chinked with mud on a foundation of local stone. The flooring is of oak, and hand-split oak shakes, four feet long, cover the roof. In 1829 the building was weatherboarded, lathed, and plastered. Originally it contained a massive balcony that was almost half as large as the main floor and was reached from the outside by a ladder. This balcony, with its cherry railing, was torn down in 1829 and the timbers were used in the construction of a barn near by. An attempt has been made in recent years to restore the meeting house. It is planned (1939) to use some of the timbers that have been preserved in the old barn in reconstructing the balcony.

Between Paris and Lexington the route is through a corner of Kentucky's horse-breeding area. Here fine country mansions stand far back from the road at the end of avenues lined with trees. The white-fenced paddocks, green grazing lands, and landscaped grounds combine to make this 17 miles resemble a large park.

GREENTREE (L) is at **56.7** *m. (see Lexington).*

At **57.1** *m.* (R) is ELMENDORF *(see Lexington).*

Across the road from the Widener estate at **57.5** *m.* is the C. V. WHITNEY FARM *(see Lexington).*

At **58.1** *m.* is (L) LLANGOLLEN *(see Lexington)* and the junction with Johnston Rd., improved.

Left on this road to BRYAN STATION, 5 *m.*, where there is a memorial, a stone wall four feet in height, octagonal in form, around the spring that supplied water to the defenders of the station when it was besieged in 1782 by a band of Indians under the leadership of Capt. William Caldwell and the renegade Simon Girty. Sweeping westward toward Lexington, the invaders, on the evening of August 15, 1782, secretly surrounded Bryan Station, anticipating an easy victory when they should attack on the morrow.

There is a story, the authenticity of which is disputed, that the little company found itself with too little water to withstand a long siege and determined to risk sending the women out in the early morning to obtain a supply; they were to act as though they did not know that the enemy was in the canebrake around the spring. According to the story, the women carried out the plan, walking out and back again without undue haste. There is no explanation of why the enemy failed to attack at this time. Later about 100 Indians appeared openly and a group of settlers came out and fired on them. Immediately the hidden Girty and the remainder of the band attempted to take the station by storm. They were met by gunfire from the post.

All that day and the next the siege continued. On the first afternoon reinforcements arrived from Lexington and Boone Station and fought their way into the fort. Girty's men, failing to take the fort within the two days, and fearing the arrival of more troops, retreated toward the Ohio River, pursued by the defending garrison and other troops. At the Battle of Blue Licks the Kentuckians were ambuscaded and cut down. In spite of this disaster the defense of Bryan Station halted the invasion of Kentucky and resulted in the withdrawal of the British allies.

Just beyond the memorial and across the railroad is BRYAN STATION HOUSE, on a hill above fields and woods. The excellent condition of this white-painted, brick dwelling, erected in 1797, belies its age. It is a story and a half high. The half story is formed by a steep shingled roof, the severity of which is relieved by three dormers. A wide porch, added in recent years, extends across the front. At the right is the original porch, which has square columns of hickory. From this porch is an excellent view of the Elkhorn Creek Valley. In the yard is the outline of the stockade surrounding the station for which the house was named.

A private driveway (L), **59.6 m.**, leads to the LEXINGTON COUNTRY CLUBHOUSE, on a knoll surrounded by an extensive, well-kept, shady lawn. It commands a broad view of the meadows around the headwaters of North Elkhorn Creek.

Opposite the clubhouse is the entrance (through Swigert Lane) to HAYLANDS *(grounds open)* (R), owned by Miss Elizabeth Daingerfield. Haylands is the home of Morvich, winner of the Kentucky Derby in 1922.

LEXINGTON, **63.8 m.** (957 alt., 45,736 pop.) *(see Lexington).*

Points of Interest: Homes of Henry Clay, Gen. John Hunt Morgan, Mary Todd Lincoln, and John Bradford; Transylvania College; University of Kentucky; loose-leaf tobacco market, and others.

Lexington is at the junction with US 60 *(see Tour 16),* US 25 *(see Tour 4),* and US 27 *(see Tour 3).*

Section b. LEXINGTON *to* BOWLING GREEN *173.5 m. US 68.*

Southwest of LEXINGTON, **0 m.,** US 68 runs through a varied country. Parklike grounds and wide bluegrass meadows contrast with the tree-crowned cliffs of the Kentucky River's majestic gorge. Along the route are towns containing fine old mansions and State parks and battlefields.

At **2.8 m.** is the junction with the Lane Allen Rd.

Right on this road to SCARLET GATE **1 m.,** now a stock farm but formerly the home of James Lane Allen. The two-story house has one-story wings, one of which is now a garage. The one-story Doric portico relieves the simplicity of the façade.

James Lane Allen (1849–1925), author of the *Choir Invisible, Reign of Law* and other widely read novels, was born in a small frame house on the Parker's Mill Rd., about six miles from Lexington. Much of his work has a Kentucky background *(see Literature).*

BEAUMONT (R), 3.5 *m.*, the 2,500-acre thoroughbred-horse farm of Hal Price Headley, is the home of such noted runners as Supremus, Pharamond II, and Epinard.

The congregation of the old SOUTH ELKHORN BAPTIST CHURCH (R), 6.2 *m.*, was founded in 1783 by Lewis Craig, pioneer Baptist minister in Kentucky *(see Tour 3).*

At 9.8 *m.* is the junction with Catnip Hill Pike.

Left on this road to LA CHAUMIERE DU PRAIRIE, 1 *m.*, built in 1800 by Col. Davis Meade, officer in the Revolutionary Army, on his 400-acre land grant. The dwelling developed as a series of rooms, some of log, others of stone, one of mud, and one—remaining today—of brick in octagonal form. Passageways of stone or brick were built to connect the units as the group was enlarged from time to time. The one-story octagonal room—built to entertain Lafayette, according to local legend—was constructed of bricks burned on the place, and the framework was put together with wooden pegs. Adjoining the octagonal room are two small "powder rooms" where wigs were dressed; one of these rooms, for the men, contained a sideboard for liquors. Four men who were or had been Presidents of the United States—Thomas Jefferson, James Monroe, Andrew Jackson, and Zachary Taylor—as well as Henry Clay, Aaron Burr, and Lafayette, were guests here at one time or another.

At 14.6 *m.* is the junction with State 29.

Left on this road is WILMORE, 2 *m.* (882 alt., 1,329 pop.). ASBURY COLLEGE, established in 1890, by Dr. J. W. Hughes of the Methodist Episcopal Church, has 16 buildings and a campus of 46 acres. The college offers both academic and religious courses and confers the A.B. degree.

Also on State 29 is HIGH BRIDGE STATE PARK *(camping facilities),* 7 *m.*, named for a railroad bridge that rises 317 feet above the water and has a span of 1,230 feet. This beautiful area is just below the confluence of the Kentucky and Dix Rivers. The Kentucky, flowing between tree-topped bluffs, has cut a deep gorge into comparatively level terrain.

South of BOONE TUNNEL, 18.8 *m.*, cut through solid limestone in the great gorge of the Kentucky River, US 68 crosses Brooklyn Bridge, which offers a view of the palisades and the deep-hued river.

SHAKERTOWN, 24 *m.* (930 alt., 50 pop.), locally called Pleasant Hill, was settled in 1805 by Shakers, or Shaking Quakers, a religious cult that came into existence in England after 1747, when Jane and James Wardley began exhorting their neighbors to a more austere manner of life. Ann Lee, then 21 years old, was converted to Quakerism, but was later expelled for nonconformity. Actuated by a revelation, she sought refuge in America, landing in New York in 1774. After two years of itinerant preaching and healing, she and her converts established a Shaker settlement at New Lebanon, New York. Later, through missionary labors, chiefly on the frontier, others were organized including this one at Pleasant Hill, which came to be known as Shakertown, and was an important center of Shaker activity. In 1812 this colony, with the acquisition of 3,000 acres of very fertile farm land, inaugurated a large-scale building program. About 20 plain, strong brick and stone structures, with walls three and four feet thick, were erected.

These included a school, a church, a general office, a post office, and a weaving house, in addition to North, East, Center, and West Houses. Each house held one communal "family."

The Shakers were notably industrious people. Next to religion, work was the chief interest of their lives. Their sleek, well-fed cattle and horses, their sheep and farm products brought high prices. Here, in addition to farming, they conducted a sawmill, a gristmill, a fulling mill, an oil mill, a tanyard, and a paper mill; their furniture and brooms were noted for their superior quality. The women wove silk and other cloth and made straw hats. Their preserves, jellies, and pickles were as renowned as the farm products of the men. The Shakers adhered to the principle of communistic living—all worked for the good of all—and the equality of the sexes, women having the same power and authority as men. Though celibates, they united in families because they believed the family unit to be the most effective. All were "brothers and sisters in the Lord." The plan of government, established prior to 1800, included a spiritual head—two elders and two eldresses—who were the final authority in all affairs, temporal as well as spiritual. They believed in the dual nature of the Deity, that Jesus had come to earth as the masculine principle, and that "Mother Ann" represented the feminine—though they did not worship either. The chief tenet of the Shaker religion was Christian socialism; in addition, they believed in the "gift of many tongues," in visions and prophecy, in communion with the spirits of the departed, and in power over physical disease, detachment from the world, and confession of sin. Sedate singing, dancing, and hand clapping accompanied their worship.

When the colony was a little more than 100 years old it was so depleted in numbers that its members were forced to sell their land and houses, with the provision, however, that their debts should be paid, and that 12 remaining brothers and sisters should be cared for during their lives. Sister Mary Settles, the last Shaker in Kentucky, died here in 1925 at the age of 87.

The Shakers' houses all have capstones bearing the dates of erection. They have no decorations of any kind and no mantels over the fireplaces. Each family house has a double entrance, one used by the men and the other by the women. Though men and women met socially, they were separated in the dining room, at work, and during worship. The houses are three and one-half stories in height with full basements; their walls, 22 inches thick at the first floor, diminish in thickness with each succeeding floor. All the brick used in these buildings was burned on the property and the stone was quarried from near-by hills.

The Shakers constructed one of the first water systems in Kentucky, a horse provided power for a force pump that raised the water from a spring to the tank house, and thence to a hydrant just outside of the buildings.

The NORTH FAMILY BUILDING (L) was built of brick in 1831.

The women's WORK SHOP *(open)* is (R) a two-story, frame, rectangular building. The stones in its foundation are exceptionally large, one of them 12 feet in length and 18 inches square.

The brick EAST FAMILY HOUSE *(open)*, now the Shakertown Inn, was built (R) in 1817. It was designed to accommodate 50 men and 50 women, contains 22 rooms and five compartments in the basement. All the woodwork is of yellow poplar and is mortised and pegged. The floors are of white ash of irregular width. Encircling the walls in each room is a peg board, 6 feet from the floor with 3-inch turned wooden pegs set 12 inches apart.

The WORK SHOP (R), a two-story brick building with a frame ell, is of more recent date.

The GUEST HOUSE *(open daily 9–5; adm. 10¢)* is (L) now a museum. This building, built of brick in 1839, has a wide doorway with side- and fan-lights; the windows have side lights with green shutters. It contains two beautiful self-supporting spiral stairways.

The MINISTER'S HOUSE (L) is a plain two-story frame building, now used as a residence.

The MEETING HOUSE (L) is a two-story rectangular frame building with the usual double entrance. Above the auditorium are rooms that were formerly used for committee and business meetings.

The CHURCH FAMILY HOUSE (R) is a two-story stone building resembling the brick family houses.

The FARM MANAGER'S HOUSE *(open)*, now called Ye Old Shaker Tavern, is (R) the oldest building of the group (1809). It is of stone, two stories in height, and has one entrance instead of the usual two.

The CARPENTER'S SHOP (L), a one-story building, is now a store.

The DOCTOR'S OFFICE (R), a two-story stone building with a single entrance door, is now a residence.

The WEST FAMILY HOUSE (R), now the Pennebaker School for Girls, an orphanage of the Presbyterian Church, is practically a duplicate of the East Family House.

In the BURYING GROUND (L), beyond the pond, the grave markers are of cast iron and of stone and contain only initials.

Left 3 *m.* from Shakertown on State 33 to DIX DAM, built in 1925 by the Kentucky Utilities Company near the confluence of the Dix and Kentucky Rivers. The dam is 1,030 feet long, 275 feet high, with a base thickness of 750 feet and a top width of 24 feet. The spillway is 3,000 feet long and 250 feet wide. HERRINGTON LAKE *(bass fishing; motor launches $1 an hour)*, formed by the dam, is 36 miles in length. In the FLOATING BASS HATCHERY at Gwinn Island in Herrington Lake, large-mouthed bass are propagated.

Between Shakertown and Harrodsburg, US 68 crosses an area of fertile Bluegrass farm land.

HARRODSBURG, 32 *m.* (871 alt., 4,029 pop.) *(see Harrodsburg).*

Points of Interest: Pioneer Memorial State Park, Old Fort Harrod, Memorial Monument, Lincoln Marriage Temple, Pioneer Cemetery, Mansion Museum, College Street, Morgan Row, and others.

Harrodsburg is at the junction with State 35 *(see Tour 5)*.

Right from Harrodsburg on the Dry Branch Pike to old MUD MEETING HOUSE, 3 *m.*, a Dutch Reformed church, now the property of the Harrodsburg Historical Society. This meeting house was built on land purchased in 1800 by a congregation organized in 1796 by the Reverend Peter LaBaugh, a missionary from New Jersey. In the adjoining yard is the GRAVE OF DOMINIE THOMAS KYLE, the first pastor. Although it is now weatherboarded and plastered, this well-preserved building was constructed in an unusual manner. Heavy log sills were laid upon a stone foundation. Into these sills squared timbers, placed at intervals of several feet, were mortised and tenoned. Pieces of hand-split hickory were mortised horizontally across the uprights, and between these puddled clay, mixed with straw, was tamped into place. When the clay hardened the whole formed a solid wall. The flooring, made of boards irregular in width, was tongued and grooved by hand, fitted together, and laid upon joists.

The name of PERRYVILLE, 42.4 *m.* (913 alt., 349 pop.), is connected chiefly with the battle fought two miles from here in the War between the States. Main Street is flanked by weather-beaten frame buildings, their stoops overhanging the sidewalks and their ells abutting on the Chaplin River, which divides the town. Many of the buildings served as hospitals or quarters during and after the Battle of Perryville.

Right from Perryville on the Mackville Pike, an improved road, to the PERRYVILLE BATTLEFIELD, 2 *m.* Here was fought the deciding engagement of the Kentucky campaign of 1862. General Bragg entered Kentucky early in September 1862 and moved far into the interior of the State, attempting to rouse, by his presence, the secessionists he felt to be predominant in the State.

General Buell, the Union commander, moved his army from Tennessee into Kentucky to checkmate the moves of the Confederates, and, if possible, to drive them out of the State.

After considerable maneuvering by both sides, the two armies met near Perryville. The battle was really an accidental collision. Neither side could claim a clean-cut victory, but the Federals held the field, while Bragg retired to Harrodsburg and presently retreated into East Tennessee. Subsequently the Confederates abandoned all attempts to bring Kentucky into the Confederacy by military means. The battlefield embraces 17 acres in which a Confederate monument was erected in 1902, and another for the Union dead in 1931.

US 68 leads past the old PERRYVILLE CEMETERY and continues in a zigzag course.

The HALFWAY INN (L), 48.4 *m.*, now a private residence, was built prior to 1792. It was so named because of its position halfway between Boonesboro and the Falls of the Ohio on the road connecting the settlements. After the Battle of Perryville many of the wounded were cared for in it.

In SPRINGFIELD, 58.9 *m.* (728 alt., 1,487 pop.), founded in 1793, is the WASHINGTON COUNTY COURTHOUSE, at Main and Cross Sts., that was erected in 1814. Among its records, which date from 1792, are the marriage bond of Thomas Lincoln, father of Abraham Lincoln, the certificate of the marriage of Thomas Lincoln and Nancy Hanks; and one of the two known signatures of Lincoln's grandmother, Bersheba Lincoln.

The JOHN POPE HOUSE, Walnut and High Sts., was built of brick in the Georgian Colonial style, about 1795, by Gen. Matthew Walton. John Pope (1770–1845), who was a representative and Senator from Kentucky and third Governor of the Territory of Arkansas (1829–1835), resided in Springfield from about 1819 until his death.

The ROBERTS HOUSE, N. Walnut St., is the home of Elizabeth Madox Roberts, author of the *Great Meadow,* the *Time of Man,* and other novels and poems *(see Literature).*

CEMETERY HILL, Walnut St., is a burying ground established in 1797.

1. Right from Springfield on State 55, an improved road, to the LINCOLN HOMESTEAD PARK *(open Apr.-Oct., 9–4; adm. 10¢),* 5 *m.,* containing a reproduction of the home of Lincoln's grandmother, Bersheba, a MEMORIAL TO NANCY HANKS, and a monument marking what is believed by some historians to be the SITE WHERE LINCOLN'S GRANDFATHER WAS KILLED by Indians *(see Tour 16).* Here, on June 12, the annual Lincoln Marriage Festival is held under the sponsorship of the Washington County Historical Society. The States of Kentucky, Indiana, and Illinois participate in a program that includes re-enactment in costume of the marriage of Thomas Lincoln and Nancy Hanks. The festivities close with a costume ball.

2. Left from Springfield on State 55 to a monument marking the GRAVE OF BEN HARDIN, 2 *m.,* the noted pioneer lawyer, of Bardstown.
Right from Springfield on State 53, a paved road, to a PREHISTORIC BURIAL GROUND, 5 *m.,* where beneath two stone mounds many fragments of prehistoric bones and artifacts were found. These are on display in the museums of the Eastern State Normal School, Richmond, and Southwestern Presbyterian University, Memphis, Tennessee. Along the same road are several earth mounds (R).

In the rolling to hilly agricultural country west of Springfield, the farms are small; erosion has taken heavy toll here.

At 60.5 *m.* is the junction with a graveled road.

Left on this road to ST. ROSE'S PRIORY (L), 1.2 *m.,* a Dominican school founded in 1806, which was attended (1816–18) by Jefferson Davis, later President of the Confederacy.

The CONVENT AND ACADEMY OF ST. CATHERINE OF SIENA (L), 61.5 *m.,* established in 1820, is a junior college for girls. In its library of 7,000 volumes are rare books. The academy also owns a number of paintings, some of them attributed to Rembrandt, Murillo, and Perugino, but probably copies. In the school museum is a small collection of local relics, Indian and prehistoric.

FEDERAL HILL *(open 9–4; adm. 25¢),* 76.6 *m.,* completed in 1818, was built as the manor house of a great plantation that belonged to John Rowan, Jr., whose cousin, Stephen Collins Foster, wrote the ballad, "My Old Kentucky Home." Now in a State park, the brick mansion, among trees some distance (L) off the highway, is one of the best examples of Georgian Colonial architecture in Kentucky. This brick house, on a stone foundation, is two stories high and is finely proportioned within and without. There is a service court between the dining room and an outside one-story kitchen. With the exception of the long narrow windows that flank the classically enframed doorway, and those directly above them, all the windows in the façade have 24 panes. The central hall is spanned by an arch with fluted colonettes. All of the rooms have beautifully carved wooden mantels.

William Rowan brought his son John (1773–1843), later the builder of Federal Hill, to Kentucky from Pennsylvania in 1783, and settled first near Louisville, then in the vicinity of Bardstown, where he placed his son in the school of Doctor Priestley. In 1795 John was admitted to the bar at Bardstown. About this time he married and brought his bride to the little brick house that is now the rear wing of the mansion. In 1804 he was appointed Secretary of State, in 1806 was elected to Congress from a district in which he did not reside, and in 1819 was appointed judge of the Court of Appeals. After he was elected to the United States Senate (1824), this house was used chiefly as a summer home and hunting lodge.

At the foot of the hill in front of the dwelling is the old stone spring house; over this, in a room of logs, was Rowan's law office in which several young lawyers received their training, and briefs on many legal cases were prepared. Tradition relates that here John Rowan, Henry Clay, and their cronies enjoyed many glasses of Kentucky whisky and played games of poker.

Rowan, who died in Louisville in 1843, was buried in the family burying ground here. His son, John, who succeeded him as the master of Federal Hill, became United States Minister to the Kingdom of Naples in 1848.

In 1852, a few months before Christy's Minstrels first sung "My Old Kentucky Home," Stephen Collins Foster (1826–64) and his wife came down the river from Pittsburgh on their way to New Orleans. It is locally affirmed that on this trip Foster visited his cousin at Federal Hill and that "My Old Kentucky Home" was written here.

At 76.9 *m.* is the junction with US 62; the two routes are united between this point and Bardstown.

BARDSTOWN, 77.2 *m.* (637 alt., 1,767 pop.), among the hills of Nelson County, is a stately old town with magnificent trees bordering broad streets on which are numerous houses in the late Georgian Colonial and the Greek Revival styles. First known as Salem, Bardstown was renamed for William Baird (or Bard) of Pennsylvania, one of the owners of the 100-acre tract on which the town was laid out. It was incorporated by the Virginia Legislature November 4, 1778, and in its youth rivaled Louisville and Lexington as a center of social and educational activities. Salem Academy was founded here in 1788 by James Priestley. Nazareth Academy, for girls, was founded near Bardstown in the early part of the nineteenth century; St. Joseph's College, a school for boys, founded in 1819, attained a high reputation.

A doubtful legend, cherished by the citizens, is that Louis Philippe, Duke of Orléans, later King of France, was a resident of the little town for a time, during which he taught French and dancing to the children of the gentry and worked at the watchmaker's trade. Louis Philippe and two brothers, on their way from the capital to New Orleans, crossed the Salt River at Pitts Fork with difficulty, on October 16, 1797, and spent the night at Captain Bean's tavern here. Though the Duke became very ill, he was left alone because the first company of stage troupers had come to town—an event causing great excitement.

The JOHN FITCH MONUMENT (R), on Courthouse Square, was erected by Congress to honor the man now acknowledged as the inventor of the steamboat. John Fitch was born in Connecticut in 1743. His first successful experiment with a boat propelled by steam was made on the Delaware River in 1787—20 years before Fulton launched the *Clermont* on the Hudson. Fitch came to Kentucky as a surveyor, and the proceeds of the sale of a map he had made of Ohio and Kentucky helped him to finance his experiments. His ideas of the possibilities of the steamboat for use in reaching the West were regarded as the ravings of a madman, and it was 1790 before he finally sold enough stock to finance the boat that carried passengers between Philadelphia and Trenton for several years. With the profits of this venture a vessel was built for operation on the Ohio, but, just as it was ready for launching, it was dashed to pieces by a storm. Unable to obtain public recognition for his engine or financial aid to promote it, he returned, in 1796, to the wilderness of Kentucky and to a life of seclusion. He came here to settle on land he had bought during a surveying trip, only to find it overrun by squatters. While he was in Bardstown he constructed a small model of a steamboat, which he floated on the town creek.

In the summer of 1798, bitter and disillusioned, he ended his life, it is said, with a dose of poison. In his journal he had written: "I know of nothing so vexatious to a man of feelings as a turbulent wife and steamboat building. I experienced the former and quit in season and had I been in my right sense I should undoubtedly have treated the latter in the same manner, but for one man to be teased with both, he must be looked upon as the most unfortunate man of this world."

Back of the jail in an old cemetery is the marked GRAVE OF JOHN FITCH.

The TALBOTT HOTEL, on Courthouse Square, has been operating since its construction about 1800. In an upstairs room, probably used originally as a banquet hall, are murals that reflect the influence of the Italian school.

The BEAL RESIDENCE (L), two blocks south of Courthouse Square, was one of the first brick dwellings in Bardstown; it was built between 1790 and 1800. One of the first race tracks in the State was on the Beal estate.

Construction of ST. JOSEPH'S PROTO-CATHEDRAL (R) was begun in 1816, the building was dedicated by Bishop Benedict Joseph Flaget in 1819. The building is a notable example of church architecture of its period. The woodwork and structural timbers, including the six massive poplar columns of the broad pedimented Ionic portico, were taken from the near-by forest; a local limestone quarry and a clay bank supplied the stone and material for the brick; the nails and hardware were wrought by local blacksmiths. The simple Greco-Roman design of the building, with its classic façade and lofty clock, and bell tower and spire, was the work of John Rogers, who moved from Baltimore to Bardstown to superintend the construction. Within the cathedral are many paintings, said to have been obtained by Bishop Flaget and his assistants, Fathers Badin and Nerinckx, from the sacked churches of Belgium and France during the Napoleonic era. Among them is the *Flaying of St. Bartholemew*, of the Rubens school; *Winged St. Mark*, *St. John the Baptist*, and *St. Peter in Chains*, believed to be by Van Dyck (1599–1641); a *Descent of the Ghost* and *Annunciation* are ascribed to Van Eyck; a *Crucifixion* to Van Bree, and a *Crowning of the Blessed Virgin* to Murillo (1617–82). Local tradition credits many of the rich interior furnishings, including the altar pieces and paintings, as well as the sweet-toned bell, to the generosity of Louis Philippe, King of France from 1830 to 1848, and to other royal donors. In 1841 the seat of the Roman Catholic see was moved from Bardstown to Louisville, and this church was thenceforth known as the Proto (Gr., *first*) Cathedral.

The BEN HARDIN HOUSE, in the southwestern part of Bardstown, is a large brick structure, irregular in form, and of no distinct style of architecture. It was erected in 1819 by Ben Hardin, one of Kentucky's greatest criminal lawyers and one of the most picturesque figures of his day. John Randolph of Roanoke, in allusion to Hardin's peculiar style, said of him, "Hardin is like a kitchen knife, whetted on a brick; he cuts roughly, but he cuts deep." He was called "Kitchen Knife" until his death.

Bardstown is at a junction with US 62 *(see Tour 14)* and US 31E *(see Tour 6)*.

Between Bardstown and a point at 135.7 *m.*, US 68 and US 31E are one route *(see Tour 6)*, and between HORSE CAVE, 139.5 *m.* (603 alt., 1,259 pop.) *(see Tour 7)*, and BOWLING GREEN, 173.5 *m.* (469 alt., 12,348 pop.) *(see Tour 7)*, US 68 and US 31W are united *(see Tour 7)*.

Section c. BOWLING GREEN *to* PADUCAH; *144.5 m.*

South of BOWLING GREEN, 0 *m.*, through the southern Knobs section of the State, the highway abounds with delightful vistas of upland forests and well-cultivated fields. This fertile agricultural area produces a high grade of dark tobacco and many thoroughbred horses.

Three brick buildings, at 14 *m.*, are REMNANTS OF A SHAKER COLONY, founded in 1800. There were formerly six large buildings and nearly 100 other structures here. The Shakers here operated a tannery, a hat factory, and a canning and preserving factory, and wove some silk produced by their own silkworms. Celibacy of the members and the lack of new recruits reduced the group to a dozen survivors who, in 1922, removed to the settlement at Lebanon, New York. The oldest building now standing bears the date 1824.

At 14.8 *m.* is the junction with State 73.

Left on State 73 to the town of SOUTH UNION, 1 *m.* (579 alt., 110 pop.), containing an old SHAKER INN of stagecoach days. The building, now unoccupied, is a three-story, rectangular, gable-roofed structure with no ornamentation, though there is a large porch at one end of the dining room. It stands among large, old trees.

Along the highway between Bowling Green and Auburn are many stone walls, most of them built by slaves. The road here has one of the most solidly built roadbeds in the State. Limestone slabs a foot or more in length were placed on end, forming a bed of an average depth of 10 inches; this old foundation has been repaved.

AUBURN, 17.9 *m.* (605 alt., 821 pop.), is on the border between the rolling fertile land and the abrupt winding knobs.

RUSSELLVILLE, 28.4 *m.* (534 alt., 3,297 pop.), is in a valley among the knobs. Trees arch above its old houses, which are surrounded with old-fashioned flower gardens. It was founded in 1790 and was at first called Big Boiling Spring. The name was changed to honor Gen. William Russell, an officer of the Revolutionary Army.

In the COKE HOUSE, SE. cor. 4th and Winter Sts., advocates of State sovereignty met in 1861 and passed an Act of Secession, declared Kentucky a Confederate State, established Bowling Green as the capital, and elected George W. Johnson Provisional Governor.

The old SOUTHERN BANK BUILDING, SW. cor. 6th and Main Sts., now a residence, is a two-story brick structure that originally served as a combined residence and a bank. The doorway of the wing which abuts on the sidewalk has an elaborately carved frame. Posing as a group of wealthy cattle buyers, Jesse James and four companions arrived here on March 20, 1868, and shocked the townspeople by suddenly robbing this bank of $9,000 and wounding its president before they fled to Tennessee. Two weeks later one of the band, George Shepherd, was captured in Tennessee, returned, and sentenced to three years' imprisonment.

West of Russellville is a broad valley with stock farms and dark-tobacco fields.

ELKTON, 43.8 *m.* (602 alt., 951 pop.), seat of Todd County, is the former home of Associate Justice J. C. McReynolds of the U.S. Supreme Court.

Right from Elkton on State 181, an improved road, to the stone entrance, 3 *m.*, of BLUE AND GRAY STATE PARK *(adm. 10¢, picnic ovens; hotel)*. The park, so named because of its intermediate position between the birthplaces of Jefferson Davis and Abraham Lincoln, consists of an 86-acre wooded area. It was established in 1925, when citizens of Todd County donated the tract to the State Park Commission. The driveway winds through a broad meadow and terminates on the brink of a woodland bluff, into the side of which a rustic hotel has been built. On three sides of the building are verandas, overlooking a wooded valley, picnic grounds, tennis courts, and Mallory Springs, source of the hotel's water supply. Many sportsmen stay at the hotel during the fall while fox hunting and shooting small game in the surrounding region.

In FAIRVIEW, 52.3 *m.* (175 pop.), is a JEFFERSON DAVIS MONUMENT in DAVIS MEMORIAL PARK (L), commemorating the birthplace of the man who became the President of the Confederacy. The concrete obelisk, in a 20-acre tract, is 351 feet high. At the base is a room, 20 feet square, containing a bronze tablet and a bas-relief panel with a life-sized figure of Jefferson Davis, the work of Frederick C. Hibbard. An elevator carries visitors to the top of the shaft, from which point is a fine view of the surrounding country. The monument, erected by the United Daughters of the Confederacy, was dedicated in 1929.

In the park near the monument stands a reproduction of the DAVIS CABIN, the two-room log house in which Jefferson Davis was born. The vestibule of the BETHEL BAPTIST CHURCH is the site of the original cabin.

Jefferson Davis was born on June 3, 1808, the son of a well-to-do planter. After a brief experience on a Mississippi plantation, the family returned to Kentucky. The lad was sent to school in Bardstown, later entered Transylvania University at Lexington, and after two years became a cadet at West Point Military Academy. After graduation his commission was signed by John C. Calhoun, then Secretary of War.

He was a field officer during the Indian wars, notably in a campaign against Black Hawk. He entered politics, became a presidential elector (1844); and in 1845 a Representative in Congress from Mississippi. During the Mexican War, in which he led a Mississippi regiment, he fought at Buena Vista and Monterey and, on his return, was sent to the United States Senate.

Though he was primarily a land-owner and his interests were those of a planter, President Franklin Pierce persuaded him to accept an appointment as Secretary of War. He had married President Zachary Taylor's daughter, who died three months later. Nine years afterward he married Miss Varina Howell of Natchez, Mississippi.

When the great controversy between the North and the South came to a head, Jefferson Davis, who had long been a secessionist, was elected President of the Confederacy virtually by acclamation. He was captured in Georgia at the close of the War between the States and was imprisoned for two years in Fortress Monroe.

After his death in New Orleans in 1889, his birthday was made a public holiday in most of the Southern States.

Right from Fairview on a dirt road to PILOT ROCK, 11 *m.*, a natural formation rising 200 feet. From its top the Jefferson Davis monument is visible.

The WESTERN STATE HOSPITAL (R), 60.9 *m.*, is one of three institutions for the mentally diseased.

HOPKINSVILLE, 63.1 *m.* (541 alt., 10,746 pop.) *(see Tour 4)*, is at the junction with US 41 and US 41E *(see Tour 8)*.

CADIZ, 83.5 *m.* (468 alt., 1,114 pop.), seat of Trigg County, is in the center of a large dark-leaf tobacco-growing area and is the home of several wealthy planters. It is known also for the number and quality of hams it ships. Trigg County was named for Col. Stephen Trigg, a Virginian who was a well-known Indian fighter.

Left from Cadiz on State 93 to the junction with State 287, 2.6 *m.*, an improved road. At 6 *m.* on State 287 is a foot trail (L) leading to the first of the BRELS-FORD'S CAVES, a series of seven caverns. Although never extensively explored, the interiors of these caves possess beauty and diversity in their formations. During the War between the States one of them was used as a hideout by bands of guerillas.

CANTON, 92.5 *m.* (200 pop.), by the Cumberland River, was once a busy landing place for river cargo-carriers. BOYD'S TAVERN, now the Canton Hotel, is an old two-story massive brick structure with joists of hand-hewn black walnut and floors of white ash. A wide hall runs through the center on each floor.

West of the Cumberland River *(toll 30¢)* is a sterile region. The 47,000-acre KENTUCKY WOODLANDS WILDLIFE REFUGE, in Trigg and Lyons Counties, is supervised by the Bureau of Biological Survey, which is demonstrating methods of utilizing lands that are unsuitable for farming by removing submarginal crop lands and devoting this area to forestry and to the conservation of wild life. Parts of the refuge have been adapted to the use of waterfowl, the upland areas are devoted to the production of deer, turkey, quail, and other small game.

At 101.3 *m.* the road crosses the Tennessee River on a State toll bridge *(toll 30¢)*.

At 102.5 *m.* is the junction with State 94, a paved road.

Left on this road through a broken and hilly region to MURRAY, 15 *m.* (480 alt., 2,891 pop.), the seat of Calloway County, named in honor of John L. Murray, a member of Congress (1830). The MURRAY STATE TEACHERS' COLLEGE was founded in 1922 and now has an enrollment of more than 1,000 students. The college, housed in seven modern buildings, has a beautiful campus.
Nathan B. Stubblefield, a native of Murray, achieved distinction here as a pioneer experimentalist in the field of wireless telephony. It is alleged locally that he was the first to transmit the human voice successfully through the medium that is now known as radio. The experiment was performed in 1902 across the swampy wood that is now the college campus. As often happens in connection with important scientific pioneering, a series of controversies, claims, counterclaims, and recriminations has arisen over the question of Stubblefield's primacy in the radio field. Stubblefield's basic patent was not recorded until May 12, 1908, six years after the climax of his experimentation and twenty years after a patent covering the same essentials had been issued to Lucius J. Phelps of New York.

An annual event that arouses great interest in Murray is the annual exhibition in October of purebred Jersey cattle. In 1929 Calloway County was awarded the prize for having made more progress in the development of the purebred Jersey than any other county in the

United States. On the fourth Monday in March, known as Mule Trading Day, animals for sale or exchange are brought here from the surrounding country.

BENTON, 119 *m.* (1,021 pop.), seat of Marshall County, is in that part of the State known as the Purchase *(see Tour 9)*, lands ceded to the United States by the Chickasaw in 1818. The town was named for Thomas Hart Benton (1782–1858), the United States Senator from Missouri, hero of those who wanted all lands taken from the Indians. The first Marshall County Courthouse was built of logs in 1843 by Francis Clayton. Two years after its construction, the building was sold to Clayton for $26; the second courthouse was built in 1847.

" 'Tater Day," celebrated for more than 50 years on the first Monday in April, like county court day in many rural sections of Kentucky, is the annual spring holiday when the countryside gathers on the streets to buy and sell sweet potatoes for seed. The transactions have been extended to include livestock, produce, guns, knives, or anything that can be swapped. The day is an occasion not only for trading, but also for meeting friends.

Old Southern Harmony Singing held here annually on the fourth Sunday in May, was established in 1884 by J. R. Lemon, a west Kentucky newspaperman. Beginning at 10 A.M., the singing continues for nearly two hours, when an old-fashioned basket dinner is eaten on the courthouse lawn. The old *Southern Harmony* used in the annual festival was one of the most widely used song books written in four notes— *fa, sol, la, mi*—of the shape note variety. Tradition relates that, in 1853, when J. R. Lemon's ancestors came over the mountains from North Carolina to Marshall County in a covered wagon, they brought with them, among their household goods, a copy of *Southern Harmony*, known then as "Singin' Billy Walker's book" and dated 1835. The songs in this book were collected in the rural sections of the South.

Between Benton and Paducah is a gently rolling farm land in which tobacco, corn, wheat, and berries are grown. This section of western Kentucky, with Paducah as the hub, has developed into the largest strawberry-producing area of the State. Benton is one of several loading points from which refrigerator cars carry crates of Dixie Aroma strawberries to midwestern, northern, and eastern markets.

At 139.5 *m.* is the junction with US 60 *(see Tour 16)* and US 62 *(see Tour 14)*.

PADUCAH, 144.5 *m.* (341 alt., 33,541 pop.) *(see Paducah)*.

Points of Interest: Paduke Statue, Tilghman Memorial, Irvin Cobb Hotel, McCracken County Courthouse, Noble Park, Marine Ways, Brazelton House, Illinois Central Shops and others.

Paducah is at the junction with US 60 *(see Tour 16)*, US 62 *(see Tour 14)*, and US 45 *(see Tour 9)*.

Tour 16

(Huntington, W. Va.)—Ashland—Owingsville—Mount Sterling—Winchester—Lexington—Versailles—Frankfort—Louisville—Henderson—Paducah—Wickliffe—(Charleston, Mo.); US 60, the Midland Trail. West Virginia Line to Missouri Line, 516.4 m.

Paved roadbed throughout.
Chesapeake & Ohio Ry. parallels route between West Virginia Line and Lexington; Louisville & Nashville R.R. between Frankfort and Louisville, and between Cloverport and Henderson.
All types of accommodations in cities and larger towns; limited elsewhere.

US 60, the longest single route in the State, winds east-west through Kentucky, revealing all its varied topography. Between Catlettsburg and Ashland it follows the Ohio River, paralleling the railroad tracks and yards through the industrial section of eastern Kentucky. Between Ashland and Louisville it passes through mountain counties that had been practically inaccessible before the highway was built in the 1920's. Between Morehead and Mount Sterling the valley widens, the hills decrease in height, and open farm and pasture lands appear. It crosses the Bluegrass section, a land of fertile chocolate-colored soil, white frame fences, and spacious ante-bellum houses whose columns are half hidden by trees. Lexington, midway between Catlettsburg and Louisville, is the center of Kentucky's saddle-horse and race-horse breeding section—the heart of tradition's "old Kentucky"—where life is still lived in the grand manner, and a knowledge of horses is of prime importance. The route crosses the Kentucky River at Frankfort, the State's capital, where the Bluegrass country meets the foothills of the northeast highlands.

Section a. WEST VIRGINIA LINE *to* LEXINGTON, *141.4 m. US 60*

US 60 crosses the West Virginia Line, 0 *m.*, 10 miles west of Huntington, West Virginia *(see West Virginia Tour 12)*, by way of a bridge *(toll 50¢)* over the Big Sandy River.

CATLETTSBURG, 0.5 *m.* (552 alt., 5,025 pop.), sprawled among the hills overlooking the junction of the Big Sandy and Ohio Rivers, is the seat of Boyd County. The business district, dominated by the courthouse and given a spacious appearance by the courthouse square, is along the waterfront. Extended back from the river are quiet streets and unpretentious brick and frame dwellings. The town and near-by

Catletts Creek were named for Sawney Catlett, who came from Virginia in 1808 and established a trading post that, for more than 50 years, served trappers and hunters of the Ohio and Big Sandy River regions. These valleys were filled with big game; early explorers, drifting down the Ohio to the mouth of the Big Sandy, then known as Chattaroy (Ind., *river of sand bars*), were frequently attacked by Wyandottes, who resented the intrusion of white men into the valley, called Oki-se-jib-kith-ke (Shawnee, *where buffalo are plenty*).

Among early white visitors, of whom there is record, was a party that arrived in 1772, led by the Reverend David Jones, afterwards an officer in the Revolutionary Army. Another member of the expedition was young George Rogers Clark. The party remained at the mouth of the Big Sandy for several weeks, exploring the lower reaches of the stream. Clark received here his first impressions of the value of the Ohio River as a waterway to the Northwest Territory, and of its importance as a line of defense. Catlettsburg continued as a trading post until 1857, when the cutting of big timber along the upper reaches of thè Big Sandy inaugurated an era of slow but steady growth. The focal point for valley trade, it ranked for several years as a very important round-timber market. During the steamboat era it became a gay and busy place. Riverside folk of the Sandy and Ohio valleys gloried in the coming of the showboat with its blaring band, its shouting captain, and jovial passengers. On the day the Cotton Blossom Floating Theater, whose fame was revived by Edna Ferber's novel, *Show Boat,* tied up at the wharf, Catlettsburg was a typical river town, with its inns, wharves, boathouses, and saloons, where drinks and free food were dispensed. With the coming of railroads and the development of the coal industry, Ashland became the metropolis of northeastern Kentucky. On the old waterfront, once the scene of great activity, are now deserted inns and fading signboards.

Between Catlettsburg and Ashland, US 23 *(see Tour 1)* and this route are united.

ASHLAND, 6.4 *m.* (552 alt., 20,074 pop.) *(see Ashland).*

Points of Interest: American Rolling Mills Plant, Ashland Coke Company Plant, Central Park, and others.

Ashland is at the junction with US 23 *(see Tour 1).*

West of Ashland US 60 winds in and out among the creeks and hollows of the hill country, climbing up and down ridges from whose tops are excellent views of the ranges of hills.

The 6,400-acre ARMCO PARK, 11.8 *m.* *(picnicking facilities),* is a part of the old furnace lands that for years lay open as "commons," on which cattle and hogs were grazed. During the 1920's, after the American Rolling Mills Company had become well established in Ashland, part of this open land was set aside for this park, but most of the enormous holdings of the old iron companies of the nineteenth century have been sold and fenced off.

WILLIAMS' HALFWAY INN (R) **20.8** *m.*, was built about 1824 by Louis Williams. The front of this low, rambling story-and-a-half log house, warped and darkened by the years, has been weatherboarded, and an extension has been added in the rear. The original clay mortar still holds between many of the squared logs. Although the structure was built as a dwelling, like many of the early homes it opened its doors to travelers; it soon became a regular stopping place on the stagecoach route between Louisville and Washington, D.C., and many travelers of early prominence stayed here. The inn is within a 22,000-acre tract belonging to the American Rolling Mills Company that is held as a game preserve.

KILGORE, **22.6** *m.* (634 alt., 50 pop.), is the trading center of a region of iron and coal country.

GRAYSON, **33.5** *m.* (752 alt., 1,022 pop.), largest trading center of an active iron district and seat of Carter County, was named for Col. Robert Grayson.

Left from Grayson on a dirt road to MOUNT SAVAGE, 3 *m.* Here is the largest of the old furnaces in this region. The folklore and songs of this area have acquired a distinctive flavor from the coal-mining industry that was introduced here in the latter part of the eighteenth century.

The story of an explosion at a mine in 1905 is told in the following ballad, composed and often sung by Aunt Molly Jackson *(see Tour 19),* who was born in the mountain region of Kentucky:

> Come all my friends and near relations
> And I will tell you if I can
> What a great and sad occurrence
> That has happened in our land.
> It was on one Monday morning
> On the 18th day of May
> Near 300 coal miners, around us
> Left their homes and marched away
> They went to labor for their families
> And for those they dearly loved
> All at once this sad occurrence
> Now, our chance to meet them is above
> Some was killed without a moment's warning
> And some wrote letters till after two
> Some wrote they would soon be in heaven
> Oh, just think if that be true.

At **44.2** *m.* is the junction with State 182, a graveled road.

Right on this road **1.2** *m.* to the junction with a graveled road; L. **0.6** *m.* to CASCADE CAVES *(open 6–8; adm. 25¢ to $1, guides),* with two electrically lighted caverns and an underground waterfall.

One of the caves, known as Cathedral Room, is 220 feet in length; the other, 720 feet long, has three chambers, one of which is reputed to have been the rendezvous of a band of counterfeiters.

Northwest of the road to Cascade Caves, State 182 passes through a rugged, almost primeval, region skirting Tygarts Creek for a short distance, and winding along the creek bottom of a tributary stream. Virgin stands of timber on the hillsides shade the narrow road. Broken and crumbling stone outcroppings add to the primitive appearance of this defile. Only a part of the extensive series of caverns in the Tygarts Creek district has been fully explored and developed.

At *5.2 m.* on State 182 is the reservation embracing CARTER CAVES AND NATURAL BRIDGES *(open 6–8; adm. 27¢ to each cave, group rates less; guides)*. Only four of the eight caves here are open to the public. A wooden bridge high in the center of a sheer rock wall gives access to X CAVE, formed of four chambers that outline the letter X. From SALTPETER CAVE came some of the crude saltpeter with which the gunpowder used by Kentucky riflemen at the Battle of New Orleans was made. Indian relics have been found here and an excavated spot was the grave of a so-called Indian "princess." BAT CAVE, so named because of the hundreds of bats that hang in clusters from the ceiling, is the largest cavern on the reservation and the only one of those open to the public that is not electrically lighted. Many of its recesses are still unexplored. LAUREL CAVE, the smallest and the one that contains the most interesting formations, is an upper cavern reached by a stairway from the cave below. It contains an outlet through a rock cliff that looks out upon Tygarts Creek, a great distance away. Carter Caves are connected with Cascade Caves by CARTER CAVE NATURAL BRIDGE, one of the largest in Kentucky. It is 219 feet long, 196 feet high, and 12 feet wide, and its top is so level that the highway leading to Carter City crosses it. There is a natural rock stairway from the bridge to the bottom of the ravine 200 feet below. This and two smaller natural bridges, Smoky and Fern, also in this reservation, are considered by geologists to be remnants of caves formed by stream erosion.

OLIVE HILL, 49.8 *m.* (752 alt., 1,484 pop.), is a brickyard town in a narrow hollow between the hills. This district is widely known for its deposits of plastic clays of superior quality; the TROUGH CREEK MINE *(visited by permit)* is (L) especially striking when the numerous furnaces are in operation.

West of Olive Hill the rugged, heavily wooded hills on each side of the highway afford exceptionally fine views.

MOREHEAD, 70 *m.* (712 alt., 825 pop.), seat of Rowan County, was the trade center for lumbermen working on extensive operations in the hills to the south. The town lies in the valley of Triplett's Creek, with surrounding mountain ridges reaching an elevation of 1,000 feet. The buildings of the MOREHEAD STATE TEACHERS COLLEGE (R) are spread out over a 75-acre campus on the wooded slope of a mountain at the eastern edge of town. The school was established in 1887 as a private denominational institution for mountain boys and girls; it was transformed into a teachers' college for eastern Kentucky in 1922. The red-brick, stone-trimmed buildings are in Tudor Gothic style.

Morehead was the first site of the Eastern Kentucky Moonlight Schools that were created in 1911 by Cora Wilson Stewart and the teachers of Rowan County. The enrollment reached 1,200 the first year, pupils ranging in age from 18 to 86 years. By the end of 1913 illiteracy in the county had been practically wiped out. This region was long known for its feuds *(see Tour 19)*, one of which is described in the local ballad, "Rowan County Troubles."

Rowan is the northernmost of the 17 counties that contributed land for the 900,000-acre Cumberland National Forest, which stretches along the western rim of the mountains in a narrow band from Rowan County south to the Tennessee Line. Within the forest are many beautiful spots that make admirable camp sites.

At 71.6 *m.*, on the western outskirts of Morehead, is the junction with a hard-surfaced road.

Left on this road to CLEARFIELD, 0.6 *m.* (705 alt., 250 pop.), a fire-clay manufacturing town. The extensive fire-clay beds here are a continuation of the Sciotoville deposit that extends southward and westward from Scioto County, Ohio. Non-refractory clays suitable for the manufacture of brick, tile, and terra cotta are also present in this region.

Right in Clearfield, at the fork of two unmarked roads on a narrow winding road 3.8 *m.* to the MOREHEAD FIRE OBSERVATORY (1,100 alt.), one of the 22 steel observation towers in the Cumberland National Forest. From the glass-enclosed observatory is a splendid view of the forested mountains. South of the observatory on an undulating ridge table is a FOREST CAMP *(camping and picnicking facilities)*.

FARMERS, 78.1 *m.* (868 alt., 290 pop.), on the Licking River, is a trade center of the clay region.

US 60 proceeds through a region of steep-sided foothills—especially striking in the spring and early summer when rhododendron and azalea are in bloom—into the Knobs area, a narrow belt of rounded or flat-topped hills almost surrounding the Bluegrass region, some of them rising abruptly several hundred feet above the lowlands.

OWINGSVILLE, 92.1 *m.* (1,025 alt., 933 pop.), seat of Bath County, lies at the top of a low hill. The main and almost the only street is lined with fine old houses. The town was named for its most prominent early citizen, Col. Thomas Dye Owings, who settled on land granted for services in the Revolutionary War, and became wealthy through the mining and processing of iron ore. When this site was selected as the county seat in 1811, it was owned by Richard Menifee and Colonel Owings, each of whom wished to bestow his name on the new town. It was decided to name the village for the man who erected the finest residence in the shortest time. Colonel Owings won with the OWINGS HOUSE *(open)*, on Main St. (L), just beyond the courthouse. This house, completed in 1812, is a two-story building of painted red brick. One end of the old house has been torn down and replaced by a commercial building. The wide front doorway, now with colored glass side lights, under a second-story Palladian window, was originally in the center of the house. All woodwork, windows, doors, and the lovely spiral stairway ascending three stories, were made by hand and brought from Baltimore by oxcart. The house, of Georgian Colonial design, has walls from three to four feet thick. This, together with its fortlike arrangement, servants' quarters in the basement, portholes and entrance to a subterranean passage concealed behind the drawing room fireplace, indicate that, with all its beauty of line and finish, safety from Indian and other attacks compelled consideration. After Owings' death the house became an inn on the stagecoach route between Lexington and Washington, D.C. It was the center of social life for the entire section during the first half of the nineteenth century. Louis Philippe and Lafayette were among the distinguished guests, and in 1826 a grand ball was given here in honor of Henry Clay, then Secretary of State and a frequent guest.

Left from Owingsville on State 36, improved, to the SLATE CREEK IRON FURNACE, 2.6 *m.*, built in 1790. A small tree grows among the ruins, which stand on the bank of Slate Creek. During the War of 1812, cannon balls, weighing about four pounds each, were cast here and sent by wagon to the Licking River and on flatboats down the Licking, the Ohio, and the Mississippi Rivers to New Orleans for the use of General Jackson in the battle with the British in 1815. From that time the furnace has usually been referred to as "Andrew Jackson's Old Thunder Mill."

On State 36 is OLYMPIAN SPRINGS (R), 8.9 *m.*, the most important of the mineral springs and baths for which Bath County was named. It was established in 1791 and was once widely known as a watering place. It was also noted for its "most pure and salubrious air." Its setting has been called a "high mountainous country, embellished with scenery of a bold romantic character." The first stage line in Kentucky ran between Lexington and Olympian Springs, then known as Mud Lick. Henry Clay, one of its early owners, changed the name to Olympian Springs.

A millstone marker (R), 104.6 *m.*, points to the old sycamore tree, on Kingston Creek, that is the traditional SITE OF THE DEATH OF CAPT. JAMES ESTILL who was killed in a hand-to-hand struggle with an Indian during the disastrous Battle of Little Mountain in 1782. This was the result of one of the British-inspired incursions that led to the Battle of the Blue Licks (*see Tour 15*). At the buffalo crossing near this tree Captain Estill and a party of 25 Kentuckians overtook but were defeated by the band of Wyandottes who had attacked Estill's Station.

MOUNT STERLING, 106.5 *m.* (934 alt., 4,350 pop.), seat of Montgomery County, is an attractive town in a winding valley and along the slopes of several hills. It was surveyed and platted by Enoch Smith, in 1793, and called Little Mountain Town, for the large mound northwest of it. Shortly afterward Hugh Forbes, a Scot living in the neighborhood, suggested Stirling, in honor of his boyhood home, and the name became Mount Stirling but was later spelled with an "e." In December, 1863, Confederate troops captured the town, burned the courthouse, destroyed nearly all the county records, and confiscated the funds of the town's only bank. In Montgomery County are 25 mounds that have yielded many relics of the mound builders.

Peter Lee Hensley (1855-1926), a Negro owner and breeder of trotters, was born in Mount Sterling. Hensley began his career at the age of 14 when he got a job as a wagon driver; by the time he was 19 he owned a grocery store and a restaurant, and a few years later he bought his first trotter. He eventually purchased the Yellow Rose Farm, just outside of Mount Sterling, and there he bred and trained his horses. Two of Hensley's most outstanding racers were Temple Bar, winner of 24 out of 25 races, and Alcyo, a stallion that won 17 consecutive events.

Mount Sterling is at the junction with State 40 (*see Tour 17*).

Left from Mount Sterling on the Spencer Rd. to SPENCER, 5 *m.* (50 pop.).
Left from Spencer, over a bridge spanning Slate Creek, then on a very narrow

loose-gravel road winding to the top of the hill where stands the OLD ROCK HOUSE OF MORGAN'S STATION (R), 6.5 *m.*, now a farmhouse. This tall two-story building of unfinished stone, commanding one of the highest elevations in the vicinity, was attacked by Indians in 1793. The crevices, originally chinked with mud, have been filled with cement. The walls of the old station house are two feet thick; its exterior, with a large stone chimney at each end, is plain, even austere. The hand-carved woodwork of ivory-painted poplar is still in excellent condition; there are coronets above the mantel and over one of the inside doorways. The wainscoting, two and one-half feet high, is a noteworthy feature.

West of Mount Sterling the highway traverses the undulating terrain characteristic of the Bluegrass section. On both sides of the highway stretch stock farms dotted with oak and beech trees and watered by streams flowing between limestone banks.

The HENRY C. BISUDEN HOUSE (R), 118.3 *m.*, a large two-story red-brick house trimmed with stone, has a three-story tower on one corner and a carriage porch. It is on a slight elevation a short distance from the road, surrounded by old trees. The house was built in 1860 by Benjamin Broom, a prosperous stock farmer who imported the English shorthorn cattle for which this region was once famous. The designs for the house were suggested by the English country manors seen by Broom on one of his purchasing trips to England. It contains 21 spacious, high-ceiled rooms, including one that can be reached only through the top tower room, which has a secret entrance. (On one occasion during the War between the States, provisions placed in this room were discovered only when a soldier drew his sword and threatened to cut the throat of the Negro cook unless she revealed the place where they had been hidden.) The west room on the first floor has a bay window between two delicate hand-carved Corinthian pilasters, and a crystal chandelier. The staircase in the central hall, also elaborately carved, winds to the second floor and forms a balcony. This estate, known for many years as Vinewood, was equipped with an extensive system that supplied the house and other buildings with running water.

WINCHESTER, 122.7 *m.* (981 alt., 8,233 pop.), seat of Clark County, is on low hills that are a part of the watershed between the Kentucky and Licking Rivers. Its spacious business and residential districts combine the appearance of a modern city with that of an old-fashioned town. The settlement, incorporated in 1793, was named for Winchester, Virginia, the former home of John Baker, its founder. Early in its history it became the marketing center of this fertile agricultural area on the margin of the inner Bluegrass. It was the shorthorn-cattle capital of the region for many decades; the highest price ever realized for a single head of cattle in this region was $45,000. Although primarily a residential town, it has several industries, including flour milling, lumbering and millworking, and the assembling of gas and farm machines. The building of the L. & N. R.R. branch from Winchester into the eastern Kentucky coal field and the discovery of oil and gas deposits have contributed to the town's prosperity. In the old CLARK COUNTY COURTHOUSE, on Main St., in the center of the business district, Henry Clay made his last speech in Kentucky. His first Kentucky speech was also made in Winchester on an immense burr-oak stump at the corner of Main and Fairfax Sts., where the Brown-Proctoria Hotel now stands.

KENTUCKY WESLEYAN COLLEGE (co-educational), on College St., founded in 1866 by the Methodist Episcopal Church, South, occupies a group of brick buildings arranged in a semicircle upon the grassy eastward slope of the campus. The Administration Building is a three-and-one-half-story structure of gray brick with a pedimented portico. Spencer Memorial Gymnasium, a $100,000 building of modern construction, with a recessed porch, is across the street from the Administration Building. The college library, an attractive one-story stone building, was the gift of Andrew Carnegie.

The HICKMAN HOUSE, NW. cor. Maple and Hickman Sts., a two-story building of red painted brick, was built in 1814. William Hickman, its first owner and occupant, was a Virginian, as were many of the pioneers who established estates and built substantial and beautiful homes in Kentucky. Although the house has been extensively repaired and reconstructed in recent years and the oldest unit has been enlarged by the addition of two wings, the design of the first structure has not been altered. The walls, 18 inches thick, are of brick. The mantels and the other woodwork are hand-carved, and the joists under the first floor of the original building are logs from which the bark has been removed.

The GOVERNOR JAMES A. CLARK MANSION, at the junction of Colby Pike and Wheeler St., is a two-story house of brick painted red. The façade has a wide porch, with Ionic columns in the center supporting a small pediment, a wide entrance with fanlights and side lights, and a Palladian window in the center of the second story. The GRAVE OF JAMES A. CLARK, marked with a tall obelisk, is a short distance from the Winchester High School upon whose grounds the mansion stands. Clark was the twelfth Governor of Kentucky (1836–39).

This town was the birthplace and early home of Joel T. Hart (1810–70), sculptor.

Winchester is at the junction with State 15 *(see Tour 2)* and US 227 *(see Tour 17A)*.

Right from Winchester on the Colbyville Rd. to the junction with Becknerville Rd. 5 *m.;* L. on Becknerville Rd. to COLBYVILLE TAVERN, 5.2 *m.* The two-story brick farmhouse was one of the three large buildings that enclosed a court into which the stagecoach could be driven, as in old English taverns. The walls of this old house are laid in Flemish bond, four bricks thick.

US 60, between Winchester and Lexington, was first known, and is still referred to, as Strode's Rd., named for a station erected about one mile west of the present limits of Winchester.

The marker on the SITE OF THE JOHN STRODE CABIN, 124.8 *m.*, commemorates the founder of this station, who came from Berkeley County,

Virginia, in 1776, and built his cabin here. In the spring of 1779 he induced a number of men from his home county, whom he found at Boonesboro, to accompany him back to this site. They built about 30 cabins and erected a stockade around them, a defense work about 300 feet long and 100 feet wide, in which they sheltered themselves against the British and Indians, and reared their children in comparative safety.

The McCORMICK SEED HARVESTER WORKS *(open to public)*, 125 *m.* (R), a one-story frame structure covered with sheet metal, manufactures machines for harvesting Bluegrass seed. The operating principle is that of the closely serrated board once used by slaves to strip the matured heads of the bluegrass of their seed. The machine, operated by one man, can harvest 10 to 15 acres a day.

In this region were formerly several famous cattle farms, which have since been broken up into smaller units. The earliest and most notable was the Matthew Patton farm on which, in 1795, were the first purebred shorthorn cattle west of the Alleghenies. At the old Renick farm, the shorthorn was brought to such a state of perfection that breeders from other countries came to it to purchase their stock.

The W. R. SPAHR HOUSE (L), 126.3 *m.*, a massive two-story red brick house, built after the War between the States, has a classic two-story portico visible at the end of an avenue of tall trees.

The JOHN WINN PLACE (L), 127 *m.*, a fine old two-story red brick house of Victorian style, was built around 1878 to replace a much older frame house. It stands in a grove, almost hidden from the road.

The DAVID PREWITT PLACE (R), 129.7 *m.*, also known as Dunreath, is typical of the estates along US 60 between Winchester and Lexington that were acquired during the early decades of the nineteenth century. The house is one-fourth of a mile from the road on a lawn shaded by locust, wild cherry, ash, maple, and walnut trees. In the 1840's, J. Howard Sheffer, then living in a log cabin, fenced off this area and gave instructions to mow around every tree shoot in order to improve the setting for the home he planned to erect. The two-story red brick building is Georgian Colonial in style with a one-story white frame porch across the front. The roof line drops several feet to that of a two-story wing at the right. The bricks, laid in Flemish bond, as well as the lime for the plaster, were burned on the place. The timber was cut from near-by woodlands, and the roofing was brought from Belgium.

The BENJAMIN GRAVES HOMESTEAD (L), 130.5 *m.*, also known as the Wilson House, is a two-story red brick structure standing in a grove a short distance from the road.

LEAFLAND (R), 132.1 *m.*, was built almost a century ago by Jacob Hughes, and is the oldest of three mansions associated with him. In his day Hughes was one of the leading farmers and stock traders in Kentucky and was Fayette County's representative in the legislature. He owned 6,000 acres of land in Fayette and near-by Clark and Bourbon Counties. The other two houses, the Prewitt House and the Benjamin Graves Homestead, were built by Hughes' sons-in-law (J. H. Howard Sheffer and Benjamin Graves). Like most of the homes in the region,

Leafland stands among beautiful trees. All the mantels are of marble and the interior trim is unusually fine.

The ALBERTI HOUSE (R), 132.4 m., is a one-story white frame building suggestive of an Italian villa, with a two-story central section that gives height to the porch. It is surrounded and partly hidden by a grove of trees. The estate was established during the second quarter of the nineteenth century by Doctor Alberti, a physician of the Bluegrass. His son, T. L. B. Alberti, owned and conducted a wagon freight line with a large business between the iron furnaces of Powell and Estill Counties and Lexington; as many as a dozen six-horse teams were in use daily for hauling pig iron from the furnaces to Lexington.

A short distance off the road (R), at 133.4 m., is the MACEDONIAN CHRISTIAN CHURCH, built in 1928 as a memorial to J. H. Graves, a farmer of Fayette County. It is constructed in the style of a Greek temple, of rough local stone. The portico has five fluted Doric columns supporting a simple pediment.

HAMBURG PLACE (L) is at 136.3 m., including THE IROQUOIS HUNT AND POLO CLUB and THE NANCY HANKS HORSE GRAVEYARD (see Lexington).

LEXINGTON 141.4 m. (957 alt., 45,736 pop.) (see Lexington).

Points of Interest: Homes of Henry Clay, Gen. John Hunt Morgan, Mary Todd Lincoln, and John Bradford; Transylvania College, University of Kentucky, loose-leaf tobacco market.

Lexington is at the junction with US 25 (see Tour 4), US 27 (see Tour 3), and US 68 (see Tour 15).

Section b. LEXINGTON *to* LOUISVILLE; *83.2 m., US 60*

West of Lexington, 0 m., US 60 passes CALUMET FARM (R), at 4.7 m. (see Lexington).

The OLD KEENE PLACE (R), 6.2 m., a stately light-painted brick mansion, was built about 1790 on an 8,000-acre tract granted to Francis Keene of Fauquier County, Virginia, by his kinsman, Patrick Henry, then Governor of Virginia. The house is symmetrical in plan and has a two-story five-bay central section and low one-story wings. Extending across the entire width of the central section is a deep portico, supported on square paneled wooden columns and topped with a bracketed cornice and latticed rail; the slender proportions of the columns are typical of the post-Colonial architecture of Kentucky. The stiff symmetry of the façade is broken by the position of the central window of the second story, which is off axis with the unusual double doorway below. The house stands on a broad, tree-shaded lawn. Lafayette was a house guest here during his visit to Lexington in 1825. Adjoining the Keene estate, which now includes but 20 acres of the original tract, is the new KEENELAND RACE TRACK (R), 6.4 m. (see Lexington).

At 10.2 *m.* is the junction with Pisgah Rd.

Right on this road to the stone PISGAH PRESBYTERIAN CHURCH (R), 0.7 *m.*, built in 1812 and later remodeled in the Gothic Revival style. An early activity of this congregation was the sponsorship of an academy from which Transylvania University grew.

At 12.5 *m.* is the junction with the Payne Mill Rd.

Right on this road to BUCK POND (R), 1.2 *m.*, the house built in 1784 by Col. Thomas Marshall, father of John Marshall, Chief Justice of the United States, on land granted for services in the Revolutionary War. On a slight elevation at the end of an avenue, this dignified old log house weatherboarded, with a tall two-story pedimented portico, has been modernized in recent years and a one-story wing has been added to each side.

At 1.9 *m.* on the Payne Mill Rd. is (R) the TOMB OF GEN. MARQUIS CALMES, a Revolutionary officer from Virginia, who designed and erected it for himself. This stone vault, with an opening in one side, is in a field on an elevation and surrounded by young trees. Near by is a stone chimney, a REMNANT OF THE CALMES HOUSE, destroyed by fire in 1937. General Calmes and Colonel Marshall settled across the road from each other on lands granted them at the close of the Revolution.

VERSAILLES, 14.1 *m.* (923 alt., 2,224 pop.), seat of Woodford County, was named by General Calmes for Versailles, France, as a tribute to Louis XVI for his timely aid in the Revolutionary War. The town was established in 1792 on the lands of Hezekiah Briscoe, an infant, the title being vested in "a number of gentlemen landowners," among whom was Gen. Marquis Calmes. The town site is a circle whose radius is 600 yards and whose center is the courthouse. On Main St. is the SITE OF WATKINS TAVERN, a noted inn of early days kept by Henry Watkins, Henry Clay's stepfather. The old landmark burned down about 1932, being, at the time, considerably more than 100 years old. MARGARET HALL (R), an Episcopal school for girls, is a fine example of the mansion of ante-bellum days. Near the eastern edge of the campus is a monument to General Calmes.

Versailles is at the junction with US 62 *(see Tour 14)*, the two routes are united for 1.3 miles.

At 26.4 *m.* is the junction with State 40 *(see Tour 17)*.

FRANKFORT, 29.1 *m.* (512 alt., 11,626 pop.) *(see Frankfort)*.

Points of Interest: State Capitol, State Cemetery, Liberty Hall, and old houses.

Frankfort is at the junction with State 35 *(see Tour 5)* and State 40 *(see Tour 17)*.

JUNIPER HILL (R), 30.7 *m.*, is a parklike estate of approximately 200 acres. The house, almost entirely hidden from view by trees and shrubs, is a large two-story stone structure. A low stone wall on the estate follows the winding highway up the hill.

THISTELTON (L), 30.8 *m.*, is better known as the old Taylor estate, having been founded by E. H. Taylor, Jr., a distiller. The three-story frame house is an excellent example of Victorian elegance. Behind the stone wall that borders the estate are sloping grounds covered with trees and shrubbery.

From the crest of a hill, 31 *m.*, is a fine view of the Kentucky River Valley including Frankfort with the State capitol.

JEPTHA KNOB (1,163 alt.), 44.9 *m.*, rising (L) abruptly from the rolling countryside, is a cryptovolcano, one that has never reached an eruptive stage.

The SITE OF CROSS KEYS TAVERN (R) is at 46.5 *m.;* it was opened in 1800 by Adam Middleton, a blacksmith from Virginia, on the Old Wilderness Rd. Bed, board, and bourbon cost "six bits." It is estimated that, between the years 1800 and 1825, Cross Keys Tavern sheltered more than 10,000 travelers on the old dirt road. Nothing remains but the former slave quarters—a row of low rambling buildings of wood and stone.

SHELBYVILLE, 51.9 *m.* (760 alt., 4,033 pop.), a lively Main Street town that is the seat of Shelby County, was founded in 1792 and named, as was the county, for Isaac Shelby, Kentucky's first Governor. The first settlement in the area was at Painted Stone, near by. There, in 1779, Squire Boone, brother of Daniel Boone, built a fort that for more than a year was the only refuge on the road between Harrodsburg and Louisville. In 1781 the settlers, warned of the approach of Indians, started for the stronger fort at the Falls of the Ohio. They were attacked near Humes Station on Long Run Creek, and dispersed after having lost 40 to 50 men, women, and children. Col. John Floyd, with 37 men, started in pursuit of the Indians, but at Eastwood, Floyd's men were ambushed and 14 of them were killed. In all nearly 100 whites were killed or captured during this raid. Shelbyville, after its turbulent early days, gradually became a placid town of pleasant homes and the trade center of a fertile agricultural area.

SCIENCE HILL *(open by permission),* 6th and Washington Sts., is a school for girls founded in 1825. The low rambling two-story structure, partly covered with ivy, has grown room by room and addition by addition since the institution was established. An octagonal cupola surmounts the roof over the enclosed court.

The two-story brick WATKINS HOUSE, painted gray, cor. of 3rd and Washington Sts., was built in 1800 for Isaac Watkins, who maintained a stagecoach inn.

Right from Shelbyville, on State 43, to CROPPER, 10.2 *m.*, a hamlet. Left from Cropper on an improved road to PLEASUREVILLE, 16.6 *m.* (822 alt., 341 pop.), where in 1784 a Dutch group endeavored to establish a communal colony on 10,000 acres of farmland purchased from Squire Boone. The colony was not a success but many of the settlers remained and much of the tract is now individually owned by descendants of the settlers.

OLD STONE INN (R), 59.4 *m.*, is a tavern that has been in operation continuously since its establishment more than 100 years ago. Although local legend says it was erected before Kentucky became a State, more reliable sources give the date as 1794. The stone used in its construction was hauled from Nelson County in an oxcart. The one-and-one-half-story tavern has three dormers in front and two stone chimneys at each end. The partition walls of stone are 21 inches thick. The original flooring, ship-oak on the first and poplar on the second floor, and the hand-grooved casings still remain. Old Stone Inn was built for a home but had to be sold before it was entirely completed.

SIMPSONVILLE, 59.9 *m.*, a hamlet dating from 1816, was named for Capt. John Simpson of Shelbyville, killed in the Battle of the River Raisin, January 22, 1813.

LINCRAFT FARM (L), 60.5 *m.*, is a 25-acre model farm, with which Lincoln Institute demonstrates the possibilities of a small farming unit with the aid of a Negro family. The farmhouse is a modern two-story white frame building with barns and outbuildings at the rear.

LINCOLN INSTITUTE (L), 60.9 *m.*, at Lincoln Ridge, is an endowed vocational and agricultural high school for Negro boys and girls—the only one of its kind in Kentucky. As the result of the law passed by the State legislature in 1904, which prohibited attendance of Negroes at institutions attended by whites, part of the Berea College endowment (*see Tour 4)* was used to establish this school for Negroes. The two institutions now have no connection, except that by tradition some of the trustees and the president of Berea College are also trustees of Lincoln Institute. The legislature, in 1937, enacted a law that requires each county where there are no Negro high schools to pay the tuition of Negro students who attend high school in some other locality; many of these are sent to Lincoln Institute. Its 444-acre farm supplies the table. On the campus there are two three-story dormitories, an administration building, an industrial arts building, and a central heating plant, all constructed of red brick and trimmed with stone.

At 64.2 *m.* is the junction with an improved side road.

Right on this road to LONG RUN BAPTIST CHURCH (R), 2.1 *m.*, on Long Run Creek, so named because of the long flight down its valley by those who escaped an Indian attack. The church, a very plain red brick gabled building, has two entrance doors. Two hundred yards north of the church is the site of the cabin of Abraham Lincoln, grandfather of Abraham Lincoln, a President of the United States. Although some historians believe Lincoln died near Springfield, it is generally agreed that beneath the wing of the old church is the GRAVE OF ABRAHAM LINCOLN'S GRANDFATHER.

When Abraham Lincoln, the grandfather, migrated from Virginia to Kentucky, between 1782 and 1784, he settled near Green River in Lincoln County; later he moved to this place, which was near Hughes Station. One day while he was working near this cabin he was killed by an Indian. Mordecai, his son, shot the attacker, saving the members of the family, among them his youngest brother, Thomas, who was to become the father of a President.

At 70.9 *m.* is the junction with old US 60.

Left on this road to MIDDLETOWN, 0.3 *m.* (772 alt., 315 pop.), founded in 1797. In the center of the town is MIDDLETOWN INN (R), built more than a century ago with 24-inch walls, of brick and stone. The double front entrance has fanlights and side lights, and the original ash floor boards are still in use. The wide veranda across the front is a later addition.

The DOUGLAS HOMESTEAD (L), **71.3** *m.,* on the crest of the hill, is a spacious country house built before the War between the States. It is a two-story structure of brick painted gray and is surrounded by large trees and shrubbery. The estate, once a stock and race horse breeding place, is now a dairy farm.

At **75.2** *m.* is the junction with State 22 *(see Tour 13).*

ST. MATTHEWS, **77** *m.* (550 alt., 2,551 pop.), is a community village that is a shipping point for large quantities of Irish potatoes.

Right from St. Matthews on the Westport Rd. to RIDGEWAY, **0.5** *m.,* a good example of the Classical Revival style of architecture. With a well-designed central section flanked by outlying wings, it bears a striking resemblance to Maryland plantation houses. The portal, protected by a portico with four delicate columns, gives entrance to a wide arched hall that leads into a cross corridor; this in turn gives access to the wings. The woodwork, including mantels in each room, is hand-carved with lightness and delicacy, characteristic of the style. The house was built in 1804 for Major Henry Massey and his bride, Helen Bullitt Massey.

US 60 passes the SOUTHERN BAPTIST THEOLOGICAL SEMINARY (R), **78.8** *m.,* housed in attractive Georgian Colonial style buildings, erected in 1926.

LOUISVILLE, **83.2** *m.* (525 alt., 307,745 pop.) *(see Louisville).*

Points of Interest: Speed Museum, Memorial Auditorium, Presbyterian Theological Seminary, Churchill Downs, Cave Hill Cemetery, Cherokee Park, and others.

Louisville is at the junction with US 31W *(see Tour 7),* US 42 *(see Tour 12),* US 31E *(see Tour 6).*

Section c. LOUISVILLE to MISSOURI LINE, *291.8 m.*

US 60, southwest of Louisville, passes through the Knobs country of Jefferson County, especially beautiful in the spring when the redbud and dogwood trees are in bloom. For much of the distance it follows the sweeping curves of the Ohio, with its verdant meadows, forest-covered hills, and old river towns.

Between LOUISVILLE, **0** *m.,* and Tip Top US 60 and US 31W are one route *(see Tour 7).*

In ST. HELEN'S, **5.8** *m.,* is the LOUISVILLE AND JEFFERSON COUNTY HOME (L) for the aged and infirm.

WAVERLY HILLS TUBERCULOSIS SANATORIUM (L), **12** *m.,* on the heights overlooking the Ohio and the blue hills beyond the river, is a municipally owned institution under the administration of a board of 10 directors, appointed jointly by the fiscal court of Jefferson County and the director of health of Louisville. It has accommodations for 515 patients. Since its incorporation in 1907, $1,500,000 has been expended on improvements.

KOSMOSDALE, **18.5** *m.* (67 pop.), is a company town of the Kosmos Portland Cement Company.

WEST POINT, 22.5 *m.* (740 alt., 697 pop.), strung along the highway at the confluence of the Salt and Ohio Rivers, is a rambling village founded in 1800. Many of its houses have double-decked galleries running completely around them. In YOUNG'S INN, on locust-shaded Main St., Jenny Lind sang for the crowd gathered in the public room during her tour of 1851. Across the road from the inn is the JAMES YOUNG HOUSE, a fine old brick structure built by the innkeeper. Also on Main St. is the LAKE HOUSE, a venerable brick residence, with an Ionic portico.

Between West Point and Muldraugh, US 60 winds over Muldraugh Hill (alt. 786), on a treacherous stretch of road *(drive carefully, especially on the curve at overhead bridge).*

MULDRAUGH, 29.1 *m.* (750 alt., 200 pop.), was at one time the central post office for mail addressed to all towns along what is now US 60 as far west as Hardinsburg. Here are storage tanks for the gas supply of Louisville.

TIP TOP, 30.6 *m.,* is at the southern junction with US 31W *(see Tour 7).*

West of Tip Top, US 60 crosses a region of wooded knobs and extensive areas of farm land. Kentucky's first natural gas was tapped in this area in 1858.

Several Indian skirmishes occurred among the knobs and groves. Many of the early settlers were of English and Scottish extraction, and the folklore and ballads of those lands still survive. An old Highland superstition persists that a male child who cries and raises one hand at birth is born to command. The belief that infants born "open handed" will be frank and bountiful and that those whose hands are tightly closed will be frugal and close-mouthed, is purely English. Another Scotch superstition, one that many old folk still cling to, is that if a child makes marks upon the furniture it is "marking himself a grave-house" and will soon die.

At 31.5 *m.* is the junction with an unimproved road.

Right on this road to GARNETTSVILLE, 2.3 *m.* (55 pop.), and the OTTER CREEK MILL, which has been in continuous operation since 1808. This hamlet is on the border of the 2,348-acre OTTER CREEK RECREATIONAL DEMONSTRATION AREA. Although most of this land is no longer suited to agriculture it is still beautiful with heavily wooded hills and valleys, varied rock formations, and large caverns through which streams flow. Otter Creek, a stream of varying width, forms a giant horseshoe 700 to 800 feet across. The National Park Service is (1939) reforesting and controlling soil erosion in this area and building log cabins, stone ovens, trailer campgrounds, and other picnicking and camping conveniences as well as many recreational facilities. Daniel Boone and his brother, Squire Boone, came here in 1774 to look over the land and Squire Boone remained and became an itinerant Baptist preacher. Adjoining the Ohio River, at the mouth of Otter Creek, on a tract of approximately 4,000 acres, Squire Boone's son, Enoch, built a house; his descendants still live in the vicinity. The Boone burial ground is near the old Buffalo Road in the northeastern corner of Meade County.

GRAHAMPTON, 33.2 *m.* (644 alt., 300 pop.), is on both banks of Otter Creek.

The GRAHAMPTON TEXTILE MILL (R), on the western bank of the creek, is a three-story structure with walls of stone set in random courses. The adjoining warehouse, formerly a gristmill, has solid oak structural columns, beams, and joists. Its founders, Graham and Sneed, operated a textile mill in Louisville, from 1829 to 1837, when they moved the machinery to this place, sending it down the Ohio River from Louisville to the mouth of Otter Creek and dragging it up the valley over an extremely steep and rough trail with the aid of oxen. This mill has been described as "probably the first mill of its kind west of the Allegheny Mountains." About 80 years ago the old frame, millrace, and dam were replaced by the present stone ones. This dam, with buttresses at each end and arch facing upstream, is of exactly the same plan as the irrigation dams under construction today. This mill from the beginning has used steam in the textile department, but for grinding grist and other auxiliary purposes water power has been utilized. During the War between the States the Grahampton mill was run at full capacity except when it was stopped to repair damages inflicted by straggling bands of soldiers.

At 42 *m.* on US 60 is a junction with a graveled road.

Right on this road to DOE RUN HOTEL, 0.6 *m.*, an old water-power mill, the main part of which was built in 1821 by Thomas Stevenson, an Englishman. The mill, which like textile mills in early days, ground grist as a side line, was built at the headwaters of Doe Run Creek. This place was a favorite hunting ground of Daniel Boone and his brother, Squire, who was nicknamed "Bible Boone." The first recorded land entry of 500 acres, made on October 15, 1780, included "four springs and a sulphur lick," and the site of this mill. The old part of the mill is three full stories high, with finished basement. The massive foundation is of local limestone. The superstructure consists of a framework of great hewn timbers of black walnut, exposed to view; the walls of field stone display the skilled workmanship. The surface of the timbers has acquired a satin smoothness, and the stone wall is colored by moss in various shades of green. The millstones were brought from France to New Orleans, thence by way of the Mississippi and Ohio Rivers to the mouth of Otter Creek. The vicinity of the old mill is a popular spot for community frolics, and a Fourth of July picnic has been held here annually since 1893.

BRANDENBURG, 45.9 *m.* (356 alt., 484 pop.), the seat of Meade County, which was formed in 1823, was named for Col. James Meade. This community was incorporated in 1825, a year after its first court had convened. It bears the name of Col. Solomon Brandenburg, an early settler who had seen service in the War of 1812. When the railroad built its line three miles from the town, the citizens saved the town's existence by building a hard-surfaced road, the first in the county, from the center to the station. When the principal highway was extended along the ridge top, leaving the business section on a side street, the commercial district began gradually to move to the highway. Brandenburg's Main Street, nevertheless, continues to thrive; the countryfolk and townspeople mingle around the stores and the courthouse, where, for generations, they and their forebears have gathered.

On a hill overlooking Main St. and the river stands the MEADE COUNTY COURTHOUSE (R), which is more than a hundred years old and contains historic records bearing on social institutions of an earlier day, such as the following: "Henry Dawes, a poor child, is apprenticed to Henry R. Turnstall on this day, April 26, 1824, to learn the mystery of carding and spinning in its several branches. Henry R. Turnstall shall provide the above named Henry Dawes with meat, drink and apparel, lodging, washing and other necessities. In addition to the above, Henry Dawes shall be taught reading, writing and common arithmetic, including the rule of three."

On Main St. is (R) the SITE OF WALNUT TAVERN, operated by Solomon Brandenburg.

Right from US 60 on a graveled street to the BUCKNER HOMESTEAD *(open)*, 0.5 *m.*, on a hillside that commands a view of the Ohio for 15 miles. The one-story frame house was built in 1855 by Col. Robert Buckner, a soldier of the War of 1812. The façade is broken by four 20-pane windows and a very wide doorway with side lights and a transom. In the roof above the doorway is a small gable with a large fanlight. The house is noteworthy for its hand-carved mantels, hand-grooved weatherboarding, and, in its main hall, a winding staircase of the quarter-turn spiral type. For a time, during the War between the States, Gen. John Hunt Morgan had his headquarters in this house. This point was admirable as a look-out, and served as a base for Morgan's operations across the river. Cannon stationed on the hillside commanded Marvin's Landing on the Indiana bank and afforded protection to troops while crossing here. When the MASONIC BUILDING (R), a two-story structure, was the Brandenburg Academy (1816–26), the surrounding property was its campus. Federal troops were housed here during the war.

The METHODIST CHURCH (R), built around 1838 on the former campus of Brandenburg Academy, has been somewhat changed externally. In 1880 the belfry was replaced by a spire and the two front entrances, one for men and the other for women, were replaced by a central entrance. The gallery for slaves has been removed and there are now chairs instead of pews.

IRVINGTON, 57 *m.* (620 alt., 764 pop.), a thriving trade center, was the scene of frequent depredations during the Reconstruction period. Bands of raiders, following the course of the Ohio, looted the rich farms of the region around Irvington, seized livestock and produce, and transported their booty to the Indiana shore.

HARNED, 69.7 *m.* (777 alt., 175 pop.), is at the junction of State 65, a graveled road.

Left on this road 2.1 *m.* to the junction with State 223; L. on State 223 to KINGSWOOD CHRISTIAN COLLEGE, 3.3 *m.*, opened in 1937 by a small fundamentalist group for the training of ministers and missionaries. The campus is on a high elevation, and the buildings consist of four plain, two-story white frame structures. In the tabernacle amphitheater, in the wooded valley below the campus, camp meetings have been held annually in the past. Dr. J. W. Hughes, who had founded Asbury College *(see Tour 15)* at Wilmore, founded a Holiness college here that ceased operation in 1932.

HARDINSBURG, 73.6 *m.* (715 alt., 805 pop.), seat of Breckinridge County, came into existence in 1780 as a fort built by Capt.

William Hardin, soldier and frontiersman, who was known to the Indians as "Big Bill." Breckinridge County was formed in 1799, and named in honor of John Breckinridge, United States Senator (1801–05) and Attorney General of the United States (1805–06). In recent years the town has become the headquarters of four firms that contract with women for the manufacture of robes, quilts, comforters, novelties, and other objects decorated with fine needlework. This is largely a cottage industry resembling that of the pre-factory days in England. Though the returns from the work are low and the women are not paid for the time spent carrying their work to and from the office or waiting for inspection of their handicraft, there is no difficulty in finding workers on the surrounding farms where cash incomes are low. The beautiful articles retail at very high prices.

Between Hardinsburg and Cloverport, US 60 follows a devious course through a hilly region.

CLOVERPORT, 85.4 *m.* (386 alt., 1,324 pop.), a river town established in 1808, is an industrial community with a roofing plant. In 1816 when the Lincoln family, consisting of Thomas, his wife, Nancy, their son and daughter, moved from Hodgenville to Indiana, they were ferried across the Ohio River here. Lincoln was driving a yoke of oxen hitched to a cart, to which a cow was tied. Several decades later Col. David R. Murray, who had been a boy living here when the Lincolns passed through, gave the description of the event: "On account of the unusual size of the oxen, a crowd soon gathered to find out who these people were and where they were going. . . . Old Minerva, a colored slave, who had been attracted to the scene, seeing the condition of the children, went back into the house and came back immediately with a plate heaped with slices of homemade bread covered with butter, a pitcher of milk, and some cups. She seated the children on the steps of my father's house and fed them. When they left Hardinsburg, they drove to Cloverport to get across the river. In those days there were no ferry boats, and passengers, whenever any came along, were set across in a canoe. When the Lincolns reached the ferry, a raft was made, with the assistance of several people, and the wagon placed upon it. With one man in the canoe to pull and one man on the rear of the raft to push with a long pole (the river was low at the time), the Lincolns were ferried across to the Indiana shore and landed. Then they came back, and the two oxen and the cow were made to swim over."

The water of TAR SPRINGS, 88.7 *m.* (R), has the odor and taste of tar. This place was formerly a popular resort.

JEFFERY CLIFF (R), 92.3 *m.*, a rocky bluff rising from the lowland near the Ohio, has a 40-acre tablelike top shaped like a huge hand; the jagged edges of its five jutting fingers are covered with a variety of trees and flowers. In the palm of the hand, many streams wind. Jeffery Cliff, once the site of a stockaded Indian village, was named for an eccentric Englishman who, for many years, lived on it.

From parking spaces (R) are exceptional views of the broad valley of the Ohio, bordered on the north by the level reaches of Indiana farm lands. Six miles upstream the river bends around a prominent highland, where the boat on which Lafayette was a passenger is said to have been wrecked in 1824. A narrow channel at the bend, bordered by dangerous rocks, gave the name of Rock Island. Downstream the view includes the Indiana towns of Cannelton, Tell City, and Troy.

INDIAN LAKE (L), 92.3 *m.*, on a high plateau surrounded by low hills, is a private resort for sportsmen. Its fishing, boating, swimming, and camping facilities are available only to members and their guests.

HAWESVILLE, 96 *m.* (423 alt., 790 pop.), seat of Hancock County, in the valley of the Ohio River, is partly surrounded by hills. Incorporated in 1836, it was named for Richard Hawes, who owned the land on which the town site was platted. The county bears the name of John Hancock, president of the Continental Congress (1775–77). From Hawesville many plants are shipped, including cabbages, sweet potatoes, peppers, tomatoes and "hands" of tobacco. Approximately 2,500,000 pounds of tobacco are mailed annually by parcel post.

Among the records in the Hancock County clerk's office at the courthouse are a mortgage lien filed in November 1855 against the Barnum and Bailey circus, by Madame Flouroies; a mortgage lien dated November 11, 1873, attaching the steamboat *Big Sun Flower,* which was built at Lewisport; a lien filed against a Negro church building for a debt of $43.15 due to the pastor; and numerous mortgages on slaves.

Down the slope from the courthouse, on a side street leading toward the river and making an abrupt turn (R) at the railroad, are two old houses. Immediately in their rear is a row of six caves. One now serves as a garage, another is used to store coal, a third to shelter implements and tools, and a fourth has become a cold storage cellar. The remaining two are utilized by the occupants of the houses as sleeping quarters in the summer. The temperature within the caves never varies from 60° F.

On a high hill directly opposite the south side of the courthouse is LOVER'S LEAP. Here on the craggy top are seven huge boulders carved with hundreds of names and dates, most of which are no longer legible. Local legends explain the name by not one but several Indian maidens who died for love in the traditional fashion. One of the heroines was called Negahnakee. Her brave was killed, probably in action. Grief-stricken, she plunged over the rocky edge.

Hawesville is connected with Cannelton, Ind., by 24-hour ferry service. Here the Lincoln Memorial Highway will cross the Ohio River in following the approximate course of the Lincoln family when it moved from Hodgenville to Indiana.

At **106** *m.* is LEWISPORT (393 alt., 574 pop.),

Left from Lewisport, on a dirt road, to the old PATE FARM HOUSE, 4.4 *m.*, where in 1827 Abraham Lincoln was brought before Magistrate Sam Pate on a charge of infringement of ferry privileges. According to local tradition, Lincoln, then employed in Indiana, was hailed before the squire after he had rowed a passenger to a boat in midstream, which was blocked from the landing by a sand bar. Though unprepared in law, the 18-year-old Lincoln served as his own counsel and was exonerated. The house in which the trial was held is a two-story weatherboarded log structure, built about 1822. Near it, in an old cemetery, is the well-marked GRAVE OF CAROLINE THRASHER (nee Meeker), said to have been a sweetheart of Lincoln's.

MACEO, 115.1 *m.* (100 pop.), is on the site of Rosebud, a village laid out by a group of railroad officials. Difficulties arose over the title to the property, and Rosebud wilted away. Later a settlement was established here and named Powers' Station in honor of Col. J. S. Powers, an official of the L. H. & St. L. R.R. When a post office was granted, the name was changed to Maceo to avoid confusion with Powers' Store, another post office in Daviess County. Maceo honors Capt. Alonzo Maceo, a mulatto, who was one of the leaders in Cuba's war for independence from Spain. Its population is made up largely of Negroes, many of whom were given land here by their masters at the close of the War between the States. The village is a shipping point for molding clay dug in the vicinity.

A time-honored occasion in almost any Negro settlement in Kentucky is the "chittlin" feast. Commonly known in this State as Kentucky oysters, chitterlings (hog intestines) may be prepared in several different ways. The old-time Negro cook usually buys them by the pail, cleans and soaks them in salt water, then either boils them until they are tender or fries them in grease. Potato salad and hard cider frequently comprise the rest of the menu. Fondness for chitterlings is not entirely confined to Negroes. One well-known Kentucky Congressman, it is said, annually made a trip from Washington to his home State for "a good mess of chittlins."

Left from Maceo on an unmarked graveled road to CARPENTER LAKE *(fishing)*, 2.5 *m.*, formed in 1937 by the construction of an earth-fill dam 377 feet long. Carpenter Lake, the mecca of anglers in this section of western Kentucky, is owned by the State and is under the supervision of the State Department of Conservation. Along its four-mile tree-bordered shore are many cottages.

OWENSBORO, 124.7 *m.* (765 alt., 22,765 pop.), second largest city in western Kentucky, is a bustling oil town on the bank of the Ohio River. It is in an agricultural area at the northern edge of the western Kentucky coal fields. Owensboro was first known as Yellow Banks, because of a six-mile stretch of unusual yellow clay on the banks of the river here. In 1815, when Daviess County was formed, Yellow Banks was chosen county seat and its name changed to Rossborough to honor David Ross, the owner of much property. A charter granted in 1866 renamed it Owensboro for Col. Abraham Owen, a Virginian who came to Kentucky, took an important part in the early Indian wars, and fell at the Battle of Tippecanoe. Daviess County was named for Col. Joseph Hamilton Daviess, also slain in the Battle of Tippecanoe. Colonel Daviess—who married Nanny Marshall, sister of John Marshall, Chief Justice of the United States—had moved to this section in 1806 and had settled on a 5,000-acre tract on a ridge overlooking the Ohio River. Here he built Cornland, a beautiful two-story brick house. The first lawyer from the country west of the Allegheny Mountains to appear before the U.S. Supreme Court, Colonel Daviess was appointed U.S. District Attorney for Kentucky by President Thomas Jefferson. While holding this office Daviess attempted to bring Aaron Burr to trial on a conspiracy charge, but was frustrated by the absence of important witnesses and finally by the judge's denying Daviess the right to appear before the grand jury. By the time of the War between the States, Owensboro had become important as a river port, and a number of skirmishes took place here. In September 1862 a Confederate regiment, under Col. Robert M. Martin, entered the town, demanding unconditional surrender of the Federals under Colonel Netter, at near-by Camp Silas B. Miller. Colonel Netter preferred to fight. After a second skirmish had taken place at Sutherland Hill on the same day, the Confederate forces withdrew from this vicinity. When Owensboro was raided by guerrillas in August 1864 and partly burned, the courthouse was destroyed.

Daviess County is next to the largest tobacco-producing county in Kentucky. In Owensboro are two Loose-Leaf Sales Floors and eight factories for processing and grading tobacco. The city has also two large distilleries and factories making radio tubes and electric light bulbs.

The PLANTERS' HOTEL, 4th and Main Sts., was built in 1846. Among the signatures on its register are those of Jenny Lind, the singer, and Mary Anderson, Shakespearean actress.

On Griffith Ave. (L) is the GRIFFITH HOUSE, built by William R. Griffith in 1828. The large hand-made locks, bearing coats of arms, were brought from Philadelphia. The house is of Georgian Colonial design, but a modern front porch has been substituted for the original columned portico.

Left from Owensboro on State 54 to SORGHO (750 alt., 120 pop.), *8.9 m.;* L. from Sorgho on State 56, to MOUNT SAINT JOSEPH (Maple Mount P.O.), *6.4 m.,* an Ursuline convent and educational institution founded in 1874. The academy connected with the convent was established in 1880, and the junior college in 1926. Both are fully accredited. Mount Saint Joseph is the mother-house of a community of Ursuline nuns, a teaching order of women founded in Italy in 1535. The 500 rolling and terraced acres are landscaped with shrubbery and flowers. The original building, a three-story brick structure painted gray, holds parlors, a library, a museum, and music and art rooms. In the museum are relics and a variety of specimens for the study of natural science. The chapel is in the Tudor-Gothic style, with stained glass windows made by Munich artists.

The highway on a bridge *(toll 30¢),* 144.6 *m.,* crosses GREEN RIVER, widely known for the beauty of its waters and for muskellunge fishing. It is the narrowest river in Kentucky that can float a full-sized steamboat for any great distance. Six locks and dams provide a

constant five-foot channel. Its name was suggested by its color, which
is caused by the depth of the water.

At 153.3 *m.* is a junction with US 41 *(see Tour 8)*, which is united
with US 60 between this point and Henderson.

HENDERSON, 154.7 *m.* (382 alt., 11,688 pop.), seat of Henderson
County, is on the high red bluffs facing the mile-wide Ohio River.
Many well-kept country estates and spacious old homes are on the
wooded hills. The town was founded by the Transylvania Company
(later known as the Richard Henderson Company) in the year 1797,
on 200,000 acres granted to the company by the State. The first settlement, made in and around the old stockaded village of Red Banks, was
named for Col. Richard Henderson, leader of the company.

On the original plat of the town, which is in the courthouse, all the
streets were 100 feet wide, and the entire river front—two and a quarter
miles long—was municipal property. Today these wide thoroughfares
and this river front, which is being made into a continuous park, are
among Henderson's most attractive features. On a hill in TRANSYL-
VANIA PARK, which divides the town, is the HENDERSON COUNTY
COURTHOUSE, a two-story building of stuccoed brick, completed in
1842. A pedimented Greek Revival portico with four Doric columns
and an octagonal cupola relieve its austerity. Six large tablets in the
courthouse record the exploits and achievements of the Transylvania
Company from the time it sent Boone to cut a trail into the wilderness
to the founding of Henderson.

John James Audubon, the ornithologist, whose home was here from
1810 to 1819, lived in a little log house near the corner of Main and
2d Sts. On the same corner was his general merchandise store and
near by his frog and turtle pond. Second St. was formerly known as
the Old Mill Rd., being the route used from the country to Audubon's
mill.

The LOCKETT HOUSE *(open)*, at the corner of Elm and Jefferson Sts.,
is a one-story frame dwelling on a brick foundation. It was built in
1856 for Judge Paschal Hickman Lockett, nephew of Capt. Paschal
Hickman, one of the heroes of the Battle of the River Raisin during
the War of 1812. In the sitting room of this house is the first coal-oil
lamp used in Henderson County. It was brought from New Orleans
by Judge Lockett in 1856. In 1862, when the news came to Judge
Lockett that the Federal soldiers had crossed the Ohio, and, under the
command of Captain Shanklin of Evansville, Ind., were stationed in
the woods near his home, he had the slaves remove part of the cellar
wall and dig a trench in which he hid valuables as well as the contents
of the smokehouse and other provender. The massive front door still
shows the scars made by the gun butts of soldiers who were attempting
to gain entrance, when Captain Shanklin, having just learned that Mrs.
Lockett was his former sweetheart, restrained them.

The LAZARUS POWELL HOUSE *(open)*, 216 South Elm St., was built
in 1818 by the father of Lazarus W. Powell, United States Senator and

later Governor of Kentucky (1851–55). The older part of the two-story frame structure, designed in the Georgian Colonial style, has two huge square rooms on each floor that flank wide central halls. The stairway, simply constructed of beautiful hardwood, is satin-smooth through long usage. The side lights beside the paneled doors are of old glass. These doors have hand-wrought butterfly hinges and two of them have the original locks bearing the arms of William IV of England. In 1857 two rooms of brick were added, one for a private study and one for a bedroom. The slave quarters are still in the back yard.

The P. J. LAMBERT HOUSE, South Main St., built about 1830, has wrought-iron balustrades and balcony, and red-brick steps.

ST. PAUL'S EPISCOPAL CHURCH, corner of Center and Green Sts., of English Gothic design, is a copy of the famous old church at Stoke Poges, England. The three stained-glass windows of the chancel, portraying scenes from the life of St. Paul, were made in Holland. There are also several memorial windows and a tablet dedicated to Bishop Channing Moore Williams, a native of Henderson, who built the first Protestant church in Japan and with the Reverend John Liggins was the first Protestant missionary in Japan.

Henderson is at the junction with US 41 *(see Tour 8)*.

Left from Henderson on State 54, a graveled road to the GREGORY PLACE (L), 2.8 *m.*, one of the oldest estates in the Pennyrile. Here, enclosed by an iron fence, is the GRAVE OF GEN. SAMUEL HOPKINS, agent and attorney for Col. Richard Henderson and often called Henderson's foster-father. On the WILLIAM D. LAMBERT ESTATE (R), 2.8 *m.*, is a stately Georgian Colonial mansion built on a lofty hill overlooking miles of green fields and pleasant valleys. It is a massive, two-story structure of red brick, with limestone trim; its lines are accentuated by the whiteness of the woodwork and its proportions remain excellent despite several additions.

At 157.8 *m.* is the junction with State 136, an improved road.

Right on this road to GENEVA, 4 *m.;* R. here to INDIAN VALLEY FARM, 11 *m.*, established in 1840 by Haywood Alves, son of Walter Alves, an original grantee of the Transylvania Company. Walter Alves and his wife Amelia Johnson Alves, whose share was one-eighth of the grant of 200,000 acres, left their miles of Ohio River frontage to their several children. Haywood, the second son, chose this site opposite DIAMOND ISLAND. The Georgian Colonial house is brick, the main part two stories, with one-story wings. On the front of the house are deep French windows and a square porch. Quantities of arrowheads and other artifacts have been found on this farm which is a part of the Old Indian Valley, a favorite camp site of tribes on hunting trips into Kentucky and Tennessee. Shortly after 1800 this site and Diamond Island were the rendezvous of the infamous Mason band, and of Little Harpe who joined Mason after Big Harpe had been beheaded *(see Tour 8)*. These land pirates preyed on travelers going down the Ohio River on flatboats. Fortesque Cuming told of stopping at beautiful Diamond Island in his *Tour to the Western Country,* published in 1810, and said that from 20 to 30 bandits lived there. . . . These pirates were finally driven out of the vicinity by a company of local "regulators." Diamond Island was approximately three miles long and a half mile wide in Mason's day. It was covered with gigantic trees and luxuriant vines and presented "so wonderful a scene" that it attracted early travelers. Today it is a cornfield, noted for its fertility.

At 172.4 *m.* is the junction with State 141, an improved road.

Right on State 141 to ST. VINCENT'S ACADEMY (R), 0.6 *m.*, surrounded by century-old trees. This Roman Catholic institution was established in 1820. First known as Little Nazareth for the mother-house of the Sisters of Charity of Nazareth *(see Tour 6)*, it was established as a girls' boarding school by three nuns who journeyed 150 miles on horseback with all their belongings sewed in a tow-cloth apron. The bricks in the old building were burned by the nuns in their own kiln and then were trundled by them in wheelbarrows to the brickmason who did the construction work. The academy consists of a coeducational graded school and a high school for girls.

MORGANFIELD, 178.1 *m.* (439 alt., 2,551 pop.), built on rolling uplands, is the seat of Union County, whose farmers early pioneered in replacing "scrub" beef stock with purebred sires and in growing the soil-enriching Korean lespedeza. Seed from this clover was shipped to many parts of the country. A 26-acre combined city park, playground, and athletic field is on the eastern edge of the town. Morganfield and the surrounding region were the scene of several skirmishes during the War between the States.

STURGIS, 189.1 *m.* (375 alt., 2,154 pop.), is the home of the West Kentucky Coal Corporation and center of the bituminous-coal industry of Union County.

MARION, 208 *m.* (1,892 pop.), seat of Crittenden County, was incorporated in 1844 and named for Gen. Francis Marion, Revolutionary War hero. The town is the principal Kentucky shipping point for fluor spar. A company, headed by Andrew Jackson and organized to mine galena for the silver it contained, in 1815 sank the first shaft in this region. When Jackson found that the galena here has a low silver content, he disposed of the thousands of acres of land to which he had acquired title. Because its value was unknown, the fluor spar was not utilized until the time of the War between the States. The industry was at its peak during the World War, when mines were operated at full capacity. About 75 percent of the production is used in the manufacture of steel products and many large steel corporations have secured holdings in this field. Fluor spar is also employed in the manufacture of artificial marble for soda-water fountains and the enamel used on bath tubs, imitation cut glass, and other glass products.

Fluor spar is mined by sinking shafts down the perpendicular vein; some mines reach a depth of 600 feet but the veins of fluor spar are believed to extend a much greater distance. A pneumatic drill breaks up the mineral which is dynamited and brought to the surface on steam hoists. Mining shafts are common throughout the region; many farmers have erected them in their own yards. Some of the crystals are exquisite shades of purple, saffron-yellow, delicate pink, blue, green, and violet.

Right from Marion on State 91, a graveled road, to FORD'S FERRY, 11 *m.*, across the Ohio River from Cave in Rock on the Illinois shore. Here on the Illinois side early in the nineteenth century, Wilson's Liquor Vault and House of Entertainment was operated. The place became infamous for deeds of villainy and licentiousness committed by a band of about 45 men who operated here and at Hurricane Island, about 10 miles down the river. Wilson finally lost his life at the hands of one of his own men, who was tempted by the large reward offered for Wilson's head.

At 208.3 *m.* is the junction with State 297, a graveled road.

Right on this road to TOLU (250 pop.), 11 *m.*, on the Ohio River. Dr. W. D. Funkhouser of the University of Kentucky has uncovered burial places as well as many ornaments and utensils of the prehistoric mound builders. Many of the beads are of local fluor spar.

SALEM, 219.1 *m.* (32 pop.), a hamlet in the center of a fertile valley, is on the western slope of a low hill. The old log houses of the early settlers who came here with their slaves from Virginia and Carolina, once dotted this region. There is nothing now in old Salem to indicate that from 1798 to 1842 it was the seat of Livingstone County. When in 1842 the county seat was transferred to Smithland most of the inhabitants, together with the county officials and lawyers, moved away.

The GRAVE OF LUCY JEFFERSON LEWIS (R), 231.2 *m.*, is marked by a granite shaft. Lucy Jefferson, only sister of Thomas Jefferson, was born in Virginia in 1752 and in 1808 moved to Kentucky with her husband, Dr. Chas. Lilburn Lewis, from Albemarle County, Virginia. She was the youngest child of the Jefferson family. The Lewises, imbued with the current enthusiasm for the West, migrated to Kentucky and settled on a lonely, rocky hillside—now known as Lewis Hill—overlooking the Ohio River, part of a military grant given Lewis as a reward for his services in the American Revolution. Dr. Lewis was said to have been of an unsociable nature, given to moods and queer mannerisms. He soon tired of his Kentucky home and left his family, supposedly to return to his large Virginia estate. It is said that Lucy Jefferson Lewis also pined for her Virginia home but she died here in 1811.

US 60 crosses the LUCY JEFFERSON LEWIS MEMORIAL BRIDGE *(toll 50¢)*, 234 *m.*, which spans the willow-hung Cumberland River, near the point where the stream ends its winding journey of 687 miles.

SMITHLAND, 234.6 *m.* (286 alt., 519 pop.), spreads along a high bluff, above the confluence of the Ohio and the Cumberland. This quiet little village was once looked upon as the coming metropolis of this entire region. Its heyday was in the days when both the Ohio and the Cumberland teemed with commerce. From Pittsburgh and from New Orleans came the floating passenger palaces and great freight carriers. Smithland's busy wharves served as a transfer point for passengers and cargoes bound for inland points.

Christian Schultz, who visited Smithland in 1807, wrote of the early town in his *Travels on an Inland Voyage:* "At the mouth of Cumberland—known by its more ancient name of Shawanese River—is a small settlement called Smith Town, consisting of only five houses. The situation, however, is extremely eligible for further improvement. . . . Most of the boats descending to New Orleans and Memphis generally make a halt here, either for hams, provisions, boats or repairs. . . . It appears to be a kind of inland port, where run-away boys, idle young men, and unemployed boatmen, assemble to engage as hands on board of any boats that may happen to call. An amusement has already been introduced at this place, which although excusable in large towns and cities, yet in a new country, and especially in an infant settlement like this, cannot be too much condemned. You will scarcely believe, that in a place just emerging from the woods, which although advantageously situated, can prosper only by the dint of industry and care, and where the girdled trees which surround its houses threaten with every storm to crush the whole settlement, you will scarcely believe, I say, that a billiard table has been established, which is continually surrounded by common boatmen, just arrived from the Salt Works, St. Louis, or St. Genevieve, who in one hour lost all the hard-earned wages of a two-months' voyage."

With the passing of the steamboat era, Smithland, which had approximately 3,000 residents, languished and dwindled. When railroads were built in the Ohio Valley, Smithland was missed eight miles. Some old houses and taverns still stand on the river front, which is gradually being washed away by the encroaching waters.

Smithland is at the junction with US 62 *(see Tour 14);* the two routes are united between this point and Paducah.

US 60 crosses George Rogers Clark Memorial Bridge over the Tennessee River *(toll 30¢)* at 246.9 *m.*

At 248.6 *m.* is the junction with US 68 *(see Tour 15).*

PADUCAH, 250.7 *m.* (341 alt., 33,541 pop.) *(see Paducah).*

Points of Interest: Paduke Statue, Tilghman Memorial, McCracken County Courthouse, Noble Park, Marine Ways, Brazelton House, Illinois Central Shops, and others.

Paducah is at the junction with US 45 *(see Tour 9),* US 62 *(see Tour 14),* and US 68 *(see Tour 15).*

KEVIL, 269.7 *m.* (439 alt., 231 pop.), is the home of Mary Lanier Magruder, writer of short stories and poems.

In BARLOW, 278.8 *m.* (614 pop.), a small village, the highway makes a right-angle turn.

Right from Barlow on the Paducah-Cairo Pike to CLEAR LAKE (R), and FISH LAKE (L), 3 *m.,* part of a chain of lakes that extend across a plain, within a great bend of the Ohio River. These lakes, probably part of a former course of the Ohio River, provide excellent hunting and fishing. Southeast of Fish Lake is BUCK LAKE, a watering place of buffalo and deer in the days when the Indian roamed the forests of Kentucky. AX LAKE, northeast of Clear Lake, is another popular fishing resort. South and north of these lie numerous small lakes and ponds that abound with fish. Lining the shores of the lakes are thousands of cypresses, their fine foliage outlined in the deep, clear water. Several of these lakes are used by the Federal Government as rearing ponds. At intervals along the banks are screened cabins of trappers, hunters, and fishermen who rent cabins and render service to those who visit the lakes.

WICKLIFFE, 286.2 *m.* (332 alt., 1,108 pop.), seat of Ballard County, is at the confluence of the Ohio and Mississippi Rivers. An eminence near the northern entrance to the town offers a view of this meeting of great waters.

An ancient BURIED CITY *(open daily, adm. $1)* is here on a lofty bluff above the junction of the two streams. Some mounds made by a prehistoric race are still intact, while others have been opened with such care that all remains are in their original positions. The burial mound, now sheltered by a modern building, contains 153 uncovered skeletons. Burials were upon, rather than within, the soft alluvial soil; and charcoal found here indicates that fire was used in some manner in connection with the burials. There are five layers of burials, one superimposed upon the other. The lower layers are in a better state of preservation than the upper ones. Three modes of burial were used: some bodies were fully extended, some were in bundles, and some had been cremated. Many articles of use and adornment found beside the bodies indicate that the race who lived here had reached a high degree of culture. Charred remains of Indian corn, the remnants of timbers used in house construction, the still existing fireplaces, and fragments of wooden furniture, all tell of a non-migratory life. No weapons, except one flint dagger, have been found. Apparently there was a flourishing trade center here before the coming of the white man.

Wickliffe is at the junction with US 51 *(see Tour 10)* and US 62 *(see Tour 14)*.

Between Wickliffe and East Cairo US 60 and US 51 are united.

At 288.5 *m.* is a junction with a trail.

Right on this trail to HUNTERS' POND, 0.9 *m.*, one of the chain of lakes in Ballard County; this lake is large and filled with water plants and trees. In the autumn sportsmen from many parts of the region stand hip-deep in the chilly waters to bring down wild ducks and geese. West of Hunters' Pond is SWAN POND covering an area of about 1,000 acres. Between Swan Pond and FIRST LAKE, the lake nearest the Ohio River, are LONG POND and MINOR LAKE, used as rearing ponds.

At 291.3 *m.* US 60 crosses the Illinois Line and a tip of Illinois to the Missouri Line, 291.8 *m.*, 16 miles east of Charleston, Mo., by way of bridges over the Ohio and Mississippi Rivers *(combination toll $1)*.

Tour 17

Warfield—Paintsville—Mount Sterling—Georgetown—Junction with US 60; 185.3 *m*. State 40.

Hard-surfaced roadbed except for graveled section between Warfield and Paintsville.
All types of accommodations in larger towns.

State 40 winds through a mountain area that was isolated until shortly after the World War, when this highway was built. Consequently the mountaineers living in this region have for the most part retained their distinctive speech, manners, customs, and modes of living *(see Tours 1, 18 and 19)*. Jagged mountains, pine groves on inaccessible pinnacles, laurel-grown cliffs with rhododendron in profusion on the upper sandstone ridges, log cabins, and tales of "hants" characterize this country. The topography changes gradually from mountainous terrain to plains as the highway crosses the Knobs belt and enters the outer rim of the Bluegrass.

WARFIELD, 0 *m*. (662 alt., 120 pop.), on the western bank of the Tug Fork of Big Sandy River, opposite Kermit, West Virginia, was established shortly after the War of 1812 when George R. C. Floyd and associates acquired title to the Ben Say Grant, established the town, drilled a salt well, and started a salt works. They later opened up coal mines, and shipped the product by water. Floyd was a brother of John B. Floyd, Governor of Virginia (1830–32).

INEZ, 10.1 *m*. (600 alt., 500 pop.), is one of the few unincorporated county seats in Kentucky; its former act of corporation was dissolved in order that the State Highway Commission might pave State 40 through the town, construction that the town could not afford. When a post office was established here, the town was to have been called Eden, but it was found that there was already a post office in the State by that name. The postmaster at Louisa, then named the post office for his daughter, Inez Frank. The first settler was James Ward, a veteran of the Revolutionary War and a companion of Daniel Boone on many of his hunting expeditions and in Indian affrays. Ward selected the site for his camp because of the proximity of several salt licks. This region is the locale of Peter Clay's *Big Sandy Poems*, published in 1890.

Left from Inez on a trail to a small NATURAL BRIDGE, 1.5 *m*., in a setting of sylvan beauty.

The highway gradually descends to the ridge dividing Martin and Johnson Counties, and to the junction, 21 *m.*, with an improved road.

Left on this road 4 *m.* to the top of SPRING KNOB, on which is a forest fire observatory.

PAINTSVILLE, 33.8 *m.* (620 alt., 2,411 pop.) *(see Tour 1)*, is at the junction with US 23 *(see Tour 1);* between Paintsville and a point at 35.7 *m.*, State 40 and US 23 are united.

In the area between Paintsville and Oil Springs mining and petroleum production are of importance, though much small fruit is harvested for shipping to outside markets.

At 36.8 *m.* is the junction with State 172, improved.

Right on this road to MUD LICK, 1.9 *m.*, a group of three separate falls between towering cliffs; the central falls has a drop of about 25 feet.

State 40 follows the course of PAINT CREEK, named for painted trees found by early settlers *(see Tour 1);* whence it passes through Road Fork Creek Valley.

At 37.5 *m.* is the junction with a graded road.

Right on this road to FISHTRAP, 3 *m.* *(camping shelters, 50¢ a week, 10¢ a day each person)*, in a deep gorge. A 4-H clubhouse has been erected here by seven counties.

OIL SPRINGS, 42.9 *m.* (892 alt., 150 pop.), named for an oil pool (L) caused by seepage, is on Mine Fork of Paint Creek, whose name was suggested by the tales of John Swift and his legendary silver mine *(see Tour 1)*.

Near the headwaters of the State Road Fork of Paint Creek, 44.6 *m.*, the highway passes through a grove long used as a CAMP MEETING GROUND. Camp meetings are still held in rural Kentucky but their character has changed much since 1800, when the first one was held on Gasper Creek in Logan County. Until the automobile brought a demand for the improvement of roads, the social life of people in the remote coves was very limited; the camp meeting offered the chief opportunity for spiritual comfort, excitement, gossip, trading, courting, and even electioneering. The pioneers, who had shaken off the Established Church during the Revolution, had not yet found a substitute on the frontier when the first itinerant preachers arrived; self-sufficient as the people were in forcing livings from the wilderness, they had a deep unrest and a feeling of insecurity that made them welcome the revivalists eagerly. The meetings were first held in houses and then, when the audiences overflowed, in groves. The men who could best stir the emotions drew the biggest crowds and the larger the crowd the more chance there was that hysteria would break out. One neurotic could swing hundreds to a frenzy. The excesses of the camp meetings soon reached a stage that caused the more settled members of communities to scorn them. In the later days when they were more staid, the meetings became strongholds of the fundamentalists, people who sang, "The old time religion is good enough for me," and meant it.

State 40 continues to climb to the watershed between the Big Sandy and the Licking Rivers. Though much of the roadway in this immediate section leads through woodland, occasional clearings permit a view of the valley below.

SALYERSVILLE, 51.1 *m.* (875 alt., 446 pop.), seat of Magoffin County, named for Beriah Magoffin, Governor (1859–62), is on the Licking River in a natural amphitheater. It was first called Adamsville for Uncle Billy Adams, a pioneer noted for his shrewdness, who operated a gristmill, a flour mill, a carding factory, a tannery, and a blacksmith shop. When Magoffin County was formed in 1860, the town's name was changed to honor Sam Salyers, the district's legislative representative. The open field behind the courthouse is the scene of old-time horse trading each Jockey Day *(see Tour 4)*, which is the first day of the circuit court term in January, April, and September.

At 51.8 *m.* is the junction with State 30.

Left on this road to ARNETT'S GAP, 2 *m.*, an area of jagged cliffs of unusual beauty, with a softening cover of pine, cedar, and mountain laurel. Here columbine and other wild flowers flourish.

State 40 passes along the winding course of the Licking River, occasionally climbing out of the valley to an elevation sufficiently high to give a commanding view of distant hills.

WEST LIBERTY, 74.4 *m.* (777 alt., 569 pop.), on the Licking River, is the seat of Morgan County, named for Gen. Daniel Morgan of Revolutionary fame. The town is a trade center for an area with deposits of cannel coal, which is richer in carbon than ordinary bituminous and highly esteemed for open-grate fires in the home. The town's buildings are of local stone, brick, dressed wood frame, and logs covered with clapboards; some have adjacent slave quarters. In West Liberty and Morgan County there were more slaves than in any of the other Kentucky uplands.

Right from West Liberty on State 7, a graded road, to the junction, 3 *m.*, with Blaze Rd.; L. on this road to YOCUM FALLS, 7 *m.*, a waterfall slightly more than 100 feet high in a setting of wild beauty. Tall trees grow around the basin into which the water falls, their tops reaching almost to the brink. Huge rocks at the foot of the falls are gray and green with lichens and other mosses, and out of the rock crevices and spray-drenched soil grow many rare plants.

RIFE SPRINGS, 8 *m.*, was once a health resort of note. The mineral spring flows into a basin hewn from the rock over which the water originally flowed. A moss-covered stone wall enclosed the spring. Near by are the RUINS OF THE RIFE SPRINGS HOTEL.

Between West Liberty and Frenchburg State 40 winds over an old buffalo trace, found by the Indians when they entered this region. The highway follows generally the branches of the larger creeks, crossing several watersheds at elevations that afford a broad view.

At 94 *m.* is the junction with an unmarked road.

Right on this road to BROKE LEG FALLS *(camping and fishing privileges, 10¢),* 0.5 *m.,* on a creek of the same name. In a wild and primitive setting of natural beauty BROKE LEG CREEK plunges from an overhanging rock ledge more than 100 feet high. Below the falls is a quiet ravine enclosed by rocky cliffs. Between these rock walls and along the banks of the creek are mountain flowers, trees, and shrubbery, seldom seen so close to a highway.

State 40 continues over the ridge tops, often permitting excellent views of the valleys below. Immediately after the World War much drilling for oil was carried on in this vicinity. Abandoned equipment and a few producing wells are noticeable.

FRENCHBURG, 103.9 *m.* (246 pop.), the seat of Menifee County, is a quiet old town in a valley so narrow that the few streets and the public square with its town pump occupy practically all available level land. Houses are wedged between the narrow sidewalk and the base of the mountain. A visitor once said it was a place where one can see in only a single direction—skyward.

State 40 follows a comparatively level course through a widening valley. A rapid change in terrain, from mountainous heights through knobs and then to hillocks, marks the approach into the Bluegrass plain.

MOUNT STERLING, 126.9 *m.* (934 alt., 4,350 pop.) *(see Tour 16),* is at the junction with US 60 *(see Tour 16).*

NORTH MIDDLETOWN, 140 *m.* (400 pop.), was first called Swinneytown for a settler who had an inn here. In 1818, when it was incorporated, the name was changed to Middletown because it was midway between Paris and Mount Sterling. The "North" was added later to distinguish it from the Middletown in Jefferson County.

XALAPA (L), 141.5 *m.,* is the estate of Edward Francis Simms, breeder of thoroughbreds. A stone wall, extending along the highway for two miles, surrounds the place and a wide gateway gives access to miles of driveways bordered with dogwood, hawthorn, oaks, maples, lilacs, and evergreens. The one-and-one-half-story brick residence is covered with Virginia creeper; the front façade has four large windows. Circular steps with old boxwood on each side lead to the small circular portico, which has slender columns and an ironwork balustrade. The paneled doorway has a delicately leaded fan transom and side lights, and there is a handsome Palladian window in the front gable. A reproduction of an old stone mill contains an immense recreation room, a ballroom, a guest room, a bath, and a kitchen. The windows overlook Stoner Creek, which winds through the estate.

The house was built in 1827–28 by William Thomas Buckner, who came from Virginia in 1820. Henry Buckner, a son, inherited the estate of 880 acres, and, after his return from service in the Mexican War, named it Xalapa in memory of the little Mexican town that the Spaniards called the "Happy Land." The estate was purchased by the father of Edward Francis Simms who after he inherited it increased the acreage to 2,700.

At 150.6 *m.* is the junction with US 68 *(see Tour 15);* between this point and Paris, State 40 and US 68 are united *(see Tour 15).*

PARIS, 151.6 *m.* (826 alt., 6,204 pop.) *(see Tour 15),* is at the junction with US 27 *(see Tour 3),* US 68 *(see Tour 15),* and US 227 *(see Tour 17A).*

Between Paris and a point at 153.1 *m.* State 40 and US 27 are united.

ROSEDALE (L), 157.1 *m.,* formerly Johnson's Inn, is shown on Filson's first map of Kentucky, published in 1784, as being on the main road between Lexington and Limestone (now Maysville). Tradition relates that as many as 50 covered wagons stood in the yards here at one time. The two-story brick house, painted white, has a one-and-a-half-story wing at one side and a porch—a later addition—across the front. The woodwork of the interior is of walnut, the mantels are carved, and the paneled doors have brass knobs. The old kitchen is still in use; its large stone fireplace is used to heat the rooms as well as cook the food. There are 11 rooms, including the old bar, which has six cupboards. The dining room, adjacent to the bar, is 30 by 18 feet, and was the scene of many brilliant social functions and dances.

Cuming mentioned stopping at this inn in 1807. He said that Captain Johnson had a fine farm and a supply of wheat and corn left over from the previous year.

At 167.9 *m.* is the junction with US 62 *(see Tour 14);* between this point and Georgetown, State 40 and US 62 are united.

GEORGETOWN, 169 *m.* (866 alt., 4,229 pop.) *(see Tour 4),* is at the junction with US 25 *(see Tour 4)* and with US 62 *(see Tour 14).*

Between Georgetown and a point at 170.1 *m.,* State 40 and US 62 are united.

At 171.6 *m.* is the junction with US 227 *(see Tour 12A).*

FORKS OF ELKHORN, 182.7 *m.* (172 pop.), a rural village, is at the forks of ELKHORN CREEK *(bass fishing),* a small river draining the central area of the Bluegrass. This river was so named because its two forks resemble the branching horns of an elk. Along the highway are pools for bass hatchery.

BLACK'S POND (R), 185 *m.,* like many waters of the Bluegrass, is believed locally to be bottomless.

The highway winds and dips as it enters the deep narrow valley of the Kentucky River.

At 185.3 *m.* is the junction with US 60 *(see Tour 16),* 2.7 miles east of Frankfort.

Tour 17A

Paris—Boonesboro—Richmond, 39.1 *m.;* US 227.

Hard-surfaced roadbed throughout.
All types of accommodations in towns; limited elsewhere.

Between Paris and Richmond US 227 winds through that part of eastern Kentucky where the inner Bluegrass gives way to the outer Bluegrass, with a hint here and there of the mountains whose foothills begin only a few miles to the east. The highway passes black locust trees near gates and roadways; wide pastures shaded with twisted oak, black walnut, and beech trees; stock farms outlined by wooden fences and old limestone walls, some made by slave labor; great barns, many with the side ventilators indicating their use for tobacco storage; and houses less over-modernized and pretentious than many found near Lexington. Spring brings out the wild locust bloom; and the honeysuckle, wild rose, and trumpet vine clamber over the fences. In the stonier sections the blue-berried red cedar comes up. There are scatterings of woodland—scraggly second-growth hickory, oak, maple, and sycamore—but the greater part of the landscape is divided into wide squares of bluegrass, corn, and such soil-improving crops as clover, rye, and alfalfa. The tobacco patches are smaller, but they grow a white burley that is thinner and finer than silk.

This region is so generous that it was among the first to draw settlers, who risked torture and death at the hands of the Indians, determined to keep their hunting grounds. Besides descendants of these first settlers, many of whom still live here, there are a few wealthy Eastern sportsmen and gentlemen farmers.

US 227 branches south from PARIS, 0 *m.* (826 alt., 6,204 pop.) *(see Tour 15),* which is at the junction with US 68 *(see Tour 15),* State 40 *(see Tour 17),* and US 27 *(see Tour 3).*

South of Paris horse farms stretch along both sides of the road. Their stone, wire, and wood paddocks run end-to-end from the edge of the highway back across the gently uneven fields dotted with oaks and other trees; a few horses can be seen in one or another of the checkerboard pastures. Unlike the big wealthy farms around Lexington, most of these farms are not show places, but the use of low, weathered stone fences for paddocks lends a special charm to the scene.

In the CLAIBORNE THOROUGHBRED STUD BARN *(open on request),* 1.3 *m.* (L), owned by A. B. Hancock, were foaled some of the greatest thoroughbreds in the history of racing, including Gallant Fox, a Derby winner in 1930 and sire of Omaha, which won the Kentucky Derby in 1935, and later won the Preakness, Belmont Stakes, and other races. Other famous Claiborne horses are Galahad III, Gallant Sir, Diavolo, Stimulus, Alcazar, Hard Tak, Reigh Count, and Sir Andrew.

The GAITSKILL FARM (R), 8 *m.*, is the birthplace of John Fox, Jr. (1863–1919), author of *The Trail of the Lonesome Pine, The Little Shepherd of Kingdom Come,* and other Kentucky stories. The house in which he was born has been destroyed by fire.

John Fox, Jr., the son of a schoolmaster, entered Transylvania University in 1878 when he was only 15. After two years he transferred to Harvard from which he was graduated in 1883, the youngest man in his class. He joined the staff of the New York *Sun* and later entered Columbia Law School, but soon abandoned law and joined the staff of the New York *Times.* After a few months, illness compelled him to move to the South.

He joined his father and brother in a mining venture in the Cumberland Mountains, where he later taught school for a time. He began his literary career with the story, "A Mountain Europa," which appeared in the *Century* of September and October 1892. It was followed by "On Hell-fer-Sartain Creek," published in *Harper's Weekly,* November 24, 1894. When the Spanish-American War was declared, Fox went to Cuba as a Rough Rider, but left the Army to act as correspondent for *Harper's Weekly.* His experiences were written into his first long novel, *Crittenden* (1900). *The Little Shepherd of Kingdom Come* (1903), *The Trail of the Lonesome Pine* (1908), and other stories followed. In 1909 he married Fritzi Scheff, the light opera star, from whom he was later divorced. He died of pneumonia on July 8, 1919, at Big Stone Gap, Virginia, where he had lived for several years. He was buried at Paris, Kentucky.

The road crosses a small, whitewashed COVERED BRIDGE, 9 *m.*, over Stoner Creek, the last of three such bridges met in a five-mile course, and leaves behind the wide, fairly open land with a thin march of trees against the distant low horizon. Moderate but repeated rolls and swells run back from the highway across large pasture fields and small corn and tobacco patches. Few trees are seen, but fences of all kinds—stone, board, and rail—mark off the uneven fields for grazing cattle and sheep. Livestock farming is good in this area, and substantial modern houses are met along the way.

WINCHESTER, 17.2 *m.* (981 alt., 8,233 pop.) *(see Tour 16),* is at the junction with US 60 *(see Tour 16)* and State 15 *(see Tour 2).*

At 24.2 *m.* is the junction with a lane.

Right on this lane to the little stone PROVIDENCE CHURCH, 0.5 *m.*, in constant use since it was built about 1787; this is one of the oldest Protestant church buildings west of the Alleghenies. It was built by members of the body known as the Traveling Baptist Church, who came to Kentucky from Spotsylvania County, Virginia, in 1781, to escape the church laws of Virginia *(see Tour 3).* It was turned over to Negro Baptists during the middle of the nineteenth century.

Winding past some rock outcroppings crowding the highway (L), US 227 meets, at 25 m., the limestone STATUE OF DANIEL BOONE (L) facing the Kentucky River at the east end of the Boonesboro Memorial Bridge *(toll 30¢)*. The short, thick-bodied figure on a spreading base, with a face resembling that of George Washington, wears a coonskin cap and carries a gun. The statue is the work of A. D. Fisher of Winchester.

From the bridge, which rides high above the Kentucky River, opens (R) one of that river's many beautiful gorges. The steep walls of carved limestone that rise perpendicularly above the water are spotted with the brown of sandstone, which indicates that the hills are not far away. Trees grope along the top of the gorge, and at the bottom, the shimmering river reflects the images of the grave masonry overhead and the tangle of beech, maple, sycamore, grapevine, thunderwood, and ironwood by its sides. The gorge ends near the bridge as the river curves through a narrow bottom land (L) past Boonesboro.

BOONESBORO, 25.3 m. (600 alt., 167 pop.), is a small resort of stilted red and green frame cottages, a hotel, and a bathing beach on the Kentucky River. The granite Daniel Boone monument is on the SITE OF FORT BOONESBORO, laid out in 1775 by Daniel Boone and his backwoodsmen under the sponsorship of Col. Richard Henderson, a man prominent in the political life of North Carolina. Fascinated by Boone's glowing stories of hunting forays in the Kentucky country, Henderson had induced Nathaniel, David, and Thomas Hart to join him in founding a great proprietary colony beyond the mountains. At first the association bore Henderson's name, but it was later called the Transylvania Company, and the proposed region was referred to as Transylvania.

At a great council, held in March 1775, the Cherokee, in return for a substantial cash payment, had ceded to Henderson for the company a vast tract in what is now Kentucky. News of the transaction aroused the Governors of Virginia and North Carolina; they denounced the proceedings by proclamation. Nothing daunted, Henderson went ahead with his plans. A party of 30 under Daniel Boone was sent over the mountains to blaze a trail and lay out the town that was to be the capital of Transylvania. Here, on a plain south of the Kentucky River, near a salt lick frequented by herds of buffalo, Boone went to work, April 5, 1775, and Fort Boonesboro began to take shape. Henderson reached the scene April 20, and at once called a convention of the people at the four stations, St. Asaph, Harrodsburg, Boiling Springs, and Boonesboro, to agree on some form of government. They met under a magnificent elm, about four feet thick, later to be known as the "divine elm." Under its spreading branches was held the first religious service in Kentucky, and the first wedding ceremony at Fort Boonesboro, that of Samuel Henderson, younger brother of the pioneer, and Elizabeth Callaway. The wedding was solemnized by Squire Boone, brother of Daniel Boone, on August 7, 1776.

When the real work of pioneering began, many of the first settlers left the settlement; some had joined the expedition merely from restlessness and a love of adventure; others found that the government in the wilderness was no more to their liking than the one back home, and returned to Virginia; and yet others became frightened by accounts of Indian activities and sought safer spots. But in the fall came new recruits, among them George Rogers Clark, later the hero of the Northwest Territory; he had been surveying for the Ohio Company and was picking out choice sections of land for himself, as was the custom of the time. Another arrival was Simon Kenton *(see Tour 15)*, who had fled into the wilderness because he thought he had killed a man in a fist-fight.

By the time the Boone women arrived in September cabins and furniture of a sort were in the making, and the women were soon busy with soap kettles and spinning wheels. They helped to lay aside supplies for the winter, while the men continued to collect pelts for trade.

Colonel Henderson soon found that purchase from the Cherokee was one thing, but recognition of that purchase by Great Britain or Virginia, quite another. His title was not confirmed. Opposition to the transaction came first from the assembly, jealous of its domain, and later from the settlers at Harrodsburg *(see Harrodsburg)*, angered at being thrust into the background by Henderson's intruders. In 1776 George Rogers Clark and John Gabriel Jones were sent from Harrodsburg to the Virginia Assembly with a petition to have Kentucky set apart as a county. The assembly ignored the protests of Henderson—who had paid the Indians 10,000 pounds and, with his men, had labored vigorously to keep Transylvania going—and granted Clark's petition. By way of consolation, the Virginia Assembly in 1778 granted Henderson 200,000 acres in the new county, between the Ohio and Green Rivers, today the county bearing his name *(see Tour 16)*.

Danger from Indians at Fort Boonesboro was meanwhile growing acute. It came to a head July 14, 1776, when two daughters of Colonel Callaway and the one daughter of Daniel Boone were captured by Indians while on the river just outside the fort. Their cries were heard; Boone and Col. John Floyd, leading a party of eight, in which were the suitors of the three girls, started in pursuit. The Indians had fled northward in the direction of their villages across the Ohio, a trail that took them close to the present Winchester, North Middletown, and Carlisle. To guide rescuers Elizabeth Callaway had broken twigs and brush and scattered them as she walked; in spite of threats, she next tore bits of clothing and let them fall on the path. Although her fellow captives had been persuaded to put on moccasins, Elizabeth kept her shoes on and, as she walked, dug her heels deep into the ground. Boone and his little band shortly overtook the Indians, who fled, leaving the girls unharmed.

Early in 1778, returning from a salt-making expedition, Boone and 15 companions were captured by the Shawnee who demanded that they be shown the way to Boonesboro. Boone, who knew how unprepared the fort was, persuaded the Indians to wait till spring, but could not get them to release their captives. Boone contrived to escape in June and, after a perilous journey, reached Boonesboro where he found he had been given up for dead and that his wife had gone back to her old home. He warned the settlers of their danger and hastened defensive measures, strengthening blockhouses, building palisades, and protecting a powder magazine in a sunken place within the fort.

The attack was made September 7 by 400 braves and 40 French-Canadians. The fort withstood a siege of 10 days and finally its small body of defenders, not more than 60 able to bear arms, drove off the Indians. Afterward Boone was brought before a court-martial on a charge of conspiracy preferred by Colonel Callaway. Speaking in his own defense he not only secured acquittal but also was promoted to the rank of major.

Although this victory brought Boonesboro fame, it could not prolong the town's existence. A small graveyard, on the river bank 100 yards or so downstream, is the only remnant of the pioneer settlement. It is believed to mark the site of one of the log forts that withstood the siege.

The early history of Kentucky is more closely identified with the name of Daniel Boone—explorer, trail maker, and Indian fighter—than with that of any other man. Boone united in an eminent degree those qualities of initiative, courage, native shrewdness, and cool self-possession in moments of emergency that inspired confidence; men of wealth and influence were willing to trust adventurous enterprises to his care. There are so many thrilling stories and legends of Daniel Boone's adventures that the simplicity of the man has been quite obscured. In his person there was nothing remarkably striking. Chester Harding, who painted his portrait when he was a gaunt, old man, described him as a dreamy person busy about his domestic labors, shunning publicity, and despising the traditional headwear of coonskin cap with bushy tail. Asked once if he ever got lost, he hesitated a moment; "not lost, so to speak," he said, "but sometimes bewildered."

Between Boonesboro and Richmond the highway passes through a productive livestock region. Every farm has its herds of cattle or its flocks of sheep. The sheep are raised for their especially fine soft wool used in the manufacture of infants' clothing. For several miles the hills, thick with trees, look down upon the road (R), while along the other side of US 227 are long, narrow corn bottoms, paralleled farther back by the willows and sycamores of Otter Creek, and by low hills beyond. After several risings and descents through small valleys, the road emerges on a rolling terrain where continuous swells and dips ripple back to the low horizon. Pasture fields border the highway; cornfields stand in the background.

RICHMOND, 39.1 *m.* (926 alt., 6,495 pop.) *(see Tour 4)*, is at the junction with US 25 *(see Tour 4)*.

Tour 18

Junction with US 23—Hindman—Somerset—Columbia—Glasgow—Junction with US 31W–68; 274.6 *m.*, State 80.

Hard-surfacing throughout being completed (1939).
Limited accommodations except in larger towns.

This route passes through a region of primitive beauty and grandeur, where stillness fills the valleys that are shadowed on all sides by blue-green mountains. Some of the patches of cultivated land—mostly corn-fields—lie on steep slopes between stands of virgin timber and end on the rims of steep cliffs; others huddle along the streams below.

Far back from the main roads and almost hidden in the coves or on mountain sides are dilapidated log cabins, which usually consist of a single large room and a lean-to, with puncheon floor, a heavy plank door, a large stone chimney, and one window with a single sash. Often there is a narrow porch in front. Built long ago of green timber, the average cabin has shrunk and sagged until there is hardly a square joint, a perpendicular face, or a level place in the structure. Puncheons have warped, leaving wide cracks in the floor, and the rived shingles have curled and been patched repeatedly. The limited amount of clothing not in use hangs from nails and pegs on the walls between bunches of dried beans, strings of peppers, dried apples, and gourds. There is usually an almanac in the cabin, but no clock, for "What does a man want with a clock when he has a good crowin' rooster?" A kerosene lamp, frequently without chimney, or a twisted rag stuck into a bottle of hog grease, furnishes illumination. Tables and chairs are home-made, and beds are few—regardless of the number of people in the family. In the yard stands an ash hopper for running lye to make soap, and a large iron kettle for boiling clothes and soap, for scalding hogs, as well as for a variety of other uses.

The woman of the mountains leads a difficult life, while the man is lord of the household. Whether he works, visits, or roams through the woods with dog and gun, is nobody's business but his own. If he converts the corn that his family laboriously cultivated on the steep mountain side into whisky, his wife never thinks of asking "the law" to force him to keep it for family support. A spirit of personal independence and belief in his rights as an individual are distinctive traits of the mountaineer. He is entirely unable to understand any interference in his affairs by society; if he turns his corn into "likker," he is dealing with what is his. In spite of extreme poverty and an environment beset with trying, often hazardous conditions, the mountaineer maintains a code of hospitality characteristic of those living in isolated regions.

The customs, speech, folk songs, child rhymes, and superstitions of the mountaineer recall eighteenth-century England (see Tours 1 and 19). The frequent occurrence of "King George" and "King Henry" in many of the play songs, the mention of "Fair Notanom [Nottingham] Town" and such lines as

"There was a rich margent
In London did dwell . . ."

are instances of the partial preservation of the rhymes and songs of his forefathers. With improved methods of transportation, however, and the establishment of modern schools, old customs, speech, and habits of thought, a gradual transformation is taking place.

Towns and streams, however, continue to bear the names given them by the pioneers, including Red Fox, Pumpkin Center, Troublesome Creek, Deadman Creek, Cut-Shin Creek, Hell-Fer-Sartain, and Polecat Creek.

State 80 branches southwest from its junction, 0 *m.*, with US 23 (see Tour 1) 9.3 miles south of Prestonsburg.

ALLEN, 0.5 *m.* (638 alt., 284 pop.), is on the west bank of the Levisa Fork at the gateway to Beaver Valley, the most populous section of Floyd County and its trade and industrial center.

Right from Allen on a paved road to the BEAVER VALLEY GOLF AND COUNTRY CLUB (open to public, fee 50¢), 0.3 *m.*, the center of social life of the better-to-do in the little valley towns.

State 80 crosses Beaver Creek on a steel span bridge and passes through Beaver Valley, where there are many small mining camps. The mountains and hills of the region are underlain with veins of coal ranging in thickness from 30 inches to 6 feet and a commercially exploited supply of natural gas. One of the first flowing oil wells in eastern Kentucky was drilled in 1892 on Right Fork of Beaver Creek at the mouth of Salt Lick Creek. This began production of the Beaver Creek Oil Pool which has been in continuous operation since that time. At present (1939) there are between 600 and 700 producing wells in the region.

GARRETT, 17.7 *m.* (1,000 alt., 1,000 pop.), is incorporated under the same charter, with the same set of public officials as Wayland. Each town has its own high school and stores.

LACKEY, 18.6 *m.* (522 pop.), is a small mining settlement.

Left from Lackey on State 7 to WAYLAND, 2 *m.* (2,436 pop.), a mining town whose public affairs are directed jointly with those of Garrett.

Between Lackey and Hindman the route passes through Troublesome Creek Valley, a region immortalized in song and story.

HINDMAN MOUNTAIN is visible (R) for miles along the highway.

At 30 *m.* is the junction with a marked road, passable in dry weather.

Left on this road, which follows Terry Fork Creek, to CANEY CREEK JUNIOR COLLEGE AND COMMUNITY CENTER at the village of PIPPAPASS, 3.5 *m.* The center, which is supported by free-will offerings, was founded by Mrs. Alice Lloyd in 1917, and consists of a 175-acre farm and 30 buildings. Its activities include clubs, a Sunday school, and health clinics; a lower-form school and a fully accredited county high school are maintained in co-operation with Knott County. The junior college is a private institution under the management of the center; it is coeducational and fully accredited. The organization makes it possible for the most promising students to attend universities.

HINDMAN, 34 *m.* (1,032 alt., 508 pop.), seat of Knott County, lies in a narrow valley at the forks of Troublesome Creek. Its main street, with a school at one end and a church at the other, stretches along the stream. Steep, rugged mountains rise precipitously above it. Hindman consisted of three houses, a store, and a water-power mill when Knott County, with a scattered population of 2,000, was formed.

One of the most notorious feuds *(see Tour 19)* of the Kentucky mountains began near the end of the eighteenth century in Hindman as a result of the killing of Linvin Higgins. Dolph Drawn, a deputy sheriff of Knott County, organized a posse and started for Letcher County with warrants for the arrest of William Wright and two other men accused of the murder. When the sheriff's men reached Daniel's Hill they were fired on by the Wright band. In the fight that followed several men were wounded and the sheriff's horse was killed. ("Devil John" Wright, leader of the Wright faction, later paid for the animal because he "regretted the killing of a fine horse.") After the first encounter Clabe Jones led Drawn's party, and at one time both Jones and Wright not only had warrants for the arrest of the other but had also succeeded in persuading the Governor to offer a reward for each other's capture. Although this feud lasted several years and was responsible for the death of more than 150 men, all of its participants who were tried in court were cleared. While the feud lasted, all the men who took part in it had a glorious time; when the enemy was not near at hand the partisans sat about cleaning guns, boasting of what they were going to do at the next encounter, rehearsing the details of past battles, and planning strategy that included travel by night, ambush, decoying tactics, and raids. Those who were killed were buried secretly to keep the enemy from knowing its score.

John Wright, who played such a prominent part in the war, had accumulated quite a fortune in the lumber business and is described as a man of "splendid mind and some education." He built a brick house that was one of the first of its kind in Letcher County, and he brought glass from Virginia to build a greenhouse in which to grow the flowers that were his hobby. John Fox, Jr. *(see Tours 17A–19)* lived in Wright's home while gathering material for his stories.

HINDMAN SETTLEMENT SCHOOL was founded in 1902 by May Stone of Louisville and Katherine Pettit of Lexington, under the sponsorship of the Woman's Christian Temperance Union. The school was organized to supply the need expressed by "Uncle Sol" Beveridge, 82 years of age, who had walked 20 miles from Hindman to Hazard to enlist the interest of the two young women who were camping there. He said: "When I was a little chunk of a shirt-tailed lad, a-hoeing corn on the steep hillside, I'd get to the end of a row and look up Troublesome Creek and wonder if anybody would ever come to larn the young 'uns. Nobody ever come in. Nobody ever went out. We jist growed up and never knowed nothin'. I can't read nor write; many of my chilluns can't read nor write, but I have grands and greats as is the purtiest speakin' and the easiest larnin' of any chilluns in the world. I want as they should have a chancet."

The school, the first of its kind in the State, was started in a little house and a near-by cottage on four acres of rented ground; today the institution owns 165 acres of land and 18 buildings. It is accredited by the Southern Association of Secondary Schools and Colleges and has an average enrollment of 400. The curriculum includes preparation for college, as well as industrial training, homemaking, and social service. Extension work—sewing and cooking classes, public health service, home demonstration, and Sunday school—is carried on in the county. Through the Fireside Industries, a phase of the school's work that has been emphasized, traditional homecrafts have been revived and today the coverlets, blankets, and other products of the loom, made by the mountain women, are on sale. The returns to the workers for this handwork are very low because of the competition with machine-made goods, but those sponsoring the movement say that the work does at least bring in some cash to those who have no other way of earning it.

On the school grounds is the "UNCLE SOL" BEVERIDGE CABIN *(open)*, restored to honor the old mountaineer whose vision inspired the establishment of the school. The cabin is furnished as it was when "Uncle Sol" lived in it, with spinning wheel and dulcimer, home-made wooden furniture, rifle and powder horn, home-made coverlets and rugs, and iron cooking utensils around the open fireplace.

The work of the school has been portrayed in the stories of Lucy Furman, a teacher here for many years. Her best known works, *Quare Women* and *Hard-hearted Barbara Allen*, preserve the racy idiom and imaginative language of the mountaineer.

DWARF, 47 *m.* (900 alt., 118 pop.), is the site of the old TUNNEL MILL, which still grinds the mountaineers' corn. Near by is a horseshoe bend of the creek, where two early settlers tunneled through the mountain in order to obtain increased force in the fall of the water for a millrace. After nine years of labor they completed the undertaking and built a sawmill, a carding mill, and a gristmill. Only the gristmill remains.

Dwarf is at the junction with State 15 *(see Tour 2);* between Dwarf and a junction at 52.7 *m.*, State 80 and State 15 are one route.

State 80 crosses North Fork of the Kentucky River at 56 *m.*

In WOOTEN, 66.7 *m.* (875 alt., 1,763 pop.), the Presbyterian Church supports a school and community center. A "listening center" for classes in agriculture is maintained here by the University of Kentucky. The school is also reviving and preserving old songs, dances, and plays.

HYDEN, 73.7 *m.* (870 alt., 1,471 pop.), seat of Leslie County, named for Preston H. Leslie, Governor of Kentucky (1871–75), is in the valley of Middle Fork of the Kentucky River. Cottages and cabins are scattered over the hillside, and on the surrounding hills are small growths of beech, oak, maple, hemlock, poplar, ash, and walnut—all that remains of the great forests of pre-lumbering days. The first white settlers, John Sizemore and his wife, Nancy Bowling Sizemore, came to the valley from North Carolina in 1817. The growth of the settlement was very slow; Leslie County was not formed until 1878. No wagon road connected Hyden with the outside world until 1880; before that "store goods" had been brought by canoe up the Kentucky from Clay's Ferry near Lexington.

In 1879 a two-room store was erected here; this log structure is unchanged though it is now a dwelling.

Within the court square, which is encircled by a stone wall, is the little-used county jail. The majority of cases tried here today are concerned with land-title disputes. Sentences for theft and robbery are rare, as the victim frequently kills the thief—an act for which he is usually acquitted or given a very light sentence. Feuds *(see Tour 19)* were formerly responsible for many shootings, and in such cases the courts were powerless. During Prohibition, when there was a demand from the outside for "moonshine" and "white mule," nearly all criminal cases resulted from the illicit sale of liquor. Whisky was made everywhere, in the mountaineers' homes, in deserted log cabins, and in caves far back in the hills. All the equipment needed to produce from 20 to 60 gallons a day was a vat for the corn mash, a boiler, and a "worm" (a coil of copper pipe).

In 1894 the Reverend D. McDonald, an evangelist and educator of New York, was sent to Hyden by the Presbyterian Church for the purpose of establishing a church school, which was dedicated in 1896. The influence of the institution has been widely felt in this remote region.

A weekly Hyden newspaper called *Thousand Sticks,* for the highest hill in the vicinity, is the only publication in Leslie County. This four-page news sheet employs the local dialect and, like other country papers, concentrates its attention on the interests of the people it serves. It dates from 1898 and has subscribers in many parts of the United States.

The FRONTIER NURSING SERVICE HOSPITAL (R) is a two-story stone building with 18 beds, a babies' ward, a dispensary, an operating room, and a wing for those suffering from infectious diseases. Built in 1928, the hospital is the only one in a large mountain area.

The Frontier Nursing Service, of which Mary Breckinridge is the founder and active leader, maintains eight nursing centers in isolated, almost inaccessible areas, co-operating with Federal and State authorities and with various health foundations. It is supported largely by voluntary contributions. Each center contains a clinic and living quarters for two nurse-midwives. These uniformed public health nurses travel on horseback, attending women in childbirth, nursing the sick, and giving instructions in sanitation, health, and hygiene. Midwifery receives primary attention. The two nurses at each center give service to an area of about 80 square miles; each carries a saddlebag, one side holding equipment for general nursing, the other for obstetrical work. Before this service was established the maternal and infant death rates in the mountains were high. Even if there had been a doctor in the area the women would not have called him because of a tradition that "borning" was the job of a woman—usually a grandmother whose qualification was the number of children and grandchildren she had "borned." Before the service was founded in 1925 charms and home remedies were the only medical resource of the 10,000 people in a 700-square-mile area where there was not a single resident physician. When Miss Breckinridge determined to provide better obstetrical service here she was faced with the fact that midwifery has only partial recognition in the United States; in but one or two places, notably in Bellevue Hospital in New York City, is it possible to take some training in the craft, and even there the training is limited to the care of normal cases. For this reason it was necessary either to import midwives trained in Europe or to send American nurses abroad for training. American nurses who wish to join the frontier staff are examined with care and tested in Kentucky for endurance and adaptability before they are sent abroad. After receiving an English or Scottish license to practice, the nurse takes public health training in the United States if she does not already have it. While great emphasis is placed on nursing and midwifery, the teaching function is equally important. She must teach the mountain women to care for their sick between her infrequent visits.

At first the mountain people were very suspicious of the "brought on women" and continued to have their babies "cotched by the grannies." But since confidence has been established, the infant death rate has been decreasing and there has not been a single death during childbirth among the clients.

The nurses are assisted by "couriers," lay volunteers who come from the cities. Clinics are held at each center, with nurses, a doctor, and a dentist in attendance, and patients are urged to come to these clinics to save the time of the staff. The usual charge for prenatal care and delivery is $5, but since the mountaineers are permitted to pay in labor or in produce, the nurses are always well supplied with chickens, eggs, and vegetables, the horses with fodder, and the cabins are furnished with quilted "kivvers" and splint-bottom chairs.

1. Left from Hyden on an unimproved road to WENDOVER *(open)*, 4 *m.*, the directing center and residence of Mary Breckinridge. The modern two-story log house with stone foundation is built on a steep slope overlooking Middle Fork of the Kentucky River. In the garden below the terrace is a collection of wild flowers from the mountains, and a stream from the spring on the hill above the house flows through.

2. Right from Hyden on an unmarked, unimproved road that follows Middle Fork of the Kentucky River to DRY HILL, 6 *m.* (34 pop.), where the Presbyterian Church maintains a community center.

The surrounding region is watered by two creeks, CUT-SHIN (R) and HELL-FER-SARTAIN (L), both confluents of Middle Fork of the Kentucky River near Dry Hill. Tradition is that when an early pioneer was coming through here with his oxtrain he found one of the creeks swollen by recent rains and the crossing difficult. While driving his oxen over, he cut his shins on the sharp rocks; hence the name, Cut-Shin. The following day he came to the other stream, more rugged, more swollen, and far more difficult to cross. When he realized his predicament he exclaimed, "Well, by jeeminy, this is hell-fer-sartain!" and the name has clung to this usually limpid beautiful mountain brook.

On Devil's Jump Branch of Hell-Fer-Sartain Creek is the mountain HOME OF WILLIE SANDLIN, the only native Kentuckian to receive the Congressional Medal of Honor for World War services. Sandlin, also a recipient of several foreign medals including the Croix de Guerre, is now a farmer.

REDBIRD CREEK, 89.8 *m.*, offers good fishing. The high ridges, with steep sides above the narrow valleys through which the route passes, are heavily timbered with oak, hickory, maple, beech, and other hardwoods.

In GARRARD, 102.8 *m.* (43 pop.), salt was made at a lick as early as 1803. A few of the old salt kettles remain at the site of the salt works.

At 103.1 *m.* is the junction with State 21.

Right on State 21 to MANCHESTER, 2.3 *m.* (860 alt., 900 pop.), seat of Clay County; it was named for the great cotton-manufacturing center in England. Built on a hill overlooking Goose Creek, a tributary of the South Fork of the Kentucky River, this town has changed little from generation to generation.

Shortly after the Revolutionary War, James White of Abingdon, Virginia, purchased the salt spring here and established a salt works. Prior to the coming of the white man, the place had evidently been known to the Indians, for the ground around the spring was littered with the shards of their clay kettles. Soon settlers were toiling over the trails from their log cabins to carry back their year's supply of salt. About 1808, when the demand outgrew the supply, wells were drilled. With the enlargement and multiplication of salt works, the Goose Creek area became an important center. Pipes, necessary to carry the brine from outlying wells to the works, were made of the trunks of small trees, bored with long augers, fitted end to end, and carefully calked. Cooperage plants were established in the near-by region, and the salt was shipped down the river from Manchester to Clay's Ferry in flatboats having a capacity of 500 to 700 barrels. During the War between the States, and for a number of years thereafter, Virginia and Tennessee, as well as Kentucky, were supplied in great measure by the Goose Creek works.

On State 21 is BURNING SPRINGS 8.3 *m.* (225 pop.), named from the natural flow of gas that burned with a steady flame for many years after its discovery in 1798 and was regarded by the pioneers as a phenomenon perhaps connected with the devil. The flame has since been extinguished; the gas that once fed it is piped to Lexington. The development of this large field began in 1907, when the century-old salt industry of the area was abandoned.

Between the junction with State 21 and London, State 80 winds between forested ridges, purple in the distance, and along creeks that meander through narrow, green valleys.

LONDON, 124.8 *m.* (1,209 alt., 1,950 pop.) *(see Tour 4)*, is at the junction with US 25 *(see Tour 4)*.

BERNSTADT, 131.9 *m.* (424 pop.), was the largest of several Swiss colonies in this region. In 1881 the Bernstadt Colonization Company, one of whose founders was Paul Schenk, son of a President of Switzerland, purchased 40,000 acres of land in Laurel County for cultivation as vineyards. The Swiss group, which at first included more than 600 persons, has declined in numbers; only about a dozen families of Swiss descent remain. The vineyards have been largely abandoned, and cheese making has become the leading commercial activity.

ROCKCASTLE RIVER *(good fishing)*, 138.6 *m.*, was so named because of the number of large rocks that in some places impede its course.

SOMERSET, 159.5 *m.* (879 alt., 5,506 pop.) *(see Tour 3)*, is at the junction with US 27 *(see Tour 3)*.

A NATIONAL CEMETERY (R), 168.7 *m.*, contains graves of both Confederate and Union soldiers killed at the Battle of Logan's Cross Roads. A stone recounting the deeds of valorous Southern troops marks the spot where more than 100 unidentified Confederates are buried.

At 171.2 *m.* is the junction with State 235, improved.

Left on State 235 to ZOLLICOFFER MEMORIAL PARK, 1 *m.*, established by the United Daughters of the Confederacy in memory of Gen. Felix K. Zollicoffer who fell at the Battle of Logan's Cross Roads, January 19, 1862.

In the late fall of 1861, General Felix K. Zollicoffer was ordered to establish an entrenched camp on the Cumberland River at Mill Springs in order to block off any attempt by the Federal troops to turn the flank of the Confederate forces in Kentucky *(see Tour 20)*.

General George B. Crittenden, who succeeded to the command of the force at Mill Springs, ordered General Zollicoffer to advance from that place and defeat the small Union detachment encamped at Logan's Cross Roads. Unknown to the Confederates, reinforcements had reached General Thomas which increased his numbers to approximately the equal of theirs.

The Confederates attacked the Federals about daylight on the 19th of January, 1862. The fall of Zollicoffer and the flanking fire of the Union troops, coupled with a bayonet charge by a Union regiment, caused the final defeat of the Confederates, who fled in disorder. Thomas followed up his advantage and forced the Southerners to abandon their fortifications and cross the Cumberland in retreat. This battle cleared the way for a Union advance into eastern Tennessee, and exposed Johnston's right flank at Bowling Green.

During the battle Union Col. Speed S. Fry ordered Zollicoffer's body removed to the rear of his lines. Because of the poor condition of General Zollicoffer's uniform, his body was reclothed in Colonel Fry's civilian clothes. The body was then sent in a wooden coffin to Lebanon. Thence it was sent, by Colonel Fry's orders, to Danville where the body was transferred to a metal coffin and forwarded to Nashville where it now rests.

NANCY, 171.5 *m.* (358 pop.), is chiefly a crossroads.

RUSSELL SPRINGS, 193.7 *m.* (1,080 alt., 500 pop.) *(see Tour 5)*, is at the junction with State 35 *(see Tour 5)*.

COLUMBIA, 207.9 m. (750 alt., 1,195 pop.), seat of Adair County, is built about the old court square. Dignified old buildings, which have been modernized, are indicative of the town's early prosperity.

The HURT HOUSE, a two-story brick structure with a gabled roof and an ell, was the home of William Hurt, a soldier in the Revolutionary War who came to Kentucky in 1793. He cleared a farm, the first in this region, and built his cabin, unprotected by blockhouse or stockade. Hurt was the first slaveowner in this region and the first possessor of a cart and a yoke of draft oxen. In 1863, when the house was occupied by Timoleon Cravens, a Captain Carter and two soldiers were killed on the Hurt House lawn during a skirmish while serving with a detachment of Gen. John H. Morgan's Confederate Cavalry.

The LINDSEY WILSON JUNIOR COLLEGE offers premedical, normal, and theological courses. It has five modern school buildings, homes for faculty members, and a library of approximately 6,000 volumes—the only public library in the county. Founded by Miss Eliza Forte, the school is operated by the Methodist Episcopal Church, South.

The annual Adair County Fair, held at Columbia late in August, sponsors agricultural exhibits, field sports, and horse racing.

In April 1862, bandits robbed the bank here. They killed the cashier and escaped with a few hundred dollars while the other members of the band held the populace at bay by firing from the town square. Legend has it that this was the Jesse James gang, but James was only 15 years old at the time.

Right from Columbia on State 61, a paved road, to GREENSBURG, 19.4 m. (583 alt., 770 pop.), seat of Green County, named for Gen. Nathanael Greene, a general of the Revolutionary Army. Greensburg is on the site of Glovers Station, established about 1777. On the public square stands the GREEN COUNTY COURTHOUSE, built in 1799, the only one of its kind remaining in the State. The builder was Thomas Metcalfe, tenth Governor of Kentucky (1828–32), known as "Old Stonehammer," because of his trade and his great vigor as a public speaker. The two-story building, constructed of random-width limestone, looks like a two-story dwelling. Housed on the second floor of the courthouse is the JANE TODD CRAWFORD LIBRARY, named in honor of the pioneer woman who traveled 60 miles on horseback through the wilderness to be operated on without anesthetics (see Tour 5). Facing the courthouse is the old BANK OF GREENSBURG, built in 1800 of hand-dressed limestone with walls three feet thick. This structure has long been used as a private home; its vault of hand-wrought iron sheets is a repository for family heirlooms. Gen. James Allen, the first lawyer admitted to the bar in Greensburg, and a veteran of the War of 1812, became president of the bank after the war. Finding its finances in a critical state, he liquidated its assets, paid off every depositor and closed the bank. Allen then made the building his home.

Between Columbia and Edmonton the route leads through a rugged region with ranges of low hills in the distance.

In BLISS, 212.4 m. (30 pop.), along Lampton Lane, once stood the home of Benjamin Lampton. Col. William Casey, who settled in this region in 1791, had a daughter, Peggy, who became the wife of Benjamin Lampton. Their daughter, Jane, married John Marshall Clemens, with whom she moved to Tennessee and afterward to Missouri, where their fourth child, Samuel L. Clemens (Mark Twain), was born.

EDMONTON, 231.2 *m.* (800 alt., 237 pop.), overlooking the Little Barren River, is an unincorporated community, but is the seat of Metcalfe County. The town is named for Edmond Rogers, a soldier of Virginia, who came to Kentucky after the Revolutionary War. He acquired 20,000 acres of land and a large number of slaves, and laid out a town here.

The TRIGG FISH HATCHERY (L), 246.8 *m.*, is the only spring-fed hatchery operated by the State.

GLASGOW, 249.9 *m.* (780 alt., 5,042 pop.) *(see Tour 6)*, is at the junction with US 31E *(see Tour 6)* and State 90 *(see Tour 20)*.

Between Glasgow and Merry Oaks the route continues through an oil field that has not been fully developed.

MERRY OAKS, 261.3 *m.* (67 pop.), is the locale of Cordia Greer Petrie's *Angeline,* stories of the rural Kentuckian's reaction to the city life of Louisville.

A quarry (R) at 265.5 *m.* produces Bowling Green oölitic limestone.

At 274.6 *m.* is the junction with US 68 *(see Tour 15)* and US 31W *(see Tour 7)* 6.7 miles east of Bowling Green.

Tour 19

(Williamson, W. Va.)—Pikeville—Jenkins—Junction with US 25E; US 119.
West Virginia Line to Junction with US 25E, 165.9 *m.*

Hard-surfaced roadbed throughout.
Louisville & Nashville R.R. roughly parallels route between Lynch and Pineville.
Accommodations chiefly in towns.

US 119 crosses a rugged and long-isolated region twisting around high mountain shoulders, where each turn of the road reveals range after range of dark green wooded slopes, beautiful in the spring with the snowy white, pink, and deep red of the rhododendron and wild azalea, and where the narrow, winding valleys echo with the sound of the waterfalls and rapids in the clear streams. At intervals along the highway are lonely little log cabins perched on ridges or half-hidden in the coves; patches of cornfields on the steep hillsides; and the unsightly shacks of small mining settlements. The northern part of the route traverses the valley of the Big Sandy and its forks, the Levisa and the Tug, a favorite hunting ground of the Shawnee, the Cherokee, and other Indians. This valley was the last section of Kentucky to be wrested from them by white settlers.

The history of the area on both sides of the Kentucky-West Virginia Line is violent. It was the scene of the notorious Hatfield-McCoy feud that began on an election day early in the nineteenth century. Stories of the origin are obscure. One is that while "Devil Anse" Hatfield and his clan from across the Tug Fork in West Virginia were carousing with the McCoys on the Kentucky side, Hatfield's son eloped across the river with Randall McCoy's daughter. When a few months later McCoy's unwed daughter returned to her Kentucky relatives with a child, a war of hatred and revenge began. The feud outlived all of those who saw its beginning, and though there were peaceful interludes, a trivial argument over such a matter as the number of notches on a hog's ear would start another series of killings. On one occasion an old man of the Hatfield clan stood alone against the McCoy tribe, and when he died cursing his enemies with his last breath, his gun was empty, his body riddled with bullets. Later, after three McCoys had stabbed a Hatfield in the back, a party of Hatfields surrounded Randall McCoy's cabin and set it on fire in order to see their targets—the McCoys trapped inside. On that night a Hatfield shot a young McCoy girl to death and then broke her mother's back. It was a great day for the McCoys when this Hatfield was hanged, many years later, before 6,000 spectators. He was the first and one of the few feudists hanged legally.

The courts were particularly ineffective in handling this feud because the participants lived in two States and the State authorities on both sides of the line were disinclined to permit extradition of their citizens, since each side laid blame on the other. Moreover, many of the sheriffs and even judges were kin to participants. About the time of the War between the States, when coal mining began in the region on a minor commercial scale, the operators found themselves much hindered by the primitive tribal warfare and put pressure on authorities to curb it. They had a reward offered for the capture of Devil Anse and forced him into semi-hiding in the hills—then bought up his land for a dollar an acre. Other Hatfields and some of the McCoys became mine operators themselves, though many of their kin eventually came down to work in the mines. But the hill people were only half tamed and the frontier habit of every man's settling his quarrels with his own gun was not easily eradicated. It was carried over into the period of industrial development.

In Harlan County big scale mining began about 1911, after the discovery of thick seams of bituminous. Northern corporations invested heavily here and a railroad was built. The real boom came with the World War. The demand for fuel by the steel mills and other plants manufacturing munitions drove coal prices high enough to make operation highly profitab even in this field, which had to ship in competition with northern fields having much more favorable freight rates. Competition for labor raised the wages of miners to abnormal heights. Men flocked down from the hills, where many of them had never seen $100 in cash in the course of a year, to earn much more than $100 in the course of a month. The companies hastily built shacks and barracks to house them and opened stores to get their trade. The new industrial workers were a bit like sailors on shore leave; cash for something to spend and there seemed no limit to the flow. Many, unaccustomed to paying rent and buying foodstuffs, spent the whole of their wages the day they received them and had to go in debt to provide themselves with room and board until the next pay day. In no time their ignorance of money-values had put them into the hands of those willing to profit by it.

The end of the boom came when the war was over and the demand for huge quantities of coal fell off. The first to suffer in the deflation of production and prices toward peacetime levels was the miner. Men were laid off and wages cut. The uprooted hill people either had no land to return to or could not face return to the isolated cabins; miners who had poured in from other fields found no other fields that wanted their labor. Bitterness flared in every coal district. The absentee owners who demanded profits were often represented locally by natives of the district or by the kind of men who always flock to boom towns, and the old feud spirit flared up with a bitterness equal to that of the most spirited days of the Hatfield-McCoy war. Strikebreakers were sent in from outside to guard closed mines or to keep mines open during strikes, and people on both sides of the struggle used guns, as they had long been accustomed to do in times of stress.

Well-meant attempts to mediate by "furriners" were notably unsuccessful, in part, because of unfamiliarity with the local people and customs, and in larger part because of the complicated economic problems involved. The post-war flare-up gradually became less violent, though the struggle continued; the economic collapse that came on after 1929 brought it to white heat again. In 1938 a Congressional Committee studying violations of civil liberties brought hill-people from the area to Washington for testimony and focused national attention on the labor-industrial warfare *(see Labor)*.

Small coal diggings with their gaping black entrances and makeshift tipples are frequently seen along the roads of this mining region. For the most part they are worked by one or two part-time miners who gain a meager livelihood by selling the coal in the vicinity or by hauling it to near-by markets.

US 119 crosses the West Virginia Line, 0 *m.*, at Williamson, West Virginia *(see West Virginia, Tour 11)*, on a bridge over the Tug Fork of the Big Sandy River, and follows Pond Creek through a drab coal-mining area. At this point the road is an artery of the area once known as "the billion dollar coal field" of which Williamson is the heart.

BELFRY, 3.6 *m.* (668 alt., 410 pop.), one of the coal-mining communities that are strung out along Pond Creek for approximately 15 miles, is typical of the numerous half-abandoned mining towns of the area. They are unincorporated and, with their unpaved streets and unpainted buildings, come into view like blighted spots on the land. They have all the inconveniences and few, if any, of the comforts of modern towns of equal size, and none of the advantages of the agricultural countryside. Small drab houses, most of them in need of repair, huddle close together along the deep valleys or stand uncertainly on the mountain sides. Most of them are of boom-time flimsiness, with one thickness of board in the walls that rest on slender, often tottering, posts, many are papered with newspapers and patched with cardboard to shut out draughts. Dark hills of coal tailings blotch the sides and bases of the larger hills. The numerous abandoned mines are marked by warped and disjointed frame tipples and entrances, weathered to a dull gray. Only the waters of Pond Creek, now littered with tin cans and other refuse, suggest the natural beauty that was destroyed by industrial development when it penetrated the formerly inaccessible places.

Since the middle 1920's the miners of the Pond Creek region, when not totally unemployed, have worked only part time. Some of the towns are slowly reviving on a new pattern. Mining, of necessity, is no longer the sole occupation. Odd jobs in lumbering, agriculture, road building, Government projects and construction, supplement the employment, mostly seasonal, that is still afforded by the mines. The groups of men clustered around a store or the local "joint" are part of the army of former miners. Life in the coal-mining towns is meager and hard. The customary diet of the miner and his family consists chiefly of beans—and more beans—corn bread made without milk, and "bulldog gravy," a mixture of flour, water, and a little grease. In the summer those fortunate enough to find a small patch may grow a few vegetables, but for the most part they grow pumpkins. There is little or no milk available even for the children. As a result diseases of malnutrition are common. Leisure is abundant and money scarce. Brawls and an occasional shooting, a bit of penny- and nickel-gambling, all of them usually enlivened with moonshine, are the recreation of the men.

US 119 at 7 *m.* begins its ascent from the valley into the mountains whose forested slopes and ridges constantly change in appearance. They are gray-green on a misty morning, a vivid green on a clear afternoon. The tender fernlike foliage of early spring, when each leaf, bud, and shoot is a delicate green, changes into the heavier, deeper-hued vegetation of summer. In the fall, the sun, which shines in many valleys for only a few hours, splashes the tree-clad mountains with light, intensifying the yellows, reds, oranges, browns, and dark greens.

One of the most impressive views on US 119 between Williamson, West Virginia, and Pikeville is at 17.2 *m.* From the top of the ridge the surrounding maze of ranges, deeply cut by narrow valleys and extending to the horizon, form a scene of wild, rugged beauty.

PIKEVILLE, 32.2 *m.* (680 alt., 3,376 pop.) *(see Tour 1),* is at the junction with US 23 *(see Tour 1);* between this point and Jenkins, US 119 and US 23 are united.

SHELBIANA, 39.2 *m.* (698 alt., 200 pop.), is a mountain hamlet at the junction with State 80.

Left from Shelbiana on State 80, an improved road, to ELKHORN CITY, 16.6 *m.* (790 alt., 995 pop.), a small coal-mining town, rambling along a bend of Russell Fork at the mouth of Elkhorn Creek. Here is the PIKE COUNTY FISH AND GAME ASSOCIATION FISH HATCHERY.

South of Elkhorn City, State 80, here an unimproved, narrow dirt road, continues through a primitive region of rugged grandeur. This dirt track leading to the plateau overlooking the Breaks of Sandy, leads through virgin stands of timber. Fragrant slender pines rise above the leafy undergrowth. Stone outcroppings, weathered smooth, are covered with moss and vine, and edged with mountain fern. The ground is soft and damp beneath the many layers of decayed vegetation.

One of the most picturesque views of the BREAKS OF THE SANDY is at 24.6 *m.* A thousand feet and more below, in the most striking water gap of the Big Sandy Valley, flows Russell Fork which begins as a thin mountain stream in Virginia and flows into the Big Sandy in Kentucky. The river has worn a deep gorge through an uplift dating from the Paleozoic era. In this great upheaval other streams that once crossed the land here in an east-west direction were thrown back upon themselves or else were diverted to form Elkhorn Creek and Pound River. In a succession of waterfalls and rapids—called "jumps" by the natives—the river plunges over and around boulders that fill the bed of the stream, and descends about 350 feet in traversing the tortuous five miles of the Breaks. Rising on each side of the turbulent stream are palisades bedecked with rhododendron, evergreens, and hardwood. In the lower reaches the gorge is shallower and the banks of the stream below, where there are numerous campsites, can be reached from the highway.

Two miles southeast of the Kentucky Line in Virginia is a great castellated sandstone formation, the TOWERS, which rise almost 1,600 feet, and guard the exit from the Breaks. These pinnacles, when seen sharply outlined against a deep blue sky and forested ridges, are among the striking features of the Cumberland Mountains.

Shawnee legend describes an immense cave in the base of Pine Mountain near the Breaks of Sandy used by the Shawnee, during a great battle with the Cherokee, for the protection of the women and children. This mythical cave also appears in the stories of Swift's fabulous silver mines *(see Tour 1)* as a cache holding the silver and gold.

Between Shelbiana and Jenkins US 119 winds through the valley, passing a few ragged mining settlements, almost lost among the mountains.

JENKINS, 71.6 *m.* (1,527 alt., 8,465 pop.), a collection of modern buildings and unsightly shacks, is surrounded by impressive mountains whose vast coal deposits make the town one of the State's principal mining centers. In contrast with the settlement farther north, this company town, strung out along the highway, gives an impression of activity. Modern buildings and facilities give evidence of some stability, though the box-like houses, the grim piles of coal tailings, and the denuded slopes clearly indicate its dependence on coal. On the southern outskirts is (R) an artificial lake in a dammed basin on the gentle slope of the mountain. The lake occupies part of the tract once owned by "Devil John" Wright, mountain feudist *(see Tour 18)*.

Jenkins is at the junction with US 23 *(see Tour 1)*.

Southwest of Jenkins the highway passes through valleys and ascends uplifts of the Cumberland plateau, a region of much beauty, and the most intensively exploited coal area in the State. Coal towns and camps are numerous.

BOONE CREEK (R), 77.9 *m.*, and BOONE HILL (R), near the headwaters of the Kentucky River, are reminders of Daniel Boone, who with several companions hunted in this county. John Fox, Jr. *(see Tour 17A)*, made the region pierced by US 119 the locale of two of his best-known stories, *The Little Shepherd of Kingdom Come,* and *A Knight of the Cumberlands.*

Many old customs and folk superstitions have survived with great tenacity *(see Tours 1 and 18)* in these mountain fastnesses. Many peculiarities of speech, song, custom, and belief are a heritage from English and Scottish-Irish ancestors. A couple contemplating marriage is "called out in meetin' " at least once prior to the marriage ceremony. So steadfast is the belief that a bride must start her new life in a new pair of shoes, that if the family is unable to buy a pair it becomes a matter of neighborhood concern, and the ceremony must wait until the bride can be newly shod.

Slat sunbonnets, of calico or any bright-colored material, are the usual headgear of the hill women; for after marriage a woman, however young, is expected to don "decent duds," discarding bows, beads, and earbobs. Dark colors are substituted for the vivid pinks, blues, reds, and lilacs proper for girls.

If horses and mules are restless at night, if they prance and snort, everyone is sure that evil spirits are trying to mount them; many persons braid corn husks into the manes to ward off this evil.

The "Elf Knight," a version of the old English ballad, the "Six Kings' Daughters," "Barbara Allen," the "Little Mohee," and "Madge Wildfire's Song" are often heard in this country.

US 119 crosses the North Fork of the Kentucky River, 80.7 *m.*, which twists and cuts its way through several hundred miles before joining the Ohio.

At 88.4 *m.* is the junction with State 15 *(see Tour 2)*.

PINE MOUNTAIN looms in the distance at 90.1 *m.* Over a part of the timbered, craggy ridge extends the Trail of the Lonesome Pine. The northern flank of the mountain, blanketed with dense stands of timber, hems in the country as far as the eye can see. The road, beginning its winding ascent of the mountain, follows a shelf below high overhangs of limestone. During the climb small mountain cabins are seen clinging to the sloping side far below, looking like doll houses in the distance.

At 93.7 *m.* is the summit of Pine Mountain (2,600 alt.). Here is a junction with a dirt road.

Left on this road 3 *m.* to a FIRE OBSERVATORY *(open)* on one of the highest points in the region. It affords a magnificent view of the Appalachians. The distant blue-veiled horizon to the east is formed by the Blue Ridge Mountains of Virginia.

Southwest of the crest of Pine Mountain, US 119 passes down the great corridor formed by Pine (R) and Black Mountains (L). For 75 miles the highway parallels the Cumberland River.

The origin of the settlers in this region is unmistakable. Their "ballets" (ballads) are relics inherited from their English and Scottish forebears, though time and place have resulted in local variations. "Sweet William and Lady Margery," "Sourwood Mountain" (named for the sourwood tree which grows in profusion on the mountains), the "Merry Golden Tree," "Hangman's Song," and "Lovin' Nancy" are popular favorites, most of them very old. A few modern ballads on mining themes, chiefly tragedies, were brought in by Pennsylvania miners, among them "Western Union Telegram" and "Down in a Coal Mine." Speech here is vivid and fresh. When all goes well a man is "happy as a 'possum up a 'simmon tree with a dog a mile off." After a really close call he will say, "If hell were biled down to a pint, it wouldn't be ez hot ez the place I war in." "Black as a wolf's mouth," "sweet-smellin' ez a plum-granite," "fine as fur in the North," are pioneer relics. "Don't fault your elders," "Wagon the deceased to the graveyard," and "She feathered him too much" are reminders of the basic English of the first American settlers from Britain. The people live in a "house-room," are patients of a "doctor-man," and a "tooth-dentist," hunt with a "rifle-gun," and go to a "jail-house."

CUMBERLAND, 112.2 *m.* (1,430 alt., 2,639 pop.), is a mining town whose civic and industrial activities have been stimulated by the building of the highway.

Left from Cumberland on State 160, hard surfaced, to LYNCH, 4.5 *m.* (1,712 alt., 7,000 pop.), a mining center at the headwaters of Looney Creek. Out of what was little more than a wilderness in 1917, Lynch has been developed by the United States Coal & Coke Company, whose 42,000 acres of coal land contain four known workable seams. The tipple (cradledump) here is unusually large. The Greeks, Italians, and Syrians, who form the majority of the small foreign population, have retained many national customs that give color to local entertainments.

The worst labor disturbance here occurred in 1934, when 700 employees were discharged and several hundred sympathizers quit. Some of the men eventually returned to the mines without working agreements; others, who refused to do this, were driven out of the mining camps.

On State 160 at 8 *m.*, BIG BLACK MOUNTAIN (4,150 alt.), the highest peak in Kentucky, is seen (R). Its tree-crowned crest is visible for miles.

At 9 *m.* State 160 crosses the Virginia Line, becoming VA. 67, which leads into US 23.

DILLON, 122 *m.* (1,248 alt., 21 pop.), is chiefly a crossroads.

Right from Dillon 2 *m.* on a dirt road to the entrance of KENTENIA STATE FOREST of 3,624 acres on the slope of Pine Mountain. This, the only State forest in Kentucky, is used for a forest nursery and is being developed for recreational purposes.

A steel OBSERVATION TOWER, 4.2 *m.*, 100 feet in height, affords an exceptional view of Pine Mountain.

PINE MOUNTAIN SETTLEMENT SCHOOL, 8 *m.* (1,756 alt.), was founded in 1913 through the generosity of William Creech—"Uncle William" as he was affectionately known in the neighborhood. The school provides education for boys and

girls of remote mountain covers, part of which they pay for by working in the
kitchen, the laundry, the garden, or on the farm. Sixteen buildings, from one-
quarter mile to two miles apart, house the students. Academic work is carried
through the eighth grade and a course is offered for prospective teachers. Extension work has been carried into the surrounding district; two smaller centers, 12
miles apart, provide medical care and other community services.

At BAXTER, 134.5 *m.*, is a monument 12 feet high, made of blocks
of coal from the 45 mines in Harlan County.

A resident of Harlan County for many years was Aunt Molly Jackson—midwife, composer and singer of ballads—three of whose four hus-
bands died in mine accidents or from mine diseases. When she was 12
years old, Molly dressed in a costume, blackened her face with charcoal,
and, with whoops and yells, ran to the neighboring farm to frighten her
playmates. News of Molly's exploit traveled throughout the county
and it was not long before the sheriff came to arrest the child, on the
strength of a law that forbade anyone to wear a mask. Molly was sen-
tenced to 10 days in jail and payment of a fine. While in jail, the girl
composed a ballad, which she sang to the jailers and to her visitors in
order to earn money towards the payment of her fine.

> The day before Christmas I had some fun
> I black my face and took my gun
> I went up to Bill Lewis' and made him run
> Mr. Cundif turn me loose.
>
> The next Monday morning Bill Lewis got out a writ
> When I found it out the wind I split
> It was just three weeks till I came back to Clay
> Cotton 'tested me the very next day.
>
> Then I thought my case would be light
> When Cotton took me before Judge Right
> For blackin' my face and putting breeches on.
>
> He listened to me till I told my tale
> And give me ten days in Mr. Cundif's jail
> Mr. Cundif turn me loose.
>
> When I went in jail they thought I was fool
> They didn't offer me a stool
> But old Mrs. Cundif treated me kind
> Because she thought I had no mind.
>
> Now what she thought I did not care
> I know I was just as smart as her
> Mr. Cundif turn me loose.
>
> .   .   .   .   .
>
> Hello, Mr. Cundif, if you'li open the door
> I won't put my breeches on no more
> Mr. Cundif turn me loose.

Left from Baxter on an improved road to HARLAN, 1 *m*. (1,197 alt., 4,327 pop.), the coal capital of the State, and seat of Harlan County. First called Mount Pleasant, the town was later renamed to honor Maj. Silas Harlan, who came to Kentucky from Virginia in 1774, and was killed while leading his command at the Battle of Blue Licks (August 19, 1782). The town, in the valley between Big and Little Black Mountains, at the confluence of the three forks of the upper Cumberland River, was a backwoods village for more than 100 years after its settlement in 1819 by a small company of Virginians under the leadership of Samuel Hoard (Howard). Since the coming of the railroad in 1911, the town has become an important lumber shipping point, as well as the center of an extensive bituminous and cannel coal area.

Up to 1930 the only labor organization represented in the district was the United Mine Workers of America. Attempts at unionization had been bitterly contested by many of the larger operators; great bitterness developed between employers and employees during the first widespread strike in 1916. The strike of 1924 closed the mines of the Black Mountain Coal Corporation, one of the larger operators, resulting in considerable suffering among several hundred families dependent on the mines for a living. In 1931, after the national economic collapse had further reduced the market for coal, the employees of the Evarts Coal Company struck to maintain wage rates that would keep miners from utter destitution. Both sides resorted to violence, and several miners were killed. The situation was investigated by a Congressional Committee, and on May 6, 1938, the National Labor Relations Board began its prosecution of 44 Harlan County coal operators and former deputy sheriffs *(see Tour 4)*. The trial ended on August 1, 1938, with a hung jury, but on September 1, 1938, a contract was signed by the Harlan County Coal Operators' Association with the United Mine Workers.

The mounds and rock shelters of this section have yielded many artifacts and skeletons. The best-known site is a PREHISTORIC BURIAL GROUND on Main St., opposite the hotel. The EVERSOLE COLLECTION OF INDIAN RELICS *(open on request)*, N. Main St., is unusually fine, including pottery, beads, arrowheads, and various other articles. At the Harlan County Fall Festival, held annually for one week in September at the HARLAN ARMORY, prize farm products and examples of handicraft are exhibited. The latter include articles made on neighboring farms, where sheep are raised. The farm wives card the wool and spin, dye, and weave it into fabric.

Between Baxter and Pineville, US 119 is called the Rhododendron Trail because of the profusion of that shrub along the way; it blooms from May or early June to late July.

At 165.9 *m*. is the junction with US 25E *(see Tour 4A)*, at a point 0.4 miles south of Pineville.

Tour 20

Burnside—Monticello—Albany—Burkesville—Glasgow; 102.3 *m*., State 90.

Hard-surfaced roadbed between Burnside and Albany; remainder graveled. Accommodations in larger towns; limited elsewhere.

This route winds through an agricultural region as diversified in topography as in the types and occupations of the people. Its farms vary widely in size and methods of cultivation. Subsistence farming predominates, but the region also contains some very fertile tracts on which the modern methods of cultivation and equipment contrast sharply with those on the neighboring submarginal farms where oxen still pull plows.

The remoteness of the area and the sparseness of population have allowed a profusion of wild flowers to survive. Evergreens abound and ferns of many varieties grow close to the roadside.

BURNSIDE, 0 *m.* (705 alt., 914 pop.) *(see Tour 3)*, is at the junction with US 27 *(see Tour 3)*.

Between a bridge *(toll 45¢)* over the Cumberland River and Burnside Hill the scenery is particularly fine, including an extensive view of the Cumberland River Valley below hills covered with pine, oak, and laurel. The road winds through rolling farms for several miles south of the river.

MILL SPRINGS, 11.5 *m.* (844 alt., 75 pop.), a few cabins at the mouth of a cove, owes its place in history to the fact that the battle of January 19 and 20, 1862, fought some 10 miles to the north of this place, is often called the Battle of Mill Springs *(see Tour 18)*. This engagement is also known as the Battle of Logan's Cross Roads, Fishing Creek, Somerset, and Beech Grove. Visible from the highway (R) are the remains of the Confederate entrenched camp, established by General Zollicoffer in November 1861 to hold the right flank of the Confederate forces in Kentucky.

Prior to the Battle of Logan's Cross Roads, General Zollicoffer had made his headquarters in the LANIER HOUSE (L). Back of the house is a WATER-POWER GRISTMILL built about 1818 and still in operation. Its original overshot water wheel, 31 feet in diameter, is said to have been the largest ever used in Kentucky.

Right from Mill Springs on the River Rd. (graveled) to a junction with a foot-path 0.5 *m.;* L. on this path about 300 yards to HOGG CAVE, a small stalagmitic formation that has yielded a large quantity of human and animal bones. Because many of the human bones bore traces of gnawing, it is believed that the burials had been shallow, and since most of them were found beneath a stalagmite nearly eight feet in diameter, the skeletons are considered very ancient. Exploration of the cave was made in 1922 when the stalagmite was removed.

At 0.8 *m.,* on River Rd., is a path leading (R) about 100 yards to COOPER CAVE in which extensive clay deposits were mined, either by early white settlers, by Indians, or by prehistoric people. Marks of tools were still plainly visible when the cave was explored. Further evidence of aboriginal occupation was the presence of ash beds, potsherds, flint chips, and kitchen middens. No graves were found in the cave.

At 1 *m.* on the River Rd. is the junction with a trail; L. here a short distance to HINES CAVE (L). An entrance 20 feet high leads to an outer chamber 145 feet long and 60 feet wide. The ceiling is proportionately high. Thousands of animal bones and numerous artifacts were uncovered here; they represent at least three distinct cultures. A number of the objects found are in the Museum of Archeology of the University of Kentucky.

Excellent farmlands border State 90 in this section; abandoned equipment once used in prospecting for oil is visible.

PRICE'S MEADOW, 12.5 *m.*, is the site selected by the Long Hunters—so called because of their long hunting expeditions—as their central camp. A company of about 40 men from Virginia and North Carolina, attracted to the wilderness for the sake of adventure and by reports of plentiful game, set out in June 1770 for Kentucky. They passed through Cumberland Gap and established their base, where they found an excellent supply of spring water. From this point the men went out in parties to hunt, and to this base they brought their furs and hides every full moon.

One evening in February 1771 a group of these hunters heard a voice singing in the forest. They cautiously approached the spot whence the sounds came, and there, stretched full length on the ground, was Daniel Boone, singing at the top of his lungs. Boone *(see Tour 17A)* joined the Long Hunters, and they were met by Squire Boone, Daniel's brother, who had gone home to get supplies. About a month later the brothers, after an absence of two years, set out for home with a large quantity of furs. At Cumberland Gap they were met by Cherokee who appropriated all the peltries. Dejected and without supplies to enable them to replace their loss, the Boones made their way home empty-handed.

While, as a whole, the Long Hunters' stay in Kentucky was profitable, it was not without several disasters. After a two-month trip away from the base, they returned to find their peltries spoiled, and their dogs, which they had left to guard the camp, a pack of wild animals.

With characteristic pioneer calm, one of the Bledsoes inscribed this memorandum on a fallen poplar: "2,300 deerskins lost; Ruination, by God."

In February 1772 some of the company became discouraged and departed for the eastern settlements. Roving Indians captured two of the remaining men and plundered the camp. These misfortunes did not discourage the hardy survivors, however, and it was not until August 1772 that the last of them turned homeward.

STEUBENVILLE, 15.6 *m.* (887 alt., 38 pop.), is in an oil region; along the highway there are numerous producing oil wells.

The GAP OF THE RIDGE BATTLEFIELD, 16.6 *m.*, is the scene of the Battle of Rocky Gap, which occurred in the summer of 1863. General Morgan had avoided a pitched battle with the Union troops encamped at Monticello by leading the Confederate cavalry past the Union encampment to this gap. The Union troops pursued, as Morgan had intended they should, but their advance was so rapid that the battle was precipitated before the Confederates were prepared to defend themselves. As a result the Confederates had 20 killed and 80 wounded, while in the Union forces only 4 were killed and 26 wounded.

The higher forested elevations form an unusual background along the highway.

MONTICELLO, 20.8 *m.* (926 alt., 1,503 pop.), named for the Thomas Jefferson estate, was settled prior to 1800 when Wayne County, of which Monticello is the seat, was formed. It is by Elk Creek at the western edge of a rolling plain. Industrial activity here consists of pencil manufacturing and the milling of cedar, flour, and meal. Monticello is a distributing center for most of Wayne and Clinton Counties. The discovery of the Sunnybrook Oil Pool in 1901 started production in the Wayne County oil field, where continuous operation has resulted in many local booms.

MONTICELLO PARK, dedicated to soldiers killed in the War between the States, has shaded benches that are always popular with the townsfolk. A DOUGHBOY MONUMENT in the square is the county's tribute to its World War soldiers. In the Burton Building (R), by the public square, is the JOHN BURTON COLLECTION *(open weekdays)*, which contains the last stagecoach used in Kentucky. After many years of service this coach made its last trip, from Burnside to Monticello, in 1912. The collection also includes Indian relics, firearms, mementoes of the War between the States, and other objects of local historical interest.

Shelby M. Cullom (1829–1914), a native of this area, was Governor of Illinois from 1877 to 1883, and United States Senator from that State from 1883 to 1913. Preston H. Leslie (1819–1907), also born in this region, was Governor of Kentucky from 1871 to 1875, Governor of Montana from 1887 to 1889, and was appointed United States District Attorney for Montana in 1894.

In the early spring frogging is a diversion of a large part of the populace of this area. Late in the evening parties in quest of frogs are seen along the road, headed toward streams and ponds, with lanterns, gigs, and gunny sacks.

At 23.8 *m.* is the junction with the Wild Goose Shoals Rd. improved.

Right on this road to the village of MURL, 3 *m.* (75 pop.). The BARNES HOUSE *(open)*, the second one beyond the post office (R), is the home of Mr. and Mrs. A. E. Barnes who undertook, in 1930, to revive home industries. They brought out, repaired, and put into operation spinning and weaving equipment which their ancestors had brought from Virginia and which had been used as long as cotton and flax were grown in the county. They produced coverlets, scarfs, and runners, in designs used by members of the family a century ago. The Barnes products soon were accorded a wide recognition for the authenticity of their patterns and the excellency of their workmanship.

State 90 traverses a very rugged and broken terrain for about four miles, following and crossing Beaver Creek, named for the beaver that were plentiful near the mouth of the stream in pioneer days. West of the valley of Beaver Creek, the land is undulating or slightly hilly. This area has some good farms with modernized houses, but most of the land is submarginal with primitive buildings of logs or slabs. Along the route are tracts of virgin timber, producing oil wells, laurel- and pine-covered hillsides, a variety of wild flowers, and an abundance of red cedar.

ZULA, 26.8 *m.* (842 alt., 20 pop.), is in a bend on the northern bank of Otter Creek, so named by pioneers because of the many otter found along the stream. A water-power GRIST AND FLOUR MILL (R) has stood here for more than a century.

The highway crosses the creek and winds up Otter Creek Hill for about two miles. Among the hills of this region are fertile valleys in which corn, hay, tobacco, and wheat are grown. Sinking creeks, sinkholes, waterfalls, and cliffs are visible from the road.

POPLAR MOUNTAIN (1,745 alt.), the most prominent elevation in this area, is (L) a spur of the Cumberlands, and forms a curve within which is Stockton's Valley (L), a fertile area named for Thomas Stockton, a pioneer.

At 39.8 *m.* State 90 passes through WADE'S GAP (1,227 alt.).

Right from Wade's Gap on a foot trail that follows the old overgrown carriage road to the Summit of SEWELL MOUNTAIN (1,720 alt.), 2 *m.* Here is RE-HOBETH SPRINGS (R), a watering place of the early days, near three chalybeate springs. Before the War between the States the springs were visited by many invalids, who proclaimed numerous benefits and cures. From the top of the mountain, on a clear day, the surrounding country is visible for a distance of about 75 miles.

At 41.8 *m.* on State 90 is the junction with Kogar Creek Rd., unimproved.

Left on this road to COPPERAS KNOB, 4 *m.* (1,715 alt.), topped with a small pond. JENNY'S KNOB, 5 *m.* (1,560 alt.), is (R) one of the highest peaks in Clinton County; FLOWER'S CAVE (L) is 1.5 miles long and has six rooms, which have been explored; BALD ROCK (R) is a gigantic treeless rock formation.

ALBANY, 44.9 *m.* (964 alt., 852 pop.), seat and principal town of Clinton County, was named for the capital of New York. Settlements near by at Paoli and in Stockton's Valley were made as early as 1790 by families chiefly from East Tennessee. An old water-power GRIST-MILL (L) on the western edge of Albany is still operated. There is an artificial lake and falls formed by the mill dam. Although an unimportant outpost during the War between the States, Federal troops took possession of the town early in 1863 and remained for 10 months. Like all the border districts, this region suffered from the operations of numerous bands of guerrillas during the war. Thomas E. Bramlette, United States district judge, 1862, and Governor of Kentucky from 1863 to 1867, was born near Albany as was S. B. Maxey (1825–95), who was a United States Senator from Texas from 1875 to 1887.

Albany is at the junction with State 35 *(see Tour 5).*

At BROWN'S CROSSROADS, 47.8 *m.,* is a junction with an unmarked road.

Left on this road to BROWN'S POND *(good fishing),* 3 *m.,* covering 25 acres.

At 49.8 *m.* on State 90 is the junction with an unimproved road.

Left on this road to CANEY BRANCH CAVE (L), 1 *m.*, outstanding among the caves in Clinton County. Within about 40 yards from the entrance is a small stream containing blindfish. Because of disuse through the generations that their ancestors have lived in the cavernous darkness, their eyes have ceased to function as organs of sight. Though the rudimentary eyeball is still in place, it is smaller in size than that of fish living in open waters, and a heavy skin covers it. About one-eighth of a mile deeper the cave divides, the left chamber extending beyond any point yet explored. Stalagmites and stalactites of blue, purple, brown, and white festoon the interior.

West of the junction with the Caney Branch Cave Rd. is the Cumberland Valley; the uplands behind the broad valleys are so dissected that the land is almost untilled and uninhabited. It is a strangely quiet but pleasant area, unlike, in physical aspect and conditions of life, either the upland Pennyrile about it or the mountainous region to the east.

A State ferry *(free)* crosses the Cumberland River at 61.9 *m.*

BURKESVILLE, 63.5 *m.* (581 alt., 885 pop.), seat of Cumberland County, was incorporated in 1810 and named for Samuel Burke, an early settler, who before coming here had been the first licensed tavern keeper in Greensburg *(see Tour 18)*. The town is on a hill overlooking the Cumberland. Steamboat traffic on the river lasted exactly 100 years. The first boat was launched in 1834, and the last one made the trip to Burnside, at the head of navigation, in 1934. On file in the county clerk's office are two bonds dated 1802 and 1804, made by Thomas Lincoln to Governor Garrard when Lincoln was constable, and in Deed Book "A" are records of two deeds of Thomas Lincoln for lands on the Cumberland River and on Marrowbone Creek.

Right from Burkesville, 3 *m.*, on State 61 to the marked site of one of the earliest oil wells drilled in the United States, accidentally discovered by Dr. John Croghan on March 12, 1829, while drilling for salt water near the bank of the Cumberland River. There is a local tradition that one of the drillers remarked that he was going to drill until he "struck salt or hell." When the bit was withdrawn, after having penetrated solid rock to a considerable depth, oil gushed out, and in a few days the flow had covered the surfaces of the Cumberland River and Big and Little Rennox creeks. The oil was ignited and the river soon became an inferno of flames, leaping to the tops of the highest trees along the banks. The well was neglected for many years until the medicinal quality of the oil was discovered.

Directly west of Burkesville, State 90 ascends BURKESVILLE HILL, one of the outstanding viewpoints in the State. A winding graveled road leads to the top from which scenes of rugged grandeur lie in every direction. On a clear day the Cumberland Mountains in the vicinity of the gap, 75 miles to the east, are visible.

The 17-mile-long MARROWBONE VALLEY, 66.5 *m.*, is some of the richest soil in the State. The valley was so named because of its fertility, which the pioneers compared with the richness of the marrow of a bone. The roadway is bordered with prosperous farms, behind which are beautiful uplands.

The terrain is less rugged at 73.5 *m.* Hilly country is interspersed with lowland farms skirting the roadside. Much of the higher ground is covered with second-growth timber.

The distinguishing features of the south central part of the State (the Pennyrile) become more pronounced at 79.5 *m.* Slopes of hills are more gentle, and elevations more uniform.

BEAUMONT, 85.6 *m.* (42 pop.), is at the junction with State 163, graveled.

Left from Beaumont on State 163 to TOMPKINSVILLE, 15 *m.* (850 pop.), seat of Monroe County; from Tompkinsville, 2 *m.* on the Park Rd. to OLD MULKEY MEETING HOUSE STATE PARK *(open daily; adm. 10¢).* In 1773 Philip Mulkey and a group of Baptists from North and South Carolina settled here. A cabin of rough-hewn logs was erected on a bluff near the present OLD MULKEY MEETING HOUSE. By 1798 this building had become inadequate for the congregation, so the present structure was erected. This is the oldest log meeting house in Kentucky. Constructed of half-hewn logs and chinked, it has 12 corners. Tradition ascribes the 12 corners as representing the Twelve Apostles, and again as symbolic of the Twelve Tribes of Israel. In all probability the design resulted from necessity. A large structure was imperative, and logs of uniform thickness were not available in sufficient length to enclose the desired space within four corners. When the number of angles was increased, shorter logs of uniform thickness could be used for the side walls and rafters. No provision for heating was ever made. In cold weather a log fire in the yard served as a warming place. During services the men took turns at keeping the fire burning and guarding against Indian attack. The CONGREGATION RECORD BOOK, which contains the names of the members written with pokeberry ink, has been preserved. Huge oak trees stand in the yard. In the adjoining burial ground is the GRAVE OF HANNAH BOONE, sister of Daniel Boone, as well as the graves of many pioneers, including several Revolutionary soldiers.

Between Beaumont and Glasgow the farms are more prosperous and have a greater diversity of crops; there are also numerous producing oil wells.

GLASGOW, 102.3 *m.* (780 alt., 5,042 pop.) *(see Tour 6),* is at the junction with US 31E *(see Tour 6)* and State 80 *(see Tour 18).*

Part IV

Appendices

Chronology

1584 Virginia charter embraces territory which eventually becomes Kentucky.

1654 Colonel Wood explores Kentucky as far as the Mississippi.

1669 John Lederer makes three trips into the Blue Ridges.

1671 Thomas Batts and Robert Fallam reach Ohio Valley.

1673 James Needham and Gabriel Arthur explore in Tennessee region.

1730 John Salling, Williamsburg, Va., first native white American to penetrate western Kentucky, is captured by Indians.

1739 M. Longueil descends Ohio River; discovers Big Bone Lick.

1742 John Howard, an Englishman, crosses mountains from Virginia.

1750 Dr. Thomas Walker and companions cross Alleghenies and pass through Cave (Cumberland) Gap on exploring expedition.

1751 March. Christopher Gist visits Big Bone Lick.

1756 First village in Kentucky established opposite site of Portsmouth, Ohio, by French traders.

Mrs. Mary Inglis is first white woman to visit Kentucky.

1769 Daniel Boone, with John Finley and four other companions, crosses Appalachian ridges into Kentucky region.

1770 "Long Hunters," led by James Knox, reach country south of Kentucky River.

1771 Simon Kenton and others visit Ohio River Valley and navigate tributary streams.

1773 June and July. Companies headed by Capt. Thomas Bullitt, Hancock Taylor, and James, George, and Robert McAfee venture into northern Kentucky. Captain Bullitt reaches Falls of the Ohio; he surveys land below falls to Salt River and up Salt to Bullitt's Lick.

August. Bullitt makes first town plat in Kentucky above Ohio Falls, on part of site of Louisville.

1774 May and June. Capt. James Harrod, Abram Hite, Jacob Sandusky, and others navigate Kentucky River into what is now Mercer County. They lay off Harrodstown (now Harrodsburg).

Daniel Boone warns Kentucky surveyors of impending Indian wars.

1775 March. Party of 30, led by Daniel Boone, reaches Rockcastle River.

Col. Richard Henderson and others acquire from Cherokees land between Ohio, Kentucky, and Cumberland Rivers and as far east as Cumberland Mountains. Virginia later refuses to recognize their right. Daniel Boone, earlier, marked road through southern wilderness via Cumberland Gap to "Cuntuckey," the first marked road in Kentucky.

April. Daniel Boone and small party build fort for settlement (Boonesboro) on southern bank of Kentucky River. Settlements made at Boiling Spring (Mercer County) and St. Asaph's (Lincoln County).

May. Simon Kenton and Thomas Williams land at mouth of Limestone Creek (now Maysville) and plant corn crop.

May. Representatives chosen by people of Transylvania meet at Boonesboro, agree on proprietary government and pass nine laws.

September. Delegate from State of Transylvania to Continental Congress refused seat by Virginia.

September. Boone and others bring wives and families to Kentucky.

October. Fort built at Royal Spring (Georgetown).

1776 George Rogers Clark moves to Kentucky. Kentucky County created out of Fincastle County by Virginia. McClellan's Fort (Georgetown) attacked by Indians.

1777 Harrodsburg besieged by Indians under Chief Blackfish. Boonesboro also attacked. Kentucky County sends representatives to Virginia House of Burgesses. First court opened at Harrodsburg (September). Harrodsburg's population 198.

Harrodsburg, Boonesboro, and St. Asaph's are only settlements withstanding Indian attacks of this year. Salt making becomes Kentucky's earliest industry.

1778 George Rogers Clark appointed to lead forces against British post in Illinois. Daniel Boone, captured by Indians near Blue Licks, escapes four months later. French and Indians besiege Boonesboro for 13 days; siege lifted by treaty. Capt. James Patton, Richard Chenoweth, and others build fort and lay foundation of Louisville.

Virginia grants Colonel Henderson and associates 200,000 acres on Ohio below Green River.

1779 Col. Robert Patterson begins fort at Lexington; town laid out. Virginia Legislature passes land law for Kentucky, permitting unsupervised surveys. Many overlapped; confusion of title results in many lawsuits.

Bryan Station (Fayette County) established.

1780 Colonel Byrd with British force compels surrender of Ruddle's and Martin's stations.

Three hundred large family boats filled with immigrants arrive at Falls of the Ohio during spring.

Town of Louisville established by act of Virginia Legislature.

Kentucky County divided into three counties: Jefferson, Lincoln, and Fayette.

1782 Capt. James Estill and eight men killed by Wyandots near Mount Sterling. Four months' drought. Bryan Station besieged by Indians. Fort Nelson built at Louisville. Battle of Blue Licks (Aug. 19).

Brig. Gen. Clark, with 1,050 men, ends Indian raids into Kentucky.

1783 Kentucky becomes a judicial district; district court opens at Harrodsburg in March. First horse race in Kentucky run at Humble's race path; second at Higgins' race path—both near Harrodsburg.

1784 First of nine conventions, in session in Danville, considers separation of Kentucky from Virginia.

1786 Towns of Frankfort, Stanford, and Washington founded.

1787 Navigation of Mississippi discussed at Danville.

June. Gen. James Wilkinson descends Mississippi to New Orleans with cargo of tobacco and other Kentucky products. Spanish Governor gives permit for marketing.

August 18. John and Fielding Bradford establish Kentucky *Gazette*, second newspaper west of the Alleghenies, at Lexington.

1788 Spanish Government offers Kentucky commercial favors "if the people of Kentucky would erect themselves into an independent state."

1790 First Federal census of Kentucky: population 73,677.

July. Ninth convention of Kentucky accepts terms offered by Virginia in 1789; fixes June 1, 1792, for independence.

1791 January. Congress creates local board of war for District of Kentucky. General Scott leads Kentucky Volunteers against Indians on Wabash. Military expeditions under Gen. James Wilkinson, Gen. Arthur St. Clair, and Gen. Anthony Wayne.

February 4. Congress authorizes Kentucky to frame a constitution.

1792 April 3. Convention meets at Danville to frame a State constitution.

May. Isaac Shelby elected first Governor of Kentucky.

June 1. Kentucky, with an area of 37,600 square miles, admitted as State into the Union.

June 4. Kentucky Legislature assembles at Lexington; selects Frankfort as capital (June 6).

August. First paper mill in Kentucky built at Georgetown (operated until 1836).

1793 September 28. Draft of Kentuckians ordered by Governor Shelby to replenish forces of General Wayne.

November 1. Legislature meets for first time at Frankfort.

November 16. First line of packets on Ohio River established at Cincinnati; monthly service to Pittsburgh; Limestone (Maysville) is made boat station.

1794 May. Citizens meet at Lexington; pass resolutions regarding free navigation of the Mississippi.

August. Edward West successfully runs a steamboat on Elkhorn Creek, near Lexington—first on mid-Western waters.

1795 Kentucky Academy established.

Spanish Governor of Louisiana sends Thomas Powers to negotiate with Kentucky.

1796 Lexington Library established with 400 volumes.

1797 July. Thomas Powers, Spanish agent "to concert a separation of Kentucky from the Union," again comes to Kentucky.

November. Henry Clay arrives from Virginia; opens law office in Lexington.

1798 February. Legislature endows each of five Kentucky academies with 6,000 acres of land.

June. John Fitch, steamboat inventor, dies at Bardstown.

November. "Kentucky resolutions of 1798," favoring nullification of alien and sedition laws, passed by legislature.

Henry Clay advocates gradual emancipation of slaves.

December. Transylvania University established by union of Transylvania Seminary (founded 1780) and Kentucky Academy (founded 1796).

1799 August. Constitutional convention meets at Frankfort.

1800 Population 220,955. Right of deposit for American trade at New Orleans suspended, creating great excitement in Kentucky. Great Revival begins in Kentucky in July.

1802 Kentucky Insurance Company chartered, with banking powers, at Lexington.

1803 First stage route from Lexington via Winchester and Mount Sterling to Olympian Springs in Bath County.

1805 State legislature charters company to construct canal around Falls of Ohio River at Louisville. Aaron Burr makes first visit to Kentucky.

John Breckinridge becomes U.S. Attorney General.

1806 July 4. *Western World,* new Frankfort weekly, describes intrigues with Spain, implicating Wilkinson, Brown, Innes, and others.

November 3. Aaron Burr, charged with high misdemeanor, appears in Frankfort court; defended by Henry Clay and acquitted (December 2). His acquittal celebrated by brilliant ball at Frankfort.

December. Bank of Kentucky organized with authorized capital of $1,000,000.

1808 Bardstown becomes seat of Catholic "mother diocese" of region west of Alleghenies.

June 3. Jefferson Davis born in Christian County.

1809 John Hutchins discovers Mammoth Cave.

Dr. Ephraim McDowell, "father of ovariotomy," successfully performs, at Danville, first operation in world for excision of ovarian tumor.

January 19. Clay and Marshall fight duel near Louisville.

February 12. Abraham Lincoln born in Hardin (now Larue) County.

1810 Population 406,511.

1811 January 31. Lands granted at 10 cents per acre to encourage building of iron and salt works in Pulaski and Wayne Counties.

November. Great earthquake, most severe in West, occurs.

Henry Clay becomes speaker of U.S. House of Representatives.

1812 Sisters of Loretto and Sisters of Charity of Nazareth founded.

February. Kentucky Legislature appropriates $12.50 "for digging stumps out of State House yard."

June 18. Congress declares war with England.

1813 May 5. Brig. Gen. Green Clay, with 3,000 Kentuckians, cuts way through enemy's lines into Fort Meigs, reinforcing General Harrison.

October 5. Gov. Shelby with 4,000 Kentuckians participates in Battle of the Thames.

November 25. Statehouse at Frankfort burned.

1814 Nazareth College founded in Nelson County.

1815 January 4. Kentucky Militia, 2,500 under Gen. John Thomas, reaches New Orleans.

February. Fayette hospital for the insane chartered.

July. First cattle show in West held at Sandersville.

1817 Lexington-Maysville, and Lexington-Louisville turnpike road companies chartered.

May 6-30. *Enterprise*, first steamboat to ascend the Mississippi and Ohio, reaches Louisville in 25 days.

June. Cornerstone of Lunatic Asylum—the first erected West of the Appalachian Mountains—is laid at Lexington.

December 12. Earthquake.

1818 Most of 46 independent banks chartered in State fail.

January. Company chartered to build canal at Falls of the Ohio.

February 4. Gen. George Rogers Clark dies near Louisville.

1819 Centre College at Danville and St. Joseph's College at Bardstown founded. Agricultural show at Lexington.

1820 Population 564,317. Former President Madison feted at Louisville (June 24).

Bank of Commonwealth, with $2,000,000 capital, chartered (Nov.).

1822 Lotteries authorized to establish medical college at Lexington and to drain ponds in Louisville.

Augusta College (Methodist) at Augusta chartered.

1823 Col. James Morrison of Lexington (d. April 23) bequeathes $60,000 to Transylvania University.

Kentucky Institution for the Deaf and Dumb established at Danville.

1824 Stage line from Maysville through Lexington and Frankfort to Louisville (two days) and to Washington, D.C. (six days) begins (April 17).

Henry Clay is candidate for Presidency.

Capitol at Frankfort destroyed by fire. (Nov. 4).

1825 Louisville & Portland Canal chartered, with capital of $600,000.

March 7. Henry Clay becomes U.S. Secretary of State.

March. General Lafayette welcomed in Kentucky.

Science Hill Academy founded in Shelby County.

1826 Clay-Randolph duel near Washington, D.C.

1828 February 13. Louisville becomes a city.

Natural gas discovered by Samuel White on Green River.

1829 Louisville & Portland Canal opens.

1830 Population 687,917.

January. Companies chartered to build railroad from Lexington to Ohio River.

January 29. Common-school law, providing for tax-supported schools, enacted.

March. Model of railway locomotive engine and coach, constructed by Joseph Bruen of Lexington, exhibited at Frankfort.

Oil discovered near Burkesville, during boring for salt; spouts 50 feet.

October 22. First rail of Lexington & Ohio R.R. is laid at Lexington.

1831 Four hundred and six steamboats and 421 flatboats and keel-boats, 76,233 tons, pass through Louisville & Portland Canal.

1832 October. Asiatic cholera epidemic in many Kentucky towns.

1833 February. Importation of slaves prohibited. Legislature adopts resolutions in favor of Union and against nullification.

March. Kentucky Colonization Society sends 102 freed Negroes to Liberia.

May and August. Asiastic cholera again sweeps State.

September. Kentucky Livestock Association holds exhibit at Lexington.

1835 January 29. First train arrives at Frankfort from Lexington—time: 2 hours, 29 minutes.

1836 Richard M. Johnson elected Vice President of the United States.

Kentucky Historical Society founded at Frankfort.

1837 Medical College of Louisville (Medical School of the University of Louisville) opened.

1838 February. State Agricultural Society organized.

1840 Population 779,828. Louisville College chartered (January).

Five locks and dams are under construction on Kentucky River (Dec.)

1841 Numerous frays between abolitionists and opponents. Temperance movement makes gains in State.

1842 February 5. Kentucky Institute for the Blind established at Louisville.

1844 October. Factory for spinning and weaving silk established at Newport.

1845 May. Methodist Episcopal Church, South, organized at Louisville.

June 4. *True American*, abolitionist journal, established at Lexington by Cassius M. Clay. Refuses (Aug. 14) to discontinue journal; press and type seized.

September 13. Body of Daniel Boone, first citizen of Kentucky, brought from Missouri, re-interred in Frankfort Cemetery.

1846 February 7. University of Louisville chartered.

1847 July 20. Kentuckians who fell in Mexican War are reburied in State Cemetery at Frankfort. (O'Hara's poem, "Bivouac of the Dead," written to commemorate this event.)

December. Telegraph lines connect larger Kentucky cities with Nashville and Cincinnati.

1848 November 7. Zachary Taylor becomes President-elect.

1849 October. Constitutional convention meets at Frankfort.

1850 Population 982,405.

1851 March. Emancipated slaves compelled to leave State.

July 19. Wire suspension railroad bridge completed over Kentucky River at Frankfort.

1852 June 29. Henry Clay dies at Washington, D.C.

1853 James Guthrie, of Louisville, becomes U.S. Secretary of the Treasury and Jefferson Davis U.S. Secretary of War.

March. Livestock importing agency organized in Lexington.

May 18. Steamboat *Eclipse* reaches Louisville from New Orleans in record time of 4 days, 9 hours and 31 minutes.

October. Sixty-three Negroes, most of them freed slaves, leave Louisville for Liberia.

December. Joel T. Hart, Kentucky sculptor, completes busts of John J. Crittenden, Charles A. Wickliffe, and Henry Clay.

1855 "Bloody Monday" election riots in Louisville; 22 persons die, much property destroyed.

1856 March 7. Kentucky Agricultural Society organized to stage annual State Fair.

November. John C. Breckinridge of Lexington is elected Vice President of the United States.

1857 October. Methodist Episcopal Church, South, in conference at Hopkinsville, votes to expunge general rule forbidding "the buying and selling of men, women and children, with intent to enslave them."

1859 October 28–29. Mob destroys the plant of the *True South,* abolition paper at Newport.

1860 Population 1,155,684. Great "Union" meeting throughout State (January). Secession feeling grows (November). Abraham Lincoln elected (November) though voted down in Kentucky.

1861 February 11. Legislature, refusing to call convention which might take Kentucky out of the Union, adjourns.

March 5. Two Kentuckians join Lincoln's cabinet: Joseph Holt as Secretary of War, and Montgomery Blair as Postmaster General.

April 15. Governor Magoffin refuses to furnish militia for Union. State remains neutral. President Lincoln promises not to attack Kentucky if it remains neutral.

May. Numerous skirmishes in Kentucky. Union and Confederate troops encamp within State, notwithstanding Kentucky's position of neutrality.

November 18. "Sovereignty Convention," at Russellville, declares Kentucky a Confederate State, with Bowling Green chosen as capital.

December 10–12. Kentucky delegates are seated in Confederate Congress.

1862 January 19. Battle of Mill Spring; Confederate General F. K. Zollicoffer killed.

March 11. Legislature rules that any person in Confederate Army or service who gives voluntary aid against United States or Kentucky, shall be expatriated and no longer be a citizen of Kentucky except by permit of State legislature.

June 1. U.S. Military Commandant of Kentucky appointed.

July. Morgan and his men conduct raids into Kentucky.

October 4. Inaugural ceremonies of Provisional (Confederate) Government of Kentucky held at Frankfort, with Richard Hawes of Bourbon County as Governor. Four hours later Provisional Government flees from Frankfort, never to return.

October 8. Battle of Perryville.

1863 January 1. President Lincoln issues Emancipation Proclamation.

December 24. First lot of sugar and molasses received at Louisville since Confederate blockade of the Mississippi was established in 1861.

1864 May. Governor Bramlette calls for 10,000 men.

July. President Lincoln places State under martial law.

November 24. First street railway line in Louisville begins operation.

1865 February. College of Agriculture, as part of Kentucky University at or near Lexington, established by legislative act.

March 12. Sue Munday (Marcellus Jerome Clark), notorious guerrilla, captured and hanged in Louisville.

April. Southern leaders surrender to Federal commanders.

November 11. General Palmer's methods in Kentucky are termed "monarchial" by General Sherman. Grand Jury later indicts Palmer for enticing slaves to leave State.

November 30. President Johnson restores privilege of writ of habeas corpus (suspended by Lincoln on December 15, 1863) to all border States except Kentucky.

December. Lead ore discovered in Owen, Henry, and other counties; oil wells drilled in many localities.

December. Legislature repeals drastic wartime acts.

1866 January. Legislature votes to restore county courthouses burned or destroyed during the war.

January. Ashland, home of Henry Clay at Lexington, bought by University of Kentucky.

February. Legislature passes acts relating to Negro welfare and education. Requests removal of Freedmen's Bureau from Kentucky.

May. National Tobacco Fair at Louisville.

1867 Legislature rejects (January) Fourteenth Amendment; passes (Feb.) Amnesty bill. Theodore O'Hara, Kentucky poet, dies (June 10) in Alabama.

1868 March 20. Jesse James and gang rob Russellville bank.

1869 March. Legislature rejects Fifteenth Amendment.

1870 Population 1,321,011.

February 18. Railroad bridge across Ohio River at Louisville is dedicated.

1871 January. Ku Klux Klan raids.

November. Enlarged Louisville & Portland Canal opened.

1872 April 27. Public Library opened at Louisville with 20,000 books and 100,000 museum specimens.

September. National Industrial Exposition opens at Louisville.

1873 October 7. First Negro high school in State opened in Louisville.

October 13. Barney Macauley's new $200,000 theater in Louisville completed.

1875 Louisville largest whisky market in world.

April. Plan to utilize water power at Ohio Falls.

May 17. First Kentucky Derby won by Aristides.

October 8. Jefferson Davis speaks to 5,000 at Christian County Fair; visits his old home at Fairview (October 10).

November 27. Mary Anderson makes debut at Macauley Theater in Louisville.

1876 May 15. Vagrant wins second Kentucky Derby. Dom Pedro, Emperor of Brazil, watches Derby.

1879 First telephone exchange in Louisville.

1880 Population 1,648,690. U.S. Government gains control of Louisville & Portland Canal, abolishing tolls.

1882 McCoy-Hatfield feud flares with renewed vigor.

1883 August. Southern Exposition opens at Louisville.

1884 May. Filson Club founded at Louisville.

1885 Local option reforms win in many counties.

1890 Population 1,858,635. Tornado (March 27) kills 120, destroys $2,500,-000 of property in Louisville. Constitutional convention meets (Sept.) at Frankfort.

1893 February. John G. Carlisle, U.S. Senator, becomes Secretary of the Treasury.

1898 Kentucky furnishes three regiments of infantry and two troops of cavalry in war with Spain.

1899 Famous "Music Hall Convention" of State Democrats held in Louisville.

William Goebel loses in gubernatorial race to W. S. Taylor (Republican). Result contested.

1900 Population 2,147,174.

January 30. Goebel, mortally wounded in front of statehouse, declared victor in election contest.

1902 First Kentucky State Fair at Churchill Downs.

1904 "Night Rider" outbreaks.

1908 Agricultural and Mechanical College becomes State University.

Legislature passes child labor law.

1910 Population 2,289,905.

1912 Kentucky Home Society for Negro orphans founded.

1916 State University becomes University of Kentucky.

1917 Camps Knox, Thomas, Zachary Taylor, and Stanley established in Kentucky. During war 75,043 Kentuckians serve in U.S. forces.

Frank L. McVey becomes President of University of Kentucky.

1920 Population 2,416,630.

1922 U.S. Hospital for service men at Outwood completed.

WHAS, first radio broadcasting station in Kentucky, established.

1925 Frontier Nursing Service founded for obstetrical and other work in Kentucky mountains.

1926 State ranks second in tobacco production for the year.

Efficiency commission appointed to study governmental structure.

1927 J. B. Speed Memorial Museum, Louisville, opened.

1928 Bowman Field purchased by Louisville for airport.

1929 January. Mammoth Cave estate, bought by Mammoth Cave National Park Association, becomes Mammoth Cave National Park.

May 8. Paducah-Brookport Bridge dedicated.

October 31. Municipal bridge connecting Louisville and Central Kentucky with Jeffersonville, Ind., dedicated.

1930 Population 2,614,589.

1932 Camp Knox becomes permanent military post known as Fort Knox.

1933 Kentucky State Planning Board organized.

1934 Miners' strike in Harlan County.

1936 March 7. Shields-Nickell Governmental Reorganization Act is approved by State legislature.

Thirty Kentucky distilleries produce more than one-third of the national output.

Gold bullion depository at Fort Knox completed.

1937 January and February. One of greatest floods in history of United States raises crest of Ohio River and its many tributary streams. Speedy relief and rehabilitation.

The University of Louisville celebrates its centennial as "the oldest municipal university in the United States."

Selective Bibliography

GEOGRAPHY AND TOPOGRAPHY

Burroughs, W. G. *Geography of the Kentucky Knobs*. Frankfort, 1926. 284 p. illus., maps, diagrs., tables, bibliog., index. (Kentucky Geological Survey. Geologic Reports. Ser. 6, v. 19.)

────── *Geography of the Western Kentucky Coal Field*. Frankfort, 1924. 211 p., illus., maps, diagrs., tables, bibliog., index. (Kentucky Geological Survey. Geologic Reports. Ser. 6, v. 24.)

Davis, D. H. *Geography of the Bluegrass Region*. Frankfort, 1927. 215 p. illus., maps, diagrs., bibliog., index. (Kentucky Geological Survey. Geologic Reports. Ser. 6, v. 23.)

────── *Geography of the Jackson Purchase*. Frankfort, 1923. 185 p. illus., maps, tables, bibliog., index. (Kentucky Geological Survey. Geologic Reports. Ser. 6, v. 9.)

────── *Geography of the Mountains of Eastern Kentucky*. Frankfort, 1924. 180 p. illus., maps, diagrs., tables, bibliog., index. (Kentucky Geological Survey. Geologic Reports. Ser. 6, v. 18.)

Jillson, W. R. *Kentucky State Parks*. Frankfort, 1927. 92 p. illus., maps, bibliog. citations, index. (Kentucky Geological Survey.) Describes proposed State park areas, as well as those already established.

────── *Topography of Kentucky*. Frankfort, 1927. 291 p. illus., maps, tables, bibliog., index. (Kentucky Geological Survey. Geologic Reports. Ser. 6, v. 30.)

Randolph, Helen. *Mammoth Cave and the Cave Region of Kentucky*. Louisville, Standard Printing Company, 1924. 156 p. illus., maps, bibliog., index. Brief, authoritative work combining history and description.

Sauer, C. O. *Geography of the Pennyroyal*. Frankfort, 1927. 303 p. illus., maps, diagrs., tables, bibliog., index. (Kentucky Geological Survey. Geologic Reports. Ser. 6, v. 25.)

GEOLOGY, MINERAL RESOURCES, AND PALEONTOLOGY

Jillson, W. R. *The Geology and Mineral Resources of Kentucky*. Frankfort, 1928. 409 p. illus., maps, diagrs., tables, index. (Kentucky Geological Survey. Geologic Reports. Ser. 6, v. 17.)

────── , et al. *Paleontology of Kentucky*. Frankfort, 1931. 469 p. illus., maps, diagrs., bibliog., index. (Kentucky Geological Survey. Geologic Reports. Ser. 6, v. 36.) Symposium by paleontologists.

Miller, A. McQ. *The Geology of Kentucky*. Frankfort, 1919. 392 p. illus., maps, charts, tables, bibliog., index. (Kentucky Department of Geology and Forestry. Geologic Reports. Ser. 5, bull. 2.) An outstanding work on the geology of the State.

Twenhofel, W. H. *The Building of Kentucky.* Frankfort, 1931. 328 p. illus., diagrs., bibliog., index. (Kentucky Geological Survey. Geologic Reports. Ser. 6, v. 37.) Study of the geological development of Kentucky from its earliest determined beginning to the present day.

PLANT AND ANIMAL LIFE

Funkhouser, W. D. *Wild Life in Kentucky.* Frankfort, 1925. 385 p. illus., maps, diagrs., bibliog., index. (Kentucky Geological Survey. Geologic Reports. Ser. 6, v. 16.) Definitive work on the reptiles, birds, and mammals of Kentucky, with a discussion of their appearance, habits, and economic importance.

Mattoon, W. R. *Common Forest Trees of Kentucky.* Frankfort, 1923. 72 p. illus. (Kentucky Department of Agriculture.) Handbook describing 70 common forest trees of the State.

ARCHEOLOGY AND INDIANS

Beckner, Lucien. "Eskippakithiki, Last Indian Town in Kentucky." Louisville, 1932. (Reprint from *Filson Club History Quarterly,* October 1932, v. 6: 355–382.) A chapter in Kentucky history never before written.

Call, R. W. *Life and Writings of Rafinesque.* Louisville, J. P. Morton & Company, 1895. 227 p. (Filson Club Publications, no. 10.) An account of the famous botanist, together with a bibliography of his writings.

Funkhouser, W. D., and W. S. Webb. *Ancient Life in Kentucky.* Frankfort, 1928. 349 p. illus., diagrs., bibliog., index. (Kentucky Geological Survey. Geologic Reports. Ser. 6, v. 34.) Brief presentation of paleontological succession with a systematic outline of the archeology of the State.

HISTORY

Brown, J. M. *The Political Beginnings of Kentucky.* Louisville, J. P. Morton & Company, 1889. 263 p. front. (Filson Club Publications, no. 6.) Good source of the pre-statehood conventions. Written partly as a defense of John Brown, first U.S. Senator from Kentucky.

Clark, T. D. *A History of Kentucky.* New York, Prentice-Hall, 1937. 702 p. illus., index. The most recent of Kentucky histories; also one of the most readable. Extensive annotated bibliography.

Clay, Cassius M. *Cassius Marcellus Clay, Life and Memoirs, Writings and Speeches.* Cincinnati, J. Fletcher Brennan, 1886. 600 p. illus. Autobiography of a Kentucky abolitionist.

Collins, L. and R. H. *History of Kentucky.* Covington, Collins & Company, and later by other publishers. 1874 and subsequent reprints. (Revision of an earlier 1-volume edition by L. Collins.) 2 v. illus., maps, indexes. Valuable Kentuckiana. Not always dependable, but indispensable, especially in county histories.

Connelley, W. E., and E. M. Coulter. *History of Kentucky.* Chicago and New York, American Historical Society, 1922. 5 v. illus., bibliog., index. Ed. by

Judge Charles Kerr. One of the most complete and scholarly works on Kentucky history; copious bibliographical and explanatory footnotes.

Coulter, E. M. *The Civil War and Readjustment in Kentucky.* Chapel Hill, University of North Carolina Press, 1926. 468 p. maps, bibliog., index. Well-rounded study giving modern emphasis to social and economic factors.

Jillson, W. R., ed. Filson's *Kentucke.* Louisville, J. P. Morton & Company, 1929. 198 p. map, bibliog., index. Facsimile reproduction of the original Wilmington edition (1784).

———*Kentucky History.* Louisville, Standard Printing Company, 1936. 96 p. illus. An annotated bibliography of Kentucky history divided into regional, State, and county histories.

———*Pioneer Kentucky.* Frankfort, State Journal Company, 1934. 152 p. bibliog., index. Describes exploration and settlement, early cartography and primitive geography.

———*Tales of the Dark and Bloody Ground.* Louisville, C. T. Dearing Printing Company, 1930. 154 p. illus., bibliog., index. A collection of papers containing some good pioneer history, including John Cowan's "Journal" and Levi Todd's "Narrative of 1774–1777."

Lester, W. S. *The Transylvania Colony.* Spencer, Ind., Samuel R. Guard & Company, 1935. 288 p. bibliog. An account of the colony's origin, aims, and accomplishments.

Marshall, Humphrey. *History of Kentucky.* 2d ed. Frankfort, G. S. Robinson, 1824. 2 v. The first edition (1812) is the second earliest history of the State, ranking second only to Filson's *Kentucke.* Includes Rafinesque's "The Ancient Annals of Kentucky."

Mayo, Bernard. *Henry Clay, Spokesman of the New West.* Boston, Houghton Mifflin Company, 1937. 570 p. illus., bibliog., index. The life of the "Great Compromiser" cast upon a panoramic and richly detailed background of the pioneer West. This is the first of three volumes.

McElroy, R. McNutt. *Kentucky in the Nation's History.* New York, Moffat, Yard & Company, 1909. 590 p. illus., bibliog., index. Contains an extensive and important bibliography.

Shaler, N. S. *Kentucky, a Pioneer Commonwealth.* Boston, Houghton Mifflin Company, 1885. 433 p. map, bibliog., index. Until the publication of T. D. Clark's *History of Kentucky* that was considered the best 1-volume historical work on Kentucky. It is written in a fluent, easy style and is very reliable.

Townsend, J. W. *Kentucky: Mother of Governors.* Frankfort, Kentucky State Historical Society, 1910. 51 p. front.

BIOGRAPHY

Biographical Encyclopaedia of Kentucky. Cincinnati, M. Armstrong & Company, 1878. 792 p. illus., index. The biographies are usually autobiographic, and perhaps are overlaudatory, but are factually correct.

Southard, M. Y., and E. C. Miller. *Who's Who in Kentucky.* Louisville, Standard Printing Company, 1936. 582 p. illus., index.

TRAGEDIES, FEUDS, AND OUTLAWS

Johnson, L. F. *Famous Kentucky Tragedies and Trials*. Louisville, Baldwin Law Book Company, 1916. 336 p. The "headlines" of the past. The Sharp-Beauchamp case described in this volume is probably the most unusual in Kentucky annals.

Mutzenberg, C. G. *Kentucky's Famous Feuds and Tragedies*. New York, R. F. Fenno & Company, 1917. 333 p. One of the best accounts of the mountain feuds.

Rothert, O. A. *The Outlaws of Cave-in-Rock*. Cleveland, A. H. Clark Company, 1924. 364 p. illus., bibliog., index. Accounts of the famous highwaymen and river pirates who operated in pioneer days.

GENERAL SOCIAL CONDITIONS

Gardner, C. *Clever Country*. Chicago, F. H. Revell Company, 1931. 159 p. illus., maps. Entertainingly written account of the Frontier Nursing Service and of the mountain people it serves.

Kentucky Department of Health. *Annual Report Cooperative County Health Work in Kentucky: 1936*. Louisville. 29 p. maps, diagrs., graphs, charts, tables. (Bulletin, v. 10, no. 1; August, 1937.)

Odum, H. W. *Southern Regions of the United States*. Chapel Hill, University of North Carolina Press, 1936. 664 p. maps, charts, tables, bibliog., index. An important source of social, economic and cultural information on Kentucky, as well as on the South as a whole.

Poole, Ernest. *Nurses on Horseback*. New York, Macmillan Company, 1932. 168 p. illus. This story of the Frontier Nursing Service is full of human interest.

Thomas, W. R. *Life Among the Hills and Mountains of Kentucky*. Louisville, Standard Printing Company, 1926. 414 p. illus., tables, bibliog. Historical, social, and economic surveys of each of the 38 mountain counties, and a general picture of cultural conditions in the mountains of eastern Kentucky.

INDUSTRY, AGRICULTURE, AND LABOR

Hasse, A. R. *An Index to Economic Materials in Printed Documents of the State of Kentucky: 1792–1904*. Washington, Carnegie Institution of Washington, 1910. 452 p. A tabulation and chronology of Kentucky documents.

Jillson, W. R. *Oil and Gas in Western Kentucky*. Frankfort, 1930. 632 p. illus., maps, diagrs., bibliog., index. (Kentucky Geological Survey. Geologic Reports. Ser. 6, v. 39.) Short introductory essay, followed by detailed accounts of drilling and production in 23 counties of this region.

Kentucky Bureau of Agriculture, Labor and Statistics. *Kentucky Resources and Industries*. Frankfort, 1929. 389 p. illus., maps, tables, charts. (Bulletin 34.) Although not up-to-date statistically, this is a good source of information, as well as an industrial directory of each of the 120 counties in the State.

Kentucky Department of Agriculture, Labor and Statistics. *Biennial Report: 1934–1935.* Frankfort, State Journal Company, 1936. 273 p. illus., tables, charts.

Kentucky State Planning Board. *Progress Report and Appendices.* Louisville, 1935. 2 v., 511 numb. maps, tables, diagrs. Mimeographed compilation of social and economic data on Kentucky; good statistical source.

Ross, Malcolm. *Machine Age in the Hills.* New York, Macmillan Company, 1933. 248 p. illus. Good study of conditions in the coal mining communities of Kentucky and West Virginia. Impartial on the whole and popular in style.

U.S. Department of Commerce. *An Aid for Analyzing Markets in Indiana and Kentucky.* Washington, Government Printing Office, 1933. 24 p. maps, tables, graphs, charts, diagrs. Presents a clear picture of the State and its counties in economic terms. Helpful in understanding the economic organization of Kentucky.

TRANSPORTATION

Ambler, C. H. *History of Transportation in the Ohio Valley.* Glendale, Calif., Arthur H. Clark Company, 1932. 465 p. illus., maps, bibliog. citations, index. The story of transportation in the Ohio Valley from the canoe to the packet-boat. Describes the advent of the railroad and the present problems of river transportation.

Clark, T. D. *The Beginning of the L&N.* Louisville, Standard Printing Company, 1933. 107 p. bibliog. The development of the Louisville & Nashville R.R. from 1836 to 1860.

———— *A Pioneer Southern Railroad.* Chapel Hill, University of North Carolina Press, 1936. 171 p. illus., map, bibliog., index. The story of the southern branches of Illinois Central R.R. told with color and filled with the lore and romance of the railroad.

Coleman, J. W. *Stage-Coach Days in the Bluegrass.* Louisville, Standard Printing Company, 1935. 286 p. illus., bibliog., index. Describes stagecoach travel and tavern days in central Kentucky between 1800 and 1900.

Kerr, J. L. *The Story of a Southern Carrier; the Louisville & Nashville.* New York, Young & Ottley, 1933. 67 p. bibliog. Outline history of a railroad which played a recognized part in the industrial reconstruction of the South.

Lafferty, M. W. *A Pioneer Railroad of the West.* Lexington, University of Kentucky, 1916. 29 p. Historical accounts, interspersed with many reminiscences, of the Lexington & Ohio R.R. (now part of the L&N R.R.), Kentucky's first railroad of importance.

Pusey, W. A. *The Wilderness Road to Kentucky.* New York, George H. Doran Company, 1921. 146 p. illus., maps, bibliog. Describes a route of travel by which early settlers arrived in the State.

Verhoeff, Mary. *Kentucky River Navigation.* Louisville, J. P. Morton & Company, 1917. 257 p. illus., maps, tables, bibliog., index. (Filson Club Publications, no. 28.) Study of navigation on the most historically and economically important tributary of the Ohio in the State.

EDUCATION

Baber, George. *Origin of Popular Education in Kentucky*. Louisville, J. P. Morton & Company, 1881. 48 p. Traces the beginnings of public education in the State.

Hamlett, Barksdale. *History of Education in Kentucky*. Frankfort, 1914. 334 p. illus., index. (Kentucky Department of Education.) Compilation of reports from State superintendents and county commissioners describing education primarily useful for research. The last chapter gives historical sketches of 39 church and endowed schools and colleges in the State.

Lewis, A. F. *History of Higher Education in Kentucky*. Washington, Government Printing Office, 1899. 350 p. illus., index. Not always dependable, but the only single volume covering higher education in Kentucky thoroughly.

Peter, Robert. *Transylvania University*. Louisville, J. P. Morton & Company, 1896. 202 p. front., bibliog. citations, index. (Filson Club Publications, no. 11.) Historical sketch (from its founding to 1865) of the institution which pioneered in higher education in Kentucky.

FOLKLORE

Mackaye, Percy. *Tall Tales of the Kentucky Mountains*. New York, George H. Doran Company, 1926. 185 p. illus. Twelve tales told in the mountain vernacular by Solomon Shell, a legendary figure.

Thomas, D. L. and L. B. *Kentucky Superstitions*. Princeton, Princeton University Press, 1920. 334 p. bibliog., index. Compilation of almost 4,000 superstitions of every type.

RELIGION

Bishop, R. H. *Outline of the History of the Church in the State of Kentucky*. Lexington, Thomas T. Skillman, 1824. 420 p. Contains the memoirs of Rev. David Rice; sketches of the origin and status of the various denominations at the time; and accounts of some of the men prominent in the early ministry of Kentucky.

Fortune, A. W. *The Disciples in Kentucky*. Lexington, Convention of the Christian Churches in Kentucky, 1932. 415 p. illus., bibliog., index. An account of the Christian Church in Kentucky by one of its ministers.

Redford, A. H. *The History of Methodism in Kentucky*. Nashville, Southern Methodist Publishing House, 1868–1870. 3 v. front. Detailed, authoritative work.

Spencer, J. H. *A History of Kentucky Baptists*. Cincinnati, J. H. Spencer, 1886. 2 v. fronts., indexes. History of the Baptist Church in Kentucky from 1769 to 1885 with more than 800 biographical sketches.

Webb, B. J. *Centenary of Catholicity in Kentucky*. Louisville, Charles A. Rogers, 1884. 594 p. illus., index. Describes Catholicism and Catholics in Kentucky up to the year of publication. An historical source book of more or less reliability.

LITERATURE

Allen, James Lane. *Flute and Violin*. New York, Harper & Brothers, 1891. 308 p. illus. Collection of Kentucky tales and romances.

Bird, Robert Montgomery. *Nick of the Woods, or The Jibbenainosay*. N.Y., Macy-Masius (Vanguard Press), 1928. 395 p. Reprint of a popular tale of the Kentucky frontier first issued in 1837; edited by Mark Van Doren.

Cobb, Irvin S. *Old Judge Priest*. New York, George H. Doran Company, 1916. 401 p. (Murray Hill Library edition.) Stories about Old Judge Priest, a homely, shrewd, lovable figure, typical of Kentucky and the Old South.

———*Kentucky*. New York, George H. Doran Company, 1924. With illus. by John T. McCutcheon. 62 p. (Cobb's America Guyed Books.) Humorous characterization of the State by Kentucky's outstanding humorist.

Combs, J. H., ed. *All That's Kentucky*. Louisville, J. P. Morton & Company, 1915. 285 p. index. First-rate anthology of poetry on Kentucky and its lore.

Dickey, Fannie Porter. *Blades o' Blue Grass*. Louisville, J. P. Morton & Company, 1892. 331 p. illus. Compilation of poems by Kentuckians with biographical sketches. "The Bivouac of the Dead" by Theodore O'Hara is the most outstanding selection.

Fox, John, Jr. *Hell Fer Sartain*. New York, Charles Scribner's Sons, 1904. 119 p. Describes a locality high up in the Cumberlands.

Furman, Lucy. *Quare Women*. Concord, Atlantic Monthly Press, 1923. 219 p. Sympathetic portrayal of the mountain people of eastern Kentucky. Mirth-provoking and penetrating.

Hall, Eliza Calvert. *The Land of Long Ago*. Boston, Little, Brown & Company, 1909. 285 p. illus. Homely short sketches of olden times in the rural districts of the Pennyrile.

Hergesheimer, Joseph. *The Limestone Tree*. New York, Alfred A. Knopf, 1931. 386 p. Chronicle of an American family in Kentucky from the eighteenth to the nineteenth century.

Johnston, Annie Fellows. *The Little Colonel Stories*. Boston, Page Company, 1930. 559 p. illus. Contains "The Little Colonel," "The Giant Scissors," and "Two Little Knights of Kentucky"; depicts child life of a quarter-century ago in the Pewee Valley neighborhood of Oldham County.

Knight, Grant C. *James Lane Allen and the Genteel Tradition*. Chapel Hill, University of North Carolina Press, 1935. 313 p. front., bibliog., index. Critical and biographical study.

Rice, Alice Hegan. *Mrs. Wiggs of the Cabbage Patch*. New York, The Century Company, 1901. 153 p. An epic of optimism.

Roberts, Elizabeth Madox. *The Time of Man*. New York, Viking Press, 1926. 328 p. Tells of the struggle of the Chessers, a family of the Kentucky hills, to better their condition.

Stuart, Jesse. *Head o' W-Hallow*. New York, E. P. Dutton & Company, 1936. 342 p. Nineteen stories about the mountain people of eastern Kentucky.

Townsend, J. W. *Kentucky in American Letters: 1784–1912*. Cedar Rapids,

Iowa, Torch Press, 1913. 2 v., index. Indispensable work on Kentucky literature. While its critical evaluations do not equal its wealth of information, it remains the most comprehensive work on Kentucky literature up to the date of its publication. Includes excerpts from each writer's work.

Venable, W. H. *Beginnings of Literary Culture in the Ohio Valley.* Cincinnati, Robert Clarke & Company, 1891. 519 p. bibliog. citations, index. A valuable collection of literary, historical, and biographical material on early western literary culture.

ART AND HANDICRAFT

Goodrich, F. L. *Mountain Homespun.* New Haven, Yale University Press, 1931. 91 p. illus., index. Folklore interwoven with a description of the home crafts, particularly weaving and spinning, of the people living in the southern Appalachians.

Price, S. W. *The Old Masters of the Bluegrass.* Louisville, J. P. Morton & Company, 1902. 181 p. illus. (Filson Club Publications, no. 17.) Biographical sketches of Jouett, Bush, Grimes, Frazer, Morgan, Hart, and Price, with portraits and illustrations of the artists' work.

ARCHITECTURE

Lathrop, Elise. *Historic Houses of Early America.* New York, Tudor Publishing Company, 1927. 464 p. illus., bibliog. Chap. XVI, pp. 387–398, includes the stories of 11 famous Kentucky houses.

Newcomb, Rexford. "The Architecture of Old Kentucky." (*Kentucky State Historical Society Register.* Frankfort, July, 1933. v. 31, no. 96, pp. 185–200.) Authoritative, indispensable article on the architecture of early Kentucky.

Simpson, E. M. *Bluegrass Houses and Their Traditions.* Lexington, Transylvania Press, 1932. 408 p. illus. Steeped in the lore and the cherished romance that cling to the renowned houses of the Bluegrass.

MUSIC AND THEATER

Campbell, O. D., and C. J. Sharp. *English Folk Songs from the Southern Appalachians.* New York, G. P. Putnam's Sons, 1917. 341 p. map, bibliog., index. An important contribution to the subject of American folk song, comprising 122 songs and ballads and 323 tunes. Contains an introduction and notes.

Cox, J. H. *Folk Songs of the South.* Cambridge, Harvard University Press, 1925. 545 p. illus., map (West Virginia), index. An annotated compilation of 185 songs and ballads with their different versions, and 26 tunes collected under the auspices of the West Virginia Folklore Society.

Jackson, G. P. *White Spirituals in the Southern Uplands.* Chapel Hill, University of North Carolina Press, 1933. 444 p. illus., bibliog., index. A pioneer work; it is also important for the history of the Negro spiritual.

McGill, Josephine. *Folk-songs of the Kentucky Mountains.* New York, Boosey & Company, 1917. 106 p. Twenty traditional ballads of the Kentucky mountain people notated and arranged for the piano.

Odum, H. W., and G. B. Johnson. *The Negro and His Songs.* Chapel Hill, University of North Carolina Press, 1925. 306 p. index. A valuable study.

Smith, Sol. *Theatrical Management in the West and South for Thirty Years with Anecdotal Sketches.* New York, Harper & Brothers, 1868. 276 p. illus. Delightful memoirs of a retired actor who often played in Kentucky. Sol Smith establishes the origin of the Jim Crow song in Louisville.

Wyman, Loraine, and Howard Brockway. *Lonesome Tunes: Folk Songs from the Kentucky Mountains.* New York, H. W. Gray Company, 1916. 102 p. front. Twenty-five folk songs, including "Barbara Allen" and "Sweet William and Lady Margery" with elaborate accompaniments.

KENTUCKY HORSES

Alves, Clinton. "Blood Will Tell." *Country Life,* April 1938.

Beer, Richard. "Lexington en Route." *Country Life,* May 1936.

Bradley, Col. E. R. "My Four Kentucky Derbies." *Saturday Evening Post,* May 8, 1937.

Estes, J. A. "The Thoroughbred in the Blue Grass." (In *Keeneland Opening Program,* 1936.)

"Life of a Derby Starter." (In *Kentucky Derby Official Program.* Louisville, 1935.)

Reed, Robert. "Big Red Comes of Age." *Country Gentleman,* April 1938.

Reynolds, Quentin. "The Sun Shines Bright." *Collier's,* May 8, 1937.

Index